DATE DUE

DEMCO 38-296

CONTEMPORARY MUSICIANS

ISSN 1044-2197

CONTEMPORARY MUSICIANS

PROFILES OF THE PEOPLE IN MUSIC

LUANN BRENNAN, Editor

VOLUME 24
Includes Cumulative Indexes

The Gale Group

DETROIT • SAN FRANCISCO • LONDON • BOSTON • WOODBRIDGE, CT

STAFF

Luann Brennan, *Editor*
Leigh Ann DeRemer, *Assistant Editor*

Mary Alice Adams, Carol Brennan, Gerald E. Brennan, Gloria Cooksey, Robert Dupuis, Mary Kalfatovic, Christine Morrison, Timothy Kevin Perry, Jim Powers, Paula Pyzik-Scott, Brenna Sanchez, Ann M. Schawlboski, Sonya Shelton, B. Kim Taylor, *Sketchwriters*

Bridget Travers, *Managing Editor*

Maria Franklin, *Permissions Manager*
Margaret Chamberlain, *Permissions Specialist*
Shalice Shah-Caldwell *Permissions Associate*

Mary Beth Trimper, *Production Director*
Deborah Milliken, *Production Assistant*
Cynthia Baldwin, *Product Design Manager*
Barbara J. Yarrow, *Graphic Services Supervisor*
Robert Duncan, Michael Logusz, *Imaging Specialists*
Randy Bassett, *Image Database Supervisor*
Pamela A. Reed, *Imaging Coordinator*
Gary Leach, *Graphic Artist*
Cover illustration by John Kleber

Contents

Introduction ix

Cumulative Subject Index 243

Cumulative Musicians Index 271

Emily Ameling 1
  Best loved soprano

Vanessa Bell Armstrong 4
  Gospel singer with an R&B flavor

Ralph Bass 7
  Great starmaker of early rock 'n' roll

Booker T. & the M.G.'s........................ 10
  Hottest R&B soul band of the sixties

Clifford Brown 14
  Best ever jazz trumpeter

Buffalo Springfield 18
  Folk/country/ rock amalgam

Caravan 22
  "Canterbury" progressive rockers

Richard Carpenter 25
  Pop music prodigy

Ray Charles 29
  Genius keeps on singing

Cherry Poppin' Daddies 33
  Swing music trend setters

Leonard Chess 36
  Founder of Chicago blues sound

Cornershop 39
  Modern-rock chart success

Crosby, Stills, and Nash 42
  Inspired lyrics with pure harmonies

Dennis Russell Davies 45
  Modern-day, globe-hopping maestro

Doris Day 48
  Post-war singing and acting sensation

Des'ree 52
  She's just gotta be

Pete Droge 54
  More that a "one-hit wonder"

Emmet Swimming 56
  Offbeat musical offering

Nesuhi Ertegun 58
  No typical record guy

Merrell Fankhauser 61
  Music of exemplary quality

Renee Fleming 64
  Preeminant lyric soprano

The Four Seasons 68
  Power doo-wop

Frankie Lymon and The Teenagers 71
  Rags to riches story ends sadly

Ghost 75
  Rock band of exotic sounds

Deborah Gibson 78
  No longer "Little Debbie"

Gerry Goffin-Carole King 81
  Successful pop music partnership

The Go-Go's 84
  Rock band with girl power

Gong 87
  Style influenced by ethnic musics

Goodie Mob 91
  Eclectic hip-hop/rap group

Patty Griffin 94
  Sings with conviction

Johnny Hodges 96
  Ellington's right-hand man

Don Howland 99
  Major force in independent music

Charlie Hunter 101
  Avant-garde jazz musician

Mississippi John Hurt 104
  Guitarist for blues aficiandos

Janis Ian 107
  American folk troubadour

Abdullah Ibrahim 110
  Fuses South African music with jazz

Jackyl 113
  Rock band for Beavis & Butthead

Skip James 116
  Reluctant performer

Kilgore 119
  Thinking person's metal band

B. B. King 121
  Blues legend

G. Love 124
  Blues with a twist of hip-hop

Yo Yo Ma 127
  Grammy award winning cellist

Yngwie Malmsteen 130
  Explosive Sweedish guitarist

Loreena McKennitt.......................... 134
  Canadian singer combines past and present

Dave McLean.................................. 137
  Quintessential blues singer

Monifah 139
  Versatile R&B artist

Van Morrison 141
  Elusive rock star

R. Carlos Nakai 145
  World''s foremost Native American flutist

Newsboys 148
  Rock band on a mission

Dolly Parton.................................... 150
  Legendary country and western singer

Pearls Before Swine 154
  Weaver's of musical magic

Phil Perry 156
  Romantic R&B singer

Quasi 158
  Unusual experimental rock duo

Queen Latifah 161
  Rapper of significant talents

Eddie Rabbitt 164
  Jersey boy with a soft heart

Radiohead 167
  Alternative band with devoted cult following

Andrew Rangell 170
  Classical pianist is legend in his own time

The Rankins 172
  Family revives Celtic roots

Reef.. 174
  Bluesy guitar-driven rock band

Roy Rogers 176
  America's singing cowboy

Richie Sambora 179
  Unpretentious blues rocker

Simon and Garfunkel 181
  Rock duo with school boy innocence

Sly & the Family Stone 184
  Pioneers of funk

Sonny and Cher 187
  Positive counter-culture image

Jo Stafford 190
  Quintessential vocalist of 40s and 50s

Ringo Starr 194
  Unknown Beatle goes solo

Richard Stoltzman 196
  Award winning clarinetist defies categorization

Surfin' Pluto 200
  Rock band rides wave of success

Clark Terry 203
  Talented trumpeter breaks color barrier

Jean-Yves Thibaudet 207
  Command performer on world stage

Michael Tilson Thomas 209
  Wunderkind of San Francisco Symphony

Ike and Tina Turner 213
  Rough and raucy R&B duo

Luther Vandross 216
  Emotionally soulful singer

Jimmie Vaughan 219
  Powerful blues presence

Muddy Waters 221
  King of the blues

Lucinda Williams 224
  Country singer catches few breaks

Brian Wilson 227
  Founding force of California surf music

Robert Wyatt 231
  Champion of underdogs

Tammy Wynette 235
  First lady of country music

Yo La Tengo 238
  Indie band receives praise

Introduction

Fills the Information Gap on Today's Musicians

Contemporary Musicians profiles the colorful personalities in the music industry who create or influence the music we hear today. Prior to *Contemporary Musicians,* no quality reference series provided comprehensive information on such a wide range of artists despite keen and ongoing public interest. To find biographical and critical coverage, an information seeker had little choice but to wade through the offerings of the popular press, scan television "infotainment" programs, and search for the occasional published biography or exposé. *Contemporary Musicians* is designed to serve that information seeker, providing in one ongoing source in-depth coverage of the important names on the modern music scene in a format that is both informative and entertaining. Students, researchers, and casual browsers alike can use *Contemporary Musicians* to meet their needs for personal information about music figures; find a selected discography of a musician's recordings; and uncover an insightful essay offering biographical and critical information.

Provides Broad Coverage

Single-volume biographical sources on musicians are limited in scope, often focusing on a handful of performers from a specific musical genre or era. In contrast, *Contemporary Musicians* offers researchers and music devotees a comprehensive, informative, and entertaining alternative. *Contemporary Musicians* is published three times per year, with each volume providing information on 80 musical artists and record-industry luminaries from all the genres that form the broad spectrum of contemporary music—pop, rock, jazz, blues, country, New Age, folk, rhythm and blues, gospel, bluegrass, rap, and reggae, to name a few—as well as selected classical artists who have achieved "crossover" success with the general public. *Contemporary Musicians* will also occasionally include profiles of influential nonperforming members of the music community, including producers, promoters, and record company executives. Additionally, beginning with *Contemporary Musicians 11,* each volume features new profiles of a selection of previous *Contemporary Musicians* listees who remain of interest to today's readers and who have been active enough to require completely revised entries.

Includes Popular Features

In *Contemporary Musicians* you'll find popular features that users value:

• **Easy-to-locate data sections:** Vital personal statistics, chronological career summaries, listings of major awards, and mailing addresses, when available, are prominently displayed in a clearly marked box on the second page of each entry.

• **Biographical/critical essays:** Colorful and informative essays trace each subject's personal and professional life, offer representative examples of critical response to the artist's work, and provide entertaining personal sidelights.

• **Selected discographies:** Each entry provides a comprehensive listing of the artist's major recorded works.

• **Photographs:** Most entries include portraits of the subject profiled.

• **Sources for additional information:** This invaluable feature directs the user to selected books, magazines, and newspapers where more information can be obtained.

Helpful Indexes Make It Easy to Find the Information You Need

Each volume of *Contemporary Musicians* features a cumulative Musicians Index, listing names of individual performers and musical groups, and a cumulative Subject Index, which provides the user with a breakdown by primary musical instruments played and by musical genre.

Available in Electronic Formats

Diskette/Magnetic Tape. *Contemporary Musicians* is available for licensing on magnetic tape or diskette in a fielded format. The database is available for internal data processing and nonpublishing purposes only. For more information, call (800) 877-GALE.

Online. *Contemporary Musicians* is available online as part of the Gale Biographies (GALBIO) database accessible through LEXIS-NEXIS, P.O. Box 933, Daton, OH 454012-0933; phone: (513)865-6800, toll-free:800-543-6862.

We Welcome Your Suggestions

The editors welcome your comments and suggestions for enhancing and improving *Contemporary Musicians.* If you would like to suggest subjects for inclusion, please submit these names to the editors. Mail comments or suggestions to:

The Editor
Contemporary Musicians
The Gale Group
27500 Drake Rd.
Farmington Hills, MI 48334-3535

Or call toll free: (800) 347-GALE

Elly Ameling

Soprano

Described by *Opera Now* as "one of the best loved sopranos of the post-war years," Dutch singer Elly Ameling's remarkable vocal control, purity of tone, and subtlety of interpretation captivated audiences from her debut in Holland in 1961 until her retirement in 1995. She attracted a legion of fans, according to Andrew Porter of the *New York Observer,* by "her freshness, naturalness, ease, and beauty of timbre." Her work displayed wide range. She performed music from the Baroque period to the modern, including Bach, Handel, Mozart, Beethoven, Bruckner, Mahler, Satie and Faure; but she is particularly renowned for her interpretations of the songs of Schubert and Brahms and for her performances of early music. In all, she has been an influential figure in vocal music of the late twentieth century.

Elisabeth Sara Ameling was born on February 8, 1938 in Rotterdam, Netherlands. As a teenager, Ameling studied voice with several Dutch teachers including Jo Bollenkamp in Rotterdam. She also traveled to Paris to study under Pierre Bernac who encouraged her to perform French songs. When she was 18, Ameling won a vocal competition at 's-Hertogenbosch in the Netherlands; two years later she won another in Geneva, Switzerland. At the age of twenty three, in 1961, Ameling held her debut recital in Amsterdam.

Ameling's recording career began in the mid-1960s when she made a series of recordings for the Deutsche Harmonia Mundi label. The albums were notable for a variety of reasons. Andrew Porter of the *New York Observer* described them as "intimate, gentle, communicative, bold, passionate, or twinkling where necessary; never forced, never exaggerated in expression and with a kind of freshness of discovery that brings each song to life." On them, Ameling showed her ability to sing in a broad palette of musical styles.

The Deutsche Harmonia Mundi records introduced Ameling as one of the premier singers of so-called early music—music composed in or before the seventeenth century, performed using original instruments and vocal techniques. Accompanied by the Collegium Aureum, one of the first early music ensembles, Ameling recorded chamber cantatas by Johann Sebastian Bach, C.P.E. Bach, Georg Philipp Telemann, and Georg Friedrich Handel. Ameling's pure voice and precise intonation was uniquely suited to singing early music and her rendering of J.S. Bach's *Wedding Cantata* has been recognized as one of the most beautiful performances of all time. In *Classical Pulse!,* David Patrick Stearns called her "the godmother" of all early music vocalists who followed.

Ameling's early recordings also introduced her as a talented interpreter of the nineteenth century German songs called *lieder.* Stearns described the qualities that made Ameling's first *lieder* recordings so effective. "[Ameling's] girlish timbre, sunny openheartedness and refusal to record anything so glitzy as opera remind us that the basis of the early 19th-century *lieder* movement was folk-inspired poetry, and she never gives it a sense of false sophistication." Ameling would record and re-record classic *lieder* throughout her career.

Ameling's English debut took place in London in 1966 and, two years later, when she was 30 years old, she held her first American performance in New York City. She returned to the United States and Britain regularly and performed in other countries throughout the world. Through her career she concentrated on concerts and vocal recitals, frequently with pianist Dalton Baldwin. She also performed opera occasionally. Her most notable role was Ilia in the Netherlands Opera's 1973 staging of Mozart's *Idomeneo,* a role she repeated with the same company in Washington, D.C. a year later.

But whatever Ameling sang, her warm, unaffected personality brought a light touch to the material. She delivered it with a technique that seemed effortless. Her interpretive freshness exuded wit and charm. Furthermore her linguistic facility further enabled her to sing with confidence lyrics written in German, French, Italian, or English. She was awarded the Edison Prize twice, in

For the Record . . .

Born Elisabeth Sarah Ameling, February 8, 1938 in Rotterdam, Netherlands; studied voice with several Dutch teachers, including Jo Bollenkamp; later studied in Paris with Pierre Bernac.

Won first competition in 's-Hertogenbosch in 1956; won competition in Geneva in 1958; gave first recital at the age of 23 in Amsterdam; made London debut in 1966 and New York debut in 1968; played Ilia in Idomeneo with the Netherlands Opera in 1973, and in Washington D.C. in 1974; performed with several accompanists, but most frequently with pianist Dalton Baldwin; released more than a dozen albums between 1970 and 1998.

Awards: Edison Prize in 1965, Edison Prize in 1970, Knight of the Order of Oranje Nassau in 1971.

Addresses: Record company—Harmonia Mundi USA, 2037 Granville Avenue, Los Angeles, CA 90025, (310) 478-1311, fax (310) 996-1389; email: info-usa@harmoniamundi.com.

Patrick Stearns described her singing as "a clear prism ... a crystal clear mirror of the composer's intentions." Critics noted that Ameling's performance on her last album, *Songs of Hugo Ball,* recorded in 1991, hinted at the reasons she chose to give up her career at age 57. She no longer possessed what she herself in *Opera News* had called "a very young voice, girlish and pure." Instead, noted David Patrick Stearns, singing the Ball songs, Ameling's voice "seems rough, worn and effortful."

Despite the inevitable changes that age brings to a singer's voice, Ameling could look back on a distinguished, prolific, and successful career. It will serve as a benchmark for future vocalists. Through her recordings she will continue to thrill both old and new fans alike with her unflinching purity of tone, her delicacy of emotion, her adroit mastery of material, and her "visceral outpouring of superb musical instinct," according to David Patrick Stearns. They offer timeless insight into the work of the world's great composers. Few vocalists have devoted themselves so completely and so successfully to the work that Ameling held dearest.

Selected discography

Johann Sebastian Bach: *Cantata No. 130,* Deutsche Harmonia Mundi, 1970.

Ludwig van Beethoven: *Mass in C,* Deutsche Harmonia Mundi, 1971.

Johann Sebastian Bach: *Cantatas No. 147 and 3 Motets,* Deutsche Harmonia Mundi, 1972.

Elly Ameling Singt Lieder von Johann Brahms, DHM, 1972, reissued as *Elly Ameling Sings Brahms Lieder,* DHM, 1977.

Johann Sebastian Bach: *Actus Tragicus,* DHM, 1973.

Johann Sebastian Bach: *Weihnachts Oratorium,* DHM, 1973.

Johann Sebastian Bach: *Actus Tragicus,* BWV 106 , DHM, 1973.

Gabriel Urbain Faure: *Melodies,* DHM, 1974.

Gabriel Urbain Faure: *Requiem,* DHM, 1974.

Ludwig van Beethoven: *Missa Solemnis,* Op. 123, DHM, 1976.

Handel's Messiah Arias and Choruses, DHM, 1976.

Christmas Songs from Europe, DHM, 1977.

Cimarosa's Requiem, DHM, 1978.

Mahler's Symphony No. 4 in G, DHM, 1979.

Christmas with Elly Ameling, DHM, 1980.

Claude Debussy's Ariettes Oubliees, DHM, 1980.

After Hours, DHM, 1982.

Sentimental Me, DHM, 1984.

Soiree Francaise, BMG/DHM, 1986.

Songs By Hugo Wolf, Hyperion, 1995.

Elly Ameling: The Early Recordings, BMG/DHM, 1995.

1965, the year of her Schubert recordings, and in 1970, the year she recorded the *Bach Cantata No. 130.* In 1971, she was made a Knight of the Order of Oranje Nassau.

Ameling was frequently in the recording studio in the 1970s and 1980s. Those recordings demonstrated the remarkable range she was capable of. Between 1970 and 1973 she released five albums of music by Johann Sebastian Bach. In 1971 and 1976 she released albums of material by Ludwig van Beethoven. She made an album of Brahms *lieder* in 1972, two albums of the *Melodies* of Gabriel Faure in 1974 and 1975, and recorded *Symphony No. 4* of Gustav Mahler in 1979. She also recorded albums of works by Claude Debussy, George Frideric Handel, Domenico Comarosa, Anton Bruckner, two albums of Christmas songs, and two collections of songs and arias.

1995 was a landmark year for Elly Ameling. She retired from music, her last record was released, and her very first records were re-released. The recordings gave critics the opportunity to look at her career in overview. *Elly Ameling: The Early Recordings, 1964-1968,* a four CD set, showed her at her best for many critics. David

Sources

Books

Orey, Leslie (ed.). *The Encyclopedia of Opera,* Charles Scribner and Sons, New York, 1976.

Periodicals

BBC Music, October 1995.
Classical FM, October 1995.
Classical Pulse!, December 1995.
Gramophone, Ii 1974.
New York Observer, July 23, 1995.
Opera Now, October 1995.

—B. Kimberly Taylor

Vanessa Bell Armstrong

Singer

Phot by Eric von Lockhart, reproduced by permission ©

Singer Vanessa Bell Armstrong has been praised for her r&b-flavored contemporary gospel music and has met with success in both the gospel and secular realms. She has often been compared with another Detroit native, Aretha Franklin. At times, Armstrong has stretched so far afield of "traditional" gospel music that in the 1980s, she was at times considered too contemporary for gospel. *Billboard*, in a 1998 review of *Desire Of My Heart—"Live,"* wrote, "A lot has changed [since 1988] and Armstrong has stood her ground, emerging with a work that is the perfect summation of gospel's rich history and its cutting-edge presence in the mix of today's R&B music.... It took a while, but the world seems to be catching up to Armstrong."

Vanessa Bell was born in Detroit, Michigan on October 2, 1953. She was raised in the Church of God in Christ, a denomination that had nurtured other gospel greats such as BeBe and CeCe Winans, Andre Crouch, Edwin, Walter and Tramaine Hawkins, and others. In 1957, when she was four years old, Vanessa began traveling with her mother, singing in various churches in the Detroit area, singing. It was clear even at that young age that she had both remarkable stage presence and the vocal control of someone considerably older.

In 1966, when she was thirteen years old, Vanessa was discovered by Dr. Mattie Moss Clark. Clark became her mentor. She began traveling with Clark, singing in her various choirs and sharing the stage with such gospel titans as Rev. James Cleveland, the Mighty Clouds of Joy, the Clark Sisters, and the Winans. Other early influences included Marion Williams, Mahalia Jackson, Inez Andrews, and Aretha Franklin. Armstrong's first recording experience was an appearance on Donald O'Connor's 1981 release, *Bring Back Birdie*. Her own recording career began in 1984 when, at the age of 31, she signed with the Onyx label and released *Peace Be Still*.

Career Took Off

In 1987 Armstrong's career took off in earnest. She beat out stiff competition—including the likes of Aretha Franklin and Patti LaBelle—for the chance to record the theme song for the popular television sit-com *Amen*. Armstrong had her Broadway debut in 1987, captivating audiences in the musical *Don't Get God Started*. She also made a guest appearance on Tom Jones' *Move Closer*.

When she signed with Jive Records in 1987, Armstrong began a period of prolific recording activity. Her eponymous album, *Vanessa Bell Armstrong,* released in 1987, yielded the crossover r&b hit, "You Bring Out the

Born Vanessa Bell on October 2, 1953, in Detroit, MI; daughter of Jesse Bell, a minister; married with five children.

Began singing in various Detroit area churches at the age of four; discovered at the age of thirteen by Dr. Mattie Moss Clark; sang with gospel performers such as Rev. James Cleveland, the Mighty Clouds of Joy, the Clark Sisters, and the Winans as a teenager; appeared on Donald O'Connor's 1981 release, *Bring Back Birdie;* released *Peace Be Still* in 1984; released *Vanessa Bell Armstrong* album in 1987; recorded the theme for the television sitcom *Amen* in 1987; appeared in the Broadway musical *Don't Get God Started* in 1987; appeared on Tom Jones' *Move Closer* in 1988; released *Wonderful One* in 1990; released *Greatest Hits* and *The Truth About Christmas* in 1990; released *Chosen* in 1991; released *Something On The Inside* in 1993; released *The Secret is Out* in 1995; released *Desire of My Heart: Live in Detroit* in 1998; featured on the 1995 compilation *A Tribute to Rosa Parks,* on John P. Kee's 1994 release, *Color Blind,* and on Kee's 1995 release, *Stand.*

Addresses: *Record company*—BMG Entertainment/ Verity Records, 1540 Broadway, New York, NY 10019, (212) 930-4000.

Best in Me". Her 1990 release, *Wonderful One,* featured a duet, entitled, "True Love Never Fails," with Jive labelmate jazz guitarist Jonathan Butler. The track was also included on Butler's acclaimed *More Than Friends* album. In 1990, Jive released a CD of Armstrong's greatest hits album along with the highly praised *Truth About Christmas.* In 1991 *Chosen* was released.

The multi-talented Armstrong branched out even further afield of gospel music in the late 1980s when she appeared with Oprah Winfrey in the *Women of Brewster Place,* a made-for-TV movie which enjoyed widespread critical acclaim. Armstrong continued her brisk recording pace; she released *Something On The Inside* in 1993, *The Secret is Out* in 1995, and her first live album, *Desire of My Heart: "Live"* in 1998. Armstrong was a featured guest on the 1995 compilation release *A Tribute to Rosa Parks,* and on two John P. Kee CDs, the 1994, *Color Blind,* and the 1995 , *Stand.*

Continual Spiritual and Artistic Growth

Armstrong has continually expanded her horizons and her audience, performing on Broadway and releasing eclectic, contemporary albums such as *Truth About Christmas, Something on the Inside,* and *The Secret is Out.* Mainstream entertainment and her music has been praised figures such as Oprah Winfrey, Anita Baker, Luther Vandross, Sheryl Lee Ralph, and Tisha Campbell; artists such as Sandra Crouch and Donna McElroy have found musical guidance and inspiration in Armstrong's music and career.

Desire of My Heart—"Live," released in 1998 on the Verity label, was recorded in Detroit's Perfecting Church, and accompanied by a live video shot during the recording session. The recording shows the spiritual and artistic growth Armstrong has undergone over the course of her career. Its title track was the first song she wrote herself. And while recording the album, Armstrong reconfirmed her life's desire, above all else, to please God. Armstrong was the record's co-producer, also a first for her.

She decided to release a live recording for two reasons: her fans had wanted one for some time, and Armstrong felt it would be a new challenge. Recording in a studio afforded her a relaxed, comfortable atmosphere; the live CD brought Armstrong's fans into the recording process and reproduced the concert experience. The CD was something of a family affair—her father, Elder Jesse Bell, contributed the track "Labor In Vain." Joining Armstrong on the live recording were the Perfected Praise Choir; Perfecting Church pastor Marvin Winans sang with Armstrong and the choir on the powerhouse track "He Is Lord."

An Enduring Classic

Armstrong's career has flourished throughout the 1980s and 1990s, and gives every indication that she will continue to challenge herself and delight listeners. *Billboard*'s gospel reviewer brimmed with praise for the live CD, calling it "an enduring classic." Darren K. Greggs of *Love Express* wrote, "It's always a pleasure to see someone continue to grow in their ministry, and that's just what sister Vanessa Bell Armstrong appears to have done. The evidence is manifested in ... *Desire of My Heart—Live.* Each song on this one is powerful and displays the talent that sister Vanessa returns to God in his service."

Whether singing urban contemporary ballads, secular material, powerhouse gospel tracks, or television theme songs, Broadway hits, or forging into completely new territory, Vanessa Bell Armstrong will continue to astound her fans and to test the limits of her seemingly boundless talent.

Selected discography

Peace Be Still, Benson, 1984.
Vanessa Bell Armstrong, Jive/Novus, 1987.
Wonderful One, Jive/Novus, 1990.
The Truth About Christmas, BMG, 1990.
Chosen, Onyx, 1991.*Something On The Inside,* Jive/Novus. 1993.
Malaco's Greatest Gospel Hits: Vol. 2, Malaco, 1995.
Desire Of My Heart—"Live," Verity, 1998.

Sources

Periodicals

Billboard, May 30, 1998.
Love Express, 1998.

Online

All-Media Guide: http://www.amg.com

Additional information provided by the publicity department at Verity Records.

—B. Kimberly Taylor

Ralph Bass

Record company executive, producer

Record company executive, producer, talent scout, and R&B pioneer Ralph Bass was aptly described by Rolling Stone's David Fricke as one of "the great starmakers of early rock & roll," a "master talent scout," and a "prolific producer" who left his own indelible stamp on the charts of pop music history. During his long and successful career as a producer and Artist & Repretoire (A&R) man for the Savoy, King/Federal, and Chess record labels, Bass was instrumental in discovering, recording, and nurturing the talents of James Brown, Hank Ballard and the Midnighters, Etta James, Moms Mabley, Johnny Otis, Little Esther Phillips, Sonny Boy Williamson, Howlin' Wolf, Clara Ward, and Muddy Waters. Fricke wrote, "During the Fifties and Sixties, Ralph Bass was one of the most successful producers and talent spotters in the independent record industry." After hearing James Brown's demo tape, which included "Please, Please, Please," Bass quickly signed Brown to King Records in 1956, after driving as fast as possible to Macon, Georgia, through a torrential rainfall in order to arrive before Leonard Chess of Chess Records to the punch. In a late 1980s interview with *Contemporary Musicians*, Bass recalled seeing Brown perform for the first time in a small club in Georgia, crawling on his belly up to women in the audience and moaning, "Please, Please, Please Me." Bass rolled his eyes, and exclaimed as though it had happened the day before, "The women were shrieking with delight! Some looked like they were going to pass out. I knew I had struck gold."

Bass was born on May 1, 1911, to Ralph and Lena (Blaus). He was raised in a liberal Jewish family in the Bronx borough of New York City. He played the violin in high school and later worked as a violinist in various New York society bands. He attended Colgate University and New York University. Bass married Alice Robbins in 1933. They had three children: Michael, Dennis, and Joanne Patricia. He grew interested in jazz and relocated to the west coast, where he took odd jobs to support his family. He worked as a part-time DJ, liquor store owner and operator, and salesman for the Arrowhead and Puritas Water Company before joining Black & White Records as talent scout and producer in the late 1930s. At Black & White, he produced such astoundingly talented musicians such as Dexter Gordon, Lena Horne, and T-Bone Walker. His first major hit was Jack McVea's "Open the Door Richard" in 1947. He later went on to produce the music of Erroll Garner, Dizzy Gillespie, Charles Mingus, and Charlie Parker while at Black & White. He racked up numerous r&b hits when he joined Savoy Records in 1948 as their west coast A&R man. At Savoy, he produced recordings by Brownie McGee, Jay McNeely, Johnny Otis, Little Esther Phillips, and Mel Walker. Bass produced three of the top ten biggest r&b

For the Record . . .

Born May 1, 1911, son of Ralph and Lena (Blaus) Bass; raised in the Bronx borough of New York City; played the violin in high school; married, Alice Robbins, 1933; married, Shirley Hall, 1960; children: (by first marriage) Michael, Dennis, and Joanne Patricia. *Education:* Colgate University, New York University.

Worked as a part-time DJ, liquor store owner and operator, salesman for the Arrowhead and Puritas Water Company in Los Angeles, CA, joined Black & White Records as a talent scout and producer, late 1930s; produced Dexter Gordon, Lena Horne, and T-Bone Walker at Black & White; first hit was Jack McVea's "Open the Door Richard," 1947; produced Erroll Garner, Dizzy Gillespie, Charles Mingus, and Charlie Parker; joined Savoy Records, 1948 as their west coast A&R man; produced recordings by Brownie McGee, Jay McNeely, Johnny Otis, Little Esther Phillips, and Mel Walker; toured the South with the Johnny Otis Revue; produced Johnny Otis, 1949; returned to New York City, 1951 to head A&R department at King Records; oversaw creation of the King subsidiary, Federal Records; recorded "Sixty Minute Man" by Billy Ward and The Dominoes, "Work With Me Annie" by Hank Ballard and the Midnighters; signed James Brown to Federal Records, 1956; moved to Chess Records in Chicago, 1960 as a staff producer; produced hits by Etta James, Ramsey Lewis, Sonny Boy Williamson, Howlin' Wolf, Muddy Waters, and The Violinaires; Chess records dissolved in 1976; Bass worked as an independent record producer after 1976.

Awards: Inducted into the Rock and Roll Hall of Fame, 1991.

Addresses: *Home*—601 East 32nd Street, Apt. 500, Chicago, ILL 60616; *Office*—2411 S. Michigan Ave, Chicago, IL 60616.

hits of the 1950s with Johnny Otis, Little Esther, and Mel Walker. After touring the South with the Johnny Otis Revue and producing Johnny Otis' material in 1949, Bass decided he preferred the raw earthiness of the blues to the the jazz of his New York City youth. His tour of the South with Otis also opened his eyes to the racism that many black musicians experienced at the time. As a white man, Bass, hadn't fully comprehended the racism until he witnessed it on the tour. The blues, r&b, earthy rock and roll, and gospel were all novel and exciting to Bass. Determined to follow his musical interests, he returned to New York City in 1951 as head of the A&R department at King Records.

While at King Records, Bass oversaw the creation of the King subsidiary, Federal Records. There he recorded "Sixty Minute Man" by Billy Ward and The Dominoes, material by the Five Royales, and the notorious "Work With Me Annie" by Hank Ballard and the Midnighters. Bass moved to Chess Records in Chicago in 1960, which was then the nation's seat of the urban Delta-based blues, and worked on hits by Etta James, Ramsey Lewis, Sonny Boy Williamson, Howlin' Wolf and Muddy Waters, as well as the pioneering pop- gospel group The Violinaires. As a staff producer at Chess, Bass interacted with and nurtured a vast array of talent, both established and budding. He was especially noted for his unrestrained enthusiasm. When Chess records dissolved in 1976, Bass retired to Miami, Florida, to work at the T.K. Record Company but stayed only two years in Miami before returning to his home in Chicago. Back in Chicago, he worked as an independent record producer, and devoted a lot of time to writing his autobiography—the working title of which was, *I Didn't Give A Damn What the Whites Thought.*

As a producer at Black & White, Bass produced Lena Horne's unforgettable "Call It Stormy Monday." However, his career and musical profile was heightened more in 1947 by a ribald, off-color comedy recording titled "Open The Door Richard"—based on an old vaudeville skit—that Bass cut with Jack McVea and his band. Bass admitted the recording was more a fluke than anything, yet in an interview with *Contemporary Musicians,* Bass recalled it as one of his favorite recordings. As a producer at Federal, Bass released Hank Ballard and the Midnighters" "Work With Me Annie." The single was banned but sold more than a million copies. Bass also produced the original version of the classic r&b standard "Kansas City," originally titled "K.C. Lovin" and recorded by Little Willie Littlefield for Federal Records.

Bass was inducted into the Rock and Roll Hall of Fame in 1991 where he was lauded for recording some of the greatest performers in black music. His career and success was fueled by a passion for the blues, r&b, gospel, and jazz, as well as a passion for the people who created the music. His charismatic personality and boundless zeal for life contributed greatly to his ability to work with a wide array of performers, and his tried-and-true "golden ear" for new talent gave the world some of the best American r&b, blues, and jazz in the twentieth century.

Selected discography

Produced on Federal/King Records

(by Jack McVea), "Open the Door Richard," 1947.
(by Billy Ward and the Dominoes),"Sixty Minute Man."
(by Hank Ballard and the Midnighters), "Work With Me Annie."

Produced on Black & White Label

(by Lena Horne), "Call It Stormy Monday."
(by Little Willie Littlefield), "KC Lovin," (better known as "Kansas City").

Selected writings

Bass, Ralph, *I Didn't Give a Damn What the Whites Thought,* (autobiography).

Sources

Books

Gregory, Hugh; *Soul Music*, Sterling Publishing Company, New York, 1991.

Periodicals

Rolling Stone, February 7, 1991.

Online

http://www.rockhall.com/induct/bassralp.html

Additional material was drawn from a *Contemporary Musicians* interview withRalph Bass in 1989.

—B. Kimberly Taylor

Booker T. & the M.G.'s

Soul band

The birth of Booker T. & the M.G.'s, one of the hottest r&b soul bands of the 1960s, began by accident. It started in the recording studio of Stax Records in Memphis, Tennessee on a sweltering summer afternoon in 1962. A group of studio musicians were assembled waiting for white rocker Billy Lee Riley to show. He had a recording session. Some say that he was too drunk to show up. In any case, he never arrived. So the musicians in the studio began jamming with a blues progression. Amazed by what they were playing, Stax owner and recording engineer, Jim Stewart, quickly switched on the recording machines. The resulting songs were "Behave Yourself" and its flip side "Green Onions." When released, the song "Green Onions" became a smash radio hit and a tune adopted by both white and black Americans. It hit number one on *Billboard*'s Rhythm & Blues charts and number three on the pop charts. Knowing a great gifthorse when he saw one, Jim Stewart began recording more of Booker T. and his M.G.'s. Songs such as "Mo' Green Onions," "Soul Dressing," "Boot-Leg," "My Sweet Potato," "Hip-Hug Her," "Groovin'," "Soul Limbo," "Hang 'Em High,"

A/P Wide World Photos. Reproduced by permission.

"Time is Tight," "Mrs. Robinson," "Something," and "Melting Pot," hit the charts as the group became a symbol as one of the coolest and hippest sounds of the era.

Three-fourths of the M.G.'s came from an earlier band called the Mar-Keys. What later became known as Booker T. & the M.G.'s had an initial lineup with Steve Cropper on guitar, Donald "Duck" Gunn on drums, Al Jackson on drums, Booker T. Jones on keyboards, and Lewis Steinberg on bass. This group was also unique in that it was a fully integrated band which existed in the South during the 1960s. Along with their own releases, the group remained the "house band" for Stax Records. They continued to back up practically every soul artist who recorded for both Stax and Volt Records, including musical great, Otis Redding. Guitarist Cropper was the one who co-write Redding's classic anthem "(Sittin' On) The Dock of the Bay", he also co-wrote the song "Midnight Hour" with Wilson Pickett, Sam & Dave's "Soul Man", Eddie Floyd's "Knock On Wood", and Albert King's "Born Under a Bad Sign."

Booker T. Jones grew up with a special love for music. He was inspired by the gospel sounds of the Southern churches of his neighborhood. He studied piano but later switched to electric keyboards and, when he was old enough, sought work as a studio musician. He was hired by Stax Records and began his rise as a successful studio musician. Steve Cropper came from Willow Springs, Missouri. His family moved to Tennessee while Cropper was still young. While he was growing up, he learned to not only master the guitar, but develop a unique playing style which would serve him quite well in later years.

Memphis native Donald "Duck" Dunn attended the same school as Cropper and Don Nix. As teenagers, the trio fell in love with the rhythm and blues music being played in the black nightclubs of West Memphis. They started a group called The Royal Spades with horn players Packy Axton and Wayne Jackson, percussionist Terry Johnson, and keyboardist Jerry Lee "Smoochie" Smith, and began performing wherever they could find work. This included playing in a lot of rowdy roadhouses and nightclubs in the greater Memphis area. Later, they changed their band name to the Mar-Keys and had a hit with the tune "Last Night, which was released by Satellite Records, the record company that would later change ownership and be renamed Stax Records.

The Mar-Keys were a hit on the local club circuits. They also toured across the country, playing at teen dances and various other venues. They tried to follow up with three more hits to the song "Last Night" but couldn't quite recapture the magic of that first song. Three years later, they disbanded. Dunn and Cropper resumed doing their studio work at Stax. Dunn's distinctive "heavy bottom" bass lines were used on most of the classic Stax hits. 1962 would become the turn around for the Mar-Keys. Fate seemed to intervene with Riley's no-show and Booker T. & the M.G.'s became known world over as the hottest hippest soul group on vinyl. All the while they were recording as a group, each musician still contributed their talents as session men for the whole host of Stax and Volt artists. Cropper began arranging and Dunn went on to become a staff producer and part owner of the label's publishing business.

In 1968, Stax Records was sold to different owners and Booker T. & the M.G.'s decided to take a long hiatus and go their own separate ways. It wasn't an official dissolution of the group but each member wanted to explore their own different musical horizons. Booker T. left for California, where he began a very successful career there. He arranged, produced, and recorded for Bill Withers such hits as "Use Me" and "Ain't No Sunshine." He also worked with the Jeff Beck Group, Rita Coolidge, Jose Feliciano, Al Green, Willie Nelson, and many others. Cropper left Stax soon after Booker T. and set up his own recording label called Trans Maximus. When Stax Records folded in the 1970s, Dunn parlayed his recording experience becoming an in-demand session man for various artists in the industry. During the 1970s and '80s he worked on albums for Roy Buchanan, Bob Dylan, Rod Stewart, and Muddy Waters. In 1975 tragedy struck as drummer Al Jackson was murdered in front of his own home during some very unsusual circumstances.

A brief Booker T. & the M.G.'s reunion happened in 1977. Alumni Willie Hall filled in for the departed Al Jackson, and the M.G.'s once again began recording. They released the album *Universal Language* on Electra/Asylum Records. Not long after that, both Cropper and Dunn signed up with Levon Helm's RCO All-Stars Band. It was during this period that they received a phone call from John Belushi and Dan Akroyd and the group became known as The Blues Brothers Band. Cropper and Dunn were some of the musicians who appeared as part of the Blues Brothers Band in the first Blues Brothers movie. Together with Belushi and Akroyd, they recorded and released three albums, with their first effort *One Briefcase Full of Blues* soaring to number one. At the same time, Booker T. was working on a solo career. He hit the charts with *"I Want You"* in 1981.

Another brief Booker T. & the M.G.'s reunion occurred as they reunited for Atlantic Record's 40th Anniversary concert at Madison Square Garden. This second reunion was marred by Booker T. who suddenly came down with food poisoning before his appearance. He was replaced by David Letterman's Paul Shaffer. The third get-together proved more successful. A new addition to the group, drummer Steve Jordan, filled the spot occupied by the late Al Jackson. A newly re-energized band showed up at the Montreaux Jazz Festival in 1987. Following reunions proved equally rousing. They were house band for Bob Dylan's Madison Square Garden concert in October of 1992. This spectacle had the group playing alongside a who's who in pop music, including Eric Clapton, Mike McCready, George Harrison, Lou Reed, Eddie Vedder and Neil Young. The M.G.'s performance inspired Neil Young to ask them to join his 1993 world tour. It was during this time that they released the first album in 17 years. *That's The Way It Should Be* in 1994. "The biggest challenge," said Steve Cropper to Columbia Records Press, "was to sound like Booker T. and the M.G.'s. It might seem easy but how do you sound like you did thirty years ago and still have it fresh, up to date, and technically together? I'd lay a rhythm pattern and Booker would put a melody on top of the pattern and then Duck would come in and put an incredible bass on it. Somehow we did it. We believed in it and it happened." Cropper added, "This latest album is something which comes from the heart. I think it's one of the best things we've ever done. It's all mint. It's very honest stuff and I think it has validity. We're not out there to try and rip people off, we're not selling some elixir. This is just the real guys playing the real stuff." According to Booker T. Jones, "As far as I'm concerned, the music is speaking. It's saying the things I want it to say. I feel really happy and fortunate that we can do that." Currently, each member of the M.G.'s are pursuing their individual careers. They occasionally still get together to record. In 1992, Booker T. & the M.G.'s were inducted into the rock and roll hall of fame.

Selected discography

Singles

"Green Onions", Atlantic, 1962.
"Soul Dressing," Atlantic, 1965.

Albums

And Now, Booker To. And the M. G.'s, Rhino, 1966.
Best of Booker T. & the M.G.'s (1962-67), Atlantic, 1968.
Groovin, Rhino, 1993.
That's the Way It Should Be, Sony, 1994.
Universal Language, Stax , 1977.

Sources

http://www.rockhall.com/induct/bookert.html, and the Sony Music Web Site at http://www.sonymusic.com/artists/BookerTandTheMGs_That'sTheWayItShouldBe.html

Additional information was provided by Atlantic Records and Columbia Records.

—Timothy Kevin Perry

Clifford Brown

Jazz trumpeter, composer

Many musicians and jazz music observers thought that, at 25, Clifford "Brownie" Brown had developed into one of the best-ever jazz trumpeters. Some felt that when Brown was cut down in a tragic automobile accident on June 26, 1956, he had already achieved top ranking. Despite an outpouring of shocked tributes from fellow musicians and writers at the time of his death, recognition of his unusual contributions continued to be written decades after his passing. As Michael Ullman wrote in 1985 for *Atlantic,* "Some time in 1954, when he was twenty-four years old, the trumpeter Clifford Brown became one of the greatest jazz soloists. His playing, already celebrated for its fluency and imagination, took on a rhythmic grace, an added ease at whatever tempo he was confronted with, and a variety that made his phrases billow and float as naturally as silk in a gentle wind. A brilliant melodist with a big, singing tone, Brown was playing with warmth, forthrightness, and a head-long swing reminiscent of the young Louis Armstrong." Further, as Daniel Okrent observed in *Esquire,* "Brown was as beloved as he was admired. (His death inspired not only profound mourning, but also one of the finest of jazz standards, Benny Golson's 'I Remember Clifford')."

Many have wondered how Brown could have attained not only such formidable skills but such maturity of concept at such a tender age. Some of this is attributable to his early training. Born in Wilmington, Delaware on October 30, 1930, Brown remembered, "My father played trumpet and violin and piano for his own amusement and from the earliest time I can remember it was the trumpet that fascinated me." After receiving his first horn around age 13, Brown began taking music lessons of a broad nature from Robert Lowery, a junior high school teacher and local bandleader. With much of the focus on ear training, he was introduced to the piano and chord changes.

After about three years with Lowery, including playing in his dance band, Brown began his most serious and important trumpet study with Harry Andrews, the choral and band teacher at Wilmington's Howard High School. Though a classically trained specialist, Andrews had led a jazz band in Europe during World War II. He introduced Brown to such disciplines as playing 16 or 32 bars of music on one breath and using the non-pressure method of applying the lips to the mouthpiece. Andrews told Hollie West of *Down Beat,* "When he came to us he was a good intermediate trumpet player. But he played the 'Carnival of Venice' as his graduation solo, and I mean he really played it.... He had great drive. Many times I'd be cleaning up my desk after school and he'd stick his head in and ask if I had time for another lesson. And we'd go at it." During this period Brown was immersing himself in harmony and theory, as well as learning to play the piano, vibraphone, and bass. Other examples of his determination and diligence abound. As his wife LaRue Brown Watson wrote, "We lived a lifetime during our brief marriage. We had fun and Clifford practiced. We traveled and Clifford practiced. We had a son, Clifford practiced. He even explained the music to his infant son, Clifford Jr., and practiced while holding him on his lap. By now I am sure you get the point."

Introduced to Big-Time

After finishing high school and playing some local gigs, Brown began playing twice a month in a house band in Philadelphia where he sat in with his main influence, trumpeter Fats Navarro. This also afforded him the opportunity to play with bebop icons Dizzy Gillespie and Charlie Parker, as well as trombonist J.J. Johnson and drum stylist Max Roach. It was Navarro, rather than Gillespie, to whom Brown is most often and most accurately compared to stylistically. Both Navarro and Brown achieved a beauty and fullness of tone that Gillespie, by his own assessment, never reached. All of these jazz leaders were encouraging and helpful to Brown, the young lion, none more than Dizzy.

Just as Brown's career and reputation were taking off, he was involved in an automobile accident, in June of 1950, while coming home from a gig. He was hospitalized for nearly a year, thinking that, at age 20, he might never play trumpet again. Gillespie was especially encouraging to Brown throughout this difficult period and helped see to it that the younger man returned to his horn. During this time, Brown developed his piano playing, causing his former teacher, Andrews, to comment, "He played very well for a guy who was just starting." After a year of recuperation, Brown resumed playing the trumpet with renewed vigor. He also began attending Delaware State College as a math major, later switching to Maryland State College on a music scholarship. Once he regained a reasonable facsimile of his former sound and agility on his horn, there was no turning back from music.

First Recordings Spread the Word

In 1952, while playing regularly with Chris Powell's Blue Flames, Brown made his first recordings. Though this was basically a rhythm and blues group, jazz lurked near the corners, especially when Brown soloed. These first recordings are included in Columbia's *The Beginning and the End.* Early in 1953, Brown played a series of gigs with bop composer/arranger/bandleader Tadd Dameron, with whose band he recorded for Prestige on June 11, 1953. Writer Ira Gitler, who supervised this session, is quoted by Stephen Stroff in *Antiques and Collecting,* "When Brownie stood up and took his first solo on 'Phillie J.J.,' I nearly fell off my seat in the control room. The power, range, and brilliance together with the warmth and invention was something that I hadn't heard since Fats Navarro." Brown's name was now being spread throughout the jazz community and he could practically pick his spots to play.

From August to December he picked the legendary leader/vibraphonist Lionel Hampton's band, about to embark on a European tour. Though recording outside the full band setting was forbidden by Hampton, the leader looked the other way while the energetic trumpeter led recording sessions of a sextet and a quartet; the former featured Brown as leader. He was also the nominal leader of a big band session, actually put together by saxophonist Gigi Gryce. It is worth noting that Brown's trumpet section mates in Hampton's band included Art Farmer and a young Quincy Jones, eventually to become one of music's great entrepreneurs.

Before going overseas with Hampton, Brown had led a Blue Note session with Gryce, tenor saxphonist Charlie Rouse, pianist John Lewis (later the leader of the Modern Jazz Quartet), and drummer Art Blakey. When he returned, Brown was snapped up by Blakey to be founding member of what would become Art Blakey's Jazz Messengers. This group, employing varying line-ups, proved to be one of the longest-running jazz combos. With Lou Donaldson on alto sax, pianist Horace Silver, bassist Curly Russell and drummer/leader Blakey, Brown recorded a live performance album with the precursor of the Jazz Messengers. Throughout these experiences Brown continued to practice and grow. Blakey's fiery, busy drumming, inspiring to many young musicians, seemed to lead Brown to play in a more frenetic manner than he was best suited to. The trumpeter could play with clarity and unbelievable articulation—the separation of each note—at any tempo and with whatever accompaniment. However, Brown's gorgeous tone, his controlled vibrato, his extended phrases, his floating, melodic lines—these qualities could be better served by a more musical, sensitive drummer.

Attained Perfection

By mid-1954, Roach was the quintessential bop drummer, having played and recorded with a who's who of jazz legends—Coleman Hawkins, Duke Ellington, Benny Carter, Dizzy Gillespie, Charlie Parker, et al—from the early 1940s. With his meticulously-tuned drum set, Roach drew accolades from his fellow-players for his careful listening and backing of soloists, urging them on to improved self expression. As Ullman wrote, "What Roach offered Brown was firm support and a clear, ringing sound in a relatively un-busy style. Roach is a melodic drummer. Where Blakey pounded and prodded, Roach let Brown's own melodies unravel." Working in California, and still enjoying a wider reputation than Brown, Roach encouraged the trumpeter to become co-leader of the Clifford Brown-Max Roach Quintet, which included Harold Land on tenor sax, pianist Richie Powell (pianist Bud Powell's brother), and bassist George Morrow. When Land left in late 1955, Roach convinced the exciting tenor saxophonist Sonny Rollins to join, finalizing one of the most celebrated jazz combos of all time.

Before the Quintet really took off, Brown recorded notable sides with a number of cool jazz greats, including drummer Shelley Manne, saxophonist Zoot Sims, and pianist Russ Freeman. But it was in the Quintet context that Brown flourished for the rest of his too-brief life. The two years between 1954-56 found this group producing much of the classic jazz of this era. Brown's playing became even more melodic, more communicative, without losing any of the fire of his earlier efforts. All jazz trumpeters took note, as did musicians of every stripe. Former co-principal trumpeter of the New York Philharmonic, Gerard Schwarz, told West, "I admired a number of things about him. His sound really got to me. I thought it was one of the most gorgeous sounds I ever heard. It was a fat, rich, beautiful sound. And the musical ideas seemed so strong to me. It seemed so right, everything that he did."

Celebrated for Example

Brown's private life seems to have been exemplary. As author Nat Hentoff wrote in the Wall Street Journal, "In interviews, musicians ... characterize Clifford Brown as 'sweet'—an attribute I've never heard applied to any other jazz musician." He took care of his body, eschewing the habits that ruined some of his important jazz predecessors like Bix Beiderbecke, Bunny Berigan, Fats Navarro, Charlie Parker, all of whom were eliminated by addiction to alcohol or drugs. Partner Max Roach told Arthur Taylor for his Notes and Tones, "Brownie was a human being who put in a lot of time, a hard worker. When we first got together and went to California, we were living in the same apartment for about six months until we took the group east. He was a man who put a lot of time in: that's why he developed himself so well at such a young age. Sometimes if I woke up at nine, I would beat him to the piano.... We knew we were involved in something and that work was the answer."

It was Roach who introduced LaRue Anderson to his "beautiful" friend Brownie when he joined the drummer in California. In a booklet that accompanied the Mosaic release of The Complete Blue Note and Pacific Jazz Recordings of Clifford Brown, she wrote touchingly of their meeting and of her original disdain for jazz music. Anderson was in fact writing a thesis whose purpose was to prove that jazz was not art. At one point, she took Brown to meet her classical music teacher who, much to her surprise, recognized the trumpeter and assured her that, "This man is a genius!" At about the same time, she wrote, "I also discovered that Max had not been referring to Clifford's physical beauty. [He] had recognized the beauty that dwelled within and exuded from him.... We found that we not only respected each other and shared a valuable friendship, we were also in love." Shortly thereafter, "He asked me to marry his music and him," which Anderson did in June of 1954.

After about six months in California, the band hit the road and the recording studios (15 times), soon to become perhaps the most important and influential group in jazz, Miles Davis notwithstanding. The new Mrs. Brown, and later the new Clifford Brown, Jr., traveled with the band. "Clifford believed that families should be together as much as possible.... We prowled the museums and art galleries, rode carrousels in amusement parks, went to historical landmarks and visited friends," she wrote. Happy in marriage and musically secure in a great quintet, Brown continued to grow in expressiveness and assurance. Sought out by younger players, the naturally shy trumpeter freely offered help and advice, just as he had received from his mentors, Navarro and Gillespie.

Success and Tragedy

Brown had completed an engagement in Philadelphia and was en route to the Blue Note club in Chicago to join Roach and Rollins. On June 26, 1956 Richie Powell's wife, Nancy, was at the wheel in a rainstorm on the Pennsylvania Turnpike. In the ensuing accident Brown and both Powells were killed—exactly two years after Brown's wedding date. In a *Down Beat* tribute Dizzy Gillespie said, "Jazz was dealt a lethal blow by the death of Clifford Brown.... There can be no replacement for his artistry, and I can only hope that jazz will produce in the future some compensation for this great loss to our cause." Horace Silver added, "I can't think of anyone who was more deserving as a musician and as a person."

While he was widely recorded, only one piece of film exists showing Brown playing. A 1996 *Detroit Free Press* article details the discovery by comedian Soupy Sales of a 1956 kinescope of Brown playing on his late night *Soupy's On* television show. It offers some compelling glimpses of the master at work. Though more than a generation of trumpeters has paraded before the jazz public since 1956, many with astounding technical facility, few if any have matched the full complement of talents Brown brought to his art. Equally at home on ballads such as "Stardust" and "Once in A While" and adrenaline-laced swingers like "Cherokee" and "Quicksilver," he brought a level of consistency and beauty rarely rivaled in jazz history. His compositions "Joy

Spring," "Daahoud," and "Sandu" have become jazz standards, as has Golson's tribute, "I Remember Clifford."

Selected discography

Alone Together: The Best of the Mercury Years (with Max Roach), CD reissue, Verve, 1995.
Clifford Brown with Strings, CD reissue, Verve, 1998.
The Complete Blue Note and Pacific Jazz Recordings of Clifford Brown, LP reissue, Mosaic, 1984.
The Beginning and the End (includes Blue Flames session, final night's performance), Columbia.

Sources

Books

Carr, Ian, Digby Fairweather, and Brian Priestley, *Jazz: the Rough Guide;*The Rough Guides, 1995.
Erlewine, Michael, et al, eds., *All Music Guide to Jazz;* Miller Freeman Books, 1996.
Taylor, Arthur, *Notes and Tones: Musician to Musician Interviews;* Perigee, 1982.

Periodicals

Antiques & Collecting, March, 1987.
Atlantic, December, 1985, pp. 93-94.
Detroit Free Press, July 28, 1996.
Down Beat, August 8, 1956; August 22, 1956; July, 1980; January, 1992; June, 1992.
Esquire, November, 1990.
Wall Street Journal, February 15, 1996, p. 12.

Additional information obtained from Notes for the booklet accompanying *The Complete Blue Note and Pacific Jazz Recordings of Clifford Brown.*

—Robert Dupuis

Buffalo Springfield

Rock group

The recording and performing career of Buffalo Spring field bore striking similarity to a flash fire. The creativity of Stephen Stills, Neil Young, Richie Furay, Bruce Palmer, and Dewey Martin sparked almost spontaneously in 1966, flared brightly for a brief period, then extinguished itself only two years and three albums later. Thanks to a series of debilitating ego trips and personality conflicts, the group's aspirations of achieving widespread commercial success always remained just out of reach.

Buffalo Springfield combined rock, folk, country-western, rhythm and blues, and even Latin music into what biographer John Einarson described in a 1997 article in *Goldmine* magazine as "a unique acoustic-electric folk/county/rock amalgam that would become known as the California sound." Despite its share of critical acclaim, the group's legacy is represented as much in the accomplishments of its members following the band's breakup, and in its guiding influence on dozens of other groups in the decades that passed after Stills, Young, Furay, and the others went their separate ways. "Our influence speaks for itself," noted Furay in *Goldmine*. "Crosby, Stills and Nash, Neil Young, Poco, Loggins and Messina ... [plus] the stake we smacked into the ground took root in bands like the Eagles and other California bands that came after us." A member of the Eagles, Randy Meisner, confirmed the importance of Buffalo Springfield when he said in Marc Eliot's 1998 biography, *The Eagles: Take It to the Limit,* that his career and the bands in which he played "shifted away from pure folk-rock and into the kind of newer, harder country thing they were doing."

The origin of Buffalo Springfield was akin to a rock and roll fairytale. The individual paths of Stills, Young, and Furay crossed in Canada and New York City during the mid-sixties. However, their "once upon a time" moment came on April 6, 1966 in a Hollywood traffic jam, when the planets finally aligned on all three, plus Palmer. It was nearly unbelievable, but only nine days later—time enough to find a drummer and have a few rehearsals—Buffalo Springfield opened for the Byrds, America's premier folk-rock band at the time, at the Orange County Showgrounds in San Bernardino, California.

The Texas-born Stills was the acknowledged leader of the band. He and Furay had performed as members of a large, East Coast folk group, the Au Go Go Singers. The group dissolved shortly after the flop of its debut album, *They Call Us the Au Go Go Singers.* Stills started a new group minus Furay, and met Young during a tour of Ontario. By 1965, Stills moved to California and even auditioned for the Monkees.

Young's first band was a Winnipeg, Manitoba quartet known as the Squires. After leaving school, he moved back to his hometown of Toronto and worked in some of the city's folk clubs. In late 1964, he visited New York in hopes of reuniting with Stills, who had already left town. Young did find Furay and shared one of his songs, "Nowadays Clancy Can't Even Sing." Then it was back to Canada, where Young joined Palmer and future funk star Rick James in the Mynah Birds, a short-lived group that recorded some unreleased material for Motown.

Furay remained in New York following Stills' departure for Los Angeles and Young's return to Toronto. In February of 1966, though, he flew to California based on the false belief that Stills had a new band and an opening for a singer. Despite the fact that there was no ready-made opportunity, Furay's trip brought the two musicians together again.

Reuinted in Traffic Jam

In late March of 1966, Young and Palmer headed for Los Angeles, arriving on April Fool's Day. They were tired and broke, but quickly began looking for Stills. Five days later and without luck, they sat in Young's old Pontiac hearse, stuck in a massive traffic tie-up on Sunset Boulevard and ready to return to Canada. But Stills and Furay were not far away. They were killing time

Members include **Richie Furay** (born May 9, 1944, Dayton, OH), guitar, vocals; **Dewey Martin** (born September 30, 1942, Chesterville, ON, Canada), drums, vocals; **Jim Messina** (born December 5, 1947, Maywood, CA), bass, replaced Bruce Palmer in late 1967; **Bruce Palmer** (born September 9, 1946, Toronto, ON, Canada), bass **Stephen Stills** (born January 3, 1945, Dallas, TX, married, Kristen Hathoway, two children by two previous marriages), lead guitar, vocals; **Neil Young** (born November 12, 1945, Toronto, ON, Canada, married, first wife Susan, divorced 1970; second wife, Pegi, three children, Ben, Amber, (with Pegi); Zeke (by Carrie Snodgrass), lead guitar, vocals;.

Group formed by Stills, Young, Furay, Palmer, and Martin in April 1966 in Los Angeles; signed with Atlantic Records (Atco); released three albums in its two-year existance, *Buffalo Springfield*, 1966,(reissued 1967); *Buffalo Springfield Again*, 1967; *Last Time Around,* 1968; only hit single, "For What It's Worth," peaked atnumber seven nationally in April 1967; performed final concert in May 1968; *Retrospective—The Best of Buffalo Springfield* released, 1969.

Awards: Inducted into Rock and Roll Hall of Fame, May 6, 1997.

Addresses: *Record company*—Atlantic Records, 75 Rockefeller Plaza, New York, NY 10019-3211.

in another vehicle caught in the same tie-up. Stills looked out and saw a black hearse, much like the one that he knew Young drove. A glance at the Ontario license plate clinched it. He and Furay hurried over and renewed acquaintances. During a jam session that night, an arrangement and performance by Stills and Furay of "Nowadays Clancy Can't Even Sing" left Young impressed. The four decided then to form a band.

Furay was designated the featured singer and rhythm guitarist, Stills and Young would handle lead guitar, and Palmer would play bass. Drummer Dewey Martin, another Canadian, was added days later. Rehearsals took place immediately. "The whole thing happened at hyper speed, warp drive," recalled Palmer in *Goldmine.*

During this nine-day period, the guys even borrowed a name, Buffalo-Springfield, that they saw on a steamroller parked outside a friend's home. They just dropped the hyphen. The booking for Buffalo Springfield to open on the Byrds' short, five-stop tour of southern California was arranged with the help of Dick Davis, who soon became the group's manager and had a hand in getting the band to open for the Rolling Stones' Hollywood Bowl concert in July. The Byrds' Chris Hillman helped set up a guest shot for Buffalo Springfield at the popular Whisky A Go Go. The group was soon signed for a six-week run as the house band. The public response was immediate, and Buffalo Springfield responded. "The first week at the Whisky was absolutely incredible," recalled Stills in *Goldmine.* "That's when we peaked ... when we were a band, when we lived together." Richie Furay was the centerpiece for the group's live performances. "He'd bounce from one end of the stage to the other on his tiptoes backward," recounted Davis in Jerry Hopkins' 1970 book, *The Rock Story.*

Signed with Atlantic Records

Buffalo Springfield signed with Atlantic Records, with the band's releases coming out on Atco, a subsidiary. Davis introduced the group to a management team that had handled Sonny and Cher, and who would produce the band's first album, *Buffalo Springfield.* The managers were not music producers, though. Despite initial sessions at Gold Star Studios in Los Angeles, the site for many of Phil Spector's legendary recordings of the Ronettes, Crystals, and Righteous Brothers, the Buffalo Springfield management team could not capture in the studio the excitement of the group's live performances. Members of the band wanted to scrap those recordings and start over, but Atlantic refused. *Buffalo Springfield* was released in December 1966, with "Nowadays Clancy Can't Even Sing" as the first single. It was the record company's decision to release the song as the A-side. The band expected Stills' "Go and Say Goodbye" to have that distinction.

The band's fortunes were at low ebb in November of 1966, when long-haired youths clashed with police in what came to be known as the Sunset Strip riots. Shortly afterward, at a Topanga Canyon party, Stills picked up his guitar and started strumming and singing. The title of the song was "For What It's Worth," but it would be better known by its lyrics, "Something is happening here, what it is ain't exactly clear," followed by the chorus, "Stop, hey, what's that sound, everybody look what's going down." Buffalo Springfield went into the studio the next day and, with Stills producing, recorded what would be their only hit single. Atlantic rush released it to early acclaim in California and a slow, 14-week ascent up the charts across the country, reaching number seven on the charts nationwide in April of 1967. Its impact was nationwide, too, as the tune, "the first explicit document of an unbridgeable generational chasm, helped consolidate the youth movement," according to editors Ed Ward, Geoffrey Stokes and Ken Tucker in the 1986 book, *Rock of Ages: The Rolling Stone History of Rock & Roll.*

On the strength of "For What It's Worth," Atlantic re-pressed *Buffalo Springfield,* adding the hit to the song lineup and dropping another number, "Baby Don't Scold Me." Album sales eventually reached a quarter-million. The fortunes for Buffalo Springfield should have been looking up, but this was a group which writer Jerry Fuentes would call in a 1987 *Goldmine* article, "arguably America's best Sixties rock band in terms of artistic impact, musical creativity, and psychodrama."

Young Left Band

Friction was developing among band members, especially between Stills and Young. Each sought to have as many of their own compositions as possible on an album, plus both were eager to not only play lead guitar but also to sing their own songs. Furay's role was diminished by this internal dissension. Despite having an abundance of talent, "the band quickly became a collection of individuals pursuing their own interests," wrote Fred Goodman in his 1997 book, *The Mansion on the Hill.* At the same time that recording sessions were underway for a second album, *Buffalo Springfield Again,* the group was touring the Midwest. Stills and Young would "walk off the stage ready to kill each other," recalled Davis in *The Rock Story.* Young left Buffalo Springfield in 1967, prior to important bookings at the Monterey Pop Festival and Newport Folk Festival. He returned later in the year, but a pattern was set that had bandmembers feeling it was only a matter of time before Young was gone for good, in favor of a solo career. Complicating matters, Palmer was in the United States illegally, and he soon faced a series of drug and immigration charges that would force him from the band, at first temporarily, then permanently by the time of Buffalo Springfield's third album, *Last Time Around.*

Buffalo Springfield Again was produced by Atlantic Records' president Ahmet Ertegun and released in late 1967. Despite the apparent disintegration of the group, the album has been praised by many, including writer Jerry Fuentes, as "the band's creative peak.... Every song is inspired and brilliantly performed." Highlights included Stills' "Bluebird" and "Rock & Roll Woman," plus Young's "Mr. Soul" and "Broken Arrow."

The recording engineer on *Buffalo Springfield Again* was Jim Messina, Palmer's eventual replacement as the group's bassist. In 1968, Furay and Messina were left to assemble *Last Time Around* from tapes submitted by bandmembers. Studio musicians filled in the holes. The album includes "Kind Woman," considered to be the best tune that Furay contributed to Buffalo Springfield.

Farewell Concert

A drug bust on March 20, 1968 nabbed Young, Furay and Messina. Martin had left moments earlier and Stills squeezed out a back window. This essentially served notice that Buffalo Springfield was ready to fold. The band's farewell concert came in Long Beach, California on May 5, 1968, barely two years following their first live performance. "We were good, even great," reflected Young in *Goldmine.* "When we started out, we thought we would be together forever. But we were just too young to be patient...."

Following the breakup, Martin toured with a group of session musicians under the name of the New Buffalo Springfield, but former members filed a lawsuit to halt that effort. In 1984, Martin and Palmer tried to resurrect the band as Buffalo Springfield Revisited, but there were few takers.

In 1969, Stills began performing with Crosby, Stills and Nash, a group that would periodically include Young. He also pursued a solo career and recorded with Chris Hillman in a group known as Manassas. Young maintained a long and storied solo career, often with his band, Crazy Horse. Furay joined Messina and Rusty Young, the latter a session musician on *Last Time Around,* in Poco, a leading country-rock band. Messina later recorded with Kenny Loggins as Loggins and Messina. In May 1997, Buffalo Springfield was inducted into the Rock and Roll Hall of Fame in Cleveland, Ohio.

Selected discography

Singles

"Nowadays Clancy Can't Even Sing" b/w "Go and Say Goodbye," Atco, 1966.
"For What It's Worth," Atco, 1967.
"Bluebird" b/w "Mr. Soul," Atco, 1967.
"On the Way Home," Atco, 1968.

Albums

Buffalo Springfield (includes "Baby Don't Scold Me), Atco, 1966, reissued (includes "For What It's Worth)," 1967.
Buffalo Springfield Again, Atco, 1967.
Last Time Around, Atco, 1968.
Retrospective—The Best of Buffalo Springfield, Atco, 1969.

Sources

Books

Einarson, John, with Richie Furay, *For What It's Worth: The Story of Buffalo Springfield,* Quarry Press, 1997.
Eliot, Marc, *The Eagles: Take It to the Limit,* Little Brown, 1998.
Goodman, Fred, *The Mansion on the Hill,* Times Books/ Random House, 1997.
Helander, Brock, *The Rock Who's Who* (second edition), Schirmer Books, 1996.
Hopkins, Jerry, *The Rock Story,* New American Library, 1970.
Jancik, Wayne, *One Hit Wonders,* Billboard Books, 1990.
Ward, Ed, Geoffrey Stokes, Ken Tucker, *Rock of Ages: The Rolling Stone History of Rock & Roll,* Rolling Stone Press, 1986.

Periodicals

Goldmine, February 13, 1987, p. 8; May 23, 1997, p. 18.

Online

All Music Guide, profiles of Buffalo Springfield, Stephen Stills, Neil Young, Richie Furay, Bruce Palmer, Dewey Martin, and Jim Messina; http://www.allmusic.com/
Rough Guide to Rock, The, Richie Unterberger: Buffalo Springfield; http://www-2.roughguides.com/rock/entries/ entries-b/BUFFALO_SPRINGFIELD.htme

—*Jim Wiljanen*

Caravan

Rock group

Caravan is one of the flagship bands of "Canterbury" progressive rock, a quirky, intelligent branch of English pop music history which has built a devoted following over the past three decades. The music by Canterbury artists is influenced as much by church hymns as jazz, r&b, and British Invasion pop, lending it a very recognizable, distinctive sound.

Caravan formed in Canterbury, England during the late 1960s. Its origins lie with the local band The Wilde Flowers, formed in 1964 and featuring Robert Wyatt, Kevin Ayers, and Hugh Hopper, future founders of The Soft Machine, and guitarist Richard Sinclair. When drummer and vocalist Wyatt wanted to concentrate on singing, Richard Coughlan joined as percussionist in 1965. Soon after, Ayers' friend Pye Hastings became second guitarist.

After surviving periodic turnovers in membership of The Wilde Flowers, the band suffered a major setback when Wyatt, Hopper, and Ayers quit to form the Soft Machine in late 1966. Pye Hastings became vocalist while Sinclair's cousin David joined as organist. Early in 1968, after several months of inactivity, the quartet renamed itself Caravan and began rehearsing and writing songs. Occasional live performances built a word-of-mouth following.

As Caravan's profile grew slowly and steadily, it was soon offered a recording contract with Verve Records.

The band members couldn't afford to live in London so they pitched tents outside their rehearsal hall in Canterbury. Caravan's self-titled debut album, released in late 1968, reflected a warm and accessible yet still experimental sound that bridged the gap between psychedelic rock and the emerging progressive rock sound. BBC DJ John Peel championed the band. Unfortunately, Verve closed its English branch soon after releasing the album; subsequently, its sales suffered from lack of promotion.

Caravan soon got new management and a recording deal with the better-established Decca Records. The title track to its second album *If I Could Do It All Over Again I'd Do It All Over You* was a minor British hit single, featuring a brief but brilliant organ solo, and Richard Sinclair was honing his songwriting chops as well as becoming a second lead vocalist. Richard explained the band's collaborative songwriting process to *Melody Maker*, "You could say Pye does most of the writing, but when he does something, we all put our ideas into it. Being good friends, we understand what he means."

The band followed with *In The Land of Grey and Pink*, balancing its ability to write extended, progressive suites as well as concise, witty pop songs. Unfortunately, at the band's creative and commercial peak, David Sinclair left to join Robert Wyatt's new band Matching Mole. He explained to *Melody Maker*, "I left Caravan ... because of musical stagnation. After three years of playing with the same band I felt the need to expand into other directions." Pianist Steve Miller and several horn players replaced David to give the band a jazzier sound. While the resulting album *Waterloo Lily* has its fine moments, it reflects the turmoil within the band and alienated a segment of Caravan's fans. Hastings recalled, "Caravan was beginning to lose the 'Caravan feel.' With Steve we were getting more involved with the solos than the songs."

Unsatisfied with the band's new direction, Richard Sinclair left Caravan in 1973 to form Hatfield and The North with former Gong drummer Pip Pyle and Matching Mole guitarist Phil Miller. Matching Mole having disbanded, David Sinclair was persuaded to rejoin Caravan when Steve Miller left. Multi-instrumentalist Geoff Richardson was added to the fold for *For Girls Who Grow Plump In The Night*, a return to form for the band. Because the album featured an orchestra to good effect on some songs, the band and producer David Hitchcock staged a concert in London with The New Symphonia Orchestra.

That performance, released as *Caravan & The New Symphonia*, was well received, although the band was

For the Record . . .

Members include **Doug Boyle** (joined c. 1996), guitar; **Richard Coughlan** (born September 2, 1947, in Herne Bay, Kent, England), drums; **Jimmy Hastings**, saxophone, flute, clarinet; **Pye Hastings** (born Julian Hastings, January 21, 1947, in Taminavoulin, Banffshire, Scotland; married Cathy Ross [a publicist] c. 1968; son, Julian), vocals, guitar; **Jim Leverton** (joined c. 1995), bass; **Dek Messecar** (bandmember c. 1977-81), bass, vocals; **John G. Perry** (bandmember c. 1973-74), bass; **Geoffrey Richardson**, (joined band c. 1972), viola, flute, guitar; **Jan Schelhaas** (bandmember c. 1975-78), keyboards; **David Sinclair** (born November 24, 1947, in Herne Bay, Kent, England, left band c. 1971, bandmember c. 1973-75, rejoined band c. 1979), organ, piano; **Richard Sinclair** (born June 6, 1948, in Canterbury, England, left band c. 1973, rejoined c. 1981-93) bass, vocals; **Mike Wedgwood** (bandmember c. 1974-76), bass, vocals.

Formed c. 1968 in Canterbury, England; released first album *Caravan* on MGM/Verve Records, 1968; recorded for Deram Records, c. 1970-4; recorded for BTM Records c. 1975-6; recorded for Arista Records c. 1977; disbanded c. 1981; original quartet reunited c. 1982; released *Back To Front* c. 1982; original quartet filmed Bedrock TV Special c. 1990, recorded for HTD Records c. 1990s.

Addresses: *Record company*—Cuneiform Records, P. O. Box 8427, Silver Springs, MD 20907.

several acts Arista culled that year, considered unprofitable.

The band was inactive for most of the eighties. The four original members of Caravan briefly reformed for an album, *Back To Front*, and several concerts. The quartet played live sporadically throughout the eighties and was featured in 1990 on a British television "Bedrock" special.

Throughout the nineties, Pye Hastings, when not working full time as a plant hire manager, has been leading Caravan for new studio recordings and live performances. Recently Caravan has released two albums, *All Over You*, a disappointing collection of re-recordings of classic material, and *The Battle of Hastings*, new songs that prove that the band is still a vital musical force. Richard Sinclair briefly led Caravan of Dreams, who recorded a fine album in 1991, before becoming a carpenter. He occasionally releases albums and plays concerts.

Richard Sinclair takes much pride in the town of Canterbury and the music that he had an active role in shaping. He was quoted in *Facelift*,: "I think it has got a particular sound.... We've sung it in our schools here ... I was part of the C of E (Church of England) choir: up to the age of sixteen I was singing tonalities that are very English. Over the last three hundred years, four hundred years, maybe, and even earlier than that, some of the tonalities go back.... People say 'what is the Canterbury scene?' I think you have to come to Canterbury and see and hear it."

Selected discography

(with Pye Hastings, Richard Sinclair, and Richard Coughlan), *The Wilde Flowers* (rec. 1965-69), Voiceprint, 1994.
Caravan, Verve, 1968, reissued HTD, 1997.
(By Kevin Ayers), "Singing A Song In The Morning", Harvest, 1970.
If I Could Do It All Over Again, I'd Do It All Over You, Deram, 1970, reissued, Mantra/Decca, 1995.
In The Land of Grey and Pink, Deram, 1971, reissued, Mantra/Decca, 1995.
Waterloo Lily, Deram, 1972, reissued, Mantra/Decca, 1995.
For Girls Who Grow Plump In The Night, Deram, 1973, reissued, Mantra/Decca, 1995.
(with Pye Hastings), Hugh Hopper, *1984*, Columbia, 1973, reissued Cuneiform, 1998.
Caravan & The New Symphonia, Deram, 1974, reissued, Mantra/Decca, 1995.
Cunning Stunts, BTM, 1975, reissued HTD, 1996.
Blind Dog At St. Dunstan's, BTM, 1976, reissued, HTD, 1996.

disappointed with the results. In the liner notes to *Canterbury Tales,* Richardson reminisced, "The gig seemed a bit tense and over-organized. I felt really constrained since it was a performance and didn't have any spontaneity."

Cunning Stunts, from 1975, followed Caravan's first American tour. That album and its follow-up *Blind Dog at St. Dunstan's* featured a more pop-oriented approach. In late 1977, when the band's record label, Arista requested new material and several band members were unavailable due to other commitments, Hastings persuaded Richard Sinclair to rejoin the band. Over an album's worth of songs were recorded but remained unreleased for over a decade as Caravan was among

Better With Far, BTM, 1977.
The Album, Kingdom, 1980.
Back To Front, Kingdom, 1982.
BBC Live In Concert (rec. 1975), Windsong, 1992.
Live (rec. 1990), Demon, 1993.
Cool Water (rec. 1977), HTD, 1994.
Canterbury Tales: The Best of Caravan 1968-1975, Polygram Chronicles, 1994.
(by David Sinclair), *Moon Over Man* (rec. 1978), Voiceprint, 1994.
All Over You, HTD, 1997.
The Battle of Hastings, HTD, 1997.
Songs For Oblivian Fishermen: The BBC Sessions (rec. 1969-73), Hux, 1997.
Ether Way: The BBC Sessions Volume 2 (rec. 1974-76), Hux, 1998.
"In The Land of The Grey and Pink" (rec. 1971) on *Supernatural Fairy Tales: The Progressive Rock Era*, Rhino, 1998.

By Richard Sinclair

Hatfield & The North, *Hatfield & The North*, Virgin, 1974, reissued, Caroline/Blue Plate.
Hatfield & The North, "Let's Eat (Real Soon)", (rec. 1974), on *Supernatural Fairy Tales: The Progressive Rock Era*, Rhino, 1998.
Hatfield & The North, *Rotter's Club*, Virgin, 1975, reissued, Caroline/Blue Plate.
Hatfield & The North, "Halfway Between Heaven & Earth", *Over The Rainbow*, Chrysalis, 1975.
(With Robert Wyatt), *Rock Bottom*, Virgin, 1975, reissued, Thirsty Ear, 1998.
Camel, *Rain Dances*, Janus, 1977, reissued Deram, 1992.
Camel, *Breathless*, Arista, 1978, reissued One Way, 1994.
Camel, *Echoes, The Retrospective* (rec. 1973-1991), Polygram, 1993.
Alan Gowen, Phil Miller, Richard Sinclair, and Trevor Tompkins, *Before A Word Is Said*, Europa, 1980, reissued, Voiceprint, 1996.
(With National Health), *Complete* (rec. 1976-82), East Side Digital, 1990.
(With National Health), *D. S. Al Coda*, Europa, 1982, reissued, Voiceprint, 1996.

(With Phil Miller), *Split Seconds*, Reckless, 1987.
(With David Sinclair), *Richard Sinclair's Caravan of Dreams*, HTD, 1992.
(With Todd Dillingham), *The Wilde Canterbury Dream*, Voiceprint, 1994.
Richard Sinclair and Hugh Hopper, *Somewhere In France* (rec. 1983), Voiceprint, 1996.
R.S.V.P., Sinclair Songs, 1996.

Sources

Books

Frame, Pete, *The Complete Rock Family Trees*, Omnibus Press, 1993.
Joynson, Vernon, *Tapestry of Delights: The Comprehensive Guide to British Music of the Beat, R & B, Psychedelic, and Progressive Eras 1963-1976*, Borderline Productions, 1995.
King, Michael, *Wrong Movements, A Robert Wyatt History*, SAF, 1995.
Martin, Bill, *Listening To The Future, The Time of Progressive Rock 1968-1978*, Open Court, 1998.
Schaffner, Nicholas, *The British Invasion*, McGraw-Hill, 1981.
Thompson, Dave, *Space Daze: The History & Mystery of Electronic Ambient and Space Rock*, Cleopatra, 1994.

Periodicals

Facelift, Issue 6; Issue 7; Issue 11; issue 15.
Goldmine, October 6, 1989; April 10, 1998.
Melody Maker, August 15, 1970; January 2, 1971; July 15, 1972; July 7, 1973; November 17, 1973; April 27, 1974.
Ptolemaic Terrascope, January, 1992.
Record Collector, June 1992.
Where But For Caravan Would I?, (September, 1996).

Online

www.alpes-net.fr/~bigbang/calyx.html, September 26, 1998.

—Jim Powers

Richard Carpenter

Pianist, composer, arranger

Musical prodigy Richard Lynn Carpenter is permanently etched into the memory of the American popular music scene as the creative force behind The Carpenters, the vastly popular singing duo of the 1970s and early 1980s. The Carpenters began when, at the age of 19, Richard Carpenter turned his talents to composing and arranging music specifically to spotlight the singing talents of his younger sister, the late Karen Carpenter Burris. Together the siblings experienced incredible popularity and sold millions of records. The two achieved international fame and won numerous awards until the untimely death of Karen Carpenter in 1983. Richard Carpenter successfully worked his way through the loss of his sister and resurfaced to embark on a solo career as well as to release a series of posthumous albums of music by Carpenters.

Born October 15, 1946 in New Haven, Connecticut, Carpenter began to collect records before he could read the labels. By age four he was already captivated by the world of music and began accordion lessons. He began piano studies at age eight, and although he favored the piano as an instrument he failed to impress his first piano teacher. It was Henry Will, Carpenter's second piano teacher, who noted that the boy was clearly engrossed with improvisation, arranging, and writing songs. Carpenter was particularly intrigued by musical scales and harmonies, and by the time he was 12, his musical talent was undeniable. "He was about twelve. The whole neighborhood knew that he was on his way to becoming a professional musician, even then," stated a family friend to biographer Ray Coleman. The boy hounded his parents incessantly to purchase records. He was not partial to any particular style; he loved all music. After three years of lessons, piano teacher Henry Will referred Carpenter for an audition at Yale Music School because of the boy's astonishing aptitude for music.

During his primary school years, Carpenter was not a popular student, especially in high school. His classmates viewed him as odd because of his advanced preoccupation with music, which ran contrary to the interests of his peers. Shunning sports and other extra-curricular activities, he started an ensemble of sax, bass, and drums with some friends. They developed an extensive repertoire and the ability to play on demand. At age 16, he participated in a professional recording session for a local New Haven group.

Early Enterprises

Carpenter was 16 years old when his family moved to Downey, California, near Los Angeles. He transferred to

---

For the Record . . .

Born Richard Lynn Carpenter, October 15, 1946, New Haven, CT; son of Agnes Reuwer Tatum and Harold; one sibling, Karen; married Mary Rudolph in Downey, CA on May 19, 1984; four daughters. *Education:* Yale Music School, California State University at Long Beach.

Formed Richard Carpenter Trio, 1966; forged song writing partnership with lyricist John Bettis, 1966; Carpenters sign contract with A&M Records, 1969; released singles "Close To You" and "We've Only Just Begun," 1970; released *Carpenters*, 1971; *Now And Then*, 1973; released first solo album after sister Karen's death, *Time*, 1987; second solo release *Pianist, Arranger, Composer, Conductor*, 1997; both on A&M Records.

Awards: Grammy Award, Best Contemporary Vocal Group, Best New Artist, 1971; Grammy Award, 1972; Hollywood Walk of Fame, "Carpenters Square," 6931 Hollywood Boulevard.

Addresses: *Record company*—A&M Records Publicity, 1416 N. La Brea Ave., Hollywood, CA 90028.

Downey High School where he was an average student. He learned to play the organ at the request of the pastor of a local Methodist Church. He also performed as a lounge act in his spare time while his was still in high school. After graduation in 1964 he enrolled in a music program at California State University at Long Beach, but becoming increasingly sidetracked by show business and performing, he abandoned his studies before earning a degree. He then formed the Richard Carpenter Trio with his younger sister on drums, and fellow college student Wes Jacobs on tuba. The group worked around the area in local restaurants, and for parties and other affairs. In 1966, at age 19, Carpenter entered his trio in the Battle of the Bands on at the Hollywood Bowl, and won prizes for the best instrumentalist and best combo leader. The recognition led to a short-lived contract with RCA records for the trio at the end of 1966.

During the summer of 1967, Carpenter performed at Disneyland with John Bettis as a banjo and piano duo. That partnership ultimately led to a long-time song writing and producing collaboration between Bettis and Carpenter. All the while the Carpenters, brother and sister, continued working in churches and performing at amateur night shows while Richard Carpenter gave piano lessons on the side, to finance a new piano. At one point the duo teamed with Bill Sissyoev on double bass for an appearance on "Your All American College Show." That performance earned them a commercial contract with Ford Motor Company.

The Carpenters' big break came when trumpet player and record producer Herb Alpert of A&M Records heard a tape of Karen Carpenter's voice in 1969. Alpert was determined to market the wholesome Carpenter siblings, despite the media's tight focus at that time with hard rock, hippies, and other more rebellious subcultures. Alpert signed the Carpenters to A&M records on April 22, 1969. Their first album, *Offering,* was released that same year. The album sold poorly, but Alpert resolved to try at least one more record. For their second release the Carpenters pulled an old Hal David/Bert Bacharach song from relative obscurity. The recording, "Close to You," became a number one best seller by the summer of 1970, and launched the duo into the big time.

Rapid Rise to Fame

The Carpenters next recorded a song that originally aired on a bank commercial. The song "We've Only Just Begun," was written by—then unknown—Paul Williams. Within weeks of its release, the song rewarded the duo with their second smash hit. Coleman quoted Williams's partner, Roger Nichols in reference to the Carpenters rapid success, "They [Richard and Karen Carpenter] had a frightening amount of musical talent drooling off them." Meanwhile the decision had been made to market the duo not as The Carpenters, but simply as "Carpenters." Carpenters' second album, *Close to You,* was released in 1970, and they embarked on a tour of the U.S. later that year.

While on tour they heard and were enamored with "For All We Know," the theme from the feature film *Lovers and Other Strangers*. The two decided almost immediately to record the song that became their third hit single. In 1971, "Rainy Days and Mondays Always Get Me Down," another Paul Williams song, was their fourth single to sell a million copies. Key to Carpenters' success was Richard Carpenter's talent for writing, selecting, and arranging songs to most effectively showcase his sister's beautiful and eloquent voice. In 1971 Carpenters were nominated for six Grammy awards, of which they won two: Best Contemporary Vocal Group and Best New

Artist. Noted composer Henry Mancini was impressed so much by Carpenters that he offered them a song with vocal and piano scores, to record on their third album. That album, *Carpenters,* earned gold certification and won a Grammy Award the following year.

Overworked, Overdosed

Richard Carpenter and his sister earned a reputation as a pair of driven perfectionists and work-a-holics, yet down-to-earth at the same time. Seemingly unaffected by fame, the Carpenter siblings treated the members of their entourage as equals. When Jerry Weintraub took over as manager of Carpenters in 1976, however, the group was faltering between Karen Carpenter's health problems—-she had developed the eating disorder, anorexia nervosa—and Richard Carpenter's addiction to sleeping pills. As the talented duo launched into stardom, they operated at breakneck pace, their schedule habitually overbooked: 145 concerts in 1971, plus a European tour; 174 concerts in 1972, plus live performances, television appearances, and an album; 174 concerts in 1973, plus an album and three television appearances. Additionally, Carpenter suffered a serious motorcycle accident that year. He broke his leg and his wrist, sprained the other wrist, and spent five months healing in casts, yet refused to slow his work pace. In 1974 there were 203 concerts and a trip to Japan, where the pair encountered massive crowds. Carpenters performed 118 concerts in 1975, toured Japan and Europe, and taped an album. Their schedule that year was too hectic even for the driven Carpenter siblings, and portions of the European tour overflowed into 1976.

Until that time Richard Carpenter's growing addiction to Quaaludes, a powerful sleeping medication, was not apparent. The Carpenters in fact were known to sip on iced tea during recording sessions and while working, but never to drink alcohol. At the peak of their stardom, during the mid-1970s, Karen Carpenter developed anorexia nervosa. Richard Carpenter, troubled by his sister's failing health, turned to alcohol, cigarettes, and increasingly frequent doses of sleeping pills. At the peak of his addiction, Carpenter was known to take as many as six pills at a time and then wake up in the middle of the night to take some more. In 1977 Carpenter was hospitalized in an unsuccessful attempt to quell the addition. His performance ability was affected, and by 1978 he turned over a significant share of his behind-the-scenes work to Peter Knight *for their* holiday album, *Christmas Portrait.* Carpenter lost the strength to perform. Lacking confidence and concentration, he canceled engagements. He underwent treatment again in 1979, and his health improved. Carpenters released

Made in America in 1981, a comeback album, and made a promotional tour in London. The album includes the Carpenter/Bettis hit "Because We Are in Love," written as a wedding song for Karen Carpenter who married Tom Burris in 1980. A second reunion album, underway in 1982, was never completed. Karen Carpenter's marriage quickly dissolved. She became increasingly ill and died of heart failure due to her anorexic condition in 1983.

Solo Career

After grieving the death of his sister, Carpenter released his first solo recording, *Time,* in 1987. For the next ten years Carpenter became involved in a variety of personal and professional projects, before emerging with his second solo album, *Pianist-Arranger-Composer-Conductor,* in 1997. Carpenter, as always, maintained extensive control over the production of his music. At live performances, Carpenter interspersed an assortment of newer songs, mixed with reprises of vintage Carpenter tunes from the 1970s, plus classics from other composers.

During the course of Richard and Karen Carpenter's careers, the siblings were hosted by President Richard Nixon at the White House to entertain West German Chancellor Willy Brandt on May 1, 1973. They won three Grammy awards and received a "Georgie" award in 1971 from the American Guild of Variety Artists for Best Musical Group. October 12, 1983 marked the dedication of a Carpenters square on the Hollywood Walk of Fame on Hollywood Boulevard. New Haven's Nathan Hale School presented a Hall of Fame Award "To Richard and Karen Carpenter" at graduation ceremonies on June 19, 1991, and California State University Long Beach Campus dedicated the Carpenter Performance Arts Center to the duo.

Selected discography

Time, A&M, 1987.
Pianist, Arranger, Composer, Conductor, A&M, 1997.

With Carpenters

Offering, A&M, 1969.
Close To You (includes "We've Only Just Begun"), A&M, 1970.
Carpenters (includes "Rainy Days and Mondays"), A&M, 1971.
A Song for You (includes "Top of the World"), A&M, 1972.
Now and Then, (includes "Sing"), A&M 1973.

Horizon, A&M 1975.
Passage, 1977.
Christmas Portrait, A&M, 1978.
Made in America, A&M 1981.
Voice of the Heart, A&M, 1983.
An Old Fashioned Christmas, A&M, 1984.
Loveliness, A&M, 1989.
From the Top, A&M, 1991.

Sources

Books

Coleman, Ray, *The Carpenters: the Untold Story,* HarperCollins Publishers, 1994.

Periodicals

Los Angeles Times, February 17, 1997.

Online

http://www.keyboardmag.com/features/carpnter/carpntr.shtml, (October 2, 1998).

—Gloria Cooksey

Ray Charles

Piano, singer, songwriter

Singer, pianist Ray Charles' popularity spans numerous generations. Toddlers may have seen Charles singing the alphabet with Elmo on *Sesame Street*. Teenagers may remember a catchy Pepsi commercial with Charles singing in his gravely voice, "You Got the Right One, Baby, Uh-huh!" Many adults, however, grew up listening to his blend of gospel, blues, and rock and roll songs that cemented Charles' name in the history books. He was one of the first soul stars and a major influence for musicians who would follow him. He has recorded all styles of music, from gospel to jazz to country western. A compilation of his work was released in 1997 titled *Genius and Soul: The 50th Anniversary Collection*. He has won countless awards, including 12 Grammy awards and induction into the Rock and Roll Hall of Fame. As he stated in his 1978 autobiography *Brother Ray,* "Music is nothing separate from me. It is me."

Ray Charles Robinson did not have an easy childhood. At five, he witnessed the death of his younger brother, George, who fell into a washtub in the backyard and drowned. Soon after, Charles contracted the degenerative eye disease glaucoma, which went untreated. He could look directly at the sun when he was four, and by age seven he was permanently blind. Born in Albany, Georgia in 1930, he was raised in Greenville, Florida in extreme poverty. His father died when he was ten. His mother died when he was 15, leaving Charles to fend for himself. Charles later told *Jet* that his mother had given

him valuable advice before she died. "My mom would say, 'You might not be able to do things like a person who can see. But there are always two ways to do everything. You've just got to find the other way.'"

An inkling of the musical talent that Charles embodied revealed itself when he was three as he sang with the Shiloh Baptist Church choir. At four, he sang in the Red Wing Cafe, where the owner let him play the piano. In 1937 Charles entered the St. Augustine School for the Deaf and Blind as a charity student. He studied classical piano and clarinet, and learned to read and write music in Braille, which he said gave him a greater understanding of music. He told Alan Paul of *People,* "Because in Braille music, you can only read so many bars at a time. You can't play it and see it at the same time, so your memory and understanding expand." When the death of Charles' mother left him an orphan at fifteen, he left school and joined a few dance bands in Jacksonville, Florida. He made enough money to help him relocate to Seattle, Washington where he entered a talent contest the first night he was there. He was offered a job playing at the local Elk's club, where he crooned, Nat "King" Cole style. He formed the McSon Trio, and planned his next move.

Genius Made

After playing several clubs in Washington, Charles and his trio moved to Los Angeles and recorded their first single, "Confession Blues," which was written by Charles. In 1949, Charles worried that his original last name, Robinson, would cause the public to confuse him with boxer Sugar Ray Robinson, so he dropped it and went by Ray Charles. The McSon Trio released several singles including "Baby Let Me Hold Your Hand," which hit the U.S. R&B chart in 1951. In 1952, Atlantic Records signed Charles to a major contract and he began recording and touring regularly. His first commercial success came when he went to New Orleans in 1953 to work with Guitar Slim. Slim's "The Things That I Used to Do" sold over a million copies and featured Charles on piano. This success gave Charles the confidence to form a larger band that included saxophonist David "Fathead" Newman.

Charles achieved commercial success with his new band and Atlantic in 1954 with "It Should Have Been Me." Charles admitted to Marc Silver of *U.S. News and World Report* that he wasn't exactly an overnight success. "When I was coming up, the record people looked at the talent. I made about four records at Atlantic before I got a hit. Ain't no way I could be with a big company today and make four records that was not hits and

For the Record . . .

Born Ray Charles Robinson, September 23, 1930 in Albany, GA, to Bailey and Aretha Robinson; divorced, 1977; nine children. *Education:* attended St. Augustine School for the Deaf and Blind.

Permanently blinded at age seven by glaucoma, 1937; attended school for deaf and blind where he learned to read music in Braille and play piano, clarinet, 1937-45; left school, joined Florida dance bands, 1945; moved to Seattle to play with local bands, 1947; composed and recorded first single with McSon Trio "Confession Blues," 1949; signed with Atlantic, 1952; recorded several singles with Atlantic, including "I Got A Woman," 1954; released debut album, *Ray Charles,* 1957; recorded first million-seller "What'd I Say," 1959; signed with ABC-Paramount, 1959-1965; recorded for his own production company, Tangerine Records, 1965-73; started production company, Crossover Records, 1973; Appeared in several films and television programs.

Awards: recipient New Star award, Down Beat critics poll, 1958, 1961-64; NAACP Image Award, number one singer, Jazz Critics Poll, 1968; twelve Grammy awards including Lifetime Achievement Award, 1987; best soul and R&B artist, *Down Beat* critics poll, 1984; Songwriters Hall of Fame honorary lifetime chairman; Rhythm and Blues Hall of Fame; four gold albums; charter inductee of Rock and Roll Hall of Fame, 1986; NAFEO Leadership award, 1991.

Addresses: *Production company*—Ray Charles Entertainment 2107 Washington Blvd., Los Angeles, CA 90018.

they'd still keep me." Luckily, Atlantic kept him. Over the next several years, Charles' popularity skyrocketed as he hit the R&B charts regularly with songs like "I Got a Woman," "Don't You Know," "This Little Girl of Mine," "Drown In My Own Tears," and "Hallelujah I Love Her So." In 1957, Atlantic released Charles' debut album simply titled *Ray Charles.*

At this stage of his career, Charles' musical style was a mix of gospel and blues. His distinctively raspy, soulful voice backed by his raucous piano became a trademark in his songs, especially the romping "What'd I Say." That song was a major hit in 1959, the first of Charles' that sold over a million copies. The song crossed over to hit the U.S. popular music chart at number six after hitting number one on the R&B chart. By now, Charles was a major name in the music industry, arranging and performing with several other artists, as well as composing his own hits. He was nicknamed the "Genius," after the Atlantic release of *The Genius of Ray Charles* in 1960. That same year, Charles' version of Hoagy Charmichael's "Georgia On My Mind" reached number one on the pop charts and sold over a million copies. In 1961 Charles won three Grammy awards, two for "Georgia On My Mind," and one for the album *The Genius of Ray Charles.*

The Genius On His Way

Executives at ABC-Paramount Records took note of Charles' crossover success and persuaded him to sign with them in 1959. Charles continued his success with the album *The Genius Hits the Road,* which reached number nine on the pop charts. Three more "Genius" albums did very well in the charts: *Genius + Soul = Jazz, The Genius After Hours"* and *"The Genius Sings the Blues."* The single "Hit the Road Jack," written by Charles' friend Percy Mayfield, reached number one and sold over a million copies. In 1962, another album, *Modern Sounds in Country And Western Music,* solidified Charles' place in music history by remaining at the top of the pop chart for 14 weeks. The album included Charles' renditions of Hank Williams and Floyd Tillman songs. One of the singles off of the album, "I Can't Stop Loving You," was the year's best selling single at over two million copies.

His versatility—and willingness to take risks—allowed Charles to record many different styles of music. As he told *Down Beat,* "My music's not about pleasing critics; it's about pleasing me." Charles forays into so many different styles—gospel, jazz, R&B, pop, and country—often gave his music the reputation of being "eclectic." Charles claimed that he always had the confidence to record any music that sounded interesting to him because he always had the backing of his record companies. He told Chris Morris of *Billboard,* "The way I look at it, I have a deal with record companies. I say, 'Look, if you don't bother me about my music, I won't bother you about your marketing, because I don't know nothing about marketing, and I don't figure you know that much about what I'm doing."

Charles spent the sixties recording and touring until he hit a bump in the road in 1964. After embarking on a world tour that included shows in Japan and Europe, Charles was arrested at Boston's Logan Airport for possession of narcotics. Customs officials found heroin and marijuana. After his arrest, Charles confessed to having been addicted to heroin since the age of 15—almost 20 years of addiction! After the confession, he checked into a rehabilitation center in California and quit heroin in four days, never to go back. By the time he faced a trial in 1966 for the arrest, he was found clean and sober by several random drug tests throughout 1965. He was convicted of possession, but given a suspended sentence, a fine, and four years' probation. In 1966, Charles responded to the ordeal with the timely single "I Don't Need No Doctor."

In 1966, Charles expanded his horizons with a cameo role in the film, *Ballad in Blue*. He also formed his own custom record company with ABC called Tangerine Records. His first hit on that label was "Let's Go Get Stoned." Later, in 1973, Charles left ABC to form Crossover Records with Atlantic, his original company. He continued to influence other musicians such as Otis Redding, Stevie Wonder, Steve Winwood, and Joe Cocker, earning numerous awards and countless hits along the way. Towards the end of the 1960s, however, his musical style had shifted from the strong gospel and r&b to softer pop, jazz, and country songs.

Lifetime Achievement

In the 1970s, Ray Charles was a major celebrity, recording an album each year of the decade, accumulating awards, and making several film and television appearances. He composed songs for films and television shows, including the theme song for *Three's Company* and "Beers to You" for the Clint Eastwood film *Any Which Way You Can*. He appeared in the film *The Blues Brothers* as well as television's *Moonlighting*. While critics claimed that his music took on a softer touch, lacking the harder edge of his earlier gospel and blues mixes, his fans continued to sell out his worldwide performances. He helped compose—and performed on—the song "We Are the World" for the United States fundraising effort for Africa (USA for Africa) in 1985.

Charles long career spawned several prestigious awards. In 1979, his rendition of "Georgia on My Mind" was officially named Georgia's state song. Charles was one of the first musicians to be inducted into the Rock and Roll Hall of Fame in 1986, and in 1988 he was awarded the National Academy of Recording Arts and Sciences Lifetime Achievement Award. In 1994, Charles was honored with a twelfth Grammy Award for his

rendition of "Song for You." A 1997 collection of his hits, *Genius and Soul: The 50th Anniversary Collection,* had critics and fans taking a trip down memory lane. Some critics thought that the 101 songs included on *Genius and Soul* weren't enough. J. D. Cosidine of *Entertainment Weekly* wrote, " given the way many sets leave listeners moaning 'enough!' isn't it nice to be left hungry for more?"

Selected discography

Singles

"Drown In My Own Tears," Atlantic, 1956.
"Hallelujah I Love Her So," Atlantic, 1956.
"Georgia on My Mind," Atlantic, 1960.
"Ruby," ABC, 1960.
"Hit the Road Jack," ABC, 1961.
"Unchain My Heart," ABC, 1961.
"I Can't Stop Loving You," ABC, 1962.
"Born to Lose," ABC, 1962.
"You Don't Know Me," ABC, 1962.

Albums

Ray Charles, Atlantic, 1957.
What'd I Say, Atlantic, 1958.
The Genius of Ray Charles, Atlantic, 1959.
The Genius Sings the Blues, Atlantic, 1960.
The Genius Hits the Road, ABC, 1960.
Genius + Soul = Jazz, ABC, 1961.
Modern Sounds in Country and Western, ABC, 1961.
Modern Sounds in Country and Western Volume 2, ABC, 1962.
Ingredients in A Recipe for Soul, ABC, 1963.
Crying Time, ABC, 1966.
A Portrait of Ray, ABC, 1968.
Doing His Thing, ABC, 1969.
Volcanic Action of My Soul, ABC, 1971.
Brother Ray Is at It Again, Atlantic, 1980.
My World, Warner Brothers, 1993.
Genius and Soul: The 50th Anniversary Collection, Rhino, 1997.

Sources

Books

Crampton, Luke and Dafydd Rees, editors, *Encyclopedia of Rock Stars,* DK Publishing Inc., 1996.
Herzhaft, Gérard, *Encyclopedia of the Blues,* University of Arkansas Press, 1997.
Romanowski, Patricia, editor, *The New Encyclopedia of Rock and Roll,* Rolling Stone Press, 1995.

Periodicals

Billboard, February 15, 1997.
Down Beat, January 1998.
Jet, February 20, 1995; September 22, 1997.
Maclean's, July 13, 1998.
People September 22, 1997.
U.S. News and World Report, September 22, 1997.

Online

All-Music Guide, 1998.
Eyeneer Music Archives, 1997.
Palo Alto Weekly, (September 26, 1997).
The Rock and Roll Hall of Fame and Museum,
    www.rockhall.com, 1998.

—*Christine Morrison*

Cherry Poppin' Daddies

Swing band

Several years before the resurgence of swing music in the late 1990s, the Cherry Poppin' Daddies combined their jazz, punk, and ska influences into a sound that became the forefront of the new trend. With such a unique sound, especially in the grunge scene of the Northwest, the group resorted to recording their music on their own label, Stone Age Bachelor Pad Records. They released three albums on their own before signing a major label deal with Mojo/MCA Records. The wide distribution resulted in a surge of popularity, riding the wave of the growing swing trend. They stood out from many of the other '90s swing bands with their prominent punk influence and cerebral lyrics.

Cherry Poppin' Daddies started out in 1989 after singer/ guitarist Steve Perry decided to quit his chemistry studies at the University of Oregon. Perry had played and performed in punk bands until that time and refused to participate in the grunge scene that was developing in the Northwest. "My mother had bought me *The Smithsonian Collection of Classic Jazz*," Perry told Chris Morris in *Billboard*. "I got it for my birthday early in life, and I listened to it all the time.... Around the late '80s, I had the idea 'hey, what if I fused [punk and swing]? What would that sound like? 'Cause I didn't want to do what everybody else was doing."

Perry found a group of musicians in Eugene, Oregon that shared his interest in jazz, swing, and punk. The group started with Perry, Brian West on drums, Brooks Brown on alto and baritone saxophone, Adrian Baxter on tenor sax, Dana Heitman on trumpet, Chris Azorr on keyboards, Jason Moss on guitar, and Daniel Schmid on bass. They originally performed their shows wearing casual clothes, like a rock band. Since they had a horn section, they usually ended up playing clubs with ska bands around Eugene. "Part of my idea of not wearing suits was to contemporize swing," Perry told *Spin*'s Erik Himmelsbach, "but I don't think people were getting what we were trying to do.... It sounds really lame, but when we started to wear suits, people got it."

The band began to develop a following around Oregon, and decided to form their own record label to release their material. Their debut album, *Ferociously Stoned*, was released in 1990 on Space Age Bachelor Pad Records. Some of the songs on the album included serious lyrics with social commentary, including "Drunk Daddy." "I wanted it to be real '90s," Steve Perry told Winda Benedetti in the *Spokesman Review*. "I wanted to put the energy of punk rock and the lyricism of the '60s bands into swing."

Ferociously Stoned also included other notable tracks such as "Cherry Poppin' Daddy Strut" and "Dr. Bones." Even with their self-released debut, they began to develop limited recognition for their new, unusual style. No one could quite find a category for their sound. Brad Jones wrote in the *Denver Westword*, "The Daddies mix everything from jazz and metal to be-bop and ska into their funky, horn-drenched sound. Yet below *Stoned*'s festive surface, there runs an underlying current of corruption and mayhem." The Cherry Poppin' Daddies continued to perform throughout the country over the next four years. In 1994, they released their next effort *Rapid City Muscle Car*, again on their own label. Perry continued his lyrical intensity with songs such as "Bobby Kennedy" and "The Search."

Although they had some frustration with their limited distribution, the band refused to give up their artistic freedom to a major record label. "It's sort of like to have what it takes means you have to surrender," Perry explained to Bill Locey in the *Los Angeles Times*. "They [record companies] seem to want one of the Seven Cliches of Rock, but this is unnatural for an artist. With our own label, Space Age Bachelor Pad, we get to express ourselves. We're poor, but happy, and we want to keep doing our own thing."

Towards the mid 1990s, the Cherry Poppin' Daddies began to undergo some lineup changes. West, Brown, Baxter, and Azorr all left the group between 1995 and 1996. Sean Oldham replaced West, but was soon

Members include **Chris Azorr** (1989-96), keyboards; **Adrian Baxter** (1989-96), saxophone; **Brooks Brown** (1989-95), saxophone; **Tim Donohue** (joined, 1996), drums; **Ian Early** (joined, 1996), baritone and alto saxophones; **Sean Flannery** (joined, 1996), saxophone; **Dana Heitman**, trumpet; **Dustin Lanker** (joined 1996), keyboards; **Jason Moss**, guitar; **Sean Oldham** (1995-96), drums; **Steve Perry**, vocals and guitar; and **Daniel Schmid**, bass; **Rex Trimm** (1995-96), saxophone; **Brian West** (1989-95), drums.

Band formed in Eugene, Oregon, 1989; created Space Age Bachelor Pad Records and released *Ferociously Stoned*, 1990; *Rapid City Muscle Car*, 1994; *Kids on the Street*, 1996; signed contract with Mojo/MCA Records, 1995; released *Zoot Suit Riot*, 1997.

Addresses: *Record company*—Mojo/MCA Records, 70 Universal City Plaza, 3rd Floor, Universal City, CA 91608.

replaced by drummer Tim Donohue. Saxophonist Rex Trimm took Brown's place. He also left the band and was replaced by Ian Early on baritone and alto sax. Sean Flannery took over the tenor sax after Baxter's departure. And finally, Dustin Lanker replaced Azorr on keyboards.

Amidst all the personnel changes, the Cherry Poppin' Daddies recorded and released *Kids on the Street* in 1996. This time, they managed to get some national recognition by reaching the top of *Rolling Stone*'s Alternative Chart. The album had sold 25,000 copies as soon as it hit the streets. They also began to get better exposure by touring the United States three times and opening for bands like the Reel Big Fish and the Mighty Mighty Bosstones.

Around this same time, Mojo Records President Jay Rifkin approached Steve Perry about signing the Cherry Poppin' Daddies to a record deal. The group negotiated a contract and had a deal by the end of 1996. The following year, they released their biggest hit album, *Zoot Suit Riot*. The LP included a mixture of tracks from their first three albums, plus four new songs. Within the year, it reached platinum sales and a spot on *Billboard*'s Top 20.

Michael Dunn described *Zoot Suit Riot* in the *Tampa Tribune* as "a high-energy hybrid of swing, ska, and rockabilly that's irrepressibly danceable." The title track reached No. 18 on *Billboard*'s Modern Rock Tracks chart. Perry wrote "Zoot Suit Riot" about the riots in Los Angeles in 1943. At the time, white servicemen had randomly assaulted Hispanics wearing zoot suits, who were marked as part of the city's growing pachuco culture. "Do people know about [what it means historically]? Not many," Perry explained to Chris Morris in *Billboard*. "I get a lot of e-mail from the Chicano community and Latino community, saying that it's great that somebody addressed the riots. Bringing it to the consciousness of the public is a good thing."

The Cherry Poppin' Daddies had definitely brought their music to a far-reaching public by 1998. In April of that year, they went on tour with Los Fabulosos Cadillacs, and that summer, they played on the Vans Warped tour. By that fall, they were nominated for Best New Artist at the MTV Video Music Awards. They also recorded a cover of Harry Belofonte's song "Jump in Line" for the 1998 film *BASEketball*.

Although they were at the forefront of the trend, the Cherry Poppin' Daddies had reservations about their place in the popularity of modern swing. "We're not a retro thing," Perry said in the group's record company biography. "Swing has to be reinvented. Use the lyricism of the 1960s, use punk-rock energy, use the stuff that can't be denied and create a new thing."

Perry also expressed his fears about the direction of the swing-style genre and how it might affect the future of the Cherry Poppin' Daddies and other bands in the same category. "It's really more about the swing dancers and not about the bands," Perry said to Randy Cordova in the *Arizona Republic*. "It doesn't matter what they're dancing to, as long as they can dance. I think that will kill the scene for sure. It will be just like disco." The Cherry Poppin' Daddies had no plans to stop swinging, irrespective of the scene's fate. They played their own style of music before it was popular, and they planned to keep on doing it as long as someone would listen—and maybe even dance.

Selected discography

Ferociously Stoned, Space Age Bachelor Pad Records, 1990.
Rapid City Muscle Car, Space Age Bachelor Pad Records, 1994.
Kids on the Street, Space Age Bachelor Pad Records, 1996.
Zoot Suit Riot, Mojo Records, 1997.

Sources

Periodicals

Arizona Republic, November 6, 1997.
Billboard, March 21, 1998.
Collegian (Kansas State University), October 17, 1997.
Denver Westword, September 14, 1994.
Idaho Statesman, October 24, 1997.
Los Angeles Times, July 20, 1995.
Oregon Daily Emerald, March 14, 1997.
San Francisco Weekly, August 6, 1997.
Spokesman-Review (Spokane, WA), April 17, 1997; July 24,
    1997; October 24, 1997.
Tampa Tribune, September 13, 1997.

Online

www.bitech.com/daddies/ (September 15, 1998).
www.musicblvd.com (September 8, 1998).

—*Sonya Shelton*

Leonard Chess

Record company owner

Leonard Chess probably had as great an impact on modern popular music as any other man in the twentieth century. For his company, Chess Records, he produced and recorded the seminal Chicago blues acts of the 1950s, performers like Muddy Waters, Howlin Wolf, Little Walter, and Sonny Boy Williamson, musicians who would in turn become major musical influences on the Rolling Stones, Eric Clapton, John Mayall, Paul Butterfield, Fleetwood Mac. He discovered and recorded Chuck Berry, whose work as a guitarist and songwriter influenced nearly every rock and roll musician who followed in his footsteps. Along the way, Chess also recorded seminal musicians in the field of doo-wop, jazz, New Orleans music, and soul. His legacy is, in a word, astounding.

Leonard Chess was born Lazar Shmuel Chez in 1917 in Poland. In 1928, his impoverished family immigrated to the United States with Leonard and his brother Phil. They settled in a Jewish neighborhood on Chicago's South Side. As adults in the 1940s, the brothers opened a chain of taverns in the black South Side of the city. The most successful of these was the Macomba, a popular night club in the heart of the Black Belt that hosted the most popular black acts of the day, including Ella Fitzgerald, Billy Eckstine, and Gene Ammons. Working the Macomba every night, Len Chess became aware of the popularity of music in the black community and the lack of companies producing records for this market.

A couple of years after the end of World War II, the Chess brothers bought into Aristocrat Records, a company owned by Evelyn Aron. Chess set to work. He seems to have been the label's Artist and Repretoire (A&R) man, scouring the city for new talent. "When I first saw Leonard Chess in 1946," piano player Lazy Bill Lucas remembered, "he had a tape recorder, no bigger than that, going around from tavern to tavern, looking for talent." The first Aristocrat records were cut in early 1947. The artists on those records played the same kind of smooth sophisticated music that could be heard at the Macomba, smooth, swinging numbers, often reminiscent of big band music, like Clarence Samuels "Lollypop Mama."

This started to change when piano player Sunnyland Slim came to record with a young guitarist from Mississippi who went by the name Muddy Waters. The two played a grittier style of blues that had its roots in the blues played in the rural south. Their first sides, Slim's "Johnson Machine Gun" and Muddy's "Little Anna Mae," were ensemble blues that hearkened back to the sparer, guitar and piano based sound of old Chicago artists like Tampa Red. They were effective, engaging blues but they did not particularly light up the night.

Not long after that first session, however, Muddy returned to the studio. This time he was accompanied only by bassist Big Crawford. The two songs that came out of that session, "I Can't Be Satisfied" and "I Feel Like Going Home" were rough and raw delta blues played through an amplifier. The sound was unlike anything that had been recorded and Len Chess didn't know what to make of it. "What the hell's he singing?" he demanded and refused to release the songs at first. His partner Evelyn, however, heard something she liked in the music and pressed Chess to give Muddy a chance. He did. The record's entire first press sold out the day the record was released.

Chess began to hear Muddy's music with new ears. "Chess began to come close to me," Muddy later said, "because I was selling so fast they couldn't press them fast enough. Muddy was so successful, Chess refused to change the formula—he insisted that Muddy record only with Big Crawford, although by that time Muddy was playing South Side clubs with a full group. Chess used his clout in various ways to combat competition. When Baby Face Leroy's "Rollin' and Tumblin'"—on which Muddy played anonymously—looked like it was going to be a hit, Chess brought Muddy into the studio and had him record the song under his own name, effectively killing sales of the other record. He was able to control radio play of songs he felt competed with his artists. Later in the 1950s he got Billy Boy Arnold's "I

Wish You Would" pulled from playlists because Chess felt it was too similar to his label's "Bo Diddley."

The label grew quickly in the wake of Muddy's phenomenal success. Len Chess was astute enough to capitalize on the new sound and recruited other "down-home" artists, like Robert Nighthawk, to Aristocrat. By 1948, the company had taken over its own distribution, and in 1950 the Chess brothers bought out Evelyn Aron's share and renamed the label Chess Records. Over the next two years, Chess began a blues renaissance as a veritable hall of fame collection of musicians joined the label, including Little Walter, Jr. Wells, Jimmy Rogers, and Baby Face Leroy. By 1953, Chess had begun to break out of Chicago and in to the national charts.

Phil Chess ran the business side of the company and concentrated on recording jazz, while Leonard looked after the blues side. With his right-hand-man Willie Dixon, he supervised all Chess recording sessions and he acquired the reputation of a ferocious perfectionist who rehearsed numbers until he was completely satisfied. "Leonard would work hard," Jimmy Rogers recalled, "sometimes he overworked! You didn't go in there too often and make numbers right away y'know— he'd be turning it around there quite a while trying to get the best you have." Chess, the Polish immigrant, even insisted on playing bass drum himself on Muddy's "She Moves Me" to get the exact sound he wanted.

When Chess wasn't making records, he made forays into the South looking for new talent. The talent he found for his record company for shorter or longer stays in the early 1950s, represents the pantheon of classic urban blues: Sonny Boy Williamson (Rice Miller), John Lee Hooker, J.B. Lenoir, Willie Mabon, Elmore James, Otis Spann, Jr. Wells, Walter Horton, Lowell Fulsom, and Willie Dixon.

Chess also set up a fruitful relationship with Sam Phillips in Memphis. First an independent producer and later the owner of Sun Records, Phillips sent a number of artist Chess's way, including Rufus Thomas, Bobby Bland, and Chester Arthur Burnett, the fabulous Howlin Wolf, who became a Chess star second only to Muddy Waters.

Another record acquired from Sun was "Rocket 88" by Jackie Brenston and His Blues Rockers, a tune some consider the first rock and roll recording. It was Chess's first involvement in this kind of music and marked an important transition for the label. By the middle 1950s, the popularity of Chicago blues had peaked and was being eclipsed by rock and roll. Leonard Chess was not left behind thanks to two discoveries in 1955. The first, singer/guitarist Bo Diddley, made a single named after himself that turned out to be a smash hit.

Even more important was a young guitarist Muddy Waters introduced to Len Chess. One of his songs, with a country flavor, had already been rejected by both Decca and Mercury. Chess recorded it as a rock and roll tune in August 1955, retitled it "Maybelline," and Chuck Berry began his career as the biggest selling artist in Chess history, penning and recording a string of hits that stretched into the early 1970s. Ironically Chess turned down an opportunity to buy Sun Records from Sam Phillips in the early fifties or they would have had then—unknown Elvis Presley on Chess as well! In 1964, the Rolling Stones, still in the early days of their musical careers, came to Chess studios to record a tribute to the music of Muddy Waters, Howlin Wolf and others that had meant so much to them.

By 1960, Chess Records had seen its heyday. It continued for nearly a decade however, producing other kinds of music in addition to rock and roll and the blues that had put the label on the map: jazz, New Orleans music, rhythm & blues, and soul, by artists like Sonny Stitt, Ramsey Lewis, Clifton Chenier, Etta James and Little Milton. The last Chess blues record to chart was "Wang Dang Doodle" by Koko Taylor in 1966.

In 1969, the Chess brothers, Len and Phil, sold Chess Records to GRT. Leonard Chess died just months later, on October 16, 1969. In 1987 he was inducted into the Rock and Roll Hall of Fame.

One of the Voyager spacecraft included, as representative of earth culture, Chuck Berry's song "Johnny B. Goode." The significance of that gesture was summed up by Marshall Chess, the son of Leonard Chess: "I tell my children it's amazing that your grandfather produced a record and it's representing earth to aliens. That's pretty good for immigrants from Poland."

Selected discography

Chess Blues: 1947-1967, Chess/MCA, 1992
Chess Rhythm & Roll: 1947-1967, Chess/MCS, 1994

Sources

Books

Erlewene, Michael, Vladímir Bogdana, Chris Woodstra, and Cub Koda. *All Music Guide to the Blues*, San Francisco: Freeman Books, 1996.

Herzhaft, Gérard. *Encyclopedia of the Blues*, 2nd edition, Fayetteville: University of Arkansas Press, 1997.
Rowe, Mike. *Chicago Breakdown*, New York: Da Capo, 1979.

Periodicals

Independent, May 21, 1997.
New York Beacon, June 25, 1997, July 2, 1997.
Independent, "The Original Blues Brothers."

—*Gerald E. Brennan*

Cornershop

Anglo-Asian alternative act

Cornershop merges elements of British club music—trance beats, distorted electric guitar, sampling—with the weaving, elliptical rhythms of traditional Indian music. Its singer and songwriter offers the occasional lyric in Punjabi, his first language, and the band has evolved from an unschooled punk outfit who did their 1-2-3-4 intro counts in Punjabi, to a smooth, solidly produced modern-rock chart success. "Brimful of Asha," their 1997 single, made Cornershop huge, but they still retained much of the iconoclastic attitude that got them there in the first place. *Rolling Stone* writer David Fricke compared their body of recorded work to "serendipity in overdrive: volatile, compelling collisions of primal guitar menace, rubbery '70s funk, budget-synth techno, ... hip-hop and Punjabi folk.... Cornershop make commercially improbable, dangerously messy music."

The creative force behind Cornershop rests in Tjinder Singh and Ben Ayres, both near thirty when "Brimful of Asha" and their third album, *When I Was Born for the Seventh Time,* met with tremendous critical and commericial success. The son of a teacher, Singh was born in England into an immigrant family that hailed from the north India state of Punjab. He grew up in the Staffordshire city of Wolverhampton, in England's center, which was perhaps an even worse place to be a foreigner than London, where Singh was assaulted on the street for having a non-Asian girlfriend as late as 1995. Singh described his youth in Wolverhampton as rife with racist incidents, and "pretty terrifying" in an interview with *Rolling Stone*'s Jon Wiederhorn. "I've always lived in an intimidating rather than happy atmosphere. It's really fueled my aggression and given me a sense that I don't belong." That malaise would spark his musical drive.

As a teen, Singh had to attend temple services, where he played such traditional Indian instruments as the dholki, a type of drum. Wolverhampton's Punjabi community rented a house of worship, however, and they shared the place with another denomination whose sacred tunes leaned toward black gospel; the simultaneous auditory experience made a profound impact on him. In college in Preston, England, Singh became friends with Ayres, a Canadian by birth. By 1992, dissatisfied with what they felt was the feebleness of the British music scene, they decided to start their own band. For a time, Singh's brother Avtar was their guitarist; he later dropped out and in time, the rest of the line-up coalesced: Anthony Saffery on sitar, harmonium, and keyboards, percussionist Peter Bengry, and a drummer, Nick Simms. Ayres had to learn to play most instruments and not just the exotic ones like the tamboura, a string instrument; he later said that in the early years he played what he assumed was an acoustic guitar, only to discover it was actually a classical guitar. Singh used a range of instruments, from the dholki to a Casio keyboard he bought at a thrift store.

Blasted Morrissey

Though Cornershop was derided early on in the British music press for lack of ability, they improved considerably. Singh became proficient on an array of instruments, both eastern and western, and also produced the tracks he and Ayres wrote. As a live act, their sound was initially limited to the size of their mode of transport. "We couldn't afford to buy a van," Singh told Fricke in *Rolling Stone,* and thus only played the instruments they could fit in a car. But from the start, Singh used the band as a vehicle to address social issues. They took their name from the British slang term for the corner convenience store. "A lot of people think that all Asians do is run cornershops," Singh told *Village Voice* writer Jon Savage, "and that they're timid and they don't socialize. We want to destroy that stereotype."

Signed to the Wiiija label not long after their first performance, Cornershop achieved notoriety in England not just for their politically charged, anti-racist songs ("How Can Any Asian Vote Tory?") but for their concrete actions: they burned Morrissey posters onstage after the former Smiths' singer and cult idol emerged with a new look in the early 1990s sporting a shaved head and new album with songs construed by some as racist. Cornershop was particularly outraged about the tracks "Asian Rut" and "The National Front Disco." The band held a press conference in front of EMI Records denouncing the record and some recent remarks Morrissey had made in the media. However, Singh and Ayres were accused of trying to engineer publicity for themselves. Singh defended the acts of protest in the 1996 interview with Wiederhorn. "We felt it was required," Singh said, noting that in the eighties the gay, vegetarian Morrissey had had a profound impact on his fans' lifestyles regarding those choices. "Now he was ... [peddling] right-wing paraphernalia. Asians bear the brunt of racist hostilities in England, and we were very grieved by that."

Cult Following Grew

For several years, Singh didn't even admit his real surname, in order to protect his family from violence. The anonymity grew increasingly difficult, however, as

Cornershop found success both in an increasingly pancultural atmosphere in Britain, and a critic-driven fan base in North America. They released several EPs, and a debut LP, *Hold On It Hurts,* on Wiiija in 1994. The record attracted the attention of former Talking Head David Byrne and he signed them to his label, Luaka Bop, in 1995. A tour for their second full-length effort, *Woman's Gotta Have It*, marked their American debut in late 1995. Byrne also introduced them to mutual fan Allen Ginsberg, and with the famed Beat poet, Cornershop made an on the spot recording of Ginsberg reciting one of his poems to their music in his New York City kitchen.

Woman's Gotta Have It, recorded for around $5,000, gave Cornershop a cult following among critics and eccentric alternative music fans inside the record industry and radio. Though not all reviewers found the album a solid, cohesive effort, most adored the front and end tracks that pay homage to Singh's family's hometown in India, "6 a.m. Jullandere Shere" and "7:20 a.m. Jullandere Shere." Fricke, called them "long, droning beauties"; *Village Voice* reviewer Richard Gehr described them as "15 minutes of levitating Punjabi grunge." The record sold nearly 10,000 copies in the United States.

Catchy Tune Made Radio Impact

Iconoclastic execs at Luaka Bop decided to use Cornershop as an opening band for a diverse array of acts, from Stereolab to Oasis; they also played the 1996 Lollapalooza tour. With their third release, however, Cornershop became the headliner. Released in the late summer of 1997, *When I Was Born for the Seventh Time* and its first single, "Brimful of Asha," were instant modern-rock hits. The song was written by Singh in homage to the small Indian cinemas that once flourished in urban England's Indian neighborhoods; they played the "Bollywood" fare—action and romance movies from Bombay—that Singh remembered for their fantastic musical scores. Before the prevalence of VCRs shuttered the theaters, people used to dance in the aisles, he recalled in one interview. A singer named Asha Bhosle was one of the most popular soundtrack singers, and Singh and the other band members collect her old 45s as well as those at other Bollywood singers from this era.

As "Brimful of Asha" became a radio hit, critics found effusive praise for *When I Was Born. Billboard*'s Doug Reece wrote that with this record, Cornershop "cemented its reputation for creating brazenly eclectic tunes that are also extremely melodic," and termed Singh's voice "hypnotically soothing." The *Village Voice*'s Savage wrote that "Singh's vocals have the insistent, distorted timbre of a muezzin or Indian Bollywood star." Wiederhorn, in the *Rolling Stone* piece, called the album "a sumptuous melting pot of politics, language and music." The music press also appreciated Cornershop's sly joke of including a cover of "Norwegian Wood (This Bird Has Flown)," the 1960s Beatles track that introduced the sitar to popular rock music. Singh sings the entire song in Punjabi, an act that "brings pop colonialism full circle," remarked *Rolling Stone* critic Neva Chonin. "Even their covers are incendiary," she declared, and called *When I Was Born* "a cohesive, finely crafted LP in which the last album's low-fi funk expands into low, fat grooves."

Singh now travels everywhere with a portable DAT machine to make samples. To accompany the Ginsberg track, "When the Light Appears Boy" (on *When I Was Born*), he recorded a street band in India for some of the background. A second single, "Sleep on the Left Side," was released over the winter, but fared less well. He and Ayres have also formed a side project called Clinton. In late 1997, Ayres still had a job behind the scenes at London's Beggars Banquet Records, and bandmate Saffery was a social worker when not on tour. Singh noted in the *Rolling Stone* interview with Fricke that his full-time band duties meant he had to forgo a day job, but confessed that his parents were still in the dark about what he did. Traditional and religious, they still "think I work at Wiiija Records," he told Fricke. "I used to pick up my phone for two years, saying `Wiiija Records,' just in case it was my dad."

Selected discography

Lock, Stock and Double-Barrel (EP) Wiiija, 1993.
Hold On It Hurts, Wiiija, 1994.
Woman's Gotta Have It, Luaka Bop, 1995.
When I Was Born for the Seventh Time, Luaka Bop/Warner, 1997.

Sources

Billboard, November 22, 1997, p. 103; February 7, 1998, p. 11.
Rolling Stone, February 22, 1996, p. 32; August 21, 1997, p. 106; October 30, 1997; December 25, 1997, p. 168.
Village Voice, November 21, 1995, p. 55; September 23, 1997, p. 69; November 4, 1997, p. 74.

—*Carol Brennan*

Crosby, Stills, and Nash

Rock band

The middle to late 1960s was a very tumultuous time all over the world. Students, women, and the disenfranchised were standing up to protest against what they felt were discriminating and oppressive societies. Culture, as a whole, was swept up and into the politically and socially relevant movements of the era. Pop music was no exception. Introspection and often times politically astute observations were not only the province of folk artists, they even managed to find homes in the works of such rock artists as Bob Dylan and Crosby, Stills, and Nash. What set Crosby, Stills, and Nash apart from other protest artists were their pure and clear harmonies. Their inspired lyrics and song writing helped to set the stage for the emergence of the singer-songwriter movement of the early 1970s.

There is some debate over the exact place where the trio first met and discovered their unique knack for creating three part harmonies. It was in late 1968, either at folk singer Joni Mitchell's place or at Cass Elliot's house. Each of the members of Crosby, Stills, and Nash had achieved a good deal of success before joining up with the others. David Crosby had played with the acclaimed folk influenced rock band the Byrds. He had been let go from the band because of his headstrong personality and because his musical direction had begun to differ from that of the rest of the band. Stephen Stills had rather recently disbanded Buffalo Springfield after much inter-band strife. Graham Nash,

who had founded the English band the Hollies, was desperate to rid himself of that band amid similar musical differences. Crosby knew Stills and introduced him to Nash.

It was in Los Angeles, in late 1968, when the band first discovered their unique style of vocal harmonizing. As Nash related on their website, "When David and Stephen were singing 'You Don't Have to Cry' they were singing the two parts and they started to show off because they wanted to show me that they had worked on it very diligently. It sounded great and I asked them to sing a second time. They looked at each other and sang it a second time. Then I asked them to sing it again and I had, by then, a rough idea of what my part would be. It turned out to be nothing short of musical magic. When we heard ourselves for the first time, it was truly astounding to us as musicians that three people from such diverse backgrounds can meld and come together with that sound."

Not long afterward, David Geffen signed Crosby, Stills, and Nash to Atlantic Records. In December of 1968, Nash finally left the Hollies and began to practice in earnest with Crosby and Stills. In June of 1969, their debut album, *Crosby, Stills, and Nash*, was released. A mere two months later, Crosby, Stills, and Nash performed their second live gig at the infamous Woodstock Music and Art Fair. Neil Young joined them with additional guitar playing and occasional vocals .

Young would perform with Crosby, Stills, and Nash off and on for the next 20 years. Shortly after Crosby, Stills, and Nash performed at Woodstock, "Marrakesh Express," their first single peaked at number 28 on the American singles chart. In November, the second single, "Suite: Judy Blue Eyes" just barely missed the American top 20. Around this time, *Crosby, Stills, and Nash* was certified gold in America. The band also opened for the Rolling Stones at the ill-fated Altamont Speedway concert in California. in December of 1969, where one fan was murdered.

In early 1970, Crosby, Stills, and Nash won the Grammy Award for Best New Artist. They also began to work on their second album. "Woodstock," the first single from their soon to be released second album charted at number eleven. May of 1970 saw the release of *Déjà Vu*, recorded with Young as a full member. *Deja Vu* was certified gold in America only one week after its release. The killing of four students by the Ohio National Guard at Kent State University prompted Young to write the anti-war protest anthem "Ohio." "Teach Your Children," the second single from *Deja Vu*, peaked at number 16, in America, over the summer. "Our House," the third

Members include **David Crosby** (born David Van Courtland, August 14, 1941, Los Angeles, CA) guitar and vocals; **Graham Nash** (born February 2, 1942, Blackpool, Lancashire, England) guitar and vocals; **Stephen Stills** (born January 3, 1945, Dallas, TX) guitar, keyboards and vocals.

Group formed in Los Angeles, CA, 1968; signed to Atlantic; released *Crosby, Stills, and Nash*, 1969; released *Deja Vu*, 1970; released *4 Way Street*, 1971; released *So Far*, 1974; released *CSN*, 1977; released *Replay*, 1981; released *Daylight Again*, 1982; released *Allies*, 1983; released *American Dream*, 1988; released *Live it Up*, 1990; released *Carry On*, 1991; released *After the Storm*, 1994.

Awards: Gold certification for *Crosby, Stills, and Nash*, 1969; Grammy Award for Best New Artist, 1970; gold certification for *Deja Vu*, 1970; gold certification for *4 Way Street*, 1971; platinum certification for *CSN*, 1977; platinum certification for *Daylight Again*, 1982; inducted into the Rock and Roll Hall of Fame, 1997.

single from *Deja Vu*, hit number 30 on the American singles chart.

By then, the group had, in effect, broken up. The stress of trying to balance such diverse and dominant personalities had taken its toll on the group dynamics within the band and each member had decided to go his own way. Commenting on the break up in their website, Nash said, "We wanted to let people know that we weren't a band in the traditional sense, that we were individuals who would come together in a group dynamic and with whomever we felt like."

Crosby, Stills, and Nash's next album was the 1971 live double album, *4 Way Street*, compiled from concert recordings from the previous year. It was certified gold upon shipment in America, and subsequently topped the charts there. There would not be another Crosby, Stills, and Nash album until the 1974 compilation *So Far*, which also reached number one in America. Late in 1976, Crosby, Stills, and Nash returned to the studio and recorded their first album of new material since *Deja Vu*. *CSN* was released in 1977, and it peaked at number

two in America in August of that year. The first single, "Just a Song Before I Go," peaked at number seven in America.

Replay, was released in 1981, and in August of 1982, Crosby, Stills, and Nash released *Daylight Again*, which would become their second platinum album. It peaked at number eight, while the first single, "Wasted on the Way," made it to number nine. The follow up single, "Southern Cross," peaked at number 18. A live album, *Allies*, was released the following year. 1989 saw the release of *American Dream*, where Crosby, Stills, and Nash had reunited with Young. It peaked at number 16. Two years later, Crosby, Stills, and Nash released *Live it Up*. *Carry On* came out in 1991, and *After the Storm* followed in 1994. In 1997, Crosby, Stills, and Nash were inducted into the Rock and Roll Hall of Fame.

Commenting on their relevance online, Nash said, "I hope our musical and social legacies go hand in hand ... We only cared about being true to ourselves ... I think we were willing to put our musical lives on the line and our physical lives on the line for things that we felt very strongly about. I think one reason why people love this band is that they see three people up there who are going through the same things and the same changes the audience are going through and doing it publicly and it takes a certain amount of courage to do that. What's important is the emotional connection between us and our audience."

Selected discography

Crosby, Stills, and Nash, Atlantic, 1969.
(with Neil Young) *Deja Vu*, Atlantic, 1970.
4 Way Street, Atlantic, 1971.
So Far, Atlantic, 1974.
CSN, Atlantic, 1977.
Replay, Atlantic, 1981.
Daylight Again, Atlantic, 1982.
Allies, Atlantic, 1983.
American Dream, Atlantic, 1988.
Live it Up, Atlantic, 1990.
Carry On, Atlantic, 1991.
After the Storm, Atlantic, 1994.

Sources

Books

Helander, Brock, ed. *Rock Who's Who*, second edition, Schirmer, 1996.
Rees, Dayfdd, and Luke Crampton, *Encyclopedia of Rock Stars*, DK, 1989.

Online

"Crosby, Stills, and Nash," http://www.alpha.nl/CSN/bio2.html (October 13, 1998).

"Crosby, Stills, and Nash," http://www.rockhall.com/induct/csandn.html (September 9, 1998).

—Mary Alice Adams

Dennis Russell Davies

Conductor

It is clear that conductor Dennis Russell Davies once hoped to make his career at home rather than abroad, but the kind of professional opportunities he sought were not to be found in the United States. So American audiences have come to know his work from guest appearances, tours with European orchestras, and recordings. He moved to Germany in 1980 and has held a series of full-time positions in Europe, including general music director of the City of Bonn. His resume once led K. Robert Schwarz to dub him "a model of the modern-day globe-hopping maestro" in the *New York Times*. Davies has also forged a reputation for being an adept symphony and opera conductor as well as a passionate, uncompromising advocate of new symphonic music. Moreover, these two spheres of interest have helped to form Davies' particular style of conducting, which stresses understanding a composer's larger emotional intent rather than becoming bogged down by the myriad of small directions in a written score.

A native of Toledo, Ohio, Davies was only three years old when he began picking out melodies on a piano. His father, a factory foreman who played the piano, was thrilled by his son's precociousness and had him taking lessons by the time he was six. Davies went on to make his professional debut on the piano in a Toledo Symphony Orchestra concert in 1961 and, soon thereafter, enrolled at the Julliard School of Music in New York City. While an undergraduate student at Julliard, the young man's interest shifted from the piano to conducting and, as a graduate student he formed the Julliard Ensemble with faculty composer Luciano Berio. The ensemble performed under Davies' direction until 1974 in forums such as the New and Newer Music series at Lincoln Center, with the express purpose of presenting twentieth-century compositions.

In 1972, Davies took on the job of music director for the St. Paul Chamber Orchestra, a position he held for eight years. According to Michael Anthony in the (Minneapolis) *Star Tribune,* Davies "built the Chamber Orchestra into a major ensemble with an international reputation for bold programming." In conversation with Anthony, Davies remarked that "St. Paul was my first real job" and remembered, "Yeah, I was considered fairly far out there.... I was quite a bit younger then, and full of self-confidence, which I guess I still have, to the extent that one has it having been tempered by experience." What made Davies exceptional or "far out" was his selection of works by contemporary composers such as John Cage, Virgil Thomson, and Hans Werner Henze, which he conducted along with the traditional staples of the orchestra's schedule, such as Mozart, Beethoven, and Bach.

The conductor's success in St. Paul, however, did not translate into a more prestigious conducting job in the United States. In 1980, he accepted a job in Germany as music director for the Württemberg State Opera in Stuttgart. Ten years later, Richard Dyer remembered this transition in the *Boston Globe,* "he was the most underappreciated American conductor, about to embark for his first full-time appointment in Europe." When the conductor received his next promotion in the musical world, it was to become the music director for the City of Bonn. This post gave him the responsibility of conducting the Bonn orchestra and opera, directing a Beethoven festival, and otherwise planning the city's classical music programs. Davies evaluated the situation in the *New York Times.* "It's pretty hard to imagine a situation in the States that could compare to that.... Basically I don't have to choose between concerts and opera; my regular work is music director of the symphony orchestra, which also plays the opera. It makes for a very rounded overview." Davies remained in this position from 1987 to 1995.

Davies has often returned to the United States, leading the Bonn and Stuttgart orchestras and as a guest conductor. He has developed long-standing relationships with the Cabrillo Festival in California and the Philadelphia Orchestra at the Saratoga Performing Arts Center. From 1991 to 1995, he was the principal conductor of the Brooklyn Philharmonic, which had just been

For the Record . . .

Born April 16, 1944 in Toledo, OH; son of Harry (a factory foreman) and Lois (maiden name, Shuller) Davies; married Molly Robison (a filmmaker), later divorced; married Renate Gola; children: (with Robison) Annabel, James, April; (with Gola) two children. *Education:* Julliard School of Music, B.A., 1966; M.A., 1968; D.M.A., 1972.

Served as Norwalk, CN Symphony Orchestra music director, 1968-72; St. Paul Chamber Orchestra music director, 1972-80; Württemberg State Opera music director, 1980-87; City of Bonn general music director, 1987-95; Stuttgart Chamber Orchestra chief conductor, 1995 to present; Vienna Radio Symphony Orchestra chief conductor, 1995 to present; also acted as regular guest conductor for the Netherlands Opera, Berlin Philharmonic, Vienna Radio Orchestra, Chicago Lyric Opera, and Stuttgart Opera; Cabrillo Music Festival music director, 1974-92; White Mountain Festival music director, 1975-77; Julliard Ensemble conductor, 1968-74; Flying Dutchman Bayreuth Festival conductor, 1978-80; Brooklyn Philharmonic principal conductor, 1991-95; American Composers Orchestra music director, 1995—.

Addresses: *Home*—Stuttgart, Germany. *Office*—American Composers Orchestra, 1775 Broadway, Suite 525, New York, NY 10019-1903.

joined with the Brooklyn Academy of Music at the time of his appointment. In a 1990 *New York Times* interview, Davies eagerly anticipated the new post, saying "I hope that the image of the Brooklyn Philharmonic will become more reflective of the work that is in the [progressive] tradition of the Brooklyn Academy. You know, times have changed, and why shouldn't our cultural institutions be in the forefront of that change?" An older alliance with the American Composers Orchestra, which Davies helped co-found in 1977, has perhaps given him a greater opportunity to showcase new music. A regular conductor with the orchestra, he became the group's music director in 1995.

Programmed New Music

In the often conservative world of classical music, it is somtimes difficult to program contemporary music, but Davies has taken a firm stance on the issue. K. Robert Schwarz commented in a 1996 *Opera News* article, "[Davies] has managed to balance his dual careers in the symphony and opera worlds, and he has never allowed the conservatism of presenting organizations to diminish his enthusiasm for the new." As if to prove his resolve on this issue, the conductor told Schwarz, "They don't have to hire me, and I don't have to work for them." Throughout his career, Davies has served to introduce the works of many contemporary composers to audiences that might not otherwise seek out such music. For example, Richard Dyer reviewed a Davies-conducted American Composers Orchestra recording of compositions by Roger Sessions in the *Boston Globe,* "Davies has taken the trouble to learn the music—so convincingly that many listeners will want to learn it too. This recording will not be a best seller, but it is truly useful, truly inspiring, and that is a rare and cherishable quality." But even Davies is aware that some of his forays into unfamiliar territory are not entirely welcome. "A good healthy boo at a concert is not necessarily a bad thing. I think there's a predictability about a lot of concerts that those of us who make programs really have to avoid."

As a proponent of contemporary classical music, Davies has had the opportunity to work with many composers, an experience that has made him a better conductor all around. He commented in the *Boston Globe,* "I've also found that working with composers is a very freeing thing. You realize that you don't have to be a slave to the score. You don't want to be untrue to the score, but being a slave is just as bad. What you have to respect is the style of the composition, its integrity, and above all, the emotional impact of the music." Schwarz gave his own take on the interplay between Davies' expertise in old and new music in *Opera News.* "Davies is no extroverted, sloppy romantic, either as an interpreter or as a conductor. He wields his stick with brisk economy, and his readings of standard symphonic works tend to be unsentimental and sharply articulated. Yet their lean textures and refreshing clarity of line are in themselves distinctive. Perhaps the experience of conducting so much new music has encouraged such precision."

Made Late Met Debut

In 1996, Davies made his Metropolitan Opera debut in New York City conducting Philip Glass's *The Voyage.* It would seem fitting that Davies was selected to direct Glass's opera, because the conductor has had a long working relationship with the American composer. But at the same time, Davies seemingly still has trouble reconciling the diversity of his interests with American audiences and concert hall managers.

In a 1990 *New York Times* interview with Schwarz, he once fumed, "Really, it has to do with the fact that for the public if you do any new music at all you're a little bit unusual. And the fact is that I'm committed to new music and I'm proud of it—but I don't think it should be a surprise that I also need and want to do older music." In 1996, *Boston Globe* critic Richard Dyer remarked that Davies "remains something of a prophet without honor." The conductor found himself newly ensconced as the chief conductor of the Stuttgart Chamber Orchestra and the Vienna Radio Symphony that same year. The demands of these two jobs left him uncertain whether he, his wife soprano Renate Gola, and two children would continue to live in Stuttgart.

Selected discography

Glass: Akhnaten, Sony, 1987.
Glass: Songs from the Trilogy, Sony, 1989.
Harrison: Chamber Works, BMG/Musicmasters, 1990.
J.C.F. Bach: Four Early Sinfonias, BMG/Musicmasters, 1991.
Copland: Appalachian Spring; Ives: Symphony No. 3, Pro Arte, 1992.
Lachrymae, BMG/ECM, 1993.
Mendelssohn: Symphonies 1-3, Hebrides Overture, BMG/Musicmasters, 1993.
Plays Thorne; Roussakis; Carter, Composers Recordings Inc., 1993.
Beethoven: Symphony no 3, BMG/Musicmasters, 1994.
Trojahn: Enrico, Cpo, 1994.
Von Winde Beweint; Ct Vla, BMG/ECM, 1994.
Music Of Colin Mcphee, BMG/Musicmasters, 1996.
Sessions: Symphonies 6, 7 & 9, Pgd/Argo, 1996.
Isang Yun: Double Concerto for Oboe and Harp, Images Camerata, 1997.
Kancheli: Caris Mere, BMG/ECM, 1997.
Mozart: Symphony in D, Discover International, 1997.
Phillip Rhodes: Memory, Art, Time and Form, Composers Recordings Inc., 1997.
A Classical Portrait, BMG/Musicmasters, 1998.
Glass: Symphony no. 2, WEA/Elektra/Nonesuch, 1998.

Sources

American Record Guide, July/August, 1997, p. 22.
Boston Globe, January 18, 1990, p. 78; April 4, 1996, p. 28; August 12, 1996, p. C7.
New York Times, January 7, 1990, p. 25; July 7, 1991, p. 33.
Opera News, March 30, 1996, p. 10.
(Minneapolis) *Star Tribune,* March 21, 1997, p. 4E.

—*Paula Pyzik Scott*

Doris Day

Singer, actress

The post World War II period brought out some of the finest musical entertainers in this century, but one of those not only enhanced her career through her singing, but also with her talent as an actress in the film industry. Doris Day was born Doris Mary Anne von Kappelhoff on April 3, 1924 in the middle class Cincinnati suburb of Evanston, Ohio to first generation American parents, Frederick Wilhelm (William) and Alma Sophia Welz, whose parents had immigrated from Germany. Her mother named her Doris after her favorite silent film star, Doris Kenyon, and her professional name "Day" was suggested by a local bandleader, Barney Rapp, because she frequently sang a requested song entitled "Day After Day" and also felt von Kappelhoff was inappropriate for a professional stage name. Doris expressed dissatisfaction with the name "Day," likening it to the headliner at the Gaiety Burlesque House in Cincinnati.

Her father was a piano and violin music teacher, St. Mark's Catholic Church organist and choral master who enjoyed classical music and listening to the opera. Conversely, her mother loved the sounds of Country and Western music as well as Hillbilly tunes and later worked in the Welz family bakery. As a child she attended ballet and tap dancing schools at the Hessler Dancing School and by 1936, she and dancing partner Jerry Doherty had won a local amateur contest enabling them to travel to Hollywood and advance their careers with the presti-

gious and professional Fanchon and Marco stage show. Her parents divorced in 1934 and her mother played a dominant role in directing her career. The family returned to Cincinnati and moved their belongings to Hollywood to further advance their dauaghters' careers by touring with the Fanchon and Marco vaudeville circuit.

On October 13, 1937, the car Day was riding in became involved in an accident with a train in Hamilton, Ohio. The accident shattered her right leg and inflicted a double compound fracture. Her condition was further exacerbated during a lengthy 14 month recuperation when she fell causing additional damage to her leg. The second injury served as a catalyst for her to begin studying singing and abandoning any hopes of furthering her dancing career. She was kept away from attending school and turned to the radio where the voice of Ella Fitzgerald helped inspire her to develop her singing voice. Her mother took her to Grace Raine, a local voice coach, where she took three lessons a week. Through contacts Raine had with local radio station WLW, Day appeared in a 1938 radio show without pay. A local band leader, Barney Rapp, heard her on the air and before long, she was appearing for $25 a week at his newly opened Cincinnati nightclub "The Sign of the Drum," choosing her over 200 artists who had auditioned for him.

In 1939, Raine also encouraged her to audition for Bob Crosby's orchestra and his "Bobcats" in Chicago at the Blackhawk Club where she remained for three months during that summer. During a later Crosby gig at the Strand Theater in New York City, she was noticed by bandleader Les Brown and his "Band of Renown." She left Crosby and joined Brown where she remained from 1939 until 1941 when she married her first husband, Al Jorden, a trombonist from Rapp's Ohio based band, who had gone to New York as a member of the Jimmy Dorsey Band. The marriage was marked by frequent physical abuse, crazed jealousy and stalking. Her only child, Terry, was born in 1942. They divorced in 1943.

Day returned to Cincinnati and again appeared on WLW radio and later rejoined Les Brown and his traveling band in 1943 in Columbus, Ohio. She remained with Brown until 1946 and during that period had two number one recordings, "My Dreams Are Getting Better All The Time" and "Sentimental Journey", which eventually became Brown's theme song. She had 12 charted hits while working with Brown.

She married George Weidler, a saxophonist musician, in 1946. She also left Brown's orchestra and went with Weidler to his home state of California in search of work in Los Angeles. Eight months later she was performing

For the Record . . .

Born Doris Mary Anne von Kapplehoff, April 3, 1924, in Cincinnati, Oh; daughter of Frederick Wilhelm (a piano and violin music teacher and a church choral master) and Alma Sophia (a homemaker and bakery worker); maiden name, Welz) von Kappelhoff; married Al Jorden (a musician) 1941 (divorced 1942); married George Weidler (a musician) 1946 (divorced 1949); married Marty Melcher (entertainment agent) April 3, 1951 died 1968; married Barry Comden (restaurant employee) 1976 (divorced 1981); children (first marriage) Terry, a son, later adopted by Melcher. *Education:* Attended Hessler School of Dancing in Cincinnati, Oh. Attended Fanchon and Marco School, Los Angeles, Ca. and studied dancing under the direction of Mr. Louis DaPron. Day received vocal lessons for Grace Raine, a local voice teacher from Cincinnati, Oh.

Performed on WLW radio, Cincinnati, Oh. 1938; Joined Bob Crosby's Orchestra, Chicago, Il. 1939; Performed with Les Brown & his Orchestra 1939-41; Returned to WLW radio in 1942; Rejoined Les Brown & his Orchestra 1943-46; Signed with Columbia Records 1947 and continued her affiliation until 1972; Made her film debut with Warner Brothers 1948; Made 38 additional films for Warner Brothers, MGM, Paramount, and Universal Studios from 1948-68. host of television programs *The Doris Day Show*, 1968 and *Doris Day's Best Friends* 1985.

Addresses: Ms. Doris Day, P. O. Box 223163, Carmel, CA. 93921.

in New York and received a devastating letter from Weidler informing her that their marriage was over. She returned to Los Angeles but they could not reconcile their differences and they divorced in 1949. Weidler later played with the Stan Kenton Orchestra and formed his own band in the early 1950s.

A Star Was Born

In 1948 she auditioned for the part of Georgia Garrett, a singer in a sleazy nightclub for the Warner Brothers film "Romance On the High Seas." She won the part after singing "Embraceable You" and it opened the doors and paved the way for her to becoming a celebrated singer and the top box office motion picture star in the late 1950s and early 1960s. Two of her biggest hits, "It's Magic" and "Put 'em in a box, tie it with a ribbon, and throw it in the deep blue sea," written by Sammy Cahn and Julie Styne were major contributions to the recording industry. Her single of "It's Magic" topped over a million in sales and remained on the Hit Parade for many weeks. "Romance On the High Seas" was also nominated for an Academy Award for its film score. Sammy Cahn recalls. "I'll remember this to my grave.... We all walked into a room to see the screen tests. The first screen test was Marion Hutton's. Then came Janis Paige. Then on the screen came Doris Day. I can only tell you, the screen just exploded. There was absolutely no question, a great star was born, and the rest is history."

Over the next 20 years, Day appeared in 39 films including at least one film each year from 1948 through her last role in "With Six You Get Egg Roll" in 1968 with actor Brian Keith. She showed her versatility by playing roles in suspense films, musicals, and a variety of comedies opposite actors such as Clark Gable, Rex Harrison, Danny Thomas, Stephen Boyd, Rock Hudson, Rod Taylor, James Cagney, Louis Jordan, Robert Cummings, James Stewart, Richard Widmark, Jack Carson, Jack Lemmon, James Garner, Peter Graves, Stephen Boyd, Kirk Douglas, Ronald Reagan, David Niven, and singer actors, Frank Sinatra, John Raitt, Ray Bolger, Gene Kelly, Howard Keel and Gordon MacRae.

In the early 1950s, actor Ronald Reagan divorced actress wife Jane Wyman and began to date Day at about the time they were making the film "The Winning Team," a biography of baseball great, Grover Cleveland Alexander of the St. Louis Cardinals. They dated but Day had already changed agents in 1950 and had become involved with her new agent, Marty Melcher, who had entered in divorce proceedings with his wife, Patty Andrews, of the famous Andrews Sisters. Melcher was a one time music song plugger from Leeds Music Company.

On April 3, 1951 they were married on her twenty-seventh birthday in a Burbank, California civil ceremony. Melcher later adopted Doris's son Terry and his name was changed to Terry Melcher. The marriage appeared initially to be made in heaven but as the years passed, many thought the reason Melcher married Day in the first place was to gain control of her money. The very fine father-son relationship that began with Marty Melcher and Terry dissolved over the years and deep resentment set in between the two men.

Films Produced Top Hits

Her work in films frequently produced top hits. In 1953 Day played the lead role in the lively western musical, "Calamity Jane", and an Academy Award was given to Sammy Fain and Paul Francis Webster for their composition, "Secret Love." Day's recording made it a top hit with sales in the seven figures. In 1955 she appeared in "Love Me or Leave Me", a biography of 1920s singer Ruth Etting opposite James Cagney. Day's motion picture soundtrack recording became a number one best seller and Sammy Cahn and Nicholas Brodszky's "I'll Never Stop Loving You" also became a hit for her. In 1956, she starred in Alfred Hitchcock's suspense drama, "The Man Who Knew Too Much" and sang "Que Sera, Sera" winning an Academy Award for songwriters Jay Livingston and Ray Evans. The song became a number one hit and sold over a million copies. In 1961, she appeared opposite actor Rock Hudson in "Pillow Talk" and received an Academy Award nomination. The awards were given for best screenplay and story for this imaginative sex comedy about two people sharing a party line without knowing each other's identity. Day turned down the role of "Mrs. Robinson" in the film "The Graduate" because she felt it was not a favorable fit with her artistic talent. Anne Bancroft later went on to win an Academy Award for the role.

At the same time Day was making Hollywood films, she engaged in recording hundreds of singles and albums for Columbia Records that began in 1947 with her first 78 rpm singles through 1972 collaborating with arranger/conductors Paul Weston and Frank DeVol. During the 1950s she frequently teamed with male artists from the Columbia label including Johnny Ray, Don Cherry, Frankie Laine, Frank Sinatra, Andre Previn and her first gold duet hit with Buddy Clark, "Confess." Clark was killed in a private airplane when it crashed on a Los Angeles street the year after their big hit "Confess." During the period 1949-55, eight of her albums charted and only one did not reach the top five.

When third husband Marty Melcher died in 1968 at age 52, she learned that he had committed her to a television show without her knowledge. But the news was even worse when son Terry acting as administrator for Melcher's estate, learned that Melcher had squandered millions of dollars of her money on "hair brain" get rich schemes and she was nearly a half a million dollars in debt. Melcher had been fooled by entrusting her financial assets to a lawyer who provided false, misleading and inaccurate financial information directly leading to the losses. Broke and needing money, she agreed to host a television series the, "Doris Day Show," on the Columbia Broadcasting System, (CBS) from 1968 to 1973 and later "Doris Day's Best Friends" on CBS from 1985-86.

In 1976 she married for a fourth time to Barry Comden, who she had met at a Beverly Hills restaurant where he worked as a greeter. After a tempestuous marriage, they were divorced in 1981. Afterward, she became very interested in the welfare of animals and formed several organizations including the Doris Day Pet Foundation and Doris Day Animal League, which is located in Washington, D. C., and serves as a direct lobbying group for the welfare of animals. Day relocated to a scenic eleven acre estate at Carmel, California, which she shares with numerous dogs and cats and affectionately calls it "Casa Loco." She has been known for her reclusiveness and rarely makes a public appearance. Her contributions to the music and film industry have made her an American icon forever.

Selected discography

Albums

Day by Day, Columbia, 1957.
Sentimental Journey, Columbia, 1965.
Love Him, Columbia, 1964.
Day by Night, Columbia, 1957.
Bright and Shiny, Columbia, 1960.
Love Me or Leave Me, Columbia, 1955.
Young At Heart, Columbia, 1955.
Cuttin' Capers, Columbia, 1959.
Listen to Day, Columbia, 1960.
Que Sera Sera, Bear Family, 1994.
Secret Love, Bear Family, 1995 .
Move Over Darling, Bear Family, 1996.

Selected filmography

Romance on the High Seas, Warner Brothers, 1948.
Calamity Jane, Warner Brothers, 1953.
Love Me or Leave Me, MGM Studios, 1955.
The Man Who Knew Too Much, Paramount, 1956.
Pillow Talk, Universal Studios, 1959.

Sources

Books

Clarke, Donald, *Penguin Encyclopedia of Popular Music*, Penguin Books Ltd. 1989.
Gammond, Peter, *The Oxford Companion to Popular Music*, Oxford Univ. Press 1993.

Guiness Encyclopedia of Popular Music, Volume 2, 1992-94

Hotchner, A. E., *Doris Day, Her Own Story,* William Morrow & Co., Inc. 1976.

Laredo, Joseph F., *Doris Day - It's Magic - 1947-50* - Bear Family Records - 1992.

Laredo, Joseph F., *Doris Day - Secret Love - 1951-55* - Bear Family Records - 1994.

Laredo, Joseph F., *Doris Day - Que' Sera' - 1956-59* - Bear Family Records - 1995.

Laredo, Joseph F*., Doris Day - Move Over Darling - 1960-67-* Bear Family Records, 1996.

Lax, Roger & Frederick Smith, *The Great Song Thesaurus,* Oxford Univ. Press, 1989.

Maltin, Leonard, *Movie & Video Guide,* The Penguin Group, 1995.

Osborne, Jerry, *Rockin Records,* Antique Trader Books, 1996.

Whitburn, Joel, *The Billboard Book of Top 40 Hits* - Billboard Publications Inc. 1996.

Online

http://www.ddal.com.

http://www.ozemail.com.au/~almoore/.

http://www.geocities.com/SunsetStrip/Amphitheatre/6146/index/html/

—*Francis D. McKinley*

Des'ree

Singer

In 1994, a singer/songwriter from England named Des'ree appear on the pop charts seemingly out of nowhere with the catchy, smooth "You Gotta Be," a paean to positive thought. The song's bridge highlighted Des'ree's astonishing voice, and it went all the way to number five on the charts. Yet it was far from the first flush of success for the 25-year-old, who had already enjoyed acclaim in Europe with a 1991 debut record. Her record company also believed it would not be her last, and gave her a leisurely four years to produce a 1998 follow-up. "We're not in the business of manufacturing cornflakes," a 550 Music executive told *Billboard's* Paul Sexton about Des'ree. "Artists have their own time frame."

At the height of her newfound fame in 1995, *People* termed Des'ree "the reigning queen of New-Age cheer." At the time, Des'ree shared a home in London, where she grew up, with her mother, Annette Norma, and sister. In the late 1970s, her parents, both West Indian by birth, took their daughters from the familiarity of their south London surroundings to a new home in Barbados so that they might learn about their heritage. Des'ree lived on the island from the age of ten until thirteen, and during that time, she was exposed to dub, calypso, and other indigenous musical genres of the Caribbean. She has said that she grew up singing, and loved Stevie Wonder and Gladys Knight and the Pips as a child. As a teenager, however, Des'ree grew shy, and turned to writing to express herself. She penned poetry and then songs, some of which later wound up on her first album.

When she was 16, Des'ree dropped off a demo tape at a record company, and someone called her at home before she'd even arrived back. But she felt "the time wasn't right," as she explained to *People,* and again trusted her instinct when six years later she "woke up one morning and said [to her then boyfriend-manager], you have to take this tape to Sony Music.'" He did and it fell into the hands of the same executive who discovered Terence Trent D'Arby, and a contract was inked with Sony's British arm. Des'ree had never been in a professional recording studio before, and immediately set to learning the business of making records. She auditioned arrangers for her songs, and did her own publicity and management work, which she continued to do for some years. After the tracks were finished, Sony put her out as opening act for Simply Red, and released "Feel So High" as a single. "Feel So High" achieved great success in Europe in 1991.

Sony/Epic signed Des'ree in 1992 and released *Mind Adventures* that same year. Though an article in *Billboard* spoke of her great promise as a performing artist—reporter Michael Gonzales wrote that she "expresses a wisdom and sensitivity that reach beyond her age"—the album barely made a dent in the charts and she remained an unknown in the U.S. As Des'ree explained rather diplomatically to *Essence* writer Deborah Gregory a few years later, back in 1992 Sony/Epic "was promoting projects from established artists such as Mariah Carey, Michael Jackson and Luther Vandross, so I had to take a back seat. My music ... got lost in the shuffle." Still, she remained a moderately successful abroad; in 1993 she cut a single with Terence Trent D'Arby, "Delicate," that charted in Britain.

It was not until the planned release of *I Ain't Movin'* in 1994 that everything seemed to fall into place for Des'ree. Sony decided to include the track "Feel So High" on this album, as it was not included on *Mind Adventures.* But it was the video for the first single chosen from *I Ain't Movin,'* "You Gotta Be," that gave the chanteuse her first meaningful American exposure. Working with director Paul Boyd, the two created a stunning black and white video that managed to showcase both the singer's good looks and haunting voice. The clip began airing on the video music channel VH1 and was an immediate success in the late summer of 1994. The song, with its positive-focused lyrics, received almost no airplay on urban R&B stations despite having a decidedly soulful feel, but it was picked up by pop radio stations, further increasing Des'ree's exposure.

For the Record . . .

Born Des'ree Weekes in London, England, 1969.

Worked in a health-food store in London in the early 1990s; signed to Sony U.K., 1991; signed to Sony/Epic (U.S.), 1992; made American debut with the LP, *Mind Adventures,* Sony/Epic Records, 1992; released *I Ain't Movin,* 550 Music, 1994; single from second album, 1994's " I Ain't Movin", reached number five on the *Billboard* Hot 100 charts in 1995; released *Supernatural,* 550 Music, 1998..

Awards: Earned gold record for *I Ain't Movin'.*

Addresses: *Record company*—Sony 550 Music, 550 Madison Ave., New York, NY 10022.

The inspiration for the title track from *I Ain't Movin'* came during a visit to Barbados. As Des'ree explained to *Rolling Stone* writer Marie Elsie St. Leger, "I thought to myself, 'The most beautiful parts of the world are where my people come from—Africa, the Caribbean, the Antilles.' And I said, 'I ain't moving from my place, from my race, from my history.'" St. Leger termed the LP "a catchy blend of Caribbean rhythms, American R&B and English cool." *Village Voice* writer Lisa Kennedy wrote that *I Ain't Movin'* "inspires hope, and not just because of her humanism and well-grounded voice. In 'You Gotta Be,' she combines an earned optimism with an I-will-survive candor; its an edge that if sharpened could cut through some of her softer sentiments to the heart of the matter."

Sony/Epic put Des'ree on tour with Seal while "You Gotta Be" sat on various charts for 44 weeks. Even four years later, the song was still heard occasionally on the radio. Its video remained in rotation on VH1 longer than any other clip from an artist in the music channel's history. Des'ree then took a break after earning her gold record for *I Ain't Movin',* and recorded duets with Steve Winwood and Babyface before moving on to her next effort. She had virtually created a new niche called "urban alternative" in the music business single-handedly, but the subtle barriers circling artists, genres, and demographics in America still baffled her. "It wasn't until I was in the States that I realized how segregated the industry was," Des'ree told Sexton. "I was disappointed that I wasn't considered `black enough' for urban radio.... That's something I could never understand." Evidence of her influence was made apparent in an odd way: her music publisher, Sony Music Publishing, initiated legal proceedings against Janet Jackson in 1998 which resulted in a sizeable settlement due to the significant resemblance between "Feel So High" and Jackson's "Got `Til It's Gone."

Sexton noted that there were two other cases of copyright infringement for Des'ree's first hit in Europe seven years back, a song relatively unheard of in the U.S., in the summer of 1998. But Des'ree, positive-minded as always, was more focused on the future: her third album, *Supernatural,* was released to excellent reviews that same summer. J. D. Considine, writing for *Entertainment Weekly,* termed it a furtherance of the qualities that made "You Gotta Be" such a success, "strong melodies, engaging grooves, powerfully understated singing.... Des'ree conveys a depth and complexity that go well beyond what's on the lyric sheet."

Selected discography

Mind Adventures, Epic/Sony, 1992.
I Ain't Movin', 550 Music, 1994.
Supernatural, 550 Music, 1998.

Sources

Billboard, September 12, 1992; September 24, 1994; January 28, 1995; June 13, 1998.
Entertainment Weekly, August 21, 1998.
Essence, August 1995.
People, May 8, 1995.
Rolling Stone, December 1, 1994.
Village Voice, April 25, 1995.

—*Carol Brennan*

Pete Droge

Pete Droge

Singer, songwriter

Pete Droge has suffered the "one-hit wonder" tag since his 1994 alternative-radio hit, "If You Don't Love Me (I'll Kill Myself)." The song helped make his debut, *Necktie Second*, a commercial success, but his record label was undergoing financial distress by the time his 1996 follow-up was released, and *Find a Door* predictably went nowhere with no marketing effort to help it. Yet singer/songwriter Droge, an interesting by product of the Northwest grunge scene who has sometimes been compared to Tom Petty, is fortunate to possess well-connected friends who have great faith in his talents.

Droge was born in the late 1960s and grew up in Seattle, Washington. His mother was a music teacher, and his father, also a music-lover, taught Droge to play his first instrument, the ukulele, at the age of four. As a young adult, Droge worked in a pizza place and befriended Mike McCready, who would later go on to fame as the lead guitarist for Pearl Jam. By the time the Seattle-based group achieved massive success in the early 1990s—second only to Nirvana—Droge had his own roots-rock outfit called Ramadillo. "We didn't have the attitude, `Let's get it perfect,' so it was `alternative,'" Droge told *Rolling Stone*'s Kim Ahearn, and said Ramadillo was just part of a "subscene" at the time that "the Artist and Repretoire (A&R) people who were flocking [to Seattle] didn't pick up on."

Droge next spent time living and playing around the Oregon city of Portland, which boasted its own thriving, though less legendary music scene. McCready, still pals with Droge, gave one of his demo tapes to Pearl Jam producer Brendan O'Brien, who liked Droge's sound so much he engineered a deal for the relative unknown with American Recordings, the label owned by rap impresario Rick Rubin. O'Brien would produce all three of Droge's releases, in between helping out artists like Neil Young and Soundgarden in the studio.

Droge's debut, *Necktie Second,* was released in 1994, and its first single, "If You Don't Love Me (I'll Kill Myself)," quickly climbed the Modern Rock charts. A somewhat insouciant, "stalker-with-a-sense-of-irony" tune, Droge had written it in the summer of 1993 in his Portland home. He would later have to endure criticism for the lightheartedness of its lyrics, which were part of its commercial success in the first place; some critics termed its lines downright absurd. Droge, who toured for a year and a half in support of *Necktie Second*, soon tired of the hassles from those who seized upon this part of the song's character. "At the time of writing a tune like that ... you don't think that somebody's going to be calling you up and asking, `So what exactly is an Eskimo freeze?'" Droge complained to *Billboard*'s Eric Boehlert in late 1994. The rest of the record offered a more diverse range of fare, and it would sell over sixty thousand copies. "The sense of quiet longing in most of his music has little in common—barring the universal subject of heartache—with the blatant goofiness of `If You Don't Love Me,'" wrote Ahearn.

With his second effort, *Find a Door*, Droge ran into some bad luck when his label, American, underwent internal difficulties. The 1996 record was given little promotion, and accordingly did not do well. Yet Droge had, by this time, assembled a permanent backing band that grounded him and certainly lent support during some rough times. The band, which was first called the Sinners, included Peter Stroud, Dave Hull, Dan McCarroll, and vocalist Elaine Summers (who would later release a solo album that Droge produced in 1997). He had also invited session musicians from the world of gospel to round it out musically. On *Find a Door,* Droge credited the band with helping him focus his talents into a specific style. "A lot of the reasons this album will work, if it indeed does work, is due to the strengths of all five of us," Droge told Douglas Reece in *Billboard*.

By this time, Droge's clear roots-rock style was earning him comparisons to up-and-comers Hootie and the Blowfish and the Dave Matthews band, but Droge was simply sticking to what he had always done, especially in his former musical incarnation of Ramadillo. "Having

For the Record . . .

Born c. 1969.

Droge had an early 1990s band called Ramadillo; Self-released independent Ramadillo LP, 1991; signed with American Recordings, c. 1993; released debut *Necktie Second*, 1994; released *Find a Door*, 1996; signed to Fiftyseven Records, c. 1997; released *Spacey and Shakin'*, 1998.

Addresses: *Record company*—Fiftyseven Records, 1770 Century Blvd., Suite B, Atlanta, GA 30345.

cut my teeth in the Seattle club scene when just about every band in town got a record deal but me, I'm not all that swayed by what's popular, and I have a hard time putting anybody in a category," Droge told Reece in the *Billboard* interview. "But, yeah, I see a lot more music that isn't hard rock beginning to reach people."

True to form, Droge ventured into new territory with his third record, the 1998 *Spacey and Shakin'*. By then, Droge had spent months opening for acts such as Tom Petty, Neil Young, and his friends in Pearl Jam, and the experience had led him away from his acoustic sound. *Spacey and Shakin'*, released on producer O'Brien's Fiftyseven Records label, put forth a much heavier electric guitar sound, which Droge explained as a natural progression for any guitarist after playing so many large venues. "You have so much adrenaline running when you hit the stage," he told *Guitar World*'s Alan Paul, "and you just want to get the audience's interest right away and keep it, especially if you're an opening act."

Despite the title, *Spacey and Shakin'* was not that far-out a record, though there was some clear nods to '60s psychedelic bands and evidence of Droge's love of the Troggs ("Wild Thing") and Bob Dylan. He recorded it with the same assemblage of musicians, now renamed the Millionaires. The alternative paper *Boston Phoenix* gave *Spacey and Shakin'* a positive review, and noted that Droge's "voice splits the difference between Jimmie Dale Gilmore and Tom Petty." *Chicago Sun-Times* writer Jim DeRogatis called it Droge's "most ambitious album" to date, and termed it one of the most outstanding examples of the year in its overcrowded "guitar-rock" category.

McCready remains one of Droge's biggest fans, and even penned a homage to him in *Guitar Player*. He praised Droge's songwriting abilities, and confessed that Droge's lyrics and plaintiff acoustic guitar riffs could easily reduce him to tears. He termed several songs from *Necktie Second* as "crucial in this generation's landscape of ideas.... Pete paints auditory pictures of everyday life in its pleasures and struggles."

Selected discography

Necktie Second, American, 1994.
Find a Door, American, 1996.
Spacey and Shakin', Fiftyseven/Epic, 1998.

Sources

Billboard, December 17, 1994, p. 73; May 18, 1996, pp. 14, 21.
Boston Phoenix, April 24, 1998.
Chicago Sun-Times, April 5, 1998.
Guitar Player, February 1995, p. 16.
Guitar World, July 1998.
Rolling Stone, March 9, 1995, p. 32.

Additional information for this profile was provided by Epic Records publicity materials, 1998.

—Carol Brennan

Emmet Swimming

Rock band

Alternative rock band Emmet Swimming combines the ease and skill of natural storytellers with compelling rhythms and hypnotic musical textures. The mixture creates a unique, offbeat musical offering. In the early 1990s the band generated an underground fan base in their hometown of Fairfax, Virginia; it then branched out performing in clubs in the Washington DC, North Carolina, and Maryland areas. Beginning in 1993, Emmet Swimming released a series of CDs, each surpassing its predecessor in sales and popularity. Their 1998 release, *Big Night Without You,* combines elements of gospel, alternative rock, dark humor, wailing, and churning rock guitars. Mark Jenkins of the *Washington Post* described their music as, "the drift of folk-rock toward a jazzier sound ... a late-night cocktail ambiance that suggests American Music Club or Tindersticks more than Emmet influence (and producer Dixon client) R.E.M."

The four band members—drummer Tamer Eid, bass player Luke Michel, vocalist and guitarist Todd Watts, and guitarist Erik Wenberg—met as students at George Mason University in Fairfax, Virginia. Eid began playing drums at the age of four, and Wenberg studied piano as a child while growing up in the suburbs of Washington D.C. Vocalist/guitarist Watts, originally from Kentucky, formed the band and remains the band's leader. The early musical influences on the band's members include the Clash and the Cars. Asked to explain the origin of the band's name, Watts told the *Washington Post*'s Eric Brace that while growing up in Kentucky, he remembered stories of the 1955 killing of Emmett Till, an African-American youth who was shot and thrown in a river for whistling at a white woman. "It's a horrible case of injustice," Watts told Brace, "it resonated for me."

The band's success can be attributed in large part to its emphasis on live performance. Emmet Swimming concerts are designed to be memorable and satisfying, and the band is devoted to touring as much as they can. The Performing Arts section of the *Washington Post,* described an Emmet Swimming concert as "an espresso overdose." Watts vocal style was called "distinctive, sometimes eerie." Watts' baritone dominates the band's material and it fluctuates from low and ethereal to rousing. The band's material is usually tinged with dark humor; it causes the listener to pause and reflect.

The band utilizes musical elements from a wide variety of styles: blues, jazz, gospel, rock, folk, surf, honky-tonk country, punk, mariachi, and even classical. Emmet Swimming is thoroughly original and thoughtful, and its mostly youthful, college-age fans are fanatically devoted. Many have created unofficial web pages for the band on the Internet, full of slogans like, "The best band in the world!" underneath photographs of the band.

Emmet Swimming released *Dark When The Snow Falls* in 1993 on their own Screaming Goddess Music label. A year later they released *Wake* on the Bloated Caribou Music/Screaming Goddess label as well as a Christmas single titled "Silver Star." The single was included in a release of local Fairfax artists presenting Christmas songs titled *Fa la la la la la la la la* in 1994, released on Loud Mouth Sound, Inc. A year later in 1995, the band had its first major label CD when Sony/Epic released *Wake*.

The *Arlington to Boston* CD, which came out in 1996, was the release that first garnered national attention for Emmet Swimming. They followed up the album's on-the-road themes by taking to the road themselves. *Arlington to Boston* received airplay on radio stations throughout the Mid-Atlantic and Southern regions and the band spent the year touring tirelessly, playing festivals and clubs along the East Coast, from New England down to Georgia. In the process, they broadened their already loyal fan base. *Arlington to Boston* was produced by Don Dixon, who had also worked with R.E.M. and the Smithereens.

In the wake of their success, in 1996, the band won the Washington D.C. Music Association's WAMMIE Award

For the Record . . .

Members include **Tamer Eid,** drums; **Luke Michel,** (born April 28, 1972), bass; **Todd Watts,** (born in KY), guitar and vocals; **Erik Wenberg,** (born July 22, 1968, Washington DC), guitar; members met while students at George Mason University in Fairfax, VA.

Eid began playing drums at the age of four; guitarist Wenberg learned piano as a child; Watts formed the band and remains the band's leader; released *Dark When The Snow Falls* in 1993 on band's own label, Screaming Goddess Music; released *Wake* on the Bloated Caribou Music/Screaming Goddess label in 1994; released a Christmas single, entitled "Silver Star," in 1994 and included in a Christmas compilation of Fairfax, VA artists, entitled *Fa la la la la la la la la,* (Loud Mouth Sound, Inc); *Wake* released on Sony/Epic in 1995; *Arlington to Boston* released in 1996; *Big Night Without You,* produced by Grammy-winner Peter Collins released in 1998,; played on the Horde Tour in 1998, Washington D.C.

Awards: Music Association's WAMMIE Award in 1996 for Top Alternative Band, Top Alternative Recording, Top Alternative Song, Top Alternative Instrumentalist (Tamer Eid), and Top Alternative Band Manager (Alan Stewart).

Addresses: *Record company*—Emmet Swimming, P.O. Box 744, Fairfax, VA 22030, (703) 913-2082; email: emmets@emmet.swimming.com; web site: http://www.emmetswimming.com.

for Top Alternative Band, Top Alternative Recording, Top Alternative Song, Top Alternative Instrumentalist (Tamer Eid), and Top Alternative Band Manager (Alan Stewart). Emmet Swimming played on the Horde Tour during the summer of 1998 to rave reviews. Their fans eagerly awaited whatever they would release next.

It turned out to be 1998's *Big Night Without You*, a record produced by Grammy-winner Peter Collins, who had also worked with Jewel, the Cardigans, Indigo Girls, Suicidal Tendencies, Rush, and Sneaker Pimps. This collaboration created a lush, urgent sound on the band's fourth album, together with its trademark musical tapes-

try of styles. The songs on *Big Night Without You* tell clear, complete stories with a moral. "Sunblock" tells the story of a lovable lout who trades in his social-climbing girlfriend for a view of the ocean, a tale that is underscored by mariachi horns, surf music, hony-tonk music, and a touch of rebellious punk. Each of the band's releases has sold three to four times as many copies as its predecessor, so the band and its label are looking forward to a prosperous future.

The members of Emmet Swimming create their distinctive brand of music by remaining true to their own vision and musical tastes, and more or less oblivious to musical trends. As a result, their lyrics, vocals, and their compositions are uncompromised and fresh. They found success by not seeking it, but by letting it find them. Their devotion to their personal perspectives is patently evident in their music. Their ability to tell a story enhances their music and keeps listeners waiting for the next tale. Some songs are like short musical films: the couple breaking up during a road trip to Reno, the man who leaves his empty-hearted lover for a trip to the ocean, and the man who confronts the passage of time and the unerring force of nature are all characters brought to life, however briefly, in song. It may be this combination of artful music and superb storytelling that fuels the success and ardent fan base of Emmet Swimming.

Selected discography

Dark When The Snow Falls, Screaming Goddess Music, 1993.
"Silver Star," Bloated Caribou Music, 1994.
Wake, Bloated Caribou Music/Screaming Goddess Music, 1994; rereleased on Sony/Epic, 1995.
Arlington to Boston, Sony/Epic, 1996.
Big Night Without You, Sony/Epic, 1998.

Sources

Periodicals

Washington Post, July 23, 1996; July 19, 1996; July 15, 1996.

Online

http://www.emmetswimming.com
http://www. themadnessofjane.com
http://www.yahoomusic.com

Additional information was provided by the publicity department at Sony/Epic Records.

—*B. Kimberly Taylor*

Nesuhi Ertegun

Producer

AP Wide World Photo. Reproduced by permission. ©

Visionary Atlantic Records partner Nesuhi Ertegun, brother of Atlantic Records chairman and cofounder Ahmet Ertegun, helped establish the label as a haven for now-classic jazz, pop, and rhythm-and-blues. Ertegun joined the label in 1955 as a partner—his brother founded the company in 1947—and was in charge of expanding Atlantic's jazz roster and of shifting the singles-oriented label into LP production. Under his direction, Atlantic's jazz roster widened to include such musical titans as Ornette Coleman, John Coltrane, Charles Mingus, the Modern Jazz Quartet, and Herbie Mann. He also oversaw the recordings of Coleman's *Shape of Jazz to Come,* Coltrane's *Giant Steps,* and Mingus's *Blues and Roots.* In many cases, the jazz recordings that musicians created with Ertegun were their initial recordings. Joel Dorn, a producer who recorded and promoted jazz for Atlantic in the 1960s, told *Rolling Stone*'s Fred Goodman, "Atlantic had the best mix of commercial and artistic music. With John Coltrane, Bobby Darin, and Ray Charles on the same label, the scope was just incredible. That was a reflection of Nesuhi's viewpoint." Ertegun oversaw Atlantic's mid-fifties move into long-playing albums, and Jerry Wexler, the former president of Atlantic Records, told Goodman, "Nesuhi opened that whoe area for Atlantic—everything from recording to packaging was done under Nesuhi's guidance." Ertegun won a 1991 Lifetime Achievement Award and was inducted into the Rock and Roll Hall of Fame that same year.

Ertegun was born in Istanbul, Turkey, and moved to the U.S. in 1939 with his family to live in Washington D.C. His father, M. Munir Ertegun, served as the Turkish ambassador to the U.S. As a young man, Ertegun and his brother Ahmet organized jam sessions with jazz musicians at the Turkish embassy, and both brothers were known to be ardent record collectors. He and his brother Ahmet would frequent the Howard Theater in Washington D.C. and scour the black community for records by their favorite musicians. Ertegun attended school at the Sorbonne in Paris and then at American University in Washington D.C. After college, he moved to Los Angeles and opened a record store; he also started his own record label, Crescent Records—later called Jazzman—which released recordings by Jelly Roll Morton, Jimmy Noone, Kid Ory, and other early New Orleans-style jazz musicians. He taught one of the earliest accredited classes in jazz music at UCLA and edited a record magazine called *Record Challenger.* While Ertegun was living on the west coast, Wexler asked him to record a session with the R&B group The Drifters as a favor, even though Ertegun wasn't affiliated with Atlantic Records at the time. When he was a producer at Atlantic, Ertegun's career extended far beyond jazz: he produced recordings by LaVern Baker,

For the Record . . .

Born Nesuhi Ertegun in Istanbul, Turkey, (died on July 15, 1989, at the age of 71 due to complications following cancer surgery); moved to the U.S. in 1939 with his family to live in Washington D.C.; son of M. Munir Ertegun, (Turkish ambassador to the U.S); brother of Ahmet Ertegun (Atlantic Records co-founder and producer); married: wife Selma; children: Leyla and Rustem. *Education:* Attended school at the Sorbonne in Paris; attended the American University in Washington D.C.

Opened a record store after college and; started his own record label, Crescent Records (later Jazzman), released recordings by Jelly Roll Morton, Jimmy Noone, Kid Ory, and other early New Orleans-style jazz musicians; taught one of the earliest accredited classes on jazz music at UCLA; edited record magazine, *Record Changer;* recorded a session with the R&B group The Drifters as a favor to an Atlantic Records executive; joined the Atlantic Records as a partner, 1955;— headed expansion of Atlantic's jazz roster and of shifting the singles-oriented label into LP production; widened Atlantic's jazz roster widened to include Ornette Coleman, John Coltrane, Charles Mingus, the Modern Jazz Quartet, and Herbie Mann; oversaw the recordings of Coleman's *Shape of Jazz to Come,* Coltrane's *Giant Steps,* and Mingus's *Blues and Roots;* produced recordings by LaVern Baker, Ray Charles, and Bobby Darin; signed Roberta Flack to the label; produced albums by Bobby Short; oversaw everything from packaging to recording during Atlantic Records' mid-1950s move into long-playing albums; after acquisition of Atlantic Records by Warner Communications in 1967, Ertegun spearheaded the creation of WEA International in 1971; created East-West Records, which specialized in jazz, 1987;: was first president of the National Academy of Recording Arts and Sciences, which presents the Grammy Awards; chairman of the International Federation of Phonographic Industries, 1981-89; helmed a campaign to stop the piracy of f records, tapes, and sheet music, particularly in his homeland, Turkey, and in Korea and Southeast Asia; founded the New York Cosmos Soccer Club, 1971.

Awards: Inducted into the Rock and Roll Hall of Fame and given a Lifetime Achievement Award both in 1991.

Ray Charles, and Bobby Darin. He was also responsible for signing Roberta Flack to the label, after Dorn brought her talent to his attention. He had a taste for sophisticated cabaret music and produced albums by Bobby Short. Dorn told Goodman, "I was stunned by how meticulous he was. When preparing an album, he'd be just as concerned about the cover art and the punctuation in the liner notes as he was with the music."

Warner Brothers chairman Steven J. Ross told Susan Heller Anderson of the *New York Times,* "He attracted the top people because he cared so much about music and musicians. Musicians were enormously responsive to him because he realized that music was a universal language." Modern Jazz Quartet pianist John Lewis told Goodman, "He was key in the development of the Modern Jazz Quartet. He was just about the only producer I worked with, and without him, the group wouldn't have happened." Lewis was one of many musicians who grew close to Ertegun after meeting and working with him. Yusef Lateef, a flutist and saxophonist with the Modern Jazz Quartet, told Goodman, "Talking to Nesuhi was like talking to a brother or a father ... when I returned to the U.S. in 1985 [from Nigeria], it was because of Nesuhi that I was able to do an album that won a Grammy."

In 1971, four years after Atlantic Records was acquired by Warner Communications in 1967, Ertegun spearheaded the creation of WEA International—a global network of record companies that rendered Warner the world's largest record company with sales in excess of $1 billion. He served as the company's chairman and CEO from 1971-87, and oversaw the creation of WEA operations in dozens of countries. He was able to bring the American music of WEA's U.S. labels—Warner, Elektra/Asylum, and Atlantic, as well as Geffen and MCA—to far reaches of the globe. Ertegun spoke several languages, and his elegant, distinguished, quiet demeanor served him well as an ambassador of music. The establishment of WEA-distributed artists such as Madonna, Prince, and U2 as international superstars would have been unlikely had it not been for Ertegun's groundbreaking work. Ertegun was also in charge of the special projects division of Warner Communications, and created his own jazz label, East-West Records, in 1987-1988. He was also the first president of the National Academy of Recording Arts and Sciences, which presents the Grammy Awards. From 1981-89, Ertegun was chairman of the International Federation of Phonographic Industries, which represents all recording companies in copywriting. During his time as chairman, he helmed a campaign to stop the piracy of records, tapes, and sheet music, particularly in his homeland, Turkey, and in Korea and Southeast Asia.

Ertegun's other passions apart from music were soccer and art. He founded the New York Cosmos Soccer Club in 1971 and brought some of the sport's best players to New York. Ertegun was a close friend of statesman Henry A. Kissenger, and Mr. Kissinger told Anderson that Ertegun was invaluable in advising him during his successful negotiations to bring the 1994 World Cup soccer championship to the U.S. He also collected books and art; his substantial collection of mostly Surrealist paintings included pieces by Max Ernst, Magritte, Dali, Bacon, and Arp. He was a member of the board of the T.J. Martell Foundation, which provided money for cancer research.

Dorn told Goodman, "He was so antithetical to the typical record guy. There were a couple of guys who were special—Nesuhi, [Columbia Records president] Goddard Lieberson, [Columbia A&R man] John Hammond—and I don't know how you replace those people. The record industry is a product of their moments." Ertegun died on July 15, 1989, at the age of 71 due to complications following cancer surgery at the Mount Sinai Medical Center in New York City. He was inducted into the Rock and Roll Hall of Fame two years later in 1991 and given a Lifetime Achievement Award that same year. He lived in Manhattan, Katonah, NY, and Biot, France. His former partner Wexler told Goodman, "He was a linguist, a philosopher, and he had studied at the Sorbonne. Malice is the aegis that his business flies under, yet there was nothing but good relations between us." When Dorn was 14 years old, long before he worked with Ertegun, he wrote a letter to Ertegun and told him that he wanted to be a producer. Ertegun wrote him back, sent him out-of-print records, and eventually let him produce his first record. Dorn told Goodman, "Anything I am, I owe to him."

Sources

Periodicals

Down Beat, August 1987.
Rolling Stone, May 7, 1989.
New York Times, July 16, 1989.

Online

Rock and Roll Hall of Fame Website, http://www.rockhall.com/induct/ertenesu.html, (September 9, 1998).

—*B. Kimberly Taylor*

Merrell Fankhauser

Guitar

Guitarist Merrell Fankhauser's career began in the early 1960s with the surf instrumental band, The Impacts. To the present day he has adapted to many of the trends in popular music along the way, each band making music of exemplary quality. Although Fankhauser has not enjoyed chart hits, he claimed that authorship of the rock standard "Wipe Out" was stolen from him and he finally won the publishing rights to it in the 1990s.

Fankhauser was born on December 23, 1943 in Louisville, Kentucky. His father played guitar and listened to country blues music. Merrell acquired a ukelele early in his teens. Around this time, his family moved to California, where young Fankhauser was intrigued by the rhythm and blues music he heard on the radio. He recalls, "I used to try to figure this stuff out on my ukelele and it was kind of interesting because there was no way you could get the same sound out of an electric or even acoustic 6-string guitar."

Soon Merrell acquired an acoustic, then an electric guitar. He and his school friend, Bill Dodd, won a local talent contest in 1960 and were invited to join the band The Impacts. After months of rehearsals, the band began playing around Pismo Beach, California. The band was one of the first bands to play upbeat, guitar-based instrumental music which would eventually become well known as "surf music."

The Impacts attracted the attention of a recording scout from Del-Fi Records in 1962. The band recorded its repertoire for the talent scout and was later surprised to see an Impacts album appear in stores. In early 1963, the band returned to the studio to record more songs, including a new arrangement of a song called "Wipe Out." After unknowingly signing away their royalties, the band members heard "Wipe Out" on the radio. Fankhauser recalled to Goldmine, though, "But when the announcer said it was The Surfaris, we all went, 'Shit, they ripped us off!'"

Merrell left The Impacts in 1963 and got a job as an airport gas boy. While strumming guitar during a break, another employee introduced Fankhauser to his son, Jeff Cotton. Jeff was another young guitarist. The two got along well and formed a band, Merrell and The Exiles, with musicians who answered a newspaper ad. The Exiles were inspired by the recent British Invasion bands. The group attracted the attention of a local record producer who released an Exiles single on his own label. The record reached the top ten at a Palmdale, California radio station alongside records by The Beatles and Jan and Dean. The band recorded more singles and were becoming popular around Los Angeles. Fankhauser left The Exiles, however, when their agent sent them on tour near a logging camp in Oregon.

Through 1966, Fankhauser was recording with local musicians in southern California while looking for a record deal. The producer who released many of the Exiles' singles released an album of current Fankhauser tracks mixed with Exiles sides under the name *Fapardokly,* a name coined from the first syllables of Merrell's band members' names. Few copies were pressed, and it eventually became one of the most collectible rock albums.

Merrell Fankhauser's next band was closest to bringing him commercial success. H.M.S. Bounty formed in 1968 featuring dual lead guitars and three part vocal harmonies. Many of the songs incorporated mystical, psychedelic ideas but Fankhauser was also capable of writing more commercial material. The band was signed to Uni Records after Merrell auditioned for the label's president.

Opening with two straightforward pop songs, *Things* twists and turns through a survey of the hip sounds of 1968, from a mystical, sitar driven ballad to heavier rock numbers. Fankhauser's producers also released a solo single, a version of "Everybody's Talkin'", which alienated his bandmates. Later, Merrell found out that he'd signed away his songwriting royalties as well.

For the Record . . .

Born December 23, 1943 in Louisville, KY; son of Reuben Fankhauser (a race car driver); married Josie c. 1965, separated c. 1976, childern: one son, Tim.

Formed The Impacts c. 1962; recorded for Del-Fi Records c. 1963; left The Impacts c. 1963; formed Merrell and The Exiles c. 1964; recorded for Glenn Records c. 1964-5; disbanded c. 1965; formed Fapardokly c. 1966; recorded for U.I.P. Records c. 1966; disbanded c. 1967; formed H.M.S. Bounty c. 1968; recorded solo and with H.M.S. Bounty for Shamley Records c. 1968; disbanded c. 1969; formed Mu c. 1970; relocated to Maui c. 1971; disbanded Mu c. 1975; recorded solo c. 1976-99; formed Fankhauser-Cassidy Blues Band c. 1990s; reunited The Impacts c. 1995; recorded *Return To Mu* c. 1990s.

Addresses: Ocean Records, P. O. Box 1504, Arroyo Grande, CA 93421.

Upon the demise of H.M.S. Bounty, Fankhauser reunited with Cotton, who had been playing with Captain Beefheart, and two former members of the Exiles. The band played under different names until Fankhauser named it Mu, from a book he found called *The Lost Continent of Mu*, about an island that sank into the Pacific Ocean centuries ago. Fankhauser became fascinated with the mythology of this lost land and has been researching it extensively since. The influence of the book permeates Mu's lyrics, with many references to mysticism, soul searching, and an island paradise.

Mu is the maturation of Fankhauser's songwriting and bandleading talents. Mu developed an otherworldly avant-blues-rock sound, but with Fankhauser's keen command of melody and surf guitarist's penchant for pithiness, it is the most hummable progressive rock ever recorded. After releasing its first album in 1971, the bandmembers relocated to Maui, Hawaii. Mu settled into the island's laid back lifestyle, but Cotton and Wimer grew wary of the islands mythology which permeated the band's existence and quit.

Without a band, Fankhauser remained on the island throughout the seventies, recording with violinist Mary Lee as a duo. His 1976 solo album was too folky for the mainland music scene and he remained in Maui for the rest of the decade. In 1983, he met former Quicksilver Messenger Service guitarist John Cipollina; they collaborated on *Doctor Fankhauser*. Merrell was getting back into recording and touring when, during a 1987 concert he felt a sharp pain in his chest. He had a heart attack on stage and was rushed to the hospital just in time. As his chances of recovery became slimmer, he repeated a Tibetan chant which improved his health.

During the 90s, Fankhauser has recorded with drummer Ed Cassidy from Spirit as well as three forthcoming albums continuing his fascination with the mythology of *The Lost Continent of Mu*, and an autobiographical disc, *Psychedelic Dreams*. Merrell Fankhauser has remained very resilient and optimistic despite the many obstacles he has encountered throughout his career. His albums, many of which hves been reissued, are classic lost treasures of American rock.

Selected discography

with The Impacts

Wipe Out!, Del-Fi, 1963, reissued, 1994.
"Blue Surf" and "Impact" (rec. 1963) on *Wild Surf*, Del-Fi, 1995.
"Torchula" on *KFWB's Battle Of The Surfing Bands!*, Del-Fi, 1963.
"Wipe Out," (rec. 1963), on *The Del-Fi Rarities*, Del-Fi, 1994.
"Steel Pier," (rec. 1963) on *The Del-Fi Rarities*, Del-Fi, 1994.
"Blue Surf," (rec. 1963) on *Big Surf Hits*, Del-Fi, 1994.
"Wipe Out," (rec. 1963) on *Big Surf Hits,* Del-Fi, 1994.
"Fort Lauderdale" (rec. 1963) on *Pulp Surfin'*, Del-Fi, 1995.
(with The Impacts and The Exiles), *Desert Island Treasures* (rec. 1963-5), Bacchus Archives/Dionysus, 1996.
The Impacts, *Surfin 101*, Gee Dee, 1996.
The Impacts, *Eternal Surf*, Gee Dee, 1997.

with Others

(with the Exiles), *The Early Years 1964-1967*, American Sound, 1994.
Fapardokly, U.I.P., 1967, reissued Sundazed, 1995.
(with H.M.S. Bounty), *Things*, Shamley, 1968, reissued Sundazed, 1997.
"Everybody's Talkin'," Shamley, 1969, reissued on *Things*, Sundazed, 1997.
"Tampa Run," Shamley, 1969, reissued on *Things*, Sundazed, 1997.
Mu, Era/RTV, 1971, reissued Sundazed, 1997.
Merrell Fankhauser, Maui Music, 1976, reissued as *The Maui Album*, Reckless, 1988.

"Sail It Over The Ocean," Free Spirit, 1979.
"Calling From A Star," Free Spirit, 1979.
A Day in Paradise, D-Town, 1985.
"Some Of Them Escaped," D-Town, 1986.
"I Saw Your Photograph," D-Town, 1986.
Doctor Fankhauser, D-Town, 1986, reissued Legend, 1994.
Message To The Universe, One Big Guitar, 1986.
Flying To Macchu Picchu, Legend, 1992.
California Live, Legend, 1994.
The Fankhauser Cassidy Blues Band, *On The Blue Road,* D-Town, 1995.
Psychedelic Dreams, Ocean, 1998.
Return To Mu, Aspen, 1999.

Sources

Books

Joynson, Vernon, *Fuzz, Acid, and Flowers: A Comprehensive Guide to American Garage, Psychedelic, and Hippie Rock 1964-1976,* Borderline Productions, 1996.
Unterberger, Ritchie, *Unknown Legends of Rock n' Roll,* Miller-Freeman, 1998.
Woodstra, Chris, ed., *The All Music Guide To Rock,* Miller-Freeman, 1995.

Periodicals

Goldmine, April 26, 1996; August 1, 1997.

Additional information was obtained from an interview with Merrell Fankhauser.

—*Jim Powers*

Renee Fleming

Opera singer

Perhaps the preeminent American lyric soprano, Renee Fleming has become one of the greatest female figures on the opera stage. She is frequently praised for her beautiful voice, which falls into the relatively rare "lyric" category, and for a charm and vivacity that make her an exceptional performer. Fleming has become most famous for singing Mozart and Strauss, but has also appeared in the premieres of several new operas, including the role of Blanch Dubois in Andre Previn's 1998 adaptation of *A Streetcar Named Desire*. Another famous professional friend was conductor Sir Georg Solti, who played a key role in starting the singer's recording career. Having now been cast in many of opera's greatest female roles in the world's most important opera houses, Fleming easily fills the traditional role of diva on stage but is otherwise a rather unconventional opera celebrity. Far from being the temperamental, ego-driven starlet of opera myth, she is known for her pleasant demeanor and her ability to juggle being a mom and wife with her booming career.

Fleming had to win several hard-fought battles before earning attention of opera house managers and kudos from critics. The soprano told the *Chicago Tribune*, "Seeing me today, everybody finds it hard to believe that I wasn't a natural, extrovert performer.... That's one of the things I had to work at very hard." As a child, Fleming was a reluctant singer. The daughter of two high school vocal-music teachers, Fleming grew up in Rochester, New York with constant reminders that she was expected to be a singer. She explained in the *New York Times*, "When I got older, we discussed singing every night at dinner. So I felt a lot of pressure. My mother was the worst kind of stage mother. She would make me and my younger sister and brother little duckling costumes and put us in kiddie shows." She continued to perform, but as Fleming recalled, "I was stolid and stone-faced.... I did everything grudgingly and became painfully shy."

Studied At Home and Abroad

At one time, Fleming fantasized about becoming a horse trainer, but she went on to study voice with Patricia Misslin as an undergraduate, and earned a bachelor's degree in music education from State University of New York (SUNY) Potsdam in 1981. Subsequently, she attended the Eastman School of Music and then the American Opera Center at Julliard, where she met her husband Rick Ross and the woman who would remain her vocal instructor for many years, Beverly Johnson. While at SUNY Potsdam, Fleming worked as a jazz singer and so impressed the famous tenor saxophone player Illinois Jacquet that he offered her a job. Fleming

Born Renee L. Flemming, February 14, 1959 in Indiana, PA; daughter of Edwin Davis Fleming and Patricia (Seymour) Alexander (both vocal music teachers); married Richard Lee Ross (an actor) on September 23, 1989; children: Amelia and Sage. *Education:* State University of New York at Potsdam, B.M. (Education), 1981; Eastman School of Music, M.M., 1983; Julliard American Opera Center, 1983-84; Fulbright scholar, Frankfurt, Germany, 1984-85.

Made professional opera debut at the Landestheater, Frankfurt, Austria, 1986; New York City Opera debut, 1989; Royal Opera at (London) Covent Garden debut, 1989; New York Metropolitan Opera debut, 1991; appeared in premiere of *The Ghosts of Versailles,* 1991; appeared in premiere of *The Dangerous Liaisons,* 1994; signed exclusive solo recording contract with Decca/London, 1995; released first solo album, *Visions of Love,* 1996; appeared in premiere of *A Streetcar Named Desire,* 1998.

Awards: Förderungs Preis, International Singing Competition, Austria, 1985; winner, Metropolitan Opera National Auditions and the George London Prize, 1988; the Richard Tucker Award, 1990; Solti Prize, Academy du Disque Lyrique, 1996; Debut Recording of the Year for *Visions of Love,* National Public Radio's *Performance Today,* 1996; Vocalist of the Year, *Musical America,* 1997; prize for *The Beautiful Voice,* L'Academie du Disque Lyrique, 1998.

Addresses: *Management*—ML Falcone Public Relations, 155 W. 68th Street, Suite 1114, New York, NY. *Record company*—London/Decca, c/o Columbia Artists Managment Inc., 165 West 57th Street, New York, NY, 10019-2276.

remarked in *Opera News*, "It's tempting to say I worked my way through college as a jazz singer ... but the truth is I didn't make much money doing it." These performances required her to tell jokes and chat with the audience, which was important in helping the singer begin to deal with her stage fright.

Fleming was granted a Fulbright Scholarship to study in Germany during 1984-85, which gave her the opportunity to take a master class with soprano Elisabeth Schwarzkopf. In 1986 she made her professional opera debut in Salzburg in the Mozart opera *Die Entufhrung aus dem Serail.* Both of these events, which had the appearance of being great opportunities, only served to shake Fleming's confidence and left her doubting if she knew how to sing. Regarding the debut performance, Fleming told *Opera News*, "I just wasn't ready for it. In retrospect I'm so grateful that it happened then, when nobody cared."

Showered with Awards

Perseverance and further training with Johnson eventually ironed out problems of vocal technique. Moreover, upon returning to the United States, Fleming got professional help with her stage fright. She remembered in *Opera News*, "for six months I went and saw a lady and we just dealt with my self-esteem issues." Fleming's new self-assurance and improved singing were confirmed by a series of awards received in the following years: a first place in the Metropolitan Opera National Auditions and the George London Prize in 1988, and the Richard Tucker Award in 1990. These honors earned her the attention of opera management and, finally, numerous of job offers.

In 1989, Fleming made her New York City Opera debut as Mimi in Puccini's *La Bohème* and her Royal Opera debut at London's Covent Garden in Cherubini's *Médée.* Her Metropolitan Opera debut came somewhat unexpectedly in 1991 when she replaced the flu-stricken Felicity Lott as the Countess Almaviva in *Le Nozze di Figaro.* This would emerge as one of Fleming's signature parts, as she noted in *Opera News*: "I was emerging in the role just as the Mozart bicentennial was about to hit, so I ended up singing a lot of Countesses." Even so, she managed to accept parts in a wide range of operas, including the premieres of John Corigliano's *The Ghosts of Versailles* in 1991 and Conrad Susa's *The Dangerous Liaisons* in 1994.

Having had this kind of exposure, it is something of a surprise that Sir Georg Solti had not yet heard of Fleming in 1994 when she was recommended as a replacement for the part of Fiordiligi in his production of Mozart's *Cosi fan tutti.* Solti was wowed by her voice and, after offering her the role, became an important advocate for the soprano. In 1996, Solti honored Fleming with the first Solti Prize, awarded by the French Academy du Disque Lyrique. The conductor was also largely responsible for the shape of Fleming's recording career, having recommended her to London/Decca. The recording company signed her to an exclusive solo contract, the first such agreement it had made with an American singer since signing Marilyn Horne in 1965. Commenting on her relationship with Solti, who died in September of 1997, Fleming told the *Chicago Sun-Times*, "I had three fantastic years with him.... The great conductors are larger than life. They have the ability, like any great leader, to inspire. What that does for me as an artist is take me beyond my own expectations, beyond what I think I can do. Solti was tough, demanding, loving. We outperform ourselves for somebody like that."

Developed Pure Lyric Sound

Many critics have perceived something rare and special in Fleming's particular soprano sound. In 1998, John von Rhein marveled in *Chicago Tribune*, "The voice, a peaches-and-cream soprano with both agility and carrying power, is in full bloom. Rarely since Eleanor Steber has America produced a full lyric soprano voice of this quality—a natural for the Mozart and Richard Strauss roles and the French repertoire that make up her *Fach* (vocal specialty)." In *Opera News*, James M. Keller said, "Fleming's voice seems custom-made for Mozart's heroines, displaying refined technique, warm timbre, authoritative articulation, lyric agility combined with requisite heft, and an expressive, malleable vibrato." Fleming herself commented on her own perception of her vocal quality in the *New York Times* when she said, "I enjoy the more floaty, exposed, elegant singing.... I don't like to sing loud. People seem to understand this about my voice, so I don't get too many ridiculous offers."

This last comment refers to an important issue for the soprano: keeping her voice fit for the kind of singing at which she excels. One such offer that Fleming regrettably accepted was the 1996 role of Eva in Wagner's *Die Meistersinger* in a Bayreuth, Germany production. The part was too low for her voice and affected her vocal placement for weeks afterwards. Fleming was forced to cancel engagements while she worked to return to a more natural mode of singing. Solti had advised her against this role and was quoted in the *New York Times*, "What I told her, speaking like a father, which I could easily be to her, is that she must not sing parts that are too heavy too soon.... Or sing too much. She has listened more or less, but it is hard to resist temptation when the whole world is coming to you."

Managed a Full Calendar

By early 1998, Fleming was booked four years in advance. At that time, Rhein described her in the *Chicago Tribune* as "the most sought-after lyric soprano of her generation, the toast of opera houses from New York to Milan, the American singer every impresario and concert manager in the world wants to engage." Just a few months later, in a review of *A Streetcar Named Desire* for the *Los Angeles Times*, Mark Swed commented, "This is to be Fleming's year. The Metropolitan Opera is staging three new productions for her, and Previn not only created Blanche for her, but might well have titled the opera "Blanche," so musically centered around her in the score." As she neared the age of 40, Fleming enjoyed a sense of maturity as a performer. In 1998, regarding her frequent role as the Countess Almaviva, Fleming told the *Chicago Sun-Times*: "[My interpretation] has changed a lot in the past 10 years.... And right here, now, I feel like I've had a breakthrough. Dramatically, I have more experience of life.... I don't feel like I'm trying to act like a countess.... It feels much more natural."

Fleming has been given ample opportunity to showcase her growing talent in her recordings. Hugh Canning, writing for *Gramophone* in 1997, opined that the soprano "has a virtual carte blanche to record what she wants." Fleming's recordings include full opera performances of *Rusalka*, *Cosi fan tutte*, and *Don Giovanni*; solo projects including *Visions of Love* (Mozart arias), *Shubert Album* (songs with pianist Chistoph Eshenbach), *Signatures* (opera scenes), *The Beautiful Voice* (songs and arias), and *I Want Magic* (American arias); and duets with Placido Domingo on *Star-Crossed Lovers*. In addition to these traditional classical CDs, Fleming sang with pop singer Michael Bolton on his 1998 album called *My Secret Passion: The Arias*. She was also making plans for a jazz album featuring Duke Ellington tunes, an old musical love from her college days.

Clearly, Fleming has managed to be selective about her projects and to put her own stamp on nearly everything she does. As *Time* reporter Terry Teachout concluded, "This thoroughly modern diva does everything her own way, from wrapping up her recitals with a group of songs by Duke Ellington to scrupulously avoiding the knife-in-the-back behavior that has given so many top singers a bad name." He further noted that she was "happily aware that in her case, the nice girl finished first."

Selected discography

Der Rosenkavalier: Final Trio, Sony, 1993.
Armida, Sony, 1994.
Cosi fan tutte, London/Decca, 1994.
Hérodiade, Sony, 1995.
Bells, Telarc, 1996.

Chansons de Jadis, Centaur, 1996.
Lulu/Wozzeck Suites, Sony, 1996.
Don Giovanni, London/Decca, 1996.
Alma Brasileira, RCA, 1997.
Elijah, London/Decca, 1997.
Four Last Songs, RCA, 1997.
Schubert Album, London/Decca, 1997.
Signatures, London/Decca, 1997.
Rosmonda D'Inghilterra, Opera Rara, 1998.
Rusalka, London/Decca, 1998.
Star-Crossed Lovers, London/Decca, 1999.

Sources

American Record Guide, July/August 1998.
Chicago Sun-Times, March 5, 1998.
Chicago Tribune, February 8, 1998.
Gramophone, April 1997.
New York Times, September 14.
Opera News, September 1994; October 1997.
Time, November 17, 1997.

—*Paula Pyzik Scott*

The Four Seasons

Pop group

With their distinctive style of music—perhaps best described as power doo-wop—The Four Seasons have enjoyed a long and extremely successful career in popular music. Coming together in the mid-1950s, they had their first major hit "Sherry" in 1962. It was followed by a string of other hit songs including "Big Girls Don't Cry," "Walk Like a Man," and "Let's Hang On to What We've Got." Along with The Beach Boys, The Four Seasons were the only American group to survive the "British Invasion" of the pop charts in the mid-1960s. Their hit songs have become pop standards and their concert tours continue to attract enthusiastic audiences made up of longtime fans and younger people whose acquaintance with the group comes from "oldies" format radio stations.

The Four Seasons have undergone numerous personnel changes over the years but the essence of the group has remained with lead vocalist Frankie Valli and songwriter/manager Bob Gaudio. Valli and Gaudio own the master tapes of all the group's recordings, the right to use the musical group name "The Four Seasons," and also own the rights to the music and lyrics of all the Four Seasons' songs. These properties have generated millions of dollars in revenue for Valli and Gaudio's joint enterprise, called the Four Seasons Partnership.

The roots of the Four Seasons can be traced to the working class neighborhoods of Newark, New Jersey in the mid-1950s when Frankie Valli (born Francis Stephen Castelluccio) joined the Variety Trio, a vocal group made up of Hank Majewski, and brothers Nick and Tommy Devito. The addition of a fourth member made the trio a quartet and so the group's name was changed to the Variatones. Though still a teenager, Valli was an experienced singer. In 1953, under the name Frankie Valley, he had recorded a few songs for Corona Records. The son of a barber, Valli had decided to be a singer at age seven. "I was always singing, as far back as I can remember. In those days, big bands would come and play in theaters like the Paramount (in New York) or the Adams Theater in Newark. My mom used to take me once a week to the Adams, so I saw every major big band at the tail end of that era," Valli recalled to Steve North of the *Two River Times*. Receiving no formal vocal training, Valli honed his voice by listening to records of favorite performers, such as the Four Freshmen, the Hi-Lo's and the Modernaires. He sharpened his falsetto by imitating female singers including Dinah Washington and Rose Murphy.

The Variatones played at clubs in New Jersey and the surrounding area. In 1956, they were signed by RCA records and renamed the Four Lovers. Their RCA recording of "Apple of My Eye" was a minor hit which earned them three appearances on the *Ed Sullivan Show*. Despite this notoriety, the group had trouble garnering many fans. "When we went out of town, we used to lie and tell everybody we were playing at the big resorts. Only we were really performing in a bowling alley in Philly," Valli told John Anderson of *SmartMoney*. Changes came to the Four Lovers in 1960 when Hank Majewski left the group and was replaced by Nick Massi. In the same year, the Four Lovers were taken under the wing of Bob Crewe, a New York-based record producer. In 1961, Nick Devito resigned from the group and Bob Gaudio joined it. In addition to being a keyboard player and vocalist, Gaudio was a talented songwriter able to supply the group with original material. As member of the Royal Teens, Gaudio had written and recorded the novelty hit "Short Shorts" in 1958. After retitling themselves The Four Seasons, taking the name from a bowling alley lounge which had refused to give them a booking, the group was set with the moniker and personnel—Valli, Gaudio, Massi, and Tommy Devito—that would take them to the top.

It was at this point, just before stardom, that Valli, who had day job as barber, and Gaudio, who worked at a printing plant, decided to form a partnership. The deal was made while they sat in Valli's parents's apartment in a low-income housing project in Newark. "We said, 'Neither of us know where we're going to wind up, but maybe we should hedge our bets. You get 50 percent

For the Record . . .

Members in the 1960s include **Tommy Devito** (born June 19, 1935), vocals, guitar; **Bob Gaudio** (born November 17, 1942 in Bronx, NY), vocals, keyboard, and principal songwriter; **Nick Massi** (born September 19, 1935), vocals, bass; **Frankie Valli**, (born May 3, 1937 in Newark, NJ), lead vocals. Earlier members included **Nick Devito** and **Hank Majewski**. Later members include **Don Ciccone**, bass; **John Pavia**, guitar; **Gerry Polci**, vocals, drums; **Lee Shapiro**, keyboard.

Began as the Variatones in early 1950s; became the Four Lovers and signed with RCA records in 1956. Recorded a minor hit, "Apple of My Eye," for RCA in 1956. Appeared on *The Ed Sullivan Show*; teamed with independent record producer Bob Crewe in 1960; songwriter and keyboardist Bob Gaudio joined in 1961; The Four Seasons, had first major hit with the Gaudio composition "Sherry," for Vee-Jay Records in 1962; other hits for Vee-Jay include "Big Girls Don't Cry," "Walk Like a Man," and "Candy Girl;" signed with Philips Records, 1964; released "Dawn," "Ronnie," "Rag Doll," "Save It for Me," "Let's Hang On!," "Working My Way Back to You," "I've Got You Under My Skin," and "C'Mon Marianne;" as the Wonder Who?; had a hit with "Don't Think Twice, It's Alright" in 1965; signed with Motown and released unsuccessful album *Chameleon* in 1972; signed with Warner-Curb Records, 1975; released "Who Loves You?" and "December, 1963 (Oh, What a Night);" rereleased "December, 1963," 1994. Frankie Valli solo hits include "Can't Take My Eyes Off of You," 1967; "My Eyes Adored You" and "Swearin' to God," 1975, and "Grease,"1978. Popular nightclub and touring act in the 1980s and 1990s.

Awards: Inducted into the Rock and Roll Hall of Fame in 1990. Bob Gaudio and Bob Crewe inducted into the Songwriters Hall of Fame in 1995.

Addresses: *Management company*—International Creative Management, 8942 Wilshire Blvd., Beverly Hills, CA 90211.

of me, and I get 50 percent of you,'" Gaudio recalled to Charles P. Alexander of *Time*. The deal, which has never been based on anything more official than a handshake, has endured. Despite ups and downs in their relationship over the decades, neither Valli nor Gaudio has seriously considered breaking the arrangement. "That would be like telling your brother that he couldn't come to dinner anymore. We're family," Gaudio explained to Alexander.

Major success came to the Four Seasons in September of 1962, when their recording "Sherry" for Vee-Jay Records went to the top of the charts. Originally called "Terry," the song had been written by Gaudio in 15 minutes. The lyrics were concocted merely as a way for Gaudio to remember the tune but producer Crewe and the other group members thought they should be retained. Only change was the girl's name in the title. "Sherry was a non-existent person.... It was just a song and the name made it easier to sing, "Sherrrry Sherry Baby." It was impossible to do that with the name Linda or Laurie. See, we were creating a sound," Valli told Tim Ryan of the *Honolulu Star-Bulletin*.

The success of "Sherry" was quickly followed by another number one hit, "Big Girls Don't Cry," another Gaudio composition. The title phrase was taken from an old movie in which the leading man (sometimes identified as Clark Gable, sometimes as John Payne), slaps the leading lady, then taunts her by saying "Big girls don't cry." Over the next five years, The Four Seasons enjoyed a string of top ten hits, most written by Gaudio. Combining simple lyrics about young romance with a driving, infectious beat, Four Seasons material appealed to that part of the audience which continued to be drawn to the East Coast street corner harmonies of the 1950s and early 1960s. Their hits include "Walk Like a Man," "Candy Girl," "Dawn," "Ronnie," "Rag Doll," "Save It for Me," "Let's Hang On," "Working My Way," "Tell It to the Rain," and "C'Mon Marianne." One non-Gaudio hit was a version of Cole Porter's "I've Got You Under My Skin," which Valli told Ryan was "the most sophisticated song we ever recorded." In 1965, the Four Seasons, billing themselves as The Wonder Who?, released a rendition of Bob Dylan's "Don't Think Twice It's Alright," with Valli singing in his highest pitched falsetto. The song went to number 12 on the *Billboard* chart. Valli abandoned the falsetto in favor of a rich baritone on his solo recording of the romantic ballad "Can't Take My Eyes Off of You," which was a hit in the summer of 1967.

It took some time for success to sink into the minds of the Four Seasons. Valli, for example, continued living with his parents in a Newark housing project. "I don't think I really believed the success until about 1964. I drove an old car until that year; I was afraid to buy a new one.... I thought someone would pinch me and I'd wake up from this wonderful dream I was having," Valli told North.

Though the Four Seasons had withstood the British Invasion of American pop music led by the Beatles in 1964, by the late 1960s their popularity began to wane. In response to this drop in public favor, the group made some false moves, most notably a socially conscious concept album called *The Genuine Imitation Life Gazette*. Released in 1968, the album featured an eight-page newspaper insert. The experimental album received a good deal of publicity but sold poorly. By the early 1970s, the Four Seasons were at a low ebb with Valli as the only original member still performing with the group. Gaudio, who had taken over management of the group in the late 1960s, stopped performing in 1971. Gaudio's retreat from the stage annoyed Valli. "Frankie felt like I'd deserted him. It was our toughest time," Gaudio told Anderson. In 1972, the Four Seasons signed with Motown Records' California-based subsidiary MoWest and released the album *Chameleon* which drew little attention.

In 1975, their contract with MoWest having expired, Valli and Gaudio took Valli's solo recording of the song "My Eyes Adored You," to Private Stock Records. Written by Bob Crewe and Kenny Nolan, the low key romantic tune put Valli back at the top of the charts. It was quickly followed by another Valli solo hit, the disco-influenced "Swearin' to God." Meanwhile, Gaudio recruited new personnel for the Four Seasons, including John Pavia, Lee Shapiro, Don Ciccone, and Gerry Polci, and signed a contract with Warner-Curb Records. In the autumn of 1975, the revised group had a major hit with "Who Loves You?" In the spring of 1976, the Four Seasons enjoyed an even bigger success with "December '63 (Oh, What a Night)." Written by Gaudio and his future wife Judy Parker, the song was a bouncy coming of age ditty that played on the nostalgic view many people in the 1970s had developed towards the 1950s and early 1960s. In an unusual turn, lead vocals on the recording were done by Gerry Polci, instead of Valli.

As a solo artist, Valli had the biggest hit of his career with the title song from the movie *Grease* in 1978. Written by Barry Gibb of Bee Gees fame, the disco-style song detracted from the early 1960s setting of the film and was not a part of the stage musical on which the film was based. Nevertheless, the *Grease* title song was a tremendous success in the summer of 1978, as was the movie itself. Although Gaudio had nothing to do with the *Grease* recording, Valli kept to their agreement and split the profits from the song with him. Similarly, Gaudio shared his earnings from outside projects with Valli.

Notable among Gaudio's other projects is the soundtrack to Neil Diamond's movie *The Jazz Singer* in 1981.

Frankie Valli and The Four Seasons are a popular attraction in nightclubs and other live entertainment venues. Though he likes the challenge of new material, Valli understands that audiences come out to hear the hits. "If I went to see someone I had admired all my life, I'd feel disappointed if I didn't hear certain songs ... a lot of people come to our shows to forget about what's going on. It's kind of like therapy," Valli told Winnie Bonelli of the *Passaic Herald & News*. Reissues of Four Seasons recordings enjoy steady sales with many purchases being made by people who weren't alive during the group's heyday.

Selected discography

"Apple of My Eye," RCA, 1956.
"Sherry," Vee-Jay Records, 1962.
"Big Girls Don't Cry," Vee-Hay Records.
"Rag Doll," Philips Records.
"December, 1963 (Oh What a Night)," Warner Curb Records, 1975, rereleased, 1994.

Sources

Books

Helande, Brock, *The Rock Who's Who*, 2nd edition. New York: Schmirmer Books, 1996.
Rees, Dafydd and Luke Chapman, *Encyclopedia of Rock Stars*, New York: Dorling Kindersley, 1996.
Stambler, Irving, *Encyclopedia of Pop, Rock, and Soul*, revised edition, New York: St. Martin's, 1989.

Periodicals

Honolulu Star-Bulletin, March 5, 1998.
Passaic Herald & News, July 10, 1992, p. B1-2.
People, July 27, 1992, p. 122.
SmartMoney, February 1997, p. 79-81.
Time, May 11, 1987, p. 54.
Two River Times (NJ), September 2, 1992, p.1-2.

Online

Rock and Roll Hall of Fame website, www.rockhall.com.

Additional information provided by International Creative Management, Inc.

—*Mary Kalfatovic*

Frankie Lymon and The Teenagers

Vocal group

Frankie Lymon and the Teenagers—like Hansen, the New Kids on the Block, the Jackson 5, and Stevie Wonder after them—all had smash pop music singles before they could legally drive. However, Frankie Lymon was, as Cub Koda stated in the *All Music Guide, Volume 1,* "the first black teenage star." From the streets corners of Harlem to the London Palladium stage, Frankie Lymon and The Teeagers, as noted in the *Encyclopedia of Pop, Rock, and Soul,* were a doo-wop vocal group whose "saga ... might be called a Cinderella story without a happy ending" as well as a song without an answer to this eternal question: "Why Do Fools Fall in Love?"

In the 1950s, a sweet-sounding musical craze swept across America—doo wop. In 1955, one group, the Ermines—school friends Herman Santiago, Joe Negroni, Sherman Garnes, and Jimmy Merchant stood on West 165th Street in New York City and harmonized because, as Merchant said in the *New Yorker,* "It was a fad at the time to be a vocal group. It wasn't just like roller skating. It was a higher-class fad—a quality fad. It tied in to being known, and getting girls." Yet, it was not until another voice, the soprano boy voice of Frankie Lymo, joined the group that the Ermines, now renamed the Coupe de Villes, became more than a fad. Lymon, had already stepped into the public spotlight by singing with the Harlemaires, his father's gospel group, but how Lymon joined the Coupe de Villes is unclear. One version suggested by reporter Calvin Trillin in the *New Yorker,* was that Lymon, passing the group on the street, overheard Santiago struggling to hit some high notes. Lymon, as Santiago told Trillin, who was "extremely talented and bright and very cocky," just jumped in with his "gospel tenor—a high strong voice of remarkable clarity."

By late 1955, the once Ermines and Coupe de Villes, changed their name again—to the Premiers. Richard Barrett, a member of another vocal group, the Valentines and a part-time record company employee, heard the Premiers singing "Lily Maebelle"—a Valentine's hit—outside his bedroom window. Barrett liked what he heard and promised to praise the group to his boss, Gee Records producer/promoter George Goldner, if they would stop waking him up every morning. Goldner, awed by one song—"Why Do Fools Fall in Love?"—asked Lymon, as quoted in the *Encyclopedia of Pop, Rock, and Soul,* "You got any sheet music for it?" Lymon replied, "Nope, we don't know anything about written-down music. This lack of "written-down music" knowledge would 30 years later create an intriguing court battle. However, on January 10, 1956, "Why Do Fools Fall in Love?" was released and as stated by Trillin in the *New Yorker,* "It was an instant, stupendous hit."

Short Ride On Success's Wave

With the success of "Why Do Fools Fall in Love?"—a gold record single—Frankie Lymon, at the age of 14, and The Teenagers, all under the age of 16, became pop music superstars. However, it was not just their smooth vocal harmonies that made them popular. In the 1950s, due to race discrimination, crossover success from the rhythm and blues charts to the pop charts by black recording artists was uncommon. Yet, as stated by Trillin in the *New Yorker,* "The Teenagers came in a squeaky-clean package—processed hair and the sort of clothes familiar from Hollywood campus movies of the forties, including letter sweaters." And with their smash hit spending 16 weeks on the pop chart, Lymon and The Teenagers rode a wave of success onto Ed Sullivan and Dick Clark's TV shows as well as onto rock 'n roll deejay Alan Freed's rock concerts and movies, such as *Rock, Rock, Rock.* In that movie, Lymon and The Teenagers debuted two new, non-intimidating singles, "Baby, Baby, Baby" and "I'm Not a Juvenile Delinquent."

By the middle of 1956, four more singles from the group's first album also hit the top ten: "I Promise to Remember," "I Want You to be My Girl," "I'm Not a Know-it-All," and "Who Can Explain?" Trillin believed that, "the Teenagers were the model—the proof that a miracle could happen." Frankie Lymon and The Teenagers, five kids from the street corners of Harlem, played concerts at London, England's Palladium theatre and cruised in luxury. Merchant told Trillin that "we [the group] were the first people to get out of long limousines with sneakers and jeans on." Moreover, as Trillin further stated, the success of this vocal group was because "The Teenagers were not considered threatening to whites—probably because of Frankie, who came across as the sassy, pint-sized kid brother who would never grow up."

Yet, the end of 1956, Lymon had grown up enough to catch a new wave—a solo wave. The Teenagers replaced Lymon but never again rode the high wave of success. Neither did Lymon, as quoted in *People,* "he [Lymon] got trapped in his child-like image"—but his voice had changed. Thus, Lymon was forced to lip-synch his hits at sock hops. Lymon also was not, as Jerry Blavat, a deejay, told Trillin, "the mischievous kid, whose idea of back stage entertainment was to hide Paul Anka's shoes just before Anka had to be on-stage"—Lymon had become a drug addict. Lymon, as quoted by *People,* admitted that the single, "I'm Not a Juvenile Delinquent" was far from autobiographical, "[I] ... had been a pimp at age 10 ... [and] had been smoking marijuana when I was in grade school. But I didn't start using [heroin] until I got into show business." Lymon tried to get clean, but failed. As quoted in *People,* Lymon said, "I didn't give a damn about drugs."

However, Lymon despite a career cut short by his voice change and drugs, married three times—first, in 1964 to Elizabeth Waters, a woman with arrests for theft and prostitution; In 1965, to Zola Taylor, the Platters girl singer, and in 1967, after a brief stint in the Army to get out of jail time, to Emira Eagle, an elementary school teacher. In 1968, Lymon attempted a comeback and had been promised a singing job in New York. Yet, on February 28, 1968, Lymon was found dead on his grandmother's bathroom floor. Lymon, only 25, had overdosed on heroin. Ten years later, two Teenagers—

Garnes and Negroni also died—Garnes from a heart attack and Negronia from a cerebral hemorrhage.

Over the next 28 years, Frankie Lymon and the Teenagers, were a forgotten doo-wop quintet, however their hit single, "Why Do Fools Fall in Love?" was not. In 1973, the song was featured in the popular coming-of-age movie, *American Graffiti*, and in 1981, Diana Ross recorded her version of the song, and it once again became a Top 10 hit on the pop music charts. In 1984, George Goldner, Frankie Lymon and The Teenagers' producer applied for an original copyright of the song to insure royalty money for Emira, Lymon's third wife. However, two questions arose with this application—first, who was Lymon's legal widow, and second, who wrote "Why Do Fools Fall in Love?"

Married Thrice But Never Divorced

Lymon's three wives—Elizabeth Waters, Zola Taylor, and Emira Eagle—had never met. That fact changed in 1997, almost 30 years after Lymon's death, when, at a Manhattan court house, the three women were called to testify. Because Lymon had never divorced Waters, Taylor, or Eagle, the question of who was Lymon's legal widow had to be answered before any royalty money was awarded. Each woman had their own memories of Lymon. Waters, as quoted in the *New Yorker*, knew "Frankie at the time [in 1961] he was a very sad, lonely person." Waters also stated that," Frankie could fool you, he could fool me, Frankie could fool God." However, Waters seemed to fool Lymon. In 1964, when Lymon and she were married, Waters was already married to someone else. Taylor, Lymon's second wife, and the Platters girl singer, had dated Lymon when he was just 14, never produced a marriage license. Eagle, only married to Lymon for eight months, remembered, as quoted in *People*, that Frankie "treated me like I was his queen."

The judge decided that only Waters, seeing that Lymon could not legally marry anyone else after marrying his first wife, and overlooking the fact that she was already married, named Waters Lymon's legal widow. However, in 1990, this decision was overturned and Eagle was named Lymon's new legal widow and therefore entitled to his estate of back royalties for "Why Do Fools Fall in Love?" However, another question had to be answered before any money was awarded—who wrote that smash single?

In the early 1990s, another court battle began—this time to decide who were the true author's of "Why Do Fools Fall in Love?" To answer this question, a time trip must be taken back through a maze of buyers and sellers (including Lymon himself). In 1956, the song's registered copyright listed Lymon and The Teenager's producer George Goldner as the hit song's writers. However, as stated by Trillin in the *New Yorker*, it was a "common practice in the fifties for an R & B record producer to tell a group that he'd have to have a writing credit if it wanted its song recorded." Richard Barrett, the man who brought Lymon and The Teenagers to the attention of Goldner further stated that, "we [doo-wop groups] had no idea of the value of a song then. We had no idea what the value of a copyright was. And they [record producers] weren't going to tell any black people about that anyway."

Three Versions of "Fools"

However, Goldner, after amassing too many gambling debts, left his partner, Morris Levy, with control of the copyright. In 1965, Lymon, by that time a heavy drug user, needed money. So he sold his rights to Levy for, as reported in the *New Yorker*, "a sum that was probably something like fifteen hundred dollars." Thus, when "Why Do Fools Fall in Love?" appeared in the 1973 movie, *American Graffiti*, and when Diana Ross covered the hit in 1981, only Levy received 100 per cent of the royalties. Yet, in the late 1980s, Jimmy Merchant and Henry Santiago—the last two surviving Teenagers—contested Levy's claim. At the trial, as stated in *People*, "witnesses testified that Merchant and Santiago were 15-year-old street corner harmonizers who came up with the tune before Lymon joined them." Merchant and Santiago also had, as reported in the *New Yorker,* an "interesting piece of evidence: the first 45-r.p.m. single of "Why Do Fools Fall in Love?" [which] listed as the song's writers not just Frankie Lymon and George Goldner but also Herman Santiago."

Furthermore, Santiago and Merchant stated in the *New Yorker* that the idea for the song came when they picked through a groupie's letters to "get ideas, just to see what we could come up with.... That's basically what we had the idea from." Yet, another version of the song's origin, as reported by Trillin, was that one of the groupie's letters included a poem. That poem had "one of its ["Why Do Fools Fall in Love?"] main lines: "Why do birds sing so gay?" [and] Santiago and Merchant ... worked the sentiments of the letters into a song lyric and then Frankie Lymon helped with the tune."

However, Lymon himself told three versions of how he wrote the song. The first version, as remembered by Emira Lymon in the *New Yorker*, said that Lymon "had written the song at twelve because he had fallen in love with a teacher and she told him that he was nothing but a kid, he was too young for her. And that is why he wrote 'Why Do Fools Fall in Love?'." Another version, as cited in the *New Yorker,* was that the song was "inspired by Lymon's seventh grade essay." Yet, Elizabeth Waters, Lymon's first wife, offered that the song was just "off the top of his [Lymon's] head." Finally, in 1992, over 30 years after "Why Do Fools Fall in Love?" hit the charts, Santiago and Merchant, along with Frankie Lymon were named the writers of the song. Merchant told *People,* "Thirty-six years is a long, long, long time. But they [record producers] never really do get away with it." However, this verdict was later overturned.

"Fools" Rose Again

In the late 1990s, Santiago, Merchant, and Lymon's brother Louis still performed as The Teenagers. Yet, it was in September of 1998, when Hollywood released *Why Do Fools Fall in Love,* a movie based on the life of Frankie Lymon and The Teenagers, that the group's doo-wop sound and hit single rose again. However, the movie, as stated in the *Milwaukee Journal Sentinel,* "missed its mark ... and never notes Frankie's voice changing ... [nor how Frankie] lost his looks and charm." Bobby Jay, the Teenagers current bassist, further commented that Lymon "was begging on the street. The drugs took a huge toll. He was missing teeth. He looked bad. It was tragic."

Even though the movie misrepresented Lymon and The Teenagers life, it had reminded the public of their sweet-sounding melodies. Moreover, as stated in the Rock 'n Roll Hall of Fame's online biography of the group, "The song ["Why Do Fools Fall in Love?"] has attained the status of a vocal-group classic owing to Lymon's agile, ingenuous and utterly charming performance." Thus, perhaps the saga of Frankie Lymon and The Teenagers and the eternal question: "Why Do Fools Fall in Love?"

was a fairy tale, albeit one without a happily-ever-after ending for Lymon—or as Santiago told *People,* "a natural superstar. There was nobody like Frankie."

Selected discography

Why Do Fools Fall in Love, Gee Records, 1956.
At The London Palladium, 1956.
The Teenagers For Collectors Only [Box Set], Collectables Records, 1994.
The Very Best of Frankie Lymon & The Teenagers, Wea/Atlantic/Rhino, 1998.

Sources

Books

Hitchcock, H. Wiley and Stanley Sadie, eds., *The New Grove Dictionary of American Music Volume Three, L-Q,* Mac-Millan Press Limited, 1986.
Stambler, Irwin, *Encyclopedia of Pop, Rock, & Soul,* St. Martin's Press, 1974.

Periodicals

Milwaukee Journal Sentinel, September 6, 1998, page 8.
New Yorker, February 25, 1991.
People, December 7, 1992; September 14, 1998.

Online

"Frankie Lymon and the Teenagers," *Rock and Roll Hall of Fame,* http:www.rockhall.com.

Additional information was provided by Music Boulevard Online Newsstand [Cub Koda's short biography].

—*Ann M. Schwalboski*

Ghost

Rock band

The Japanese rock group Ghost has been mystifying audiences with its invigorating brew of exotic sounds emanating from The Ghost House in Tokyo, as well as temples and other open-air locations. As a youth at a private junior high school, bandleader Masaki Batoh was exposed to rock music during field trips with his music teachers. He reminisces to *Wire*, "One of these places was Jazz Kizza, a small coffee shop that used to play jazz records. Through them [his teachers] I was awakened to the music of Bob Dylan, Pink Floyd, Velvet Underground, Beatles, and Rolling Stones." Batoh also listened to English folk-rockers The Third Ear Band, German rock groups Can, Amon Düül, Popol Vuh, and traditional Japanese folk music.

Batoh founded Ghost with several of his college friends in Tokyo during the early 1980s. From the beginning, the band's lineup was in a state of flux. Batoh explains to *Ptolemaic Terrascope*, "In the beginning, we used to play far-out long freak-outs in small college gigs. But the members of Ghost were always so changeable, mainly because the ideas of each one's methods had always swayed between materialism amd spirituality ... some wanted to express themselves through ordinary rock music while others wanted to make music through the philosphical, idealist way."

Ghost had a different name for the first several years of its existence. However, in 1989, prior to the release of its first album, the band was asked by its record company to change its name. Batoh told *Ongaku Otaku*, "The boss of P.S.F. said our previous name, from 1983, was not suitable for our sound then. 'How do you feel about changing the name?' he asked. Okay.... So I was thinking, thinking, and one time when I took the train, I saw a poster for the movie Ghost. And I arrived, then, at our name. It sounded nice, it's cool."

Ghost's self-titled first album was released in 1991. The material on the album was more song-oriented than the band's live performances, which bandmembers called *sokyo*, or improvisations. Batoh explained the changes in Ghost's style to *Ongaku Otaku*, "When we thought to make an album, we played many *sokyo*. But when we listened to it, the sound was not interesting.... At first we played the same ways, then we tried to make some tunes. Easy ones, two chords or three chords, using our instruments and sometimes banjo or Japanese instruments.... Finally, we cut the songs up with long improvisations."

The band's next album, *Second Time Around*, was more folk and folk-rock influenced. Ghost began to attract attention around the world, and critics began describing its music using other bands as reference points. This did not bother Batoh, as he told Ongaku Otaku, "We don't make music, it's born from inside us. If our music sounds like some other bands Quicksilver, Amon Düül it's all right. We don't care at all. It was born from our inside, naturally and gradually constructed in its production."

Ghost first toured the United States in 1995. Following the live album *Temple Stone,* the band released its American debut album, *Lama Rabi Rabi,* on the Drag City label. In underground rock circles, Ghost was regarded as a major new player. The *Wire* said of the group, "It is [the] diversity of musical influences (many of which are stirred into the same song) that give Ghost their charm and individuality. It seems that anything that can be adapted to fit into their complex musical tapestry so long as it is strange or interesting enough to attract their imagination."

Soon after *Lama Rabi Rabi,* Batoh released a solo album *Collected Works,* of unreleased demos and other material. Batoh did not originally intend to release the material, but was persuaded to by friends. He elucidates to The *Wire,* "One day I went into the studio and gathered up all the material I had for songs that had been left there for several years. At the same time I found odd demos with fragments of songwriting, singing, sound effects, and field recordings from various places. I edited together a tape for myself, for my secret joy. When I played it for some friends at Ghost House they suddenly stopped talking, and I thought they must have been disturbed by this rough, ominous sounding music. But as soon as I moved to stop the tape they asked me to leave it playing, they liked it [and] urged me to release the tapes as soon as possible. I never used to listen to other people's advice about my own music but this time I obeyed."

Another Ghost-related side project is Cosmic Invention, featuring a varying line-up of members of various Japanese underground rock groups. Batoh is very supportive of the underground rock scene in Japan, but never enjoyed pop music from his homeland. He told *Ptolemaic Terrascope,* "The situation regarding popular music in Japan just makes me feel sadness. I never say it's hopeless, but almost all Japanese popular music has never produced any impression on my mind except for traditional folk. Although there has been a great number of groups, I have found none of them to be unique or interesting. They're content on following on from American and European movements."

In 1997, Ghost played a concert featuring a surprise appearance by Damo Suzuki, the Japanese vocalist for the German band Can during the 1970s, a major influence on Ghost. The following year, members of Ghost toured America with the folk-rock duo Damon and Naomi and Tom Rapp, leader of the 1960s folk-rock group Pearls Before Swine, another of the band members' favorite performers. Those three performers shared the stage at the Terrastock West Festival, sponsored by the U.K. magazine *Ptolemaic Terrascope.* The set ventured from gentle ballads to avant-garde noise, and was a highlight of the three-day event.Ghost continues to amaze and delight a growing number of fans worldwide, mixing disparate musical traditions and influences into an earthbound yet otherworldly musical stew.

Selected discography

Ghost, PSF, 1991, reissued Drag City, 1997.
"Improvised Yama Tura," (on *Tokyo Flashback Volume 1*), PSF, 1991.
"Sun Is Tangging" (on *Tokyo Flaskback Volume 2*), PSF, 1992.
Second Time Around, PSF, 1992, reissued Drag City, 1997.
Temple Stone, PSF, 1993, reissued Drag City, 1997.
"Images of April" (on *From The Dead In Space: A Tribute To Tom Rapp)*,Magic Eye , 1997.
Lama Rabi Rabi, Drag City, 1997.
"Return To Coimbula" (excerpt on *Succour*), Flydaddy, 1997.
"Return To Coimbula" (on *Alms*), Fleece, 1997.
"Moungod Air Cave"/ "Guru In The Echo", Now Sound, 1997.

Masaki Batoh solo

Masaki Batoh, *A Ghost From The Darkened Sea*, Now Sound, 1996.

Masaki Batoh, *Kikaokubeshi*, Now Sound, 1997.

Masaki Batoh, *Collected Works*, Now Sound, 1997.

(With Masaki Batoh and others), *Cosmic Invention, Help Your Satori Mind*, Now Sound, 1997.

Sources

Periodicals

Ongaku Otaku, Issue 3.

Ptolemaic Terrascope, April, 1993; September, 1997.

The Wire, January, 1997; August, 1997.

Online

http://www.terrascope.org, (September 28, 1998).

http://www.allmusic.com, (September 28, 1998).

Additional information was obtained through press materials from Drag City Records.

—*Jim Powers*

Deborah Gibson

Singer, songwriter

Ever since she could walk, Debbie Gibson had music in her blood and theater in her heart. As a young child she played both roles of Baby June and Baby Louise in a 1982 Long Island production of Gypsy. She also performed with the Metropolitan Opera. Yet all the while she kept singing and composing her original pop songs on the side. Diligently writing her songs and recording them for her own personal enjoyment and those of her neighborhood friends, she knew that it was only a matter of time before she could make this secret dream a reality. As a teenager, she convinced her parents to help convert the family garage into a high-tech recording studio. What followed was some serious music making. At age 16, she cut "Only In My Dreams" on a 12 inch disc in her own little production shack and sent the demo to Atlantic Records. Atlantic was surprised at her genius and gave her a recording contract. The single "Only In My Dreams" skyrocketed onto the top 40 charts and introduced Debbie Gibson's talent to the world.

After another more months of preparation, she released her debut album, Out of the Blue, in 1987. The songs "Foolish Beat" from Out of the Blue, and "Lost in Your Eyes" from the double platinum Electric Youth, catapulted into number one hits, earning her the 1989 ASCAP Songwriter of the Year Award. An award she shared with Bruce Springsteen in a tie. But it gave the teenage Gibson the distinction of being the youngest artist in entertainment history to write, produce and perform such a feat. "Being versatile bridges the gap between the recording studio and the theater," she told Billboard's Chuck Taylor. "It's really the perfect match." Her most rabid fans call themselves "Debheads."

A series of award winning albums followed in lightning succession. In 1990, she went gold with Anything Is Possible. At the same time, she continued in theater, entertaining Broadway audiences with her portrayal of the tragic Eponine in Les Miserables, the rock and roll tart Rizzo in Grease, the romantic lovelorn Belle in Beauty and the Beast, and as Fanny Brice in Funny Girl. During this time, she even made guest appearances on television in such shows as Beverly Hills 90210 and Street Justice. However, Gibson was not one to neglect her original music and she hit the pop charts again with Body Mind Soul in 1993, and Think With Your Heart in 1995. Grown into a mature young woman, Gibson decided to make some changes, dropping the name Debbie for the more adult Deborah. And in a surprising musical lark, audiences were stunned to hear Deborah singing back up on a Circle Jerks album. Doing the accompanying vocals to "I Want To Destroy You," she excited the Circle Jerks and their producer so much that they wanted her to go touring with them and work on the entire album. "People were shocked," she told Detour Magazine's Dennis Hensley. "I loved putting myself to that extreme. I can let my hair down and rock with the best of them. I have a gutsy side, and I have a sensual side, everyone has." She declined the Jerk's invitation but appeared with them one night in New York's punk mecca CBGB's. The moshers became wilder as Deborah egged them on. She climaxed the performance by diving headfirst into the mosh-pit. "I stage dove into the crowd," she told Detour's Hensley, "You're floating on a sea of hands, on a lot of Mohawks and piercings."

After all this, she decided it was finally time she started her own recording label. Many successful musicians have attempted to do so in the past but with mixed results. She chose to think positive thoughts and started Espiritu Records. The company's first releace was the self-titled Deborah in 1997. A track from this effort, "Only Words," is a hard, powerful dance remix which recently made Billboard's Hot Dance-Music/Club Play's Top 40. But most critics panned this latest album as they have her previous three efforts. Even so, a small number of critics were surprised to hear the depth and maturity of this new production but were hesitant to endorse it for fear of being labeled a Debhead. Gibson feels that many critics as well as audience members still can't get that perky teenage Electric Youth image out of their heads. "I don't know how to be put into a little box or category," she told Dance Music Authority's Jeffrey L. Newman.

For the Record . . .

Born April 31, 1970, Brooklyn, NY, Religious denomination:daughter of Joe and Diane Gibson, mother is manager of the career.

Singer, composer, Broadway and television actress; made acting debut as a child actor on the Long Island stage playing both the roles of *Baby Jane* and *Baby Louise* in the musical *Gypsy;* as a child she also performed with the Metropolitan Opera; released debut album, *Out of the Blue,* 1997; released second album, *Electric Youth,* 1989; appeared in Beverly Hills 90210, 1991; appeared in *Street Justice,* 1992; starred as Eponine in the Broadway production of *Les Miserables,* 1992; starred as Sandy in the London West End production of *Grease,* 1993-94; starred as Rizzo in the U.S. National tour of *Grease;* appeared in episode *Step By Step,* 1995; played the title role of the stripper Gypsy Rose Lee in *Gypsy* at the Paper Mill Theater, Milburn, NJ, 1998.

Awards: Double platinum status for *Out of Blue,* 1997 New York Music Award for Debut Artist of the Year, 1989; New York Music Award for Debut Album of the Year, 1989; double platinum status for *Electric Youth,* 1989; ASCAP Songwriter of the Year Award-(tied with Bruce Springsteen) 1989; New York Music Award for Song of the Year, "Lost in Your Eyes," 1990; American Music Award nomination for Best Female Pop Vocalist, 1990; American Songwriter Award for Rock Producer of the Year, 1990; People's Choice Award nomination for Favorite Female Music Performer, 1992; St. Mary's Children & Family Services Humanitarian Award Recipient, 1998.

Addresses: *Record company*—Atlantic Records, 1290 Avenue of the Americas, New York, NY 10104; Espiritu Records, 666 Avenue of the Americas, Suite 302, New York, NY 10103; *Website*—The Official Deborah Gibson Web Site: http://www.deborahgibson.com/.

Now, at the age of 28, having sold over 16 million albums worldwide, with enough gold records, and musical awards to fill half a dozen livingroom mantlepieces, Gibson reflects on her whirlwind career. "My perspective has changed quite a lot over the years," she told Taylor. "I try to hold on as much as possible to that raw enthusiasm. That's what makes it enjoyable. I've learned a lot about people, some good, some bad. But the most important thing I know is it's most satisfying to be yourself, accepted or not. I'm doing this the way I want to do it."

Gibson still maintains her mother Diane as manager. Also, she regularly includes her sisters in various production aspects of her career. Family has always been an important part of Deborah's life. The Gibson family shares a very loving, atmosphere together. That is why Deborah is able to maintain such a caring, positive family-oriented personality.

She also believes in supporting charities. Along with her musical and theatrical careers, there is another side to Deborah Gibson, one of concern for the less fortunate. She also understands the tragedies which hardships can bring. Her own father, Joe Gibson, had a hard life as a young man and even spent some time in an orphanage. She has done work and continues to do work for the Pediatric Aids Foundation, the Make-A-Wish Foundation, and St. Mary's Children & Family Foundation. The St. Mary's Children Foundation is a special concern for Gibson, since her father spent several years there as a child. It involves providing a caring home for abused, orphaned, and otherwise neglected children. At present, she is still single, but wishes to eventually marry and have her own children, as well as adopting several others.

While waiting for that one special romance to happen, Gibson occupies herself by more work. Ever the energetic, she finished a six-week run of *Gypsy* at the Paper Mill Playhouse in Milburn, New Jersey during the 1998 fall season. Also, she recently wrapped up several acting roles starring in two as of yet unreleased movies, *Wedding Party,* and *My Girlfriend's Boyfriend.* In addition, she has completed some songs for the soundtrack of Ethan J. Todd Anderson's film *Naked Man,* is recording a concept album for *Z, The Masked Musical.* Presently she is working on an original musical called *Skirts* that will hopefully premiere on Broadway.

Selected discography

Anything Is Possible, Atlantic Records, 1990.
Body Mind Soul, Atlantic Records, 1993.
Deborah, Espiritu Records, 1996.
Electric Youth, Atlantic Records, 1989.
Greatest Hits, Atlantic Records, 1995.
Out of the Blue, Atlantic Records, 1987
Think With Your Heart, Atlantic Records, 1995.

Sources

Billboard, August 16, 1997.
Cosmopolitan, September 1998.
Dance Music Authority, August 1997.
Detour Magazine, April, 1996.
In Style Magazine, October 1998.
National Enquirer, August 18, 1998.
People Magazine, August 17, 1998.

Additional information provided by Espiritu Records publicity materials, 1998, and from Deborah Gibson sites on the World Wide Web.

—Timothy Kevin Perry

Gerry Goffin-Carole King

Pop music composers

The songwriting team of Gerry Goffin and Carole King is one of the most successful partnerships in pop music. The songs they co-wrote together as part of the Brill Building musical dynasty are so successful that they are still played on radio stations throughout the country. The Beatles were so impressed and influenced by the Goffin-King duo that they were the first people they wanted to meet at the Brill Building in New York City, when they arrived in America.

During the late fifties and early sixties, the Brill Building became one of the foremost music publishers of the world and it fostered a group of young songwriters who were original and brilliant in their talents. The greatest ones were the teams of Gerry Goffin/Carole King, Barry Mann/Cynthia Weil, Jerry Leiber/Mike Stoller, and Jeff Barry/Ellie Greenwich. The couples mentioned here are responsible for writing most of the pop songs from the late 1950s to the early 1960s. Many were still in their teens when they started cranking out gold records for a who's who of rock and roll artists and performers. Instead of performing the songs they wrote and being out in front of the stage lights themselves, the Brill group preferred to work behind the scenes. However, as the Beatles' British invasion took hold of America's youth, the types of songs as well as the sound itself began changing and the success of the Brill Building began to decline. Another vital factor to Brill's decline was that many of the new musical groups arriving on the scene wrote their own songs and didn't have a need for hired tunesmiths. Most of the Brill songwriters saw what was coming and branched out into other kinds of songwriting. Ellie Greenwich became a jingle-song writer for commercials, some wrote musicals, Jeff Barry wrote the songs for the Archies, and Burt Bachrach began drifting towards the jet-set bossa nova songs he is now primarily associated with.

Gerry Goffin was born on February 11, 1942, in Queens, New York. He became interested in music at an early age and, as he grew older, progressed in his songwriting abilities. Goffin had a unique talent and style that only seemed to get better as he grew up. After high school, he attended Queens College. While at college, Goffin became part of a loosely based group of very talented, upcoming musicians and songwriters. It was here where he also met his future wife and musical songwriting partner Carole King.

Carole King was born on February 9, 1942 in Sheepshead Brooklyn, New York. A very talented girl, Carole grew up singing, playing piano, and became entranced by the emerging new musical genre of rock and roll. Full of confidence, she told herself that she could write songs as good or even better than the stuff she was hearing on the radio. At the age of 16, she began travelling regularly to Manhattan after school to knock on the doors of the music publishers and record companies. Eventually, her perserverance paid off and she was accepted into the Brill Building as a songwriter. What followed was "Oh Neil," an answer to the popular Neil Sedaka hit "Oh Carol" written in her honor, a parody of Annette Funicello's "Tell Paul" which became "Short Mort," "The Right Girl/Goin Wild," and "Baby Sitter/Under the Stars," all these songs written while still in high school. Later, she began showing up with famous DJ Alan Freed at his local rock and roll shows. Upon graduation from high school, she attended Queens College and continued her songwriting. Along with meeting Goffin, it was here at Queens College where she likewise became friends with Paul Simon. Already a successful Brill writer, she married Goffin and began her most famous award winning collaborations as part of the writing team of "Goffin-King." Once married, it wasn't long before they had a child. They named the baby daughter Louise.

The Hitmakers

The first song Goffin-King wrote together "Will You Love Me Tomorrow" was initially turned down by Columbia Record's chief Mitch Miller. Undeterred by this rejection, they went to the Scepter label and released the

For the Record . . .

Gerry Goffin (born February 11, 1942, Queens N.Y.); **Carole King** (born February 9, 1942); married each other in the early 1960s; children: one daughter, Louise. *Education:* Both attended Queens College in NY.

Began working at the Brill Building and wrote a series of number one hits "Will You Love Me Tomorrow" performed by the Shirelles in 1961, "Take Good Care of my Baby" performed by Bobby Vee released in 1961, *The Loco-Motion*" performed by Little Eva, released in 1961, "Up on the Roof " performed by the Drifters released in 1963; "I'm Into Something Good" performed by Herman's Hermits in 1966, "Don't Bring Me Down" performed by the Animals in 1966, "A Natural Woman" performed by Aretha Franklin in 1967, and a "Pleasant Valley Sunday" performed by the Monkees in 1967.; Goffin started writing with new songwriting partner Barry Goldberg; King released first solo album *Writer,* 1970; released *Tapestry,* 1971, two songs off *Tapestry* gained became hit singles, "So Far Away" and "It's Too Late" ; released "Music," in 1971 which went to number one and had hit single "Sweet Seasons;" released *Rhymes & Reasons,* 1972; released *Simple Things* in 1977; released *Pearls,* 1980; released *Speeding Time,* 1983; released *Color of Your Dreams* 1993; Gerry Goffin released solo album *Backroom Blood,* 1993.

song in 1960. The song also became a number one hit in 1961 for an all-girl group, The Shirelles. Their next tune "Take Good Care of My Baby" was performed by Bobby Vee in 1961 and became a number one hit as well. Their next effort was "The Loco-motion" was sung by their own babysitter Little Eva. Along with having had success as a number one hit in the early sixties, that song also re-emerged over a decade later to enjoy more hit success as a raucous hard rock piece performed by Grand Funk Railroad.

Another great Goffin-King classic during this early-sixties period was "One Fine Day" recorded by The Chiffons. Goffin and King went on to a fast rollercoaster ride of chart topping successes in the period of the early sixties. In 1962, King tried to launch a solo career but only had one hit, "It Might As Well Rain Until Septem-

ber". In the mid-sixties, columnist Al Aronowitz joined King and Goffin as partners in a new record company called Tomorrow Records which turned out to be a commecial flop.

Mid-Sixties Haze

As the mid-sixties became wilder in dress, politics, and music, the commercial songwriting market went through tremendous changes. No longer did the radio listening/record buying public want happy, late fifties-early sixties pop songs about high school love and crusing in convertibles. Even the mop top "yeah, yeah, yeah" of Beatlemania had long since passed. The trend in the music business was geared toward albums instead of single hits. The sound, tenor, and angry political tones of this new musical scene was an entirely different situation. However, despite all the socio-political changes, Goffin-King scored more musical gold. They wrote the number one hit, "I'm Into Something Good," for Herman's Hermits in 1964, "Don't Bring Me Down," performed by the Animals in 1966, "A Natural Woman," recorded by Aretha Franklin in 1966, and "Pleasant Valley Sunday," for the Monkees in 1967.

Eventually, the Goffin-King marriage dissolved. Goffin started writing with musical songwriting partner Barry Golberg. They scored the hit "I've Got to Use My Imagination" for Gladys Knight and the Pips in 1974. King married her second husband Myddle Class' bassist Charles Larkey and moved west. They founded a group called the City; a trio completed by New York musician Danny Kortchmar. They released a debut album *Now That Everything's Been Said.* The album failed. Some believe it was because of King's stage fright. However, three songs from that album went on to later commercial successes; "Wasn't Born To Follow" became a hit for the Byrds, "Hi-De-Ho" became a hit for Blood, Sweat & Tears, and "You've Got A Friend," became a hit for singer-songwriter James Taylor.

King became close friends with Taylor who encouraged her to embark on a solo career. A shy, sensitive woman, King eventually agreed with Taylor's advice and released her first solo album, *Writer,* in 1970. It flopped. She tried again by releasing her second solo album *Tapestry* in 1971. Three hits came from this effort, "So Far Away", "It's Too Late", and "I Feel The Earth Move." The album remained on the charts for six weeks and became the most popular, best-selling album of that early seventies period. Her next work, *Music,* was released in 1971. It went to number one, too, with the song "Sweet Seasons." Next, she released *Rhymes & Reasons* which reached number two on the charts in

1972. She put out *Wrap Around Joy* in 1974 which had "Jazzman". The song reached number one.

Worked with Old Friends

King reunited with Goffin in 1975 to write the album *Thoroughbred*. It wasn't a romantic reunion, it was simply a reunion of two very successful songwriters who wanted to collaborate once again to work their special magic. Key artists on this work were long-time friends David Crosby, Graham Nash, and James Taylor. Public reaction was subdued.

King's next project was the album *Simple Things* which she released in 1977. For this effort, she mounted a tour with a backup group called Navarro. During this period she married a third time. This trip around the altar was to songwriting partner Rick Evers. Tragedy struck when he died of a heroin overdose a year later. She put out an album called *Pearls* in 1980. It was a collection of song performances written during her Goffin-King days. It proved to be her last great hit. After this, she retreated from the fast paced music lifestyle and moved to a small mountain village in the state of Idaho. There King became actively involved in the environmental movement while still writing her songs. She released the album *Speeding Time* in 1983. After this album she took a six-year hiatus.

Wrote in the Nineties

King graced the world of music again when she re-emerged with her album *City Streets*. *City Streets* featured an impressive guest performance by Eric Clapton. She released *Colour of Your Dreams* in 1993 with a cameo from Guns N' Roses' Slash. Having spent a long, successful career as a singer-songwriter, King

decided to enter a new venue. In the 1990s she started working on various projects for the musical theater. In 1994, she made her Broadway debut in the tense, exciting drama *Bloodbrothers*. At present, King continues to write her music and explore different ways of expanding her creative horizons. Currently, Gerry Goffin continues to write his music. His most recent release was *Backroom Blood* in 1996.

Selected discography

Singles

"Will You Love Me Tomorrow," 1960.
"Take Good Care of My Baby," 1961
"The Loco-motion."
"One Fine Day," 1962.
"It Might As Well Rain Until September," 1962.

Albums

(Carole King solo album,) *Tapestry*, Epic Records, 1971.
My Greatest Hits:Songs of Long Ago, Ode/CBS Records, 1987.
Brill Building Sound, Era Records, 1993.
(Goffin solo album), *Back Room Blood*,, Genes Records, 1996.
(Carole King solo album), *Carnegie Hall Concert: June 18, 1971*, Sony Records, 1996

Sources

http://www.rockhall.com/induct/goffgerr.html.

Additional information was provided by CBS/Ode Records and Epic Records.

—*Timothy Kevin Perry*

The Go-Go's

Rock band

After blasting onto the Hollywood punk scene in 1978, the Go-Go's made their own way as the first female pop band to sell records and rule the charts by writing and playing their own material. What started out as a goof ended up making it big. "We formed a band for laughs and it turned into this huge thing," lead singer and founding member Belinda Carlisle told *People* in 1986. The Go-Go's created their own pop world by combining the New Wave style of the time with their own brand of what came to be known in the 1990s as "girl power."

Carlisle met Jane Wiedlin on the Hollywood punk club circuit, where Carlisle had been hanging out since she left high school . Carlisle was going to be the drummer for the seminal punk band The Germs but was replaced before she started by a drummer who actually owned a drum kit and knew how to play, neither of which Carlisle did. Wiedlin was attracted to Carlisle's punk attitude and bubbly demeanor, just as Carlisle was to Wiedlin's free spirit and snappy attitude. The two became fast friends and started a band with Charlotte Caffey on lead guitar, Elissa Bello on drums and Margot Olaverra on bass. Carlisle's bouncy, "chipmunk" voice fronted the band and Wiedlin's spunky guitar rhythms filled out the band's sound. Bello and Olaverra dropped out and were replaced by Gina Schock on drums in 1979 and Kathy Valentine on bass in 1980.

After being noticed by—and touring with—British ska outfit Madness, the Go-Go's released their debut album, *Beauty and the Beat*, on I.R.S in 1981. By the spring of 1982, the album was number one on the *Billboard* charts, where it stayed for six weeks, and "We Got the Beat" and "Our Lips Are Sealed" had become hits with staying power. *Beauty and the Beat* ended up earning a double-platinum certification for sales of over two million, and was by far the Go-Go's biggest success. Their next two albums, *Vacation* in 1982 and *Talk Show* in 1984, produced three hit singles. "Vacation" was a top ten hit in 1982, and "Head Over Heels" and "Turn to You" made it to number eleven and number 32, respectively, in 1984.

As *Rolling Stone*'s Christopher Connelly wrote in 1984, the Go-Go's had created a girls' world of fun, fun, fun. "Welcome to the world of the Go-Go's, where women are girls, men are boys, everyone is fair game and no one ever stops smiling. If you can't have fun with the Go-Go's, maybe you can't have fun, period." Laughter and the effervescent sound of their own music was the soundtrack to the lives of the Go-Go's.

For a group who was known for their girlish, upbeat personalities, the Go-Go's were plagued by very serious, grown-up problems. In addition to the almost-constant man troubles of one member or another, the business of being a successful commercial entity began to wear on them. In 1982, Ginger Canzoneri, the band's inexperienced but energetic manager, left the band. To start 1983, when they received their semiannual financial statement from their record label, they found they were owed over a million dollars in royalties for *Beauty and the Beat* but the label didn't have the money to pay them. After a lawsuit was filed, the dispute was handled out of court, with the royalties being paid and the band remaining on I.R.S.

Those problems remedied, the physical troubles started. As The Go-Go's were ready to start recording again, Caffey was diagnosed with a case of carpal tunnel syndrome that pained her for four months and stalled the creative momentum the band was ready to build on. *Talk Show* was released in 1984 and, with things looking up and a tour on the horizon, drummer Gina Schock was diagnosed with a congenital heart defect. She underwent open-heart surgery that left her with a scar running from her collarbone to her navel. During all of this, the band was living the rock and roll high life. Drugs, alcohol, and weight problems only increased the scope of their battles.

Despite the band's obvious troubles, Connelly quipped at the end of a lengthy, in-depth story in July of 1984,

"This party ain't over yet." But the boding of another fate could be read from Wiedlin's words, despite the story's cheerful interpretation of them. "I don't think this band's longevity is going to be decided by how many records we sell," she said. "I think it's going to be decided by how well people get along with each other, and how much people are willing to adjust to changing times and moods." Optimism did not prevail for the group this time. For all intents and purposes, the party, as The Go-Go's had known it was, in fact, over.

By October of 1984, Wiedlin, who'd already recorded one solo album, left the group in search of artistic freedom and a solo career that allowed her to sing her songs as she wished. The rest of the band rallied to stick together after Wiedlin left, moving bassist Valentine into the vacant guitarist's spot and hopeful to find a replacement bassist. Caffey told *People* in 1984, after Wiedlin's break, "My woman's intuition tells me it's going to be a good thing for both Jane and the band." Her intuition was wrong, and the Go-Go's were officially done by May of 1985.

Gina Schock told *People* in 1984, "You pay a price for making the Go-Go's the most important part of your life." After the break up of the first all-female rock band to top *Billboard* charts, the price each Go-Go paid became evident. Carlisle's was the most public. "It was a fairy tale," she told *Life* in 1988, long after the Go-Go's heyday. "I've had to start all over again." And start over she did. Although each band member had some success on her own, Carlisle's was the most commercially viable. Wiedlin made a handful of solo records; Caffey joined the Graces in 1985; Valentine started the Delphines; Schock released a record with her own band, *House of Schock*, and went on to join the Delphines in 1997. But Carlisle, with the support of her new husband, Morgan Mason (son of actor James Mason), overcame drug and alcohol dependency, lost 25 pounds, and released *Belinda*, a 1986 success. Carlisle's solo debut earned her a nomination for best female performance at the Grammy awards and a number three hit with "Mad About You."

The group reformed in 1990 for a relatively successful reunion tour in support of *Go-Go's Greatest*, a collection of the band's hits. Ten years after the band burst out onto the pop scene, they were back playing colleges and theaters—deemed more realistic venues, sizewise, to reintroduce the group. In 1991, a decidedly more mature, slick looking Go-Go's were featured in a lengthy spot during the Super Bowl to promote Bugle Boy Jeans. Despite the fact that the spot was targeted at men 18-24 years old, who were too young to have experienced the girl group first hand, marketers saw timeless appeal in their spunk.

The Go-Go's returned in 1994 with *Return to the Valley of the Go-Go's*, a retrospective two-CD set that included very early garage recordings of the group as a tough little punk outfit alongside three new pop songs. The release was filled out by classic Go-Go's hits. The band toured to support it and publicized that they'd stick together as a band.

Selected discography

Beauty and the Beat, I.R.S., 1981.
Vacation, I.R.S., 1982.
Talk Show, I.R.S., 1984.
Go-Go's Greatest, I.R.S., 1990.
Return to the Valley of the Go-Go's, I.R.S., 1994.

Sources

Books

Romanowski, Patricia and Holly George Warren, editors, *The Rolling Stone Encyclopedia of Rock & Roll*, Fireside/Simon & Shuster, 1995.

Periodicals

Adweek, Jan 28, 1991.
Amusement Business, November 12, 1990.
Entertainment Weekly, October 21, 1994; May 29, 1998.
Guitar Player, April 1995.
Life, March 1988.
People Weekly, June 16, 1986; December 19, 1994.
Rolling Stone, April 12, 1984; July 5, 1984.

Online

"Go-Go's," *All-Music Guide,* http://www.allmusic.com (September 20, 1998).
"Go-Go's," *Trouser Press,* http://www.trouserpress.com (September 20, 1998).

—*Brenna Sanchez*

Gong

Pop band

For the past 30 years, Gong has lingered on the fringes of pop music's consciousness, building a following via word-of-mouth. Gong is as much about a unique political and spiritual world view and philosophy as it is about a unique style of music that draws influences from psychedelia, jazz, folk and various ethnic musics. Gong began in the early 1950s in Melbourne, Australia, in the mind of the eccentric youngster, Daevid Allen. A self-described freak since childhood, he was beaten up frequently by classmates at the exclusive Australian Public School. Inspired by Beat poetry, Allen traveled the world after graduation.

During 1960, Daevid Allen emigrated to England with wife Gilli Smyth. The room he rented in London was part of a mansion owned by the Wyatt family. Daevid Allen struck up a close friendship with young Robert Wyatt, as well as Robert's school chums in Canterbury. After playing guitar with several short lived avant-garde jazz groups, the nomadic Allen traveled Europe, working with writer William S. Burroughs and composers Terry Riley and LaMonte Young.

Allen returned to England in 1966, luring Wyatt from his rock band The Wilde Flowers to join The Soft Machine. Allen's tenure with the Soft Machine was brief. He and Gilli Smyth remained in Paris following a tour of Europe in 1967. The duo played psychedelic-styled jazz in clubs, finding steady collaborators along the way. In 1969, Allen and Smyth recorded their first album *Magick Brother Mystic Sister* as Gong, a name derived from Indonesian gamelan music.

By the early 1970s, the band's lineup stabilized with Allen as guitarist and vocalist, vocalist Smyth, drummer Pip Pyle, bassist Christian Tritsch, and Didier Malherbe on woodwinds. Its 1971 album, *Camembert Electrique*, was a cohesive blend of psychedelic rock and jazz topped with ambiance and tape loops, with solid song-writing throughout. The bandmembers created a mystique by their unorthodox appearances and adopting whimsical stage names and singing about gnomes who inhabited the Planet Gong and traveled in teapots.

After Gong's English debut at the 1971 Glastonbury Fayre, Pyle and Tritsch departed. They were replaced by Francis Moze and Laurie Allen. Guitarist Steve Hillage and synthesist Tim Blake also joined, giving the band a spacier ambiance. Gong released the first album of its Radio Gnome Invisible Trilogy, *Flying Teapot*, on the fledgling Virgin label in 1973. The trilogy is a humorous allegory for world peace. The ideal peaceful state that the planet Earth could attain was similar to that on the "Planet Gong." The Planet Gong was inhabited by little green men called pot head pixies who travel around in flying teapots communicating telepathically through the ether wind of Radio Gnome Invisible. Allen created a corollary to the planet earth in Zero the Hero and Captain Capricorn, space travelers from earth who encounter cosmic vibrations from Planet Gong but aren't sure what to do.

Moze and Laurie Allen left Gong after *Flying Teapot* and were replaced by Mike Howlett and Pierre Moerlen. Daevid Allen and Smyth quit soon after and the band continued as Paragong. Daevid Allen and Gilli's departure was temporary, however, as they returned to Gong in mid-1973 to record *Angel's Egg, Radio Gnome Invisible Part II*, a high water mark for the band, both artistically and commercially. The collection, recorded in the back garden of the band's French countryside home, continues the story of Zero The Hero, The Pothead Pixies, and Radio Gnomes on the Planet Gong in the band's unique jazz-steeped psychedelic "space rock" style. The band toured constantly, improvising its material into free flights of fancy in concert.

Despite its successes, Gong was fraught with tension. Smyth left after the *You* album to care for her children. She was replaced by Steve Hillage's girlfriend Miquette Giraudy. Daevid Allen, who had recently quit using drugs was finding himself increasingly at odds with other bands members who continued to use them. *You* is the most polished of Gong's albums. There are more

Members include **John Alder**, (a.k.a. Twink, band member c. 1994), synthesizers; **Daevid Allen**, (a.k.a. Bert Camembert, The Dingo Virgin b. January, 1938 in Melbourne, Australia), vocals, glissando guitar; **Kevin Ayers**, (b. August 16, 1945 in Malaysia), vocals, guitar; **Keith Bailey**, (a.k.a. Keith The Missile Bass, bandmember c. 1992), bass; **Tim Blake**, (a.k.a. Hi T. Moonweed, b. February 2, 1952 in Hammersmith, West London, England, bandmember c. 1972-5, rejoined c. 1994), synthesizers; **Graham Clark**, (a.k.a. Albert "No Parking" Parkin, bandmember c. 1992-4), violin, vocals; **Miquitte Giraudy**, (a.k.a. Bambaloni Yoni, bandmember c. 1976), vocals; **Steve Hillage**, (a.k.a. Steve Hillside, b. August 2, 1951 in London, England, bandmember c. 1973-6), guitar, vocals; **Rachid Houari**, (b. Morocco, bandmember c. 1969-70), drums; **Mike Howlett**, (a.k.a. Mr. T. Being, b. April 27, year unknown, Lautoka, Fiji, bandmember c. 1972-6, rejoined c. 1994), bass, vocals; **Shyamal Maïtra**, (a.k.a. Banana Ananda, bandmember c. 1992), tablas, percussion; **Didier Malherbe**, (a.k.a. Bloomdido Bad de Grass, b. January 22, 1943 in Paris, France, bandmember c. 1969-76, rejoined c. 1992), saxophone, flute, woodwinds; **Pierre Moerlen**, (a.k.a. Pere Cushion de Strasbourger, b. October 23, 1952, Colmar, France, bandmember c. 1973-9, rejoined c. 1995), drums, percussion; **Pip Pyle** (a.k.a. Pip The Heap, b. April 4, 1950 in Sawbridgeworth, Hertfordshire, England, bandmember c. 1970-1, rejoined c. 1992), drums; **Gilli Smyth**, (a.k.a. Shakti Yoni, b. Wales, bamdmember c. 1969-75, c. 1994-8), "space whisper" vocals; **Christian Tritsch**, (a.k.a. The Submarine Captain, bandmember c. 1969-73), bass.

Band formed c. 1969, Paris France; released debut album *Magick Brother, Mystic Sister*, 1969 on Byg Records; made English debut c. 1971 at Glastonbury Fayre Festival; signed with Virgin Records c. 1972; released *Radio Gnome Invisible Trilogy*, c. 1973-5; disbanded c. 1976; reformed c. 1992; released *Shapeshifter* on Celluloid Records, c. 1992; toured Europe, United States, Japan, c. 1994-8.

Addresses: *Record company*—Cleopatra Records, 13428 Maxella Ave., Suite 251, Marina Del Rey, CA 90292.

instrumentals, as Daevid Allen's influence in the band was waning, but he still managed to tie up loose ends of the Pothead Pixie and Zero the Hero story.

In 1991, Daevid Allen explained the Radio Gnome Invisible Trilogy to interviewer Jason Rubin. "There was the first level, which was the playful silliness and just having fun. But it is also the code both for a political manifesto and a spiritual teaching. But what is interesting is that while the story that we told originally appears to be just talking about little green men with pointed hats, every single thing in the Planet Gong mythology has a deeper meaning for those who want to peel away the layers and get to the chocolate center. I can't say much more than that, it's really something you need to come and check out for yourself."

After *You*, Smyth departed, followed soon by Daevid Allen in 1975. The band was led by Steve Hillage, backing him on his solo album *Fish Rising*. Hillage's influence waned on the 1976 release *Shamal*, afterwhich he quit Gong for a successful solo career. As Pierre Moerlen's Gong, the band soldiered on for several instrumental albums before disbanding in the early 1980s.

Daevid Allen went to Majorca upon leaving Gong in 1976 and joined the local acoustic band Euterpe for *Good Morning*. Subsequent solo albums of the 1970s, including the punk influenced *About Time*, belied his lack of direction. Daevid Allen and Smyth separated in 1978. She founded Mothergong, representing the feminine side of Gong. Allen retired from the music business in 1981 and returned to Australia, in time to see his father before he died. Allen drove a taxi in Australia until 1989 when enough contact from fans convinced him to return to public life.

Since the early 1990s, Allen has been recording prolifically solo, with Shimmy Disc founder Kramer, and Mothergong. He reunited Gong in 1994 for a 25th birthday celebration concert in London. On the strength of consistent touring and a well-organized fan network, The Gong Appreciation Society, Gong keeps going strong into the next millennium, picking up new 'family members' along the way.

Selected discography

Magick Brother Mystic Sister, Byg, 1970, reissued Decal, 1990.
Continental Circus, (soundtrack). Philips, 1971, reissued Giacomo, 1996.
(with Dashiell Hedayat), *Obsolete*, Shandar, 1971, reissued Mantra, 1994.

"Est-Ce Que Je Suis (Garcon ou Fille)"/ "Hyp Hypnotise You", Byg 129021, 1970, reissued on *Je Ne Fume Pas Des Bananes*, (rec. 1969), Legend, 1996.

Camembert Eclectique, (rec. 1970), Gong Appreciation Society, 1994

Camembert Electrique, Byg, 1971, reissued, Decal, 1991.

(with others), *Glastonbury Fayre*, Revelation, 1972.

Flying Teapot, Virgin, 1973, reissued Decal, 1991.

Angel's Egg, Virgin, 1973.

You, Virgin, 1974.

Shamal, Virgin, 1976.

Live Etc. (rec. 1973-6), Virgin, 1977.

Gong Est Mort, Vive Gong, Tapioca, 1977, reissued Celluloid, 1993.

(Pierre Moerlen's Gong), *Expresso II*, Virgin, 1978.

New York Gong, *About Time*, 1979, reissued, Decal, 1991.

Gong Maison, Demi Monde, 1989.

Gong Maison, *Live At Glastonbury 1989*, Gong Appreciation Society, 1994.

History and Mystery of the Planet Gong, (circa 1964-89), Thunderbolt, 1989.

Shapeshifter, Celluloid, 1992, reissued Viceroy, 1996

Live au Bataclan 1973, Mantra, 1993.

Live At Sheffield 1974, Mantra, 1993.

25th Birthday Party, Gong Appreciation Society, 1994.

Pre-Modernist Wireless, The Peel Sessions 1971-74, Strange Fruit, 1995.

"Perfect Mystery" (rec. 1974) on *Supernatural Fairy Tales: The Progressive Rock Era*, Rhino, 1996.

Daevid Allen solo projects

(with Freaks of Nature), "People! Let's Freak Out"/ "Secret Police", Island, 1966.

(with Soft Machine), "Love Makes Sweet Music"/ "Feelin' Reelin' Squealin'", Polydor, 1967, reissued on *Rare Tracks*, Polydor, 1975.

(with Soft Machine), *Rock Generation Volumes 6 & 7* (rec. 1967), Byg, 1971.

Banana Moon, Caroline, 1971, reissued Decal, 1992.

(with Euterpe), *Good Morning*, Virgin, 1976.

Now Is The Happiest Time of Your Life, Tapioca, 1977, reissued, Charly, 1992.

N'Existe Pas, Charly, 1979.

Invisible Opera Company of Tibet, Voiceprint, 1987.

Australian Years (rec.81-88), Voiceprint, 1991.

The Death of Rock (rec. 1982), Voiceprint, 1991.

(with The Magick Brothers), *Live at the Witchwood 1991*, Voiceprint, 1991.

Twelve Selves, Voiceprint, 1991.

Trio, *Live 1963*, Voiceprint, 1993.

(with The Magick Brothers), "Trial by Headlines" on *Passed Normal Volume 5*, Fot/Ponk, 1993.

Daevid Allen and Kramer, *Who's Afraid*, Shimmy-Disc, 1993.

Daevid Allen and Kramer, *Hit Men*, Shimmy-Disc, 1994.

Je Ne Fume Pas Des Bananes, (rec. 1969), Legend, 1996.

Dreamin' A Dream, Gong Appreciation Society, 1996, reissued Cleopatra, 1998.

(With Solid Space), "Visions of Angels" on *The Fox Lies Down, A Tribute To Genesis*, Purple Pyramid/Cleopatra, 1998.

(with Pip Pyle), Brainville, Knitting Factory Works, 1999.

Gilli Smyth and Mothergong projects

(with Pip Pyle), Gilli Smyth, *Mother*, Charly, 1978.

Fairy Tales, Charly, 1979.

Robot Woman, Butt, 1981.

Robot Woman 2, Shanghai, 1982.

Robot Woman 3, Shanghai, 1989.

(with Daevid Allen), *Magenta / She Made The World*, Voiceprint, 1993.

Every Witches Way, Voiceprint VP, 1993.

"Spiral Dance" on *Passed Normal Volume 5*, Fot/Ponk, 1993.

Radio Promo, Voiceprint, 1994.

Wild Child, Demi-Monde, 1994.

Eye, Voiceprint VP, 1994.

Politico-Historico-Spirito, Voiceprint, 1995.

The Best of (rec. 1978-94), Purple Pyramid/Cleopatra, 1997.

"In The Beginning" on *The Fox Lies Down, A Tribute To Genesis*, Purple Pyramid/Cleopatra, 1998.

Pip Pyle solo projects

Hatfield and the North, Virgin, 1974.

(with Hatfield and the North), "Let's Eat (Real Soon)" (rec. 1974) on *Supernatural Fairy Tales: The Progressive Rock Era*, Rhino, 1996.

(with Hatfield and the North), *The Rotters' Club*, Virgin, 1975.

National Health, Charly, 1978.

National Health, *Of Queues and Cures*, Charly, 1979.

National Health, *D.S. Al Coda*, Europa, 1982, reissued on Voiceprint, 1996.

National Health, *Complete* (rec.1978-1982), East Side Digital, 1990.

(with Steve Hillage), National Health, *Missing Pieces* (rec. 1976-78), East Side Digital, 1997.

Soft Heap, Charly, 1979.

(with Didier Malherbe), *Pip Pyle's Equip'Out*, 52 Rue Est, 1985.

(with Phil Miller), *Split Seconds*, Reckless, 1987.

(with Phil Miller), Digging In, Cuneiform, 1991.

Pip Pyle's Equip'Out, *Up*, Gimini/NTI, 1991.

(with Didier Malherbe), Short Wave, *Live*, Gimini, 1993.

(with Didier Malherbe), *Seven Year Itch*, Voiceprint, 1998.

Other Gong members' projects

(with Didier Malherbe), Kevin Ayers, *Whatevershebringswesing*, Harvest, 1972, reissued BGO, 1992.

(with Steve Hillage), Kevin Ayers *Bananamour*, Harvest, 1973, reissued BGO, 1992.

Paragong, *Live 1973,* Gong Appreciation Society, 1995.

Paragong, "Pentagramaspin", *V*, Virgin, 1975.

(with Tim Blake, Mike Howlett, Didier Malherbe, and Pierre Moerlen), Steve Hillage, *Fish Rising*, Virgin, 1975.

(with Mike Howlett), Strontium 90, *Police Academy* (rec. 1977), Pangea, 1997.

(with Tim Blake), *New Jerusalem*, Mantra, 1978.

with Tim Blake), *Crystal Machine*, Mantra, 1979.

(with Pip Pyle), Didier Malherbe, *Fetish*, Votre, 1990.

(with Tim Blake), *Magick*, Voiceprint, 1991.

Sources

Books

Allen, Daevid, *If Words Were Birds*, Outposts Publications, 1964.

Allen, Daevid, *Gong Dreaming part 1*, Gong Appreciation Society, 1995.

Allen, Daevid, *Gong Dreaming part 2*, Gong Appreciation Society, 1996.

Allen, Daevid, *A Pocket Introduction To The Planet Gong*, Byg, 1971.

Cutler, Chris, *File Under Popular*, Autonomedia, 1994.

Joynson, Vernon, *Tapestry of Delights: The Comprehensive Guide to British Music of the Beat, R & B, Psychedelic, and Progressive Eras, 1963-1976*, Borderline Productions, 1996.

King, Michael, *Wrong Movements: A Robert Wyatt History*, S.A.F., 1994.

Miller, Bill, *Listening To The Future: The Time of Progressive Rock 1968-1978*, Open Court, 1998.

Smyth, Gillian, *The Nitrogen Dreams of A Wide Girl*, Outposts Publications, 1966.

Thompson, Dave, *Space Daze: The History and Mystery of Electronic Ambient Space Rock*, Cleopatra, 1996.

Woodstra, Chris, editor, *The All Music Guide To Rock*, Miller-Freeman, 1995.

Periodicals

Facelift, Issue 11.

Goldmine, October 6, 1989; April 10, 1998.

Melody Maker, April 27, 1974; October 19, 1974; November 9, 1974; April 19, 1975; April 26, 1975; June 19, 1976; September 26, 1976; July 16, 1977; January 12, 1980.

Option, July, 1992.

Record Collector, June, 1992.

Sound Choice, No. 17.

Voiceprint News, Spring, 1994.

Online

http://www.alpes-net.fr/~bigbang/calyx.html (October 22, 1998).

http://musart.co.uk (September 26, 1998).

http://www.ice.net/~ponk (September 26, 1998).

http://www.terrascope.org (September 28, 1998).

Additional information was obtained through The Gong Appreciation Society and interviews with Gilli Smyth, Pip Pyle, and Mike Howlett.

—Jim Powers

Goodie Mob

Hip-hop band

Eclectic hip-hop/rap group Goodie Mob combines rhythm-and-blues, gospel, trip-hop, hip-hop, rock, soul, and acid jazz with positive messages to achieve a unique sound. *Billboard*'s Shawnee Smith wrote, "[Goodie Mob] goes against the grain of what is being presented in the majority of contemporary hip-hop lyrics, which is what makes the group's music appealing." Since the group's first appearance on *Southernplayalisticadillacmuzik* in 1994—an album that went platinum and the first release of the Atlanta group, Outkast—Goodie Mob has had two hit singles and released two albums. More importantly the band has combated the growing negativity of much rap and hip-hop with messages of hope and respect for its young, largely black audience.

All of the group's members, T-Mo (Robert Barrett), Cee-lo (Carlito Green), Khujo (Willie Knighton), and Big Gipp (Cameron Gipp), were raised in the Southern Baptist church. Both of Cee-lo's parents were ministers, a fact evident in Cee-lo's soulful choruses and charismatic delivery. Khujo told Smith, "Our real background is struggle. Being from the South, we've been oppressed. So it's not like we said we gonna be real positive; we just soaked up our environment—the old values we was taught and the new values we just being taught as we come of age."

Those long-standing Southern values of family, hard work, and community are often at odds with the gap in values between the generations, as well as with the culture of violence in the rap community. Goodie Mob hoped to counteract some of the uglier trends in hip-hop with their music. "Beautiful Skin," for example, is a song in praise of African-American women that encourages them to respect themselves. "The Experience" is a song that explores whether either rappers or their audience should be using the word "nigga." "Distant Wilderness," reminds listeners that life is a temporary and sacred journey.

In speaking of the group's influences, Cee-lo told *Spin*'s Zev Borow, "I listened to all types of music growing up. Run D.M.C., Sugar Hill Gang, 2 Live Crew, but I also liked Al Green, Led Zeppelin, and yeah, Billy Idol." Band members met while attending Benjamin Elijah May High School in southwest Atlanta. T-Mo and Khujo went to Morris Brown College and began performing together as the Lumberjacks. Big Gipp had joined a band called the East Point Chain Gang. They started getting together at a basement home-studio, dubbed "The Dungeon," that belonged to the group Organized Noize. Goodie Mob was finally formed in 1993. The name stands for "Good Die Mostly Over Bullsh*t," although it has also been said to stand for "God Is Every Man of Blackness" and "A Goodie Bag of Musical Messages and Flavas."

After its 1994 debut on *Southernplayalisticadillacmuzik*, Goodie Mob released its first album, *Soul Food*. *Spin*'s Borow described the record as, "a smooth collection of harmonious jams infused with live instrumentation and a resilient, if at times preachy, hope for the future." Atlanta itself influenced the band members' perspective. *Allstar*'s Jay W. Babcock wrote, "When you participate in pop culture, you can write about what you know or what you think people want. Goodie Mob choose the former. What they know is the ghetto in general, and Southwest Atlanta (S.W.A.T.S.) in particular." T-Mo told Borow, "In New York, in L.A., it's money, business, all the time. But in Atlanta it's about soul, the civil rights movement, Martin Luther King Jr., Elijah Mohammed. We have more of a spiritual influence, and that shows in what we say."

When Goodie Mob released *Soul Food* in 1995, with its Organized Noize-produced conspiracy-theory hit single "Cell Therapy," both locals and listeners outside of the South raised their ears. And their second CD, *Still Standing,* garnered nationwide praise. *Allstar* called it "the richest, most urgent socially conscious hip-hop in recent memory. *Spin*'s Charles Aaron wrote, "*Soul Food* was a patchy primer, but ... *Still Standing* jolts you like a future-funk manifesto-sophisticated, shifty production underlying hardscrabble, spiritually haunted rants

For the Record . . .

Members include **Robert Barrett**, (T-Mo, born 1972); **Cameron Gipp** (Big Gipp, born 1973); **Carlito Green** (Cee-lo, born 1976); and **Willie Knighton** (Khujo born 1973). Green's parents were both ministers.

Members met at Benjamin Elijah May High School in southwest Atlanta; first appeared on *Southernplaylisticadillacmuzik*; released debut CD *Soul Food,* with the hit single "Cell Therapy" in 1995; single "Decisions, Decisions" included on *DJ Muggs: The Soul Assassins—Chapter 1* in 1997; released *Still Standing* in 1998, which reached number two on *Billboard's* Top R&B Albums chart, and number six on the *Billboard* 200.

Addresses: *Record company*—LaFace Records, One Capital City Plaza, 3350 Peachtree Road, Suite 1500, Atlanta, GA 30326-1040; (404) 869-404; fax (404) 869-4980; email.sanabria@bmge.com.

... funk-rock groove (guitar, drums, bass, keyboard, backup singers) with the kind of explicit moral imperative that Chuck D now chokes on."

Gipp told *Billboard*, "We just care a lot. A lot of artists who learn the game may not care. But we care about the music and about the people." He added that the band hoped listeners would give thought to the choices they make and to the consequences of their actions. "We're not going to change just because people want to dance in the clubs," he said. "After you dance in the clubs, then what?... There's got to be another mission."

Goodie Mob stresses the importance of education and self-motivation. "If party music is all the young kids hear on the radio," Big Gipp told Smith, "they will get the impression that that's all there is to think about.... We have to give them something bigger than that to do. They need positive things to get through what they have to deal with in life." According to Big Gipp, Chuck D and other 1980s musicians set good examples for him and his generation. "They helped us understand where we wanted to go," he told *Billboard*. The members of Goodie Mob are comfortable being role models for the generation that follows theirs. They are aware of the effect their lyrics have. T-Mo told Smith, "For us to put out a rap album that was something other than positive would be a transgression. Nobody lives forever, and in the end we all got to answer to God."

The group's music is directed primarily at African-American youth. "I got to deal with the problems in my house," Khujo explained to Smith, "before I go out and tell my next-door neighbor what to do." However, sources at the LaFace label told *Billboard* that the band's message reaches listeners of all races, in both urban and rural areas. LaFace General Manager Dorsey James told Smith, "[Goodie Mob's music] crosses the cultural lines in much the same way that a lot of rap does, because it provides a window into the black community. And people in general are voyeurs and like to look into places they can't go, and Goodie Mob provides that view." The bulk of the band's audience is located in the South, Midwest, and West Coast and, in an effort to win new fans, the band toured the Northeast with The Roots in 1998.

Allstar described *Still Standing* as, "68 minutes of anger, empathy, love, and soul." Cee-o raps on it: "I don't sell dope. I sell hope." Babcock continued, "[*Still Standing*] is a deeply detailed, local, slang-filled, heartfelt reportage that dares to critique its subjects and itself, to ask how things got so bad for both poor folk and hip-hop.... But unlike, say, Public Enemy's third album, *Still Standing* is socially conscious hip-hop that is not really directed toward an audience outside of the ghetto.... This music should move you—and, perhaps, inspire you to learn." Summing up Goodie Mob's perspective, Cee-lo told *The Source's* Michael Gonzales, "To me, music is so powerful and beautiful that if you take a picture of it, I believe that's what God would look like. For me, music is both medicine and ministry."

Selected discography

Soul Food, LaFace, 1995.
Still Standing, LaFace, 1998.

Compilation

DJ Muggs Presents: The Soul Assassins—Chapter 1, Columbia Records, 1997.

Sources

Periodicals

Allstar, May 1998.
Billboard, July 25, 1998; May 2, 1998; April 18, 1998; April 11, 1998.

Los Angeles Times, April 25, 1998.
Puncture, Summer 1997.
Rap Sheet, December 1995.
Request, May 1998.
The Source, May 1998; April 1998.
Spin, August 1998; May 1998.
Washington Post, May 29, 1998.
XXL, Issue #3, 1998.

Online

http://www.musicblvd.com

—*B. Kimberly Taylor*

Patty Griffin

Singer, songwriter

Folk and rock singer Patty Griffin burst onto the national music scene in 1996 with her stark, emotional acoustic CD *Living with Ghosts*. Called a "stunning piece of work, an unprecedented major-label debut by a relative unknown featuring just her naked vocals and acoustic guitar, with no overdubs" by Seth Rogovoy in *Hotwired,* the album introduced a singer-songwriter of uncommon power. John Scheinman writing in the *Fairfax Journal* said, "Here's this woman from Old Town, Maine ... making the kind of record only Bob Dylan gets to make anymore.... [But] Griffin doesn't need a band to fill the spaces because the songs come out of her gut with a conviction that's more than enough."

Her second album, *Flaming Red,* proved Griffin a musician of remarkable versatility and range, capable of hard rockers, contemplative ballads, melancholy country tunes and bright pop songs. Far from alienating her fans, *Flaming Red* solidified Griffin's position as an important talent. It revealed her as a musician willing to challenge her listeners rather than simply fulfilling their expectations.

Griffin was the youngest of seven children—three sisters and three brothers—in a struggling family in Old Town, Maine, a town near Bangor. Her father taught high school physics and chemistry, and her mother kept house and raised the children. Griffin grew up among singers. Her mother had a beautiful singing voice, her grandparents often sang on their porch in the evening as the sun went down, and from an early age Patty knew she wanted to be a singer. Her parents, however, convinced her the wish was frivolous, and hoping to shield her from disappointment, did not support her.

But they did buy music for her. Her father gave her her first record, the Beatles' *Sgt. Pepper's Lonely Hearts Club Band.* Griffin's other early musical influences, for lyrical imagery in particular, included Bruce Springsteen, Rickie Lee Jones, Elvis Costello, America, Tom Petty and the Heartbreakers, and Stevie Nicks. When she was 16, Griffin bought herself an inexpensive guitar and started writing songs. She didn't know if she *could* sing, but she did know she *wanted* to sing.

After graduating from high school, Griffin moved to Florida where she lived for two years. There she concentrated mostly on sports. She eventually applied the self-discipline and goal-setting required in athletics to her work as a musician. In an interview with Philip Van Vleck of the *Raleigh Spectator,* she compared music and sports. "It's a lot like what an athlete goes through," she said. "A lot of repetition, a lot of repetition, and then at some point, hopefully, it all starts to work for you." Eventually Griffin moved to Boston and married. But she spent most of her time there as a waitress and was not able to pursue her music career in earnest.

At the end of 1992, she was jolted into performing when her husband told her he wanted a divorce. Single again, Griffin started performing in various Boston clubs. At the same time she was shopping around a demo tape she later admitted was overproduced. The demo was recorded in a kitchen in Nashville and in a room near Boston City Hospital, and the sound of ambulance sirens could be heard behind the music. Nonetheless Griffin caught the attention of a scout from A&M Records, who invited her to audition. Overwhelmed by her raw, natural talent, he persuaded her to re-record a second, stripped-down tape with just her voice and a guitar. Six months later she landed a deal with the label. Most of her demo tape was used on her debut release, *Living With Ghosts.*

Griffin described the ten emotionally turbulent tunes on *Living With Ghosts* to Rogovoy as "pretty honest, pretty close to what I really am." They reveal her roots in soul, pop, and country, and range over topics as elememtal as poverty, loneliness, anger, and the dissolution of love. Because of her music's themes and passionate intensity, Griffin has been compared by music critics to Kurt Cobain and Alanis Morissette. Van Vleck wrote of

For the Record . . .

Raised in Old Town, ME; the youngest of seven children; father taught high school physics and chemistry, mother was a home-maker; lived in Florida for two years after high school; moved to Boston where she married and worked as a waitress.

After divorce in 1992, began performing in clubs in the Boston area; caught the attention of A&M Records scout; released debut album *Living With Ghosts* in 1996; performed in Lilith Fair concert tour in 1997; released *Flaming Red* in 1998; singles used in the films *The Newton Boys* and *Niagra, Niagra*.

Addresses: *Record company*—A&M Records, 595 Madison Avenue, New York, NY 10022, (212) 826-0477; 1416 North La Brea, Los Angeles, CA 90028, (213) 469-2411.

Living With Ghosts, "A spare piece of work ... nothing but Griffin, an acoustic guitar and 10 very potent, very intimate songs. The minimalism of the album gives Griffin no place to hide, but that's also the beauty of it. Her strengths are the immediacy of her performance and the emotional depth of her lyrics."

Even after Griffin had long left behind the personal experiences that resulted in *Ghosts,* new listeners continued to discover and identify with the record. "The album ... is a collection of tunes from a time in my life when I definitely needed to express what was going on inside," Griffin told Van Vleck. "I keep remembering that people are hearing these songs for the first time and I draw from that knowledge when performing.... I may not be as close now to the experience that made me write those songs, but there are other things to draw from, that's the art of performance."

A&M's decision to release Griffin's album in an obvious state of minimalism was unusual for a major label. "Realizing [A&M was] attached to those solo performances made me appreciate the strength of them and gave me the guts to ask if they'd put them out that way," Griffin told Van Vleck. "And they did." John Scheinman praised A&M's insight in the *Fairfax Journal.* "*Living With Ghosts* is such a startling debut. The label left well enough alone and just let Griffin be herself. She can wistfully talk-sing with the ache of Rickie Lee Jones,

rock with the force of Bonnie Raitt, moan the blues, hiccup the country, turn a phrase about pain that makes you need to hear it twice." Since *Living With Ghosts* far exceeded expectations at A&M in terms of sales, the label quickly stepped up its promotion machine for Griffin and supported the making of her second release in every way possible.

In 1998, after playing the all-woman Lilith Fair concert tour, Griffin's second CD, *Flaming Red,* was released to great critical and popular acclaim. In startling contrast to her acoustic debut release, *Flaming Red,* produced by Jay Joyce, saw Griffin backed by a full band, including Joyce on guitar and powerhouse rock drummer Kenny Aronoff from John Mellancamp's band. The album included a wide variety of musical forms as well: ballads, rock and roll, and pop singles. "Even when Griffin rocks her hardest ... her crystal voice commands the high ground," wrote *People.* "And she never allows the sound to drown out the lyrics of these 13 well-crafted songs."

Flaming Red included a tribute to a deceased friend, songs about the suicide of an ostracized gay boy, a young girl's love for her red pumps, and the romantic tribulations of the late Christina Onassis. Griffin's work was included in the soundtracks for two films: she played with Bad Liver on the single "Copenhagen" in Richard Linklater's *The Newton Boys,* and her singles "Not Alone" and "Regarding Mary" were featured in the soundtrack to *Niagra, Niagra.* An unpredictable, honest musician with natural talent, Griffin will continue to surprise her audience and to chart new musical terrain.

Selected discography

Living With Ghosts, A&M Records, 1996.
Flaming Red, A&M Records, 1998.

Sources

Boston Phoenix, March 7, 1997.
Fairfax Journal (Virginia), March 14, 1997.
Fort Worth Star Telegram, April 19, 1997.
People, July 20, 1998.
Raleigh Spectator (North Carolina), March 6, 1997.

Online

A&M Records website: http://www.a&mrecords.com

—B. Kimberly Taylor

Johnny Hodges

Saxophone

Photo by Frank Driggs. Archive Photos, Inc. Reproduced by permission. ©

Johnny Hodges is best remembered as the lead saxophone player of the legendary Duke Ellington band. Hodges, a soloist in his own right, was one of the first great saxophone players in the history of modern jazz. Adept at arranging as well as playing both soprano and alto saxophones, for 40 years Hodges played on almost every album Duke Ellington made and held a reputation as Ellington's stalwart right-hand man. Hodges and his teacher, Sidney Bechet, are credited as two of the most significant soprano saxophone players in the history of twentieth century jazz. Many critics observed that Hodges effectively achieved a quasi-vocal quality with his instrument. He turned "Jeep's Blues" into a jazz classic, and is remembered as one of the earliest and greatest jazz saxophonists.

John Cornelius Hodges was born in Cambridge, Massachusetts on July 25, 1907. His family later moved to Hammond Street in Boston. Hodges played both piano and drums as a child before taking up saxophone at age 13. A few days after he acquired a soprano saxophone, Hodges forced an opportunity to meet Sidney Bechet backstage at a burlesque house in Boston. Bechet heard Hodges play "My Honey's Lovin' Arms," and encouraged the young saxophonist. Soon after, Hodges acquired an alto sax, which he preferred to the soprano. He experimented on his own, and took lessons sporadically for several years due to lack of funds. After he encountered Bechet a second time, Hodges's interest in the soprano saxophone was rekindled and Bechet's respect for Hodges's talent was renewed. Hodges studied and worked with Bechet and eventually performed as a warm-up to Bechet's act at Club Bechet in New York City. The young and talented Hodges also shared the spotlight with Bechet as they performed duets. Hodges, who emulated Bechet's style, continued his association with Bechet later when the two appeared separately but on the same bill at the Rhythm Club in 1924 and together again at Club Basha in 1925. Hodges also studied with the late Benny Waters for a time before joining forces with Ellington. Waters and Hodges played in a band together around 1920 in Boston, at a time when Waters taught saxophone in between gigs and radio shows. Waters recalled Hodges as a truly natural talent on the saxophone.

Joined Ellington Orchestra

It was outside of Massachusetts that Hodges eventually took up with Ellington, after playing around Boston and New York during the early 1920s. Hodges joined the legendary Duke Ellington band on May 18, 1926. Despite a stoic on-stage demeanor and distinct inability to project his personality during performance, Hodges also earned a reputation for his whimsical sense of humor. The audience, on occasion, overheard Hodges' spontaneous asides through the stage microphone: calling a bet with a fellow band member; airing a curt grievance at another musician; expressing momentary displeasure.

He developed a massive following based on sheer talent. An enormously talented young man, he developed his skills with the Ellington band and in time achieved recognition as a solo artist. The original Hodges style was to play very fast, in double time, and very frequently on the soprano saxophone. After 1940, his style evolved and took a much slower pace at which point Hodges focused almost exclusively on playing the alto saxophone, which he did with great poise. Indeed Ellington not only arranged some of Hodges solo recordings, but played back up piano for Hodges as well.

Hodges toured around the world as a member of the Ellington band. In the 1920s and early 1930s the group played New York's Apollo Theater and the Cotton Club, the London Palladium, and Europe's Trocadero. They performed for royalty and met with the same. The band toured the southern United States on various occasions, including Texas and New Orleans. Despite the precarious racial climate of the United States during those years, Ellington's son, Mercer, reported that they, "... were feted like ... heroes." An overseas tour in 1939 took the band to Scandinavia.

Parted with Ellington

During the 1940s the band's movements were limited because of political restrictions associated with World War II. Several of the members became restless and, in 1951, Hodges made a decision to break out on his own. He started his own group and brought it to New York. The band included Harold Land and Richie Powell. During this hiatus from Ellington, in June of 1952, Hodges made an album called *Just Friends* with the great Charlie Parker, who was an ardent fan of Hodges. The two collaborated in a studio jam for an album, along with Benny Carter and Ben Webster. Hodges also recorded with Dizzy Gillespie, in 1953. In August of 1955 Hodges returned to Ellington's band, to the mutual benefit of all. The late Mercer Ellington, in a memoir of his father, stated that the contributions of Johnny Hodges "... were highly important and ... enriched the band's tonal fabric." In the years after his reunion with the Ellington band, Hodges continued to make solo albums and to tour and perform with the Ellington group.

Hodges was virtually illiterate from a musical standpoint, mostly due to a lack of formal lessons when he first learned to play as a child. Although his reading skills improved as he played with Ellington's band, Hodges preferred, whenever possible, to play by ear or from memory—and to improvise—rather than to follow the written parts. Despite his poor musical literacy, Hodges was highly disciplined and played directly from the heart. He further displayed a natural ability to embellish and accent the music he played for maximum emotion. His eloquent style elicited praise from his contemporaries as well as from modern historians of the jazz genre. Hodges influenced many prominent jazz and new age saxophonists including John Klemmer and the late John Coltrane.

Private Glance

Personally, Hodges was known as an epicure and was well received in the most elite restaurants, where chefs were known to prepare special dishes exclusively for him and his companions. Hodges was himself a culinary whiz. Yet, despite Hodges's reputation as a connoisseur, he nonetheless earned the nickname Rabbit, because of his unique fondness for bacon, lettuce, and tomato sandwiches—sans bacon. Hodges also held a reputation as a lucky gambler, winning large keno jackpots and poker hands with apparent ease.

As the years passed Hodges suffered from heart problems, which he refused to address. He died suddenly on May 11, 1970. Hodges's passing was painful to Duke Ellington, who's eulogy of Johnny Hodges was quoted freely, "[O]ur band will never sound the same."

Selected discography

Masters of Jazz, Vol. 9, Storyville (Denmark), 1960.
At the Berlin Sportpalast, Pablo, 1961.
Everybody Knows, Impulse, 1965.
Caravan, Prestige, 1992.
Johnny Hodges with Lawrence Welk's Orchestra, Ranwood Records, 1994.
Classic Solos (1928-42), Topaz Jazz, 1994.
Hodge Podge, Columbia, 1995.
Jeep's Blues, Living Era, 1996.
Used To Be Duke, Verve.
Triple Play, RCA Victor.
Vol. 35—Verve Jazz Masters, Verve.
(with Duke Ellington Orchestra), Jazz Party in Stereo, Columbia.
(with Duke Ellington Orchestra) Blues in Orbit, Columbia.
(with Duke Ellington Orchestra) Side by Side, Verve.

Sources

Books

Dance, Stanley, *The World of Duke Ellington,* Charles Scribner's Sons, New York, 1970.
Ellington, Edward Kennedy (Duke), *Music Is My Mistress,* DaCapo Press, Inc., New York, 1973.
Ellington, Mercer with Stanley Dance, *Duke Ellington in Person: An Intimate Memoir,* Houghton Mifflin Company, Boston, 1978.

Periodicals

Jazz Rambler, March/April 1998.

—*Gloria Cooksey*

Don Howland

Rock performer

Don Howland became a major force on the independent musical scene. Originally from Columbus, Ohio, it was here in the city of his birth that Howland began learning the guitar and dreaming dreams of rock and roll greatness. He grew up during the era of mid-seventies punk. But he knew that it might take quite a long time for his rock and roll dreams of success became reality, so in order to pay the bills, he decided on getting a degree in education. All the while, though, he kept writing and perfecting his original songwriting abilities and performing talents. After graduation from college, Howland began a dual life of alter-egos. In the daytime, he worked as a teacher in an inner-city Columbus junior high school. It was a place where he was a person in position of authority and was regularly called "Mr. Howland." But at night, Howland continued in his musical pursuit. Skillfully managing a precarious schedule, he eventually arranged a situation where he could work as a teacher in the day and play club dates at night with his band.

The first group he joined was The Great Plains. This was a local Columbus, band which attracted some favorable criticism as well as attracting a good share of the nightclub audiences. Howland didn't use his real name but played bass with this group under the peculiar pseudonym of Frank O' Hare. In the mid-1980s, Howland was ready to explore working with a different group. Even so, he had to maintain his day job as school teacher. He was married with two small children to support. Nevertheless, he perserved in his dream. And along with his hard-edged New Wave upbringings, Howland was heavily influenced by country blues. This was how he met up with a local band, The Gibson Brothers. They were playing a kind of punk-rockabilly subgenre that is labelled "psychobilly." Personalities clicked as did their musical synchronicity. What followed was months of touring and gaining national recognition as they continued to develop their unique style. They released their debut album , *Build A Raft* in 1986. Other albums included, *Big Pine Boogie*, 1988, *Dedicated Fool*, 1989, *Punk Rock Drivin' Song of a Gun*, 1990, *The Man Who Loved Couch Dancing* and *On the Riviera* , 1991, and *Memphis Sol Today!* in 1993.

Howland needed some time to muse over his musical alternatives. This meant finding a new record label as well. While he was doing that, he decided to fill in and help out each of his former bandmates as he pursued his own music. For a brief period, he went to work for Jeff Evans then Doug Edwards. Still though, Howland wanted to make his own unique mark on the indie rock scene, but he couldn't find just the right vehicle to make the specific statements he wanted to make. He also realized that the only way to really do what he wanted was to start his own group. Naming the new band poved to be controversial, but fitting, in a punky sort of way. The name was found on the wall in a restroom at a local bar. Someone had taken a profane phrase and wrote over the first letter "a" making it a "b" instead. "I just thought, if I ever got another band, that's what I'm going to call it," Howland told Greg Baise of the Detroit *Metro Times*.

Such were the nihilistic beginnings of The Bassholes. In another unusual move, Howland found himself with only a drummer and decided the two would work as a duo. The next item on his agenda was to find the right record label. Howland found In The Red Records from Anaheim, California, whose founder, Larry Hardy, is a unique mogul. He has a self-professed love for vinyl instead of cds. He's alos one of a small but growing number of independent record labels that release single seven inch EPs and other vinyl creations along with the more commercial profitable cd versions. Howland's work impressed Hardy and he particularly liked the material Howland wrote for The Bassholes. Negotiations were made and a contract was signed. Hardy's In The Red released the Bassholes debut album *Haunted Hill* in 1995. Other releases for the label included, *Deaf Mix, Vol. 3* and *Blue Roots* in 1997, and *When My Blue Moon Turns Red Again*, and *Long Way Blues 1996-98* in 1998.

Abandoning some of the cheesier, self-conscious psychobilly satire, Howland came up with a sound that is

For the Record . . .

Born in Columbus, OH; married; children: two.

First group was The Great Plains; his second group was The Gibson Brothers; group signed with Old Age Records, released debut album *Build A Raft*, 1986; group signed with Homestead Records; released *Big Pine Boogie,* 1988; *Dedicated Fool,* 1989; released *Punk Rock Drivin' Song of a Gunn,* 1990; released *The Man Who Loved Couch Dancing*, Positive Records, 1991; released *On The Riviera,* Mango Records, 1991; released *Memphis Sol Today!,* Sympathy For the Record Industry Records, 1993; left The Gibson Brothers and formed The Bassholes; signed with In The Red Records; released Bassholes debut album *Haunted Hill,* 1995; along with his Bassholes work also spent time working with group Gaunt, and Ross Johnson; released *Deaf Mix Vol. 3*, In The Red, 1997; released *Blue Roots*, Matador label, 1997; started another band, Ego Summit; signed with Old Age/No Age Records, released Ego Summit's debut album *The Room's Not Big Enough,* 1977; released *When My Blue Moon Turns Red Again* and *Long Way Blues 1996-1998,* released EP "Lion's Share/Jesus Book," In The Red Records, 1998; released EP "Problem/ Change Had to Come," In The Red Records, 1998.

Addresses: *Record company*—In The Red Records, 2627 E. Strong Pl., Anaheim, CA 92806, TEL-(818)-841-2473/ FAX: (818)-841-2713, Mr. ; Don Howland *Website*—http://www.cpedu.rug.nl/~evert/bands/gh/howlandd.htm.

stripped down garage-recorded hard rock with lyrics frequently harsh and heavy on dark themes. "To me the Germs song off of the Cruising soundtrack, which we covered, and a Blind Willie McTell song have pretty much the same vibe-very dark, sexually maladjusted and pretty in a very ugly way," he told Baise. Howland's unique style involves adopting old blues lyrical motifs to quirky rock progressions, taking Bob Dylan songs and making them unrecognizable and creating what many music critics have called a "dark surrealism."

Throughout the last half decade, The Bassholes began making a niche for themselves in the indie alternative rock market. While doing this, Howland decided to start creating more branches in his ever expanding musical

repretoire. However, Howland has to maintain his day job as a teacher. This is a situation which causes him a lot of tension, grief, and upset. "I don't think the Bassholes' records would sound the way they do if I didn't have a really frustrating job," Howland told Baise. His job became even more frustrating in 1998 when two of his students committed several high-profile murders which gained a lot of sensational press and further depressed Howland. When asked about the crimes of his ex-students, he simply gave a one sentence dead-pan reply to Baise; "It was a bad year for Columbus, Ohio."

Howland not only works his teaching job during the day and his music at night, he also has the energy to involve himself with outside musical projects for up and coming independent rock bands. Besides working with Gaunt and Ross Johnson, he with the infamous band Southern Culture On The Skids, appeared on "Los Falanas," and has recently recorded four-seven-inch singles for the Sympathy For The Record Industry opus. However, his most recent sidework is a new band called Ego Summit. This latest Howland effort has teamed him up with old Gibson Brothers alumni, Ron House and Tommy Jay. The group's debut album, *The Room's Not Big Enough*, was released in 1997. It features Howland at his musical best with songs like "Ego's Bridge", "We Got it All," and "Black Hole". It appeared that Howland is doing the impossible on many fronts, but is increasingly commercially successful. He also appears to be doing well in his day job, but one day, he hopes to be able to support himself solely from his musical work.

Selected discography

Best of Gibson Brothers, Unidisc, 1993.
Deaf Mix, Vol. 3, In the Red, 1997.
Haunted Hill, In the Red, 1995.
Long Way Blues 1996-98, Matador, 1998.
Punk Rock Drivin' Song of a Gun, Homestead, 1990.
The Room's Not Big Enough, Ego Summit, Old Age/No Age Records, 1997.

Sources

Periodicals

Metro Times (Detroit), July 15-21, 1998.

Online

All-Music Guide Web Site, http://www.allmusic.com.

—*Timothy Kevin Perry*

Charlie Hunter

Guitar

As the "hip-hop" or "acid jazz" movement of the mid-1990s gained momentum in the United States, Charlie Hunter was leading it in the San Francisco Bay Area. Young groups of avant-garde jazz musicians were mixing traditional jazz with hip-hop, funk, and rock. Hunter was the first out of the pack of groups of the area to be released on CD. "We study the past and practice the present," Hunter told *Down Beat* in 1994. That blend of past and present was what Hunter used to push several incarnations of his own bands, including his trio, quartet, and T.J. Kirk—a separate Hunter group altogether—through a number of successful releases and tours. His inventive use of a custom guitar earned him astute musicians as fans, and his talent for creating infectious hip-hop dance grooves made Hunter's live shows guaranteed good times for college crowds.

Born in 1968, to Greenwich Village bohemians in Rhode Island, Hunter was raised in Berkeley, California, by his mother, who fixed instruments at Subway Guitar, a Berkeley guitar shop. He started playing electric guitar at 13, on an amp his mother made for him. At 14, he started taking lessons from now-famous guitarist Joe Satriani, a Subway instructor at the time. Satriani was demanding of Hunter, building in him the discipline that he lacked. The eclectic Bay Area environment also molded his musical talents. "Growing up in Berkeley, we were exposed to all kinds of music from the Dead Kennedys and Parliament/Funkadelic to Art Blakey," he explained to *Down Beat*. "As for my playing, Charlie Parker and John Coltrane are big influences. So are Stevie Wonder and old country blues players like Robert Johnson and Lightnin' Hopkins."

Hunter met Michael Franti, of the disbanded hip-hop group the Beatnigs, when Franti was working at Subway in 1991. Franti liked Hunter's developing style, and so the guitarist joined Franti's new group, Disposable Heroes of Hiphoprisy, as an accompaniment to Franti's raps. Hunter played on the Heroes' *Hiphoprisy is the Greatest Luxury* in 1992 and toured with them, most notably opening for Irish pop icons U2 and alternative-funk stars Primus. He left the band shortly before it dissolved completely and set out to create his own sound with his own musicians. "It wasn't what I wanted to do," Hunter told *Guitar Player* in 1994, the year after he left Disposable Heroes of Hiphoprisy. "It was great to see the world in that rock and roll environment, but it makes me realize how good I have it now, writing and playing what I want with musicians who can make me feel small every night."

If Charlie Hunter felt small every night when he played with his Charlie Hunter Trio, it didn't show. They recorded their first record, *Charlie Hunter Trio*, in Primus

For the Record . . .

Born Charles Hunter 1968, RI; grew up in Berkeley, CA.

Started playing guitar at age 12; took lessons from Joe Satriani at age 14; joined Disposable Heroes of Hiphoprisy, 1991, played on the group's 1992 release *Hiphophrisy is the Greatest Luxury;* toured with U2 and Primus; released *Charlie Hunter Trio,* Mammoth label, 1993; played second stage on the Lollapalooza tour in San Fransisco, 1993; released *T.J. Kirk* with T.J. Kirk, on Warner Brothers, 1994; signed to Blue Note; released, *Bing, Bing, Bing!,* 1995; released with T.J. Kirk, *If Four Was One,* Warner Brothers, 1996; released *Ready Set Shango!* on Blue Note in 1996; released remake of Bob Marley's *Natty Dread,* Blue Note, 1997; released *Return of the Candyman* with his group, Pound for Pound, Blue Note, 1998.

Addresses: *Record company*—Blue Note Records, 304 Park Avenue, 3rd Floor, New York, NY 10010.

frontman Les Claypool's basement and released it in 1993 on Claypool's brand new Prawn Song label. Hunter garnered attention with the bassless trio by providing simultaneous bass lines, melodies and chords as well as for his style that was more like that of an organist than a guitarist.

Hunter's hallmarks are his custom, guitar-bass hybrid Novak eight-string instrument and the way he uses it. He was into playing a seven-string guitar until a friend suggested he check out Larry Young's organ playing. Young played bass parts with his left hand and melodies and chords with his right. To Hunter, Young's style made sense and set him to design the instrument he became known for using. "The bottom three strings are tuned E, A, D, like the lower three strings on a bass," he explained to *Guitar Player* in 1995. " The top five are tuned A, D, G, B and E, as on guitar. I send the bass strings directly to a bass amp. The guitar strings go through a Korg G4 Leslie speaker simulator, a volume pedal, a wah, and then into the guitar amp." He does it all with his bare hands. "Picks are for kids," he told *Guitar Player* in the same article. "I don't mean to dis people who use a pick, but it doesn't work for me. Fingers are the way to go."

Hunter's singular style also caught the attention of legendary jazz label Blue Note, who signed him on the merit of his first release. He was simultaneously signed to Warner Brothers as part of T.J. Kirk—formerly known as James T. Kirk, until trademark concerns were raised by *Star Trek* producer Paramount. Fronted by three guitarists—Hunter, John Schott and Will Bernard—T.J. Kirk was as successful with its 1994 release *T.J. Kirk* and its subsequent tours as was Hunter's trio. "It's a total guitar nerd's fantasy band," Hunter told *On the One* in 1995 of T.J. Kirk.

In 1993, the Charlie Hunter Trio performed on the second stage at traveling alternative-rock fest Lollapalooza in San Francisco. For a group still new to the rock world, "it was scary," Hunter admitted to *Guitar Player*. But he also felt that his trio brought something to the festival that was new and different, yet easy for crowds to get into. "We put out hard-hitting energy, and people our age related to it because we related to them. And if they go out and buy a Charlie Parker or John Coltrane record after hearing us and realize how vital it is—not the de-clawed, sugar-factory stuff on mainstream jazz radio—that's great."

In 1995, Hunter was juggling his two major record deals, a new release, *Bing, Bing, Bing,* on Blue Note and still was arranging all his own shows. "20 gigs a month, ten phone calls a gig, work it out for yourself," he joked with *On the One* about his hectic schedule. Yet he still found time to record *Ready Set Shango!* for Blue Note and *If Four Was One* with T.J. Kirk on Warner Brothers, both for 1996 release.

In 1997, Hunter, this time with the Charlie Hunter Quartet, got involved with the Blue Note Cover Series, reinterpreting Bob Marley's classic *Natty Dread,* alongside Everette Harp covering Marvin Gaye's *What's Going On* and Fareed Haque doing Crosby, Stills, Nash and Young's *Deja Vu.* Although the series wasn't reviewed favorably, Hunter declared his good intention on the Blue Note Website. "It's culturally the duty of the younger generation to help the music evolve," he said.

Hunter teamed up with drummer Scott Amendola, percussionist John Santos, and Blue Note vibraphonist Stefon Harris in 1998 for *Return of the Candyman* by Charlie Hunter and Pound for Pound. Hunter composed all the tracks on the release, save "Electric Relaxation," by Ronnie Foster. Critical reviews were lukewarm. *Down Beat* opined in a 1998 review that the CD "may satisfy his fans, but to someone not familiar with Hunter's music, it's fair to say his self-penned tunes hover somewhere between pop's idea of jazz and jazzy sketches at best." But despite the album's lack of critical praise, Hunter and the group toured for the release successfully.

Selected discography

Charlie Hunter Trio, Mammoth, 1993.
Bing, Bing, Bing!, Blue Note, 1995.
Ready Set Shango!, Blue Note, 1996.
Natty Dread, Blue Note, 1997.
Return of the Candyman, Blue Note, 1998.
(With Disposable Heroes of Hiphoprisy)*Hiphoprisy is the Greatest Luxury*, 4th & Broadway, 1992.

With T.J. Kirk

T.J. Kirk, Warner Brothers, 1994.
If Four Was One, Warner Brothers, 1996.

Sources

Periodicals

On the One, Spring 1995.
Down Beat, June 1994; May 1998.
Musician, July 1998.
Stereo Review, June 1997.
Guitar Player, June 1994; November 1995.
Village Voice, September 26, 1995.

Online

"Charlie Hunter," *All-Music Guide,* http://www.allmusic.com (September 20, 1998).

Additional information was provided by Blue Note publicity materials, 1998.

—*Brenna Sanchez*

Mississippi John Hurt

Guitar

John Hurt was born and lived most of his life in a remote corner of Mississippi Delta country. By the time he passed away, he had touched a generation of folk music fans and influenced countless guitar players interested in fingerpicking styles. He had two separate careers as a professional musician, separated by 35 years, and both must have seemed a little like a dream to him. When he was in his middle thirties, a recording contract fell in his lap out of nowhere, taking him to Memphis and New York. Within a year, the Great Depression hit and he slipped back into obscurity. But blues aficionados rediscovered Hurt in the early 1960s and he toured the country to great popular acclaim until his death in 1966.

Hurt was born in Teoc in Carroll County, Mississippi sometime between early 1892 and 1894, though March 8, 1892 is usually given as his date of birth. As a child he moved to Avalon, Mississippi where he was raised with seven brothers and two sisters. Hurt attended school until the fourth grade, long enough to learn to read and write. He grew up in a family of music lovers, and around the time he was nine his mother gave him a guitar which he taught himself to play using an intricate fingerpicking style in which the thumb played rhythm on the bass strings and three fingers played melody or chords.

Around 1910, Hurt played his first public performances. These were most likely parties or informal get-togethers of friends and neighbors who gathered to listen to music and relax. Blues historian Stephen Calt points out that Hurt probably did not play at dances like most other Mississippi bluesmen often did. His guitar style was too intricate to provide the insistent rhythm needed for dancing, and his singing was too restrained to cut through the noise of a Saturday night juke joint on the Delta.

Discovered by Okeh

During his early adult life, Hurt worked first as a sharecropper, then as a day laborer, which included five months laying train track. There, it is believed, he learned railroad songs like "Spike Driver Blues." Around 1923 Willie Narmour, a white farmer in Avalon who played fiddle at local square dances, asked Hurt to play with him when his regular guitarist could not. This was a remarkable tribute to Hurt's musical ability, considering the degree of racial segregation that existed in Mississippi at the time. A few years later, Narmour won a fiddling contest in Carroll County and attracted the attention of a scout for the Okeh record company, Tommy Rockwell.

Companies were combing the south, in the middle 1920s, looking for artists to record for the popular new medium of the phonograph. When Rockwell met Narmour in Avalon, he asked about other musicians in the area who might be good enough to make records. The fiddler told him about John Hurt and not long afterwards Narmour and Rockwell drove over to Hurt's house to set up an audition. Hurt played a song. Halfway through the second, Rockwell told him to stop, he had heard enough. Hurt was invited to go to Memphis for a recording session. On February 14, 1928, John Hurt became Mississippi John Hurt. He recorded eight songs and that same year, two of them were released on Okeh 8560, "Frankie" and "Nobody's Dirty Business."

What happened next is in dispute. Some writers say the record sold so well that Hurt was offered a second recording session; others say the record flopped, but that Rockwell was convinced that Hurt had something that would sell records. At any rate, in December 1928 John Hurt traveled to New York City where he recorded songs for five more 78s. Even though Hurt was in New York City for the first time in his life—it was only the second time he had traveled more than 20 miles from Avalon—even though he met Lonnie Johnson, the most popular blues guitarist in America, it was Christmas time and Hurt felt like a poor boy a long ways from home. He missed his wife, he missed Mississippi. In the last song recorded at the session, "Avalon Blues," he sings "Avalon's my home-town/always on my mind." That song would have enormous repercussions later in Mississippi John Hurt's life.

Bad Sales, Hard Times

Hurt's records were a disappointment for Okeh, each selling only a few hundred copies. Some believe Okeh was ultimately responsible for their failure. First, they gave the records titles like "Candy Man Blues" and "Stack o' Lee Blues," when the songs had nothing in common with the true Mississippi blues being invented just a few miles from Hurt's front door. They were actually ragtime songs dating from an older folksong tradition. Second, because Hurt was *not* singing blues, because he came from the songster tradition, which was much closer to country music, he could have been popular among white audiences. Okeh, however, insisted upon listing his records in their "race" catalog of exclusively black artists.

It was all moot anyway. Less than a year after Hurt's second recording session, the Great Depression hit America. The poor audiences at whom Hurt's kind of music was aimed, black and white alike, could no longer afford frivolities like records. Hurt just settled down with Jessie Lee, his second wife, back in Avalon. He raised a family, found worked regularly, played guitar around town when he could and forgot about any career in music—and was forgotten by the rest of the world in return.

Interest in Mississippi John Hurt reawoke in the early 1950s following the release of Harry Smith's monumental *Anthology of American Folk Music.* The six-record set included two Hurt songs "Frankie" and Spike Driver Blues." Like most of the musicians on the *Anthology,* Hurt was a mystery. In fact, most listeners, according to the notes included with the 1997 *Anthology* reissue, assumed that John Hurt was white. Guitar players, in particular, were fascinated with his fingerpicking style and struggled to learn the songs, first from the *Anthology,* and later off old 78 records that began resurfacing. According to one story, one of Andres Segovia's students brought a record by Hurt for the master to hear. After listening to Hurt, Segovia reportedly asked who was playing the second guitar on the song. Hurt played solo on all his recordings.

Rediscovered at Avalon Home

In the early 1960s, two young folk musicians in Washington, D.C., Tom Hoskins and Mike Stewart, heard "Avalon Blues" on a tape a record collector had given them. What if there was a city called Avalon in Mississippi, they wondered. And what if Hurt still lived there? They couldn't find Avalon on any contemporary maps, but the tiny town finally turned up in an atlas published in 1878. When they went to the Delta with their tape recorder, they discovered that Avalon wasn't much more than a general store on the road between Grenada and Greenwood. They asked some men sitting in front of the store if they had ever heard of a Mississippi John Hurt. One pointed and said "A mile down that road, third mailbox up. Can't miss it." When Hoskins and Stewart arrived, Hurt was out in the fields on his tractor. They introduced themselves, explained that they were interested in music, and pulled out their tape recorder.

From there Hurt's second career in music snowballed quickly. Back in Washington, Hoskins released two albums of songs he had recorded at Hurt's farm. Not long after, Hurt came to Washington to play local folk clubs. He was a smash at the 1963 Newport Folk Festival, and later the same year, at the Philadelphia Folk Festival. Suddenly, at age 71, Hurt was one of the top stars in the American folk music scene. For the next three years, he toured festivals and folk clubs throughout the country, released albums on the Piedmont and Vanguard labels—this time the records were very popular—and entranced fans with his broad repertoire of ballads, ragtime numbers, old pop tunes, and religious songs, his storytelling, and his gentle personality.

Hurt's fingerpicking style is unusual among black players of his time. Only Elizabeth Cotten—another self-taught guitarist—used a similar technique. Nonetheless his playing has had an enormous impact on guitar players from the 1960s onward and echoes of his playing can be heard in the work of musicians like Leo Kottke and Stefan Grossman. John Fahey, a player who took many of Hurt's techniques into uncharted, new realms, composed and recorded a moving tribute, "Requiem For Mississippi John Hurt," on his Vanguard album *Requia*. But Hurt's influence pervades *all* guitar playing. When beginning guitarists first begin to finger-pick, almost invariably the first tunes they learn are Hurt's, pieces like "Louis Collins" or "Stack O' Lee Blues."

John Hurt was unfazed by the abrupt end of his first career as a professional musician in 1929; at the end of his life he seemed equally undaunted by the stardom that had burst upon him, out of nowhere as far as he was concerned. Once asked if he knew how good his music

was he answered almost with embarrassment. "Yeah... I know it ... and I been knowin' it, but I never dreamed things would've turned out like they have...never dreamed it." Mississippi John Hurt died in Grenada Mississippi on November 2, 1966.

Selected discography

1928 Sessions, Yazoo 1965.
Mississippi John Hurt Today! Vanguard (VSD 79220), 1966.
The Immortal Mississippi John Hurt, Vanguard (VSD 79248), 1967.
The Best Of Mississippi John Hurt, Vanguard (VSD 19/20), 1970.
Mississippi John Hurt Rediscovered, Vanguard, (79519-2) 1998.
Last Sessions Vanguard (VSD 79327).

Sources

Books

Erlewene, Michael, Vladimir Bogdano, Chris Woodstra, and Cub Koda. *All Music Guide to the Blues,* San Francisco: Miller Freeman Books, 1996.
Herzhaft, Gérard, *Encyclopedia of the Blues,* 2nd ed., Fayetteville, Arkansas: University of Arkansas Press, 1997.

Online

http://home.t-online.de/home/t_maria.wagner/jhurt.htm
http://www.eyeneer.com/America/Genre/Blues/Profiles/mississippi.john.html

Other

Calt, Stephen, *Mississippi John Hurt, 1928 Sessions*, liner notes.
Ward, Ed. *Mississippi John Hurt Rediscovered,* liner notes.

Additional materials provided by Vanguard Records.

—*Gerald E. Brennan*

Janis Ian

Singer, songwriter

A new generation of female musicians developed in the 1990's. Some of them looked tough, some fresh-faced and beautiful. Some were talented songwriters, while still others possessed angelic voices. Janis Ian was a little of each of them, but she cleared the way for them all. Ian has been called an American folk troubadour, and her consistent staying power has earned her nominations for at least one Grammy award from the 1960s-90s. And she started in 1966, when she was just 15.

While waiting to see a high-school guidance counselor, the former Janis Eddy Fink, daughter of a music teacher, wrote a song about interracial romance called "Society's Child (Baby I've Been Thinking)." After she recorded and released it, the controversial song was ignored by most radio stations, and outright banned by others. Things changed for the song, and for Ian, when conductor Leonard Bernstein featured her on his TV show *Inside Pop: The Rock Revolution,* calling her a "marvelous creature." She performed the song backed by the New York Philharmonic Orchestra. The song charted at number 14 in 1967.

Photo by Tim Paul. Archive, Photos, Inc. Reproduced by permission.

For the Record . . .

Born Janis Eddy Fink, April 7, 1951, New York, NY; married and divorced photojournalist Peter Cunningham. *Education:* attended High School of Music and Art, Manhattan.

Composition "Hair of Spun Gold" appeared in *Broadside* magazine, 1964; released debut, "Society's Child (Baby I've Been Thinking)" in 1966; released *Janis Ian* and was nominated for a Grammy award; appeared on *The Tonight Show* and in *Time, Life* and *Newsweek*; released *Between the Lines* in 1975.

Awards: Grammy awards for "At Seventeen," 1975; "Silly Habits" with Mel Torme as Best Vocal Duet, 1981; and *In Harmony 2*, in 1982.

Addresses: *Record company*—Windham Hill Records, PO Box 9388, Stanford, CA 94309; (415) 329-0647; fax (415) 329-1512; *email*—whinfo@windham.com.

After quitting Manhattan's High School of Music and Art as a junior, the year after "Society's Child" was released, she released her first album, *Janis Ian*, on Verve, in 1967. She released three more for Verve, *For All the Seasons of your Mind* in 1967; *The Secret Life of J. Eddy Fink* in 1968 and 1969's *Who Really Cares*. In 1974 and 1975, Ian released *Stars* on One Way, and *Between the Lines* and *Aftertones* on Columbia. Roberta Flack later recorded "Jesse" from *Stars* and topped the charts with it. *Between the Lines* included "At Seventeen," a single that went to number three on the charts and earned Ian a Grammy award for Best Female Vocal. 1975 was Ian's most successful year—she sold over $5 million in records—which was important to her. After "Society's Child," she felt she needed to dispel the notion that the single was a fluke, that she was washed up by age 18. Her next several albums recorded from 1977-79, *Miracle Row*, *Janis Ian*, and *Night Rains*, didn't garner much attention at all.

As a young star, Ian faced hurdles in an industry that can be difficult even for adults to deal with. "Well I was fourteen so that's already a problem," she recalled in a 1993 interview with Lydia Hutchinson of *A&R Insider*. Being underage meant that she couldn't sign her own contracts, book her own musicians, or run her own sessions. Being a young female musician in the late sixties only complicated things further. "I remember violent arguments with TV people in [Los Angeles] when I was fifteen about wearing pants or dresses," she told Hutchinson. Her wardrobe wars were only the start of her gender-related battles. She also remembered having a tough time getting credit as the leader of her three-person group. "There's this assumption that if you're male and have a band—it's your band.... But if you're female, they're pickup musicians. I don't know why that is."

Ian acknowledged that the music business is a tough road for everyone, but it was extraordinarily tough for a young, emotionally developing girl. "The hurdles weren't that different from anyone else," she said, "except when you are an adolescent, it's so hard just existing, that the added pressure of expecting yourself to be brilliant and to communicate and to become a whole and honest person is a lot." She remembered rock veteran and notorious substance abuser Janis Joplin sending her home from a party where drugs were being used.

In overcoming her growing pains, Ian only faced more complicated gender issues as an adult. She went under fire by some feminists because she didn't have any other women in her band. "I got really offended because it's a three-piece band," she said, in which she plays guitar, piano, and sings. "Outside of me there's just two other people, so we have a 33 percent ratio. But it was like I wasn't in the band. There was this assumption on some weird level that as a female and as a singer I was not a serious musician." Although she still felt pressure as a female musician in a man's world, Ian knew things had changed for her over the years. "Well, the dress thing's not an issue," she told Hutchinson, laughing. She started receiving credit from musicians she respected. "Chick Corea thinks I'm a wonderful pianist, Chet Atkins thinks I'm a wonderful guitarist. And that beats it to me. How much does the rest matter?"

Even as a young musician, Ian always stayed true to her own material. Except for a few commercial jingles, she only recorded songs she had written. "I did turn down 'You Light Up My Life,' and I would have done a good job on it," she admitted to *A&R Insider*, "but it seemed real important at the time, since there were so few women writers, to prove the point." And prove the point she did, releasing 13 albums—consisting mostly of her songs—from 1967-81. The next 12 years, however, would see only two albums from Ian.

Ian's 12-year hiatus before *Breaking Silence*, in 1993, was due to a series of major personal and financial problems that kept her from recording, but strengthened her resolve and self-worth as a musician, nonetheless. A former accountant had botched her taxes, her health failed, her marriage ended, and she lost her house. She sold her instruments for money to live on, but she kept writing music. "The knowledge kept hitting me in the face that everybody could take everything away from me," she told Richard Johnston in *Guitar Player* in 1997, "but they couldn't take my talent."

"It's good in a lot of ways because I didn't want a lot of those years on record," she told Hutchinson. "I didn't like what I was writing. It took me a while to find my voice again, I think." The voice she found was stronger, more mature, than the one her fans had last heard. It was with this hard-earned personal resolve that Ian also revealed her homosexuality. With *Breaking Silence*, she seemed renewed and empowered, taking on the issues that she'd been missing out on for over a decade. The laid back folk sound of Ian's new material belied the strong lyrics on such heady subjects as battered wives, eroticism, the Holocaust, and '60s nostalgia.

When new-age and classical record label Windham Hill approached Ian's manager, they were told she didn't trust major labels. "I certainly didn't want to be with Windham Hill and make 'zither' music," Ian told *Billboard* in 1997. But they "wined and dined" her and treated her "like royalty"—a refreshing change for an older female artist, she said. Grace Newman, of Windham Hill marketing, professed the label's feeling about Ian to *Billboard* in the same story. "She's a pioneer in the female musician arena, which started out decades ago and went underground—then exploded with everybody from Shawn Colvin to Jewel to Sarah McLachlan." The label released *Hunger* shortly thereafter. Windham Hill also predicted that the respect she'd garnered as a woman over the years would attract long-time fans, as wells as those of the new generation of female musicians.

Ian approached independent female rocker Ani DiFranco—a sort of Janis Ian for the X Generation—to work on *Hunger*. Ian had listened to DiFranco's *Not a Pretty Girl* album and found a kindred spirit in the younger artist. Ian, in fact, was taken aback. "I thought I should find something else to do with my life!" she told *Billboard*. "She was pushing the envelope in ways I wanted to do." DiFranco was tentative, as she'd only produced her own material. Thinking that she'd feel intrusive in someone else's recording studio, it took Ian a year to convince her. The result was the track "Searching" and "the nicest producer experience of my life," Ian said. Ian's new sound, which she termed "techno folk" was strong, or as

Johnston called it—"Stark social commentary, vivid imagery and unflinchingly personal meditations.

Selected discography

Janis Ian (Verve), Verve, 1967.
For All the Seasons of Your Mind, Verve, 1967.
The Secret Life of J. Eddie Fink, Verve, 1968.
Who Really Cares, Verve, 1969.
Present Company, One Way, 1971.
Stars, One Way, 1974.
Between the Lines, Columbia, 1975.
Aftertones, Columbia, 1975.
Miracle Row, Columbia, 1977.
Janis Ian (Columbia), Columbia, 1978.
Night Rains, Columbia, 1979.
The Best of Janis Ian, CBS, 1980.
Restless Eyes, Columbia, 1981.
Uncle Wonderful, Grapevine, 1983.
Stars/Night Rains, CBS, 1987.
Breaking Silence, Morgan Creek, 1993.
Live on the Test 1976, BBC Worldwide, 1995.
Society's Child: the Verve Recordings, Polydor, 1995.
Hunger, Windham Hill, 1997.

Sources

Books

Romanowski, Patricia and Warren, Holly George, editors, *The Rolling Stone Encyclopedia of Rock & Roll*, Fireside/Simon & Shuster, 1995.

Periodicals

Billboard, August 30, 1997.
Guitar Player, December 1997.

Online

http://imusic.interserv.com (September 27, 1998).
http://www.songs.com (September 20, 1998).
http://www.jacksonville.com (September 20, 1998).
http://www.taxi.com (September 20, 1998).
http://www.allmusic.com (September 20, 1998).
http://www.cdnow.com (September 20, 1998).

Additional information was provided by Windham Hill publicity materials, April, 27 1998.

—Brenna Sanchez

Abdullah Ibrahim

Piano, band leader, composer

Abdullah Ibrahim is noted for his fusion of South African musical culture with freeform American jazz, and for his highly original film scores and the operas he has composed. Ibrahim also plays synthesizer, cello, soprano saxophone, and flute. His distinctive sound combines a jubilant jazz feel with a wide range of African influences. His diverse compositions display his complex, multi-layered talent. He has recorded with Enja Records for over 20 years and explained the musical philosophy of his band in one of the label's press releases. "We hope it will bring some happiness."

Ibrahim was born Adolph Johannes Brand in 1934, in Cape Town, South Africa. He was steeped in traditional African songs, jazz, and religious music as a child which became the underpinnings of his compositions. He began playing piano at the age of seven and was largely self-taught using church music, jazz on the radio, and the collection of records in his home as his teachers. He began his career in earnest in 1949, at 25, when he adopted the stage name Dollar Brand. He began playing the popular music of the mid-1950s with two bands, the Tuxedo Slickers and the Willie Max Big Band. In 1959, he met alto saxophone player Kippi Moeketsi who convinced him to devote his life to music.

By, 1960 Ibrahim had formed a jazz band called the Jazz Epistles that included Hugh Masakela, Jonas Gwangwa, and Kippie Moeketsi. They released *Jazz Epistles: Verse One* in 1960 on the French label, Celluloid. This release was the first appearance of South African jazz on a long playing record. Many of Ibrahim's former accompanists in South Africa went on win great success, notably saxophonist Basil Coetzee who became a star of modern Cape jazz. When Ibrahim's anti-government stance and political activities drew the attention of the U.S. authorities in 1962, he embarked upon a long trip to Europe with the jazz singer Sathima Bea Benjamin, whom he would marry in 1965.

Discovered by Duke Ellington

One night during the band's 1962 European tour, Duke Ellington caught the Dollar Brand Trio at the Africana Club in Zurich. Ellington was impressed with the style and craftsmanship of Ibrahim, bassist Johnny Gertze and drummer Makaya Ntshoko, and arranged for a recording session at Reprise Records. The result of the sessions was the album *Duke Ellington Presents the Dollar Brand Trio*. Ellington also provided contacts for the Dollar Brand Trio that led to appearances at major European festivals as well as on television and radio shows in 1963 and 1964.

Brand played the Newport Jazz Festival in 1965, which he followed up with by his first U.S. tour. A year later, he led the Duke Ellington Orchestra and told the Enya label, "I did five dates substituting for [Ellington]. It was exciting but very scary, I could hardly play." He moved to New York and played with the era's free jazz leaders, including Don Cherry, Ornette Coleman, and John Coltrane. He spent six months playing with the Elvin Jones Quartet.

Cut Off from Roots

It was around 1968, when Ibrahim converted to Islam. He adopted the name Abdullah Ibrahim and pursued his interest in politics and religion. Ibrahim returned to South Africa to record, but the ban on the African National Congress made it difficult for him to maintain close ties with his homeland. In spite of this political separation, he continued to explore his musical roots and the ways in which they could be fused with American jazz. In 1968, he made a solo piano tour, after which he continued to tour extensively in the United States, Europe, and Japan. He appeared at major music festivals throughout the world, including the Montreux Jazz Festival, the North Sea Festival, and festivals in Berlin, Paris, and Canada. Much of his music from the 1960s and 1970s defines those eras in American jazz. Ibrahim returned to South Africa in the mid-1970s, but he found the political climate so oppressive that he returned to New York City in 1976, where he continued to hone his music alongside many of the city's jazz titans. He was prolific during the years 1965-98, often releasing as many as four albums a year. He released both *Anatomy of A South African Village* and *The Dream* in 1965, and *Hamba Khale* with Gato Barbieri in 1968. The much-lauded *This Is Dollar Brand* and *African Piano* came out in 1973. Noteworthy releases of the late 1970s included, *Mannenberg* in 1974, *Banyana* in 1976, and *Tears and Laughter* and *Echoes from Africa* in 1979. Ibrahim's impressive output continued for the next two decades. From the mid-1980s on, Ibrahim performed with his seven-piece band, Ekaya. They released a series of albums that included *African River, Zimbabwe, Mantra Mode,* and *Yarona.* In 1996, Ibrahim and Ekaya released the album *Capetown Flowers.* Reviewing the record, *Newsday* wrote, "Giants still walk the earth and Abdullah Ibrahim is among them. This South African composer, a discovery and disciple of Duke Ellington, is playing with an authority that is close to regal."

Broadened Musical Range

In the early 1980s, Ibrahim expanded his musical palette to include a broader range of music. He began composing operas and *Kalahari Liberation* was presented to much acclaim throughout Europe. In 1988, Ibrahim wrote the soundtrack for the film *Chocolat* (the American release was entitled *Mindif*), and followed with the soundtrack to the film *No Fear, No Die* in 1990. Ibrahim returned to South Africa to live in 1990, following the end of apartheid, but he maintained a residence in New York City as well. In 1997, he collaborated with legendary jazz drummer Max Roach for a televised concert at the Baltica Festival. Swiss composer Daniel Schnyder arranged Ibrahim's compositions for a 22-piece string orchestra in 1997 and 1998. The finished product, *African Suite,* was broadcast over six days, first on Swiss television and later worldwide.

Ibrahim was the featured soloist with the Munich Radio Philharmonic Orchestra, and several other orchestras expressed interest in performing his work, which placed Ibrahim in the major classical venues of the world. In 1997, Switzerland's Innovative Music published the *Abdullah Ibrahim Song Book,* and in January of 1998, the Adbullah Ibrahim Trio performed with the Munich Radio Philharmonic Orchestra under American conductor Barbara Yahr. That concert at Munich's Herkules Saal concert hall was recorded for release on CD.

Since it began, Abdullah Ibrahim's long career has combined musical forms into fascinating new hybrids of south African music, jazz, and classical and world music. It will be exciting to hear what new forms he creates.

Selected discography

Duke Ellington Presents the Dollar Brand Trio, Reprise, 1963.
Anatomy of a South African Village, Reprise, 1965.
The Dream, Reprise, 1965.
(With Gato Barbieri) *Hamba Khale,* Reprise, 1968.
This Is Dollar Brand, Reprise, (recorded 1965) 1973.
African Piano, BMG/ECM, 1973.
Good News from Africa, Enja, 1974.
African Space Program, Enja, 1974.

Mannenberg, Celluloid (France), 1974.
Banyana, Enja Records (Germany), 1976.
Tears and Laughter, Enja, 1979.
Echoes from Africa, Enja, 1979.
African Marketplace, Sire/Discovery Records, 1980.
Live at Montreux, Enja, 1980.
African Dawn, Enja, 1982.
Desert Flowers, Enja, 1982.
South Africa, Enja, 1983.
Water from an Ancient Well, Tiptoe Records, 1985.
Mindif, Chocolat soundtrack, Enja, 1988.
African River, Enja, 1989.
No Fear, No Die, Tiptoe, 1990.
Zimbabwe, Enja, 1990.
Mantra Mode, Tiptoe, 1991.
Knysna Blue, Tiptoe, 1993.
Yarona, Tiptoe, 1995.

Sources

Books

Burton, Kim, David Muddyman, and Richard Trillo. *The Rough Guide to World Music,* Penguin Books, New York, 1994.
Sweeney, Philip. *The Virgin Directory of World Music*, Henry Holt & Co., New York, 1991.

Online

http://www.cdnow.com (September 18, 1998).
http://www.enjarecords.com/abdullah_ibrahim.html (September 15, 1998).

—B. Kimberly Taylor

Jackyl

Rock band

Marry heavy metal raunch to the traditional Southern rock boogie, and the baby will look something like Jackyl. The band's debut album, *Jackyl,* sold more than 1.2 million copies, due in part to the inclusion of a chainsaw solo on the single "The Lumberjack." The record remains one of the most consistently selling rock releases of the 1990s. Their second release, *Push Comes To Shove,* was awarded a gold record, the band appeared on the Beavis & Butthead soundtrack which went platinum, and their recording *Woodstock '94,* also went gold. Jackyl worked with AC/DC's frontman Brian Johnson on the single "Locked and Loaded," the first time a member of AC/DC had collaborated with another band.

Founded in 1990, Jackyl is comprised of vocalist Jesse James Dupree from Georgia, drummer Chris Worley and guitarists Jeff Worley and Jimmy Stiff from South Carolina, and bassist Tom Bettini from Tennessee. The band is part of a Southern powerhouse lineage that extends back to Lynyrd Skynyrd and the Allman Brothers. Jackyl rates higher on the raunch-o-meter than most of their Southern forebears however, evident in their list of influences which spans the greats of heavy metal as well as their ambition. As Dupree told Alex Richter of Rocknet, "We want to get up there with Metallica and Aerosmith."

Jackyl's first release was *Jackyl* in 1992, a record which went on to sell sold more than 2.1 million copies. Their 1994 second album, *Push Comes To Shove,* went gold despite the fact that there was no video, no MTV airplay, and no hit single. The album's success was a tribute to the power of Jackyl's touring and its attention to keeping its fanatic fan base satisfied. And it proved what Jackyl knew all along—that there were lots of fans out there. "Most bands get supported at, say, MTV or radio...then the people say the TV or the radio stations program the people because the people see it or hear it so much that they go for it," Dupree told Gargano. "Ours has been kind of reversed from all that, we have forced people to deal with us because they know the [audience] is there for us ... at Woodstock '94 ... because of the numbers we were doing touring, they couldn't deny that there were people there to see us."

Jackyl attracted a broad audience, well, a broad audience of metal heads. It's not unusual to see a teenager in a heavy metal T-shirt sitting next to someone twice his age sporting a Hank Jr. or Rolling Stones T-shirt. A number of factors contributed to Jackyl's popularity. For one thing, they don't mess with the heavy metal formula. "Think balls-to-the-wall vocal delivery, with Jackyl's guitar-driven and blues-hued-musical fury, and you've got a clue what to expect," wrote Paul Gargano in *Metal Edge.* "When this fox runs through radio's henhouse, more than feathers are going to get ruffled ... just the stuff we've come to expect from Jackyl." And like metal mentors Kiss and AC/DC, Jackyl has never hesitated to behave outrageously whether giving their songs outrageous titles guaranteed to put off parents, feminists, and all the other forces of decency, performing naked, or even posing in the buff for *Playgirl* magazine. Dupree told Gargano, "We are what we are ... and we'll continue doing what we do because we are what we are, and we're not trying to change."

Another reason for the devotion of Jackyl's fans is the band's relentless tour schedule. Besides backing up established bands with a built-in metal following, like Aerosmith, Kiss, ZZ Top, and Ted Nugent, Jackyl embraces a work ethic that is outright puritan. In 1998, the band demolished the Guinness Book of World Records mark for most live performances in the shortest period held by George Thorogood and The Destroyers. Thorogood had played 52 shows in 50 days; Jackyl played 100 performances in 50 days in 27 different states! On October 2, 1998, in Abilene, Texas, the band played 21 gigs on a single day, which must also be some kind of record.

The band's members take their live shows very seriously and will do nearly anything to entertain the crowd. Even if it means firing up a chainsaw or blasting Dupree

For the Record . . .

Members include **Tom Bettini,** (born in TN), bass; **Jesse James Dupree**, (born in GA), vocals; **Jimmy Stiff**, (born in SC), guitar; **Chris Worley**, (born in SC), drums; **Jeff Worley**, (born in SC), guitar.

Band formed, 1990; released debut album, *Jackyl,* Geffen, 1992; debut sold more than 1.2 million copies; released *Push Comes To Shove,* 1994; released *Night of the Living Dead,* Mayhem, 1996; released *Cut the Crap,* Epic, 1997; collaborated with AC/DC's frontman Brian Johnson on the single "Locked and Loaded" for *Cut The Crap* in 1997, the first time a member of AC/DC collaborated with another band; released *Stayin' Alive,* Epic Records, 1998; appeared on the *Beavis & Butthead* soundtrack which went platinum; *Stayin' Alive* appeared in 1998; released *Choice Cuts,* 1998; surpassed George Thorogood and The Destroyers *Guinness Book of World Records* mark of 52 shows in 50 days as most live performances in the shortest amount of time, delivered 100 performances in 50 days in 27 different states in 1998.

Awards: Gold certification for *Stayin' Alive* and *Woodstock '94.*

Addresses: *Record company*—Epic Records, 550 Madison Avenue, New York, NY 10022-3297, (212) 833-7442, fax (212) 833-5719; 2100 Colorado Avenue, Santa Monica, CA 90404, (310) 449-2870, fax (310) 449-2559.

out of a cannon as they did in 1998, no sacrifice is too great. Audience members often become part of Jackyl's show as well, and it isn't unusual for Dupree to pull an audience member up on stage with him.

If there's one thing Jackyl isn't, it's a bunch of sensitive poets singing to a cultivated, delicate audience. Dupree admitted to Geffen Records that Jackyl wasn't interested in providing "introspective soul-searching, political commentary, or onstage self-righteousness." The type of thing Jackyl is interested in, for example, is chainsaws.

"Dupree's father attended one of Jackyl's early concerts," Jeff Worley told journalist Georgia Lecorchick, "and said, 'You boys are makin' enough of a racket, you oughtta bring a chainsaw on stage.' So we did." Jackyl took a camera and a chainsaw down to the local Long Horn Steak House where they planned to shoot a video for their single "The Lumberjack" in 1998. No one bothered to inform diners what was about to come off. When Dupree fired up his chainsaw in the restaurant and attacked a table with it, nervous patrons dove for cover.

Dupree explained the band's approach. "Real America is where people work for a living," he is quoted on Oberheim's *Main Event* website. "When the day is over and they spend their hard- earned money on rock and roll, they deserve to get their money's worth... It's just a fact that you're always going to have trends. Trends are cute, but we're proud that we're not the flavor of the day. We're just a straight up rock band." Band members are as loyal to Jackyl as its fans are. They have stuck together since the band's inception in the early 1990s. "It would be real hard for us to ever think of replacing anyone," Dupree told Richter, "because we're so close as a band and kind of close in our personal lives."

Since 1998, Jackyl has released three albums. Its third record, *Night of the Living Dead,* released in 1996, was a Jackyl project from start to finish. The band wrote, recorded, packaged, and released the album themselves on their own label—with the help from the people at Mayhem. *Cut the Crap* followed in 1997, and both *Stayin' Alive* and *Choice Cuts,* which featured covers of Grand Funk Railroad's "We're An American Band" and "I Am the Walrus" by the Beatles, appeared in 1998..

The band's straight-ahead, in-your face-and-groin, sound will continue to rock metal heads of all ages. And while it's unlikely that Jackyl will ever redefine its sound, the band will surely find new ways to entertain, shock, and deafen its fanatically loyal audiences.

Selected discography

Jackyl, Geffen, 1992.
Push Comes to Shove, Geffen, 1994.
Night of the Living Dead, Mayhem, 1996.
Cut the Crap, Sony/Epic, 1997.
Stayin' Alive, Sony/Epic, 1998.
Choice Cuts, Geffen, 1998.

Sources

Periodicals

Metal Edge, September 1997.

Online

AMG All Media Guide, 1998: http://www.amg.com

Lecorchick, Georgia, *Rock Me, Roll Me, Jackyl Me Off,* 1998; http://www.geffen.com

The Main Event magazine: Jackyl's Jesse James Dupree: Playing for Real America, www.oberheim.com/magazines/amplifier/199717/mainevent.

Woods, John: *ROC Talk: Rock Me, Roll Me, Jackyl Me Off,* 1994; http://www.geffen.com

Yahoo.com/music/jackyl

Additional source material was provided by the publicity department of Epic Records.

—B. Kimberly Taylor

Skip James

Guitar, piano

Skip James was unique among blues players. He was accomplished on two instruments, guitar and piano. While many lesser musicians made pests of themselves in their attempts to be recorded, James refused his offer to be recorded and embraced his rediscovery in the 1960s only halfheartedly. Rather than the deep, rough shouts associated with many early male blues singers, James sang in a high thin wail. But his otherworldly voice, haunting guitar, and staccato piano bursts contributed to some of the greatest blues sides ever recorded.

Nehemiah Curtis James was born on June 21, 1902 in an African American hospital in Yazoo City, Mississippi. He was raised on the Woodbine plantation just outside Betonia, Mississippi. He was drawn to music from an early age. As a child he heard musicians Henry Stuckey and Rich Griffin play a frolic—a Saturday night dance party—in Betonia. Afterwards, he sang the songs he had heard constantly until his mother finally bought him a $2.50 guitar. As a teenager, he played his aunt's organ, and his mother encouraged his interest by sending him to a couple of piano lessons. However, James was a natural musician, his talent far outstripped the educational resources available to a young African American growing up on a southern plantation. He taught himself piano after watching a rural pianist in a barrelhouse, and he developed his guitar style on his own after Henry Stuckey showed him how to tune his guitar to an open E minor chord. Both James' guitar and piano sound are totally unique in blues.

James left Betonia around 1919 and led the life of an itinerant worker for the next few years. He worked a series of jobs, both legitimate and illegitimate, including lumberman, rail splitter, minister, sharecropper, gambler, bootlegger, and pimp. James was the product of a violent, lawless milieu where practically anything was permitted—as long as it did not erupt into the surrounding white society. He carried a gun from an early age and did not hesitate to use it. He had once emptied his weapon into a romantic rival, he told biographer Stephen Calt proudly. Calt speculated that James' nickname may have had its roots in his criminal activities not his dancing abilities as he often claimed—James often had to "skip" town in a hurry.

Young Skip James gave little thought to becoming a professional musician. At first he was interested only in playing for himself and his friends. Throughout most of the 1920s he lacked the financial incentive to play for money; he was a successful bootlegger under the protection of a white plantation owner. He earned far more from making illegal whiskey than he could hope to earn in the dangerous world of the Southern jukehouse. In 1927, Okeh Records approached him about making some records. James refused. Calt believes James' shadowy criminal side may have been the reason—records would simply have brought him too much unwanted publicity. James was finally persuaded to see H.C. Spier in February of 1931.

Spier was a furniture and record dealer, and a master scout who had single-handedly discovered most of the great Mississippi bluesmen of the 1920s and early 1930s, including Tommy Johnson, Ishmon Bracey, Bo Carter, and the legendary Charlie Patton. James played a little bit of "Devil Got My Woman," and Spier was convinced. The next day he presented the singer with a contract and a train ticket to Wisconsin, where Paramount Records had a studio. In Grafton, Wisconsin, James apparently recorded 18 tunes—he would later remember doing 26. Either way, it was a sign of how he had impressed Spier and Paramount—he recorded more sides in his session than any other Paramount artist, except Charlie Patton.

Records Classic Blues, Finds God

Accompanying himself, James laid down pieces that were later acknowledged as classics in recorded blues: "Devil Got My Woman," "I'm So Glad," "Hard Time Killin'

Born Nehemiah Curtis ("Skip") James, June 21, 1902, Yazoo City, MS; died October 3, 1969; learned guitar and piano as a child; married three times: Oscella Robinson, Mabel James, Lorenzo Meeks.

Recorded for Paramount Records February 1931; rediscovered by blues enthusiasts Bill Barth, John Fahey, and Henry Vestine and played Newport Folk Festival, 1964; recorded first post-discovery record, the album *Skip James: Greatest of the Delta Blues Singers* in July 1965.

Awards: Voted into Blues Foundation Hall of Fame in 1992.

Floor," "Special Rider Blues" on his weird modal guitar, and "If you Haven't Any Hay, Get On Down The Road" and "22-20 Blues" on piano that utilized abrupt pauses and explosive fills. The first record released by Paramount in the spring of 1931 was "Hard Time Killin Floor Blues" backed with "Cherry Ball Blues." Only 650 copies were issued. No more than 300 copies of James' other records were put out by Paramount, however, including his fifth 78 "I'm So Glad" backed with "Special Rider Blues," which Calt has called "probably the greatest double-sided blues 78 ever issued." But it was the height of the Depression, and the audience for blues had been hit harder than any, and Paramount was about to go out of business.

Not long after his recording session, James met his father again for the first time since his childhood. The senior James was a Baptist minister. He asked Skip to go to Dallas to attend his divinity school and study for the ministry. James accepted the invitation. The most serious implication of his new-found religion was relinquishing blues, which was considered "the Devil's music." Spier approached James in 1932 about recording for Victor Records, but James refused. For the next fifteen years, the only music Skip James would play would be spirituals.

However obscure his music was it did not go forgotten. Other blues artists recorded his music during the 1930s. Charlie and Joe McCoy recorded "Devil Got My Woman" for Decca in 1934, for instance. In 1943, two white jazz collectors obtained a test pressing of "Little Cow And Calf is Gonna Die Blues" and subsequently re-released

it on their own label. It was the first re-issue of a blues song for the white collectors market and sold about 300 copies—as many as Paramount had pressed of its version.

In 1948 James quit a job with a mining company in Birmingham and returned to Betonia, planning to resume his blues career. But the African American population in Mississippi was dwindling. Tastes in blues had changed, as well. Electric blues, so-called "Chicago blues," were in vogue. Time had passed Skip James and his acoustic guitar by. He was only able to play an occasional party in town. Eventually James vanished from Betonia. He apparently skipped town again after cashing in a cotton crop raised with $500 his cousin had lent him and headed to Memphis where he tried to open his own honky-tonk.

Rediscovered in Hospital

By the 1950s collectors had made Skip James records valuable commodities; by the early 1960s a blues revival was underway and three of his songs had been reissued on anthologies of early blues. Young blues aficionados set out to track down James and the other men who had made the old, exotic, scratchy records. James proved difficult to find. It was not until 1964 that guitarist John Fahey and two friends located him in Tunica, Arkansas, where he lay in a hospital suffering from cancer. Finally coaxed back to performing, his first public appearance was the Newport Folk Festival that year. He played a mere nine minute set, four songs in all, but his performance according to Calt in *I'd Rather be the Devil*, was "to many blues devotees, the most dramatic moment of the festival."

In constant pain from the as yet untreated cancer, James was unable to record at first, despite interest from various record companies. In July of 1965, he received $200 for a session for Melodeon Records, which later that year resulted in an album entitled *Skip James: Greatest of the Delta Blues Singers*. He would later record two LPs for Vanguard, *Skip James Today!* and *Devil Got My Woman*. During the last four years of his life he occasionally played gigs at coffeehouses up and down the northeast coast. But his unrelentingly depressing music made the clubs loathe to book him. His records were not particularly successful either.

Another factor contributing to his lack of success late in life was his decline in musical quality. He had forsaken blues music at the time of his religious conversion. Calt wrote in *I'd Rather be the Devil*: "Before his death, James was to tell the author that he had considered blues sinful to perform. As a compromise, he had played with his 'thinkin' faculties' but had deliberately refused to 'put my heart in it.' What James feared above all was becoming the mesmeric blues performer he had been in 1931 and thus infecting others with the sin that blues represented. 'Feelin' in music is electrifyin,' he said. 'It'll infect people'." Star-struck audiences were satisfied with whatever he did, hearing more what he represented than what he was actually playing.

Living in Philadelphia with his third wife, James was chronically broke during his last years. Until the group Cream recorded "I'm So Glad" and gave James the songwriter's credit, that is. As a result, he received a royalty check for nearly $10,000. Skip James died of cancer on October 3, 1969, in Philadelphia. He was inducted into the Blues Foundation Hall of Fame in 1992.

Selected discography

78s

"Hard Time Killin Floor Blues," Paramount.
"22-20 Blues," Paramount.
"Illinois Blues," Paramount.
"How Long 'Buck," Paramount.
"Devil Got My Woman," Paramount.
"I'm So Glad," Paramount.
"Four O'Clock Blues," Paramount.
"Jesus is a Mighty Good Leader,"Paramount.
"Drunken Spree," Paramount.

Albums

Skip James Today!, Vanguard, 1966.
The Devil Got my Woman, Vanguard, 1968.
The Complete Early Recordings of Skip James—1930, Yazoo 2009.

Video

Devil Got My Woman: Blues At Newport 1966, Vestapol 13049.

Sources

Books

Calt, Stephen, *I'd Rather Be the Devil: Skip James and the Blues*, Da Capo, 1994.
Guralinick, Peter. *The Listener's Guide to the Blues,* Facts on File, 1982.

Online

http://www.hub.org/bluesnet/artists/skip.james.html
http://www.biograph.com
http://www.eyeneer.com/America/Genre/Blues/Profiles/skip.james.html
members.xoom.com/sardine/skipbio.html

—Gerald E. Brennan

Kilgore

Heavy metal band

Kilgore, the Providence, Rhode Island-based metal band, has earned a reputation as the thinking person's metal band along with its reputation for aggressive, high-energy music. Named after the character Kilgore Trout in the Kurt Vonnegut classic, *Breakfast of Champions,* Kilgore is noted for lyrics that suggest a literate songwriter. The band started out with the name Smudge in 1991, switched to Stain in 1994, to Kilgore Smudge in 1995, and finally settled upon Kilgore in 1998. Jerry Rutherford of *Metal Maniacs* magazine wrote, "[Kilgore is reminiscent of] early Clutch, Mindset, Honkyball, Chum, and Only Living Witness ... [the band] manages to balance rhythmically piledriving riffstomp and a remarkable—though not commercially minded—songwriting flair without sacrificing one for the other." Gerri Miller of *Ozzfest '98* magazine described their sound like this, "[Kilgore offers] a molten dish of aggressive yet melodic metal." Kilgore is one of the rare bands that doesn't render the term 'melodic metal' an oxymoron, and the band's material stretches far beyond the ordinary. On that note, Rutherford continued, "[There's] rarely a moment resembling filler or an instance that finds the band falling on its collective force."

The band is comprised of vocalist and primary songwriter Jay Berndt, bassist Marty O'Brien, guitarist Mike Pelletier, and drummer Bill Southerland. Berndt met the original members of Kilgore—with the exception of

O'Brien and Pelletier, later additions to the at the Catholic LaSalle Academy high school in a music class. The school offered a unique program that allowed students to pay five dollars each in order to see three school bands perform. This allowed the future Kilgore members (then called Smudge) to play covers of metal, rock, and blues standards for their peers. Berndt, a loner in junior high and high school, read numerous books by Beat Generation authors and other authors such as Charles Bukowski, Fyodor Dostoevsky, Edgar Allen Poe, Kurt Vonnegut, and Franz Kafka. The aggressive, alienated sound sometimes found in Kilgore's music stems more from these literary influences than from musical ones. Berndt continued on to college as an English major but found the experience intellectually stifling since he felt his thoughts on literature usually differed from the norm. The band, still named Smudge, made a demo tape called *Spill* in 1994 and, as Stain, another called *Die Cast* in 1995.

In 1995, after band members graduated from high school, Kilgore signed to Revolution Records subsidiary Unsound Records and released *Blue Collar Solitude* as Kilgore Smudge. *Blue Collar Solitude* combined a gritty, working class attitude with hard-driving rock and metal and the stories and poems of various literary legends. The release was also infused with emotion-filled aggression and musical artistry and sophistication.

Kilgore Smudge perfected their intense live performances by touring as often as possible and by opening for bands such as Marilyn Manson, Biohazard, and Sublime. Their fan base grew through extensive touring, and O'Brien and Pelletier eventually replaced the band's original bassist and guitarist. Before the departure of two of the band's original members, Berndt had written all of the band's songs. After O'Brien and Pelletier joined the band, everyone decided it would be best if everyone had input into songwriting. This decision gave the band a new sense of purpose and direction and offered more flexibility and creative input into their songwriting. Soundgarden proved to be a major musical influence for Kilgore's members, since Soundgarden also progressed from early basic, slamming grunge to intricate, sophisticated songwriting.

A Search for Reason was released on Revolution Records in 1998, under the name Kilgore. The band also marked the release by performing at New York City's Coney Island High club, which was the first live performance for O'Brien. Rutherford described *A Search for Reason* as, "a record with an exceptional dynamic range." Katherine Turman of *Metal Edge* magazine describes the release , "Longing for a slightly punkier,

For the Record . . .

Members include **Jay Berndt**, vocals, songwriter; **Marty O'Brien**, bass; **Mike Pelletier**, guitar; and **Bill Southerland**, drums; based in Providence, RI; Berndt and Southerland formed band while in high school at LaSalle Academy in Providence.

Named after the character Kilgore Trout from Kurt Vonnegut's *Breakfast of Champions*; started with the name Smudge in 1991; released demo tape *Spill*, 1994; changed name to Stain, 1994; signed to Revolution Records subsidiary Unsound Records, 1995; released demo tape, *Die Cast*, 1995; changed name to Kilgore Smudge in 1995, released *Blue Collar Solitude*, 1995; final name change, Kilgore in 1998; opened for Marilyn Manson, Biohazard, and Sublime; released *A Search for Reason*, Revolution Records, 1998; toured Europe, 1998; named Band of the Month in December 1998 at the web site http://www.bandindex.com.

Addresses: *Management company*—Kilgore Management, 7144 Senalda Road, Los Angles, CA 90068.; *email:* http://www.kilgore.com or http://www.revolution-online.com.

no less heavy Pantern? A dash of Danzig in the vocals? A provocative lyrical outlook? Then search no further than Kilgore's ... brutally aggressive yet dynamic outing, *A Search for Reason*." The release was produced by Ed Stasium, who had also worked with Biohazard, the Ramones, and Living Colour. Turman added, "[Biohazard, the Ramones, and Living Colour are] three bands whose influence can be gleaned in the multi-faceted but cohesive Kilgore sound.... Undeniably hard and heavy, Kilgore are strong songwriters; their musical inflections, melodies and time changes making for an aural experience that's equal parts energetic riffing 'n' headbanging and provocative melody."

Kilgore also toured Europe for the first time in 1998. Tall, tattooed vocalist Jay Berndt cut a memorable figure during live performances both in the U.S. and overseas by stalking around the stage, growling out lyrics with an ominous air, and glowering at the audience. The much-touted literate side of the band's performances usually makes itself felt with inspirational, albeit headbanging songs such as "In Media Res" (Latin for "in the middle of") and "Never Again" (a reference to Berndt's college experience).

Kilgore was named Band of the Month in December 1998, at the web site http://www.bandindex.com, beating out other heavy metal and hard rock bands such as Megadeath, Incubus, Sevendust, and Fear Factory. Kilgore's future grew more successful and secure with each subsequent release and tour. Turman summed the band up most succinctly when writing, "Look for Kilgore to make deserved inroads in the consciousness of hungry mortal mongers the world over." The winning combination of a hard-edged metal sound and intelligent lyrics with some meat on them may prove to elevate Kilgore far above the heavy metal/hard rock fray. The band's purposeful approach to songwriting and performing renders their 1998 title *A Search for Reason* an especially apt one for Kilgore's members, and could be the key to their success.

Selected discography

Spill (under band name Smudge), demo tape, 1994.
Die Cast (band name Stain), demo tape, 1995.
Blue Collar Solitude (Kilgore Smudge), Unsound Records, 1995.
A Search for Reaso, Revolution Records, 1998.

Sources

Metal Maniacs,, November 1998.
Metal Edge, October 1998; September 1998, July 1998.
Ozzfest,, 1998.

Online

http://www.flash.net.
http://www.geocities.com/sunsetstrip/underground/2572/links.html.
http://www.kilgore.com.
http://www.imusic.com/showcase/indie/kilgore.html.
http://www.revolution-online.com/kilgore/.
http://www.skateboard-marketing.com.
http://www.themusiczone.com.
http://www.ubl.com/ubl/cards/009/5/00.html.

—*B. Kimberly Taylor*

B.B. King

Guitar, singer

In the late 1940s Riley B. King worked his way from the cotton fields of Mississippi to Memphis, Tennessee, where he was dubbed B.B. (short for Blues Boy) and earned a reputation as a first class blues man. For more than 50 years the name B.B. King would remain synonymous with blues music everywhere. King started his career on Memphis's Beale Street and became a blues legend. He became known as the King of the Blues, a rank of music royalty he would share with another Memphis legend, Elvis Presley, the King of Rock and Roll. There are, in fact, ten-foot high bronze statues of both Kings—B.B. and Elvis—on Beale Street. King, with the help of his guitar "Lucille," developed a singular musical style. Without the fullness of chords, King combined just the right combination of guitar picking, string stretching, and powerful singing to emote his blues message. King's art stems from the powerful sentiment of his life and times, which he renders through his music.

King was born on September 16, 1925, in the Mississippi Delta area—a place which he called in his autobiography as "the most Southern place on earth." By some reports King was born in Indianola, Mississippi, and by others he was born in Itta Bena. The truth, according to King, is that he was born between Indianola and Greenwood, near Itta Bena, "[O]n the bank of Blue Lake." King, was named Riley by his father, Albert Lee King, in memory of a deceased brother. Although B.B. King had a younger brother, the sibling died in infancy, and King was raised as an only child. King's mother, Nora Ella, left his father when King was very young, and the two moved in with her family. While there, King was raised by three generations of kin: his great grandfather and great grandmother who were former slaves, his grandmother, and his mother. The family lived as sharecroppers on a cotton plantation. King learned as a youngster that music was a trademark of his ancestors and not simply a way to pass the hours of backbreaking cotton picking. On a southern plantation, music was an exclusive means of communication between the African American community, a language not totally understood by the white society.

King worked on the plantation from early boyhood. At age six he milked cows every morning and every night, and he attended the nearby one-room Elkhorn Schoolhouse in between chores. King's mother died when he was ten years old, and his grandmother died shortly thereafter, leaving King to fend for himself. He elected to live in solitude in the cabin he once shared with his mother, working for a tenant farmer. After five years on his own, King moved back to Indianola to live with his father and stepmother Aida Lee. While at his father's home King attended Ambrose Vocational High School, but he soon returned to the Mississippi Delta, to a cotton plantation where he lived with his aunt, uncle, and his cousin, fellow blues singer Bukka White. It was here that King's uncle introduced him to the guitar.

At age 14 King fell in love with a neighbor girl named Angel. The relationship ended tragically when Angel along with her entire family were killed in a terrible accident. Emotionally isolated once again, King, who bought his first guitar at age 12 only to have it stolen, bought another guitar and joined the Famous St. John Gospel Singers. He played music constantly as a means of expression, perhaps because of a speech impediment. Surprisingly, King found he could sing easily without stuttering.

The Indianola city life eventually beckoned King, and he laid claim to a street corner where he played his guitar and sang songs for the passers-by. Initially he sang gospel music, but he came to the realization that the simple modification of lyrics from "Lord" to "baby" transformed gospel songs into blues fare. He learned quickly that people on the street paid to hear blues songs, not gospel music.

In 1943—during World War II—the 18 year old King enlisted in the army. He was released after basic training because he drove a tractor, an essential civilian skill during wartime. When King grew increasingly frustrated with the tiresome life in Mississippi, he hitched a ride on a grocery truck to Memphis in 1947. Just 20 years old, he was awed and inspired by the big city. He left Memphis after a few months, but vowed to return one day as a blues singer after settling his accounts in Indianola.

Return to Memphis

King returned to Memphis, and good fortune, in 1948. Almost immediately upon his arrival he found work singing on commercials at the African American radio station WDIA, where he would later become a disc jockey. His nights were spent performing at local clubs with his band, which included Solomon Hardy, Earl Forrest, Ford Nelson, and Johnny "Ace" Alexander. King's free time was spent on Beale Street. Industrious and healthy, he often picked cotton between radio shows and gigs. He made a recording for Bullet Records, and in time he was known as the Beale Street Blues Boy, soon shortened to Blues Boy, then simply B.B.

King eventually purchased a Gibson electric guitar and an amplifier. He dubbed the guitar Lucille after a fateful performance at a dance in a Twist, Arkansas, barn in December of 1949. A fight broke out between two men over a woman named Lucille, during which a kerosene stove was knocked over, setting the barn aflame. King escaped the fire, but leaving his guitar behind, he risked his life entering the burning structure to salvage the instrument. Ever afterward he would call his guitars Lucille. While the original Lucille was stolen soon after the fire, King has played at least 17 Lucilles during the decades of his career. The guitar has become so synonymous with King that Gibson manufactured a Lucille model in his honor.

By now an up and coming blues man, King spent the early 1950s on the road. He played wherever blues fans gathered—clubs, roadhouses, and barns—sometimes sleeping in his car, in the hopes of building a reputation. In 1951, Sun Records founder Sam Phillips produced King's first single, "3 O'Clock Blues," which held the number one position on the *Billboard* R&B chart for several weeks. By 1952, his reputation had grown to the point where he was now performing at an elite circuit of clubs, including the Apollo Theater in Harlem. A few years later King teamed up with the successful producer and musical arranger Maxwell Davis, assembled a band, and purchased a bus called "Big Red." As the 1950s came to a close, however, blues music slowly lost its appeal with large audiences. The popular music of the times evolved from the simple southern music style proliferated by King, into a lively rock and roll beat with catchy lyrics. King's popularity waned, his style of music now characterized as "urban blues."

The Thrill Arrived

In 1961, King inked a recording contract with ABC Records. He released three albums for ABC, *Mr. Blues* in 1963, *B.B. King Live at the Regal* in 1965, and *Confessin the Blues* in 1966, before company executives moved him to their Bluesway label. In 1969, King seemed to truly come into his own with the breakthrough album *Completely Well*. That album featured the single "The Thrill Is Gone", which would prove to be one of his biggest hits and launched King into the collective American musical conscience. Later that year, King released the successful *Live and Well*, which *Downbeat*'s James Powell called, "the most important blues recording in a long time."

King's career continued unabated during the 1970s as he managed to gain favor among young people and other musicians. *Guitar Player* magazine called him the world's best blues guitarist in 1970. He became a perennial entertainer on college campuses and emerged as an icon for many young musicians of that era, even touring for ten days with the Rolling Stones. King's influence on the blues and rock guitarists who followed him is inestimable. From the Rolling Stones' Keith Richards to blues man Albert King, who only half-jokingly claimed to be King's half-brother, his staccato picking style, bent notes, and numerous riffs have been borrowed copiously.

As for his own influences, King lists jazz legends Charlie Christian and Django Reinhardt, as well as blues men T-Bone Walker and Lonnie Johnson. His musical tastes, in fact, were even more varied. "I was crazy about the Hawaiian guitar, and I'm equally crazy about the country lap steel guitar," King told *Musician* in 1998. "And all those other guys who could use the bottleneck [slide], I loved that sound." Despite the wide diversity of musical influences, or perhaps because of it, King forged a sound and style that was unique.

Private Interests

King married for the first time at age 17, to Martha Lee of Europe, Mississippi. The marriage dissolved eight years later, from the strain of constant separation caused by King's musical career. He married Sue Hall in Detroit in 1958 at a wedding presided over by Reverend C. L. Franklin (father of singer Aretha Franklin). In 1966, that marriage also ended in divorce, for similar reasons. King sired no children from either marriage, yet in 1949, he fathered a son out of wedlock—the first of 15 children that he would father by 15 different women.

King's popularity and legendary status continued to grow with each passing year. His *70th Birthday Bash* on October 27, 1995, at the Orpheum Theater was orchestrated as a benefit for children with sickle cell anemia. The four-hour celebration featured an array of popular entertainers and attracted a sellout audience. Such an extravagant affair might have seemed strange for the humble blues king, or maybe not. As he told *Time* in 1969, "Blues is what I do best. If Frank Sinatra can be tops in his field, Nat Cole in his, Bach and Beethoven in theirs, why can't I be great, and known for it, in blues?"

Selected discography

B.B. King Live at the Regal, ABC, 1965.
Confessin' the Blues, ABC, 1966.
Blues on Top of Blues, Bluesway, 1968.
Completely Well, Bluesway, 1969.
B.B. King Live at the Apollo, GRP, 1991.
There Is Always One More Time, MCA, 1991.
B.B. King—King of the Blues, MCA, 1992.
(With others) *Blues Summit*, MCA, 1993.
The Best of B.B. King, Vol. 1, Virgin.
King of the Blues, MCA.

Sources

Books

King, B. B., with David Ritz, *Blues All Around Me: The Autobiography of B. B. King*, Avon Books, New York, 1996.
Santelli, Robert, *The Big Book of Blues: a Biographical Encyclopedia*, Penguin Books, New York, 1993.

Periodicals

Business Wire, November 17, 1997.
Downbeat, Aug 7, 1969.
Star Tribune, 20 August 1996.
Time, Jan 10, 1969.
Tri-State Defender, 25 October, 1995; 8 November 1995.

Online

MCA Records—"B.B. KING", htt://www.mca.com/mca_records/library/copy/bbking.copy.html.
http://www.island.net/~blues/bb.html

—Gloria Cooksey

G. Love

Singer

Combining blues and hip-hop into what he termed "ragmop," G. Love rose from the streets of Philadelphia into the American music scene in 1994. At the beginning of his career, he fused his vocal and guitar talents with his band Special Sauce—acoustic bass player Jimmy "Jazz" Prescott and drummer Jeffrey Clemens. As G. Love and Special Sauce, they released such popular singles as "Cold Beverage" and "Baby's Got Sauce." Love went on to work with other bands, as well as playing and recording with Special Sauce. His good looks, smooth vocal delivery, and unfailing dedication to touring provided a steady climb to notoriety. Kevin Klein described Love's persona in Weekly Alibi as "the Elvis Presley of hip hop: part [blues singer] John Lee Hooker and part [actor] Christian Slater."

Born Garrett Dutton in Philadelphia, Pennsylvania, his father, L. Garrett Dutton, Jr., was a banking lawyer, while his mother, Mike Dutton, worked as a professional cook. The Duttons exposed their son to music early, and took him to see the Blues Brothers when he was just eight years old. That same year, he began learning to play the guitar. Garrett Dutton went to school at Germantown Friends, a private school in Philadelphia—uncommon roots for a blues/hip-hop singer. His parents supported his interest in music and prepared him for its challenges throughout his life. "He's a very strong individual," his father told Tom Moon in the Philadelphia Inquirer. "I've seen him deal with the Sony [Music] people, the business people, and he's not intimidated by any of it. He was always a strong, independent, self-willed kid. We encouraged that."

When he was a teenager, Dutton met Waco Smith, who played the blues on the streets of Philadelphia. Smith introduced Dutton to the music of blues artists like Blind Lemon Jefferson, Slim Harpo, John Hammond, and Muddy Waters. In the meantime, his friends at school were listening to groups rap like Run-DMC. Inspired by the music, Garrett Dutton taught himself how to play the blues on guitar and exhibited his growing aptitude in his school's talent shows. At the age of 16, Dutton split his time between his two main interests, basketball and music. He practiced and performed his music on the streets. When people began to throw money into his guitar case, he was inspired to focus on music even more, but he wasn't quite ready to name it as his future. After he graduated from high school, Dutton went to Skidmore College in upstate New York with a plan to study either English or anthropology. After one semester, he came to the conclusion that he did indeed want to pursue a career in music.

Cooked Up Special Sauce

Dutton moved to Boston, Massachusetts, and became known as G. Love in 1992. He played for passersby on the street and at open-mike nights in clubs. In January of 1993, Love met drummer Jeffrey Clemens when he was performing at a bar called The Tam. The two began working together and set out to find a bass player to join them. After several auditions, they settled on Jimmy Prescott. The trio became Love and Special Sauce, and began performing and recording together. "When I left Philadelphia ... to go to Boston and figure out the ways of the world and try to make the best music I knew how.... That's all I wanted to do," Love told Jason Birke in the Daily Pennsylvanian. "Just keep on learning and growing through the music."

In 1994, Love had the opportunity to get his next lesson in the music business. He signed a long-term recording contract with Epic/OKeh Records. Michael Caplan, the record company executive who signed him, told him that the best way to expand his audience was to perform constantly. His advice not only improved Love's exposure, but his music as well. "I wasn't really all together when we started," Love told Moon. "I just loved it so much. It took playing every night, and trying things out in a bunch of situations for me to get decent."

Not long after the ink was dry on the record contract, G. Love and Special Sauce released their self-titled debut.

For the Record . . .

Born Garrett Dutton on October 3, 1972, in Philadelphia, PA; son of L. Garrett Dutton, Jr. and Mike (mother). *Education:* attended Skidmore College in New York.

Formed G. Love and Special Sauce in 1993; members include: Jeffrey Clemens, drums, and Jimmy "Jazz" Prescott, bass. Signed recording contract with Epic/OKeh Records and released self-titled debut, 1994; released *Coast to Coast,* Epic/Okeh, 1995; *Yeah, It's That Easy,* Epic/Okeh, 1997, recorded and performed; with various other bands, including the Philly Cartel, the New Orleans' Kings Court, and the All Fellas Band, 1996-97.

Addresses: *Record company*—Epic Records, P.O. Box 4450, New York, NY 10101-4450.

Rather than spend the money and time immersed in the studio, they recorded the entire album live at Studio 4 in Philadelphia. As Moon wrote in *Rolling Stone,* "Reinventing the blues, G. Love arrives with a message that's far more eloquent—and bone-chillingly funky—than anything the gangstas have said in ages." Soon, the trio had two noteworthy singles, "Baby's Got Sauce" and "Cold Beverage." The latter song gained the group some popularity through a video on MTV. Overall, the album achieved most of its sales through G. Love and Special Sauce's incessant touring. In 1995, they landed a spot on the first H.O.R.D.E. tour with artists such as Dave Matthews, Rusted Root, Joan Osbourne, and Blues Traveler.

Later that same year, G. Love and Special Sauce released their next album, *Coast to Coast Motel.* This time, the band traveled to New Orleans to record the album. The city's blues and jazz influence was apparent throughout the record. "Being around good music like that makes you wanna play it," Love told Birke. "If we hadn't been in New Orleans, we probably would not have recorded half the songs on that album."

With two records in the stores, Love received some criticism for his blues style without the experience of its heritage and culture. Love responded to the criticism in a interview with Elysa Gardner in *Rolling Stone,* "Blues is just a feel of what's going on, whether you're an old black man in Mississippi or a white kid in Philly. I can only write about what I see and feel."

Experimented With Different Recipes

The next two years brought Love both challenges and musical growth. He began playing with other bands, including the Philly Cartel, the New Orleans' Kings Court, and the All Fellas Band. The members of Special Sauce, Jimmy Prescott and Jeffrey Clemens, had issues with Love's new associations along with the division of the band's finances. The strife resulted in a split between G. Love and Special Sauce. Love looked at the struggle like all the challenges in his life and career– "just surf it." He explained his philosophy to Moon in the *Philadelphia Inquirer,* "When the waves get rough, I try to think like a surfer. You just ride through the stuff. You fall off; you get back on your board quickly. There are bumps. The key is how you ride them." Love's theory worked out well for him in his relationship with Special Sauce. His next album, *Yeah, It's That Easy,* included tunes with the other bands he worked with, as well as some with Special Sauce. The album also featured a guest appearance by blues pianist Dr. John. "He made the record he wanted to make," Clemens said to Moon. "We were there for him, and that's all we can do. We're hoping to have more input when we go into the studio next time."

Love's outlook on the situation with Special Sauce remained positive. "It wasn't so much turmoil over the past year," Love told Klein. "It's more that I was experimenting with different kinds of bands. I think that it's real important to play with different people so you can keep your music and ideas fresh. This [Special Sauce] is the first band I ever played with."

The results of the experiment worked out well for Love. The album's first single, "Stepping Stones" reached the Top 50 on *Billboard*'s Modern Rock chart. The second single, "I-76," soon followed. The song expressed Love's perceptions of Philadelphia's Interstate highway 76, its side streets, and its basketball team. In an unusual career move, Love filmed the entire video for the song during half-time at a Philadelphia 76ers basketball game. *Yeah, It's That Easy* also contained another significant song to the city of Philadelphia – "Slipped Away (The Ballad of Luretha Vard)." This track was a tribute to the first female Philadelphia police officer killed in the line of duty. She was shot during an armed bank robbery in 1996 by rappers named Steady B and Cool C. "It was so sad," G. Love recalled in an interview to Birke. "We just wanted to put something down so that she would always be remembered."

By the end of 1997, Love had set a strong foundation for his career. He had released three albums and formed a record label with his manager, Jonathan Block, Philadelphonic Records, to give exposure to local talent. In October of that year, G. Love and Special Sauce had sold over 250,000 records in the U.S., and continued to sell an average of 1,000 more copies every week. And they accomplished all that with very little support from radio airplay or video exposure. Love assessed his career in his record company bio. "Technically, anybody can play the blues," he said. "You just learn the three chords. But if you get way inside our music, it rings true like no other music.... I can't say I've lived the blues, and I'm not trying to be a homeboy by rapping—but I do love the music."

Selected discography

G. Love & Special Sauce, Epic/OKeh Records, 1994.
Coast To Coast Motel, Epic/OKeh Records, 1995.
Yeah, It's That Easy, Epic/OKeh Records, 1997.

Sources

Periodicals

Billboard, January 21, 1995; September 27, 1997.
Entertainment Weekly, September 22, 1995; November 7, 1997.
Guitar Player, August 1994.
Rolling Stone, June 16, 1994; October 19, 1995; November 27, 1997.

Online

http://www.mtv.com, (September 18, 1998).
http://www.epiccenter.com, (September 18, 1998).
weeklywire.com (September 18, 1998).
http://users.ids.net/~kiselka/g-love, (September 18, 1998).
http://www.dailypennsylvanian.com, (September 18, 1998).

Additional information for this profile was obtained from Epic Records press materials, 1997.

—*Sonya Shelton*

Yo Yo Ma

Cello

Ten-time Grammy Award winning cellist Yo Yo Ma possessed astounding technical brilliance and an awe-inspiring artistic sensibility. He virtually defined the standard for future cellists, and during his prolific career recorded more than 45 albums, between 1983 and 1998. Ma never hesitated to explore fresh musical terrain and the music of other cultures, and often explored the musical forms outside of the Western classical tradition. Ma immersed himself in projects as diverse as native Chinese music and it's distinctive instruments, the music of the Kalahari bush people in Africa, and tango music. Ma became one of the most sought-after cellists of his time, appearing with eminent conductors and orchestras throughout the world. He also gained a deserved reputation as an ambassador for classical music and its vital role in society.

Ma was born in Paris in 1955 to Chinese parents, and he began his cello studies with his father at the age of four. Ma gave his first public recital at the age of five. He eventually studied with Janos Scholz and then, at the age of seven, Ma became a pupil of Leonard Rose at the Juilliard School of Music in 1962. By the time Ma was nineteen, he was compared with masters such as Rostropovich and Casals. He graduated from Harvard University in 1977, and in 1978, at the age of 23, Ma received the prestigious Avery Fisher Prize. Ma gained international recognition as soloist and chamber musician. He performed as a soloist with symphony orches-

tras around the world, including those of Boston, San Francisco, Philadelphia, Toronto, and Minnesota, as well as the New York, Israel, and Los Angeles Philharmonics.

Ma earned his first Grammy award in 1984 for Best Classical Performance—Instrumental for *Bach: The Unaccompanied Cello Suites*. A year later he garnered two more Grammy Awards, one for *Elgar: Cello Concerto, Op. 85*, and one for Best Chamber Music Performance for *Brahms: Cello and Piano Sonatas in E Minor,* with Emanuel Ax. Ma's long-standing partnership with pianist Ax resulted in the lion's share of his recordings as well as numerous recitals. Their partnership became one of the music world's most successful and prolific collaborations. They recorded the complete cello sonatas of Beethoven and Brahms in addition to works by Britten, Chopin, Prokofiev, Rachmaninov, Strauss, and others. In 1986 Ma won two more Grammys, along with Ax and producer James Mallinson, in the Best Classical Album and Best Chamber Music Performance categories for *Beethoven: Cello and Piano Son. No. 4*. Two years later in 1988 Ma won a Best Classical Instrumental Performance Grammy for *Brahms: Double Concerto in A Minor*, a year later he won another in the same category for *Barber: Cello Concerto, Op. 22*. and a Grammy for Best Chamber Music Performance for *Shostakovich: Trio No. 2 for Violin, Cello & Piano* with Ax and violinist Isaac Stern.

In 1991 the Massachusetts Institute of Technology (MIT) hyperinstrument team designed a special hypercello for Ma, and Tod Machover composed a special piece titled "Begin Again Again" for Ma to be performed on this new instrument. The hypercello permitted Ma to control an extensive array of sounds through performance nuance. Ma also received an honorary doctorate from Harvard in 1991. A Grammy Award for Best Classical Instrumental Performance was awarded to Ma for his work on *Tchaikovsky: Variations on a Rococo Theme* in 1991, in addition to a Grammy for Best Chamber Music Performance for *Brahms: Piano Quartets* the same year. Ma continued to win Grammy awards in 1992, 1993, 1994, 1995, and 1997. During the 1995-1996 season, Ma and Ax celebrated the 20th anniversary of their partnership with a recital tour culminating at Carnegie Hall, as well as aspecial concert at Lincoln Center's Alice Tully Hall for an episode of PBS's *Live from Lincoln Center*.

Ma balanced his solo performances with orchestras around the world with his recital and chamber music activities. He drew inspirations from a diverse and far-reaching circle of collaborators, working with musicians such as Daniel Barenboim, Pamela Frank, Emanuel Ax,

Born in 1955, in Paris, to Chinese parents; began his cello studies with his father at age four; gave his first public recital at age five; studied with Janos Scholz and at age seven; became a pupil of Leonard Rose at the Juilliard School of Music in 1962; graduated from Harvard University in 1977; gained international recognition as soloist, and chamber musician; performed as a soloist with symphony orchestras around the world, including Boston, San Francisco, Philadelphia, Toronto, and Minnesota; won first Grammy award, 1984; won nine more Grammy awards between 1984 and 1997; released more than 45 albums between 1984 and 1998.

Awards: Received Avery Fisher Prize in 1978; Grammy Awards: Best Classical Performance—Instrumental, 1984-85,1989,1992; Best Chamber Music Performance, 1986, 1988, 1991-94, 1997 ; Best Classical Album, 1988, 1997; Best Classical Performance, 1991; Best Instrumental Soloists, 1995.

Addresses: Record company—Sony Classics, 550 Madison Avenue, 16th floor, New York, NY 10022, (212) 833-8000.

Stephane Grappelli, Jeffrey Kahane, Young Uck Kim, Jaime Laredo, Bobby McFerrin, Edgar Meyer, Mark O'Connor, Peter Serkin, Isaac Stern, Richard Stoltzman, and Kathryn Stott. Each collaboration was generated by interaction between the musicians and often resulted in pieces that extended far beyond the boundaries of classical music or of any particular music classification. Ma joined Ax, Stern, and Laredo for performances and recordings of the piano quartet repertoire of Beethoven, Brahms, Dvorak, Faurve, Mozart, and Schumman.

Ma released Hush with vocalist Bobby McFerrin in 1992, followed by the soundtrack to the Gary Oldman film, Immortal Beloved, both of which were certified gold by the Recording Industry Association of America. In 1995 Ma presented the first in a series of films of Bach's Six Cello Suites, exploring the relationship between Bach's music and other artistic disciplines. The premier film, presented at the Edinburgh Festival in Scotland, featured the original choreography of Mark Morris set to the Third Cello Suite. Subsequent multimedia presentations/films by Ma, released throughout the late 1990s, incorporate the work of Kabuki artist Tamasaburo Bando, Italian architect Piranesi, Boston-based garden designer Julie Moir Messervy, Olympic ice-dancing champions Jane Torvill and Christopher Dean, and Canadian film director Atom Egoyan. In 1996 Ma released Peter Lieberson's chamber work King Gesar, a compilation of concertos by Kirchner, Rouse, and Danielpour with David Zinman and the Philadelphia Orchestra. In 1996 Ma also released Appalachia Waltz, an album of original music recorded in Nashville, Tennessee with fiddle player Mark O'Connor and bassist Edgar Meyer. In 1997 Ma recorded new material by Andre Previn, set to words by author Toni Morrison, featuring soprano Sylvia McNair and Previn as pianist.

American contemporary composers have been featured prominently in Ma's repertoire. Ma premiered works by William Bolcom, John Corigliano, John Harbison, Ezra Laderman, Peter Lieberson, Christopher Rouse, Bright Sheng, and John Williams, among others. Ma devoted time to working with young musicians in programs at Interlochen, Michigan, and other music camps. He often included educational outreach programs in his touring schedule, through master classes and informal interaction with student audiences.

In 1997 Ma recorded the soundtrack of Liberty!, a PBS documentary series about the American Revolution. Ma performed the music of the late Argentinean composer Astor Piazzolla on the release Soul of the Tango in 1997, and performed for the music video for director Sally Potter's feature film, The Tango Lesson, in which Ma plays Piazzolla's "Libertango". On Soul of the Tango, Ma played with Argentinean tangueros, which included a rock "duet" with Piazzolla—achieved by recording over one of the master bandoneonist's—a sort of accordion—final recordings. Ma steeped himself in Piazzolla's music and background by studying a tape of Rostropovich rehearsing "Le Grand Tango" for Piazzolla, and by traveling to Buenos Aires to tour tango clubs. Ma told Billboard's Bradley Bambarger. "The whole experience of researching and recording [Soul of the Tango] was a thrill. Like a lot of people, I'm so irresistibly drawn to Piazzolla's music. It's very sophisticated, yet it's also very primal. And you can say that about Beethoven, Stravinsky—all the good stuff feeds the mind, the body, and the soul."

Selected discography

Bach: The Unaccompanied Cello Suites, Sony, 1984.
Elgar: Cello Concerto, Op. 85, Sony, 1985.

Brahms: Cello & Piano Sonatas in E Minor and F Major, Sony, 1985.

Beethoven: Complete Sonatas for Piano and Cello, Sony, 1987.

Boccherini: Cello Concerto, Sony, 1987.

Bolling: Suite for Cello and Jazz Trio, Sony, 1987.

Japanese Melodies, Sony, 1987.

Schumann: Cello Concerto, Sony, 1988.

Dvorak: Great Cello Concertos, Sony, 1989.

Portrait of Yo Yo Ma, Sony, 1989.

Shostakovich: Trio No. 2 for Violin, Cello & Piano, Sony, 1989.

Saint-Saens: Concertos, Sony, 1991.

Tchaikovsky: Variations on a Rococo Theme, Sony, 1991.

Faure: Piano Quartets Nos. 1 & 2, Sony, 1993.

Chopin: Polonaise Brillante, Sony, 1994.

Appalachia Waltz, Sony, 1996.

Goldenthal: Fire Water Paper—A Vietnam Oratorio, Sony, 1996.

Lieberson: King Gesar, Sony, 1996.

From Ordinary Things (with Andre Previn), Sony, 1997.

Liberty, Sony, 1997.

Seven Years in Tibet, Soundtrack, Sony, 1997.

Soul of the Tango: The Music of Astor Piazzolla, Sony, 1997.

Music for Strings & Piano Left, Sony, 1998.

Tavener: The Protecting Veil, Wake Up...and Die, Sony, 1998.

Sources

Periodicals

Billboard, December 6, 1997.

Online

Boston Symphony Orchestra website: http://www.bso.org, (November 4, 1998).

MIT website: http://www.brainop.media.mit.edu, (November 3, 1998).

Music Boulevard website: htt://www.musicblvd.com, (October 30, 1998).

Sony Music website: http://www.sonyclassical.com, (November 5, 1998).

Videoflicks website: http://www.videoflicks.com, (October 28, 1998).

—*B. Kimberly Taylor*

Yngwie Malmsteen

Guitar

Yngwie Malmsteen took the hard rock scene by storm in the 1980s with his lightning-fast, explosive guitar style. He garnered significant attention through his work with such bands as Steeler, Alcatrazz, and his own Rising Force. However, his popularity grew more significantly as a solo artist, performing instrumental pieces and songs with guest vocalists. Despite several personal setbacks, Malmsteen continued recording and performing his own style of neoclassical rock well into the late 1990s.

Malmsteen was born Lars Johann Yngwie Lannerback in Stockholm, Sweden, in 1963. His mother, an artist named Rigmor, and his father, an army captain, divorced not long after Yngwie was born. He was the youngest of three children, including his sister Ann Louise and his brother Bjorn. Yngwie discovered his love for music at a very young age. He took piano and trumpet lessons as a child, and his mother had bought him an acoustic guitar when he was just five years old, but he didn't touch it until he was seven.

On September 18, 1970, seven-year-old Yngwie Lannerback watched a television special on the death of guitar legend Jimi Hendrix. It was on that day that he picked up his guitar. "As a kid, you think it's cool to be a soldier, a policeman, or something, and I thought Jimi Hendrix was my hero type of guy," Malmsteen told Jas Obrecht in *Guitar Player*. "I took the guitar down off the wall and started playing. I remember playing until my fingers got all sore, and I put Band-Aids on them and kept going."

When he turned ten, Yngwie decided to change his last name to his mother's maiden name, Malmsteen. Around the same time, he skipped school often and focused all of his energy into music and improving his guitar playing. His mother recognized his talent early on and allowed him to stay home from school with his records and his guitar.

As his passion for guitar playing grew, so did his interest in both rock and classical music. He explored the sounds of bands like Deep Purple and composers like Bach, Vivaldi, Mozart, and Beethoven. "Bach is my god," Malmsteen explained to Obrecht. "Classical was the peak of the musical history of man. Music hasn't developed since classical music; it stopped being creative." Malmsteen discovered one of his major influences, Nicolo Paganini, through Russian violinist Gideon Kremer's performance of *24 Caprices*. Malmsteen used these influences to combine his love for classical music with rock guitar.

Malmsteen began playing in bands even before he became a teenager. His brother Bjorn played drums in a few of the early bands, such as Burn and Power. By 1976, he settled into a spot with a band called Powerhouse, which lasted two years. Powerhouse focused their music and show around their guitar virtuoso, performing long instrumental breaks. However, their Swedish audiences, used to more pop-flavored bands like ABBA, didn't respond favorably. Malmsteen continued his journey in hard rock with a vengeance. By the age of 15, he had lost all interest in school and quit for good.

Three years later, the Swedish army attempted to recruit Yngwie Malmsteen as an officer, based on his high intelligence test scores. He fought the enlistment by pretending to be crazy. He held a gun to his head and swore that he would kill himself before joining the military. The recruiters believed him and sent him on his way. That same year, the 18-year-old Malmsteen and several of his friends recorded a three-song demo tape for Swedish CBS Records. The tape included the songs "You're Going to Break Them All" and "Horizons." The record company asked Malmsteen to record the songs over again with Swedish lyrics instead of English. The guitarist refused and continued his quest for representation and distribution.

In 1982, Yngwie Malmsteen sent a demo tape to a music xecutive, Mike Varney, who had a column in *Guitar Player* magazine and owned his own record label called Shrapnel Music. Varney was impressed by the tape, and not only wrote a favorable review in his column, but invited Malmsteen to Los Angeles, California, to begin recording a solo album. Varney had planned to unite Malmsteen with bassist Billy Sheehan and drummer Leonard Haze. Yngwie Malmsteen began making the arrangements to move to the United States when he received an offer to join a band called Steeler, also on the Shrapnel Music label.

He accepted the offer and moved to Los Angeles in February of 1983. Steeler was formed around singer Ron Keel, so Malmsteen couldn't contribute much to the band beyond his guitar solos. But those alone brought him quite a bit of attention in the rock scene. "When I was in Steeler, I turned L.A. totally upside down," Malmsteen told Bill Ebner in *Foundations.* "Nobody could believe the way I played. They had never heard anything like it."

Malmsteen didn't enjoy being in a band where he couldn't contribute to the songwriting and left the group before their self-titled debut had even reached the stores. From there, he joined forces with singer Graham Bonnett to form another band called Alcatrazz. This time, he had the opportunity to write all the music, while Bonnett wrote all the lyrics. Before the end of 1983, Alcatrazz had released *No Parole for Rock & Roll* and *Live Sentence* on Rocshire Records. Still, Yngwie Malmsteen felt stifled. He left Alcatrazz and decided that it would be best for his career to embark on a solo career.

Broke the Speed Barrier

The following year, he released his first solo effort as Yngwie Malmsteen's Rising Force. The album *Rising Force* was mostly an instrumental recording. Despite the fact that it received almost no radio airplay, it reached number 60 on the *Billboard* album charts. The album featured the work of Malmsteen's longtime friend keyboardist Jens Johansson. Malmsteen and Rising Force performed around the world and established Malmsteen's popularity as a guitar virtuoso. Tim Holmes wrote in *Rolling Stone,* "This kid's obviously very serious about cracking the notes-per-second barrier and doesn't mean to be taken as some heavy-metal clown."

Yngwie Malmsteen's popularity increased over the next few years with the albums *Marching Out* and *Trilogy.* However, his career almost came to an end after a tragic car accident on June 22, 1987. He hit a tree with his Jaguar and broke the steering wheel with his head. He was in a coma for almost a week, then woke up unable to use his right hand. Doctors discovered that he'd suffered a concussion from the ordeal, which damaged the nerves running into his right hand.

Malmsteen refused to give up his career without a fight. He began intensive physical therapy in an effort to regenerate the nerves in his hand. However, he had to fight more than the pain in his body. During the same year, Malmsteen's mother and his main inspiration died of cancer in Sweden. He also discovered that his manager had squandered all of his money, just as he was facing rising medical bills. As he had always done, though, Malmsteen relied on his music to bring him through the tough times. By 1988, he returned with another album, *Odyssey,* and the hit single, "Heaven Tonight," featuring former Rainbow singer Joe Lynn Turner. In February of 1989, Yngwie Malmsteen and Rising Force performed unprecedented sold-out shows in both Moscow and Leningrad. The final performance was recorded and released as the video *Live in Leningrad/Trial By Fire* and the live album *Trial By Fire.* Not long after the tour, the band Rising Force decided to disband, and Malmsteen retired the name.

He moved to Miami, Florida, where he recruited a new band of fellow Swedes for the release of his next solo album *Eclipse*. In March of 1991, he left Polygram Records and signed a deal with Elektra Records. Two months later, on May 8, he married Swedish pop singer Erika Norberg; the marriage lasted less than a year.

In 1992, Malmsteen was able to fulfill one of his lifelong dreams. On the album *Fire & Ice,* he recorded with a full orchestra. The LP debuted at number one in Japan and sold gold and platinum all across Europe and Asia. However, his popularity in the U.S. had begun to wane.

Faced Challenges and Tragedies

In 1993, Malmsteen faced another year of tragedy. His manager of four years, Nigel Thomas, died of a heart attack in January. Elektra dropped Malmsteen from their label two months later. In July, he broke his right hand in an accident, and in August he was arrested for a false accusation that made international news. His fiancée's mother had called the police and said that Malmsteen was holding her daughter Amberdawn Landin hostage with a gun. Malmsteen claimed Landin's mother made up the story because she didn't want her daughter to marry him. The charges were dropped a month later. By the end of the year, Malmsteen had begun to rebound. His hand healed completely, and he signed a new recording contract with a Japanese label called Pony Canyon Records. On December 26, 1993, he and Landin got married in Stockholm, Sweden. Malmsteen returned to the studio and released *The Seventh Sign* in Japan. After the album sold triple platinum there, CMC International Records picked up the distribution rights for Europe and North America. However, Yngwie Malmsteen still didn't resurrect his popularity in the U.S. "I really resent people who say I'm stagnating," Malmsteen told *Guitar Player*'s Greg Rule. "Think about it like this: Everybody who has a recognizable sound—AC/DC, ZZ Top, whatever—continues to use it. As far as I'm concerned, I've never written better songs or had better arrangements."

Later that year, Malmsteen released two EPs on Pony Canyon, *Power and Glory* and *I Can't Wait*, and built a recording studio called Studio 308 in Miami, Florida. "It's a pretty lax vibe, which helps aid in the creativity since there is no 'clock' pressure," Malmsteen told Scott Rubin in *Musician.* "I never played in any studio as well as I do here."

Regained U.S. Opportunities

Malmsteen continued his recording pace with another release in 1995 called *Magnum Opus*. The following year, he recorded a tribute album of some of his greatest influences, including such bands as Deep Purple, Rainbow, Kansas, Scorpions, Rush and of course, Jimi Hendrix. Several guest artists such as Joe Lynn Turner, Jeff Scott Soto, David Rosenthal, Marcel Jacob, and Mark Boals joined him on the album. By 1998, he began to receive more recognition in the U.S. He signed another record contract with Mercury Records, a division of his former label Polygram, and released *Facing the Animal*. However, Malmsteen had yet to garner the notoriety and sales that he received in the 1980s.

"The U.S. doesn't support a wide variety of styles," Malmsteen told Ebner. "If anything, it's extremely trend-oriented. If you're not following what's hot, you're considered old hat. It's not like that overseas. They have a great loyalty for the artists." Whether he gained back his popularity in the U.S. or not, it didn't really matter to Malmsteen. As long as he had the opportunity to record and perform his own music, he claimed that was reward enough.

Selected discography

Albums

Rising Force, Polygram Records, 1984.
Marching Out, Polygram Records, 1985.
Trilogy, Polygram Records, 1986.
Odyssey, Polygram Records, 1988.
Trial By Fire, Polygram Records, 1989.
Eclipse, Polygram Records, 1990.
Fire & Ice, Elektra Records, 1992.
The Seventh Sign, Pony Canyon/CMC International Records, 1994.
Magnum Opus, Pony Canyon/Viceroy Records, 1995.
Inspiration, Foundation Records, 1996.
Facing the Animal, Mercury Records, 1998.

EPs

Power & Glory, Pony Canyon, 1993.
I Can't Wait, Pony Canyon, 1993.

Sources

Periodicals

Audio, August 1998.
Entertainment Weekly, March 20, 1992.
Foundations, April 11, 1994.
Guitar Player, March 1984; May 1985; December 1986; July 1988; August 1994; January 1996.

Musician, May 1998.
Rolling Stone, September 12, 1985.
The Witching Hour Magazine, Winter 1996.

Online

http://pd.net/yngwie/biography/index.html (September 23, 1998).
http://www.lewisentertainment.com/yngwie/ (September 23, 1998).

—Sonya Shelton

Loreena McKennitt

Celtic folk singer

Although she grew up in a rural Canadian community, Loreena McKennitt was credited as one of the artists responsible for resurrecting Celtic folk music. She reached into her own modern environment to create an unusual musical combination of past and present. "In her realm, Celtic tradition joins with contemporary influences to forge an ethereal symbiosis of song," Anil Prasad wrote in *Dirty Linen*. "It is not uncommon to hear threads of jazz, pop, classical, and Asian music in her pieces."

By the late 1990s, McKennitt's music had reached a wide international audience and could be heard everywhere—from the radio to film soundtracks. She reached the peak of charts across the world, while still managing her own career and her own record label. She used her various talents to take the music industry by storm, not only through her recordings and performances, but through her business savvy, as well.

McKennitt was born and raised in the small town of Morden, Manitoba in Canada. Somewhat isolated, the community included a blend of descendants from Ireland, Scotland, Germany, and Iceland. "It was a very modest community," McKennitt recalled in her record company biography. "People came from immigrant stock. Survival was the order of the day, and in some ways, broad cultural exposure was limited. Although my family's ancestors for the most part came from Ireland, there was very little overt 'Celticness' to my upbringing in the sense of music or storytelling."

Raised by her mother, Irene, who worked as a nurse, and her father, Jack, who raised and traded livestock, Loreena McKennitt and her brother Warren were exposed to music from a young age. She first began performing as a Highland dancer, even before she started school. When she broke her leg in a car accident at the age of five, she began studying music. She took lessons in classical piano for the next ten years and took voice lessons for five years.

As McKennitt developed musically, she played the piano and organ and sang for various choirs. Some of her childhood classmates couldn't share her passion for music and performing, making it difficult for her to maintain many social relationships. "I went to school with students who weren't allowed to have television in their house or wear makeup or dance," McKennitt told Salem Alaton in *Chatelaine*.

Her adolescence brought even more challenges, not all of them musical. Along with her love for music, Loreena McKennitt had also discovered a strong interest in sports and athletics. "I wasn't kind of a real social creature like a lot of other girls my age," she recalled to Peter Feniak in *Saturday Night*. "And because I felt older and different from many of my school chums, I spent time with my [physical education] teachers."

She developed a friendship with her seventh grade physical education teacher, and the two spent time together outside of school. Members of the community thought the friendship was suspect, and rumors began to circulate about a lesbian affair or sexual abuse. Although McKennitt defended her teacher and explained that their friendship was above board and strictly platonic, the teacher was dismissed over the relationship. The following year, she developed a similar friendship with her eighth grade physical education teacher. He and McKennitt had long conversations after school about music and philosophy. Soon, the same questions arose, and he was also dismissed from his job for a platonic friendship with an unusually mature student.

Discovered Celtic Roots

In 1975, McKennitt moved to Winnipeg, Manitoba, where she worked part-time in her father's Winnipeg trading office. She attended the University of Manitoba, where she began studying to become a veterinarian, while at the same time continuing to pursue her interest

For the Record . . .

Born in Manitoba, Canada, the younger of Jack and Irene McKennitt's two children; studied at the University of Manitoba, 1975-1977.

Began performing professionally as a singer, 1976; began playing the Celtic harp, 1984; formed Quinlan Road Records, 1985; released three albums, 1985-89; signed distribution deal with Warner Bros. Records, 1991; released two LPs and one EP, 1991-95; released hit album *The Book of Secrets*, 1997.

Addresses: *Record company*—Quinlan Road, P.O. Box 933, Stratford, Ontario, Canada N5A 7M3

in music. She found an informal folk society that introduced her to Celtic folk music. The sound sparked something inside her that was the beginning of a major change in her life's direction. "I heard a recording called *The Renaissance of the Celtic Harp* by Alan Stivell," McKennitt told John Diliberto in *Tower Pulse.* "And when I heard that recording, I was very much smitten by the sound that was created by the harp."

McKennitt performed her music in clubs around town at night. When she began to make some money from it, she left school to pursue a career as a singer. In 1981, she traveled to Stratford, Ontario, to sing in the chorus for a festival production of *H.M.S. Pinafore*. During her stay there, she dated an actor and singer named Cedric Smith, who performed on McKennitt's first two albums. McKennitt decided to move to Stratford permanently and performed regularly in the city's famed Shakespearean Festival.

Stepped Onto Quinlan Road

McKennitt decided she wanted to visit the land of her inspiration and made an excursion to Ireland in 1982. Feniak described what an impact the trip had on McKennitt saying, "It may have taken her two more years, and a trip to England to find her Celtic harp and teach herself to play it, but the trip to Ireland was her turning point . Born Irish at the age of 24." McKennitt found her harp in London, England. She was in a hospital, and saw it in a music shop window across the street. It was a second-hand harp, and she knew

immediately that it was the one for her. She borrowed the money from some friends, bought it, and started teaching herself to play.

In 1985, McKennitt decided to take her career's future into her own hands. She asked her family to lend her $10,000 to set up her own record company called Quinlan Road. She recorded *Elemental,* a nine-song cassette, and sold copies at performances. That same year, she also wrote the musical score for the Canadian film *Bayo*. She began to get a little discouraged a few months later and sunk into a short bout of depression.

She decided to become an activist for the Stratford Heritage Trust, and continued her music as a street performer at the St. Lawrence Market in Toronto, Ontario. After reading Diane Sward's book *How to Make and Sell Your Own Recording*, McKennitt got her motivation back and started compiling a mailing list wherever she played. Once she had a large enough list, she also approached local record stores with the evidence of her already established fan base and convinced them to carry her tape.

In 1987, McKennitt released her next recording, *To Drive the Cold Winter Away*, which included rare Celtic winter songs and some Christmas carols. Two years later, she came out with *Parallel Dreams*, with which she introduced a musical group into her work. By the end of the 1980s, she was selling more than 30,000 through her fan mailing list and local record stores. Since she produced everything herself, she made almost 70 cents profit on every dollar her records made. Her notoriety resulted in a commission from the National Film Board of Canada to score the music for the acclaimed film series *Women and Spirituality*.

McKennitt made a discovery in 1991 that would again affect her musical direction. She attended an exhibition of international Celtic artifacts in Venice, Italy. Up to this point, she thought that Celts only came from Ireland, Scotland, and Britain. As she walked through the exhibition, she found Celtic art from placeslike Hungary, Ukraine, Spain, and Asia Minor. "It was like a huge door had opened up for me creatively and as a source of inspiration," McKennitt told Kirsten A. Conover in the *Christian Science Monitor*. "So I've used that pan-Celtic history as a creative springboard."

Major Label Gave Final Boost

Before the release of her next album, McKennitt signed a worldwide distribution deal with Warner Bros. Records. She negotiated a contract that allowed her to keep her own record label, manage her own promotion, and maintain creative control. In November of 1991, she released *The Visit* in over 35 countries. With her new distribution deal, *The Visit* reached more people around the world, resulting in gold albums in the U.S., Spain, Italy, Greece, Australia, and Norway.

McKennitt continued touring across the globe and released her next album, *The Mask and Mirror*, on March 22, 1994. The album was inspired by her travels and research of Galacia, the Celtic corner of Spain. Explaining her goal for *The Mask and Mirror*, she told Feniak, "This recording, I'm going to shine this flashlight I've got on Spain. I'm going to shine it on Morocco, I'm going to shine it on the Gnostic Gospels ... on the Knights of Templar. We're going to talk about astronomy and mathematics."

The following year, McKennitt released an EP called *A Winter Garden*, and spent the next two years preparing for her next recording. In 1997, she released *The Book of Secrets*, her most popular album to date. She used her travels again as inspiration for the album, with research in Italy and on a trip on the legendary Trans-Siberian Express. "The songs on this recording have been assembled like a mosaic, with disparate pieces collected from many places and fitted together one by one," McKennitt said in her record company biography.

The single "Mummers' Dance" soon took over airwaves all over the world. In this song's lyrics, she combined the ideas behind the work of a marionette maker she met in Palermo, Sicily, with the "hobby horse" of the May Day celebrations in Padstow, Cornwall, and a Sufi order in Turkey. She took the chorus and the final verse from an original mummers' song in Abingdon, Oxfordshire.

By the release date of *The Book of Secrets*, her record company had expanded its locations with offices in both Stratford, Ontario, and London, England. The album went multi-platinum in 1998 in several countries, including the U.S., Canada, Spain, Italy, France, Turkey, New Zealand, and Greece. That same year, DNA's Nick Batt remixed the song "Mummers' Dance" in a techno style. Quinlan Road released the remix as a single in February of 1998.

McKennitt used her endless curiosity and interest in history, archaeology, environmental studies, and more,

as the fuel for her musical creativity. Her constant ambition and drive paid off into worldwide success without compromise. As Kevin Pope wrote in *Canadian Performing Arts*, "Partly thanks to her frequent peals of infectious laughter, Loreena McKennitt gives every appearance of being a woman who is doing exactly what she wants to do, and fortunately for us, she does it all very well."

Selected discography

Elemental, Quinlan Road, 1985.
To Drive the Cold Winter Away, Quinlan Road, 1987.
Parallel Dreams, Quinlan Road, 1989.
The Visit, Quinlan Road/Warner Brcs. Records, 1991.
The Mask and Mirror, Quinlan Road/Warner Bros. Records, 1994.
A Winter Garden, Quinlan Road/Warner Bros. Records, 1995.
The Book of Secrets, Quinlan Road/Warner Bros. Records, 1997.

Sources

Periodicals

Billboard, October 19, 1991; December 12, 1992; March 5, 1994; August 23, 1997.
Canadian Performing Arts, Summer 1992.
Chatelaine, March 1995.
Christian Science Monitor, October 1, 1997.
Entertainment Weekly, November 14, 1997; February 20, 1998.
Maclean's, March 28, 1994; December 26, 1994; December 1, 1997.
People Weekly, January 12, 1998.
Playboy, October 1994.
Publishers Weekly, November 21, 1994.
Saturday Night, February 1994.
Tower Pulse, November 1997.

Online

http://www.innerviews.org (September 23, 1998).
http://www.quinlanroad.com (September 23, 1998).

—*Sonya Shelton*

Dave McLean

Singer

Quintessential blues singer and guitarist Big Dave McLean contributed primarily to the blues from behind-the-scenes between 1970-98, but it was his 1998 release, *For The Blues ... Always,* that pushed him more to the forefront of the blues arena. The Canadian-based singer/guitarist released one other album before 1998, titled *Muddy Waters For President*. It was recorded in 1989 at the Bud's on Broadway club in Saskatoon. Billboard's Larry LeBlanc wrote in 1998, "At 45, the Winnipeg, Manitoba-based singer/guitarist [McLean] has done more to shape western Canada's blues scene than perhaps any other artist. He has been a significant influence on such leading Canadian blues-styled acts as singer guitarist Colin James, who produced 'For The Blues...Always,' and young Atlantic Records trio Wide Mouth Mason." James told LeBlanc, "Dave's so good at the that acoustic [blues] stuff. He's something else with a National Steel (slide guitar)." Wide Mouth Mason singer/guitarist Shaun Verrautt added, "Any aspiring blues musicians from west of Winnipeg has likely seen Big Dave perform several times. He's the real deal."

McLean was born in 1951 in Yorton, Saskatchewan. His father was a Presbyterian minister, and lived he in Moose Jaw, Manitoba, before relocating at the age of ten to Winnipeg. His brother Grant had an extensive record collection, and when McLean was a teenager, his brother introduced him to folk, jazz, and blues music.

McLean told LeBlanc, "I was a big Bob Dylan fan and really liked Woody Guthrie, Pete Seeger, and Lead Belly. We also listened to...Dave Brubeck, John Coltrane, and (Rahsaan) Roland Kirk and to Lead Belly and Sonny Terry and Brownie McGhee, who did country blues and folk songs. When I heard ... Mance Lipscomb, Robert Johnson, Sleepy John Estes, Bukka White, and Yank Rachell, that's when the door really opened. All my friends would go, 'C'mon man, let's go see Led Zeppelin.' I'd go, 'C'mon over my house and listen to Sleepy John Estes or Furry Lewis'."

McLean and his brother went to Toronto to attend the Mariposa Folk Festival in 1969, where American singer John Hammond gave McLean—then 18 years old—an informal guitar lesson. Hammond taught McLean how to play Bo Diddley's 1955 R&B hit "I'm A Man". McLean told LeBlanc, "I drove my parents nuts for the next six months playing it." McLean then worked for several years in folk and blues-styled duos; one duo was with his brother Grant and the other was with guitarist/singer Dave Marnoch, before striking out on his own. He initially performed as a solo acoustic folk and blues act, then he performed with numerous backing bands, including Black Betty, Cross Cut, and the Muddy-Tones. McLean paired up with Calgary-based guitarist Tim Williams in 1998 to record an acoustic blues album titled *Fellow Travelers* on the Cayuse Records label. McLean told LeBlanc, "I was just getting ready to fly to Vancouver for sessions with Colin [sessions for For *The Blues ... Always*] when Tim phoned, offering me this other album. Tim said, 'I guess it's a two-album day for you.' I said, 'It's been a long time since I've had a two-album day. Never, actually'."

McLean plays guitar, slide guitar, and harmonica on *Fellow Travelers,* and plays a heady mixture of Delta, Piedmont, and early Chicago blues, as well as originals that sound absolutely in sync with the material. "I don't butcher my voice trying to sound like Howlin' Wolf, and I've never learned a Muddy Waters tune the way Muddy Waters did it," McLean told LeBlanc, "I want to take their songs and put my feel into them so people say, 'That sounds like McLean' rather than watered-down Howlin' Wolf or Muddy Waters." Richard Flohill, the director of the Toronto Blues Society, wrote of McLean, "He's a player who gives equal justice to Elmore James, Mississippi John Hurt, and Little Walter. It's the sort of thing he does every week in his home town, sometimes solo, and sometimes with a solid little four-piece band."

Colin James told Flohill, "Dave McLean has been stalwartly keeping up the blues tradition for years. I first heard him when I was 9 and he blew me away then, and he still does today. He's one of the great undiscovered

For the Record . . .

Born 1951, in Yorton, Saskatchewan; son of a Presbyterian minister.

Attended Mariposa Folk Festival, 1969, where American singer John Hammond gave McLean an informal guitar lesson setting him on his course; worked for several years in folk and blues-styled duos; performed as a solo acoustic folk and blues act, then performed with numerous backing bands, including Black Betty, Cross Cut, and the Muddy-Tones; released *Muddy Waters For President,* King Alley Productions, 1989; paired up with Calgary-based guitarist Tim Williams in 1998 to record acoustic blues album *Fellow Travelers,* Cayuse Records; released *For The Blues ... Always,* Stony Plain Records, 1998.

Addresses: *Record company*—Stony Plain Recording Company, Stony Plain, Alberta Canada T72 1LA.

blues men and people ought to hear him." James produced McLean's *For The Blues ... Always* as a result of his great admiration for him. James's mother, a social worker, worked in the kitchen of the Regina Folk Club when James was a child. McLean was often the main attraction and form of entertainment at the club. At the age of nine, James would hang out in the kitchen and flat-pick on own his guitar, sometimes drawing a bigger crowd in the kitchen than in the dining area. They became friends through that experience at the Regina Folk Club and often played together over the years. McLean's release marked James's first experience as a record producer.

McLean told Flohill, "I love those old Delta guys who made their music with one voice, one guitar, and one foot stompin' on the floor. That's very special music, and I love to do it. At the same time, I love the way the band can get people moving. You do what you have to do, and I have to play the blues." McLean resided in Winnipeg throughout his entire career of playing and recording. Winnipeg was described by Flohill as, "one of the most remote cities in western Canada." McLean explained to Flohill that although he loved to play in Vancouver, Toronto, and the larger American cities, he considered Winnipeg home and enjoyed a regular playing circuit

there for 28 years. He said to Flohill, "If you play the blues, it's hard to find a place where you can afford to buy a home and raise a family, and I like being home in the day with the kids. And you can do these things [in Winnipeg], you can have a house and a yard and all normal things.... of course ... the next gig is 600 miles away in any direction."

McLean explained to LeBlanc, "Recording wasn't the reason I got into the music business. I just wanted to play the blues. I only put that (*Muddy Waters For President*) live album out so fans would have something to listen to when I wasn't around." McLean recorded the 18 songs on *For The Blues ... Always* in three days at Colin James's home studio in Vancouver, backed by James on acoustic, slide, and electric guitars, as well as by notable Vancouver musicians Norm Fisher on bass, Eric Webster on piano, Chris Norquiest on drums, and Johnny Ferriera on saxophone. The ten songs selected for the album were the McLean track, "Always," Willie Dixon's "Little Red Rooster" —popularized by Howlin' Wolf and The Rolling Stones— "Just Your Fool," Elmore James's "Dust My Broom," Jimmy Reed's "Going to New York," Taj Mahal's "Cakewalk Into Town," Muddy Water's "Rollin' And Tumblin'," and St. Louis Jimmy Oden's "Had My Fun." James told LeBlanc, "Although some of these songs are a little overdone [by the blues artists], Dave has made them his own over the years."

Selected discography

Muddy Waters For President, King's Alley Productions, 1989.
For The Blues...Always, Stony Plain, 1998.
Fellow Travelers, Cayuse Records. 1998.

Sources

Periodicals

Billboard, July 25, 1998.

Online

"Big Dave McLean," http:/www.geocities.com/Athens/Academy/2334/dave.htm, (January 19,1999).
"Dave McLean and Tim Williams," *The Salmon Arm of Folk Music Society,* http:www.jetstream.net/users/sspence/mcl_will.html, (January 19, 1999).

—B. Kimberly Taylor

Monifah

Singer

Rhythm and blues singer Monifah instantly scored a hit with the single "I Miss You (Come Back Home)"—which was featured in the *New York Undercover Soundtrack*—from her debut release, 1996's *Moods...Moments*. Her music was also featured in the soundtracks for *To Wong Foo* and *Dangerous Minds*. Monifah is noted for being an especially versatile r&b artist and is able to deftly cover hip-hop, gospel, and rap territory, as well. After the release of her debut album, *People* magazine's Jeremy Helligar wrote, "This preternaturally sophisticated 23-year old could emerge as leader of the pack. Although her debut album essentially equals the sum of her musical peers' best parts—Brandy's bubbly enthusiasm plus Monica's no-nonsense strut plus Faith's sanctified blues—it's a platinum formula nonetheless." In an *Upscale Magazine* review, Monifah's singing style was described as,"a bubbling synthesis of blues, jazz, hip hop and, of course, r&b" Charles Aaron of *Spin Magazine* wrote, "That voice, like Mary J. Blige if she'd paid attention in charm school, is enough to start a shootout between Jodeci and R. Kelly's road crews."

Born in 1972, Monifah Carter was raised in the Spanish Harlem section of New York City along with two older brothers. Her mother, Eleanor Carter, was a grants administrator for the Episcopal Church Center in New York, and in an interview with *Sister 2 Sister* magazine,

Monifah said, "I didn't grow up in a middle class home or family. The only difference was, mentally and culturally, my mom wanted more for me.... We did a lot of cultural things together. So, I knew there was a whole world out there besides the four corners of my block. I saw a lot more than the kids that I grew up around, but I was also right there, so I had the best of both worlds." Monifah's father worked at Harlem Hospital as an administrator who handled all of the paperwork for transfer patients in the ambulatory area. As a child Monifah demonstrated an interest in singing and performing and was cast in *Free To Be You and Me* and as Hermia in an Off-Broadway production of *A Midsummer's Night Dream*. Her parents separated when Monifah was nine, yet she remained close to her father until he died of a drug overdose shortly before Monifah's tenth birthday.

Monifah began her career in the early 1990s singing in a band called Rapture, which included her future manager, Charisse Louallen. Monifah met successful rapper Heavy D, then president of Uptown Records, while she was recording a demo for Rapture. The two hit it off and discovered that they shared mutual friends, and forged a long friendship that eventually led to a recording contract. Monifah began singing and touring as a back-up singer for Maxi Priest, which enabled her to broaden her horizons by seeing New Zealand, Brazil, Australia, Japan, Guam, and the Middle East.

After Monifah completed a tour with Maxi Priest, Heavy D asked her to record a reference vocal for one of his artists. A reference vocal is a tape that producers use to illustrate how a song should sound. Monifah told *Sister 2 Sister* magazine that when she had completed the reference tape, Heavy D liked it so much that he said, "You know what? You just started your album. Be here tomorrow at one."

Vibe wrote of Monifah's debut album *Moods...Moments* in 1996, "Steeped in the tradition of women who wield their gifts like whips, Monifah is always in command of her most intoxicating gift: That Voice." Producer Heavy D infused her debut album with his infectious style of songwriting. Monifah's voice and smooth delivery combined with Heavy D's songwriting, hip-hop dance sensibility, and production experience resulted in a remarkably strong first album. After the release of *Moods...Moments,* Anne Raso of *Word Up!* magazine wrote, "The name Monifah is the buzzword in the r&b world these days—her shooting star seems to be overshadowing female r&b legends like Mary J. Blige, SWV and TLC." Monifah first created a buzz when her single "You" went to number 16 on the *Billboard* Top 40 r&b singles chart and number 40 on their pop chart.

Born Monifah Carter in 1972; raised in the Spanish Harlem section of New York City; mother Eleanor Carter, (Episcopal Church Center worker in New York); father (Harlem Hospital administrator); two older brothers; daughter Akemi Denee born in 1991.

Demonstrated an interest in singing and performing as a child and was cast in *Free To Be You and Me* and as Hermia in an Off-Broadway production of *A Midsummer's Night Dream*; attended the LaGuardia High School of the Performing Arts in New York City; began her career in the early 1990s by singing in a band called Rapture; began singing and touring as a back-up singer for Maxi Priest in early 1990s; debut album *Moods...Moments* released 1996; her single "You" reached number 16 on *Billboard's* Top 40 R&B chart and number 40 on their pop chart; single "I Miss You (Come Back Home)" featured in the *New York Undercover* soundtrack; her music was also featured in the soundtracks for *To Wong Foo* and *Dangerous Minds*; released *Mo'Hogany*, 1998.

Addresses: *Record company*—Universal Records, 1755 Broadway, 7th floor, New York, NY 10019.

Much of Monifah's success can be attributed to her wide appeal to R&B audiences of all ages, as well as her ability to cross over into the pop category. She covered gospel songs such as "Jesus is Love," sultry ballads, and spiritual music such like "It's All Right," in addition to rollicking dance numbers and straight R&B material. Monifah also appealed to music lovers across educational and socio-economic groups. Despite her urban American roots she never offered the typical "I'll steal that man from you" fare. Monifah's songs contained thought-provoking, sensitive, and, considering that she was just 24 when she released her debut album, surprisingly mature lyrics. Her albums featured live instrumentation, as opposed to the synthesized orchestrations of other R&B artists.

Monifah released *Mo'Hogany* in 1998, featuring collaborators such as Queen Latifah, Mario Winans, Vincent Herbert, Heavy D, Tony Dofat, and Queen Pen. Her sophomore release was a deeply focused and peaceful collection of songs, five of which she helped write, making the collection more personal than her previous material. Monifah fashioned the material on the album from the grist of her personal life, recounting tales of love, self-awareness, loss, maturation, lust, and new beginnings. She relocated from New York City to Los Angeles. Paula T. Renfroe of *Time Out New York* wrote, "Monifah's strength is her ability to speak volumes without making a lot of noise ... she manages to embrace love, accept blame, shun infidelity, and handle rejection, all the while getting us to move our groove things, explore our minds and touch our souls."

Selected discography

Moods...Moments, Uptown/Universal Records, 1996.
Mo'Hogany, Universal Records, 1998.

Sources

Billboard, July 25, 1998; August 31, 1996.
Detroit News and Free Press, June 23, 1996.
Elegance, October 1996.
Entertainment Weekly, May 31, 1996.
Mad Rhythms, June 1996.
People, June 3, 1996.
Sister 2 Sister, September 1996.
Spin, September 1996.
Time Out New York, May 22-29, 1996.
Upscale, August 1996.
USA Today, June 4, 1996.
Vibe, September 1996.
Village Voice, June 4, 1996.
Word Up!, August 1996.

—*B. Kimberly Taylor*

Van Morrison

Singer, songwriter

Van Morrison remains one of the most elusive rock stars of the modern age. Despite the fact that he has released an album every year for three decades, he does not do many interviews. This elusiveness and his moodiness during live appearances often make Morrison seem distant, even gruff. His music is not easily defined by critics; he certainly will never be pigeon-holed. Morrison himself is often at a loss for words when asked to describe one of his songs. His blend of spirituality and mysticism in his lyrics suggests that maybe he has divine intervention. One of his band members, Georgie Fame, suggested that people don't need to know everything about Morrison. He told Jeff Gordinier of *Entertainment Weekly*, "He's a wonderful Irish poet and a great musician. What else do you want?" The song "Brown Eyed Girl" is perhaps Morrison's best known, but critics agree that *Astral Weeks* is one of the best albums in rock history.

Many great musicians' styles cannot be labeled. Ray Charles' music is often described in print with a string of adjectives: jazz, pop, r&b, soul, country, etc. Morrison, who idolizes Charles, also creates music that is hard to categorize. His music is described in print with words like Irish-Celtic mysticism, folky rock, soul, r&b, and country. His creativity may have come from a background rich in musical styles. Morrison was born in Belfast, Ireland, in 1945. His father introduced him to jazz, blues, and folk music at a young age. His mother was a jazz singer. Morrison also listened to country musicians like Hank Williams. By fifteen, Morrison played guitar, harmonica, and saxophone, and he quit school to pursue music full time. He joined several different bands like the country group Deanie Sands and the Javelins before hooking up with an r&b band in 1961 called the Monarchs. Morrison played saxophone and harmonica for them as they toured Europe. When the band finished touring, Morrison settled in Germany to act in a movie. The movie project failed, and Morrison returned to his hometown of Belfast.

In 1963, Morrison formed a band he called Them with some members from the Monarchs and some of his school buddies. Them was a turning point in Morrison's music career. He was the lead singer and songwriter for the r&b quintet as they became a locally renowned band. Their local fame led them to a recording contract with Decca Records. They recorded their first single in 1964 called "Don't Start Crying Now." In 1965, Them had a hit in Britain called "Baby Please Don't Go." The band settled in London to work with producer Bert Berns. In London, they recorded "Here Comes the Night," which broke the British and American charts. Another single, "Gloria," written by Morrison was not a major hit, but several rock artists like Shadows of Night, Patti Smith, and U2 released their own versions of the classic. Two albums were released by Them, *Them* and *Them Again*. In 1966, the band toured for several months in the United States but when Morrison became upset at the record company's marketing ploy to label the group as rough young rebels, he stopped performing and returned to Belfast. *Them* was released as *The Angry Young Them* in the United States. Morrison quit the band. This was the first sign of his unwillingness to comply with the record companies.

By 1967, Berns had formed his own record company in New York called Bang Records. When Berns heard that Morrison had quit Them, he begged Morrison to come to New York to record some singles. Morrison did, and "Brown Eyed Girl," released in 1967, marked the beginning of his solo career. "Brown Eyed Girl" was a major hit in the United States, so Morrison decided to tour again. While Morrison was on tour, Berns collected all of the new recorded singles and released them as Morrison's first solo album, *Blowin' Your Mind*. Berns didn't inform Morrison, who became irate when he learned that he had no part in the release. Berns died suddenly of a heart attack in December of 1967 and Morrison left Bang records.

Morrison eventually signed with Warner Brothers in 1968 while living in Cambridge, Massachussetts and touring the East Coast with a jazz trio. Morrison' s first solo

that of a mystic. Morrison is known as an introvert who has no interest in achieving empathy with an audience. Cocks wrote, "Morrison, whether singing on the bright side of the road or deep from the heart of his dark and beautiful vision, does not hold out a helping hand to an audience. Reaching down into himself seems more important to him than reaching out."

Morrison's work in the seventies solidified his legendary status in the music world. *His Band And The Street Choir,* released in 1970, produced two top ten hits, "Domino" and "Blue Money." In 1971, Morrison moved to California with his wife, Janet Planet. That same year Morrison released *Tupelo Honey,* which eventually went gold and had the hit "Wild Night." *Tupelo Honey* reflected Morrison's happiness with marriage, containing many love songs to his wife. In 1972, *St. Dominic's Preview* was released to rave reviews and contained two very mystical songs. What makes Morrison's songs mystical are the lyrical journeys they take through spiritual discovery, a common theme in all of his music. Two more critically acclaimed albums were released in the early seventies, *Hard Nose the Highway* and a performance album *It's Too Late To Stop Now. Hard Nose the Highway* featured the Oakland Symphony Orchestra and had a hit with "Autumn Song." *It's Too Late To Stop Now* was a Morrison performance backed by an orchestra he formed called the Caledonian Soul Orchestra.

Morrison's personal life took a turn in 1973 when he divorced his wife and went back to his hometown of Belfast. He spent months in Ireland reflecting on his life and expressing it by writing new material. The result was the very personal *Veedon Fleece* in 1974, which some critics proclaimed was his best work since *Astral Weeks.* David Browne of *Entertainment Weekly* rated it an A and remarked that *Veedon Fleece* was "achingly moody, pitch-dark-night-of-the-soul ruminations on success and love." Morrison did not record another album until 1977. Some said he had writer's block, but he was in the studio often during those three years without an album. He returned in 1977 with *A Period of Transition,* co-produced by Dr. John, who also played piano on the album. Two more albums were released in the late seventies, *Wavelength* and *Into the Music.* The albums of the seventies were creative blends of Celtic music, r&b, and soul. Morrison was influenced not just by musicians like Ray Charles, but also by poets like William Blake. His live performances were inconsistent, sometimes temperamental, but he made his mark in the seventies, earning the respect of critics and colleagues alike.

The eighties and nineties went much the same way for Morrison. He released an album just about every year that critics positively reviewed, yet almost always with

album with Warner Brothers, *Astral Weeks,* was released in October of 1968. *Astral Weeks* took only two days to record but had a lasting impact. The album did not initially generate many sales, but it is known today as one of the most dynamic records of the sixties. David Browne of *Entertainment Weekly* called it "a veritable folkjazz mass full of incanatory power." Jay Cocks of *Time* said that *Astral Weeks* set a pattern for Morrison's music: "wild record, wild-eyed reviews, loyal but limited audience." The *All-Music Guide's* William Ruhlmann wrote, "*[Astral Weeks]* failed to chart but seems to have made every critic's all-time Top Ten list ever since." Many critics today believe that *Astral Weeks* was Morrison's most powerful album.

Morrison's first commercially successful album came in 1970 with the release of *Moondance.* The album sold over a million copies that year before eventually going platinum. *Moondance* was written and produced by Morrison, who by now had proven himself a true musical artist with an inclement temperament to match. One of the singles, "Into The Mystic," yielded the label that Morrison would carry with him throughout the seventies,

lukewarm sales. Each album is composed with personal and spiritual themes like the 1983 album, *Inarticulate Speech of the Heart,* which mentioned Morrison's respect for L. Ron Hubbard's Scientology. However, with the release *No Guru, No Method, No Teacher* in 1986, Morrison seemed reluctant to accept his media label of spiritual mystic. Morrison finally had a breakout sales success with the release of *The Best of Van Morrison,* which sold two million copies in 1990. *Hymns to The Silence* went gold in 1992, much to the critics pleasure. Morrison teamed with the popular Irish band the Chieftains on *Hymns to The Silence* and on *Irish Heartbeat* in 1988.

Perhaps Morrison's biggest success is the respect bestowed upon him by leaders of the music industry. His admirers range from Bob Dylan to John Lee Hooker to Bono. Many of these industry giants have not only appeared as guests on Morrison's work but have remade many of his tunes, taking them to great heights in sales. Two examples are John Mellencamp's version of "Wild Night," which hit number three in 1994, and "Have I Told You Lately," recorded by Rod Stewart in 1993, earning Morrison thousands of dollars in royalties. Morrison has produced several albums for friends over the years as well. In 1993, Morrison was inducted into the Rock and Roll Hall of Fame.

Morrison's reputation as a cantankerous personality continues today, but his live performances in the nineties have earned him new respect onstage. One of those performances was documented on the 1994 release *A Night in San Francisco,* which critic Marc Judge of *America* called, "the spirit of rejuvenation and rebirth." Morrison even seemed friendlier to the press in the nineties, but denied that he is more open to the public. He told Clive Davis of *Down Beat,* "More extroverted? I don't think so. I thought I was more that way in the early seventies." Morrison does seem more settled these days as he continues to release critically acclaimed albums like *The Philosopher's Stone* in 1998. His hair may have grayed, but Dan Ouellette of *Down Beat* noted the timelessness of Morrison's music. He said, "What's remarkable about *The Philosopher's Stone* is how well these songs, some recorded over a quarter of a century ago, have aged."

Selected discography

Singles

"Mystic Eyes," Polygram, 1965.
"Brown Eyed Girl," Bang, Warner Brothers, 1967.
"Domino," Warner Brothers, 1970.

"Tupelo Honey," Warner Brothers, 1972.
"Jackie Wilson Said," Warner Brothers, 1972.
"Moon Dance," Warner Brothers, 1977.
"Wavelength," Warner Brothers, 1978.

Albums

Them, Parrot, 1965.
Them Again, Parrot, 1965.
Blowin' Your Mind, Bang, 1967.
The Best of Van Morrison, Bang, 1968.
Astral Weeks, Warner Bros., 1968.
Moondance (includes "Into the Mystic"), Warner Bros., 1970.
His Band and the Street Choir, Warner Bros., 1970.
Tupelo Honey, Warner Bros., 1971.
St. Dominic's Preview, Warner Bros., 1972.
Hard Nose the Highway, Warner Bros., 1973.
It's Too Late to Stop Now, Warner Bros., 1974.
TA Period of Transition, Warner Bros., 1977.
Wavelength, Warner Bros., 1978.
Into the Music, Warner Bros., 1979.
Common One, Warner Bros., 1980.
Beautiful Vision, Warner Bros., 1982.
Inarticulate Speech of the Heart, Warner Bros., 1983.
A Sense of Wonder, Mercury, 1985.
Live at The Grand Opera House, Belfast, Polydor, 1985.
No Guru, No Method, No Teacher, Mercury, 1986.
Poetic Champions Compose, Mercury, 1987.
Irish Heartbeat (with the Chieftains), Mercury, 1988.
Avalon Sunset, Polydor, 1989.
Enlightenment, Mercury, 1990.
The Best of Van Morrison, Mercury, 1990.
Hymns to The Silence, Polydor, 1991.
The Bang Masters, Epic, 1991.
Too Long in Exile, Polydor, 1993.
The Best of Van Morrison Volume 2, Polygram, 1993.
A Night in San Francisco, Polydor, 1994.
Payin' Dues, Charly, 1994.
Days Like This, Polydor, 1995.
Songs of Mose Allison: Tell Me Something, Polygram, 1996.
How Long Has This Been Going On?, Verve, 1996.
The Healing Game, Polygram, 1997.
The Philosopher's Stone, Polydor, 1998.

Sources

Books

Crampton, Luke and Dafydd Rees, editors, *Encyclopedia of Rock Stars,* DK Publishing Inc., 1996.
Herzhaft, Gérard, *Encyclopedia of the Blues,* University of Arkansas Press, 1997.
Romanowski, Patricia, editor, *The New Encyclopedia of Rock and Roll,* Rolling Stone Press, 1995.

Periodicals

America, October 29, 1994.

Down Beat, May 1996; August 1998.

Entertainment Weekly, March 7, 1997.

Time, October 28, 1991.

Online

All-Music Guide, http://www.allmusic.com1998.

Eyeneer Music Archives, 1997.

Palo Alto Weekly, (September 26, 1997).

—Christine Morrison

R. Carlos Nakai

Flute

Hailed as the world's foremost Native American flute performers, R. Carlos Nakai was one of the firsts to meld his ancestral sounds with contemporary music and electronic instrumentation. By 1998, he had released more than 30 albums and sold more than 2.5 million units all over the world. Nakai not only recorded his own albums, but also collaborated with a number of artists, including guitarist William Eaton, classical pianist Peter Kater, and his own groups Jackalope and the R. Carlos Nakai Quartet.

Born Raymond Carlos Nakai in Flagstaff, Arizona, he was inspired to pursue success by renowned Native American artist R.C. Gorman. When Nakai was around seven years old, Gorman left Flagstaff, saying that he was going away to make something of himself. Gorman eventually became one of the most successful artists in the Southwest. "I was so impressed by what he said," Nakai told Paul Brinkley-Rogers in the *Arizona Republic*. "I remember I made a transcript of it.... R.C. would come back to us sometimes, but then he stopped coming back. I guess he got famous." Gorman's accomplishment encouraged Nakai to pursue his own dreams and artistic talent.

R. Carlos Nakai began his interest in music early in life. He learned to play trumpet as a child, and later played in the Flagstaff High School band. At the same time, he also developed an interest in his Navajo-Ute heritage and culture. His family spent many weekends visiting relatives on the Navajo Reservation or with Mojave or Chemeheuvi Indian friends on the Colorado River. During these weekends, Nakai learned more about the Native American culture.

After he graduated from high school, Nakai was drafted for the Vietnam War in 1966. He went to Albuquerque, New Mexico, to enlist in the U.S. Marines, but when the Marines discovered that he weighed just 97 pounds, they turned him down. So he joined the U.S. Navy instead. The following year, he did a tour in Vietnam. His goal was to join the U.S. Navy Band as a trumpet player, but he was never accepted. Nakai's return home from the war was even more discouraging. He was showered with eggs and tomatoes as he walked down the street of his hometown. Around this same time, Nakai's father, also named Raymond, became the Navajo Tribal Chairman. Because of his father's position, Nakai decided to drop his name and use just his first initial.

After he left the Navy in 1971, R. Carlos Nakai decided to go to college. He studied music at Northern Arizona University in Flagstaff, and then at Phoenix College in Phoenix, Arizona. Although the majority of his studies centered on the trumpet and coronet in classical and jazz music, he also began researching Native American music and traditional instruments. He discovered that his ancestors, the ancient Dine of Northwestern Canada, had a tradition of playing the wood flute. The tradition was dropped somewhere in their migration from the Canadian Plateau and the American Southwest in the 15th century. Later, Nakai went on to receive a masters Degree in American Indian Studies from the University of Arizona.

In 1972, Nakai attended an Indian art fair in Santa Fe, New Mexico, where he met a man who collected and traded flutes. He purchased a traditional wood flute from the man and started learning how to play it. After playing the flute for some time, he decided to craft his own wood flutes. He made three out of oak and twoout of pinewood, but he couldn't get them to sound the way he wanted.

Eventually, he met a flute craftsman who taught him that cedar was the only wood that sounded right. He also learned how to carve the flute to fit the hand and finger measurements of the flutist, which makes each instrument sound slightly different from any other. After creating several cedar wood flutes, Nakai said in his record company biography that he viewed them less as a musical instrument and more "as a sound sculpture— a piece of art that also creates sound." By 1980, Nakai

For the Record . . .

Born Raymond Carlos Nakai on April 16, 1946, in Flagstaff, AZ; married to Pam Hyde-Nakai; received Master's Degree in American Indian Studies from University of Arizona;

As a child, studied trumpet and coronet, 1967-72; bought and created his first cedar wood flutes, 1972; made his first studio recording, 1980; signed contract with Canyon Records, 1981; released debut *Changes*, 1982; began collaboration with pianist Peter Kater, 1989; formed R. Carlos Nakai Quartet, 1996.

Addresses: *Record company*—Canyon Records, 4143 N. 16th St., Suite 6, Phoenix, AZ 85016

had practiced enough to go into the studio for his first recording. He made his own cassette tapes and sold them himself all around the Southwest. Within two years he was noticed by Arizona independent label, Canyon Records, who, in 1982 released his debut album, *Changes*.

The release was the beginning of his widespread notoriety and intensified recording schedule. He mixed his musical training and his expertise on the cedar flute into a combination of a variety of musical genres, including jazz ensembles, piano and guitar collaborations, symphony concerts, and contemporary electronic music with synthesizers and digital effects. "In the music of the cultural tradition that I was raised in, and even the traditions that were taught to me by others, you must begin to express yourself from *your* perspective of *your* philosophy," Nakai explained to Richard Simonelli in *Winds of Change*.

After releasing his own music for several years, he decided to collaborate with classical pianist Peter Kater in 1989. They released *Natives* in 1989, *Migrations* in 1992, *Honorable Sky* in 1994, and *Song for Humanity* in 1998. *Migrations* won the National Association of Independent Record Distributors (NAIRD) Indie Award for Best New Age Album. That same year, Nakai became the second Native American to receive the Governor of Arizona's Arts Award. Nakai released more than 30 albums over nearly two decades. He formed a band called Jackalope, with William Clipman, J. David Muniz, and Larry Yanez that combined modern instruments with a variety of traditional, ethnic instruments. He

collaborated with guitarist William Eaton on the 1991 release *Carry the Gift* and *Ancestral Voices* in 1993. The latter was nominated for a Grammy Award for Best Traditional Folk Music.

The following year, Nakai teamed up with a Japanese group called the Wind Travelin' Band of Kyoto to record *Island of Bows*. The band played acoustic and traditional Japanese instruments with Nakai's own cedar flute. "The variety of collaborative activities is endless," Nakai told Simonelli. "It's just being able to find a satisfactory way to communicate together. Interpersonal communication is what musicians should have anyway if they intend to work together." Nakai also received an honorary doctorate degree from Northern Arizona University and the Arizona Board of Regents in 1994. They honored him for his "exceptional achievements and contributions to humankind."

R. Carlos Nakai released one of his most successful albums in 1995 called *Feather, Stone & Light*. The album includes collaborations with William Eaton and percussionist William Clipman. *Billboard* named it one of its critic's choice selections, and it spent 13 weeks on *Billboard*'s Top New Age Albums chart. Jon Andrews wrote in *Down Beat* that, "*Feather, Stone & Light* continues the progression of Nakai's music, from haunting solo works to collaborations that extend Nakai's worldview, finding affinities in different genres."

In the mid-1990s, Nakai formed the R. Carlos Nakai Quartet with percussionist William Clipman. saxophone and keyboard player "Amo" Chip Dabney, and bassist J.David Muniz, who was later replaced by bassist and singer Mary Redhouse. The quartet released *Kokopelli's Cafe* in 1996, which blended Native American sounds with Latin rhythms and ethnic jazz. Andrew Means wrote in *Rhythm Music*, "*Kokopelli's Cafe* is a benchmark in placing cedar flute firmly within the context of mainstream contemporary jazz." The R. Carlos Nakai Quartet also released *Big Medicine* on September 15, 1998. Nakai explained his musical philosophy of fusing ethnic and traditional music with modern sounds to Paul de Barros in the *Seattle Times*. "I build on the tradition of my culture," said Nakai, "but not 'This is what happened to these people way back when.' This is what's happening to us today."

Beyond his music, Nakai continued his research into Native American history and culture. He published a book called *The Art of Native American Flute* and gave lectures throughout the United States. Through his music and his lectures, he attempted to send a message that he credits for his worldwide success. "I think the reason why people respond well to my music and the events that I perform at is because I tell them how unique and wonderful and good they are," Nakai told Simonelli. "No one says that to anyone any more."

Selected discography

Changes, Canyon Records, 1982.
Earth Spirit, Canyon Records, 1988.
Desert Dance, Canyon Records, 1990.
Sundance Season, Canyon Records, 1991.
Emergence, Canyon Records, 1992.
Journeys, Canyon Records, 1992.
Canyon Trilogy, Canyon Records, 1992.
Cycles, Canyon Records, 1993.
Spirit Horses, Canyon Records, 1993.
(with William Eaton) *Ancestral Voices*, Canyon Records, 1993.
Island of Bows, Canyon Records, 1994.
Feather, Stone & Light, Canyon Records, 1995.

With Peter Kater

Natives, Silver Wave Records, 1989.
Migrations, Silver Wave Records, 1992.
Honorable Sky, Silver Wave Records, 1994.

With R. Carlos Nakai Quartet

Kokopelli's Cafe, Canyon Records, 1996.
Big Medicine, Canyon Records, 1998.

Sources

Periodicals

Arizona Republic, October 17, 1993.
Down Beat, October 1995.
Seattle Times, January 29, 1998.
Winds of Change, Autumn 1992.

Online

www.hinman.oro.net/~bmsweb/html/music.html (September 20, 1998).
www.silverwave.com (September 20, 1998).
www.canyonrecords.com (July 7, 1998).
www.hershelfreemanagency.com (September 20, 1998).
www.indianmarket.com (September 20, 1998).

—Sonya Shelton

The Newsboys

Christian rock band

The early days of The Newsboys were filled with rough and critical barbs. Some critics felt the group relied too much on lyrical religious cliches. Undaunted by such attacks, they forged ahead in what they believed to be a mission. Each musician was a seasoned professional who could work in the secular rock market had they wanted to. Yet they each wanted to combine their professional talents with their personal spiritual beliefs and decided to start a Christian rock band. Well known for their wild, high-energy live-show performances and high-tech production numbers, The Newsboys are an example of a unique musical phenomenon. They are a Christian rock group that has managed to break into into the cross-over market of secular pop music, following such talents as Amy Grant, Audio Adrenaline, Matthew Sweet and others., The group itself formed in the late 1980's with an original lineup of lead vocalist John James, guitarists Roscoe Meeks and Phillip Urry, and drummer Peter Furler. They are considered to be one of the most popularly known Christian rock bands of the 1990s

Star Song/Virgin Records also believed in their potential and gave them a recording contract. The Newsboy's debut album, *Hell Is for Wimps,* was released in 1990 to a mild response. They released *Turn* in 1991 to much of the same. Undaunted, they continued with *Not Ashamed, Boys Will Be Boyz,* and *Read All About It* in

1992. They received a Grammy nomination for Rock Album of the Year in 1993, however, their first big success came with 1994's *Going Public.* It hit the charts like a bullet and became their first gold record. The next public accolade came from the Christian music sector when they received a Dove Nomination for Best Short Form Video in 1994 for "I Cannot Get You Out of My System. Their public expanded exponentially and since they were now approaching the crossover horizon, they wanted to maximize the impact of their deeply held spiritual beliefs. To do this in the most effective way possible, they teamed up with a Dallas-based evangelical organization called Teen Mania. Teen Mania regularly schedules weekend events and The Newsboys chose to use this venue and reach out to Christian teenagers. The following years reaped even sweeter harvests. They released *Take Me To Your Leader* in 1996. It went gold, making *Take Me to Your Leader* their second gold record in as many years.

On November 1, 1997, The Newsboys made contemporary Christian Music History. Their Houston Astrodome concert held over 33,000 people. Also, over 900,000 fans showed up to attend the *Take Me To Your Leader* Tour. The latter tour had the distinction of being named both *Christian Contemporary Music*'s *Release Magazine*'s favorite live concert of 1997.

It was at this time that vocalist John James decided to quit. According to Furler and Joel, he left the group in pursuit of other interests and for all concerned it was an amicable parting of the ways. Producer Steve Taylor that left during this period as well. Taylor was starting to launch a new record label of his own, Squint Entertainment, and he no longer had the necessary amount of time to devote to other projects. These absences left a large void to fill. "Peter really streched us," Joel told *Billboard*'s Deborah Evans Price. These problems are what the group had to contend with as they developed their latest album. Drummer Furler took over as front man. He also assumed the producer's responsibilities. True to their destiny, what seemed like insurmountable problems turned into very good solutions. Furler's emergence as lead vocalist gave the group a powerful new sound.

"It's like a cheeky way of saying both 'let the chips fall where they may'," Furler told the Newsboys Website, "and at the same time, for the fans and the youth group leaders and the like, showing them that on this record, we've gone through a lot of self-examination. We've been thinking about 'why did Jesus die on the cross? And more important, 'why do we believe what we believe? The phrase 'Step Up To The Microphone' obviously means 'make your statement'. But to me, it

For the Record . . .

Members include **Jody Davis**, guitar; **Jeff Frankenstein**, keyboards; **Peter Furler**, drums, lead vocals; **John James**, (left group, 1997), lead vocals; **Phil Joel**, bass.

Group formed in late 1980's; released debut album *Hell Is For Wimps*, Star Song, 1990; released *Not Ashamed, Boys Will Be Boyz*, and *Read All About It*, 1992; *Going Public* , 1994; *Take Me To Your Leader*, Chordant, 1996; *Step Up To The Microphone*, 1998.

Awards: Gold record for album *Going Public* in 1994; Gold record for album *Take Me To Your Leader*, 1996.

Addresses: Virgin Records America-338 N. Foothill Rd., Beverly Hills, CA. 90210, (310)-278-1181.

also means 'what are you going to say when you get there?"

After putting on the finishing touches on their latest album, *Step Up To The Microphone* was released in 1998. A week before it hit the streets, the band promoted the event by headlining the annual Creation Fest held in Mount Union, Pennsylvania. Audience reception was positive. The fans seemed to love Furler as the lead singer. Though the differences in style were apparent, it was a positive one. Because of the radical personnel changes, the Newsboys knew they had a lot to prove to their long-time fans. It was a given that the audience would make the inevitable comparisons between lead singers. Some would probably even judge the overall production tone of their album, the signature of a producer. Another change for the group was the collaborational effort of their new album, the whole band took part in writing all of the songs together. "We all stepped up and took on a whole lot more," said Joel to Price. "I

can't say it was a shock that James moved on, so it didn't rock the boat immensely. Peter has a great voice. He's had to take on being a front man and he's doing a great job." "There were a lot of challenges going into this record." Furler added, "But I think that made us more creative. I'm really proud of the lyrics. It's really a very personal record."

Having faith in their potential for reaching an even wider secular cross-over audience, Virgin Records launched a massive promotional campaign to back *Step Up To The Microphone*. They also worked through EMI Christian Music Group Distribution to release the album into mainstream outlets. Special promotional events were launched in over twenty key market areas and, for the first time in their decade long career, the crossover became a great success. Along with having their songs played on the traditional alternate Christian radio stations, they also started appearing on the playlist of major top 40 radio stations across the country. Their 120 city *Step Up To The Microphone* Fall Tour surpassed initial expectations. Everyone was pleased with the results. The tour has even surpassed the success of Amy Grant's *Age to Age Tour*. It looks like the Newsboys' mainstream crossover is here to stay.

Selected discography

Hell Is For Wimps, Star Song, 1990
Boys Will Be Boyz, Star Song, 1992
Going Public, Star Song, 1994
Take Me To Your Leader, Chordant, 1996
Step Up To The Microphone, Star Song/Virgin Records, 1998

Sources

Periodicals

Billboard Magazine, pg. 14, June 6, 1998

Online

All Music Guide Web Site-http://www.allmusic.com/cg/x.exe
The Official Newsboys Web Site-http://www. newsboys.com

—*Timothy Kevin Perry*

Dolly Parton

Singer, songwriter

AP/Wide World Photo. Reproduced by permission. ©

Legendary country-and-western singer/songwriter Dolly Parton is one of the few American country and western musicians to achieve international acclaim; in fact, her career is virtually unprecedented in music history. With twenty-two number one hit singles and ten gold and platinum albums to attest to her talent, Parton has moved far from her humble East Tennessee roots to become a cultural icon. She pursued entrepreneurial business and philanthropic endeavors and performed in numerous films and television shows. Although she began performing at the age of 12, her career began to blossom in 1967, and by 1999, she was known throughout the world as a premier country singer and American music/film media celebrity along the lines of Elvis, Madonna, and Cher. By 1999, Dolly Parton Enterprises became a $100 million media empire. Earlier, in 1986, her company opened a sprawling theme park, Dollywood, in Tennessee that celebrated her Smoky Mountain upbringing. Nominated for 70 music awards between 1968-99, she has won 34 of them. She was also nominated for an Oscar for composing the title song for the film *9 to 5* in 1980. Her ascent to fame, both impressive and unprecedented, has generated at least 16 books—one autobiography—as well as countless articles and numerous web sites.

Born Dolly Rebecca Parton in Servier, Tennesee, on January 19, 1947, she was the fourth child of twelve born to Robert Lee Parton and Bessie Elizabeth Rayfield. She was raised in Locust Ridge, only a few miles from Pigeon Forge, Tennessee, the area of the Smoky Mountain country where her theme park, Dollywood, is now located. Her 1971 autobiographical single, "Coat of Many Colors," details her poverty as one of twelve children growing up on a run-down farm. Parton first began singing by joining the gospel choir in her grandfather's church as a young child. In 1959, at the age of twelve, Parton had appeared on Knoxville television as a singer and by the age of thirteen she was recording on the small label Gold Band and appearing at the Grand Ole Opry. She released her debut album *Puppy Love* in 1960 at the age of thirteen. After graduating from high school, Parton moved to Nashville to launch her career as a country-and- western singer. There she met Carl Thomas Dean, her future husband, at a laundromat. They married in Ringgold, Georgia on May 30, 1966.

National Media Celebrity

In 1967, Parton released *Hello I'm Dolly* on the Monument label, followed by *Just Between You and Me* with Porter Wagoner the following year on RCA/Victor. Wagoner had liked her 1967 single, "Dumb Blonde," and hired Parton to appear on his television show, where

For the Record . . .

Born Dolly Rebecca Parton on January 19, 1947, in Servier, TN; fourth child of twelve; father, Robert Lee Parton; mother Bessie Elizabeth Rayfield; married Carl Thomas Dean on May 30, 1966; children: one daughter Virginia.

Began by joining the gospel choir in her grandfather's church as a young child; appeared on Knoxville television as a singer by the age of 12; began appearing at the Grand Ole Opry at 13; released *Puppy Love,* Gold Band Records, 1960; moved to Nashville after graduating from high school; released *Hello, I'm Dolly,*1967; released *Just Between You and Me* with Porter Wagoner the following year; appeared on Wagoner's television show, where their duet performances became popular; released 21 albums between 1968-72; saw 22 number one hit singles; received ten gold and platinum albums between 1968-98; appeared frequently on television specials and talk shows in the late 1970s; made her film debut in *9 to 5,* 1980 and received an Oscar nomination for composing the film's title song; opened Dollywood, 1986; formed the Dollywood Broadcasting Company,1990; composedWhitney Houston's number one R&B single, "I Will Always Love You," 1994.

Awards: Received five Academy of Country Music (ACM) Awards; five American Music Awards (AMA); eight Country Music Association (CMA) awards;four Grammy Awards; ten Music City News (MCN) awards; two Nashville Songwriters Association, International (NASAI) awards ;

Addresses: Home—Dolly Parton, Crockett Road, Route #1, Brentwood, TN 37027; *Manager*— Jim Morey, Morey & Associates, 245 North Maple Drive, Suite 300, Beverly Hills, CA 90210, (310) 278-0808; fax (310) 205-6199.

their duet performances became popular. She released an astounding 21 albums between 1968-72. When her *Joshua* album reached number one in 1970. Parton's fame soon overshadowed Wagoner's. Although she continued to release albums with Wagoner periodically over the course of her long career, she struck out on her own as a solo recording artist and songwriter in 1974. By

1974, she had released 28 albums and had won seven music awards, one of them—a Music City News Award (MCN) in 1968—for Most Promising Female Artist. The Country Music Association (CMA) nominated her as Female Vocalist of the Year every year between 1968-72, and again from 1974-79.

Parton appeared frequently on television specials and talk shows in the late 1970s, which further fueled public interest in her celebrity. Her cheerful disposition, good looks, flamboyant conversational and dress style, and winning smile endeared her to millions of viewers and her immense country music vocal/songwriting talent endeared her to millions of listeners. She made her film debut in 1980 in *9 to 5,* co-starring with Lily Tomlin and Jane Fonda.Two years later, in 1982, she appeared in *The Best Little Whorehouse in Texas,* and, in 1984, she starred with Sylvester Stallone in *Rhinestone,* a film in which the two sang a duet. The single "Tennessee Homesick Blues" from the film earned Parton another Grammy nomination.

Parton released *The Best of Dolly Parton* in 1975, which went RIAA Gold in August of 1978, and released *Here You Come Again* in 1977, which successfully blended country with pop and dance music, and crossed most musical lines. *Here You Come Again* was Parton's second gold album. It went platinum in April of 1978. Her third gold album, *Great Balls of Fire,* was released in 1979. She released her fourth gold album, *Dolly Parton's Greatest Hits,* in 1982 and this album also went platinum. The next album to reach gold status was 1984's *Once Upon A Christmas,* which also went platinum. 1987's *Trio* went gold and platinum; 1989's *White Limozeen* went gold; 1991's *Eagle When She Flies* reached gold and platinum status, as did 1993's *Slow Dancing with the Moon.* Her last release to reach gold and/or platinum status was *Dolly Parton: Her Greatest Hits* in 1998. Where many musicians are hard-pressed to attain even an eighth of her musical output, Parton managed to released 87 albums between 1960-98.

Legend Continued

Parton continued to garner awards after her first nomination in 1968, and was nominated for awards almost yearly up until 1997. She collaborated with numerous other musicians other than Porter Wagoner over the years including, Kitty Wells in 1980 for *Dolly Parton and Kitty Wells,* Kris Kristofferson, Willie Nelson, and Brenda Lee in 1982 for *Kris, Willie, Dolly and Brenda: The Winning Hand,* Kenny Rogers in 1984 for *Once Upon a Christmas,* Linda Rondstadt and Emmylou Harris in 1987 for *Trio,* Billy Ray Cyrus, Tanya Tucker,

Kathy Mattea, Mary Chapin-Carpenter, and Pam Tillis in 1993 for *Romeo*, Loretta Lynn and Tammy Wynette in 1994 for *Honky Tonk Angels. Honkey Tonk Angels. Honky Tonk Angels* also garnered a Country Music Award (CMA) Vocal Event of the Year nomination.

Parton began the new year in 1999 with the January release of *Dolly Parton*. She also opened the addition of the Southern Gospel Music Hall of Fame and Museum at Dollywood. The museum was a fitting addition to her theme park, considering that Parton's grandfather was a preacher and she first starting her singing career in his church.

Parton, a devoted philanthropist, used the 20 dollar annual membership dues for her extensive Dollywood Ambassador Fan Club to support education in Tennessee. In 1997, she dismantled her own fan club after some members complained that she didn't perform often enough for them at Dollywood. She even sent membership dues back to all of her fans. Her reasoning behind this was that she felt many of her fans weren't interested in supporting her charitable pursuits and, instead, were merely supporting her fan club. She requested that her fans send money directly to Dollywood Foundation projects. It's this spirit of giving and caring that has characterized both Parton's professional and private life. Her endless stream of material and awards over the years reveals how gifted and prolific she is. Her ability to build and maintain a multimillion dollar empire within the short span of one lifetime—starting with nothing but the basics and musical ability—renders Parton nothing less than legendary.

Selected discography

Puppy Love, Gold Band, 1960.
Hello, I'm Dolly, Monument, 1967.
Just Between You and Me (with Porter Wagoner), RCA Victor, 1968.
Just Because I'm A Woman, RCA Victor, 1968.
Just The Two of Us (with Porter Wagoner), RCA Victor, 1968.
In the Good Old Days When Times Were Bad, RCA Victor, 1969.
My Blue Ridge Mountain Boy, RCA Victor, 1969.
The Fairest of Them All, RCA Victor, 1970.
Porter Wayne and Dolly Rebecca, RCA Victor, 1970.
As Long As I Live, Monument, 1970.
A Real Live Dolly, RCA Victor, 1970.
Once More (with Porter Wagoner), RCA Victor, 1970.
The Best of Dolly Parton, RCA Victor, 1970.
Golden Streets of Glory, RCA Victor, 1971.
Two of A Kind, RCA Victor, 1971.
Joshua, RCA Victor, 1971.

Coat of Many Colors, RCA Victor, 1971.
The World of Dolly Parton, Monument, 1972.
Touch Your Woman, RCA Victor, 1972.
Together Always (with Porter Wagoner), RCA Victor, 1972.
Just The Way I Am, RCA Camden, 1972.
My Tennessee Mountain Home, RCA Victor, 1973.
Love And Music (with Porter Wagoner), RCA Victor, 1973.
Bubbling Over, RCA Victor, 1973.
Mine, RCA Camden, 1973.
Jolene, RCA Victor, 1974.
Porter 'n' Dolly, RCA Victor, 1974.
Love is Like a Butterfly, RCA Victor, 1974.
The Bargain Store, RCA Victor, 1975.
Best of Dolly Parton, RCA Victor, 1975.
Dolly: The Seeker & We Used To, RCA Victor, 1975.
All I Can Do, RCA Victor, 1976.
New Harvest—First Gathering, RCA Victor, 1977.
Here You Come Again, RCA Victor, 1977.
Heartbreaker, RCA Victor, 1978.
Great Balls of Fire, RCA Victor, 1979.
Dolly Parton and Kitty Wells, Exact, 1980.
Dolly, Dolly, Dolly, RCA Victor, 1980.
Sweet Harmony: Porter and Dolly, RCA Victor, 1980.
9 to 5 (and Odd Jobs), RCA Victor, 1981.
Heartbreak Express, RCA Victor, 1982.
The Best Little Whorehouse in Texas, MCA Records, 1982.
Dolly Parton's Greatest Hits, RCA Victor, 1982.
Kris, Willie, Dolly & Brenda: The Winning Hand, (with Kris Kristofferson, Willie Nelson, and Brenda Lee) RCA Victor, 1982.
Burlap and Satin, RCA Victor, 1983.
Songbook, Exact, 1984.
The Great Pretender, RCA Victor, 1984.
Rhinestone, RCA Victor, 1984.
Once Upon a Christmas (with Kenny Rogers), RCA Victor, 1984.
Portrait, RCA Victor, 1985.
Real Love, RCA Victor, 1985.
Dolly Parton (Collector's Series), RCA Victor, 1985.
Think About Love, RCA Victor, 1986.
The Best There Is, RCA Victor, 1987.
The Best of Dolly Parton, Volume 3, RCA Victor, 1987.
Trio (with Linda Rondstadt and Emmylou Harris), Warner Brothers, 1987.
Rainbow, CBS Records, 1987.
White Limozeen, CBS Records, 1989.
Best of Dolly Parton, RCA Victor, 1990.
Home for Christmas, CBS Records, 1990.
Eagle When She Flies, Sony (CBS), 1991.
Straight Talk, Hollywood, 1992.
Slow Dancing with the Moon, Columbia, 1993.
Heartsongs: Live from Home, Columbia, 1994.
Honky Tonk Angels, (with Loretta Lynn and Tammy Wynette), Columbia, 1994.
Something Special, Columbia, 1995.

The Essential Dolly Parton, RCA Victor, 1995.

I Will Always Love You and Other Greatest Hits, Columbia, 1996.

Treasures, Rising Tide, 1996.

Peace Train (CD Single), Flipit, 1997.

I Believe, BMG Special Projects, 1997.

Here You Come Again (from 1977), DCC Records, 1998.

Honky Tonk Songs (CD Single), UNI/DECCA, 1998.

Hungry Again, UNI/DECCA, 1998.

Trio 11 (with Linda Rondstadt and Emmylou Harris), Asylum, 1998.

Dolly Parton, BMG Special Projects, 1999.

Sources

Books

Amdur, Richard, *Dolly Close Up/Up Close,* Putnum, 1983.

Berman, Connie, *The Official Dolly Parton Scrapbook,* Grosset and Dunlap, 1978.

Bufwack, Mary A. and Oermann Robert K., *Finding Her Voice: The Illustrated History of Women in Country Music,* Henry Holt & Company, 1993.

Fleischer, Leonore, *Dolly: Here I Come Again,* Zebra Books, 1978.

James, Otis, *Dolly Parton: A Personal Portrait,* Quick Fox, 1978.

Krishef, Robert, *Dolly Parton,* Lerner Publications Company, 1980.

Nash, Alanna, *Behind Closed Doors: Talking with the Legends of Country Music,* Alfred A. Knopf, 1988.

Parton, Dolly, *Dolly: My Life and Other Unfinished Business,* Harper Collins, 1994.

Parton, Willadeene, *In the Shadow of a Song: The Story of the Parton Family,* Bantam Books, 1985.

Saunders, Susan, *Dolly Parton: Goin' to Town,* Viking, 1985.

Online

http://bestware.net/spreng/dolly/index.html

http://decca-nashville.com/dollyparton

http://www.dolly.net

http://estanley.simplenet.com/dolly/links/html

http://expressnet.lycos.com/entertainment/celebrities/celebs/Parton.html

http://www.flip.it.records.com

http://members.aol.com/dlyboy/index.html

http:/personal.cfw.com/~herlanh/97timmy/97timmy1.html

http://smokykin.com/

—B. Kimberly Taylor

Pearls Before Swine

Rock group

*A*mong the profusion of musical groups arising from the counterculture of the 1960s, Pearls Before Swine offered some of the most poetic and surreal lyrics of the day. While it was not unusual for music at that time to make social statements, Pearls Before Swine used poetry and metaphor to weave multiple layered lyrics that have earned them a following among musicians.

According to *Goldmine* magazine "[Pearls Before Swine was] really more a fictional entity than a genuine working band, the group consisted of singer/songwriter Tom Rapp and a rotating cast of supporting talent". None of the original band members would remain past the third album. However, Rapp pulled together many talented musicians throughout his career to help weave musical magic. Hence, although the band boasted many members, Tom Rapp and Pearls Before Swine have become synonymous.

Rapp was born in Bottineau, North Dakota, near the Canadian border. His earliest musical influences included his grandfather who could learn any instrument in a matter of minutes and his mother who sang radio commercials as a child. He learned to play the ukulele from a neighbor and guitar from a country singer name "Red" in Northfield, Minnesota. As a child he played country songs. Talent shows were Rapp's earliest live performances. In the *Washington Post*, Rapp recalls leafing through his mother's scrapbook and finding the

results of a show in Rochester, Minnesota. Tom had placed second, and an older boy named Bobby Zimmerman, who would later be known as Bob Dylan placed fifth.

Between 1958-65, Rapp thought little of music until he heard Peter Paul and Mary playing "Blowing in the Wind" and felt compelled to play the song. Upon discovering that the original was by Bob Dylan, he tracked down most of his songs and began once again to play. He learned picking styles from a Joan Baez songbook and formed a band with some high school friends in Melbourne, Florida. They made a demo tape, sent it to ESP Records, and were invited to New York to make an album; Pearls Before Swine was born.

In an article for *Goldmine* Rapp recalls, "I think the first real song that I ever wrote was 'Another Time', which is the first song on the (first) album. I was in a car accident when an Austin Healey Sprite flipped over a couple of times. I was thrown out, but essentially uninjured. I found myself standing in the road with the car turned around and the windshield up in a tree. I can remember just having the overpowering feeling that the universe didn't care at all. Nothing was really holding you up and whether you lived or died was just pure chance." Such was the case with many Pearls songs, arising from circumstances, shaped by Rapp. In an interview with *Goldmine*, Rapp discusses his method of songwriting: "My sense of writing a song was that you started with a mood or a feeling and you just chipped away everything that wasn't that feeling and in the end you'd have something that had crystallized it somehow. You know the theory of making a statue by starting with a piece of stone and chipping away what isn't the statue"

Pearls Before Swine's debut album, *One Nation Underground,* was recorded in four days in 1967. In addition to "Another Time", it featured a rich repertoire of songs about timely issues. "Uncle John" was one of the first about the Vietnam War, and "Playmate" was a playful song with the words of a children's nursery rhyme. Its next album, *Balaklava,* was an anti-war album; its cover was a powerful painting by Breughel the elder titled *The Triumph of Death*.

After receiving no financial compensation from ESP, Rapp record his next five albums with Reprise. *These Things Too* was recorded in 1969, followed by *The Use of Ashes.* Notable on this album is the song "Rocket Man" which inspired Elton John's song of the same name.

Around the time *Ashes* was recorded, Pearls Before Swine did its first live performance. Most live shows

For the Record . . .

Members include **Tom Rapp** (born Thomas D. Rapp, March 8, 1947, in Bottineau, ND), guitar, vocals; included several other musicians over the years.

Formed by Tom Rapp; signed to ESP Disk; released debut album *One Nation Underground*, 1967; *Balaklava*, 1968; signed to Reprise Records; released *These Things Too*, 1969; *City of Gold*, 1971; *Beautiful Lies*, 1971; signed to independent label Blue Thumb; released *Stardancer*, 1972; *Sunforest*, 1973; Rapp left music business; studied law, Northeastern University; performed benifit concert for fanzine *Ptolemaic Terrascope*; released tribute album *For the Dead in Space*, Magic Eye Singles, 1997.

were on the folk circuit with artists such as Dave Van Ronk, Odetta and John Hartford. However, the band also opened for Pink Floyd, and is reputed to have been invited to perform at Woodstock, but Rapp was living in the Netherlands at the time.

Rapp continued to record for Reprise with *City of Gold*, *Beautiful Lies*, and *Familiar Songs*. He did not fit neatly into any one genre; his manager and Reprise hardly promoted his work so his last two albums were released on the small label Blue Thumb. On these albums, Rapp had the artistic freedom he had desired and recorded under his own name. By this time however, he was tired of being broke and quit performing in 1976. He sold popcorn in a movie theater and went to college. He received a Bachelor's degree (Magna Cum Laude) in Economics from Brandeis and studied Law at Northeastern University. Rapp became an attorney for a law firm that tries civil rights cases. Most are cases in which the client is disabled or sick and their employer has chosen to discriminate. One of his cases is currently slated to go before the Supreme Court.

In 1995, it seemed to Rapp that his musical career was long behind him. Others, however, had not forgotten him and were still listening to and covering his songs, many assuming the artist had long since disappeared. In the spring of 1997, a small English fanzine *Ptolemaic Terrascope* asked him to perform at a benefit concert. Rapp performed his own set along with his son David who has a band of his own. Magic Eye Singles released

For the Dead in Space, a tribute album featuring many who count Rapp among their inspirations. In the end, whether Tom Rapp will be known as a great musician or a great lawyer remains to be seen; perhaps this song will be seen as one and the same.

Selected discography

Morning Song / Drop Out!, ESP Disk, 1967.
I Saw The World / Images Of April, ESP Disk, 1968.
Suzanne / There Was A Man, ESP-Fontana (Holland), 1969.
Rocket Man / The Jeweler, Warner/Reprise, 1970.
Marshall / Why Should I Care?, Blue Thumb, 1972.
Translucent Carriages (alt.) / The Cowboy Who Ate Vietnam / Ring Thing (alt.), Ptolemaic Terrascope, 1993.
One Nation Underground, ESP Disk, 1967.
Balaklava, ESP Disk, 1968.
These Things Too, Warner/Reprise, 1969.
The Use Of Ashes, Warner/Reprise, 1970.
City Of Gold, Warner/Reprise, 1971.
Beautiful Lies, Warner/Reprise, 1971.
Familiar Songs, Warner/Reprise, 1972.
Stardancer, Blue Thumb, 1972.
Sunforest, Blue Thumb, 1973.
Best Of Pearls Before Swine, Adelphi (2LPs), 1980.
(with various artists*) For the Dead in Space*, (Includes one previously unreleased song by Tom Rapp, "Hopelessly Romantic") Magic Eye Singles, 1997.

Sources

Books

Joynson, Vernon, *Fuzz, Acid, and Flowers: A Comprehensive Guide to American Garage, Psychedelic, and Hippie Rock 1964-1976*, Borderline Productions, 1996.

Periodicals

Goldmine, October 28, 1994
Washington Post, Sunday May 17, 1998
Dirty Linen, Feb/Mar 1994

Online

http://www.allmusic.com, (September 28, 1998).
http://www.terrascope.org, (September 28, 1998).

Additional information was obtained from an interview Tom Rapp in October 1998.

—Jim Powers

Phil Perry

Singer

Vocalist Phil Perry distinguished himself by blending soul with smooth, sophisticated rhythm-and-blues. After Perry's third solo release, *One Heart, One Love*, Atlanta's *Upscale* magazine wrote, "This work solidifies his mastery of the r&b genre What the album (offers) is a smooth sensual sound." This "easy-listening" r&b sound is Perry's trademark, often geared to lovers and the romantic, and reminiscent of legendary r&b vocalist Al Green. Perry pays homage to Green in *One Heart, One Love* by creating a medley of classical songs from Green's repertoire. Perry told *Upscale* magazine, "All too often, legendary performers retire before we (as artists) get to say 'thanks' this is my way of showing my appreciation for Green and his music." Perry's approach is firmly rooted in gospel, accessible, and thoroughly romantic. He is also noted for having worked as a session singer with Quincy Jones, Barbra Streisand, Patti LaBelle, and Lee Ritenour.

Perry was raised singing gospel music in his local church in East St. Louis. He branched out into r&b by joining a local vocal group called the Montclairs, and they recorded two albums, generating hits such as "Dreamin' Out of Season," and "Make Up for Lost Time". They also toured with the high-profile artists Rufus & Chaka Kahn, The Ohio Players, and The Miracles. In 1979 Perry and fellow Montclairs member Kevin Sanlin joined forces to record two albums for Capitol Records

but the duo disbanded after only the two releases and Perry began working as a background vocalist in Los Angeles. He worked primarily at local clubs as a vocalist for lauded guitarist Lee Ritenour. His reputation as a superb vocalist prompted friend and singer James Ingram to introduce Perry to composer Quincy Jones. Through his connection with Jones, Perry began to work with a wide array of musicians, including composer Michel Colombier, George Duke, Sergio Mendes, Barbra Streisand, and Patti LaBelle, which boosted his reputation, provided useful contacts, and broadened his musical horizons. Perry was featured on the soundtrack for the comic-romance film *Arthur II*, and he began to tour globally around 1988. He performed in Japan, the Pacific Rim, Europe, and Brazil.

Perry attended a Hollywood Bowl concert with Ritenour and executives from Capitol Records. The executives heard Perry's demo tape and the result was the debut solo release, *The Heart of The Man* in 1989. The album was a consistent seller and its single, "Call Me," topped the r&b charts. Perry's emotional, deft cover of Aretha Franklin's "Call Me" led to performances across the country, several with saxophonist Dave Koz. By 1995, Perry had toured again in Southeast Asia, contributed to *The Benoit/Freeman Project* for GRP Records, and had contributed to the group Fourplay's gold-selling release, *Between the Sheets* for Warner Brothers.

Performances with the GRP record label co-founder Dave Grusin and his brother Don resulted in Perry switching labels and releasing *Pure Pleasure* in 1994. *Pure Pleasure* contained the hit singles "If You Only Knew," a cover of Patti LaBelle's 1984 hit, and "Love Don't Love Nobody". Perry then made his seventh trip to Indonesia, toured Malaysia, Japan, and other Pacific Rim countries with Ramsey Lewis, and performed in the Caribbean and The Bahamas. Perry released *One Heart, One Love* in 1998. His vision for the record was that it would sound distinct and that he would maintain his unique vocal stylings. *Upscale* wrote of *One Heart, One Love*, "Perry again enters the music scene with another album based purely on the soulful power of good r&b music."

Perry's third solo release marked his debut for Peak Records and the Windham Hill Group. *One Heart, One Love* featured an array of romantic R&B ballads, smooth singles, and soulful jams: "Pretty Lady" was reminiscent of a quiet storm, "Do What Comes Natural" was upbeat and inspiring, and "Mind Blowah", which features the group Portrait on background vocals, was infectious and provocative. The deep soulfulness of the single "Sorry" underscored the pervasively moody-yet-rhythmic tone of the release. Perry's wife Lillian was

Born in East St. Louis, MO.

Sang in church choirs throughout his childhood; branched out into R&B by joining a local vocal group called the Montclairs and recorded two albums, generated hits such as "Dreamin' Out of Season," and "Make Up for Lost Time"; band toured with high-profile artists Rufus & Chaka Kahn, The Ohio Players, and The Miracles; Perry and fellow Montclairs member Kevin Sanlin joined forces to record two albums for Capitol Records, 1979, duo disbanded after two releases; began working as a background vocalist in Los Angeles, 1980; worked primarily at local clubs as a vocalist for guitarist Lee Ritenour; friend and singer James Ingram introduced Perry to composer Quincy Jones, which led to work with a wide array of musicians, including composer Michel Colombier, George Duke, Sergio Mendes, Barbra Streisand, and Patti LaBelle; featured on the soundtrack for the comic-romance film *Arthur11*; released debut solo, *The Heart of The Man*, 1989; its single, "Call Me," topped the R&B charts; contributed to *The Benoit/Freeman Project* for GRP Records, 1994; contributed to the group Fourplay's gold-selling release, *Between the Sheets* for Warner Brothers, 1994; released *Pure Pleasure*, 1994; *One Heart, One Love*, 1998.

Addresses: *Record company*—The Windham Hill Group, 8750 Wilshire Boulevard, Beverly Hills, CA 90211-2713; (310) 368-4800, fax (310) 358-4501.

reggae beats, or guest appearances from the realm of alternative, hip-hop or rap music.

The messages found in Perry's music stem from traditional, timeless themes such as love, deeply committed relationships, and the importance of spending quality time with those you love. As a result, Perry developed a reputation as an r&b vocalist for lovers, and it's a reputation he cherishes. Perry was particularly inspired by Al Green, a vocalist with roots in gospel music, and also a vocalist devoted to romance and positive messages in his material. Like Al Green, Perry uses his natural interpretive skills to create a musical mood, to convey an emotion, and tell a riveting story. Perry is also noted for replacing vocal grandstanding with genuine feeling. Perry collaborated with Nick Caldwell of The Whispers for his third release. He's also collaborated with George Duke, Magic, Grady Wilkins, Rickey Smith, and singer/songwriter Gary Brown. *One Heart, One Love* reached number five on the *Billboard* Contemporary Jazz chart for the week ending May1, 1998 and his single, "One Heart, One Love," reached number five on the same chart in July of 1998. Perry is devoted to the notion that relationships should be deep, fulfilling, and timeless—much like his music.

Selected discography

The Heart of A Man, Capital Records, 1989.
Pure Pleasure, (includes single "If only you knew"), GRP Records, 1994.
"Love don't love anybody," GRP, 1994
One Heart, One Love, The Windham Hill Group, 1998.

Sources

Periodicals

Upscale (Atlanta, GA), May 1998.

Online

"Entertainment News: The R&B Page," http://www.rbpage.com/news07-25.html
"Galactica Tracks," http://www.galactica.it/101/black/tlvdntl.html
"The 1998 Kansas City Blues & Jazz Festival," http://www.kcbluesjazz.org
"Windham Hill: Phil Perry: *One Heart, One Love*," http://windham.com/recordings/01005-82163-2.html

—*B. Kimberly Taylor*

featured in a duet in "Do Not Disturb." The single "We Belong Together" and "Hold On With Your Heart" were both dedicated to her.

Perry attempted to combine the playful with the soulful, the solemn with the upbeat, and the romantic with the rhythmic on *One Heart, One Love*, and succeeded. *Upscale* magazine noted that Perry spent nearly two decades singing on numerous records, and asked him if he ever considered changing his style to please a wider audience. He responded with, "I'm not changing my style, I'm still doing romantic music. There may not be much of a market for real traditional r&b anymore, but that's what I do best. I'm thankful that I have built an audience with my previous records." As a result, Perry's albums have not featured special remixes, hip-hop or

Quasi

Rock band

Along with groups like Built To Spill, Harvey Danger, and Sleater-Kinney, Quasi is part of what the Village Voice calls the "Fabulous Sounds of the Pacific Northwest." Quasi is an unusual combination in rock music. This experimental rock duo of guitarist and roxichord player Sam Coomes and his ex-wife, drummer Janet Weiss, has attracted a variety of listeners although they have only three releases. The roxichord can best be described as a kind of cheap harpsichord sound, which Coomes electronically augments with some distorted overdrive. The duo also like to add strange electronic sounds and noises to the mix, such as video game bleeps, recorded chirping of birds, boats, and robots. The lyrical content is dark and moody, exploring the depths of male-female relationships to the background of catchy uptempo pop music with a weird, quirky offbeat edge.

Back in the 1980s, Sam Coomes was the frontman for San Francisco's Donner Party. The band released two albums. The first album had a punk sound with lyrics about getting lost in New Jersey, and the general ups and downs of life in the modern world. His lyrical tone was dark and obsessive even in those days. He seemed to be unaware at times of the revolting shock value of some of his songs. The second Donner Party album had a Coomes' song with the title: "When You Die Your Eyes Pop Out." Shortly after their second album, Coomes

moved to Portland, Oregon. It was here that he met and married Janet Weiss. He would still work with Heatmiser's Elliot Smith occasionally, as would Weiss.

The other half of Quasi, drummer Janet Weiss, who ironically shares the name of the clean-cut preppie girl in the *Rocky Horror Picture Show,* was born in Hollywood, California. Music was her first love and Janet tried various instruments, hoping to find the one that best suited her personality. She decided on the drums, because she enjoyed the combination of rhythm and melody. "Besides, it was just fun," she told *Drummergirl's* Chaia Milstein, "a lot of fun, and I kind of felt that I was good at them, which always helps to keep you interested." Soon, Weiss developed a powerful talent at percussion and became a dedicated, hard-working performer. She had moderate success finding work and even auditioned once for the Lemonheads.

While she found the fellow musicians and audiences of the San Francisco club scene supportive, she didn't find the same kind of support among club owners. "Things changed when I got asked to go on tour with a band," she explained to Milstein. "I had never played a sit-down (drum) kit before, and I had about two weeks to decide. I got their record and kind of tried to figure out most of the basic beats. I just went for it. I went on tour and was forced to play every night, which helped me get better out of fear of embarrassment."

Touring was a great educational experience for Weiss. It was where she honed her drumming skills. One day she heard a classified ad for a drummer and soon found herself drumming for the hard rocking Sleater-Kinney band. Eventually, she crossed paths with Sam Coomes.

While Weiss went on playing drums for Sleater-Kinney, she also began an acquaintanceship with Commes as they began experimenting with sounds. They began rehearsing in the basement, making amateur tapes on inferior recording equipment. They continued in their music, but Coomes still had to maintain his day job. In various interviews, he has spoken about having to spend three years working in a Kinko's copy shop just to pay the bills. Weiss held a number of low-paying physically draining jobs as well.

In 1992, Coomes talked to Weiss about forming a professional group. They named it Motorgoat and began working with a revolving door of musicians. "Sam and I used to play with this guy named Brad in a group named Motorgoat," Weiss told Milstein. "But then Brad kind of moved back to San Francisco, and Sam and I decided that we would play as a two-piece. We had

For the Record . . .

Members include **Sam Coomes**, guitar, Roxi chord, vocals; **Janet Weiss**, (born in Hollywood, CA), drums, vocals; Coomes and Weiss married, divorced 1995.

Weiss and Coomes formed the group Motorgoat, changed name to Quasi, 1992; went through a revolving door of band members until just the pair remained; released first album *Early Recordings*, Key Op label, 1995; an unusual arrangement existed where Weiss played in two bands at the same time, played and recorded in Quasi with Coomes while at the same time played for the Sleater-Kinney band; Quasi signed on with Up Records; released second album *R&B Transmogrification*, 1997; released *Featuring "Birds,"* 1998.

Addresses: *Record company*—Up Records, P.O. Box 21328, Seattle, WA 98111-3328.

already done a lot of recording at home, so we started playing as a two-piece and adding our friends to play with us at shows, and we would learn the songs."

After changing their band's name to Quasi, they released their first album, *Early Recordings*. *Early Recordings* was self-produced and self-released and is an uneven work which documents the couple's emotionally disturbing divorce. Coomes expresses his pain sharply enough, but Weiss also vents her own demons, even to the point of self-mockery with songs like "I Never Want To See You Again", "The Poisoned Well,", and "Nothing From Nothing." From listening to the melody patterns, it easy to see that both Coomes and Weiss' musical influences include not only Sid Vicious but Lennon-McCartney as well.

However, as things were progressing musically, there were personal troubles in the Coomes-Weiss marriage. These problems escalated until the inevitable occurred. The couple divorced in 1995. Coomes explained how they could still work so closely together in the midst of their personal turmoil. "There were many awkward moments. There were many times when it wasn't very comfortable. But it's hard to find someone to play music with that works out good. You know self-interest can gather much strength. It's amazing how much self-interest can override any kind of other considerations if

you let it." Weiss adds, "The music also stayed good." You know it's odd. Our music (together) was just starting to get good when we split apart. It would have been a shame to dump it right there so we tried to just split that off from whatever feelings we had and for the most part it worked out."

Their second released was titled *R&B Transmorgification*. The album explored the theme and explanation of Coomes's divorce to Weiss. "There's not much of a tradition in pop music of dealing with these social issues," Coomes explained to Kristy Ojala of *The Stranger*. "The perennial themes are love and death. It'll eventually devolve back to that."

They started working in a Washington state recording facility called Jackpot Studio for their next two releases. Quasi's third album, *Featuring "Birds"* was released in 1998 and is perhaps their most all-round commercial effort to date. They decided on the bird theme because of Coomes' obsession with birds. The title of the album is a reference to one of the tracks, an 81-second interlude taken from an Audubon Society field recording. Besides its top recording quality, the production values here are their most professional to date. This album was a special delight for Coomes and Weiss because it marks the first time they had 16 tracks on the album instead of the eight tracks of previous efforts.

The lyrics concentrated on the pain the average blue collar worker struggles with as he or she is forced to work like slaves at mind numbing jobs. "The work oriented songs on this record are actually older songs, from when I worked at Kinko's over a three-year period," Coomes told Ojala. "It definitely was a source of those kinds of ideas, watching the company tighten and clamp down on workers such as myself."

"Quasi has been functioning more like a conventional band now for quite some time," Coomes told the *CMJ New Music Report*. "But if we felt like taking a different approach to things—experimenting with formats in performance or recording—we could do so more easily than most "band" bands. So, I'm reluctant to characterize Quasi strictly as a conventional type band."

Their performances are controversial. A recent show at a club called Satyricon found a musically charged Coomes and Weiss stripping down to their underwear as Coomes started assaulting his roxichord and Weiss kept the beat on her drum kit. Because of this kind of and similar grandstanding, Quasi began getting a reputation as one of the Pacific Northwest's most explosive, offbeat rock acts. "You know the song is dead when you're playing it and thinking, 'I'm kinda hungry.

I think I saw a burrito place down the street," said Coomes.

"If it's all going well, you're not thinking too much," Weiss explained to Richard Martin of *Willamette Week*. "The main difference is that we recorded in one chunk of time, spending almost every day for three weeks together, recording, working on music with few distractions. In the past, because we've done it at home, we could spend however much time we needed, and it tended to stretch out and be less focused."

"We have more resources," adds Coomes, making reference to Quasi's contract with Up Records in Seattle. "This is the first time anybody's ever given us money to make music." Coomes also explained that he is concentrating more on the thematic aspects of his work. He's also trying to better arrange the tracks in order to have a tighter rein on the "man vs. machine, man vs. woman, man vs. death motifs" which he speaks about. Currently, Coomes and Weiss still will collaborate when possible. Coomes frequently fills in on bass for Heatmiser. Weiss continues to drum for the group Sleater-Kinney.

Selected discography

Early Recordings, Key Op Records, April, 1996.
R&B Transmorgrification, Up Records, March, 1997.
Featuring "Birds," Up Records, 1997.

Sources

The Boston Phoenix, August 1. 1998.
CMJN Music Report, April 13, 1998.
Drummer Girl Magazine.
The Stranger, April-May 1998.
Willamette Week.
Village Voice, June 16, 1998.

—*Timothy Kevin Perry*

Queen Latifah

Rapper, actress, producer

During the late 1980s, Queen Latifah emerged as one of the most significant artists to enter the scene of rap recording and earned a reputation as one of the most vital female artists of the following decade. In a recording media characterized by the belligerence of the gangster culture, Queen Latifah established herself as a pillar of female strength and developed a reputation as a role model for her generation.

Queen Latifah was born Dana Owens on March 18, 1970 in Newark, New Jersey. Her parents, Lance and Rita Owens, separated in 1978. After the breakup, Latifah lived in High Court in East Newark with her mother, a schoolteacher. She also maintained ties with her father, a police officer. At age eight, she was dubbed Latifah—from the Arabic for delicate and sensitive—by one of her cousins of Muslim background. Owens embellished her nickname with the "Queen" appellation on her own.

The intellectually gifted Latifah first began singing in the choir at Shiloh Baptist Church in Bloomfield, New Jersey. She added popular music, especially rap, to her

Photo by Yukio Gion. AP/Wide World Photo. Reproduced by permission.

For the Record . . .

Born Dana Owens on March 18, 1970, in Newark, NJ; daughter of Lance, a police officer, and Rita Owens, a teacher. *Education:* Attended Borough of Manhattan Community College.

Released first rap single, "Wrath of My Madness"/ "Princess of the Posse," 1988, Tommy Boy Music; European tour and appearance at the Apollo Theater, 1989; released first album, *All Hail the Queen,* 1989; other releases include, *Nature of a Sista,* Tommy Boy Music, 1991; *Black Reign,* Motown, 1993; *Order in the Court* (includes "Bananas), Motown, 1998; CEO of Flavor Unit Entertainment Company (recording management).

Awards: Best New Artist, New Music Seminar of Manhattan; 1990, *Soul Train Music Awards,* Sammy Davis, Jr. Award for Entertainer of the Year, 1995. Grammy Award, Best Rap Solo Performance, 1995.

Addresses: *Record company*—Motown Records, Publicity & Media Relations, 825 8th Ave. 28th floor, New York, NY 10019.

repertoire around the time she entered Irvington High School, where she also played power forward on her school's championship basketball team.

Latifah's love of rap inspired her to form a group called Ladies Fresh along with two of her friends, Tangy B and Landy D. The trio sang in talent shows and made other appearances. They eventually changed their name to Flavor Unit. The three young rappers attracted the interest of a local disc jockey and basement record producer named Mark James, which led to a contract for Latifah's with Tommy Boy Music in 1988. Tommy Boy released Latifah's first single, "Wrath of My Madness," and the record proved highly successful. By the time Latifah graduated Irvington High School and entered Borough of Manhattan Community College, her first two single releases already had sold 40,000 copies.

In 1989, Latifah undertook a European tour and released her first album, *All Hail the Queen,* a diverse collection combining hip-hop, reggae, and jazz. The album espoused a number of socio-cultural themes including apartheid, women's rights, and poverty. *All Hail the*

Queen sold over one million copies. During the early days of her career Latifah always sported her trademark queen's crown, wearing it at all public appearances.

In 1993, she released her first album on Motown, *Black Reign,* dedicated to the memory of her late brother, Lance Latifah, Jr. A police officer like his father, he was killed tragically in a motorcycle accident in 1992. The incident, by Latifah's own admission, left her devastated and, in 1993, she was harshly criticized for producing Apache's "Gangsta Bitch" release. She defended herself in classic rap rhetoric and argued that the music reflects reality and creates neither the situations nor the problems. Yet by the mid-1990s Latifah developed an association with an informal consciousness raising rap network, the Native Tongues, involving such groups as the Jungle Brothers, De La Soul, and Tribe Called Quest. The Native Tongues maintained an outspoken stance against violence—especially in rap.

In 1997, Latifah released her second album with Motown, *Order in the Court.* The album included the hit single "Bananas," with Apache. "Bananas" was listed on *Billboard*'s Best in August of 1998. Despite her youth, Latifah showed prudence and invested her earnings from early record sales. Soon she established herself as an entertainer, and as an entrepreneur as chief executive officer of Flavor Unit Management. Latifah owns the recording management firm in Jersey City, along with a partner, Shakim Compere. With Motown Records as a distribution channel, Flavor Unit Management has managed a number of rap artists and groups.

Acting Career

After achieving major success as a rapper, Latifah gained similar notoriety as an actress, mainly through her own hit television show, *Living Single. Living Single* aired for five years on the Fox Network, beginning in 1993. Although she found it necessary to live much of the year in Los Angeles, during the taping of the show, Latifah maintained a home in Wayne, New Jersey, and never ceased to consider New Jersey her home. Latifah also appeared on Fox's "Smart Kids" in December of 1994, a program to encourage and empower contemporary youth.

Among Latifah's early movies, *House Party 2* was released in 1991 and featured Martin Lawrence. While *House Party 2* was widely panned, she received wide acclaim for her role as Cleo Sims, a tough lesbian bank robber, in the film *Set It Off,* with Vivica A. Fox. Latifah also recorded with Organized Noize for the title sound track of the picture. It was the controversial nature of the role of Cleo Sims, however, that left the public-at-large to speculate impertinently about Latifah's real-life sexuality. Latifah rebuked the invaders of her privacy with a sound determination to keep such personal matters private, asserting that details of her sexuality would never be of anyone's concern but her own.

Latifah's work as an actress runs the gamut of critical approval from an artistic standpoint. Her acting talents inevitably are praised, even when a movie or an album is panned. In September of 1994 she appeared on NBC's *Met Life Presents the Apollo Theatre Hall of Fame*, and as a presenter at the 1994 Essence Awards. In 1997, she had a small role in the film "Hoodlum," the story of Ellsworth "Bumpy" Johnson, an Harlem gangster from the depression era. In February of 1998, she starred in Warner Brothers' *Sphere* with Dustin Hoffman and Sharon Stone.

Honors and Awards

In 1990, Latifah won an award as Best New Artist from the New Music Seminar of Manhattan. In April of 1994, she was nominated as solo artist of the year in the First Annual *Source* Hip-Hop Awards. Although she lost the award to Snoop Doggy Dogg, she came back in March of 1995 to win a Grammy award for Best Rap Solo Performance. Also in 1995, at the *Soul Train Music Awards* she won the Sammy Davis, Jr. Award for Entertainer of the Year. Latifah performed at the American Music Awards in January of 1995, and in January of 1997 she was nominated for two Image Awards,

including Best Actress in a Motion Picture for her role in *Set It Off*.

Although she is a hero of feminists in particular, she prefers to not be labeled. She believes in making some compromises, but not in the sacrifice of self worth for money. Latifah cultivates varied interests. Her associates include many prominent personalities. In 1997, she undertook to write a book about self-esteem, for publication by William Morrow and Company.

Selected discography

Singles

"Wrath of My Madness," Tommy Boy Music, 1988.
"Dance for Me,"/ Tommy Boy Music.

Albums

All Hail the Queen, Tommy Boy Music, 1989.
Nature of a Sista, Tommy Boy Music, 1991.
Black Reign, Motown, 1993.
Order in the Court (includes "Bananas), Motown, 1998.

Sources

Entertainment, September 4 1992.
Essence, May 1, 1995.
New York Beacon, March 26 1997.
Source, August 1998.

—Gloria Cooksey

Eddie Rabbitt

Singer, songwriter

Singer/songwriter Eddie Rabbitt, a New Jersey boy with a soft heart, smooth voice, and the talent to create uplifting melodies, pioneered the expansion of country music onto the pop charts. Both country and pop music fans loved Rabbitt's no nonsense style of songwriting and made Rabbitt a superstar with 26 number one country hits and eight Top 40 pop hits. This crossover success was unheard of in 1980, but with such hits as "I Love A Rainy Night," "Drivin' My Life Away," "I Just Want to Love You," and "Step by Step," Rabbit became a crossover country/pop music pioneer.

Eddie Rabbitt was born Edward Thomas on November 27, 1941 in Brooklyn, New York. His parents, Irish immigrants, soon moved to Orange County, New Jersey where Rabbitt's father worked days as a refrigeration engineer in an oil refinery, and played fiddle and accordion nights at New York City dance halls. Rabbitt followed in his father's musical footsteps and learned to play the guitar at 12. He also quit school at 16—later passing an equivalency exam. His mother Mae told *People* that Eddie, "was never one for school. His head was too full of music." In the late 1950s, Rabbitt, like his father, picked up a day job as a mental hospital attendant before landing a nightly singing gig at the Six Steps Down club in East Orange, New Jersey. In 1964, Rabbitt signed his first recording contract with 20th Century Records and released his first single, "Next to the Note" backed with "Six Nights & Seven Days". However, for the next four years, fame and fortune alluded Rabbitt.

In 1968, Rabbitt, as noted in his online biography, hopped a bus to Nashville, Tennessee with "$1,000 in his pocket and no music business contacts." He told *People*'s Tim Allis that he soon realized "[that] singers were a dime a dozen [in Nashville]. But there weren't a lot of good songs." Hoping to fill that void, Rabbitt began writing his own songs, and on his first night in Nashville penned "Working My Way Up to the Bottom." Grand Ole Opry artist, Roy Drusky, recorded the song in 1968. Success would not be overnight, and Rabbitt was forced to work a variety of odd jobs including truck driver, soda jerk, and fruit picker to survive. Yet, Rabbitt continued writing and knocking on record and publishing company doors. A door finally opened for Rabbitt at the Hill & Range Publishing Company where he was hired as a staff writer with a weekly salary of $37.50.

Jewel in the King's Crown

With a little help from the King of Rock and Roll, Elvis Presley, Rabbitt finally hit it big in 1970. Presley recorded Rabbitt's song, "Kentucky Rain," which became his fiftieth gold record. For Rabbitt, this song, as noted in Contemporary Musicians, Volume 5, "showed the earmarks of future Rabbitt hits—it had country emotions interwoven with a pop melody—and it suggested the young songwriter might be a candidate for crossover success." Yet, Rabbitt told People that he credited his Irish roots for his emotion and inspiration, "Country music is Irish music. Appalachian music was brought over by the Scotch and Irish. I think the minor chords in my music give it that mystical feel." Rabbitt later shared this mystical feel with the world by recording "Song of Ireland"—an Irish jig-like tune with lyrics reflecting Rabbitt's love of the Emerald Isle with its "shamrock hills and 40 shades of green."

In 1974, Rabbitt wrote another hit, "Pure Love," this time for country star Ronnie Milsap. The song was Milsap's first number one single, and Elektra Records, seeing Rabbitt's potential for hit-making records, signed him to a recording contract. In 1976, Rabbitt not only scored a number one single, "Drinkin' My Baby (Off My Mind)," but he also married, as he told People, "a little thing about 5 foot tall, with long, black beautiful hair, and real pretty face. She looked like an angel to me."

Cross-Over Hit Maker

In the late 1970s, Rabbitt became a top ten single writing and recording machine with a string of number one hits including, "Rocky Mountain Music," "Two Dollars in the Jukebox," "Drivin' My Life Away," and "I Just Want to Love You". In 1977, the Academy of Country Music named Rabbitt the Top Male Vocalist of the Year. In 1979, Rabbitt hopped over to the pop music charts with the theme to Clint Eastwood's movie, Every Which Way But Loose. Yet Rabbitt kept a foot in country music and was named Music City News Country Songwriter of the Year. Rabbitt's popularity in both country and pop music not only grew, as noted by Alanna Nash in Entertainment Weekly, but "his blend of feel-good melodies, jangly rhythms, and tight vocal harmonies [also] helped usher in the urban cowboy era of the '80s."

In 1980, BMI named Rabbitt's song, "Suspicions" as their Song of the Year, and Rabbitt amazingly topped both the pop and country charts with his smash hit, "I Love A Rainy Night." Yet Rabbitt, as quoted by Tony Russel in The Guardian, never thought about crossing over, "I came to Nashville with nothing in mind about pop music. I was country and it just so happened that the kind of music I was making crossed over to the pop charts." In 1982, Rabbitt crossed over again with "You & I," a duet with Crystal Gayle, and after signing with RCA, scored another number one country hit duet, "Both to Each Other," with Juice Newton. However, one year later Rabbitt disappeared.

Backed Out and Came Back

In 1983, with the birth of his second child, Timmy, Rabbitt stepped out of the country and pop music spotlight. Rabbitt backed out because Timmy was born with biliary atresia, a disease that attacks the liver. Timmy's only chance of survival was a liver transplant. So Rabbitt, "against the advice of his manager, mothballed his career to stay near his son," wrote Allis. Rabbitt felt he had "to be there if I'm any kind of man." Sadly, in 1985, after an unsuccessful liver transplant, Timmy died. Rabbitt told Allis that Timmy's death took "the cockiness out of [my] walk."

In 1989, Rabbitt released the album *I Wanna Dance With You*. In the early 1990s, after short recording contracts with Universal and Capitol, Rabbitt released two albums: *Jersey Boy* and *Ten Rounds*. However, Rabbitt left Capitol in 1992 to focus on touring with his band, Hare Trigger. Rabbitt, as stated in *Contemporary Musicians, Volume 5*, had "become a wholesome performer without sacrificing his popular offbeat sexiness." Rabbitt himself commented, "I don't ever get down and dirty. I think the stage is no place for that. I think you have to be very careful as an entertainer about what you bring to the stage because some people try to think of you as more than human. I figure if we're going to be role models for people, we should at least try to be good role models."

Beatin' the Odds

In the late 1990s, Rabbitt became a role model off stage by becoming a spokesperson for many charities including Special Olympics, Easter Seals, and the American Council on Transplantation. In 1996, Rabbitt was once again noted for his musical contributions when BMI honored Rabbitt with their Three Million-Air award for "I Love A Rainy Night" and Two Million-Air award for "Kentucky Rain". Moreover, Presidential candidate Bob Dole adopted Rabbitt's song, "American Boy" for his campaign song. But it was the release of *Welcome to Rabbittland*, Rabbitt's first children's album that was his dream come true.

January of 1997 brought both good and bad news to Rabbitt. He signed a new recording contract with Intersound Records, but soon after that he was diagnosed with lung cancer. After completing his first round of chemotherapy and just four days before surgery to remove part of his left lung, Rabbitt released a new album, *Beatin' the Odds*. While recuperating, Rabbitt

began working on his second children's album, *Songs from Rabbitt Land*. Rabbitt described the album to Diane Samms Rush of *The Milwaukee Journal Sentinel*, as "17 songs, jokes, and stories I wrote for my kids as they were growing up.... Who knows? The rest of my career I might be known as Mister Wabbitt!"

Rabbitt once stated, "We all have to dance with our devils, but I lead." Rabbitt, however, could not beat the odds against one of life's cruelest devils, succumbing to cancer on May 7, 1998 at the age of 56. Yet, Rabbitt not only danced with many devils—the rough road to success, the sad death of his son, the hard struggle for a musical comeback, and cancer—he also lead country music to its now common, crossover pop chart success.

Selected discography

Eddie Rabbitt, Elektra.
Rocky Mountain Music, Electra.
I Wanna Dance With You, RCA, 1989.
Greatest Hits of Eddie Rabbitt, RCA.
Jersey Boy, Capitol.
Welcome to Rabbittland, Intersound, 1997.
Beatin' the Odds, Intersound, 1997.

Sources

Books

LaBlanc, Michael, ed.,*Contemporary Musicians, Volume 5*, Gale Research, 1991.

Periodicals

Entertainment Weekly, June 22, 1998.
The Guardian, May 22, 1998, p. 22.
Milwaukee Journal Sentinel, October 10, 1997, p. 7; May 9, 1998, p. 6.
People, April 17, 1989; May 25, 1998.

Online

www.country.com

—Ann M. Schwalboski

Radiohead

Alternative rock band

Arty English rockers Radiohead have found themselves starring in one the most unusual success stories in alternative music. Dismissed as one-hit wonders for their unexpected 1993 hit "Creep," in subsequent years the band slowly accrued critical adoration and a devoted cult following; by late 1997, their third album, *OK Computer,* appeared on year-end lists of one of the most outstanding releases of the year in publications as diverse as *People* and the *Village Voice.*

"This is one of the few bands in recent years to surf a brief wave of post-Nirvana success in the early `90s, watch it die and then paddle out again in search of the big one," wrote *Rolling Stone*'s Matt Hendrickson of Radiohead. Much of the group and its musical persona is centered upon lead singer Thom Yorke. Born in 1968 and once described as a cross between onetime Sex Pistol Johnny Lydon and comic actor Martin Short, the gaunt, orange-haired Yorke grew up in both Scotland and Oxford, England. He also spent time at a boys' boarding school, institutions that are somewhat notorious in the British Isles for their sadistic atmosphere.

Photo by Tom Sheehan. EMI Ltd. Reproduced by permission.

called themselves Radiohead, borrowing the name from a Talking Heads song.

Radiohead quickly became a fixture on the Oxford club scene. Most bands in the British Isles, after some hometown success, head to London to play what is called "showcase" gigs in the city's thriving club scene; the venues in London are frequented by Artist and Repretoire (A&R) people from labels looking for new acts to sign. Radiohead refused advice to play London and stubbornly stayed put; buzz about them and their sound grew so loud that at one Oxford gig, thirty record-industry people from London were in attendance. Later in 1991, they signed to Parlophone, part of the EMI family, who put them on tour. They played a hundred shows around Britain in 1992. They also headed into the studio to record their debut album, *Pablo Honey*. The album was released in the United States in 1993 and went gold only because of the success of "Creep," a wry homage to Yorke's personal demons. "I wish I was special," he laments in its chorus. "I don't belong here." He later tired of interviews that wanted to discuss the song and his self-esteem. "Self-loathing is something we can all relate to," guitarist Ed O'Brien explained to *Billboard*'s David Sprague about the impetus for the song. "Every day, we see people who are better-looking or richer or more worthy than we feel."

The Bends a Critical Success

The other tracks from *Pablo Honey,* when released as subsequent singles, failed to make a similar impact on the American modern-rock charts and, by the time of their 1995 release, *The Bends,* few were expecting a repeat of "Creep." Though it sold nowhere near as many copies as their debut, *The Bends* established them as a solid, lyrical force. "Alternately quivering with heart-rending insecurity and self-deprecating anguish," wrote *Rolling Stone*'s Jon Wiederhorn, the record "is an emotional seesaw that never remains balanced." Singles such as the title track and "Fake Plastic Trees" hit a good nerve with music-industry insiders, and the alternative press penned homages to Radiohead and their record that were almost unanimous in approval. Wiederhorn called *The Bends* "dynamic and passionate," granting that it was a bit less accessible than their debut, but termed it an "amalgam of experimental noise and meditative beauty."

That same year, Radiohead was paired as an opening act for R.E.M., a contact that made a profound influence on the way they would handle their creative/business career from then on. They also opened for Alanis Morissette during 1996, which presumably made less of

Yorke was thin, suffered from a lazy eye, and was often pummeled. His father, an industrial salesman, had once been a champion boxer, and had tried to teach Yorke the sport, but usually succeeded only in flattening him. These traumas of his youth led Yorke to form his first band around the age of ten, in which he played guitar while a friend destroyed television sets. But later, at the detestable boarding school, he taught himself to sing in the rehearsal rooms there.

It was also at school that he met fellow boarder Colin Greenwood. The duo formed a punk band called TNT before graduation. Back in Oxford, Yorke and Greenwood put together another band called On a Friday" in 1987 with friends Ed O'Brien and Phil Selway. At their first gig, Colin's younger brother Jonny sat near the stage with his harmonica until he was finally invited on stage. The band dissolved a short while later after most members departed to different universities in England. Yorke studied English literature at Exeter University, where he became politically active in the anti-fascist movement, which once again made him an easy target for battery. In 1991, he found himself back in Oxford and reassembled his friends once more; this time they

an impact but gave them great exposure. The band returned to England to record a third album, much of which was done in a gothic manse near Bath that actress Jane Seymour often rents out to bands for extended stays. "Everyone said, `You'll sell six or seven million if you bring out *The Bends, Part 2*,'" O'Brien recounted to *Rolling Stone*'s Hendrickson. "And we're like, `Yeah, right.' But we're *not* going to do that. The one thing you don't want to say to us is what we *should* do, because we'll kick against that and do exactly the opposite."

Near-Unanimous Accolades

When *OK Computer* was finished, their record company did an unusual and expensive publicity stunt to promote it: an advance cassette was glued into a Walkman and sent out to critics. It was an almost unnecessary act, though: the music press frothed over it. *Entertainment Weekly* named it "Album of the Year" for 1997, as did numerous other year-end polls and lists, and its music critic David Browne called it a "subtly resplendent opus.... No other piece of music this year so eloquently captured fin de siecle wariness." Eric Weisbard of the *Village Voice* compared Radiohead to Pink Floyd, as had some other critics, and wrote that "the sounds on *OK Computer* ... range from twinkly-tone steely guitar lullabies to jarring crash landings, often within the same number," and lauded it for the "gorgeous mood of elegy that takes over toward the close."

Hendrickson, writing in *Rolling Stone,* found *OK Computer* "a glorious piece of moody, spaced-out art-rock madness," and his magazine named Radiohead Band of the Year, as did its competitor *Spin* magazine. The latter's Pat Blashill described *OK Computer* as "full of spindly guitars and freaked-out noise, poppy songs with Beatles in-jokes and other numbers that ramble on for minutes before they actually become songs, and it's especially full of mystery. Nothing is explained, everything is suggested." The band said influences for some of the bizarre tunes—"Subterranean Homesick Alien" and "Karma Police" among their titles—ranged from Miles Davis to seventies-era German experimentalist rockers Faust to overblown Genesis albums they despised.

The Lovable Creep

Yorke seemed more comfortable handling the press and dumb interview questions after a few years' experience. Indeed, some have noted that the real impetus behind Radiohead and its unusual, though accessible, music,

has its origins in the frontman's cantankerous persona. "A self-described perfectionist and control freak, Yorke is also a moody codger," wrote Hendrickson. "It is this unpredictability that drives his band mates, who feed off the singer's mania and channel it into an explosive, complex and melodic mix of guitar rock and electronics." The rest of the band have also won critical recognition for their musicianship and daring. "Thom writes these songs that sound like a slightly more sinister Elvis Costello," Colin Greenwood told Wiederhorn in *Rolling Stone,* "then I come in and add extra structures and chords to make it more interesting. I have such a low boredom threshold that I need something more than good songs to keep my attention."

In 1998, Radiohead released the mini-EP *Airbag/How Am I Driving?,* the first of which was a single from *OK Computer*. Vehicles and automobile accidents remain somewhat of a songwriting fixation for Yorke. When asked about this and some other previous songs about car crashes, Yorke explained to *Spin*'s Blashill, "I just think that people get up too early to leave houses where they don't want to live to drive to jobs where they don't want to be in one of the most dangerous forms of transport on earth. I've just never gotten used to that." The rest of the band seems to agree. "The record company always wants to send us limos," Colin Greenwood told *Rolling Stone*'s Hendrickson. "I hate them. It's much better to have a van. There's no cachet anymore with limos. What's the point?"

Selected discography

Pablo Honey, Capitol, 1993.
The Bends, Capitol, 1995.
OK Computer, Capitol, 1997.
Airbag/How Am I Driving?, (EP), Capitol, 1998.

Sources

Billboard, May 15, 1993, pp. 17, 20.
Entertainment Weekly, December 26, 1997.
Rolling Stone, September 7, 1995, pp. 19, 21; October 16, 1997, pp. 64-69; January 22, 1998; May 28, 1998, p. 58.
Spin, January 1998, p. 64.
Village Voice, August 26, 1997, p. 63.

Additional information for this profile was provided by Capitol Records publicity materials, 1998.

—*Carol Brennan*

Andrew Rangell

Piano

A legend in his own time, classical pianist Andrew Rangell was praised by music critics for his fresh, contemporary interpretations of Bach, Beethoven, Schoenberg, and even Charles Ives. Born in Chicago in 1948, Rangell was soon uprooted from the midwest when his family moved to Colorado. It was here that he began studying piano as a young child. His parents strongly stressed the value of classical music and the fine arts, so young Rangell was exposed the European classical masters at an early age. He seemed quite receptive and became a diligent student. It is important to note that he comes from one of the most unique musical families in the United States. While some families have one or two celebrities in their family tree, the Rangell family has produced a quartet of powerful and original musical performers.

However, no matter what their musical taste, all of the siblings looked up to their big brother. They all understood the value of the classical training they had received as part of their family tradition. And while Rangell has dabbled in jazz—he released an album of a musical duo fantasy between Bill Evans entitled *Conversations with Bill Evans*—he remained dedicated to providing fresh interpretations of the classics. Rangell's strength was in making old music sound new vibrant, and relevant to contemporary audiences. Rangell's performances were known to cover a wide range of periods in classical music history. As the *New York Times* wrote, "There are so many pianists before the public today that the category, 'atypical pianist' has itself become typical. But Andrew Rangell genuinely stands out, at once free spirited and precise, he has the mark of an original artist. The audience receives his intimate artistry with enthusiasm and gratitude."

As a young man, Rangell attended the prestigious Juilliard School, where he earned a doctoral degree in piano under Beveridge Webster. Some time later, he made his debut in New York as winner of the Malraux Award of the Concert Artists Guild. As his career blossomed, Rangell performed in recitals throughout the United States, with memorable highlights at the Metropolitan Museum of Art, the 92nd Street Y and Columbia's Miller Theater. He made his Boston debut in 1977, where he would play a vital role in that city's musical life. From 1977- 85, he was resident artist and chief piano instructor at Dartmouth College. He was also a regularly occurring guest for a number of New England's prominent performing groups and festivals.

Rangell's repertoire covers a wide range of interests and affinities. He has recorded works taken from many periods in the history of the classics; great works from Bach to Schoenberg to Ives. From 1984-85, he performed as a member of a musical quintet in a series of Bach programs at Boston's Gardner Museum. This included keyboard concertos, the six partitas and the *Goldberg Variations*. Rangell has received critical laurels from many critics and the listening public alike for his work with the *Goldberg Variations,* one of his most well known and admired performances. "Rangell plays his *Goldbergs* with flair and nimbleness (Var. 12, for e.g.)," wrote music critic Freddie Sng, of the J.S. Bach's Home Music Page, "His Bach is entertaining and he is able to hold the listener's interest throughout. No repetition is made at all, but the "Toccato" in F-sharp minor and the two "Ricercares" from the *Musical Offering* compensates for it. A very well and systematic presentation of the sleeve notes comes with this equally superb digital recording."

Rangell's interpretations of the Ives' sonatas are a pleasure to hear as well as being a musically challenging to the intellect. One of the most unique aspects of Rangell's performances was his unconventionality while playing almost sacrosanct classical works. For instance, twenty years ago when he first started playing "The Carillon Nocturne" before audiences he shocked the crowd by whistling the song as he played it, the whole act being perfectly in tune. Rangell is most renown, however, for his interpretations of Beethoven's

Just as Rangell was reaching his creative peak, tragedy struck in 1991. Chronic nerve and muscle problems in his hands forced Rangell to take a temporary retirement. What followed was a trying period of both physical and mental pain for Rangell as he battled the potential crippling effects of the problems that attacked his hands. Yet this temporary rest period ultimately proved to be a most welcome hiatus for Rangell. The time he spent in recuperation seemed only to have made him a stronger, more determined performer than before.

He made a gradual re-emergence onto the stage again as he continued in his therapy. Because of his condition, Rangell had to make certain changes in the way he played. These technical changes lent themselves to the innovative pianist and he continued to play in this manner even after his hands were completely healed. As his strength began returning, he started slowly increasing the public appearances. Richard Dyer of the *Boston Globe* made this observation about Rangell. "One never thought of him as a colorist; but he used articulation and rhythmic manipulation to suggest color. He still does, but there is a wider spectrum now, and color of course isn't there for its own sake but as another manifestation of psychology."

Selected discography

A Recital of Intimate Works, Dorian, 1997.
Bach: The Goldberg Variations, Dorian, 1992.
Beethoven: The Late Piano Sonatas Vol. 1, Dorian, 1992.
Beethoven: The Late Piano Sonatas Vol. 2, Dorian, 1992.

Sources

Periodicals

The Boston Globe, June 9, 1998.

Online

http://www.classicalinsites.com
http://www.classicalinsites.com/live/fountain/recommen/
    rangell/su_rangbio.html

—Timothy Kevin Perry

works. During the 1986-89 seasons, Rangell performed a seven-concert sequence of Beethoven's thirty-two piano sonatas. He also had a memorable appearance at Lincoln Center's Mostly Mozart Festival. Altogether, his recitals throughout the United States have included ten cycles of the complete sequence of Beethoven's 32 sonatas and a five concert series.

The Rankins

Folk group

Music is something The Rankins were born into. Their parents weren't musicians and they don't come from a long line of musically inclined individuals. Yet the seventh generation Scot-Canadian family fivesome has become one of the most-lauded musical acts in Canada by keeping alive their Celtic roots.

Raised in the small town of Mabou, Cape Breton Island, in Iverness County, on the Gulf of St. Lawrence in Nova Scotia, the Rankin kids were raised with Celtic music in their home, shared by 12 Rankin children and their parents, Kathleen (Kaye) and Alexander Rankin. "It's the first music we were exposed to," John Morris Rankin said of their Celtic-hearted sound to *Performing Arts & Entertainment in Canada* in a 1993 story. "Our parents were very influential in that area." Five of the Rankins broke out from the clan as musically talented. Cookie, Heather and Raylene found their places as vocalists, while Jimmy became not only guitarist for the group, but a singer-songwriter, as well. John Morris plays keyboard and fiddle.

They got their start entertaining at family parties and weddings, step dancing and playing a blend of country, pop and Celtic-folk music. Kaye worked for her children's success, driving them to The Rankin Family concerts, selling their early records and tapes from the back of her car and taking care of their ever-growing fan club. They decided to seriously pursue their musical careers in 1989, when they started playing well-received shows on the Canadian folk-festival circuit. John Morris told *Performing Arts & Entertainment in Canada* that they decided to "broaden our audience and hope to make a living." They developed a "repertoire that moves easily from traditional Gaelic ballads, jigs and reels to original songs with a country-rock flavor," observed *Maclean*'s in a 1998 story.

When the English conquered the Scots, clan tartans, the Gaelic language and other Celtic-Scot mainstays were banned. Exodus ensued, and many Scots fled to the Nova Scotia region of Canada. It is estimated that though there were 100,000 Gaelic speakers in the area in the 1800s, only 800 to 1200 were fluent in the language in the late twentieth century, most of those being native to Scotland. The group's use of the near-extinct Gaelic language and traditional fiddle tunes celebrated their heritage and the history of Cape Breton.

The Rankins knew from the start, that the business might be tough for a group with such a traditional sound. "When we started out, we said, 'okay, we're going to sing Gaelic songs'," Cookie told Steen. "We didn't think that we'd get farther than our front doorstep with it, but we thought we'd do it because it's something that we'd learned and personally liked."

They also worked the almost-lost art of step dancing into their act, and it became an audience favorite. "When we travel to folk festivals in Canada, or the US or UK, we're really surprised to find that (the Gaelic) goes over as well as everything else does," John Morris told *Performing Arts & Entertainment in Canada*. "To take it even further, the step dancing always goes over well. A lot of the time, that's what really gets the crowd going."

Their blend of old and new must have been the right one as the Rankins became a huge success in Canada. They played sold-out performances, sold nearly two million albums and earned a number of Junos, the Canadian equivalent to the Grammys. They were unable to reach the same level of success in the United States. Their debut, *The Rankin Family* released in Canada in 1989, was never released in the United States and their subsequent effort, *Fare Thee Well Love*, was quietly released in the United States by Liberty Records. *North Country*, and *Endless Seasons* met similar fates. Their 1998 release, *Uprooted*, was taken over, along with their entire catalog, by the Grapevine label, with the intent to release them in the United States.

The Rankins were lucky to find professionals in the music industry who respected their traditional sound and encouraged it. Their record label, EMI, had ideas

For the Record . . .

Members include **Cookie Rankin**, vocals; **Heather Rankin**, vocals; **Jimmy Rankin**, vocals, guitar; **John Morris Rankin**, piano, fiddle; **Raylene Rankin**, vocals; all born to Kathleen (Kaye) and Alexander (Buddy) Rankin.

Began playing family parties in Mabou, Cape Breton Island, Canada; started playing folk festivals as The Rankin Family, 1989 ; released two independent cassettes; U.S. debut *Fare Thee Well Love*, Capitol, 1992 with; signed to EMI, 1992; released *North Country*, 1994; *Endless Seasons*, 1996; *Uprooted*, 1998; became The Rankins in 1998.

Awards: Canadian Juno Award for Group of the Year, People's Choice for Canadian Entertainer of the Year, Single of the Year for "Fare Thee Well Love" and Country Group of the Year, 1994.

Addresses: *Home*—Halifax, Nova Scotia, Canada. *Record Company*—EMI Canada.

similar to the group's and *North Country*, their first EMI release, Cookie and John Morris spoke about the artist-label relationship they shared. "They haven't influenced what we put on the album and they haven't influenced how we put things on the album," Cookie told Steen and John Morris added, "I think [the group] and the record company [were] quite concerned about not changing our sound too much." That relationship has been successful for both. The Rankins released their next two records with EMI, both to rave Canadian critical and public response.

Still all in their 30s at the time of the *Uprooted* release, the members were still evolving individually. But there was a change in the image of the group as a whole. As Diane Turbide of *Maclean's* noted in 1998, "Changes in hair, clothes, and even the CD's moody design reflect a shift from wholesomeness to a darker, more edgy look." The magazine even pointed out an "almost funky quality to a couple of the Celtic-flavored tunes." This progression and the record's title may have stemmed from the loss of their mother a few months before the release was completed.

For a long time known as The Rankin Family, the group streamlined their stage name for *Uprooted*. Turbide concluded that they seemed "less inclined to trade off the family aspect of their act, preferring to think of themselves as five musicians who happen to be siblings." That said, the family aspect of the group is still the tie that ultimately holds them together. They also have in common that four out of the five of them earned arts-related university degrees, Raylene being the only exception. She was a practicing lawyer before she dedicated herself to music full time.

When asked the inevitable question about what it's like to work and travel with one's brothers and sisters. John Morris explained to Steen that he found a balance. "It's got more advantages than disadvantages. If you're brought up in the same house, I think you have similar ways of looking at music."

Selected discography

Fare Thee Well Love, Capitol, 1992.
North Country, EMI, 1994.
Endless Seasons, EMI, 1996.
Uprooted, EMI Music Canada, 1998.

Sources

Periodicals

Billboard, May 20, 1995; May 9, 1998.
Maclean's, May 18, 1998.
Performing Arts & Entertainment in Canada, Fall 1993.

Online

"The Rankin Family," *All-Music Guide*, http://www.allmusic.com (October 3, 1998).
"The Rankin Family," *Great American Country*, http://www.countrystars.com (August 10, 1998).

—Brenna Sanchez

Reef

Rock band

Reef, from England's West Country in Somerset, astounded even their staunchest fans in 1997 by attaining the number one position on the British charts with their second album, *Glow*. This feat was foreshadowed by two back-to-back top ten singles, "Place your Hands" and "Come Together," before the release of *Glow*. The *Los Angeles Daily News* included Reef's *Glow* on their "Best of '97 Music" list and described the release as, "Bluesy, guitar-driven rock from Britain of the sort the Rolling Stones used to make." Jim Farber of the *New York Daily News* wrote, "(Reef) clearly recalls the early-'70s rock-soul of Humble Pie and Spooky Tooth . Reef's not as slavishly retro as, say, the Black Crowes or Primal Scream—even though they share the same producer."

Vocalist Gary Stringer and guitarist Kenwyn House were raised in Somerset, England near Glastonbury. Bassist Jack Bessant and drummer Domenic Greensmith were raised in nearby towns. Stringer told *Live* magazine's Tom Lanham, "When I was fourteen and living in Glastonbury—7,000 people, real small town—there were no cool clubs to go to, nothing to do. So I went over to my mate's house and noticed he had a guitar. My other mates had a drum kit and a bass so I started shouting, which turned into singing—it was just something to do. From then on, I never, ever *thought* of being a singer. I *was* a singer." Lanham described Stringer's vocal style

as "a unique blend of Joe Cocker and Van Morrison, with a little scratchy Howlin' Wolf thrown in for good measure." Stringer and Bessant met while studying at Strode College, where they formed a band that eventually became known as Chief. Chief included future Kula Shaker drummer Paul Winterhart. Stringer told Lanham that his friends all chuckled when he quit college to work for the equivalent of $125 a week at a local newsstand, but he knew what he wanted. He was saving up for a P.A. system.

When Chief disbanded, Bessant went first to Canada, and then to America. He bought an acoustic guitar and began to write his own material. Stringer took a three-month trip to Morocco and began crafting his own songs, as well. When Stringer and Bessant returned to Somerset they formed a new group. After relocating to London, they met drummer Greensmith, who introduced the duo to House. House was already somewhat familiar to Stringer from a pool hall in Glastonbury, where House was perceived as a bit of a pool hustler. The four began playing together in 1993 as Naked, and were soon signed to Sony's S2 label. After hearing the band's demo tape, Paul Weller invited them to join his tour as an opening band. Stringer told Lanham, "We used to pick fruit on the farms in the mornings to make ends meet. We'd cut our hands up from picking so much, and we'd be real dirty as well. (We would) straight away dive into the sea and catch those waves. Then we'd go onstage at night with wet hair. Wicked laughs, wicked times."

After changing their name to Reef, the band's second single, "Naked," rose to number eleven on the British chart. Their debut release, *Replenish*, followed soon after and established a trademark sound for Reef , characterized by tough, solid guitar riffs, relaxed drums, and a soulful, scratchy vocal style. Their popularity blossomed after non-stop touring, which included high-exposure tour dates with the Rolling Stones and Soundgarden. *Replenish*, reached the British top ten in 1995 and Reef performed for the first time in the U.S. later that year. After their U.S. tour, the band toured Europe for the remainder of 1995, and then toured Japan and Australia at the start of 1996.

Reef teamed with American producer George Drakoulias, in 1996 for their sophomore release, *Glow*, on Epic. Drakoulias had previously worked with such diverse musicians as Black Crowes, the Beastie Boys, Maria McKee, and Charlie Rich. Reef's members were initially skeptical about working with Drakoulias because they wanted to avoid comparisons with the Black Crowes, but the match proved to be ideal. The sessions for *Glow* began in England and were finished in Los Angeles,

Members include **Jack Bessant** (born, 1972), bass; **Domenic Greensmith** (born, 1971), drums; **Kenwyn House** (born, 1971), guitar; **Gary Stringer**, vocals.

Stringer and Bessant met while studying at Strode College, where they formed a band that eventually became known as Chief and included future Kula Shaker drummer Paul Winterhart; the four band members began playing together in 1993 and were signed to the Sony label under the name Naked; toured with Paul Weller; after changing their name to Reef, the band's second single, "Naked," rose to number 11 on the U.K. chart; released debut album, *Replenish*, 1995; toured with the Rolling Stones and Soundgarden; debut release *Replenish* reached the U.K. Top Ten in 1995; performed for the first time in the U.S. in 1995; released *Glow*, 1997; *Glow* reached number one on the English charts in 1997.

Addresses: *Record company*—Epic Records, 550 Madison Avenue, New York, NY 10022-3297.

since Drakoulias wanted Reef to work with his engineer, Jim Scott. Drakoulias and Scott inspired Reef by playing "Proud Mary" and other hits by Creedence Clearwater Revival. Reef's *Glow* reached number one on the English charts in 1997.

Glow's first single and video, "Place Your Hands," revealed a new direction for Reef: the fusion of a gospel choir with a reggae beat, and sad, poignant lyrics. That song was written about the devastation Stringer felt after the death of his grandfather. "Place Your Hands"— meant to ease the pain of death—reached number six on the U.K. charts. Farber, writing about the band's new sound, said, "Without accompaniment Gary Stringer begins "Place Your Hands" by aping the most salacious phrasings of Mick Jagger—only knocked down an octave to recall the gritty drawl of Otis Redding." *Glow*'s second single, "Come Back Brighter," reached number eight on the U.K. charts. Reef toured the U.S. in 1997, traveling from the east coast across the Midwest. The band's video for "Place Your Hands" was directed by David Moulder and features band members on pulleys and wires to create an aerial dance. MTV chose the video for its coveted "Buzz Bin," which prompted Epic to push up *Glow*'s release. *Glow* pushed Reef squarely into the mainstream, and Stringer revealed the bands' outlook and basic tenet when he told Lanham, "I always believed that if you just make a good record, then people are gonna pick up on you at some time or another."

Selected discography

Replenish, Sony, 1995.
Glow, Epic Records, 1997.

Sources

Bass Player, May 1997.
CMJ, September 1997.
Live!, July 1997.
Los Angeles Daily News, December 28, 1997.
New York Daily News, July 7, 1997.

—B. Kimberly Taylor

Roy Rogers

Singing cowboy

Photo by Roy Rogers, Jr. Reproduced by permission. ©

Roy Rogers, King of the Cowboys, was the stage appellation and legal name of the former Leonard Slye, one of the most celebrated singing cowboy personalities in the history of Hollywood. In 1947 he married his co-star, Dale Evans, and together the couple created an enduring legend of American, both through their professional and private lives. The sound of Rogers and Evans crooning their popular theme song, "Happy Trails," has brought a tear to the eyes of generations of Americans.

Roy Rogers was born Leonard Franklin Slye on November 5, 1911 at 412 Second Street in Cincinnati, Ohio. Slye (Rogers) was the son of Andy and Mattie Slye and the only boy among the couple's four children. He lived with his family on a houseboat in Portsmouth for several years, and eventually the Slye family moved to a farm in Duck Run. The boy who would become Roy Rogers had a great empathy for other people and their problems and a strong respect for life and a desire to help his fellow man. As a youngster he aspired to be a doctor, but he never did very well in school, in part because he was burdened with the unending chores of maintaining the Slye family farm, because his father worked in a shoe factory all day to make ends meet. Rogers, who never finished high school, was fully-grown when the family, along with cousin Stanley Slye, moved to California in search of better economic conditions. The frustrating endeavor proved fruitless, and the Slye family ended up working as migrant farm labor.

During that difficult time, the Slye family found solace in the evenings around a campfire, singing songs and strumming their instruments, a guitar and two mandolins, around a campfire. Eventually Rogers decided to pursue a career as a professional musician. He started by playing and singing with groups too numerous to mention, in general without pay, although he hoped to be heard by the right ears.

The first tangible glimmer of hope came in the mid-1930s when Rogers' Pioneer Trio was heard on the radio and labeled among the "Best Bets of the Day" by *Los Angeles Examiner* columnist Bernie Milligan. That notation led to a steady job singing for a local radio station, and the Pioneer Trio eventually added more instruments and musicians, and renamed themselves Sons of the Pioneers. Rogers remembered in his memoir, *Happy Trails,* among his earliest "gigs" was a performance with the well-loved humorist Will Rogers in San Bernardino, California. The engagement turned out to be Will Rogers's last before his untimely death in a plane crash in 1935. Although Leonard Slye adopted the stage name Dick Weston in 1937, it was from Will Rogers's name that he derived the popular identity of Roy Rogers which ultimately brought him fame. The name of "Roy Rogers" was coined by studio executives at Republic Pictures Inc.in the late 1930s. The Roy Rogers name was derived as a combination of the late Will Rogers's surname preceded by a Westernized version of "Roi," the French word for king. The trademark, "King of the Cowboys" however came some time later. Along with the name change, Republic Pictures invented a legendary past for the singing cowboy character Roy Rogers.

Over and over Rogers was cast in movie scripts as a cow hand named Roy Rogers. A fictional biography issued by the movie studio maintained that Roy Rogers was born on a cattle ranch in Wyoming and worked as a ranch hand before he was discovered by movie producers in California. The concept was a new approach by Hollywood, in that the actor/singer Roy Rogers always played "himself" in the form of the legendary character conceived by the studio. Leonard Slye changed his name legally to Roy Rogers in 1942. A movie called "King of the Cowboys" and starring Roy Rogers was released in 1943, which sealed his new title

and reputation. Roy Rogers, according to studio legend, rode a magnificent palomino horse named Trigger, and the studio rented such an animal from a nearby stable. Roy Rogers the actor purchased the horse Trigger from the stable in order to work more closely with the magnificent steed. The famous horse was a lifelong friend to Rogers.

In 1944 the studio teamed Rogers with a new heroine and co-star named Frances Octavia Smith, who became known as Dale. His first wife, Arlene Wilkins, whom he married in 1936, died from complications following the birth of their son, Roy Rogers Jr., in 1946. In all, the couple made 35 films together and eventually married in in 1947. Their partnership on and off the screen is a legend of Hollywood history. The couple's theme song, "Happy Trails," excites great nostalgia among generations of Roy Rogers's fans.

The Roy Rogers screen image evoked a classic American hero. Between 1943-54, Rogers was the foremost cowboy movie star in terms of box office draw. Rogers, the man, contributed to the persona of the on-screen fictional character as the quintessential "good guy," a true humanitarian. Rogers and Dale Evans along with their assorted sidekicks, Gabby Hayes and later Pat Brady (on the television show) spent all of their time righting wrongs. In a gun battle Rogers never killed his opponent, instead he would shoot the weapon from an assailant's hand.

Together Roy Rogers and Dale Evans raised the three children from his former marriage, plus Dale Evans' own son, and four children adopted after their marriage. The couple also had a child of their own, who died in infancy. Their children, as much as possible, were raised on ranches away from public view. Ultimately the family settled on a ranch in Apple Valley. Two of the Rogers children were killed in tragic accidents.

Rogers and Evans established the Roy Rogers-Dale Evans Museum in 1965. The museum, a non-profit organization, is located in Victorville, California and houses the memorabilia of the many years of their professional liaison. When Rogers's palomino, Trigger, died in 1965 at age 33, the horse's body was preserved by a taxidermist and placed on display at the museum. "Trigger" is kept saddled and receives a vacuum cleaning regularly.

Off screen Roy Rogers easily earned a reputation as one of the most caring celebrities of his time. Altogether Rogers adopted six children. Some of the children suffered emotional or developmental disabilities including Robin Rogers, who was born with Down's syndrome in 1950 and died days before her second birthday. She was the natural daughter of Roy Rogers and Dale Evans. Rogers was conscientious to a fault about answering his overwhelming abundance of fan mail which flowed in from all over the world. In order to show his gratitude to the paying public, who held him in high esteem, he took personal responsibility to see that every piece of mail was answered. The studio refused to assist Rogers with the cost of postage for answering the fan mail, so Rogers footed the bill himself. The postage bills were overwhelming, given the immense popularity enjoyed by Roy Rogers.

After he retired from his movie career, Rogers spent a great deal of his time on his ranch and at the Roy Rogers-Dale Evans Museum where he habitually welcomed the public in appreciation of their support. It was said that tourists were frequently brought to tears at the nostalgia of Rogers's warm welcome at the museum. In 1991, Rogers recorded the *Roy Rogers Tribute* album with Emmylou Harris, Clint Black, Willie Nelson, and others. In 1994 he reunited briefly with the current Sons of the Pioneers in Tucson Arizona and sang together with them.

Roy Rogers and Dale Evans celebrated their 50th (golden) wedding anniversary on December 31, 1947.

Barely six months later, on July 6, 1998, Roy Rogers died in sleep at his home in Apple Valley.

Selected discography

Roy Rogers Tribute , 1991.
Roy Rogers (with Emmylou Harris, Clint Black, Willie Nelson, and others), MCA, 1992,
The Country Side of Roy Rogers, Capitol.
A Man From Duck Run, Capitol.

Sources

Books

With Carlton Stowers, *The Story of Roy Rogers and Dale Evans: happy trails,* Word Books, Waco, 1979.

Periodicals

Artists and music, 18 July 1998.
People, August 27, 1987, p. 66; July, 20 1998.

—*Gloria Cooksey*

Richie Sambora

Rock guitarist

Though Bon Jovi fans know him best as that group's revered lead guitarist, Richie Sambora has also established himself as a solo artist with a far different style than the arena-rock riffs that made him famous and helped Bon Jovi sell 75 million records since the mid-1980s. Sambora has released two solo albums in the 1990s that allow him to explore new territory. Studio whiz Don Was produced the latest of the two and expressed admiration for both Sambora's talent and his work ethic: "Here's a guy who could spend the rest of his life cruising around on a boat!," Was remarked in a press release accompanying *Undiscovered Soul*'s debut. The producer failed to note further evidence of Sambora's good fortune (or good sense)—his marriage to television actress Heather Locklear, with whom he has a daughter.

Sambora was born in Perth Amboy, New Jersey in 1959 and grew up in nearby Woodbridge. He began playing the guitar at the age of twelve, in the early 1970s, and was lucky to have his formative musical years marked by the active recording and touring of many influential bands who created the "metal" genre, such as Led Zeppelin. When he was offered a chance to join a band that seemed to hold potential, Sambora dropped out of college, a decision that upset his parents. But the Bruce Foster Band went nowhere and Sambora hit a low point in his life. In time, he joined another New Jersey act, Bon Jovi, as their lead guitarist, and by 1985 the band was being booked on tour dates overseas. With their 1986 album *Slippery When Wet* and the song "Living on a Prayer," Bon Jovi became one of the biggest rock successes of the decade.

Bon Jovi went on to sell literally millions of records and play to sell-out crowds of screaming fans on hundreds of occasions, but Sambora felt constrained. By the early 1990s, he knew he needed a break from the idolatry, especially after the band finished exhaustive world tours. "Playing the same ... songs every night can drive a guy crazy," Sambora told Greg Rule in *Guitar Player*. "I had to break free. I needed to refine my craft, become a better musician.... I needed to find out who I was." Such desires were not easy to fulfill, though, simply because of Bon Jovi's huge international success and the group's living legend status was a mixed blessing of sorts for Sambora when it came time to do his own project. "Because of those sales, I'm expected to live up to a lot," he told *Guitar Player*. "To tell you the truth, I kind of ignored the living up to a lot' part. I kept the record company out of the studio. I gave people the same tape for seven months, and some would say things like, I love the changes you made to that song.' I found out who was [real] and who wasn't."

While he was on tour in the early 1990s, Sambora wrote song fragments in his spare time. When he decided to make his solo record, he purchased several new guitars, and had to teach himself how to play them—a strategy he knew would help him make that stylistic break from metal that he wanted. He later admitted that he was nervous about singing, since he had not done much of it in recent years with the exception of Bon Jovi back-up vocals, though he used to be the front man in his pre-Bon Jovi bands. "After the first set of basic tracks, I was really happy with the way things were sounding," Sambora told Rule in *Guitar Player*. "Everything was a lot more comfortable from that point."

Before making what would become his solo debut, 1991's *Stranger in This Town,* Sambora had the good fortune to meet one of his idols, Eric Clapton. Sambora had once been the presenter at a music-awards show and met him then, and later was invited to sit in on a live session with Clapton, Lou Reed, Buddy Guy, and Bo Diddley. When Sambora was in the process of making *Stranger,* he sent Clapton a note asking him if he was interested in helping out on a track. To his surprise, Clapton was happy to guest on "Mr. Bluesman," a song Sambora wrote about his guitar heroes such as Clapton and Robert Johnson. For some of the tracks, Sambora drew upon his early, pre-arena-concert songwriting forays when he was a New Jersey college dropout; both "The Answer" and "One Light Burning" had their creative origins in the years before he joined Bon Jovi.

For the Record . . .

Born July 11, 1959, in Perth Amboy, NJ; son of Adam and Joan Sambora; married to actress Heather Locklear; children: Ava. Attended King College, late 1970s.

Sambora's first band was the Bruce Foster Band; since 1984 he has been Bon Jovi's lead guitarist and co-written four number one hit singles; released first solo album, *Stranger in a Strange Land,* Mercury, 1991; released *Undiscovered Soul,* Mercury, 1998.

Addresses: *Record company*—Mercury Records, 825 Eighth Ave., New York, NY 10019, (212) 333-8000, Fax (212) 333-8245.

Sambora also drew upon even more ancient experiences for another track, "Ballad of Youth." The first single off *Stranger,* Sambora wanted to send a message to fans about pressures and teen angst. "I was thinking how hard it was for me to decipher being a teenager," he told Melinda Newman in *Billboard.* "Now I'm in my 30s and I want to say to kids, 'Hey man, don't be so hard on yourself because the world's a tough place. Give yourself a break'." Themes of "lost love and alienation" seemed to bind *Stranger in This Town,* wrote *Billboard's* Newman. "The result is a record that sounds more chunky, dense, and raw than typical Bon Jovi fare."

Sambora went back to Bon Jovi, who continued its successful formula of platinum-selling rock records and sold-out concert tours. During this time, Sambora was also introduced to the woman who would later become his wife, *Melrose Place* vixen, Heather Locklear. By the time the pair had wed and were expecting a daughter in 1997, Sambora decided to try his hand at another solo album. His solo debut, Sambora would later recollect, "was a real murky record because it was a murky time in my life," he told *Billboard's* Deborah Evans Price. He and his bandmates, he said, "were just mere shells of the guys we were," and he felt that exhaustion had been evident on *Stranger.*

This time around, Sambora and his Bon Jovi label, Mercury, enlisted the help of famed producer Don Was. Records from acts as diverse as Bob Dylan to Jewel to

the B-52s had benefited from Was's talents, but the Grammy-winning studio genius admitted he had reservations about working with Sambora. As Price wrote in *Billboard,* Was almost "expected him to pull up in a limo and fall out in the producer's driveway with a bottle of Jack Daniels." Yet Was found working with Sambora both a professional and enjoyable experience; he praised the guitarist's songwriting talents and his voice. "He can dive into the well of inspiration and hold his breath for a long time," Was told Price. "I learned a lot about making records working with him."

Undiscovered Soul, released in early 1998, was made intermittently over the course of the previous year. Was took some time off to work with the Rolling Stones in the studio, and Sambora devoted time to his wife and the arrival of their daughter. Locklear was enlisted to sing back-up for one track, and her Maltese dogs, Harley and Lambchop, are thanked in the liner notes of *Undiscovered Soul.* The notes also express gratitude to the studio musicians who helped out, including Billy Preston, who once worked with the Beatles late in their career, and Chuck Leavell, on loan from the Rolling Stones tour. A *People* review was less than complimentary, noting that though Sambora himself is "appealing" and a decent singer, the album shows evidence of his "eager embrace for every cliché in the rock-and-roll thesaurus." Yet New Jersey's *Asbury Park Press* cast a less critical eye on the hometown favorite: Sambora, wrote Kelly-Jane Cotter, "is a likable performer with unmitigated enthusiasm for the guitar. His voice has never sounded better. And his approach to blues-rock is unpretentious and brisk."

Selected discography

Stranger in This Town, Mercury, 1991.
Undiscovered Soul, Mercury, 1998.

Sources

Asbury Park Press, February 20, 1998.
Billboard, September 7, 1991, p. 66; September 14, 1991, pp. 38, 39; January 24, 1998, pp. 14, 24.
Guitar Player, March 1992, pp. 29-33.
People, March 9, 1998; March 16, 1998.

Additional information for this profile was provided by Mercury Records publicity materials, 1998.

—Carol Brennan

Simon and Garfunkel

Rock duo

Arguably one of the most popular and successful duos of all time, Simon and Garfunkel were the preeminent poetic pop spokespersons in the United States during the heady and turbulent period of the mid to late 1960s. Simon and Garfunkel's music transcended genres as it effortlessly blended folk music with pure pop savvy, courtesy of Paul Simon's uncanny knack for creating and writing good hooks and melodies, but this was only part of the story. Art Garfunkel's sweetly soaring, heavenly bound vocals brought an innocent warmth to Simon's lyrics and music and helped to give it an innocent school boy appearance.

Simon and Garfunkel first met in the Forest Hills area of Queens, New York when they were performing in a sixth grade production of "Alice in Wonderland." They met again in 1955 when they were teenagers. It was around this time that they secured their first copyright when they registered their composition "The Girl for Me." The duo began to intermittently write and record songs together under the name Tom and Jerry. They recorded a demo at Sande's Recording Studio in New York City for

Photo by Reed Saxon. AP/Wide World Photo. Reproduced by permission.

For the Record . . .

Members include: **Art Garfunkel** (born November 5, 1941 in Forest Hills, NY) vocals; **Paul Simon** (born October 13, 1941 in Newark, NJ) guitar and vocals.

Duo formed as Tom and Jerry in New York City, 1955; signed to Big Records and released "Hey Schoolgirl," 1957; released "Our Song," 1958; released "I'll Drown in My Tears," 1961; released "Surrender, Please Surrender," 1962; disbanded and reunited as Simon and Garfunkel, signed to Columbia and released *Wednesday Morning 3 AM*, 1964; released *Sounds of Silence*, 1966; released *Parsley, Sage, Rosemary and Thyme*, 1966; contributed to film soundtrack for *The Graduate*, 1968; released *Bookends*, 1968; released Bridge Over Troubled Water, 1970; released *Greatest Hits*, 1972; released *Concert in Central Park*, 1982.

Awards: Gold certification for "Sound of Silence," 1966; Gold certification for "Mrs. Robinson," 1968; Grammy Award, Record of the Year: "Mrs. Robinson," 1969 and "Bridge Over Troubled Water," 1971; Grammy Award, Best Pop Performance Vocal Duo for "Mrs. Robinson," 1969; Grammy Award, Song of the Year for "Bridge Over Troubled Water," 1971; Grammy Award, Best Contemporary Song for "Bridge Over Troubled Water," 1971; Grammy Award, Best Arrangement Accompanying Vocalists for "Bridge Over Troubled Water," 1971; Grammy Award, Best Engineered Record for *Bridge Over Troubled Water*, 1971; Grammy Award, Album of the Year for *Bridge Over Troubled Water*, 1971; Brittania Award (England) for Best International Album and Single released between 1952-77 for *Bridge Over Troubled Water*, 1977; inducted into the Rock and Roll Hall of Fame, 1990.

the song "Hey Schoolgirl." A copy of the song managed to find its way to a representative of Big Records. They signed with Big and released "Hey Schoolgirl" in 1957. The single peaked at number 49 in America, enabling them to perform on the popular television program *American Bandstand*. Over the next five years, Tom and Jerry released three more singles on Big. Neither 1958's "Our Song," 1961's "I'll Drown in My Tears" nor 1962's "Surrender, Please Surrender" managed to chart.

As time wore on, they drifted apart and pursued solo careers.

In 1964, Simon and Garfunkel reunited and decided to have another go at the music business. Dropping their earlier name, Tom and Jerry, the duo decided to use their real names They signed to Columbia Records in late 1964 and released their debut album *Wednesday Morning 3 AM* in autumn of that year. Initially, *Wednesday Morning 3AM* fared poorly until Tom Wilson, who has signed the pair to Columbia, re-mixed one of the acoustic cuts on the album and released it as a single. Without the duo's knowledge, the song "Sound of Silence" was re-mixed with percussion and electric guitars in late 1965, and by January 1966, had topped the pop singles chart in America. A little over one month later, "Sound of Silence" was certified gold for sales of one million copies in America.

In March of 1966, Simon and Garfunkel's second album, *Sounds of Silence*, which included the re-mix of "Sound of Silence," hit number 21 on the American album chart, while a reissue of their debut album peaked at number 30. Their next single, "Homeward Bound," which was dedicated to Simon's girlfriend, peaked at number five on the American singles chart, and reached number nine in Britain. In October of 1966, Simon and Garfunkel released *Parsley, Sage Rosemary and Thyme*, which featured the singles "Homeward Bound," "Scarborough Fair/Canticle," and "Dangling Conversation." The album itself peaked at number four in December. Their next single, "Hazy Shade of Winter" peaked at number 13 that month, as well.

The duo continued to solidify their place in the pop music world throughout 1967. "At the Zoo" crashed the top 20 American singles chart in April, and on June 16, they closed the first day of the Monterey International Pop Festival in California. That August, their next single, "Fakin' It," made it to number 23 in America. It was around this time that Simon and Garfunkel were asked to contribute to the soundtrack for the film *The Graduate*. Bolstered by the inclusion of Simon and Garfunkel tracks, including "Mrs. Robinson," *The Graduate* soundtrack topped the American album chart late in the spring of 1968. May witnessed the release of the next Simon and Garfunkel album, *Bookends*, which contained "Fakin' It," "Hazy Shade of Winter," and "Mrs. Robinson." *Bookends* knocked *The Graduate* soundtrack out of the number one spot on the American album chart, in May of 1968.

By June of 1968, "Mrs. Robinson" had topped the American singles chart, and was certified gold a month later. The tremendous success of "Mrs. Robinson" earned Simon and Garfunkel their first of many Grammy Awards in 1969. "Mrs. Robinson" won Grammys for Record of the Year and Best Contemporary Vocal Performance by a Vocal Duo. The soundtrack for *The Graduate* won the Grammy for Best Original Score for a Motion Picture. Simon and Garfunkel's next single, "The Boxer," was a top ten hit in both America and England. They released their seminal album *Bridge Over Troubled Water* in early 1970. The phenomenal success of both the album and the title track would surpass the success of both "Mrs. Robinson" and *The Graduate*.

By the end of February, "Bridge Over Troubled Water" was a certified gold selling single and topped the American singles chart for the next six weeks. The album from which the single was culled from managed to top the American album chart by early March, where it stayed for the next ten weeks. In England, the album reached number one in late February and the single did likewise one month later. By the end of March, Simon and Garfunkel managed to top both the album and singles charts in Britain and America. "Cecilia" went top five in America in May and was certified gold the following month.

Simon and Garfunkel dominated the 1971 Grammy Awards ceremony. Their single, "Bridge Over Troubled Water," took top honors for the Record of the Year, Song of the Year, Best Contemporary Song, and Best Arrangement Accompanying Vocalists. The album *Bridge Over Troubled Water* won for Best Engineered Album and Album of the Year. Before the ceremony, however, Simon and Garfunkel had disbanded, due in no small part to Garfunkel's burgeoning acting career. As Garfunkel related to *Rolling Stone*, "I think that when I went off to make *Catch 22* [in 1970], Paul was left feeling out of it and uncomfortably dependent. Looking back, I know, too, that I felt envious of Paul's writing and playing." After the break up both of them went solo to varying degrees of success.

Their *Greatest Hits* album was released in 1972 and made the top five in both America and England. After this, Simon and Garfunkel would periodically reform for live performances. In 1977, the duo was awarded the Britannia Award for the Best International Album and Single released in Britain between 1952-77 for *Bridge Over Troubled Water*. Five years later, Simon and Garfunkel reunited for the Concert in Central Park. This contract resulted in a live double album, released on Warner Brothers in 1982. In 1986, *The Concert in Central Park*, *Parsley, Sage, Rosemary, and Thyme*, *Bookends*, and *Bridge Over Troubled Water* were all certified multiplatinum, in America. Simon and Garfunkel were inducted into the Rock and Roll Hall of Fame, in 1990.

Selected discography

Wednesday Morning 3 AM, Columbia, 1964.
Sounds of Silence, Columbia, 1966.
Parsley, Sage, Rosemary and Thyme, Columbia, 1966.
The Graduate, Columbia, 1968.
Bookends, Columbia, 1968.
Bridge Over Troubled Water, Columbia, 1970.
Greatest Hits, Columbia, 1972.
Concert in Central Park, Warner Brothers, 1982.

Sources

Books

Helander, Brock, ed. *Rock Who's Who*, second edition, Schirmer, 1996.
Rees, Dayfdd, and Luke Crampton, *Encyclopedia of Rock Stars*, DK, 1989.

Periodicals

Musician, January, 1994.
Rolling Stone, March 18, 1982.

Online

"S&G Discography," http://www.discographynet.com/simongar/simongar.html (October 4, 1998).
"Simon and Garfunkel," http://www.rockhall.com/induct/garfsimo.html (September 9, 1998).

Mary Alice Adams

Sly & the Family Stone

Funk band

Record blazing pioneers of a new type of exciting popular music called "funk," Sly and the Family Stone made musical history by creating a new genre of pop music. A mix never really heard before, it was a blend of psychedelic rock, James Brown's wild soul, rhythm and blues, and gospel. In addition to leading this trend setting band, founding member and leader Sylvester "Sly" Stewart also helped produce other well-known pop artists like Grace Slick & The Great Society, Billy Preston, Bobby Freeman, and the female soul group Little Sister, which was fronted by Sly's real-life little sister Vaetta Stewart.

Born Sylvester Stewart in Denton, Texas on March 15, 1944, the young musician and his family moved west when Sly was still quite young. His formative years were spent in the grim industrial suburbs of Vallejo, California, located just across from the San Francisco Bay. Music was the one great love of Sylvester's life. While pursuing an education at Vallejo's public high school, he was also hard at work perfecting his singing and songwriting talents. By the time he attended Vallejo Junior College, he started singing in a doo-wop quintet called the Viscaynes. The Viscaynes scored a big local success with their version of the song "Yellow Moon." This inspired Sly to cut the songs "Long Time Away" and "Help Me With My Broken Heart" for the G&P label. At the same time, he began a career as a D.J., first for radio station KSOL-AM then the famous KDIA-AM. At KDIA, people began to take notice of this energetic young dj. As good fortune would have it, Tom "Big Daddy" Drake and Bob "Mighty Mitch" Mitchell of KYA-AM decided to quit the station and start their own recording label, Autumn Records. Impressed with Sly's talents, they hired him as studio musician. Besides being able to write and arrange, Sly was also a very good guitar player, keyboardist, and drummer. He was given a contract for his talents at the outset. Sly's own Autumn recordings were "I Just Learned To Swim." "Scat Swim," and the industrial strength "Buttermilk." These songs were intended to make money off the latest dance crazes. As house producer, Sly managed to take Bobby Freeman's single "C'mon & Swim" all the way up to number five nationwide.

Besides this activity, Sly formed his own band called Sly and the Stoners, a band which frequently played local San Francisco clubs. Brother Freddie had started a group called Freddie and the Stone Souls. When Sly's Stoners began falling apart, Freddie suggested joining forces with his brother who proposed taking the most talented players from each group to merge into one. This formation, later to be called Sly and the Family Stones, featured Sly on keyboards and vocals, Freddie on guitar with backup vocals, trumpeter Cynthia Robinson from the Stoners and Freddie's drummer Greg "Handsfeet" Errico. They also added sax player Jerry Martini and bassist Larry Graham. Martini was a well-known session musician and Sly's friend and Graham was famous for the wild way he played his bass. He created the idea of "slapping", "plucking", and "thumping" the strings. This created a slap-bass effect that became the standard bass sound for funk and soul recordings. One night after hearing him play at an Oakland nightclub, Sly made Larry the offer to join the Family Stones. Larry agreed. After listening to the group, Epic promotional executive David Kapralik signed this newly formed group to the Epic label. He also became a co-partner and business manager.

After the debut album, *A Whole New Thing*, Stewart asked his talented little sister Vaetta to join the ensemble. She added her excellent keyboard talents. Their landmark blend of r&b, psychadelica, and rock quickly caused a local stir in the San Francisco bay area music scene. In 1968, their first nationwide hit "Dance to the Music" cracked the charts with a bullet. Yet superstar prominence didn't come for the group until their legendary musical moments at Woodstock in 1969. Many music critics think the Family Stone's performance there was one of the best of the entire concert.

Another "first" in pop music occurred when a drum machine was featured for the first time. Sly used it for his

For the Record . . .

Members include **Greg Errico** (left group, 1971) drummer; **Larry Graham** (left group, 1972), bass; **Jerry Martini**, sax player; **Cynthia Robinson**, trumpet; **Freddie Stewart**, guitar; **Sylvester Stewart** (a.k.a. Sly, born March 15, 1944, Denton, TS), arranger, composer, guitarist, keyboardist, manager; **Vaetta Stewart**, keyboards, vocals.

Group formed in 1965; merger between Sly & the Stoners and Freddy and the Stone; Sylvester continued to write, arrange, produce, and perform for this group, released debut, *A Whole New Thing*, Atlantic Records, 1967; *Dance To The Music*, Atlantic Records, 1968; *Life*, Atlantic Records, 1968; *Stand!*, Atlantic Recorde, 1969; released *Greatest Hits*, Atlantic Records, 1970; group music was featured on the *Woodstock* soundtrack, 1970; released album There's A Riot Goin' On in 1971, released album Fresh in 1973, later as Sly using a totally different band he released *Sweet Talk*, 1974; *High Energy*, 1975; *Heard Ya Missed Me Well I'm Back*, 1976; Everything You Always Wanted To Hear, 1976; *Recorded in San Francisco 1964-67*, 1977; *Wanted: Vintage Sly*, 1977; *10 Years Too Soon*, 1979; *Back On The Right Track*, 1979; *Anthology*, 1981; *Ain't But the One Way*, 1982; *Encore Appearance*, 1989; *Family Affair*, 1991; *Dance To The Music*, 1991; featured artist in Club Epic: A Collection of Classic Dance Mixes Vol. 2, 1991; *Do the Rattle Snake Snake & More Psychadelic Soulsongs*, 1991; *The Best of The Best: Sly's Stone's Greatest Hits*, 1992; *Take My Advice*, 1992; *Oh! What A Night*, 1992; *Star Box*, 1993; *Remember Who You Are*, 1994; *Musical Magic*, 1994; *Woodstock Diary*, 1994; *In the Still of the Night*, 1995; *Slyest Freshest Funkiest Rarest*, 1996.

Addresses: *Record Company*—Atlantic Records, 1290 Avenue of the Americas, New York, NY 10104; *Website*—Sly & the Family Stone Official Web Site:http://www.slyfamstone.com

made music side by side. They also released various songs which spoke about the possibility of racial harmony and tolerance like "Different Strokes," and "Everyday People." The latter song rose to a be a number one hit in 1969. Two other number one hits followed shortly thereafter with "Thank You," Everybody Is a Star," and "Family Affair" in 1970. However, in contrast, as if possessed by a love/hate political schizophrenia, the band also released militant songs which spoke about racial violence and destruction. In 1971, Sly and his group released the provocative *There's A Riot Goin' On'*, which had an ominous threat to it. The militancy which came through in that song made some wonder exactly where Sly and the Family Stone were going with such calls for revolution. Also, Sly was becoming increasingly erratic with excessive consumption of drugs like cocaine. This eventually led to an unrealibility of showing up for concerts late or even not at all. After some rocky months, Sly moved from San Francisco to Los Angelse scene. The end result of all of this was that some of the Family Stones became restless and felt it was time to break and move on.

Errico left the band in 1971 during a production of *There's A Riot Goin' On*. He decided to go into producing as well as being a studio drummer. Shortly thereafter, Errico's solo efforts proved fruitful. He started producing work by the band War's Lee Oskar and vocalist Betty Davis. Errico also did some gigs drumming for Carlos Santana, Peter Frampton, the Grateful Dead's Mickey Hart, David Bowie, even Josef Zawinul's Weather Report.

Graham quit the band in 1972 after *Riot* was released. Graham went on to form the very successful Graham Central Station. Undaunted by these two desertions, Sly went on and continued to produce and play the music he wanted to. He received some scathing criticisms from music critics and record company people who thought his work was heading downhill. In 1974, Sly married actress Kathy Silva onstage during a sell-out Madison Square Garden concert. Some critics even said Sly did it as a publicity stunt to boost his image. Six months later the couple divorced. 1974 was a year of even more dissolutions. Long time manager and business partner David Kapralik decided to call it quits as well. Although the split was amicable, management duties were quickly assumed by Ken Roberts.

Most members of the original Family Stone have gone in diverse directions but still manage to maintain very successful careers. Freddie became a pastor and delivers Sunday sermons as well as occasionally playing electric guitar for his congregation. He regularly

little sister Vaetta's group Little Sister. Yet a third groundbreaking trend of Sly's group started was one that transcended music. It was a social innovation. Black, white, and Latino, male and female performers

holds court at the Evangelist Temple Fellowship Center in Vallejo, California. Greg Errico presently plays with Quicksilver Messenger Service as well as doing various gigs in the Bay area where he is still in high demand. His latest appearance has been in the radio documentary *I Want To Take You Higher*, hosted by ex-Doors keyboardist Ray Manzarek. Errico's musicianship can also be heard on television and radio commercial such as Taco Bell, Sprint, Bryer's Ice Cream, even Matell Matchbox Cars. Graham is working on a new Graham Central Station CD and has recently worked with The Artist Formerly Known As Prince. Martini still plays his sax even at the age of 56. Lately, he's played in a rock band in Wakiki, Hawaii on Lewers Street at a place called Irish Rose. Robinson released some work on Funkadelic's *The Electric Spanking Machine* released in 1981. Since then, she is divided her time between raising her two daughters and playing with a local Sacramento band called Burgandy Express. She also plays trumpet licks with Larry Graham's band on occasion.

As for the leader, founder, producer, and arranger himself, Sylvester "Sly" Stewart still continues to make and releasing records. Arrested for drug and alimony charges, Sly went to jail for a period. He tried several comeback tours but no tour clicked with the old successes that he and his original group previously enjoyed. Still, Sly's tenacity is remarkable. He has continued to release an album every year or so. "I've been blessed with the gift of writing songs," Stewart told David Letterman in a 1992 interview. "And for me not to make use of this gift would be the same as not contributing to society."

Selected discography

A Whole New Thing, Atlantic Records, 1967.
Dance To The Music, Atlantic Records, 1968.
Life, Atlantic Records, 1969.
Stand!, Atlantic Records, 1969.
Greatest Hits, Atlantic Records, 1970.
There's A Riot Goin' On, Atlantic Records, 1971.

Sources

The Official Sly & the Family Stone Web Site, http://www.slyfamstone.com
The Rock & Roll Hall of Fame & Museum Web Site, http://www.rockhall.com/induct/slyfam.html

—*Timothy Kevin Perry*

Sonny and Cher

Pop duo

AP/Wide World Photo. Reproduced by permission. ©

Sonny and Cher, the pop-rock hippie duo of the late 1960s and early 1970s, created a positive, non-threatening image of the American counterculture of their time. Sonny Bono in his distinctive bobcat vest, together with the tall, lean, and dark-haired Cher played the role of the misplaced hippie couple to the hilt—and to the delight of both teens and parents of that era. In 1971 Sonny and Cher, who were married in real life, hosted their own television show, the *Sonny and Cher Comedy Hour*, which was an uncontested hit until their marriage broke up in 1974. At that point the beloved couple separated, and each went on to bigger and greater stardom—an award-winning career in movies for Cher, and a budding career in national politics for Bono until his untimely death in 1998.

Salvatore "Sonny" Bono was born on February 16, 1935 in Detroit, Michigan to Jean and Santo Bono. Bono's mother was an American-born Italian who married at age 14; Bono's father, an immigrant, was born in Montelabre, Sicily. Bono was the youngest of three children, and the only boy. Bono was still in grade school when the family moved to Hawthorne, California, outside of Los Angeles, where Santo Bono found work as a truck driver. Jean Bono ran a beauty shop in the family home.

Never an exceptional student, Bono decided early in life to become an entertainer. He was fond of writing skits, cracking jokes, and pantomime. Undaunted by the reality of his grinding, granular, nasal voice, Bono loved music in particular and hoped to sing professionally. At Los Angeles's Inglewood High School he teamed up with a fellow student, a piano player, to entertain after high school football games. After graduation in 1952 however, he worked as a bagger in a grocery store, and then drove a tug in an aircraft plant, all the while writing songs in his spare time. In 1955 he recorded his first song, an abysmal flop, and continued working at odd jobs pouring cement and delivering meat. Bono married a waitress named Donna Rankin in February of 1954, with whom he fathered a child before the marriage fell into shambles and ended in divorce.

Rose to Fame

When Crystal Records offered one of his songs to Frankie Lane, Bono's rise to fame had begun. To his surprise, Crystal was impressed and asked for more songs. Soon Bono moved on to Specialty Records, and in time he veered into the production arena. When his job at Specialty was eliminated due to cutbacks, he started his own record label, Gold Records. In that venture Bono's clients were few; he spent much of his time recording his own songs under pseudonyms. Bono

For the Record . . .

Members include **Salvatore "Sonny" Bono**, vocals; Born February 16, 1935 in Detroit, MI; married Donna Rankin, February of 1954; divorced, 1960; one daughter, Christy, 1960; married Cherilyn Sarkisian LaPiere, 1964; divorced, 1974; one daughter, Chastity, March 4, 1969; married Mary Whitaker, 1986; two children Chesare and Chianna; died in skiing accident, January 5, 1998. **Cher,** vocals; Born Cherilyn Sarkisian, May 20, 1946, El Centro, CA; mother, Jackie Jean Crouch (aka Georgia Holt); father, John Sarkisian; married Gregg Allman, June of 1975; son, Elijah Blue; divorced; changed name legally to "Cher."

Started as backup singers for Phil Spector, early 1960s; sang together as Caesar and Cleo, 1964; sang together as Sonny and Cher, 165; "Sonny and Cher Show," 1971-74. Sonny Bono: started the Bono restaurant, West Hollywood, CA, 1982; Mayor of Palm Springs, 1988; U.S. 104th Congress, 1994, re-elected to Congress 1996. Cher: Broadway: *Come Back to the Five & Dime, Jimmy Dean, Jimmy Dean,* 1981; Films: *Silkwood, 1984; Moonstruck,* 1987.

Awards, Cher: Oscar, Best Actress for *Moonstruck,* 1987; Cannes Film Festival, Best Actress for *Mask,* 1985; Golden Globes, Best Performance by an Actress in a Motion Picture—Comedy/Musical for *Moonstruck,* 1988; Best TV Actress-Musical/Comedy for "Sonny and Cher Comedy Hour," 1971;

Addresses: *Management*—William Morris Agency, 151 El Camino Drive, Beverly Hills, CA 90212.

Even after the child returned home, Holt and John Sarkisian, Cher's father, carried on a tempestuous love-hate relationship during much of Cher's early life. The couple divorced and remarried twice, and ventured a third romance before the relationship ended permanently.

Cher's mother, a part-time model and waitress, then married John Southall. The couple had a daughter together in 1951, but the marriage ended in divorce, as well. Holt and her two daughters lived in dismal poverty until 1961 when Holt married once more, to Gilbert LaPiere. LaPiere, a man of means, adopted the two girls and gave them a comfortable home, but by that time Cher was already rebellious. A star-struck teen-ager, she dropped out of school at age 16.

Sonny and Cher, the Duo

Cher and Bono met in 1963. Bono, some years older than Cher and possessed of certain show business savvy, impressed the naive teenager. Bono helped her to secure work as a backup singer for the Ronettes and other artists, and eventually conceived of the notion that the two of them should form a duo. The couple originally billed themselves as Caesar and Cleo, but that image failed, as did their first record. Eventually they came up with the Sonny and Cher act, which evoked a cute hippie persona. The couple married legally in 1964, an event which undoubtedly cemented their image as Sonny and Cher.

Soon the couple was a hit. Their first number one record, "I Got You Babe," written by Bono, was released in 1965. Sonny and Cher lasted through six albums, two movies, and a musical variety television show, before they divorced, at which point the act went by the wayside along with the marriage. The couple had one child, a daughter named Chastity, who was born on March 4, 1969. Chastity Bono continued to live her mother, but maintained a very close relationship with her father as well.

Solo Careers

In 1982 Bono opened his Bono Restaurant in West Hollywood, California. Just prior to the opening, on December 31, 1981, he married Susie Coelho, an aspiring actress. Bono's long work schedule at his new restaurant, however, put stress on the new marriage and the couple separated permanently in June of 1984. In 1986 Bono opened a second restaurant in Palm Springs, California. A short time later he married for the fourth and final time, to Mary Whitaker. The couple had two children, Chesare and Chianna.

closed the door on Gold Records for the last time when he moved into a public relations job with Record Merchandising, promoting up-and-coming artists including Gene Pitney and Chubby Checker. Slowly he learned his way through the maze of the Southern California record business of the 1960s. Around that time Bono met Cher Sarkisian LaPiere, an underage runaway.

Cher was born Cherilyn Sarkisian on May 20, 1946 in El Centro, California. Her early life was very unstable. When Cher was still an infant her mother, who is most commonly known as Georgia Holt, placed the baby in the custody of a nunnery for approximately one year.

As a Palm Springs entrepreneur, Bono became involved in civic issues. In 1988 he was elected the mayor of Palm Springs, in a landslide election—the largest margin in the history of that city. In 1994 Bono ran successfully for a seat to the 104th Congress, as a representative from the 44th Congressional District. He was re-elected in 1996, but he died tragically in a skiing accident on January 5, 1998. Bono was hailed as a gifted public official and was remembered for his warmth and human compassion, as well as for his undying sense of humor. After his death, Bono's widow ran successfully for the congressional seat held by her late husband.

After the breakup of Sonny and Cher, Cher continued recording, and in time she established herself as a serious movie star as well. She earned an Academy Award nomination for her first film, *Silkwood*, in 1984, and won the Academy Award for Best Actress for her role in *Moonstruck* in 1987. She tied for the best actress award at Cannes in 1985, and she won three Golden Globe Awards. In 1996 Cher directed an trilogy for the Home Box Office (HBO) on cable television. The movie starred award winning actresses Demi Moore, Sissy Spacek, and Anne Heche, with Cher herself in a supporting role. Cher continued to devote her career to films. In 1998 she went on location to Italy to film a motion picture with Franco Zeffirelli.

After Cher's divorce from Bono, the tall and willowy singer/actress became a tabloid favorite. Her personal life often overshadowed her professional accomplishments. In June of 1975 she married singer Gregg Allman. The couple had one son, Elijah Blue Allman, a guitar player and singer. The Allman marriage faltered almost immediately as Greg Allman displayed symptoms of serious drug addiction. Although his wife committed herself to helping him, the challenge was more than she could shoulder, and the marriage did not survive. She was then associated with a virtually unending stream of beaus. Cher's attraction for handsome young Hollywood males—Val Kilmer, Tom Cruise, and Rob Camilletti—continued through the years, even as she matured into her fifties. As a result her personal moves became big business for the paparazzi photographers who followed her.

For all her talent, Cher was always renowned for her striking physical appearance. Her youthful appearance and slim silhouette solicited persistent speculation over rumored cosmetic surgeries. Cher's lavish lifestyle was equally as attention grabbing as her physical image and her romantic trysts. In 1988 she bought a $7 million home in Los Angeles, and in 1990 she paid $1.6 million for a co-op apartment in New York. She bought an adobe retreat in Aspen, Colorado in 1991, and near the end of 1996 she sold her Miami, Florida beach home when she realized that a tour boat was bringing gawkers by her house.

Image aside, she was known personally as an exceptionally industrious woman, a hard worker, and family-oriented. In 1998 Cher was asked to give the eulogy at Sonny Bono's funeral. She later taped *Sonny & Me: Cher Remembers*, a tribute to Bono, which aired on CBS on May 20, 1998.

Selected discography

"I Got You Babe," Atco, 1965.
"Bang Bang (My Baby Shot Me Down), Atco, 1966.
The Wondrous World of Sonny and Cher, 1966.
"The Beat Goes On," Atco, 1967.
The Best of Sonny and Cher, 1967.

Sources

Books

Bono, Sonny, *The Beat Goes On,* Pocket Books, New York, 1991.
Quirk, Lawrence J., *Totally Uninhibited: The Life and Wild Times of Cher,* William Morrow and Company Inc., New York, 1991.

Periodicals

People, May 25, 1998.

Online

http://northcountrynotes.com/remembrance/bono, October 7, 1998.

—*Gloria Cooksey*

Jo Stafford

Singer

In the fall of 1917, Grover Cleveland Stafford, his wife Anna York and their two daughters left their farm community of Gainesboro, Tennessee for the oil fields of California, hoping to improve their station in life. They settled in a small company owned house on a tract of land called "Lease 35" in Coalinga, California , near Fresno. Stafford had worked on a farm in Tennessee and Anna was noted for her prowess as a five string banjoist. Two months later on November 12, 1917, Anna gave birth to her third daughter, Jo Elizabeth. Another daughter would be born seven years later. Jo Stafford would later become the quintessential vocalist of the 1940s and 1950s. She is one of the finest in her profession to stand behind a microphone in this century and sing popular songs. She can easily be characterized as warm, open and a personable lady devoted to her family, and cherishes good friends and popular music.

In 1921, the family moved to Long Beach, since a new oil field had been discovered at Signal Hill. Stafford attended Hamilton Jr. High School and Polytechnic High School. She began to sing at twelve and trained for five years to be an opera singer. While singing in the glee club in high school, she took voice lessons from Foster Rucker, a local announcer at KNX radio, who later married her sister, Pauline. Pauline remarked, "Rucker was a very fine instructor and she sometimes might go

six months without actually singing a song but instead practicing breath control and other vocal exercises." In 1929, she made her first public appearance singing "Believe Me If All Those Endearing Young Charms" for a meeting of Jobs' Daughters and at 16 she sang an aria from the opera "Rigoletto" at the Long Beach Terrace Theater.

Her two older sisters, Christine and Pauline, began to appear on a local radio station, KNK, in Hollywood in a Country and Western singing trio as the Stafford Sisters. When Stafford finished high school, she joined her sisters in the hour-long country and music radio show heard five nights a week and called "The Crockett Family of Kentucky. The trio also appeared on their own 15 minute program heard three nights a week on KHJ. They performed popular songs and supplied background vocals for all the major motion picture studios in nearby Hollywood. They were also were regulars on David Broeckman's California Melodies radio show on KHJ, Los Angeles.

The Pied Pipers

In 1938, Twentieth Century Fox put together a major motion picture that required many back-up vocal groups since a large choral group was needed. The film, *Alexander's Ragtime Band,* was an entertaining musical that chronicled the ups and downs of the aristocratic bandleader and was highlighted by a score of Irving Berlin songs including the title tune. Stafford recalls, "We had to do a lot of waiting and sitting around between takes, so seven boys from a group called the Esquires and another called The Rhythm Kings began harmonizing with one another," What started out as trying to kill some time and have some fun turned out to be the start of the Pied Pipers.

Their newly formed sound caught the attention of two of the King Sisters, Alyce and Yvonne, who encouraged their boyfriends, Paul Weston and Axel Stordahl to listen to the newly formed octet. At that time, Weston and Stordahl were the chief arrangers for Tommy Dorsey's orchestra and helped produce his New York based radio program, *The Raleigh-Kool Show.* Subsequently the new group, who called themselves the Pied Pipers, were invited to perform on Dorsey's Show for a singular performance. The original group was comprised of Hal Hopper, Chuck Lowery, John Huddelston, Woody Newbury, George Tait, Dick Whittinghill and Bud Hervey. Stafford recalls, "Knowing we were only guaranteed one night of work, we drove all the way to New York and made a pact that we would save just enough money for a ticket home in case things didn't work out." They stayed on the show for nearly two months and managed to remain in New York for several more months before their money ran out. Some of the members were married and had families in California, so they disbanded and the group ended up becoming a quartet returning on the train to Los Angeles.

After returning home, Stafford was unable to find work. As her employment benefits were about to run out , she received a call from Tommy Dorsey asking her to join him at the Palmer House in Chicago. It was December of 1939 and the new Pied Piper Quartet consisted of her first husband John Huddleston, Chuck Lowery , Clark Yocum, a Dorsey guitarist and vocalist, and Stafford when they rejoined Dorsey. In 1940, the Pied Pipers were joined on by a new singer from Hoboken, New Jersey, who had worked for a short time with Harry James before jumping to Dorsey's band. Frank Sinatra would not only prove to be a fine soloist but frequently provided backing to the Pied Pipers. The Sinatra pairing with the Pied Pipers resulted inthe number one hit "I'll Never Smile Again." It remained on top for 12 weeks and nearly five months on the charts. Tommy Dorsey later gave Jo Stafford the opportunity to sing a solo and in 1942 her first solo recording ,"Little Man with a Candy Cigar," was released on Columbia Records. Columbia Records later recognized her with a Diamond Award as the first recording artist to sell 25 million records.

For the next three years, the Pied Pipers traveled with the Dorsey Band for mostly one night stands by bus and sometimes by train with an occasional stop of three or four weeks in one city. The Pied Pipers stayed with Dorsey until 1942 when Dorsey fired Lowery. However, the Pied Pipers had already established themselves and went out on their own and performed on various radio shows with Bob Crosby, Johnny Mercer, Frank Sinatra and others. Huddleston and Stafford were divorced in 1943.

Pursued Solo Career

In April of 1944, the Pied Pipers signed with Capitol Records, and Huddleston who had left the group to join the war effort, was replaced by an original octet member, Hal Hooper. Early in 1944, Stafford left the Pied Pipers to pursue a solo career with Johnny Mercer. She signed on with his newly formed Capitol Records and crossed paths again with Paul Weston, Capitol's music director. She recorded such hits as "Candy," "Serenade of the Bells," "That's for Me," and "The Tennessee Waltz." Her first recording for Capitol Records, "How Sweet You Are," reached number 14 on the charts in February of 1944. She later went to New York and performed at the Club Martinique, which was the first and only time she appeared in a night club.

Stafford was also very popular among serviceman during World War II. They dubbed her "G. I. Jo" and she was voted the favorite vocalist by many service personnel. Stafford could frequently be seen visiting military bases and hospitals around the United States. Her rendition of Irving Berlin's "I Lost My Heart at the Stage Door Canteen" easily invokes memories of that time and shows why she was so highly admired. She has the unique distinction of being voted the favorite female vocalist of service personnel of both the Korean War and World War II. One amusing story came about when she met two American pilots who told her that they were almost court marshaled because of her. They were flying back to England from Germany after a mission, when against military regulations they began listening to Armed Forces Radio. Over their home field, they changed their flight pattern by listening to a band that was playing one of her selections. Instead of turning to the correct band so they could receive their landing instructions, they waited until her song was completed.

By 1946 she had her own radio show, *The Chesterfield Supper Club,* after a close association with Perry Como. She remained with Capitol Records until 1950 then signed on with Columbia Records. Subsequently *The Jo Stafford Show,* sponsored by Revere Camera, was added followed by feature roles on the *Carnation Hour* and *Club 15* radio shows. During the 1940s she placed nearly 40 songs in the top 20 charts.

The Cold War played another significant part in Stafford's career. In 1950, she was hired to aid the Truman administration's anti-Communist effort by becoming a broadcaster at the American funded Radio Luxembourg, working there for nearly three years. The 200 watt station, Europe's only commercial station, beamed out over 400 of her broadcasts to over 350 million people with an anti-Communist message to Europe. Another Stafford weekly half hour musical show was also beamed over Europe's most powerful station. During this period, Frank Lee, then British Director of Radio Luxembourg, said, "In her own quiet way Stafford is selling America to Europe." She also worked for "Voice of America" as a disk jockey and frequently had top name guests, playing their music. In 1952 she headed a bill at London's prestigious Palladium.

Married Weston

On February 26, 1952 Stafford married Paul Weston and nine months later, their son, Tim was born, followed by a daughter, Amy in 1956. In 1954, she introduced her own television show *The Jo Stafford Show* on CBS-TV. During her work on television she attended a party of an entertainment executive who was married to Richard Rodger's sister. Rodgers and his wife were also there and she was given a Rodgers & Hammerstein songbook and asked to sing. One of Rodgers fetishes was disdain for vocalists, who tried to style his music to fit their audiences and not the way he had written the music. With Rodgers at the piano, Stafford sang one of his selections and at the end both Rodgers and his wife indicated their pleasure with her vocal delivery indicating she had sung it exactly as he had written the ballad.

Stafford was later awarded plaques on Hollywood's Walk of Fame for her records, radio and a third for television. Some of her major hits include: "You Belong to Me," "Shrimp Boats," written by husband Paul Weston, "Make Love to Me," "Jambalaya," "Hey Good Lookin'" with Frankie Laine, "Good Night Irene," "Keep it a Secret," and one of her favorite songs, Jerome Kern's

"All the Things You Are." Between 1944 and 1954 she had 75 charted hits.

By the late 1950' Stafford began to reduce the amount of time spent entertaining others by devoting more time to her two young children. Around this time her husband, Paul Weston, then music director of Columbia Records attended a convention in Key West, Florida. Later one evening he was in the bar playing the piano and began playing a comedy routine using the name Jonathan. Two executives from Columbia Records heard his satire and encouraged him to make a recording when he returned to California. He partnered with his wife and called her Darlene. For their comedy routine they selected renditions of popular songs they disliked. The outcome was a series of Jonathan and Darlene Edwards recordings. The results of their second album *Jonathan and Darlene in Paris* earned them a Grammy Award for Best Comedy Album in 1960.

In 1961 the Weston family moved to London for the summer and Stafford did a television series for ATV British network, which was seen in the United States, Australia, New Zealand, Canada, as well as in Great Britain. Her guests included Ella Fitzgerald, who she considers the world's greatest female singer, Bob Hope and comedian Peter Sellers.

Sang Folk Songs

Stafford has also teamed up with such notable performers as Frankie Laine, Gordon MacRae, Johnny Mercer, Dick Haymes and others. She combined with Paul Weston to record folk songs from the Appalachian Mountains entitled *Jo Stafford Sings American Folk Songs* and it marked the first time anyone had recorded folk songs using strings and an orchestra. Folk singer, Judy Collins remarked "Jo Stafford is one of the greatest singers of all time. Her recording of 'Barbara Allen' changed my views from Mozart to 'Both Sides Now'." It was so popular that the American Folklore Society established a Jo Stafford Prize in American Folklore as an endowment for students involved in the study of folklore and folk music that ran for several years in the early 1950s and a folk scholarship at UCLA.

She continued to make recordings up until the mid-60s when she retired because she felt she could not sing the current contemporary music being introduced to the American public. When asked what inspired her over the years, she said "It was the wonderful songwriters and songs that were being created. The music was the cream." She once wrote, "If I had to come up with a one word description of this whole era, it would be 'Fun'. We had such fun. I think because we took our work very seriously but not ourselves."

Stafford and Weston were involved in philanthropic activities prior to Weston's death on September 20, 1996. She was president of SHARE, one of Hollywood's best known charitable organizations which specializes in helping mentally handicapped children. For many years, Weston was active in helping the Crippled Children Societies of California. Today, Jo Stafford lives in Beverly Hills, California and enjoys the pleasure of her four grandchildren.

Selected discography:

Sings Broadway's Best, Columbia, 1953.
Songs of Faith, Capitol, 1954.
Ski Trails, Columbia, 1956.
Happy Holidays, Columbia, 1955.
This Is Jo Stafford , Dot, 1956.
Ballad of the Blues, Columbia, 1959.
I'll Be Seeing You, Columbia, 1959.
Ballad of the Blues, Columbia, 1959.
I Only Have Eyes For You, Columbia/Snowy Bleach, 1950's.
Jo + Jazz, Columbia, 1960.
Jo + Blues, Columbia, 1960.
Once Over Lightly, Columbia, 1965.
Getting Sentimental Over Tommy, Reprise, 1965.
Look at Me Now, Bainbridge, 1982.
The Hits of Jo Stafford, Capitol, 1984.
Ski Trails, Corinthian, mid 80's.
Jonathan & Darlene's Greatest Hits, Corinthian, mid 80's.
Jo Stafford, The Portrait Edition, Corinthian & Sony, 1994.
G. I. Jo, Corinthian, 1995.
Broadway Revisited, Corinthian, 1995.

Sources

Clarke, Donald, *Penguin Encyclopedia of Popular Music,* Penguin Books Ltd., 1989.
Eugene, Charles Claghorn, *Biographical Dictionary of American Musi,c* Parker Publishing Co., 1973.
Falzarano, Gino, *Jo Stafford, the Portrait Edition, Liner Notes*
Gammond, Peter, *The Oxford Companion to Popular Music,* Oxford Univ. Press 1993.
Larkin, Colin, *Guinness Encyclopedia of Popular Music, Volume 5,* Guinness Publishing Ltd. 1995.
Lax, Roger and Frederick Smith - *The Great Song Thesaurus,* Oxford Univ. Press, 1989.
Lees, Gene, *Singers & the Song,* Oxford University Press, 1987.
Maltin, Leonard, *Movie & Video Guide,* The Penguin Group, 1995.
Osborne, Jerry, *Rockin Records,* Osborne Publications,1999.
Stambler, Irwin, *Encyclopedia of Popular Music,* 1966.
Warner, Jay, *The Billboard Book of American Singing Groups, a History 1940-1990,* Billboard Books 1992.

Online

www.corinthianrecords.com , (January, 1999).

Additional information was obtained through two interviews with Jo Stafford on October 25, 1998 and November 1, 1998

—Francis D. McKinley

Ringo Starr

Drummer

Drummer Ringo Starr earned a place in musical history in 1962 at the age of 22 years, when he accepted a position with a then unknown band called the Beatles, which was destined to become one of the most popular groups in the history of rock and roll. During the Beatles' concert performances Starr was the most easily recognizable of the group, as he sat toward the back of the stage, pounding a steady rhythm behind singers John Lennon, Paul McCartney and George Harrison. A collection of gaudy rings adorned Starr's fingers, which earned him the nickname Ringo. When the Beatles dissolved during the early 1970, Starr re-emerged in an acting career, and he continued his musical career as a solo artist.

Starr was born Richard Starkey, Jr. in a dingy Liverpool slum, on July 7, 1940 to Richard Starkey, Sr. and Elsie Gleave. His childhood was filled with an endless series of setbacks and tragedies. His parents were poor bakery workers, and Starr's father deserted the family during World War II. His mother later remarried, to Harry Greaves, a house painter. Starr's childhood was plagued by a series of personal illnesses. At age six he was hospitalized for one year when he lapsed into a ten-week coma from peritonitis brought on by a ruptured appendix. At age 13 he suffered pleurisy so severe that he was confined to a sanitarium for two years. Starr's miseries were compounded when he developed an alcohol addiction early in life, which caused him to suffer blackouts from the age of nine.

By 1955 Starr was hopelessly behind in his schoolwork, so he quit school altogether and took a job as a messenger for British Railways. He lost the job, not surprisingly, when his employer received the results of Starr's physical examination. After a stint as an apprentice carpenter, Starr, who played drums as a child, acquired a new drum kit and found work as a professional drummer. He joined Ed Clayton's skiffle group for a time and then joined a band called Rory Storm and the Hurricanes.

It was in Hamburg, Germany, when Starr was performing with the Hurricanes that he became acquainted with the Beatles' John Lennon, Paul McCartney, George Harrison, and their drummer Pete Best. The Beatles, who were relatively unknown at the time, called on Starr a short time afterward to join their group to replace Best. As Peter Brown and Steven Gaines said in *The Love You Make,* "[Starr] was an unlikely candidate to sign on as a character player in the greatest bit part ever written. He was ... unassuming, with sad blue eyes ... [but he] was fun-loving and uncomplicated and got along well with everyone in the group." When Beatlemania exploded throughout the world in 1963, Starr, along with his Beatle bandmates, achieved instant fame; and for Starr, the sickly boy from the dockside Dingle tenement, the recognition brought particular gratification.

As drummer for the Beatles, Starr rarely took over the microphone, and he almost never sang in the background. His very deep singing voice was restricted by poor tone and by an extremely thick, Liverpudlian accent. Starr's voice was heard nonetheless on a selected few of the early Beatles recordings, including "Boys," "Honey Don't," "Matchbox," and "Act Naturally." In time, Beatles songwriters Lennon and McCartney composed and arranged certain pieces specifically as solos for Starr. He sang the title song in the Beatles' cartoon film, *Yellow Submarine,* and Starr good-naturedly furnished a rendition of the homely Beatles ballad, "With A Little Help From My Friends" on the 1967 album *Sergeant Pepper's Lonely Hearts Club Band.* Starr did not receive critical acclaim as a drummer, but his steady, driving beat earned him respect among fellow musicians. Starr also dabbled in composition, contributing his song, "Don't Pass Me By" to the 1968 album, *The Beatles—* more commonly referred to as *The White Album.*

In 1970 the Beatles disbanded, yet Starr rebounded quickly. He was already involved in a budding film career, and he took the opportunity to embark on a solo singing career as well. Starr's acting skills impressed

Born Richard Starkey, Jr., July 7, 1940, in Liverpool, England; mother Elsie Gleave, bakery worker; father, Richard Starkey, Sr., bakery worker; married Maureen Cox, February 11, 1965; children: Zak, Jason, and daughter Lee, one granddaughter; married Barbara Bach, 1981.

Drummer with Ed Clayton Skiffle Group, 1959; Rory Storm and the Hurricanes, 1960; Beatles, 1961-70; began solo career, 1970; formed All-Starr Band, 1990.

Addresses: *Record company*—Mercury Records, West Coast Office, 11150 Santa Monica Blvd., Los Angeles, CA 90025.

---

the critics on a par with his vocal skills, but as with everything Starr attempted, he offered a certain soulful, child-like allure that could never be denied. His first solo film role (without the other Beatles) was in 1967's *Candy*, and in 1969 he appeared in *The Magic Christian*. Starr's other film credits include *That'll Be the Day* in 1970 and *Stardust* in 1975. In 1981 he starred in *Caveman*, with actress Barbara Bach, whom he later married. He also dabbled in film direction with *Born to Boogie*, the story of T. Rex singer, Marc Bolan.

Starr's first solo album, *Sentimental Journey*, was released in 1970, and as the name implies, it was a Tin Pan Alley collection. His next release was a country music album, *Beaucoup of Blues*. Starr also on John Lennon's *Plastic Ono Band* and with George Harrison on his solo album *All Things Must Pass*. Starr's other solo ventures included a number of hit singles. He earned his first gold record for "It Don't Come Easy," which rose to number four on the charts. His singles "Photograph" and "You're Sixteen" each reached the number one spot, and "Back Off Boogaloo" peaked at number nine. From time to time the other members of the Beatles joined Starr on his LP recordings. Starr established his own recording label, Ring O' Records, in 1975.

In the late 1980s Starr formed his All-Starr band, a dynamic and versatile group. The All-Starr band— whose lineup rarely remained constant—has included Billy Preston and Dr. John, Peter Frampton, and assorted other musical celebrities. By 1998 the All-Starr band was in its fourth incarnation. Ringo's All-Starrs have toured extensively and joined in the Jam Against Hunger organized by former Beach Boy Brian Wilson in 1995. Starr's 1998 album, *Vertical Man,* featured, among others, Starr's own son Zak, young chanteuse Alanis Morissette, and former Beatles George Harrison and Paul McCartney. Overall Starr's record sales have exceeded 10 million worldwide from his first nine solo album releases.

Selected discography

Sentimental Journey, Apple, 1970.
Beaucoups of Blues, 1973.
Ringo, 1973.
Goodnight Vienna, 1975
Blast from Your Past, 1975.
Ringo's Rotogravure, Atlantic, 1976.
Ring the Fourth, 1977.
Bad Boy, 1978.
Stop and Smell the Roses, Boardwalk, 1981.
Time Takes Time.
Ringo Starr and His All-Starr Band, Rykodisc, 1990.
Vertical Man, Mercury Records, 1998.

Sources

Books

Brown, Peter, and Steven Gaines, *The Love You Make: An Insider's Story of the Beatles,* McGraw-Hill Book Company, New York, 1983.
Pareles, Jon, and Patricia Romanowski, eds., *The Rolling Stone Encyclopedia of Rock & Roll,* Rolling Stone Press, New York, 1983.
Stambler, Irwin, *Encyclopedia of Pop, Rock, and Soul,* St. Martin's Press, New York, 1974.

Periodicals

People, August 28, 1989.

Online

www.elibrary.com/s/hotbot

—*Gloria Cooksey*

Richard Stoltzman

Clarinet

Clarinetist and two-time Grammy Award winner Richard Stoltzman defied categorization and dazzled critics and audiences with his masterful performances in all genres of music. He worked as a soloist with more than a hundred orchestras, as a recitalist and chamber music performer, as an innovative jazz artist, and as an exclusive RCA recording artist. Stoltzman earned an international reputation as a clarinetist who opened up unforeseen possibilities for the instrument, expanding the musical envelope for all musicians in the process. In 1986, he was the first wind player to be awarded the Avery Fisher Prize, and he delivered the first clarinet recital in the history of both the Hollywood Bowl and Carnegie Hall. He has performed with jazz masters such as Gary Burton, Chick Corea, Eddie Gomez, Keith Jarrett, George Shearing, Wayne Shorter, and Mel Torme. His discography numbers nearly 40 releases, and he was a founding member of the noted ensemble TASHI, which made its debut in 1973. Stoltzman is noted for his double lip embouchure, wide vibrato, and ability to mimic the sound of a human voice on his clarinet. He combines traditional and contemporary classical and jazz material with his own unorthodox style, and the result is a constant forging of new musical territory.

Richard Leslie Stoltzman was born on July 12, 1942 in Omaha, Nebraska, to Leslie Harvey Stoltzman and Dorothy Marilyn Spohn. Stoltzman's father worked for the Western Pacific Railroad and soon moved his family to San Francisco, California after Richard was born. Stoltzman's first exposure to music came through his father, an avid fan of big band music. Stoltzman's father played the big band music of the 1940s at home on the radio and performed in a dance band during his spare time. Stoltzman began studying the clarinet at the age of eight with a teacher at a local school, and he began playing with his father in the Stewart Memorial United Presbyterian Sunday School Orchestra and at community functions within a few years. When Stoltzman was in junior high school, he began developing the jazz techniques of improvisation and he enjoyed jamming with his father at home. Benny Goodman was his earliest musical mentor, and remained a strong influence throughout his career.

Stoltzman told Allan Kozinn of the *New York Times*, "(When) I was seven years old ... I found these wonderful cylindrical objects in a nice leather case. I enjoyed playing with them ... and I vaguely remember dangling them from the second-story window of our house. That caused quite a stir, because they turned out to be my father's clarinets. But instead of punishing me, he decided that I had an interest in the instrument and rented an indestructible metal clarinet for me to start on." His family moved to Cincinnati, Ohio, and Stoltzman continued studying the clarinet in high school but was

AP/Wide World Photo. Reproduced by permission. ©

Born Richard Leslie Stoltzman, July 12, 1942 in Omaha, NE; son of Leslie Harvey Stoltzman (worked for the Western Pacific Railroad) and Dorothy Marilyn Spohn; married Lucy Jean Chapman (violinist), June 6, 1976; children: Peter, John, Margaret, Anne. *Education:* Ohio State University: B.A. mathematics, music; Teachers College of Columbia University: M.A. music, PhD Yale University.

Began studying the clarinet at the age of eight; accepted at the Marlboro Music Festival in Vermont, 1967; stayed at the festival for ten years; joined the California Institute of Arts, 1970; began playing informally with violinist Ida Kavafian, cellist Bill Sherry, and pianist/composer Bill Douglas, 1973 at the New School for Social Research in New York City; quartet named Tashi; first recording and performance as a grou; *The Messaien Quartet for the End of Time,* RCA,.1973; soloist debut, New York, 1974; recording debut *A Gift of Music for Clarinet,* 1974; became a fixture at the Lincoln Center's Mostly Mozart Festival beginning in the late 1970s; performed often with the New York Philharmonic, the Pittsburgh Symphony, and the orchestras of Atlanta and Louisville; overseas bookings in Britain, Italy, Germany, Hong Kong, Japan, and Austria; debuted at La Scala in Milan, Italy, 1981; first person to perform a solo clarinet recital at Carnegie Hall in 1982; performed with jazz greats such as Gary Burton, Chick Corea, Eddie Gomez, Keigh Jarrett, George Shearing, Wayne Shorter, and Mel Torme.

Awards: Martha Baird Rockefeller Award in 1973, Avery Fisher Recital Award in 1977, Avery Fisher Prize in 1986, Grammy Awards in 198 and 1996.

Addresses: *Home*—6 Lincolnshire Way, Winchester, MA 01890-3048; *Office*— 201 W. 54th Street, Apt. 4C, NY, NY 10019-5521; *Record company*—BMG/RCA Victor, 1133 Avenue of the Americas, New York, NY 10036; (212) 930-4000.

rejected when he applied for scholarships at the Eastman School of Music in Rochester, New York, and the Jullliard School in New York City. He went to Ohio State University in 1960 and majored in mathematics and music. He also played Sousa marches in the school's concert band and Dixieland jazz at a local tavern.

Discovered Classical Music in College

Stoltzman was introduced to classical music at Ohio State University, and told an interviewer for *Symphony Magazine,* "Someone gave me a ticket to a concert by the Julliard Quartet. They played the Lyric Suite of Alban Berg, and I was so knocked out. I didn't know there was music like that ... played with such intensity and precision and emotion. That's when I realized that it wasn't enough to play jazz or just enjoy music. You had to give blood." Dentistry had been a possible career choice for Stoltzman, but a series of lessons with Cleveland Orchestra clarinetist Robert Marcellus prompted him to choose graduate work in music instead. He entered Yale in 1964 with a graduate scholarship in music and studied with Keith Wilson. He told Robert Stock of the *New York Times* that his formal introduction to chamber music was hearing the Brahms clarinet quintet, and by the time he graduated in 1967, his passion for jazz had been replaced by classical music.

In an interview with Annalyn Swan of *Time* magazine, Stoltzman said, "Not only did I come to feel that music was essential to life, but I was surrounded by people who tried to play like a voice singing, something neglected by clarinetists." He set out to broaden the range of timbre and tonal color available to the clarinet, and to draw them closer to the sonorities of stringed instruments. He auditioned twice for the Marlboro Music Festival in Vermont while at Yale, and was turned down both times. Then, he began work on his doctorate at Teachers College of Columbia University in 1967 and studied with Kalman Opperman, who helped him gain insight into some of his shortcomings as a clarinetist. Stoltzman told Swan, "One of the first things he [Opperman] told me was that I moved my fingers like a country bumpkin—and I already had a master's degree from Yale." Opperman changed a lot of things in the way Stoltzman played, and with renewed confidence, Stoltzman auditioned again for the Marlboro Music Festival and was accepted. He stayed at the festival for ten years, where he was given the freedom to explore music in every dimension.

Forged a Difficult Career Path

The Marlboro experience granted an opportunity for Stoltzman to study with world-class figures such as Harold Wright, Rudolf Serkin, Marcel Moyse, and Pablo Casals. Stoltzman told *Symphony* magazine that when Casals beckoned him over to his chair one night after a performance and said, "You are an artist," it was a pivotal moment for him—he knew he had something special and that he also had a responsibility to develop further. Stoltzman joined the newly-established California Institute of Arts in 1970, and remained there for six years. He tried auditioning for orchestras, but his fiercely distinctive playing, musical risk-taking, and propensity to experiment were stumbling blocks, and he was turned down after each audition. He decided to forge a career as a solo clarinet recitalist, but had to overcome the limitations of the instrument itself: The clarinet is generally considered too reedy and nasal to be played solo for a great length of time. He persevered and did overcome its limitations. Stoltzman began playing informally with violinist Ida Kavafian, cellist Bill Sherry, and pianist and composer Bill Douglas in 1973 at the New School for Social Research in New York City. The four players took the name Tashi, which is Tibetan for "good fortune." Tashi was formed for one concert, but they were so well received that they continued performing and recording as a group.

The Messaien Quartet for the end of Time became Tashi's first recording on the RCA label in 1973, and they followed the release with more traditional chamber music works by Beethoven, Stravinsky, and Mozart. Among the composers who have written material specifically for Tashi are Toru Takemitsu, Bill Douglas, Peter Lieberson, William Thomas McKinley, and Charles Wuorinen. Stoltzman made his debut as a solo recitalist in New York in 1974, and he made his recording debut the same year with the release of *A Gift of Music for Clarinet* for the Orion label. Whether playing solo or with an orchestra, Stoltzman does not add new notes to existing compositions, but instead reshapes the dynamics of the score.

Stoltzman won the Martha Baird Rockefeller Award in 1973. Shortly after, he met his future wife, violinist Lucy Jean Chapman. Chapman was one of numerous musicians attracted to Tashi, entered the group, and married Stoltzman in 1976. The couple formed part of the quartet's floating membership whenever their separate careers permitted it. Stoltzman became a fixture at the Lincoln Center's Mostly Mozart Festival beginning in the late 1970s, and he often performed with the New York Philharmonic, the Pittsburgh Symphony, and the orchestras of Atlanta and Louisville. His overseas bookings took him to Britain, Italy, Germany, Hong Kong, Japan, and Austria. Stoltzman won the Avery Fisher Recital Award in 1977 and debuted at La Scala in Milan, Italy, in 1981. He was the first person to perform a solo clarinet recital at Carnegie Hall in 1982, and won the Avery Fisher Prize in 1986; he was the first wind player to win the honor. He also garnered Grammy Awards in 1982 for *Brahms: The Sonatas for Clarinet, Opus 120*, with Richard Goode an another in 1996. Throughout his career, Stoltzman successfully circumvented the constrictions of the traditional clarinet repertoire and broke new musical ground.

Selected discography

Solo releases

Begin Sweet World, BMG/RCA Victor, 1986.
Mozart: Clarinet Concerto, BMG/RCA, 1989.
Richard Stoltzman: Romance—Debussy, Poulenc, Saint-Saens, BMG/RCA, 1990.
Brasil, BMG/RCA, 1991.
Finzi: 5 Bagatelles—Clarinet Concert, BMG/RCA, 1991.
Richard Stoltzman: The Essential Clarinet, 1992.
Copland: Clarinet Concerto—Bernstein, Gersnwin, Stoltzman, BMG/RCA, 1993.
Richard Stoltzman: Dreams, BMG/RCA, 1994.
Basic 100, Vol. 55: Mozart Clarinet Concert, BMG/RCA, 1994.
Visions, BMG/RCA, 1995.
Spirits, BMG/RCA, 1996.
Foss, Englund, McKinley: Clarinet Concertos, BMG/RCA, 1996.
Open Sky, BMG/RCA, 1998.

Collaborative releases

Messiaen: Quartet for the End of Time/Serkin, Stoltzman, BMG/RCA, 1988.
Innvervoices: Stoltzman and Judy Collins, BMG/RCA Victor, 1989.
Marlboro Festival: 40th Anniversary/Mozart Serenade, Sony, 1990.
The Essential Clarinet: Mozart, Stoltzman, Tokyo String Quartet, BMG/RCA, 1991.
Marlboro Festival: 40th Anniversary/Beethoven, Sony, 1991.
Dinner Classics: Just Desserts, Sony, 1992.
Mozart in Hollywood, BMG/RCA, 1992.
Classical Music for People Who Hate Classical Music, BMG/RCA, 1994.
Takemitsu: Cantos/Richard Stoltzman, BMG/RCA, 1994.
Ax, Stoltzman, Ma: Brahms, Beethoven, Mozart—Trios, Sony, 1995.
Brahms Weber: Clarinet Quintets—Stoltzman, Tokyo Quartet, BMG/RCA, 1995.
Debussy, Ravel: Impressions/Toyko String Quartet, BMG/RCA, 1995.
Donald Erb: Concertos/Stoltzman, Fried, Ordman, Comet, Koss Classics, 1995.
Out Classics, BMG/RCA, 1995.
Amber Waves: American Clarinet Music/Stoltzman, Vollecio, BMG/RCA, 1996.
Classical Ecstasy: Classics for a New Age, BMG/RCA, 1996.
O Holy Night: Christmas Favorites, BMG/RCA, 1997.
Adagio: Greatest Hits, BMG/RCA, 1997.
Alchemy: McKinley, Fenner, Carbon, Stoltzman, Master Musicians Collective, 1997.
Barber's Adagio, BMG/RCA, 1997.
Carol of the Drum: A New Age Christmas, BMG/RCA, 1997.

Classics Go Jazz!, BMG/RCA. 1997.
Autumn Classics, BMG/RCA, 1998.
Spring Classics, BMG/RCA, 1998.
Summer Classics, BMG/RCA, 1998.

Sources

New York Times, July 31, 1983; November 13, 1983.
Symphony Magazine, February/March 1982.
Time, August 14, 1978.

Online

http://www.musicblvd.com

—B. Kimberly Taylor

Surfin' Pluto

Rock band

Surfin' Pluto's sound has been favorably compared to Blues Traveller and the Dave Matthews Band. There is a similarity in the exploration of looser rhythms and sophisticated instrumental flourishes. Yet the comparisons end there. This unique band has developed a fresh, powerful style that is strong without being overpowering, and light without being lightweight. Their press kit describes the band as being synonymous with fun, satire, and sincerity or the act of riding a wave on a surfboard, over the solar planet Pluto.

According to bass player and co-founder Gene Catallo, the band's mission has three main directives, to be fun, upbeat, and melodic. They're not interested in promoting morbid death culture pessimisms. "We're interested in writing memorable melodies that won't promote depression," Gene Catallo told *Contemporary Musicians* writer Timothy Perry. This Michigan quintet grew up absorbing the current trends in music and culture, selecting what they liked and discarding what they didn't. "The influences that made me want to play guitar and write music," Catallo told Perry, "were The Beatles, Kiss, Springsteen, and The Who. The first professional band I started playing in was called Hatchek. Man, the stories I could tell you. Talk about paying your dues. I remember one time we were playing at this club in Detroit called The Falcon Lounge. The bartender would not turn down the radio that was blasting through the bar while we were playing! I got so frustrated that I decided to do my best Pete Townsend impersonation and smashed the head of my bass through a monitor that sat innocently in front of me busting every macine head off my guitar. I still don't think he ever turned it down. But our band has a wide range of influences. One member's preference doesn't represent the whole band. We feel the diverse background of Surfin' Pluto is the reason we meet in the middle and get the sound that we do. I sometimes like to say that the basic inspirations range from Van Morrison to Van Halen. Also, our present-day tastes have generally changed."

The group of five originally formed in 1991 under the name Nobody's Heroes. Gene Catallo used to be a "runner," working as part of the production staff of the Pine Knob and the Palace Music Theaters in Clarkston, Michigan. "There were so many nights I sat by the side of the stage watching whoever was there that night," Catallo told Perry, "knowing that our band could do it better. And even though it was a great feeling to see so many bands, I was frustrated that it wasn't us on the stage," explained Catallo to Perry. "It wasn't long before we found Brian [Lancaster] to play drums. What's really unusual is the first time Gene and Chris got together with Brian was the day the Gulf War broke out. Hopefully, that wasn't an omen of things to come," he chuckles. The group went on to develop their unique style. This first group incarnation was a hard driving metal sound with dark lyrics.

Eventually, the band landed opening act gigs for some of heavy metal's most famous names. "As Nobody's Heroes, we were writing glass shattering metal. But when we opened up for Vince Neil (lead singer from Motley Crue) the audience didn't want anything to do with us. All they wanted to see was Vince. I can remember a guy in the front row viciously looking at us and giving us the finger in a fit of rage. We ended up cutting down our set just to get the hell off the stage. The real funny part was that Michael (our lead singer) was so flustered by the whole situation that after we ended what became the last song he made a mistake and said, 'David Lee Roth will be out shortly.' This while we were opening up for Vince Neil instead!"

After two years of playing together, Lancaster left the band and guitar player Chuck Hart was found to replace him. Chuck also began writing songs with Chris Gene. The band also held auditons for a lead singer and found Michae Soucie in 1994. Soucie is also a drummer and fills in on percussion if needed. Nobody's Heroes didn't last long, but it gave the musicians invaluable experience as well as establishing themselves as a presence in the Michigan music scene. They were recognized as WDZR FM's "Best New Band" in 1994.

Members include **Chris Catallo** (born December 22, 1966), keyboards ; **Gene Catallo** (born February 6, 1964), bass; **Chuck Hart** (born October 3, 1965), guitar; **Brian Lancaster** (born March 6 1967), drummer. **Michael Soucie** (born February 21, 1961), vocals.

Group first formed as Nobody's Heroes; changed the name of their group to Surfin' Pluto, 1997; played as opening act for Chicago, David Lee Roth, REO Speedwagon, 38 Special, Eddie Money, Paul Rodgers (Bad Company), Robin Trower, The Smithereens, and Marshall Crenshaw. Surfin' Pluto's song *"Millionaire"* was released on the *Kool H.O.R.D.E. Band to Band combat of the East* cd, 1998; released debut CD *Surfin' Pluto,* Overture Records, 1998.

Awards: Winner of the Kool H.O.R.D.E. Band to Band Combat for the city of Detroit, 1998.

Addresses: Gene Catallo-51407 Morowske, Shelby Township, Michigan, 48316, (810)-739-0951; *Website*—http://www.surfinpluto.com; email:splash@surfinpluto.com;*Email*—splash@ surfinpluto.com.

In early 1997, the group made another serious career decision. All felt it was time to change the direction of the band. They first changeed the band's sound. Before, they were very heavy on the metal overdrive with pessimistic lyrics. Each member grew tired of the depression-oriented flavor of what they were doing. Catallo explained to Gary Graff of the *Oakland Press*, "I think what we wanted to do was to go into an entirely different direction in writing, less big guitar, so to speak, and more songs that were melody driven with substance and a little more off-the-cuff storytelling. Times were changing. We had to make a mark in a certain era and we kinda wanted to head in a new direction for the times." The next thing the band did was change their name to Surfin' Pluto. They also changed their image and style of music as well. Nobody's Heroes was more heavy guitar oriented and the lyrics were darker. They also changed to writing more upbeat and melody based songs for their live show. "We wanted to concentrate on more upbeat melodies," Catallo explains further. "We're a real fun band. And the music represents that kind of attitude. Althought the lyrics may be serious, most of the stuff that we play stays quite upbeat."

Their onstage live shows continued to be successful. Their greatest success so far has been in winning the 1998 H.O.R.D.E./KOOL "Band to Band Combat" for the city of Detroit. At first they didn't think they had won anything but were thinking the complete opposite. "When we performed at the first Kool/H.O.R.D.E. Band to Band Combat," said Catallo to Perry, "we thought that our performance was so sub-standard that we had already started loading our equipment back into the van with the intention of leaving. My brother Chris and I were almost outside the side stage door when we heard them announce the winner. We stopped, dropped our equipment and looked at each other with huge eys and exclaimed: 'Holy shit we won!' The next thing I knew we were jumping around onstage with this giant size $10, 000 check!" This feat won them a spot on the H.O.R.D.E./Kool *Band to Band Combat* CD which was released in 1997. Their song "Millionaire" was featured on it. Being winner of the Band to Band Combat also gave the group the opportunity of playing on the road with Barenaked Ladies and Blues Traveller on *The H.O.R.D.E. Festival* at Pine Knob Music Theater, in Michigan, along with other selected tour dates.

In addition, they were also the H.O.R.D.E./Kool Midwest representatives for a concert at The House of Blues in Chicago. Important career establishing dates followed in quick succession. The next half of 1998 found Surfin' Pluto as the opening act for Chicago, David Lee Roth, REO Speedwagon, 38 Special, Eddie Money, Paul Rodgers [Bad Company], Robin Trower, The Smithereens, and Marshall Crenshaw.

The next project was to release a debut CD of their own. After they landed a distribution deal with Overture Records, they released their debut album, *Surfin' Pluto* in 1998. Audience reaction has been positive. It has been getting repeated radio play on a number of rock radio stations in the Michigan area. Songs like "Apathy," "Millionaire," "Wanna Be One," and "Deflowered," have roots in a pop oriented sound with strong melodies that have humorous lyrics. "Our main long-term goal is to be able to make a living doing what we all love so passionately. I'm talking about writing, recording, and performing our music. Our short term goals at this point in time are to find the right record label that will support us and h elp us achieve our long term goal. We feel that if you believe 100% in what you're doing and the music you make, (and for the first time we do), then that will be passed on to the audience or listener. If you don't believe in yourself and your music then why would anyone else?"

Selected discography

H.O.R.D.E./Kool Band to Band Combat East, (contributor), H.O.R.D.E. Corporation, 1998.
Surfin' Pluto, Overture Records, 1998.

Sources

Oakland Press, May 1998.

Additional information was obtained from an interview with Gene Catallo and from the Surfin' Pluto Press Kit.

—*Timothy Kevin Perry*

Clark Terry

Trumpet, bandleader

For more than six decades Clark Terry was a musician admired by his peers and honored by his public. Terry was known for several impressive gimmicks: playing his trumpet upside down; playing jazz phrases on just his mouthpiece; playing the flugelhorn and trumpet at the same time. But it was not these entertaining tricks that distinguished Terry. Though humor was never far away when Terry played, he brought to his craft a package of skills and a maturity that allowed him to share his wonderful gifts with colleagues, listeners, and aspiring musicians.

Born into poor circumstances in St. Louis, Missouri, December 14, 1920, Terry constructed his first trumpet out of a piece of garden hose, a funnel, and a cut-off piece of pipe for the mouthpiece. As Terry told *Down Beat*'s Mitchell Seidel, "the neighbors got sick of me blowing that horrendous noise on that gadget, so they chipped in and collected the $12.50 and bought me a trumpet from a pawn shop." While attending Vachon High School, he would rehearse with Ernie Wilkins, later to become one of Count Basie's principal arrangers and

AP/Wide World Photo. Reproduced by permission.

Born December 14, 1920 in St. Louis, MO, one of 10 children; first wife, Pauline, date of marriage and divorce unknown; married Gwendolyn Paris, 1992; stepson Gary Paris.

Made first "trumpet" out of crude materials; played with "Dollar Bill and Small Change," Rueben & Cherry Carnival, blues singer Ida Cox's "Darktown Scandals" show, and Fate Marable; 1942-45 played with U.S. Navy band at Great Lakes Naval Training Center, IL; played with Lionel Hampton, George Hudson, Charlie Barnet, Eddie "Cleanhead" Vinson, Charlie Ventura; joined Count Basie's big band and smaller combo, 1948-51; joined Duke Ellington orchestra, 1951-59; NBC staff musician, including "Tonight Show," 1960-1972; co-led combo with trombonist Bob Brookmeyer; formed big band, 1973; taught as clinician in high schools and colleges throughout the country; served as State Department jazz ambassador.

Awards: *Down Beat* "Talent Deserving Wider Recognition," 1963; Beacon in Jazz Award, New School of Music, New York, 1991;

Addresses: *Home*—218-14 36th Avenue, Bayside, NY 11360.

a member of his sax section. Terry played in a local drum and bugle corps before moving in with an older sister, where he helped pay the bills by hauling ashes. At about the same time he realized that his childhood dream of becoming a boxer did not mesh with the stronger desire to play the trumpet.

Worked His Way Up

"I always enjoyed practicing," he told Larry Birnbaum of *Down Beat*. "A lot of kids like to swim and roller skate, but I found that practicing was fun for me. Later, in the navy, I used to practice out of a clarinet book, because I always wanted to play fast passages, and I noticed that the clarinet books had faster things to play." Terry was determined to dispel the prevalent myth of his youth that the ability to read and play with technical precision interfered with the jazz feel. His practicing led to good things. After high school he played with a group

called Dollar Bill and Small Change; he traveled with the Rueben & Cherry Carnival; he played for blues singer Ida Cox's "Darktown Scandals;" he worked with pianist/leader Fate Marable who worked the Mississippi River on riverboats.

In 1942 he began a three-year stint in the United States Navy, playing with the elite band at the Great Lakes Naval Training Center near Chicago under the leadership of alto saxophonist Willie Smith. Among his bandmates there were Wilkins and trumpeter Gerald Wilson, who was later to become the leader himself of several notable bands. After leaving the Navy, Terry spent a few months with Lionel Hampton's band, then returned to St. Louis for a tour with George Hudson at Club Plantation. The band earned gigs and praises in New York, but after 18 months, the trumpeter moved to California where he played with the Charlie Barnet band for nearly a year. While on the coast he played with singer/saxophonist Eddie "Cleanhead" Vinson, with whom he made his first commercial recordings. He also played for a while with reedman Charlie Ventura.

Played with Royalty

In 1948, Terry joined the legendary Count Basie orchestra. Terry joined the trumpet section of the big band, but when economic stress struck, Basie was forced to reduce to a much smaller unit, usually an octet. The trumpeter returned for a while when Basie was able to reinstate the full band, which he led until his death. Terry convinced Basie to hire Wilkins as a reedman, but more importantly for his contributions to the band's songbook. Wilkins arranged such hits as the Joe Williams vocal showcase, "Everyday I Have the Blues." As Terry said in *Jazz Spoken Here*, "Basie taught us to slow down and play a note and use the space. Use the rhythm section. All that space in between is still a part of your solo. So Basie was very, very influential to me."

Jazz pioneer Duke Ellington heard Terry play with Basie in 1951, and decided he wanted Terry's sound in his band, but did not want to appear to be stealing from Basie's band. Terry feigned illness, as he explained to Birnbaum; "Duke said he would put me on salary, and that I should go home to St. Louis and wait until the band came through, and I would just happen to join them there. So I gave my notice to Basie—he took back the raise he had just given me—and I went to St. Louis and joined Duke." Terry often refers to his nearly nine-year stay with Duke as "attending the University of Ellingtonia," and the Basie experience as "prep school for acceptance" into that university. Ellington incorporated Terry's unique voice into his sonic palette just as he had with other stars, like saxophonists Johnny Hodges and Harry Carney, trumpeters Cootie Williams and Bubber Miley, and trombonists Lawrence Brown and "Tricky Sam" Nanton. Terry also did some writing and arranging for Ellington.

Broke Color Barrier

Upon leaving Ellington in 1959, Terry joined Quincy Jones' orchestra to play Harold Arlen's blues opera, *Free and Easy*. Its lukewarm reception actually led to Terry being hired by the National Broadcasting Company (NBC) in March of 1960. In a 1995 *Jazz Times* cover story celebrating Terry's 75th birthday, he told Bob Blumenthal how this came about. The Urban League had inquired of NBC why they had so few black employees, only to be told that there were no black people qualified to play music on television. The League sent out questionnaires seeking musicians who could "play studio music, read music, play in a section, play first trumpet, solo.... My name happened to come up on all the questionnaires," related Terry. The folding of "Free and Easy" allowed the trumpeter to accept NBC's offer.

Soon he became a fixture in the "Tonight Show" band, with which he was often featured in the "stump the band" segment, sometimes performing what had become somewhat of a trademark, his "Mumbles" act. Describing this act in *Jazz Lives*, Gene Lees wrote, "[Terry] is, as well, the most inventively humorous scat singer I've ever heard. His 'lyrics' tread to the edge of the salacious, then decay into the incomprehensible. This practice has earned him the nickname Mumbles." While at NBC, Terry maintained a breakneck pace that included a regular, daily shift of commercial shows for both radio and television as well as the "Tonight Show." Concurrently he co-led a quintet with trombonist Bob Brookmeyer at the Half Note club, which often ended at 3:00 or 4:00 a.m., sometimes followed by an 8:00 a.m. call at the studio. Gradually, however, network musical staffs decreased drastically.

When the "Tonight Show" moved to California in 1972, leader/trumpeter Doc Severinson offered Terry a chance to move with it, but he decided to remain in New York. He formed his Big B-A-D Band, staffed mostly by younger players and blessed by the arrangements of colleagues Ernie Wilkins, Frank Wess, Frank Foster, Phil Woods and others. The band recorded a live concert at Carnegie Hall and toured Europe, proving musically successful but a drain financially. Beginning in 1972, Terry joined promoter Norman Granz for a stint with the Jazz at the Philharmonic, as usual maintaining a broad schedule of free-lancing, which later included a series of tours to foreign countries as a musical ambassador under the auspices of the Department of State.

Professor Terry

While at NBC, Terry began an activity that has become a major focus of his efforts for more than two decades when he and other members of Severinson's band were invited to visit local schools. As Terry related to Blumenthal, "The jazz education scene was just taking off, it was very much in its infancy. It grew, and I just stuck with it. It's one of the most enjoyable things I do." His jazz education efforts included: the formation of the Harlem Youth Band; countless appearances at high schools and colleges throughout the country; regular summer camps for youth; and the establishment of the Clark Terry Institute of Jazz Studies at Tiekyo University near Sioux City, Iowa.

Among those he has mentored are the Marsalis brothers, trumpet sensation Wynton, and saxophonist Branford, who eventually succeeded Severinson as the leader of the "Tonight Show" band. In 1997 Terry was selected, along with other outstanding clinicians, to participate in JazzFest USA, an educational festival in Orlando, Florida, presented by *Down Beat*, the Thelonious Monk Institute of Jazz, and Universal Studios.

Introduced and Designed Flugelhorn

Most trumpeters credit Terry for re-introducing the flugelhorn to jazz. The larger-bored, softer-sounding horn had virtually disappeared until, as Terry told Blumenthal, "I got in contact with Keith Eckert, who was technical advisor for Selmer Brass, and we developed the first flugelhorn that Selmer put out in this country." Flugelhorns became a common sight on jazz bandstands and Olds produced the "CT" model, made to the specifications of Clark Terry. Terry was also partly responsible for trumpeters earning "doubling" pay when required to play both horns, just as almost all reed players receive if they play more than one instrument.

Though the flugelhorn requires more breath to fill it, Terry was as agile with it as he is with his trumpet. A master of triple-tonguing, he also utilized circular breathing, which allows one to play seemingly endless phrases without pausing to take a normal breath. Terry's major influence was Louis Armstrong. In his 1988 album *Portraits*, Terry honors other trumpeters he admires: Bunny Berigan, Roy Eldridge, Miles Davis, Harry Edison, and Harry James.

Selected discography

Duke with a Difference (with Johnny Hodges), Riverside, 1957.

In Orbit (with Thelonious Monk), Riverside, 1958, reissue OJC, 1987.

Oscar Peterson Trio Plus One (includes "Mumbles," "Incoherent Blues"), Mercury, 1964.

The Happy Horns of Clark Terry, Impulse!, 1964, reissue 1994..

Gingerbread Men (with Bob Brookmeyer), Mainstream, 1966.

Oscar Peterson and Clark Terry, Pablo, 1975.

Portraits, Chesky, 1988.

The Clark Terry Spacemen, Chiaroscuro, 1989.

Sources

Books

Enstice, Wayne and Paul Rubin, *Jazz Spoken Here: Conversations with Twenty-Two Musicians;* Louisiana State University Press, 1992.

Erlewine, Michael, et al, eds., *All Music Guide to Jazz;* Miller Freeman Books, 1996.

Gitler, Ira, *Swing to Bop;* Oxford University Press, 1985.

Holtje, Steve and Nancy Ann Lee, Eds., *Music Hound Jazz: The Essential Album Guide;* Visible Ink Press, 1998.

Lees, Gene, *Jazz Lives: 100 Portraits in Jazz;* Firefly, 1992.

Periodicals

AARP Bulletin, June, 1998.

Down Beat, September, 1981; June, 1986; April, 1989; October, 1994; June, 1996; July, 1997.

JazzTimes, October, 1995.

Jet, June 24, 1991; May 24, 1993.

—*Robert Dupuis*

Jean-Yves Thibaudet

Piano

Classical pianist Jean-Yves Thibaudet has become a command performer much in demand on the world concert scene. He is known for his beautiful poetic musical interpretations, and his skill at evoking the atmospheric textures, colors, and moods of the music he plays.

Born in Lyon, France to a family that heartily encouraged their children's participation in the fine arts, he began piano lessons at age five and worked hard to develop his skills. Talent showed in his seemingly effortless ability to play with an extraordinary gracefullness. At age seven, he gave his first public performance. While still a child, he apprenticed with Lucette Descaves, the great friend and collaborator of the composer Ravel. Thibaudet entered the Paris Conservatory as a twelve year old boy. Here, he studied music under the tutelage of Aldo Ciccolini. As he entered his teenage years, he won prizes for his piano playing and, at age 15, he won the Premier Prix du Conservatoire. At age 18 he won the 1981 Young Concert Artists Auditions.

Upon graduation, Thibaudet landed a contract with London/Decca Records and has remained with them ever since. He has performed in and released over 20 classical CDs throughout his career. In 1992, he released a watershed two-CD set of Ravel's complete piano works. It went over to great success. This work won Thibaudet Germany's illustrious *Schall-plattenpreis*

award and also garnered him a Grammy nomination. In addition to the Ravel works, he also released a rendering of Olivier Messiaen's Turangalila Symphony masterwork that same year. He was backed by the Royal Concertgebouw Orchestra conducted by Riccardo Chailly. The CD won the Edison Prize as well as the French *Diapason D'Or* award.

In 1993, Thibaudet released a CD with Miss Fassbaender of Wolf's *Morike Lieder* and he received many public accolades. He won the Grammaphone Award for *Morike Lieder* as well as another Edison Prize. In 1994, he released a command performance CD of Liszt's Opera Transcription, also to great critical success.

The year 1996 marked one of many future crowning achievments for Thibaudet. He made his Metropolitan Opera debut in Giordano's *Fedora*. A live April 1997 radio broadcast tape still exists of this great moment in classical piano playing. In a telecast shortly after, Thibaudet shows up in a the cameo role as the concert pianist/spy playing opposite Placido Domingo and Mirella Freni. Other U.S. season highlights were a debut recital on the *Great Performers* series at Avery Fisher Hall in 1997, with a number of dual recitals with Joshua Bell nationwide. The highest point during the tour was the performance at Carnegie Hall.

During 1997, Thibaudet played in a season of performances at the London Proms accompanied by the BBC Philharmonic. He returned to London in April of that year to preside over a mini "Thibaudet Festival" at Wigmore Hall. He also played and currently plays with the Orchestre Philharmonique de Monte Carlo, Prague Radio Symphony, the Ensemble Orchestral de Paris and the Royal Scottish National Orchestra. The next round of solo recitals took him to Paris, Bergamo, Rotterdam, Amsterdam, Glasgow and as far in the orient as Seoul, Korea. He also held a series of solo recitals throughout South America. Afterward, Thibaudet put in pleasing performances at the Pacific Music Festival in Japan accompanied by the London Symphony Orchestra. Michael Tilson Thomas conducted this performance.

For the last fifteen years, Thibaudet has played piano with every major orchestra in the United States and overseas. He has had the privilege of working with the greatest conductors of our time including Vladimir Ashkenazy, Riccardo Chailly, Charles Dutoit, Valery Gergiev, Mariss Jansons, Raymond Leppard, James Levine, Michael Tilson Thomas and Edo de Waart. All attest to his stellar artistry and knack at bringing a fresh interpretation to the work he plays. Without exception, his interpretations are always inspiringly original yet remain in keeping with the composer's intended spirit;

For the Record . . .

Born in Lyon, France; began studying classical piano at age five; studied with Lucette Descaves; studied at the Paris Conservatory under tutelage of Aldo Ciccolini.

Released a two-set cd of Ravel's complete piano works in 1992; released Olivier Messiaen's *Turangalila Symphony* with the Royal Concertgebouw Orchestra, 1992; released a cd of Wolf's *Morike Lidre* with Miss Fassbaender, 1993; released a cd of Liszt's Opera Transcriptions in 1994; debuted with the Metropolitan Opera performing Giordano's *Fedora*, 1996; released *Conversations with Bill Evans*, 1997; performed debut recital on *Great Performers* series at Avery Fisher Hall, 1997; performed at Carnegie Hall, 1997; contributor to soundtrack *Portrait of a Lady*.

Awards: Premier Prix du Conservatoire Award; Young Concert Artists Auditions Award, 1981; Germany's Schall-plattenpreis Award, 1992; The Edison Prize, 1992, 1993; the French Diapason D'Or Award, 1992; Grammaphone Award, 1993; French Diapason D'Or Award, 1993.

Addresses: *Record company*—Dorian Music, P.O. Box 285, Ayelsbury, HP22, 4SX, UK.

London Proms. Additional festival concerts have included Adelaide, Blossom, Caramoor, Casals, Hollywood Bowl, Istanbul, Mann Music Center, Prades, Prague, Ravinia, Saratoga, Schleswig-Holstein, Stavanger, and Tanglewood. Recent award winning releases are *Debussy Preludes Book I* and *II*, which won the Diapason d'Or award, recordings of Rachmaninoff's complete piano concertos *[Concerto No. 4]*, and a Brahms/Schumann recording with the Cleveland Orchestra. Appearances with Vladimar Ashenazy in several Ravel concertos with the Montreal Symphony under Charles Dutoit followed. Later in 1997, Thibaudet began work on the next two installments of his survey of the complete works of Debussy for solo piano. He also started work on Saint-Saens' *Carnival of the Animals* with conductor Sir George Solti. In addition, he worked with Herbert Blomstedt and the Leipzig Gewandhaus Orchestra as they undertook the Mendelssohn concertos.

In an effort to further expand his musical horizons, Thibaudet decided to try his hand at recording jazz. Over the years he had enjoyed listening to the best of the classical jazz greats. One artist he especially admired was the experimental pianist Bill Evans. Long known for a distinct quirky style of jazz piano playing, Evans was a musical subject Thibaduet wanted to explore in his recordings and, in March of 1997, he released a CD paying homage to this late jazz great. Later in the year, Thibaudet wanted to explore another musical avenue by recording movie soundtracks. He was featured in Nicole Kidman's movie, *Portrait of a Lady*, where he played two Schubert impromptus.

Selected discography

Ravel: Complete Works for Solo Piano, London/Decca Records, 1992.
Messiaen: Turanglia Symphony, London/Decca Records, 1992.
Rachmaninov Piano Concertos 1&3, London/Decca Records, 1993.
Debussy and Preludes, London/Decca Records, 1996.
Conversations with Bill Evans, London/Decca Records, 1997.

Sources

Jean-Yves Thibaudet Biography provided by the classicalinsites web site: hhttp://www.classicalinsites.com

—*Timothy Kevin Perry*

not an easy feat to pull off considering the complexities of some of the composers Thibaudet has chosen to work with and include in his recorded repertoire.

Along with performing with various world orchestras, Thibaudet also gives regular solo recitals. He has entertained the discriminating ear from London Wigmore Hall to Avery Fisher Hall in New York. He is also one of the most asked for performers and many other classical artists want to do duets with him. In response to this demand, as well as having a desire to expand his musical horizons, this multifaceted talent recently sought to expand his solo recitals by including duo recitals with violinist Joshua Bell, Olga Borodina, and Dmitri Hvorostovsky.

A regular performer at various summer festivals, Thibaudet has performed for the last 15 seasons at Italy's Spoleto Festival, and for the last six seasons at the

Michael Tilson-Thomas

Piano, conductor, composer

Formerly hailed as a "wunderkind" and, less flatteringly, as the "bad boy" of conducting, Michael Tilson Thomas has been a prominent figure in the classical music world since the late 1960s. Considered a top talent among American conductors for decades, it was not until 1995, when he was named musical director and principal conductor of the San Francisco Symphony, that Tilson Thomas became a full-time leader of a major American orchestra. Tilson Thomas' charismatic personality and advocacy of unfamiliar twentieth-century music—especially that of American composers—have helped to make the San Francisco Symphony an excitingly revitalized organization. "Regular pilgrimages to California have become necessary for anyone who means to keep track of the national scene. The Eastern bias of American music—monumentalized by the false cliché of a Big Five group of orchestras, in Boston, New York, Philadelphia, Cleveland, and Chicago—is collapsing under pressure from the West. It's not that these five orchestras have gone into decline: they still put a handsome frame around the nineteenth-century repertory. But they do not deliver surprises, and they do little to reflect the cities and cultures in which they live. The great Midwestern orchestras, in Cleveland and Chicago, are bolder: their programming shows an awareness that the twentieth century is happening, not to mention ending. But San Francisco has gone further

and done the job better," wrote Alex Ross in the *New Yorker*.

Michael Tilson Thomas was born in Los Angeles in 1944. His father, Ted, was a screenwriter and film producer. His mother, Roberta, was a schoolteacher. Tilson Thomas' paternal grandparents were Boris and Bessie Thomashefsky, renown performers in New York City's Yiddish theater in the early decades of the twentieth century. Ted Thomas shortened the family name to Thomas, but Tilson Thomas has contemplated going back to the name Thomashefsky to honor his grandfather. Although Tilson Thomas did not know his grandfather, who died in 1937, he feels a strong connection to him and uses his approach to the wide-ranging content of Yiddish theater as a model for his eclectic concert programming.

An only child, Tilson Thomas grew up in Hollywood with his parents and their friends who provided a stimulating cultural atmosphere. At age three, he began taking piano lessons. "I heard a lot of diverse music at home. I listened to everything—theater music, popular music, jazz, Stravinsky, medieval music, Beethoven quartets. I guess this contributed to the pluralistic view that I have of music," Tilson Thomas told Sheryl Flatow of *A&E Monthly*. At the University of Southern California Prep School, Tilson Thomas studied music with Dorothy Bishop. "Everything I am doing today is based on what I learned from Dorothy Bishop.... I started studying with her when I was ten. She appeared to be a scattered, elderly woman. She was, in fact, a tremendously imaginative educator," Tilson Thomas told Allan Ulrich of the *San Francisco Examiner*. Not surprisingly, Tilson Thomas is a strong supporter of increasing and improving music education in schools.

During high school, Tilson Thomas was drawn to a number of subjects besides music, including science and Asian culture. It was Tilson Thomas' broad range of interests that led him to attend the University of Southern California rather than a conservatory of music. His parents considered music a risky profession and hoped he would pursue a science-related career. Tilson Thomas told Katrine Ames of *Newsweek* that he insisted to his parents — "No, I have to make music."

Tilson Thomas entered USC as an advanced placement student in 1962 where he studied piano with John Crown. He graduated with a master's degree five years later. In the summer of 1968, Tilson Thomas studied conducting at the Berkshire Music Festival, run by the Boston Symphony Orchestra, where he won the Koussevitzky Prize as most promising young conductor. Tilson Thomas' impressive showing at the Berkshire Festival

Born December 21, 1944 in Los Angeles, CA; son of Ted Thomas (a screenwriter) and Roberta Thomas (a teacher). *Education:* University of Southern California, Los Angeles, CA; M.A. in music, 1967. Also studied at the Berkshire Music Center, Lenox, MA, summers of 1968 and 1969; and in master classes with violinist Jascha Heifetz, cellist Gregor Piatigorsky, and conductor Pierre Boulez.

Initially trained as a pianist. Began conducting career with the Young Musicians Foundation Debut Orchestra of Los Angeles 1963; production assistant at the Wagner Festival, Bayreuth, Germany, 1966; chief conductor, Ojai Music Festival, Ojai, CA, 1967; assistant conductor, Boston Symphony Orchestra, 1969-70; associate conductor, 1970-71; principal guest conductor, 1972-74; music director and principal conductor, Buffalo Philharmonic Orchestra, 1971-79; music director, New York Philharmonic Young People's Concerts, 1971-77; principal guest conductor, Los Angeles Philharmonic Orchestra, 1981-85; music director and principal conductor, London Symphony Orchestra 1987-95, principal guest conductor, 1995 to present. San Francisco Symphony Orchestra, music director and principal conductor, 1995 to present. Also founder and artistic director, New World Symphony, Miami, FL, 1987 to present; guest conductor at orchestras around the world. Works as a composer include "From the Diary of Anne Frank," 1990, and "Showa/Shoah," 1995. *Short Symphony, Symphonic Ode,* San Francisco Symphony, 1996; Hector Berlioz, *Symphonie Fantastique,* San Francisco Symphony, 1997; George Gershwin, *The 100th Birthday Celebration,* San Francisco Symphony, 1998.

Awards: Koussevitzky Prize for student-level conductors, 1968; *Musical America* Musician of the Year, 1971, Conductor of the Year, 1995; Ditson Award for contribution to American music, 1994; Chevalier des Arts et des Lettres (France), 1996; several Grammy awards.

Addresses: *Home*–Pacific Heights, San Francisco, CA; *Business*–San Francisco Symphony Orchestra, Davies Symphony Hall, San Francisco, CA 94102.

led to his being named assistant conductor of the Boston Symphony Orchestra in the fall of 1969.

Tilson Thomas' rise to fame began shortly after his appointment with the Boston Symphony when the orchestra's principal conductor, William Steinberg, became ill during a performance at New York City's Lincoln Center. Tilson Thomas took his place. The response from both the audience and critics toward the young conductor was highly favorable. Tilson Thomas' sudden thrust into notoriety, his highly physical manner at the podium and his dark good looks, led to comparisons with Leonard Bernstein. Tilson Thomas is flattered by the comparisons to Bernstein, who became his close friend and mentor. Bernstein even likened Tilson Thomas to his younger self, but some commentators don't see the similarities. "Comparisons to Bernstein are nonsensical, because in temperament Tilson Thomas is almost his opposite. His style is bright-toned, pointed in rhythm, devoted to the melodic line. It's really Franco-Russian.... Bernstein, for all his jazz panache, was Germanic," wrote Ross.

In 1970, Tilson Thomas was named associate conductor of the Boston Symphony Orchestra, and the following year became musical director and principal conductor of the Buffalo Philharmonic Orchestra, while continuing his association with the Boston Symphony as principal guest conductor. Under Tilson Thomas' direction, the Buffalo Philharmonic became an important venue for avant-garde works. However, the young conductor's brash personal style, his arrogant statements to the press, and his cultivation of a disco-hopping celebrity image were not universally appreciated. Disgruntled musicians took to calling him Michael Tinsel Tushy. An older and wiser Tilson Thomas acknowledges his youthful hauteur: "Back then, I thought the way to improve an orchestra was to fire a lot of the players," Tilson Thomas told Schiff.

Renewed Commitment to Music

In 1978, Tilson Thomas' supreme self-confidence was shaken by a drug arrest. Customs inspectors at Kennedy Airport in New York City found small amounts of marijuana, cocaine and amphetamines in his luggage. Tilson Thomas plea bargained and ended up paying only a $150 fine. Although the drug incident had no major effect on his professional reputation, it did lead Tilson Thomas to reassess his personal behavior and attitudes. "Some of the statements that I made years back about symphony orchestras being old fossils and about certain social scenes that were intolerable —

those were in some ways accurate observations of what was going on. But they were also manifestations of my frustration at the time. My God, I was booked up then, giving eight million concerts all over the world.... There was no place for any personal existence. I had to resolve that so I wouldn't resent what I do, which I don't. So what I'm trying to say is that I am now a very serious and committed musician," Tilson Thomas said of his life in the 1970s to Roddy in 1980.

In 1979, Tilson Thomas left Buffalo to freelance with orchestras around the world, including the New York City Opera, whose artistic director and premiere soprano, Beverly Sills, became one of his biggest fans. "He's got a non-stop mind. He's open to new ideas, and he's a delight to make music with," Sills said of Tilson Thomas to Birnbaum. In 1981, Tilson Thomas became principal guest conductor of the Los Angeles Philharmonic. Despite a successful four years in the post, he was passed over in favor of Andre Previn when the position of musical director and principal conductor opened in 1985.

Ironically, when Tilson Thomas took over the London Symphony in 1987, he was assuming a post formerly held by Previn. Time and experience had given Tilson Thomas maturity as both a conductor and a person. He enjoyed a good relationship with his associates in London. "He's a fantastic musician. He's helped us a lot. He's a stickler on the box [podium], and he hears everything," London Symphony senior concertmaster Lennie MacKenzie told Birnbaum in 1990. Tilson Thomas guided the London Symphony through rigorous touring and recording schedules and helped bring the orchestra back to the high standards it had maintained under Previn in the 1970s. "I think the LSO and I joined forces at just the right moment for both of us. And eight years there were important ones for me, as they really were the years of my mid-life crisis – when I had to come to terms with both my parents passing away – as well as that time when I stopped being a young musician," Tilson Thomas explained to Douglas Kennedy of Classic FM.

Success in San Francisco

In 1995, Tilson Thomas' returned to the United States as musical director and principal conductor of the San Francisco Symphony, an orchestra which he had guest conducted dozens of times over the previous 20 years. He took the baton from Herbert Blomstedt, who became the San Francisco Symphony's conductor laureate. "It was time for me to come back to the U.S., in my prime, or at least my majority. I find myself rediscovering all

the love I had for music in the beginning, except that now I have experience as well," he explained to Michael Walsh of Time. His arrival in San Francisco sent a shock wave through the city's cultural establishment. Symphony subscriptions went up by ten percent as the orchestra underwent a transformation from an unadventurous Old Guard organization to a vibrant musical force offering fresh renditions of familiar works and introducing new compositions. One of Tilson Thomas' innovations was to include an American work in nearly all of his concert programs. As he explained to Anthony Tommasini of the New York Times, "I have a passion for American twentieth-century music not based on dogma but on my instincts."

Tilson Thomas' inaugural season ended with An American Music Festival, a two-week celebration of American music featuring works by John Adams, Aaron Copland, John Cage, Leonard Bernstein, and others. "A marathon concert of avant-garde showpieces was capped by a dissonant jam session in which Tilson Thomas joined surviving members of the Grateful Dead. No one who was there will forget the sight of Davies Hall overrun with Deadheads, or the sound of them cheering Varese's Ionisation and Henry Cowell's Quartet Euphometric. Most wonderfully, the festival lacked the condescension that so often poisons classical-pop crossover schemes. It was an authentically festive day — topsy turvy, at times sublime," wrote Ross of An American Festival. To close his second season, Tilson Thomas presented a musical event called Celebrations of the Sacred and Profane which offered a wide variety of musical luminaries in eclectic combinations including Mozart, Bach, Schubert, Berlioz, and Kurt Weill. In June of 1998, Tilson Thomas and the orchestra presented an internationally acclaimed festival focusing on the works of Gustav Mahler. "The San Francisco Symphony has been a distinguished orchestra for many years, but the appointment of Michael Tilson Thomas as music director in 1995 served to confirm its stature as one of the country's more virtuosic and creative ensembles," wrote Tim Page of the Washington Post in 1998.

In addition to his duties in San Francisco, Tilson Thomas serves as artistic director of the Pacific Music Festival in Sapporo, Japan, an event which he co-founded with Leonard Bernstein in 1990. He also maintains a relationship with the London Symphony as principal guest conductor and is the artistic director and co-founder of the New World Symphony. Based in Miami Beach, the New World Symphony is made up of musicians who are beginning their professional careers. Tilson Thomas told Birnbaum that the New World Symphony is a "very important expression of my idealism. We can give these kids a foundation at the very beginning, so they won't burn out and so they can keep their souls together. I've told them that whoever has his soul at the end of fifty years of music making will be the winner."

Wine and Song

Tilson Thomas lives in a 1908 house in San Francisco's Pacific Heights section. The turn-of-the-century house reflects Tilson Thomas' interest in that time period. "Because of my grandparents and because of my involvement in the music of Ives and Mahler, I've always had a fixation about the years 1880 - 1910. So to discover this eclectic Edwardian American house was just fantastic," Tilson Thomas told Kennedy. In his non-working hours, Tilson Thomas enjoys fine food and wines. He likened great music to great wine. "Music is a psychological landscape, with all sorts of indefinable things. Wine is the same way. It has tastes that are very hard to define. The Chinese say that true flavor can only be defined by itself. When I drink a great wine, I get a sense of breadth—it's like a chord sounding and echoing," Tilson Thomas told Harvey Steiman of *Wine Spectator*.

In the future, Tilson Thomas would like to spend more time on composing. His major compositions so far are "From the Diary of Anne Frank," which premiered in 1990 with narration by Audrey Hepburn, and "Showa/Shoah," written to commemorate the atomic bombing of Hiroshima, Japan in 1945 and first performed at a fiftieth anniversary observance of the bombing in 1995. He would also like to delve further into conducting opera. "Until now my efforts in opera were rather negative. The time came when the necessary singers were not available, or when the stage directors acted crazy. But now such friends as Thomas Hampson and Renee Fleming are urging me to a new start with opera. Maybe this time things will go better," Tilson Thomas told Klaus Geitel of *Die Welt*. Most of all Tilson Thomas would like to find a balance between his enthusiasm for work and his personal need for peace and reflection. As he explained to Kennedy: "Quiet is so hard to find. When you have to react to so many different things as I do, you're just grateful for a little time to yourself at the end of the day. And what you want most of all is silence. You really need to stop yourself sometimes in order to remember what silence is like. And to hear the notes again."

Selected discography

With the Boston Symphony Orchestra

Carl Ruggles, *Sun-Treader*, 1970.
Igor Stravinsky, *Le Sacre du Printemps*, 1972.

With the San Francisco Symphony Orchestra

Serge Prokofiev, *Romeo and Juliet*, 1995.
Aaron Copland, *Orchestral Variations, Short Symphony, Symphonic Ode*, 1996.
Hector Berlioz, *Symphonie Fantastique*, 1997.
George Gershwin, *The 100th Birthday Celebration*, 1998.

With Others

(Cleveland Orchestra and Chrous) Carl Orff, *Carmina Burana*, 1974.
(New York Philharmonic) George Gershwin, *Rhapsody in Blue, An American in Paris*, 1975.
(Buffalo Philharmonic) Carl Ruggles, *Complete Works*, 1976.
(Los Angeles Philharmonic) Serge Prokofiev, *Lieutenant Kije Suite, Love for Three Oranges* Suite, 1978.
Gershwin Live! with Sarah Vaughan, 1982.
(Mormon Tabernacle Choir, Utah Symphony) Aaron Copland, *Choral Works*, 1985.
Richard Strauss, *Ein Heldenleben, Till Eulenspiegel*, 1988.
(Chicago Symphony) Charles Ives, *Symphony No. 1, Symphony No. 4*, 1989.
Leonard Bernstein, *On the Town*, 1992.

Sources

Periodicals

A & E Monthly, June 1996.
Classic fm, November 1997.
Fi: The Magazine of Music and Sound, January/February 1996.
Newsweek, October 2, 1995, pp. 82-83.
New Yorker, November 17, 1997, pp. 118-126.
New York Times, June 17, 1997.
New York Times Magazine, August 20, 1995, pp. 29-31.
Opera News, July 1975, pp. 18-19.
People, April 14, 1980, pp. 111-116.
San Francisco Examiner Magazine, August 6, 1995.
Sunday Times (London), November 3, 1996.
Time, April 16, 1990, pp. 66-68; April 1, 1996, p. 74.
Die Welt, November 15, 1996.
Washington Post, March 13, 1998, p. C1, 3.
Wine Spectator, November 15, 1997.

Online

http://classicalinsites.com

Additional information provided by the San Francisco Symphony Orchestra public relations office.

—*Mary Kalfatovic*

Ike and Tina Turner

Rhythm and blues duo

Combining gospel inspired vocals with rough, raunchy, and seductively sexy rhythm and blues (R&B), Ike and Tina Turner burst on to the musical scene in the early 1960s. At first, their sex-soaked soulful music captivated a mainly African American dominated audience. Slowly, however, mainstream white America began to warm to them, most notably through their R&B hits that successfully crossed over to the pop charts. Covering songs like Creedence Clearwater Revival's "Proud Mary,"—their only American top ten pop hit—didn't exactly hurt their careers, either. Despite the rather tepid reception they received in their American homeland, Ike and Tina Turner were revered in Europe, counting among their many admirers the Rolling Stones.

During the 1950s, Ike Turner was fronting an R&B band called the Kings of Rhythm. The band had become the house band of the East St. Louis, Missouri based club called the Manhattan. During their tenure as the house band of the club, they had achieved the reputation of one of the better rhythm and blues bands in the area. At the same time, 17-year- old Anna Mae Bullock began accompanying her sister to the Manhattan. She became entranced with Turner and his band, and would regularly attend the club to see the Rhythm Kings. Bullock repeatedly asked Turner if she could sing with the band, but to no avail. One day, the band's drummer offered the microphone to Bullock's sister who declined to opportunity to get up and sing with the band. Leaping at the chance she had been waiting for, Bullock leapt on stage and belted one out with the band. Turner was amazed with what he heard and told her that she could sing with the band as one of their vocalists. Not too long after this, Turner and Bullock began to date.

Bullock and Turner married in 1958. Soon after, Turner then re-christened his new bride calling her Tina after Sheena, the so-called queen of the jungle. When a session singer, who was to record Turner's song "A Fool in Love" was unable to show up, Tina took over the vocal duties, and the song became the first single by Ike and Tina Turner. The single, which was released on the Sue label in 1960, climbed to number two on the American R&B chart, and peaked at number 27 on the pop chart. The Rhythm Kings now became members of the newly formed Ike and Tina Turner Revue. The Revue also featured the Ikettes, who were Tina's backing singers and dancers. The Ikettes and Tina infused the Revue with a seductive sexuality as they strutted across the stage in short skirts and high heels.

Their next single "I Idolize You" made the R&B top five while languishing in the lower reaches of the pop chart, in December of 1960. Ike and Tina Turner's next single, "It's Gonna Work Out Fine," an R&B number two hit,

For the Record . . .

Members include: **Ike Turner** (born Izear Luster Turner, Jr., November 5, 1931 in Clarksdale, MS), guitar; **Tina Turner** (born Anna Mae Bullock, November 26, 1939 in Brownsville, TN), vocals.

Group formed in St. Louis, MO, 1956; signed to Sue Records and released "A Fool in Love," 1960; released "I Idolize You," 1960, released "It's Gonna Work Out Fine," 1961; released *The Soul of Ike and Tina Turner*, 1961; released *Don't Play Me Cheap*, 1962; released It's *Gonna Work Out Fine*, 1962; signed with Warner Brothers and released *Live! The Ike and Tina Turner Show*, 1965; signed with Phillies and released "River Deep, Mountain High," 1966; signed to Pompeii and released *Ike and Tina Turner Show Vol. II*, 1967; released *So Fine*, 1968; signed to A&M and released *River Deep, Mountain High*, 1969; signed to Blue Thumb and released *Outta Season*, 1969; released *The Hunter*, 1969; signed to Minit and released *In Person*, 1969; released *Come Together*, 1970; released *Workin' Together*, c. 1970; released *Live from Carnegie Hall/What You Hear is What You Get*, 1971; released *'Nuff Said*, 1971, released *Feel Good*, 1972; released *Nutbush City Limits*, 1974.

Awards: Gold certification for "Proud Mary," 1971; gold certification for *Live from Carnegie Hall/What You Hear is What You Get*, 1972; inducted into the Rock and Roll Hall of Fame, 1991.

for Tina, provided that Ike had no input on the song, contacted them. Ike was reluctant at first but then changed his mind when Spector offered to put both his and Tina's names on the record. Spector paid him $20,000 for Tina's services. The resultant single "River Deep, Mountain High," was, in effect, Tina's first solo recording, despite the fact that Ike was also named on the record. Released in 1966, the single failed to ignite the American singles chart and languished at number 88. On the *Fans of Tina* website, Tina was quoted as saying that the reason "River Deep, Mountain High, had not done so well in America was that "it was too black for the pop radio stations and too pop for the black stations."

All of her hard work was not for naught, though, as "River Deep, Mountain High" rocketed up the British singles chart and landed at number three. All of a sudden, the Ike and Tina Turner Revue was the next big thing in Europe, where they were treated as major celebrities. In America, however, they were still relegated to playing solely the R&B circuit. In October of 1966, the album *River Deep, Mountain High* cracked the British top thirty. The Ike and Tina Turner Revue were then asked to open for the Rolling Stones on their 1966 tour of England. They continued to tour and released *The Ike and Tina Turner Show Vol. II* in the spring of 1967. Their next record, *So Fine*, was released on Pompeii, in 1968.

Signing to a two-album contract with Blue Thumb Records, Ike and Tina Turner released *Outta Season* and *The Hunter*, in 1969. They also signed a long-term contract with Minit and released the live *In Person* in 1969. Three years after it was released in England, *River Deep, Mountain High* was released in America by A&M. It peaked at number 102. Another supporting slot with the Rolling Stones, this time in America, brought the busy year of 1969 to a close for Ike and Tina Turner.

Come Together featuring a cover of the Beatles' song of the same name, and a cover of the Sly and the Family Stone song "I Want to Take You Higher" was released in 1970. The following year, Ike and Tina Turner finally made it big, in terms of success, on the American pop chart as their R&B based cover of the Creedence Clearwater Revival song "Proud Mary" cracked the top five. The album it was culled from, *Workin' Together*, made it to number 25 on the American album chart, as did their live double album *Live from Carnegie Hall/What You Hear is What You Get,* both of which were released in 1971. In late 1971, *'Nuff Said* was released, but failed to gain the success of its predecessors.

Throughout most of their career and marriage, Ike abused Tina, both physically and emotionally . After a

crashed the pop top 20 and landed at number 14, in the autumn of 1961. A few months later their debut album, *The Soul of Ike and Tina Turner,* was released. In 1962, the Ike and Tina Turner Revue released two more albums on Sue, *It's Gonna Work Out Fine* and *Don't Play Me Cheap*. Although a consistently popular act on the R&B circuit, in America, the Ike and Tina Turner Revue did not manage to parlay its tremendous success on to the predominantly white pop market in America. They signed with Warner Brothers, in 1965, and released *Live! The Ike and Tina Turner Show*.

The dawn of 1966 marked a turning point in the fame and fortune of Ike and Tina Turner. Recalcitrant record producer Phil Spector, who offered to produce a single

bloody fight on July 2, 1976, Tina decided that she had had enough and walked out on her husband. She left with a gas card and less than 40 cents to her name. In October of 1976, their professional partnership was officially dissolved. Two years later, their divorce became final. Ike and Tina Turner were inducted into the Rock and Roll Hall of Fame in 1991.

Selected discography

The Soul of Ike and Tina Turner, Sue, 1961.
Don't Play Me Cheap, Sue, 1962.
It's Gonna Work Out Fine, Sue, 1962
Live! The Ike and Tina Turner Show, Warner Brothers, 1965.
Ike and Tina Turner Show Vol. II, Pompeii, 1967.
So Fine, Pompeii, 1968.
River Deep, Mountain High, A&M, 1969.
Outta Season, Blue Thumb, 1969.
The Hunter, Blue Thumb, 1969.
In Person, Minit, 1969.
Come Together, Liberty, 1970.
Workin' Together, Liberty, c. 1970.
Live from Carnegie Hall/What You Hear is What You Get, United Artists, 1971.
'Nuff Said, United Artists, 1971.
Feel Good, United Artists, 1972.
Nutbush City Limits, United Artists, 1974.

Sources

Books

Helander, Brock, ed. *Rock Who's Who,* second edition, Schirmer, 1996.
Rees, Dayfdd, and Luke Crampton, *Encyclopedia of Rock Stars,* DK, 1989.

Online

members.aol.com/fansoftina/english/lifestory.html (October 13, 1998).
http://www.rockhall.com/induct/turnike.html (September 9, 1998).
http://www.tristatenet.org/cpb/MSWritersAndMusicians/musicians/Turner.html (October 4, 1998).

—*Mary Alice Adams*

Luther Vandross

Singer, songwriter

Rhythm and blues singer Luther Vandross is best known for his soulful renditions of emotionally charged love ballads. Vandross' wide singing range runs from lush tenor to robust baritone and represents only one of his various talents. He has won numerous Grammy awards, while maintaining complete artistic control of his work. His musical compositions and arrangements have been recorded by many of the greatest American pop singers. Vandross, in addition to his fame as a solo artist, gained notoriety as one of the most talented backup singers in modern music. He released an astonishing 13 platinum albums in succession, beginning with his first major release.

Vandross was born in New York on Manhattan's Lower East Side on April 20, 1951. The youngest of four siblings, he was the son of an upholsterer who died from diabetes when Vandross was just eight. As a result, Vandross developed a close relationship with his mother, Mary Ida Vandross. The Vandross children were musically inclined, a trait that they inherited from their parents. His mother recognized Vandross' particular musical bent and saw to his musical education when he was still very young, beginning his piano lessons at age three.

One of Vandross' older sisters sang with the Crests as a teen-ager, and although she left home while Vandross was still a child, he cultivated a particular love and respect for the female singing styles. He was drawn in particular to the late 1960's moods of Diana Ross, Dionne Warwick, and Aretha Franklin. Vandross saw the unrestrained emotion of female singers was a magnificent faculty rarely found in the work of male pop vocalists. When Vandross was 13 he moved with his mother to the South Bronx in New York where he attended Taft High School. His interest in music became overpowering by his senior year, and although he enrolled at Western Michigan University in Kalamazoo, he abandoned his formal education after by the end of his second semester, opting instead to embark on a musical career.

From that point Vandross achieved prominence through a delicate combination of talent and luck. One of his compositions, "Everybody Rejoice," was incorporated into the score of the Broadway musical *The Wiz* in 1972. Two years later he attended some taping sessions for rock star David Bowie in the company of a friend who worked as part of the Bowie entourage. As Vandross observed the taping sessions he expressed personal observations about Bowie's musical arrangements. Vandross used his own voice to illustrate his ideas, and his comments were taken seriously by Bowie, who encouraged Vandross to join the company as a backup artist on Bowie's album *Young Americans*.

Eventually Vandross was invited to tour with Bowie, as a warm up for Bowie's act. Vandross accepted the offer, but soon complained that the experience was exhausting, and expressed apprehension. The stress of performance caused him to be nervous and overwrought. He felt anxious at the thought of facing an audience of strangers. Bowie, convinced of Vandross' potential, influenced Vandross to persevere, emphasizing to Vandross that the experiences of live performance would be critical to his future success as an entertainer.

In time Bowie referred Vandross to Bette Midler who arranged to hire Vandross as a backup singer. Vandross embarked on a career as a backup singer for many popular artists including Carly Simon, Barbra Streisand, and the Average White Band. He also made a lucrative living singing jingles for television commercials. During this time Vandross sang with the disco band Change and created a group called Bionic Boogie, a studio production of sound mixes, all performed by Vandross—a virtual one-man band.

Vandross formed his own R&B group, Luther, in 1975. With the influence of Arif Mardin the group Luther signed to record with Cotillion Records. Luther was a short-lived enterprise, their records falling well short of expecta-

Born April 20, 1951, in New York; father, an upholsterer; mother, Mary Ida Vandross; youngest of four siblings. *Education*: Attended Western Michigan University, Kalamazoo, MI.

Career: wrote "Everybody Rejoice" for *The Wiz*, 1972; backup singer on David Bowie's *Young Americans;* toured with David Bowie, 1974; Atlantic Records, backup vocalist for Bette Midler, Carly Simon, Barbra Streisand, Roberta Flack, and others, 1974-81; singer/songwriter of commercial jingles, started group, Bionic Boogie and sang with Change, 1974; signed group, Luther, with Cotillion records, 1975; signed with Sony's Epic Records, released 13 consecutive platinum selling albums, 1981-1997; performed "In the Spotlight" from Royal Albert Hall for Public Broadcasting System, 1994; first release with Virgin Records in 1998.

Awards: National Academy of Recording Arts & Science Most Valuable Player—Best Male Vocalist, 1979; Grammy awards: Best R&B Song, Best R&B Male Vocal Performance, 1990; Best R&B Male Vocal Performance, 1998.

Addresses: *Record company*—Virgin Records, 338 North Foothill Road, Beverly Hills, CA 90210.

album in 1995, featuring seven new co-written songs, along with a variety of classic carols. In 1996 Vandross performed at the Essence Music Festival. Vandross received the honor of singing the national anthem at the 1997 NFL Super Bowl, and that same year went on a five-city U.S. tour beginning in Las Vegas and culminating in Washington D.C.

Vandross parted ways with Epic in 1998, after a 16-year partnership during which Vandross released 12 hit albums and sent 22 of singles into the top ten of the R&B charts. The separation from Sony—attributed to a dispute over artistic freedom—led to a new contract for Vandross with Virgin Records. His first album for Virgin, 1998s *I Know,* featured a bevy of stars including Stevie Wonder, "Precise," Cassandra Wilson, and Bob James. The album received generally excellent reviews. Despite achieving super-stardom as a solo artist, Vandross continued to sing as a back up from time to time for a number of notable singers.

Vandross received five Grammy awards from 1990-98, including two for "Power of Love." He received three Grammys for Best R&B Male Vocal Performance, and also one for Best R&B song. All together he received three Grammy nominations in 1994, four nominations in 1995; three nominations in 1996, and three in 1997. Vandross made an acting debut in 1993 in the Robert Townsend film *The Meteor Man* and co-hosted the Soul Train Music Awards.

Selected discography

Never Too Much, Epic, 1981.
Forever, for Always, for Love, Epic, 1982.
The Best of Luther Vandross, The Best of Love, 1989.
Songs, Epic, 1994.
Luther Vandross 1981-1995 Greatest Hits, Epic, 1995.
This is Christmas, Epic, 1995.
Your Secret Love, Epic, 1997.
One Night With You: The Best of Love II, Epic, 1997.
I Know, Virgin Records, 1998.

Sources

Books

Clarke, Donald, ed., *The Penguin Encyclopedia of Popular Music,* Viking, 1989.
Rock On: The Illustrated Encyclopedia of Rock n' Roll, the Video Revolution, 1978-present, Volume 3.
Stambler, Irwin, *Encyclopedia of Pop, Rock & Soul,* revised, St. Martin's Press, 1989.

tions. Vandross, meanwhile, aspired to a recording contract that would allow him complete creative control over his recordings. Vandross signed with Epic Records in 1981 and his popularity, both as a singer and a songwriter, flourished steadily from that point forward.

Over the years Vandross wrote songs for Aretha Franklin, Diana Ross, Dionne Warwick, while his own singing career blossomed steadily. By 1991 his double album, *The Best of Luther Vandross, The Best of Love,* became a double platinum seller, and Vandross' success was assured. In 1991-92 Vandross embarked on a U.S. tour that culled a total attendance of 650,000 spectators nationwide and earned $15 million in box office receipts. In 1994 he performed a television special for the Public Broadcasting System called *In the Spotlight,* from Royal Albert Hall in London. He released a Christmas

Periodicals

Arizona Republic, December 19, 1997.
Baltimore Afro-American, November 30, 1996.
Detroit News, September 1, 1998.
Gannett News Service, November 27, 1994.
Independent, March 7, 1997, p. 10(2).
Rocky Mountain News, September 5, 1997, p. 18D.
St. Louis Post-Dispatch, September 4, 1997, p. 5.
Sacramento Observer, January 22, 1997.
Tulsa World, August 7, 1998.

Online

www.virginrecords.com/artists/
   VR.cgi?ARTIST_NAME=Luther_Vandross,
(October 5, 1998).
www.sonymusic.com/artists/LutherVandross/
   biography.html (September 23, 1998).
www.dotmusic.co.uk/MWtalentluther.html (September 10,
   1998).

—*Gloria Cooksey*

Jimmie Vaughan

Guitar, singer

Texas guitarist and vocalist Jimmie Vaughan estab lished himself as a powerful blues presence as a member the Fabulous Thunderbirds, and later as a solo artist. A native of Dallas, Texas and longtime resident of Austin, Texas, he offers contradictory blues that celebrate being alive as opposed to the usual "My-baby-done-left-me" blues commiseration. As the older brother of rock 'n' roll icon Stevie Ray Vaughan, who died in a tragic accident at the peak of his fame, he was noted for his musical craftsmanship more than the type of super-stardom his brother had achieved.

Vaughan covered his own material as well as songs such as Johnny Guitar Watson's "Motorhead Baby" and other traditional Southwestern blues classics. The *Houston Chronicle*'s Marty Racine wrote, "Think Freddie-King-meets-Booker T and the MGs. It's a mid-South circuitry that deviates from the usual Mississippi Delta/ Chicago lineage and enriches the blues (much as Robert Cray did...) with an icy craftsmanship dedicated more to composition than form." Vaughan refers to his music as "Dallas music" because it reminds him of the music that overwhelmed him when he was a child. His music reflects the Top 40 blues and r&b flavor of Texas in the 1950s and 1960s, with the addition of his own unique, soul-drenched style.

James Lee Vaughan was born in 1953, and by the time he was 14, he had already started sneaking out of his home and taking cabs to a local blues club in Dallas called the Empire Ballroom. One of the employees there would let Vaughan in through the back door and keep an eye on him. Vaughan saw performers such as Freddie King, T-Bone Walker, and other blues legends. By the time he was 15, he was playing lead guitar in a Dallas-based blues-rock band called the Chessmen. The Chessman covered the psychedelic, overblown sounds of Jimi Hendrix, Cream, and the Yardbirds. *Guitar World*'s Alan Paul wrote of Vaughan, "His ability to play note-perfect versions of the day's hits helped make ... [the Chessmen] one of the city's top club and college-circuit draws." Vaughan told Paul, "I was making 300 bucks a week, more money than my dad .... Everyone else in the band was 21, and I was this little kid with attitude and a Telecaster. I knew all the licks."

When Vaughan was 15 or 16, he opened for Jimi Hendrix as part of the Chessmen; since the band was known for its covers of Hendrix and Cream, the band couldn't play half of its repertoire and opened with Cream's "Sunshine of Your Love". Vaughan told Paul, "[Hendrix's] the Experience all came out of their dressing room to watch us, because they thought we were funny. Here they were in Texas, listening to a Cream cover band, and the guitarist is this little kid wearing a big jacket with feathers all over it. I was just trying to be as much like Hendrix as I could."

Vaughan was a founding member of the Fabulous Thunderbirds. The group released five albums in six years, beginning in 1986 with the platinum *Tough Enuff* and its top ten single. Four years later in 1990, Vaughan enjoyed his last appearance with the band in Fort Hood, Texas. By the time Vaughan left the band, he had completed his first studio collaboration with his younger brother Stevie Ray. The album, *Family Style,* was released in 1990. A few weeks before the album's release, Stevie Ray Vaughan died in a helicopter crash in Wisconsin at the age of 35, plummeting his older brother Jimmie into a depression that lasted for roughly for two and half years.

In 1992, Eric Clapton asked Vaughan to open a series of concerts for him at London's Royal Albert Hall. Although Vaughan hadn't felt like touring or making an album since his brother's death, he later explained to Epic, his label, that the reason he agreed to open for Clapton was, "I just didn't have the guts to tell him no." The audience response to this series of concerts was so positive that Vaughan returned home and began work on his first Epic solo album, *Strange Pleasure,* which was nominated for a Grammy Award in 1993.

Strange Pleasure featured eleven songs, including "Six Strings Down," a paean to his brother and other blues

For the Record . . .

Born James Lee Vaughan, 1953, in Dallas, TX.

Began playing as lead guitarist in a Dallas-based blues-rock band the Chessmen at the age of 15; opened for Jimi Hendrix as member of the Chessmen; founding member of the Fabulous Thunderbirds; left the Fabulous Thunderbirds in 1990; completed first studio collaboration with his younger brother, Stevie Ray, *Family Style*, 1990; Stevie Ray died in helicopter accident a few weeks before the album's release; opened a series of concerts for Eric Clapton at London's Royal Albert Hall, 1992; released his first solo album, *Strange Pleasure*, 1993; organized and directed *A Tribute To Stevie Ray Vaughan* for PBS, 1995; released *Out There*, 1998.

Awards: Grammy Award for Best Rock Instrumental Performance for "SRV Shuffle," 1996.

Addresses: *Record company*—Epic Records, 550 Madison Avenue, New York, NY 10022-3297.

foot pedals, which gives him a unique roadhouse vibe. In 1998 Vaughan released *Out There* and returned to touring. *Musician Magazine*'s Ted Drozdowski wrote of *Out There*, "The depth and simplicity of his performance recalls the Buddhist notion that the universe's secrets can be found in a single blade of grass." After the release of *Out There*, Racine wrote, "Unlike Little Brother's [Stevie Ray] stratospheric rock 'n' roll-ish bleed-all-over-the-frets confessions, Vaughan is grounded like a lightning rod." Vaughan's remarkable continuity established a bona fide trademark sound. Although Vaughan had been playing since the 1960s, he didn't begin singing until the 1990s. He told Paul that he was scared to sing: "I was scared to death .... I would sound like a 12-year-old kid.... So I just never did it. Now I'm starting to enjoy it, and I have some nights where I think I'm actually pretty good at it."

Vaughan told Paul that when he was 18 and just starting out in the music business, he assumed a record deal was the reward for hard work and for being a good musician. "And it was a real rude awakening when I found out that it had to do with all this other stuff, like who your manager was and what you looked like." Vaughan eventually came to accept the ways of the music industry world—and the challenges of life—telling Drozdowski, "You know the little RCA dog? Well, that's where I'm at, with my ear cocked up and listening. Freedom and honesty are where it's at for me. I'm discovering things."

legends, co-written by Vaughan with Art and Cyril Neville of the Neville Brothers. Vaughan and his Tilt-A-Whirl Band toured extensively as both headliner and supporting act, and performed on the *Conan O'Brien Show* as well as *Late Night With David Letterman*. Two years later, in 1995, Vaughan organized and directed a one-time concert event in Austin called *A Tribute To Stevie Ray Vaughan*, featuring performances by Eric Clapton, Robert Cray, Buddy Guy, Dr. John, B.B. King, Art Neville, and Bonnie Raitt. The concert was released as an album and a videocassette, and the single "SRV Shuffle" earned Vaughan a Grammy Award in 1996 for Best Rock Instrumental Performance.

Vaughan's sound is defined by the presence of a swinging drummer and an organist playing bass with

Selected discography

Family Style, Epic Records, 1990.
Strange Pleasure, Epic, 1993.
Out There, Epic, 1998.

Sources

Guitar World, August 1998.
Houston Chronicle, June 28, 1998.
Musician, August 1998.
Request, August 1998.

—B. Kimberly Taylor

Muddy Waters

Blues singer

Born in the area of rural Mississippi that spawned the first and greatest recorded bluesmen—Charley Patton, Son House and Robert Johnson—Muddy Waters electrified the sounds of rural blues and brought them to Chicago. At his peak in the 1950s, he was the undisputed King of the Blues, a moniker he went so far as to have printed on his calling cards. His name eventually became synonymous with the Chicago blues, and by the time of his death he was the most famous and beloved bluesman in the world.

Muddy Waters was born McKinley Morganfield on April 4, 1915 in Rolling Fork, Mississippi, deep within cotton country. Sometime as a boy he was given the nickname Muddy Waters, for reasons no longer known. His share-cropper father, Ollie, played guitar but Muddy never had the chance to learn anything from him. After his mother's early death, he was sent away to be raised by his grandmother in Clarksdale. Muddy worked the farm as a boy, but music was his real interest. "I always thought of myself as a musician," he said. "If I wasn't a good musician then, I felt that sooner or later I would be a good musician. I felt it in me."

Muddy's first instrument was the harmonica, which he took up when he was around 13. He played country suppers for tips and food with a guitarist friend. Guitars were all around him in the Mississippi Delta country, however, and while still a teenager Muddy saw greats Charley Patton and Son House perform. House was an especially strong influence on Muddy's playing. He showed the youngster the rudiments of playing slide guitar with a bottleneck and impressed young Muddy with his powerful, emotional singing. Muddy began playing guitar when he was 17.

He learned quickly and was soon playing local events. In the early 1940s, he joined a group that included the singer Big Joe Williams that played around town. Muddy Waters' encounter with destiny took place in summer 1941 when Alan Lomax and John Work, two folklorists from the Library of Congress came to Clarksdale. The two men were looking for the legendary blues guitarist, Robert Johnson. Johnson, however, was dead, murdered years before. Instead, on Son House's recommendation, they found Muddy Waters at Stovall's plantation. Muddy recorded two songs for the Library of Congress, "I Be's Troubled" and "Country Blues."

The songs impressed Lomax and Work enough that they returned to Stovall's two years later and recorded Muddy again. His ambition and perhaps his confidence spurred by his two recording experiences, Muddy got his first job as a professional musician, playing harmonica in the Silas Green Carnival for a short time. Clarksdale couldn't satisfy the Muddy's needs though, and in May 1943 he packed his bags and took the train north to Chicago.

Times were good in Chicago and Muddy quickly found work and an apartment. Big Bill Broonzy, who had been part of the Chicago music scene for years, introduced him around. With Jimmy Rodgers, a guitarist and harp player, he began playing house parties around the South Side. "Little Walter, Jimmy Rodgers and myself," Muddy later recalled, "we would go around looking for bands that were playing. We called ourselves The Headhunters, 'cause we'd go in and if we got a chance we were gonna burn 'em."

Muddy's New Sound

It was three years before Muddy was finally able to record in Chicago. But the results of the sessions were just warmed over versions of the urban jump blues that were already a decade old and the record companies, 20th Century and Columbia, did not release any as records. Muddy got another chance when pianist Sunnyland Slim, with whom he had been performing around Chicago, was offered a session with Leonard Chess' Aristocrat Records. According to legend, Muddy was delivering venetian blinds when he heard that Slim wanted him to play the session. Muddy is said to have told his boss that he needed the rest of the day off—his cousin had been found dead in an alley. Slim and Muddy recorded two numbers each.

The music wouldn't have gone anywhere, except for the presence of a black music scout who arranged for another session, which resulted in a record for Muddy, "I Can't Be Satisfied" and "I Feel Like Going Home." The songs were nothing like the smooth blues that had been popular in Chicago. Backed only by Muddy's electric bottleneck guitar and Big Crawford's bass, they were raw, the delta blues transplanted to the city. Leonard Chess didn't like it. "I can't understand what he's singing," he complained to his partner. She insisted that the music had some indefinable something and pushed for its release.

The single, "Aristocrat 1305," came out on a Saturday in April 1948. It was a smash hit. By 2 o'clock in the afternoon the first pressing had sold out completely. Muddy Waters went down to a record store on Chicago's Maxwell Street, he found his record being sold for $1.10 instead of the list price 79¢. To make matters worse, the record was so popular the store would only sell customers one copy, despite Muddy's protestation "But I'm the man who made it!"

The unexpected success of the record forced Len Chess to reconsider his opinion of Muddy's music. Muddy was playing Chicago clubs regularly with Jimmy Rodgers and Baby Face Leroy. Chess did not want to give up a good thing. When new sessions were arranged, they were with Muddy and Big Crawford again. They produced a string of classics nonetheless, including "You're Gonna Miss Me," "Little Geneva," and "Rollin' Stone." When Muddy recorded with groups it was on the records others were making. He played on Baby Face Leroy's popular "Rollin' And Tumblin'" for example. When Leonard Chess found out he was incensed—he had hoped to keep Muddy's trademark slide sound restricted to Aristocrat Records. He responded by having Muddy record his own version of the song.

Got Mojo Workin'

In 1950 Aristocrat Records became Chess Records, and Little Walter, perhaps the greatest blues harp player in history, joined the Muddy Waters band. Mike Rowe, in his history of the Chicago blues, *Chicago Breakdown,* wrote "The Muddy Waters records of 1950 and 1951 represent the purest and most successful strain of the new country blues." The songs they made include "Louisiana Blues," "Early Morning Blues," "Sad Letter Blues," and "Long Distance Call." Muddy's sound continued to evolve, however. He and Rodgers refined the interaction of their two guitars, Junior Wells replaced Little Walter on harp, Otis Spann came in to play piano.

By the middle 1950s, he had all but abandoned the spare instrumentation of his earlier hits and replaced it with the rollicking sound of the songs that would come to be most closely associated with Muddy: "Hootchie Cootchie Man," "Mannish Boy," and "I Got My Mojo Workin'." The first record sold 4000 copies in its first week in stores and stayed at the top of the charts for most of summer 1954.

The middle 1950s represented Muddy Waters' peak as a recording artist. The musicians he recorded with during that period are a roster of the greats of the Chicago blues: harp players Big Walter Horton, Junior Wells, and James Cotton, guitarists Buddy Guy and Matt Murphy, pianists Otis Spann and Pinetop Perkins, drummer Fred Below and bass player Willie Dixon. Dixon was responsible for composing many of the songs Muddy recorded in the latter half of the fifties.

New Audiences, New Sidemen

With the rise of rock and roll, Muddy's music—and blues music in general—entered a period of decline that would last until the end of his life. He continued to perform and make records during the 1960s. His performance at the 1960 Newport Folk Festival was electrifying and showed off his music to a whole new audience of young, white fans. He would continue to direct his music at this new audience and his 1960s albums, like *The London Sessions* which saw him team up with British rock musicians, like Eric Clapton and Steve Winwood, and *Fathers and Sons*, with Paul Butterfield and Mike Bloomfield, reflected his new focus.

Muddy's career experienced a kind of renaissance in the 1970, when blues-rock guitarist Johnny Winter became his manager. Recording and touring with Winter, Muddy cut four albums that recaptured some of the old excitement, in particular a live effort, *Muddy "Mississippi" Waters,* mostly on the Columbia label. When Muddy Waters died suddenly of a heart attack in Chicago on April 30, 1983 an era in the blues came to an end forever. Muddy was inducted into the Blues Foundation Hall of Fame in 1980 and into the Rock Hall of Fame in 1987

Selected discography

Muddy Waters at Newport, MCA/Chess, 1960
The Real Folk Blues, MCA/Chess, 1965
More Real Folk Blues, MCA/Chess, 1967
Hard Again, Blue Sky, 1977
Muddy "Mississippi" Waters, Blue Sky, 1979
The Chess Box, MCA/Chess, 1990

Sources

Erlewene, Michael, Vladímir Bogdana, Chris Woodstra, and Cub Koda. *All Music Guide to the Blues*, San Francisco: Freeman Books, 1996
Herzhaft, Gérard. *Encyclopedia of the Blues*, 2nd edition, Fayetteville: University of Arkansas Press, 1997
Rowe, Mike. *Chicago Breakdown*, New York: Da Capo, 1979

—Gerald Brennan

Lucinda Williams

Singer, songwriter

By the time Lucinda Williams released *Car Wheels on a Gravel Road* in 1998—her first release of any kind in six long years—she'd been in the music business two decades. Between a history of delays due to a string of record-label debacles and her own notorious perfectionism, the record was only her fifth. *Car Wheels* was met with the kind of critical fanfare Williams had become used to. *Rolling Stone* called it a "country-soul masterpiece" in 1998, but also noted that, "beyond print media, where she's lionized whenever she sticks her head out of her lair, Lucinda Williams can hardly catch a break."

While Williams lacked a huge fanbase and impressive record sales, she caught quite a few breaks from other musicians. Many noteworthy artists respected her talents as a vocalist and songwriter enough to have wanted her on their own projects. They appreciated her "fantastically wrecked" voice and songs that blended rock, blues, gospel, country and folk. Add some heartbreak, a lot of wanderlust and perfect honesty, and Emmylou Harris, Tom Petty and Mary Chapin Carpenter—who recorded the Grammy-winning version of Williams' "Passionate Kisses"—eagerly covered her songs. Buddy Miller, Terry Allen and Steve Earle are among the artists who've sung duets with her. Her inclusion on countless compilations, including 1993's *Sweet Relief*, a benefit album for Victoria Williams (no relation), a musician afflicted with multiple sclerosis, is testimony to the respect she garnered from fellow musicians.

The Williams children were born moving. Lucinda was born in Lake Charles, Louisiana in 1953 to Lucille and poet Miller Williams, who read at President Clinton's second Inauguration. Her parents divorced when she was eleven and, in the custody of their father, the Williams children, including younger siblings Robert and Karyn, lived in nine cities—Jackson, Vicksburg, Atlanta and Macon, Georgia; Baton Rouge and New Orleans, Louisiana; Fayetteville, Arkansas; Mexico City, Mexico and Santiago, Chile—wherever their father found teaching work.

That momentum kept Williams on the move in her adult life and was a heavy influence on her as an artist. "I get restless," she told *People* in 1998. "I've always got one foot out the door." So she bounced back and forth between New York, Austin and Houston, Los Angeles and Nashville. Her penchant for movement was clear in *Car Wheels*. The title song evokes imagery that was almost literal. For a young girl whose home essentially was the road, that sound of car wheels on a gravel road would become quite familiar. Miller Williams looked back at his family's travels with *People* in 1998. "I dragged the children with me and didn't realize what rootlessness that might create." Williams, on the other hand, insisted in the same article that "it wasn't this huge, traumatic thing. I never remember getting bummed out about it. I didn't grow up in a mom-and-pop, Ozzie and Harriet type of environment, but who did?"

What Miller Williams felt he lacked for his children in stability, he made up for with the nature of the creative and stimulating environment he provided for them. Williams was inspired by a host of her father's friends, including writers James Dickey, Allen Ginsberg, Charles Bukowski and Flannery O'Connor. She picked up the guitar at age 12 and decided on a musical future early on. Williams even, as *Spin* noted in 1998, works "like a writer of what she pronounces *poor-tree*" in her Southern drawl, writing as a poet does, using a "process of elimination, of removing all but the essential parts."

Spin declared in 1998, "Williams doesn't casually slap together anything." What's more important to her than getting a record out, is getting it out right. She makes no excuses for her reputation. As she posed to *Spin* in 1998, "I've been called a neurotic, a demanding diva, a perfectionist. Okay, I'm a perfectionist." Both *Car Wheels* and her previous release *Sweet Old World* took three years in production alone to release. Williams recorded and re-recorded each of the albums and tinkered with production, drawing the process out even more. For *Car Wheels*, Williams initially recorded all the songs in Austin, Texas, with her longtime guitarist and producing

Born January 26, 1953, Lake Charles, LA; daughter of Miller Williams (deceased) and Lucille Morgan; siblings: Robert, Karyn.

Started playing guitar at age 12; released first album, of cover songs, *Ramblin' on My Mind*, on Folkways label, 1979; released *Happy Woman Blues*, Folkways, 1980; signed with Rough Trade label and released *Lucinda Williams*, 1988, released EP *Pasionate Kisses*, 1989; signed with Chameleon, released *Sweet Old World*, 1992; made *Car Wheels on a Gravel Road* for American Recordings, record was bought by Mercury and released in 1998.

Awards: National Academy of Recording Arts and Sciences Grammy award for songwriting "Passionate Kisses," 1994.

Addresses: *Record company*—Mercury Records, 825 Eighth Avenue, New York, NY 10019. *Home*—Nashville, Tennessee.

└───┘

partner, Gurf Morlix. But she wasn't happy with it. "It's hard to explain," she told *Rolling Stone* in 1998. "Something was missing." Later, when she heard the sound of her voice on a duet she recorded with Steve Earle, she realized that he'd created the sound she wanted. She set out with Earle to re-record a few vocal tracks for her record, but "Boom," she explained to *Rolling Stone*, "We got on a roll. Everything sounded so great and cool and edgy. So we ended up recutting everything."

Williams' sporadic releases cannot all be blamed on her need for perfection. After signing a one-page deal for $250 and spending one day at Malico Studios in Jackson, Mississippi, Williams released her debut album on the Folkways record label—a label that seemed a good fit for her crossbred style—in 1979, called *Ramblin' On My Mind*. In 1980, she followed it with *Happy Woman Blues*, also on Folkways. Then, Rough Trade, a label better known for its punk releases than its country selection, caught up with Williams in 1988. That relationship was short lived, as the label crashed after producing *Lucinda Williams* in 1988 and the *Passionate Kisses* EP in 1989. After that, Williams's career was plagued by record-label problems. A shot with alternative label Chameleon produced only one release, *Sweet Old World*, in 1992, then the label folded.

Williams had more trouble finding and sticking with a label than a critically acclaimed artist should. The problem was always that no label could pigeonhole her sound. It was the same problem she'd had before — everyone liked her style but no one could figure out what to do with it. "It fell in the cracks between country and rock," she told *People* in 1998. It seemed like she had a secure deal with Rick Rubin's American Recordings, but sure enough, after all the trouble she'd had recording, re-recording, and finally completing *Car Wheels*, the label's uncertain switch from TimeWarner distribution to Sony only delayed the record's release further. That's when Mercury stepped in, bought the record outright from American, and finally got it out. Mercury's president and C.E.O. Danny Goldberg told *Newsweek* in 1998, "I think it could be her time," he said. "Bonnie Raitt, Tracy Chapman, Shawn Colvin—a number of artists have had major success with unorthodox records, just by sheer emotion and talent."

Selected discography

Ramblin' on My Mind, Folkways, 1979.
Happy Woman Blues, Folkways, 1980.
Lucinda Williams, Rough Trade, 1988.
Passionate Kisses (EP), Rough Trade, 1989.
Sweet Old World, Chameleon, 1992.
Car Wheels on a Gravel Road, Mercury , 1998.

Sources

Books

Romanowski, Patricia and Warren, Holly George, editors, *The Rolling Stone Encyclopedia of Rock & Roll*, Fireside/ Simon & Shuster, 1995.

Periodicals

Entertainment Weekly, July 10, 1998; August 14, 1998.
New York Magazine, June 29, 1998.
New York Observer, June 29, 1998.
Newsweek, July 6, 1998.
People, August 17, 1998; September 21, 1998.
Rolling Stone, July 9, 1998; August 6, 1998.
Spin, July 1998.
Village Voice, June 30, 1998.
Wall Street Journal, August 21, 1998.

Online

"Lucinda Williams," *Music Contemporary Showcase*, http//imusic.interserv.com (September 27, 1998).

"Lucinda Williams," *All-Music Guide,* http://www.allmusic.com (September 20, 1998).

"Lucinda Williams," *Trouser Press,* http://www.trouserpress.com (September 20, 1998).

Additional information was provided by Mercury Records publicity materials, 1998.

—*Brenna Sanchez*

Brian Wilson

Singer, producer, songwriter

Photo by Neal Preston, Giant. Reproduced by permission. ©

Brian Douglas Wilson is widely recognized as the founding force behind the California "surfin'" singing style of the Beach Boys, a rock and roll band dating back to the 1960s. Wilson is revered by his contemporaries as a genius of the American popular music scene. He was largely responsible for composing and producing the Beach Boys' numerous hit songs and albums.

Wilson was born in Ingelwood, California on June 20, 1942. Wilson's father was an abominably abusive man and his mother, an alcoholic, was ineffectual and complacent. The elder Wilson beat and defamed his own children regularly with little protest or interference from his wife. After the birth of Wilson's brother, Dennis Wilson, in 1944, the family moved to Hawthorne, California. Carl Wilson, the youngest of the three siblings, was born in 1946. As a result of the persistent abuse, Brian Wilson and his brothers developed a mutual inability to communicate effectively among themselves, even into adulthood when they earned renown as the Beach Boys.

Wilson's musical ability surfaced in infancy, when his father, a frustrated songwriter, noticed that Wilson could hum entire tunes from memory, even before he was old enough to walk. He wrote his first song at age five, in part as an attempt to emulate his father. Although Wilson is deaf in his right ear he taught himself to play the piano by watching his father play, and by observing the patterns and chord progressions that were involved. He also had the ability as a child to play songs from memory upon hearing them only once, as was discovered by his music teacher during a short-lived stint of accordion lessons. As Wilson approached adolescence he used his music increasingly as an escape. He played the piano at home to drown out the bickering among his parents and his brothers; he also used music as a means to avoid social situations. Although he played some sports in high school, overall he withdrew into music. Wilson was especially inspired the first time he heard the Four Freshmen singing on the radio. It was their harmony that "struck a chord" with Wilson.

The evolution of the Beach Boys began during Wilson's senior year at Hawthorne High School. After graduation in 1959, he first began singing at social affairs with his cousin, Mike Love. The two assembled a larger group consisting of Wilson and Love, Wilson's two siblings (Dennis, and Carl) and Wilson's college football teammate, Al Jardine. The five musicians originally billed themselves as the Pendletones. Their first recording session, held on October 3, 1961, resulted in the hit single "Surfin'" which was released on December 8, 1961. It was not until after the record's release that the Pendletones discovered that record distributor Candix Records had renamed the group and called it the Beach

Born Brian Douglas Wilson, June 20, 1942, Ingelwood, CA, son of the late Audree Neva (Korthof), homemaker, and the late Murry Gage Wilson (heavy-equipment supplier); older brother of Dennis and Carl; married Marilyn Rovell, December 7, 1964 (divorced 1979); married Melinda Ledbetter, 1995; children: (with Marilyn) Carnie (born April 29, 1968) and Wendy (born October 16, 1969);(adpoted with Melinda) Daria, Delanie. *Education:* Attended El Camino Junior College.

Founder and leader of the Pendletones, 1960-61; renamed the Beach Boys, 1961; recorded and toured as a Beach Boy 1962-65; recorded for Candix Records, 1961-62, Capitol Records, 1962-69, Warner Brothers Records, 1970-82; partner with Murry Wilson in Sea of Tunes Publishing Company, 1962-69; formed Brother Records Incorporated, 1966; producer and songwriter for the Beach Boys, 1961-82; collaborated with lyricists Gary Usher, Bob Norberg, Roger Christian, Tony Asher, Van Dyke Parks; solo career, 1988. Non-musical ventures: owner/manager of the Radiant Radish Health Food Store, 1969-70.

Awards: Inducted into the Rock and Roll Hall of Fame with the Beach Boys, January 1988 (Third Annual Rock and Roll Hall of Fame Awards).

Addresses: *Record company*—Giant Records, 3500 W. Olive Ave., Suite 600, Burbank, CA 91505.

Boys. The Beach Boys' "Surfin'" single made the local top 40 charts in the Los Angeles area during the first month after its release. The song peaked eventually at number 75 on the *Billboard* chart in February of 1962. The hit single is associated with the start the California "surfin' sound" in pop music of the early 1960s.

The Beach Boys' then signed with Capitol Records. Their first release with Capitol was "409"/"Surfin' Safari" on June 4, 1962. That single sold nearly one million copies and peaked on the charts at number 14; and the Beach Boys swiftly rose to become one of the most popular bands in Southern California. Brian Wilson's Beach Boys realized their first top-ten record in May of 1963 with "Surfin' U.S.A." *The Beach Boys' Concert*

album released late the following year was the first Beach Boys album to reach the number one position on the charts. In 1970, the Beach Boys released, *Sunflower,* their first album under the Warner Brothers label.

Depression and Drugs

By 1965, Brian Wilson was absorbed with the pressures of success and became increasingly apprehensive about traveling and touring. His unfounded fear, in retrospect, was a precursor to the onset of a severe mental breakdown. Wilson's condition was manifest through extended bouts of depression and paranoia, and episodes of drug addiction, gluttony, and chain smoking which lasted on and off for approximately 20 years. Wilson's phenomenal catapult to fame as a teenager was more than he could manage. He was drinking heavily by the age of 20.

Early in 1965, Wilson descended into a drug-induced depression. He stopped touring with the band, under the auspices of composing, arranging, producing, and singing at studio sessions, all of which he did. The band's subsequent hits, including the number one single, "Help Me, Rhonda," released in 1965, was written during the onset of Wilson's extended bout with narcotic drugs. He wrote "California Girls" in the "afterglow" of an initial experience with the hallucinogenic drug LSD. Also, while Wilson was fully enamored with recreational drugs, the smash hit "Good Vibrations" was released on October 10, 1966—as was *Pet Sounds,* an album which received critical acclaim from Wilson's contemporaries. In 1968, he became addicted to cocaine. Years passed and Wilson's drug addiction went undiagnosed, while friends attributed his behavioral quirks to creative genius.

During the six years from 1962-68, Wilson produced 14 albums and wrote over ten dozen songs. In so doing he kept the Beach Boys in competition with recording legends such as Phil Spector and the Beatles. In all, Wilson produced about one-half of the Beach Boys' single hits, three of which were number one sellers.

Early on, Wilson teamed up with Gary Usher, a veteran of the record trade in New York City, as a songwriting team on songs including "409," "In My Room," and "The Lonely Sea." Later he collaborated with a roommate, Bob Norberg, on some songs including "Your Summer Dream." Wilson collaborated with Los Angeles disc jockey Roger Christian for lyrics on a number of songs including "Little Deuce Coupe," and "Shut Down." He worked with Tony Asher on *Pet Sounds* and also wrote songs with Van Dyke Parks.

During the Beach Boys' climb to stardom in the early 1960s, Brian Wilson's father, Murry Wilson, became increasingly involved with the group as a self-appointed and controlling manager. Meanwhile Wilson formed Sea of Tunes Publishing Company, to hold the copyrights to his songs; and the Beach Boys together formed their own production company, Brother Records. By November of 1982, Wilson had lost control of Sea of Tunes Publishing, and he was subsequently fired by his own company, Brother Records, after years of turbulent relationships between himself and the rest of the band.

Family and Friends

Wilson's parents separated in 1964. Despite his unpleasant childhood, he said the divorce left him, "feeling like a ship whose anchor had disappeared." By the end of that same year, on December 7, 1964, Wilson married Marilyn Rovell whom he had been acquainted with for several years. The marriage faltered quickly, in part because of Wilson's inappropriate affections for Rovell's sisters, and because of his worsening drug addiction, which began with the use of marijuana escalating to LSD experimentation during the first year of the marriage. In April of 1967, the Wilsons purchased a lavish and impressive 24-room Spanish style home in Bel Air, formerly owned by Edgar Rice Burroughs. The couple had two daughters—Carnie, born on April 29, 1968, and Wendy, born on October 16, 1969. At that time, Wilson admitted that he was ineffectual as a father; he was too involved in drug addiction and music production.

Wilson's private life deteriorated rapidly. Early in 1968, he was introduced by his brothers to, and became enamored with, Beatles' guru Maharishi Mahesh Yogi, the transcendental meditation teacher considered by many to be a charlatan. Late in 1968, he was introduced to cocaine by a fellow musician and became addicted immediately. He had a brief stint as the owner of a short-lived health food store, the Radiant Radish in West Hollywood, in 1969-70, and the following years were a blur of drug parties and withdrawal from society. Eventually a man named Charles Manson befriended Dennis Wilson and began to frequent Brian Wilson's residence. Not long afterward, Manson was arrested and convicted for the grizzly Tate-LaBianca murders that shocked Hollywood during that time.

The close brush with Manson left the Wilsons unnerved. It was Marilyn Wilson, in 1975, who contacted the unorthodox clinical psychologist Dr. Eugene Landy, to treat Brian Wilson's drug abuse. By the summer of 1976,

Wilson's level of rehabilitation permitted him to make public appearances on television's *Saturday Night Live* and the *Mike Douglas Show*. An unfortunate proliferation of overconfidence, however, led Wilson's family and friends to dismiss the therapist Landy prematurely and against the doctor's own advice. Almost immediately, during the early months of 1977, Wilson began a gradual regression into his former drug habit and mental illness. Once again, Wilson was chronically depressed and given to drug binges. He ignored his family and eventually topped the scales at 340 pounds and binged on literally thousands of dollars of heroin and cocaine on a regular basis. Marijuana, alcohol, and multiple packs of cigarettes figured prominently into Wilson's daily fare. By 1978, his life again was in shambles. On September 15 of that year he separated from his wife; they divorced in 1979.

As Wilson's personal affairs deteriorated, he developed an eccentric habit of misplacing huge royalty checks around the house. When the checks would eventually be located he used the money, thousands of dollars, to purchase drugs. The Beach Boys albums released during that era were relative flops, many were shelved by the promoters for lack of potential. In 1983, Wilson once again submitted to a long and intensive program of unconventional therapy under he direction of Dr. Landy. That second episode of treatments lasted longer and met with much greater success.

Solo Career

The year 1988 brought an upturn in Wilson's waning career. In January of that year, at the third annual Rock and Roll Hall of Fame awards dinner, the Beach Boys were inducted into the Hall of Fame at a ceremony at New York City's Waldorf-Astoria Hotel. Later that year, the rehabilitated Brian Wilson embarked on a solo career beginning with the release of his album *Brian Wilson*, which received excellent reviews. Wilson published an autobiography, *Wouldn't It Be Nice,* in 1991, and in 1998 he released a second solo album, *Imagination*, with ten new songs. The sophisticated album, including nearly 100 tracks—all sung by Wilson himself—was greeted with praise.

In 1995, Wilson married Melinda Ledbetter. Soon after the couple adopted two daughters, Daria and Delanie. Wilson and his family make their home in suburban Chicago, in St. Charles, Illinois. Wilson's two older daughters, Wendy and Carnie, each developed careers as professional singers in their own right, and together as former members of the popular Wilson Philips trio.

Selected discography

Singles

"Surfin'," Candix Records, December 8, 1961.
"Help Me, Rhonda," Capitol, 1965.
"Good Vibrations," Capitol, October 10, 1966,

Albums

With the Beach Boys

Shut Down, Capitol, 1963.
Shut Down, Volume 2, Capitol, 1964.
All Summer Long, Capitol, July 1964.
The Beach Boys' Concert, Capitol, 1964.
The Beach Boys Today!, Capitol, 1965.
Summer Days (And Summer Nights) (includes "California Girls"), Capitol, June 28, 1965.
Pet Sounds, Capitol, 1966.
Sunflower, Warner Brothers, 1970.
Endless Summer, Capitol, June 1974.

15 Big Ones, Warner Brothers, 1976.

Solo

Brian Wilson, 1988.
Imagination, Giant Records, 1998.
I Just Wasn't Made for These Times, (includes "Do It Again," with Wendy and Carnie Wilson).

Sources

Books

Wilson, Brian, with Todd Gold, *Wouldn't It Be Nice: My Own Story,* HarperCollins Publishers, 1991.

Periodicals

Los Angeles Times, 12 July 1998.
People, 20 July 1998.

—*Gloria Cooksey*

Robert Wyatt

Singer, songwriter

Robert Wyatt is one of the key members of the Canterbury school of British progressive rock. One of pop music's most thought-provoking lyricists, he has developed his unique musical style without bowing to commercial pressures. Wyatt's childhood home was filled with music. He attended the Simon Langton Grammar School in Canterbury; among his schoolmates were the Hopper brothers, Hugh and Brian, Michael Ratledge, and the Sinclair cousins, Richard and David.

During the early 1960s, Hugh Hopper, the Sinclairs, and Wyatt, along with another school friend Kevin Ayers, spent their time at Wyatt's parents' mansion reading poetry, listening to jazz, and practicing music. The Wyatts took boarders; the most significant was Australian Daevid Allen. Despite being six years older, Daevid got along well with Robert through a mutual love of jazz and similar iconoclastic spirits. After Allen emigrated to Paris in 1964, Wyatt and friends formed a rock band, The Wilde Flowers.

In 1966, Daevid Allen returned from a trip to Majorca with Kevin Ayers intending to form The Soft Machine, a rock band financed by an eccentric millionaire they met on the island. Wyatt was convinced to leave The Wilde Flowers and join as drummer and vocalist, while recent Oxford graduate Ratledge became the organist. The quartet released its debut single "Love Makes Sweet Music" in 1967, while the remaining Wilde Flowers renamed themselves Caravan.

The Soft Machine toured throughout Europe in 1967, building a long-lasting Continental following for the band. Allen was forced to leave the group due to visa problems and returned to England. He eventually formed [psychedelic-progressive rock band] Gong. As a trio, the Soft Machine was the opening act for two world tours with Jimi Hendrix. Following the release of its self-titled debut album, Ayers left and was replaced by Hugh Hopper.

In 1969, The Soft Machine was augmented by a four piece horn section. Due to the financial difficulties in supporting a seven-piece band, three members left, though sax player Elton Dean became a permanent addition. The Soft Machine was shifting toward a jazzier sound and de-emphasizing vocals, much to Wyatt's chagrin. "Moon In June," Wyatt's sidelong piece on the band's *Third* album, was almost entirely a solo recording. Dissatisfied with the direction of The Soft Machine's music after the *Fourth* album, Wyatt departed in 1971 to form Matching Mole, named for the French pronunciation of "Soft Machine".

Matching Mole released two acclaimed albums and toured England and Europe incessantly until Wyatt

For the Record . . .

Born Robert Wyatt Ellidge, January 28, 1945, in Bristol, Somerset, England; son of Honor Wyatt (a broadcaster and teacher) and George Ellidge (an industrial psychologist); married Pam Howard c. 1960, divorced c. 1971, married Afreda Benge (an artist) July 26, 1974; children: one son Samuel.

Began playing drums c. 1961; formed band The Wilde Flowers c. 1963; joined band The Soft Machine c. 1966; released albums and toured with Soft Machine c. 1967-71; played drums with bands Kevin Ayers and The Whole World, Symbiosis, Centipede, and The Amazing Band, c. 1971; left The Soft Machine c. 1971; founded Matching Mole c. 1972; disbanded Matching Mole c. 1972; fell from window and broke spine, paralyzed from waist down c. 1973; released *Rock Bottom* on Virgin c. 1974; recorded for Rough Trade c. 1980-91; recorded for Thirsty Ear c. 1998.

Awards: Meilleur Disque, Leisure For Youth Best Record of The Year Award, France, 1969 for Soft Machine, *Volume Two* ; Academie Charles Cros Grand Prix du Disque Record of The Year Award, France, 1974 for *Rock Bottom*.

Addresses: *Record company*—Thirsty Ear, 274 Madison Ave, Suite 804, New York, NY 10016.

dissolved the band in late 1972 due to financial difficulties and the stress of leading a band. He was in the process of reforming Matching Mole when, during a party on June 1, 1973, he fell drunkenly from a fourth floor window and broke his spine; this accident left him paralyzed from the waist down. In *Wrong Movements*, Wyatt explains his perspective on the event, "People think I must have problems talking about my accident.... What I have problems talking about is what happened **before** the accident.... My adolescent self, the drummer biped, I don't remember him and I don't understand him.... I see the accident now as being a sort of neat division line between my adolescence and the rest of my life."

Without the use of his legs, Robert concentrated on singing and playing keyboards. *Rock Bottom*, released in 1974, is a landmark progressive rock album. Unlike previous efforts, *Rock Bottom*'s arrangements are given plenty of breathing space, and possess a clarity rarely heard before in his music. Many listeners thought that *Rock Bottom* was a sad album, since it was recorded soon after his accident, however, most of the material was written before his fall. A version of "I'm A Believer" became a surprise chart hit in Britain that year. He appeared on the BBC TV show *Top of the Pops* but was disgusted by the producer's reluctance to have a performer in a wheelchair.

Ruth Is Stranger Than Richard is a jazzier sounding album than *Rock Bottom*. In the mid-1970s, Wyatt went into semi-retirement, disillusioned by the music business. He explained to *Creem*, "You were getting to funny stages, where people who deliberately maimed themselves on-stage were selling themselves as brave and courageous, whereas you had someone like Victor Jara in Chile, who because he sang for democracy in Chile, was tortured to death. If we're going to talk about brave rebels in the music business, let's talk about Victor Jara, not people who mutilate themselves on groovy videos."

Wyatt returned to the public eye in 1980 with four singles, later compiled as *Nothing Will Stop Us*, each pairing songs dealing with freedom. In 1982, inspired by those singles, Elvis Costello wrote an anti-war song about the Falkland Islands conflict, "Shipbuilding", which he thought would be the perfect vehicle for Robert Wyatt. Costello produced Wyatt, backed by his band the Attractions, and the result was Robert's second United Kingdom-charting single.

In 1985, Robert Wyatt participated in a project with the South-West African People's Organization. "Winds of Change" was released to bring attention to the liberation movement of Namibia, which had been illegally occupied by South Africa. Robert commented about the political nature of his recent work in *Wrong Movements*, "I want to show you something which is my finger pointing.... Now there are two interesting things about a pointing finger. First of all, you can look at the finger, and secondly, you can look at where the finger is pointing.... I would only be happy if people looked at what I was pointing at."

Aside from numerous cameo appearances, Robert Wyatt was absent from the music business for several years following his 1991 recording *Dondestan*. He made a welcome return to the public eye in 1997 with *Shleep*. The album, named for a fit of insomnia during which he wrote the album's lyrics, arrived like a thought-provoking letter from an old friend who doesn't write often. Wyatt's lyrical candor and championing of the underdog has gained him an appreciative worldwide following and respect among his musician peers.

Selected discography

End of An Ear, CBS, 1970.
Rock Bottom, Virgin, 1974, reissued Thirsty Ear, 1998.
"I'm A Believer"/ "Memories," Virgin, 1974.
Ruth Is Stranger Than Richard, Virgin, 1975, reissued Thirsty Ear, 1998.
"Yesterday Man" on *V*, Virgin, 1975.
"Arauco"/ "Caimenera," Rough Trade, 1980.
"At Last I Am Free"/ "Strange Fruit," Rough Trade, 1980.
"Stalin Wasn't Stallin'"/ "Stalingrad," Rough Trade, 1980.
"Grass"/ "Trade Union," Rough Trade, 1980.
Nothing Can Stop Us, Rough Trade, 1981, reissued Thirsty Ear, 1998.
"Shipbuilding"/ "Memories of You," Rough Trade, 1983.
The Animals Film Soundtrack Rough Trade, 1984, reissued Thirsty Ear, 1998.
Old Rottenhat, Rough Trade, 1986, reissued Thirsty Ear, 1998.
Dondestan, Gramavision, 1991, reissued Thirsty Ear, 1998.
The Peel Sessions (rec. 1974), Strange Fruit 8336, 1991.
Mid-Eighties (rec. 1982-86), Gramavision, 1993.
A Short Break, Voiceprint, 1994.
Flotsam & Jetsam (rec. 1968-90), Rough Trade, 1994.
"Shipbuilding" (rec. 1983) on *Bespoke Songs, Lost Dogs, Detours and Rendezvous: The Songs of Elvis Costello*, Rhino, 1995.
Shleep, Thirsty Ear, 1997.
Canterburied Sounds Volume 1, (recorded 1962-70), Voiceprint, 1998.
Canterburied Sounds Volume 2, (recorded 1962-70), Voiceprint, 1998.
Canterburied Sounds Volume 3, (recorded 1962-70), Voiceprint, 1998.

With others

"Love Makes Sweet Music" b/w "Feelin' Reelin' Squealin'," Polydor, 1967, reissued on *Rare Tracks*, Polydor, 1975.
Soft Machine, ABC-Probe, 1968, reissued by One Way, 1991.
Volume Two, ABC-Probe, 1969, reissued by One Way, 1991.
Third, Columbia, 1970, reissued by BGO, 1993.
Fourth, Columbia, 1971, reissued by One Way, 1991.
Rock Generation Volume 7 (rec. 1967), BYG, 1971.
Rock Generation Volume 8 (rec. 1967), BYG, 1971.
Live at the Proms 1970, Reckless, 1988.
Turns On: The Peel Sessions (rec. 1969-1971), Strange Fruit, 1990.
Live At the Paradiso 1969, Voiceprint, 1995.

Spaced (rec. 1969), Cuneiform, 1996.
Virtually (rec. 1971), Cuneiform, 1997.
Matching Mole, CBS, 1972, reissued BGO, 1991.
Little Red Record, Columbia, 1972, reissued BGO, 1991.
BBC Live In Concert (rec. 1972), Windsong, 1990.
Joy of a Toy, Harvest, 1969, reissued BGO, 1991.
Shooting for the Moon, Harvest, 1970, reissued BGO, 1991.
Whatevershebringswesing, Harvest, 1972, reissued BGO, 1991.
Bananamour, Harvest, 1973, reissued, BGO, 1991.
June 1, 1974, Island, 1974.
Singing The Bruise: The BBC Sessions 1970-1972, Band of Joy, 1996.
with The Daevid Allen Trio), *Live 1963*, Voiceprint, 1993.
(with The Wilde Flowers), *The Wilde Flowers* (rec. 1965-1969), Voiceprint, 1994
(with Daevid Allen), *Banana Moon*, BYG, 1971, reissued by Charly, 1991.
(with Syd Barrett), *The Madcap Laughs*, Harvest , 1970
(with Lol Coxhill), *Ear of the Beholder*, Ampex, 1971.
(with Centipede), *Septober Energy*, RCA, 1971.
(with Keith Tippett), *Dedicated To You, But You Weren't Listening*, Vertigo, 1971.
(with Hatfield & The North), *Hatfield & the North*, Virgin, 1973.
(with Brian Eno), *Taking Tiger Mountain By Strategy*, Virgin, 1974.
(with Brian Eno), *Another Green World*, Virgin, 1975.
(with Phil Manzanera), *Diamond Head*, Island, 1975.
(with Brian Eno), *Before and After Science*, Virgin, 1977.
(with Michael Mantler), *The Hapless Child*, Watt, 1975.
(with Henry Cow), *Concerts*, Caroline, 1976, reissued by East Side Digital, 1996.
(with the SWAPO Singers), "Wind of Change," Rough Trade, 1985.
(with Ultramarine), *Every Man and Woman !s a Star*, Rough Trade, 1992.
(with Ultramarine), *United Kingdoms*, Blanco Y Negro, 1992.
(with John Greaves), *Songs*, Resurgence, 1995.
(with Hugh Hopper & Kramer), *A Remark Hugh Made*, Shimmy-Disc, 1995
(with Fish Out of Water), *Lucky Scars*, Stream, 1996.
(with Gary Windo), *His Master's Bones* (rec. 1971-1984), Cuneiform, 1997.

Sources

Books

Frame, Pete, *The Complete Rock Family Trees*, Omnibus Press, 1993.
Joynson, Vernon, *Tapestry of Delights: The Comprehensive Guide to British Music of the Beat, R & B, Psychedelic, and Progressive Eras 1963-1976*, Borderline Productions, 1995.

King, Michael, *Wrong Movements, A Robert Wyatt History*, SAF, 1995.

Martin, Bill, *Listening To The Future, The Time of Progressive Rock 1968-1978*, Open Court, 1998.

Schaffner, Nicholas, *The British Invasion*, McGraw-Hill, 1981.

Thompson, Dave, *Space Daze: The History & Mystery of Electronic Ambient and Space Rock*, Cleopatra, 1994.

Periodicals

Billboard, November 30, 1985.

Creem, January, 1987.

Down Beat, October 5, 1967; April 15, 1971; November 25, 1971; April, 1986; March, 1992.

Facelift, Issue 6; Issue 7; Issue 11; Issue 15.

Goldmine, October 6, 1989; April 10, 1998.

Jazz & Pop, April, 1971.

London Times, June 5, 1970; August 13, 1970; August 15, 1970.

Melody Maker, July 5, 1969; November 8, 1969; February 14, 1970; January 2, 1971; July 3, 1971; September 21, 1974; November 9, 1974; April 16, 1976; March 15, 1980; September 20, 1980.

New Musical Express, January 25, 1975; February 1, 1975.

Ptolemaic Terrascope, January, 1992.

Record Collector, June 1992.

Rolling Stone, January 16, 1975.

Online

http://www.alpes-net.fr/~bigbang/calyx.html, (September 26, 1998).

—*Jim Powers*

Tammy Wynette

Singer

Throughout her long-standing musical career and turbulent lifetime, Tammy Wynette was known with great fondness as the "first lady of country music." During the course of a career that spanned 32 years, Wynette recorded over 50 albums and sold in excess of 30 million records. Her distinctive voice and singing style was characterized frequently as the ideal of country soul. She was noted and remembered as the embodiment of the Nashville country music sound, both because of her twangy, heart wrenching voice and her memorable musical arrangements which featured the classic country sounds of steel guitars mixed with strings.

Wynette's personal life, too, reflected the country music paradigm of triumph over tragedy. Born Virginia Wynette Pugh in Itawamba County, Mississippi during World War II, she was not yet one year old when her father, William Hollice Pugh, died of a brain tumor. Her mother, Mildred Faye, worked for the war effort in Memphis. In time Mildred Pugh remarried, to Wynette's chagrin. Wynette was persistently at odds with her stepfather

AP/Wide World Photo. Reproduced by permission.

ist, and in a shoe factory to survive. Later she attended beauty school and worked as a beautician in Birmingham, Alabama, yet all the while she fostered an intense desire to sing professionally. Whenever time permitted she traveled to Nashville, in an effort to procure work as a singer. She knocked on the doors of major country music record producers with an unending determination. Her persistence paid off, on one of her trips to Nashville she caught the ear of the legendary country music star Porter Wagoner. He hired her to sing backup for him, which ultimately led to her meeting with producer Billy Sherrill. Sherrill was impressed with her talent, but he suggested she change her name to Tammy Wynette. She agreed to the change, and with Sherrill's influence she signed with Epic Records in 1966.

During one of her numerous trips to Nashville in 1965 Wynette met Don Chapel, a would-be country star with connections around Nashville. They were married in 1967, but not long afterward Wynette was shocked and repulsed to learn that Chapel had exploited her. She was grateful and relieved later to discover that a legal technicality made the marriage unlawful, and so it was annulled. Ironically it was Chapel who introduced Wynette to her girlhood idol and future husband, the popular country singer George Jones. In time the two singers, Jones and Wynette, developed a professional relationship as well as a close personal friendship. Wynette and Jones performed as a couple and recorded many songs together. They were married in 1969. Their professional collaboration continued until 1978, although their marriage ended in divorce in 1975. Despite the untimely ending to their marriage, the synergy between the two singers was almost legendary, and years later in 1996, they made a reunion album entitled *One.* It was well received, although it lacked the spark of their musical liaisons of earlier years. Jones and Wynette had one daughter, Tamala Georgette, born in 1970.

Following her breakup with George Jones, Wynette was both married to and divorced from realtor Michael Tomlin during the course of 1976. She was also linked romantically with actor Burt Reynolds briefly in 1977, but it was her marriage to singer/songwriter George Richey in 1978 that finally brought happiness and stability to Wynette's private life.

She published an autobiography, *Stand by Your Man,* in 1979, and although she continued to work and to perform, her career began to wind down throughout the 1980s. She went on to record with KLF, a dance-rap duo; and she sang with Sting and Elton John. In 1986, she accepted a recurring role on the CBS soap opera *Capitol.* Wynette played the part of Darlene Stankowsky, a former country singer turned waitress.

and as a result opted to live with her grandparents on their cotton farm. In the tradition of country music cliches, Wynette grew up picking cotton as a youngster, in order to survive. She also learned to play several instruments including guitar and piano, at the bidding of her father to her mother before he died. She was an avid basketball player in high school, although she was expelled in 1959, just a few month short of graduation because she married her adolescent sweetheart, Euple Byrd, against the school district rules—which was unfortunate because Wynette's infatuation with Byrd was short-lived. The young couple lived in dire poverty and the marriage collapsed after five years. At the time of their break-up Wynette was pregnant with their third daughter, Tina. The couple divorced in 1965.

During the mid-1960s, on her own and with her children to support, Wynette worked as a waitress, a reception-

Wynette, who suffered many tragedies throughout her life, maintained that she had no complaints and that she felt greatly blessed. Her house was bombed and severely damaged in 1975, and she was also victimized for some time by a stalker. In Nashville, in 1978, she was mysteriously kidnapped from a shopping center and badly beaten. Wynette's health was also a source of suffering for the singer. She developed a chronic inflammation of the bile ducts and was intermittently hospitalized, from 1978 until her death in 1998. As a result she developed a dependency on painkillers in the late 1970s. She became critically ill with a liver infection at the end of 1994. Pamela Lansden of *People* quoted Wynette's personal spin on life's tribulations as follows: "The sad part about happy endings is there's nothing to write about."

Wynette won three awards from Country Music Association as Female Vocalist of the Year, in 1968, 1969, and 1970; and she won a Grammy award for "I Don't Want to Play House" in 1967. Wynette also won a Living Legend award in 1991. In all she had 27 Country Music Award nominations. As her career wound down in the 1990s Wynette had amassed eleven number one albums and 20 number one singles. Her greatest hit was her signature song, "Stand by your Man," which she wrote along with Billy Sherrill, and which won a Grammy award in 1969.

Tammy Wynette died peacefully, in her sleep, on April 6, 1998 of a pulmonary blood clot. She was 55. Despite her persistent illnesses, she continued to perform until shortly before her death and had other performances scheduled in the offing. Wynette's funeral was held on April 9, 1998 and, at the same time, a public memorial service was underway at Nashville's original Grand Ole Opry building (Ryman Auditorium). Her death solicited commentary such as songwriter Bill Mack's commentary, quoted in the *Dallas Morning News*, that she was a "class act," and "irreplaceable," and that, "She never knew a flat note." Lee Ann Womack was quoted also; she said of Wynette, whose songs often evoked strength and controlled passion, "You knew she knew what she was singing about. You can put her records on and listen

and learn so much." Wynette was survived by her husband George Richey, five daughters, a son, and seven grandchildren. In September of 1998, shortly after her death, Wynette was inducted into the Country Music Hall of Fame.

Selected discography

Singles

"Apartment #9," 1966.
"I Don't Wanna Play House," 1967.
"Stand by Your Man," 1968.

Albums

Higher Ground, 1987.
Without Walls, 1994.
(with Dolly Parton and Loretta Lynn) *Honky Tonk Angels*, 1993.
(with George Jones) *One*, 1996.

Sources

Books

Wynette, Tammy with Joan Dew, *Stand by Your Man*, Simon and Schuster, New York, 1979.

Periodicals

Dallas Morning News, 7 April 1998.
People, 29 September 1986; 20 April 1998, pp. 54-59.

Online

"Tammy Wynette," *Great American Country*, http:// testpo.jic.com/ countrystars/artists/wynette.html, *(October 7, 1998).*

—Gloria Cooksey

Yo La Tengo

Rock band

Yo La Tengo guitarist Ira Kaplan declared, in no uncertain terms, to Jeff Salamon of *Spin* magazine in 1997, "I one hundred percent reject the notion that we're a critics' band." Strong words from a former rock critic about a band that has, since its inception in 1984, received far more words of praise in the media than it has sold records. Named for a phrase yelled by a hispanic New York Mets fielder, Yo La Tengo was started and has always consisted of guitarist and vocalist, Ira Kaplan and his wife, drummer and vocalist, Georgia Hubley. What started as a side-project for a rock critic and his percussion-wise mate became one of independent rock's most-championed bands. They'd sold only 50,000 records from their first release in 1986 to their 1997 album but their credibility in the indie-rock genre was rock solid.

For the first six years of songwriting, recording and touring, the band was essentially a two-person show, with practical contributions over the years from bassists Al Greller, Gene Holder, Mike Lewis, and Stephen Wichnewski. Guitarist Dave Schramm's input was key to

the group's 1986 debut, *Ride the Tiger* and again on *President Yo La Tengo* in 1989 and *Fakebook* in 1990. There has always been a floating third member of Yo La Tengo, and not until bassist James McNew joined the group in 1991 did the lineup ever solidify.

It is no coincidence that Kaplan and Hubley, married since 1987, have always remained the core of the trio. Chris Norris of *New York* said in 1997, "Hubley and Kaplan's music has everything to do with their relationship—would not, in fact, exist without it—and it has everything to do with the subculture that sustains them." Their common love of popular music, baseball and hanging out with other musicians works its way from their marriage into their music. That the couple has been called "pop culture's best advertisement for marriage" only illustrates the way their belief in rock and roll as more than a vehicle for attention-starved show offs comes across to fans.

Creative Upbringing Raised Grounded Rockers

While recognized as part of New York bohemia, whose genealogy can be traced back past the Velvet Underground—whom Yo La Tengo portrayed in the 1996 film *I Shot Andy Warhol*—they seemed a little more grounded than "a whole tradition of left-leaning, humanist-minded, Jewish-identified artists who have thrived in

New York's margins for 50 years." The difference Norris pointed out was that "what Hubley and Kaplan took from late-sixties art rock wasn't the emphasis on glamour, sex, drugs, and thanatos but a belief that rock could be more than teen culture, that you could keep exploring, keep experimenting." Hubley and Kaplan were deemed, unlike their self-destructive predecessors, able to find an "adult bohemia."

It seemed that Yo La Tengo had defied the rock and roll school of success and gone about eeking out a rock existence that was more stable. In a 1997 review *Spin*'s Robert Christgau said, "not all the music emanating form Yo La Tengo is perfect. That's intentional—this paradise not only has room for error, it revels in the human-scale joys of inexpertise."

Hubley grew up in a household that saw the likes of Dizzy Gillespie, Quincy Jones and Paul Simon pass through its doors. Her parents were animators—her late father John invented the character Mr. Magoo—and brought her up in a creative environment. Hubley's mother, Faith, let the neophyte drummer practice in her warehouse studio on Madison Avenue. The manager of the Carlyle Hotel, located across the street, once attempted to bribe Mrs. Hubley into stopping Georgia from practicing at night. Mrs. Hubley recalled her reaction to Norris in 1997, "I said, 'No, no, no, no. She's pursuing her art and she has the right to do that, and we don't need your money, thank you very much."

Kaplan's beginnings as a rock critic cloaked his talents as a musician. Of those days, Kaplan told Carl Swanson the *New York Observer* in 1997, "It was a way of staying close to music. I was definitely the cliché music writer who would rather be a musician." Even his father, Abraham, knew. "I remember he spent one entire summer sitting around trying to become skillful on the guitar," he told Norris. "From the earliest on, I knew it would never be a hobby."

From Bedroom Shows to Indie Success

His talent not in question, Kaplan was terrified to perform publicly—Georgia was his only audience for quite a while. One by one, the couple invited people in and at their debut performance, Kaplan opened his mouth to sing the second song—the first was an instrumental—and nothing came out.

Kaplan eventually learned to play through his performance anxiety, and Yo La Tengo became as known for their frequent live shows as for their recordings. Fans and critics reveled in the unpredictability of the Yo La

Tengo live experience. "Yo La Tengo make regular excursions into the unknown on stage, and, like any performance, the results can be pretty hit or miss. But when they pull it off, it is something to behold," commented Swanson.

Kaplan is known to tire of and become noticeably uncomfortable during press tours and interviews. Yet he performs his public responsibilities dutifully. His interests apparently lie in exposing Yo La Tengo to as many people as possible. Based on his observations, the band's relentless, though reluctant, self-promotion has paid off. "We're fortunate in that we've only gotten more popular," he told Dawn Sutton of the *College Music Journal* (*CMJ*) in 1997. "Not that we're selling a billion records, but every record does a little better than the one before and every tour does a little better than the one before, and I think that helps. I think we are very self-motivated and inner-directed and all sorts of jargony things, but at the same time it's pretty rewarding when there are all these people out there."

Three Hearts as One

The group's 1997 release, *I Can Hear the Heart Beating as One*, exhibited how the band, once a two-person operation, had evolved into an even balance of power. Adam Heimlich of the *New York Press* noted in 1997 that "not since Rush has a trio shared power as evenly as Yo La Tengo … it's easy to let the 33-and-a-third percent contributions … calibrate the whole experience." Bassist James McNew's contributions to the band went from hired hand on his first record being part of all the songwriting with them on their fourth album, *I Can Hear the Heart Beating as One*.

Critics were wowed by what they heard, the new sound of their pet band. Reviews called the record "a more subdued listen," "a more varied sound" than their previous releases. Most reviews centered on the more pronounced balance—always somewhat present on Yo La Tengo recordings—between sonic assault and heartfelt melodies, their "ability to express the pedestrian or the sublime in a single phrase," as Joe Donnelly of *Raygun* summarized in a 1997 review. Kaplan characteristically played down their reactions to *CMJ*'s Sutter. "Sometimes what may seem like a different influence is really just a different button on the drum machine," he said.

The evolution of Yo La Tengo did not go unnoticed by Kaplan, however he may have tried to play it off to journalists. As he told Salamon, the Yo La Tengo that had just released *I Can Hear the Heart Beating as One* and the one he'd known previously were "two different bands." Hubley agreed. "Now, I feel like the three of us are more like one personality," she said. "Almost a separate personality."

Selected discography

New Wave Hot Dogs/President Yo La Tengo, Twin/Tone, 1989.
Fakebook, Bar/None, 1990.
May I Sing With Me, Alias, 1992.
Upside Down, Alias, 1992.
Painful, Matador/Atlantic, 1993.
Camp Yo La Tengo (EP), Matador, 1995.
Electr-O-Pura, Matador, 1995.
Genius + Love = Yo La Tengo, Matador, 1996.
Ride the Tiger, Coyote, 1986; Matador, 1996.
New Wave Hot Dogs, Coyote, 1987; Matador, 1996.
President Yo La Tengo, Coyote, 1989; Matador, 1996.
Autumn Sweater (EP), Matador, 1997.
I Can Hear the Heart Beating as One, Matador, 1997.
Sugarcube/The Summer/Looney Toons (EP), Matador, 1997.
Little Honda (EP), Matador, 1998.

Sources

Periodicals

College Music Journal, May 5, 1997.
Entertainment Weekly, October 8, 1993; May 2, 1997.
Guitar Player, October 1997.
New York, May 12, 1997.
New York Observer, May 12, 1997.
New York Press, May 1997.
New York Times, November 5, 1997.
Rolling Stone, May 1, 1997; October 2, 1997.
Spin, January 1998.
Village Voice, October 19, 1993; April 29, 1997.

Online

"Yo la Tengo," *Trouser Press*, http://www.trouserpress.com (September 20, 1998).
"Yo la Tengo," *Pitchfork Review Archive*, http://www.live-wire.com (August 9, 1998).
"Yo la Tengo," *All Music Guide*, http://www.allmusic.com (October 3, 1998).

Additional information was provided by Matador Records publicity materials, 1998.

—Brenna Sanchez

Cumulative Indexes

Cumulative Subject Index

Volume numbers appear in **bold**.

A cappella
Brightman, Sarah **20**
Bulgarian State Female Vocal Choir, The **10**
Nylons, The **6**
Take 6 **6**
Zap Mama **14**

Accordion
Buckwheat Zydeco **6**
Chenier, C. J. **15**
Chenier, Clifton **6**
Queen Ida **9**
Richard, Zachary **9**
Rockin' Dopsie **10**
Simien, Terrance **12**
Sonnier, Jo-El **10**
Yankovic, "Weird Al" **7**

Ambient/Rave/Techno
Aphex Twin **14**
Chemical Brothers **20**
Deep Forest **18**
Front Line Assembly **20**
KMFDM **18**
Kraftwerk **9**
Lords of Acid **20**
Man or Astroman? **21**
Orb, The **18**
2 Unlimited **18**
Shadow, DJ **19**

Bandoneon
Piazzolla, Astor **18**
Saluzzi, Dino **23**

Banjo
Bromberg, David **18**
Clark, Roy **1**
Crowe, J.D. **5**
Eldridge, Ben
  See Seldom Scene, The
Fleck, Bela **8**
  Also see New Grass Revival, The
Hartford, John **1**
Johnson, Courtney
  See New Grass Revival, The
McCoury, Del **15**
Piazzolla, Astor **18**
Scruggs, Earl **3**
Seeger, Pete **4**
  Also see Weavers, The
Skaggs, Ricky **5**
Stanley, Ralph **5**
Watson, Doc **2**

Bass
Brown, Ray **21**
Bruce, Jack
  See Cream
Carter, Ron **14**
Chambers, Paul **18**
Clarke, Stanley **3**
Collins, Bootsy **8**
Dixon, Willie **10**
Entwistle, John
  See Who, The
Fender, Leo **10**
Haden, Charlie **12**
Hill, Dusty
  See ZZ Top
Hillman, Chris
  See Byrds, The
  Also see Desert Rose Band, The
Johnston, Bruce
  See Beach Boys, The
Jones, John Paul
  See Led Zeppelin
Kaye, Carol **22**
Lake, Greg
  See Emerson, Lake & Palmer/Powell
Laswell, Bill **14**
Love, Laura **20**
Mann, Aimee **22**
McBride, Christian **17**
McCartney, Paul **4**
  Also see Beatles, The
McVie, John
  See Fleetwood Mac
Meisner, Randy
  See Eagles, The
Mingus, Charles **9**
Ndegéocello, Me'Shell **18**
Porter, Tiran
  See Doobie Brothers, The
Rutherford, Mike
  See Genesis
Schmit, Timothy B.
  See Eagles, The
Shakespeare, Robbie
  See Sly and Robbie
Simmons, Gene
  See Kiss
Sting **19**
  Earlier sketch in CM **2**
Sweet, Matthew **9**
Vicious, Sid
  See Sex Pistols, The
  Also see Siouxsie and the Banshees
Was, Don **21**
  Also see Was (Not Was)

Waters, Roger
  See Pink Floyd
Watt, Mike **22**
Weymouth, Tina
  See Talking Heads
Whitaker, Rodney **20**
Wyman, Bill
  See Rolling Stones, The

Big Band/Swing
Andrews Sisters, The **9**
Arnaz, Desi **8**
Bailey, Pearl **5**
Basie, Count **2**
Beiderbecke, Bix **16**
Bennett, Tony **16**
  Earlier sketch in CM **2**
Berrigan, Bunny **2**
Blakey, Art **11**
Brown, Lawrence **23**
Calloway, Cab **6**
Carter, Benny **3**
Chenille Sisters, The **16**
Cherry Poppin' Daddies **24**
Clooney, Rosemary **9**
Como, Perry **14**
Cugat, Xavier **23**
Dorsey, Jimmy
  See Dorsey Brothers, The
Dorsey, Tommy
  See Dorsey Brothers, The
Dorsey Brothers, The **8**
Eckstine, Billy **1**
Eldridge, Roy **9**
Ellington, Duke **2**
Ferguson, Maynard **7**
Fitzgerald, Ella **1**
Fountain, Pete **7**
Getz, Stan **12**
Gillespie, Dizzy **6**
Goodman, Benny **4**
Henderson, Fletcher **16**
Herman, Woody **12**
Hines, Earl "Fatha" **12**
Jacquet, Illinois **17**
James, Harry **11**
Jones, Spike **5**
Jordan, Louis **11**
Krupa, Gene **13**
Lee, Peggy **8**
McKinney's Cotton Pickers **16**
Miller, Glenn **6**
Norvo, Red **12**
Parker, Charlie **5**
Prima, Louis **18**

Puente, Tito **14**
Rich, Buddy **13**
Rodney, Red **14**
Roomful of Blues **7**
Scott, Jimmy **14**
Severinsen, Doc **1**
Shaw, Artie **8**
Sinatra, Frank **1**
Squirrel Nut Zippers **20**
Stafford, Jo **24**
Strayhorn, Billy **13**
Teagarden, Jack **10**
Torme, Mel **4**
Vaughan, Sarah **2**
Welk, Lawrence **13**
Whiteman, Paul **17**

Bluegrass
Auldridge, Mike **4**
Bluegrass Patriots **22**
Clements, Vassar **18**
Country Gentlemen, The **7**
Crowe, J.D. **5**
Flatt, Lester **3**
Fleck, Bela **8**
   Also see New Grass Revival, The
Gill, Vince **7**
Grisman, David **17**
Hartford, John **1**
Krauss, Alison **10**
Louvin Brothers, The **12**
Martin, Jimmy **5**
   Also see Osborne Brothers, The
McCoury, Del **15**
McReynolds, Jim and Jesse **12**
Monroe, Bill **1**
Nashville Bluegrass Band **14**
New Grass Revival, The **4**
Northern Lights **19**
O'Connor, Mark **1**
Osborne Brothers, The **8**
Parsons, Gram **7**
   Also see Byrds, The
Reverend Horton Heat **19**
Scruggs, Earl **3**
Seldom Scene, The **4**
Skaggs, Ricky **5**
Stanley Brothers, The **17**
Stanley, Ralph **5**
Stuart, Marty **9**
Watson, Doc **2**
Wiseman, Mac **19**

Blues
Allison, Luther **21**
Ayler , Albert **19**
Bailey, Pearl **5**
Baker, Ginger **16**
   Also see Cream
Ball, Marcia **15**
Barnes, Roosevelt "Booba" **23**
Berry, Chuck **1**
Bland, Bobby "Blue" **12**
Block, Rory **18**
Blood, Sweat and Tears **7**

Blues Brothers, The **3**
Broonzy, Big Bill **13**
Brown, Clarence "Gatemouth" **11**
Brown, Ruth **13**
Burdon, Eric **14**
   Also see War
   Also see Animals
Cale, J. J. **16**
Charles, Ray **24**
   Earlier sketch in CM **1**
Clapton, Eric **11**
   Earlier sketch in CM **1**
   Also see Cream
   Also see Yardbirds, The
Collins, Albert **4**
Cray, Robert **8**
Davis, Reverend Gary **18**
Diddley, Bo **3**
Dixon, Willie **10**
Dr. John **7**
Dupree, Champion Jack **12**
Earl, Ronnie **5**
   Also see Roomful of Blues
Fabulous Thunderbirds, The **1**
Fuller, Blind Boy **20**
Fulson, Lowell **20**
Gatton, Danny **16**
Guy, Buddy **4**
Handy, W. C. **7**
Hawkins, Screamin' Jay **8**
Healey, Jeff **4**
Holiday, Billie **6**
Hooker, John Lee **1**
Hopkins, Lightnin' **13**
House, Son **11**
Howlin' Wolf **6**
James, Elmore **8**
James, Etta **6**
Jefferson, Blind Lemon **18**
Johnson, Lonnie **17**
Johnson, Robert **6**
Jon Spencer Blues Explosion **18**
Joplin, Janis **3**
King, Albert **2**
King, B. B. **1**
King, Freddy **17**
Leadbelly **6**
Led Zeppelin **1**
Little Feat **4**
Little Walter **14**
Lockwood, Robert, Jr. **10**
Mayall, John **7**
McClinton, Delbert **14**
McDowell, Mississippi Fred **16**
McLean, Dave **24**
McTell, Blind Willie **17**
Muldaur, Maria **18**
Patton, Charley **11**
Plant, Robert **2**
   Also see Led Zeppelin
Professor Longhair **6**
Raitt, Bonnie **23**
   Earlier sketch in CM **3**
Redding, Otis **5**
Reed, Jimmy **15**

Rich, Charlie **3**
Robertson, Robbie **2**
Robillard, Duke **2**
Roomful of Blues **7**
Rush, Otis **12**
Shaffer, Paul **13**
Shines, Johnny **14**
Smith, Bessie **3**
Snow, Phoebe **4**
Spann, Otis **18**
Sunnyland Slim **16**
Sykes, Roosevelt **20**
Taj Mahal **6**
Taylor, Koko **10**
Thornton, Big Mama **18**
Toure, Ali Farka **18**
Turner, Big Joe **13**
Ulmer, James Blood **13**
Van Zandt, Townes **13**
Vaughan, Jimmie **24**
Vaughan, Stevie Ray **1**
Waits, Tom **1**
Walker, T-Bone **5**
Wallace, Sippie **6**
Washington, Dinah **5**
Waters, Ethel **11**
Waters, Muddy **24**
   Earlier sketch in CM **4**
Wells, Junior **17**
Weston, Randy **15**
Whitfield, Mark **18**
Whitley, Chris **16**
Whittaker, Hudson **20**
Williams, Joe **11**
Williamson, Sonny Boy **9**
Wilson, Gerald **19**
Winter, Johnny **5**
Witherspoon, Jimmy **19**
ZZ Top **2**

Cajun/Zydeco
Ball, Marcia **15**
Brown, Clarence "Gatemouth" **11**
Buckwheat Zydeco **6**
Chenier, C. J. **15**
Chenier, Clifton **6**
Doucet, Michael **8**
Landreth, Sonny **16**
Queen Ida **9**
Richard, Zachary **9**
Rockin' Dopsie **10**
Simien, Terrance **12**
Sonnier, Jo-El **10**

Cello
Casals, Pablo **9**
Gray, Walter
   See Kronos Quartet
Harrell, Lynn **3**
Jeanrenaud, Joan Dutcher
   See Kronos Quartet
Ma, Yo Yo **24**
   Earlier sketch in CM **2**
Rostropovich, Mstislav **17**

Children's Music
Bartels, Joanie **13**
Cappelli, Frank **14**
Chapin, Tom **11**
Chenille Sisters, The **16**
Harley, Bill **7**
Lehrer, Tom **7**
Nagler, Eric **8**
Penner, Fred **10**
Raffi **8**
Rosenshontz **9**
Sharon, Lois & Bram **6**

Christian Music
Anointed **21**
Ashton, Susan **17**
Audio Adrenaline **22**
Champion, Eric **21**
Chapman, Steven Curtis **15**
dc Talk **18**
Duncan, Bryan **19**
Eskelin, Ian **19**
4Him **23**
Grant, Amy **7**
Jars of Clay **20**
King's X **7**
Newsboys, The **24**
Paris, Twila **16**
Patti, Sandi **7**
Petra **3**
Point of Grace **21**
Smith, Michael W. **11**
Stryper **2**
Waters, Ethel **11**

Clarinet
Adams, John **8**
Bechet, Sidney **17**
Braxton, Anthony **12**
Byron, Don **22**
Dorsey, Jimmy
  See Dorsey Brothers, The
Fountain, Pete **7**
Goodman, Benny **4**
Herman, Woody **12**
Shaw, Artie **8**
Stoltzman, Richard **24**

Classical
Ameling, Elly **24**
Anderson, Marian **8**
Arrau, Claudio **1**
Baker, Janet **14**
Bernstein, Leonard **2**
Boyd, Liona **7**
Bream, Julian **9**
Britten, Benjamin **15**
Bronfman, Yefim **6**
Canadian Brass, The **4**
Carter, Ron **14**
Casals, Pablo **9**
Chang, Sarah **7**
Clayderman, Richard **1**
Cliburn, Van **13**
Copland, Aaron **2**

Davis, Anthony **17**
Davis, Chip **4**
Fiedler, Arthur **6**
Fleming, Renee **24**
Galway, James **3**
Gingold, Josef **6**
Gould, Glenn **9**
Gould, Morton **16**
Hampson, Thomas **12**
Harrell, Lynn **3**
Hayes, Roland **13**
Hendricks, Barbara **10**
Herrmann, Bernard **14**
Hinderas, Natalie **12**
Horne, Marilyn **9**
Horowitz, Vladimir **1**
Jarrett, Keith **1**
Kennedy, Nigel **8**
Kissin, Evgeny **6**
Kronos Quartet **5**
Kunzel, Erich **17**
Lemper, Ute **14**
Levine, James **8**
Liberace **9**
Ma, Yo Yo **24**
  Earlier sketch in CM **2**
Marsalis, Wynton **6**
Masur, Kurt **11**
McNair, Sylvia **15**
McPartland, Marian **15**
Mehta, Zubin **11**
Menuhin, Yehudi **11**
Midori **7**
Mutter, Anne-Sophie **23**
Nyman, Michael **15**
Ott, David **2**
Parkening, Christopher **7**
Perahia, Murray **10**
Perlman, Itzhak **2**
Phillips, Harvey **3**
Rampal, Jean-Pierre **6**
Rangell, Andrew **24**
Rostropovich, Mstislav **17**
Rota, Nino **13**
Rubinstein, Arthur **11**
Salerno-Sonnenberg, Nadja **3**
Salonen, Esa-Pekka **16**
Schickele, Peter **5**
Schuman, William **10**
Segovia, Andres **6**
Shankar, Ravi **9**
Solti, Georg **13**
Stern, Isaac **7**
Stoltzman, Richard **24**
Sutherland, Joan **13**
Takemitsu, Toru **6**
Thibaudet, Jean-Yves **24**
Tilson Thomas, Michael **24**
Toscanini, Arturo **14**
Upshaw, Dawn **9**
Vienna Choir Boys **23**
von Karajan, Herbert **1**
Weill, Kurt **12**
Wilson, Ransom **5**
Yamashita, Kazuhito **4**

York, Andrew **15**
Zukerman, Pinchas **4**

Composers
Adams, John **8**
Allen, Geri **10**
Anderson, Wessell **23**
Alpert, Herb **11**
Anka, Paul **2**
Atkins, Chet **5**
Bacharach, Burt **20**
  Earlier sketch in CM **1**
Badalamenti, Angelo **17**
Beiderbecke, Bix **16**
Benson, George **9**
Berlin, Irving **8**
Bernstein, Leonard **2**
Blackman, Cindy **15**
Bley, Carla **8**
Bley, Paul **14**
Braxton, Anthony **12**
Brickman, Jim **22**
Britten, Benjamin **15**
Brubeck, Dave **8**
Burrell, Kenny **11**
Byrne, David **8**
  Also see Talking Heads
Byron, Don **22**
Cage, John **8**
Cale, John **9**
Casals, Pablo **9**
Clarke, Stanley **3**
Coleman, Ornette **5**
Cooder, Ry **2**
Cooney, Rory **6**
Copeland, Stewart **14**
  Also see Police, The **20**
Copland, Aaron **2**
Crouch, Andraé **9**
Curtis, King **17**
Davis, Anthony **17**
Davis, Chip **4**
Davis, Miles **1**
de Grassi, Alex **6**
Dorsey, Thomas A. **11**
Elfman, Danny **9**
Ellington, Duke **2**
Eno, Brian **8**
Enya **6**
Esquivel, Juan **17**
Evans, Bill **17**
Evans, Gil **17**
Fahey, John **17**
Foster, David **13**
Frisell, Bill **15**
Frith, Fred **19**
Galás, Diamanda **16**
Gillespie, Dizzy **6**
Glass, Philip **1**
Golson, Benny **21**
Gould, Glenn **9**
Gould, Morton **16**
Green, Benny **17**
Grusin, Dave **7**
Guaraldi, Vince **3**

Hamlisch, Marvin **1**
Hammer, Jan **21**
Hancock, Herbie **8**
Handy, W. C. **7**
Hargrove, Roy **15**
Harris, Eddie **15**
Hartke, Stephen **5**
Henderson, Fletcher **16**
Herrmann, Bernard **14**
Hunter, Alberta **7**
Ibrahim, Abdullah **24**
Isham, Mark **14**
Jacquet, Illinois **17**
Jarre, Jean-Michel **2**
Jarrett, Keith **1**
Johnson, James P. **16**
Jones, Hank **15**
Jones, Quincy **20**
  Earlier sketch in CM **2**
Joplin, Scott **10**
Jordan, Stanley **1**
Kenny G **14**
Kenton, Stan **21**
Kern, Jerome **13**
Kitaro **1**
Kottke, Leo **13**
Lacy, Steve **23**
Lateef, Yusef **16**
Lee, Peggy **8**
Legg, Adrian **17**
Lewis, Ramsey **14**
Lincoln, Abbey **9**
Lloyd, Charles **22**
Lloyd Webber, Andrew **6**
Loesser, Frank **19**
Loewe, Frederick
  See Lerner and Loewe
Mancini, Henry **20**
  Earlier sketch in CM **1**
Marsalis, Branford **10**
Marsalis, Ellis **13**
Martino, Pat **17**
Masekela, Hugh **7**
McBride, Christian **17**
McPartland, Marian **15**
Menken, Alan **10**
Metheny, Pat **2**
Miles, Ron **22**
Mingus, Charles **9**
Moby **17**
Monk, Meredith **1**
Monk, Thelonious **6**
Montenegro, Hugo **18**
Morricone, Ennio **15**
Morton, Jelly Roll **7**
Mulligan, Gerry **16**
Nascimento, Milton **6**
Newman, Randy **4**
Nyman, Michael **15**
Oldfield, Mike **18**
Orff, Carl **21**
Osby, Greg **21**
Ott, David **2**
Palmieri, Eddie **15**

Parker, Charlie **5**
Parks, Van Dyke **17**
Peterson, Oscar **11**
Piazzolla, Astor **18**
Ponty, Jean-Luc **8**
Porter, Cole **10**
Post, Mike **21**
Previn, André **15**
Puente, Tito **14**
Pullen, Don **16**
Reich, Steve **8**
Reinhardt, Django **7**
Ritenour, Lee **7**
Roach, Max **12**
Rollins, Sonny **7**
Rota, Nino **13**
Sakamoto, Ryuichi **19**
Salonen, Esa-Pekka **16**
Sanders, Pharoah **16**
Satriani, Joe **4**
Schickele, Peter **5**
Schuman, William **10**
Shankar, Ravi **9**
Shaw, Artie **8**
Shorter, Wayne **5**
Silver, Horace **19**
Solal, Martial **4**
Sondheim, Stephen **8**
Sousa, John Philip **10**
Story, Liz **2**
Stravinsky, Igor **21**
Strayhorn, Billy **13**
Styne, Jule **21**
Summers, Andy **3**
  Also see Police, The
Sun Ra **5**
Takemitsu, Toru **6**
Talbot, John Michael **6**
Tatum, Art **17**
Taylor, Billy **13**
Taylor, Cecil **9**
Tesh, John **20**
Thielemans, Toots **13**
Threadgill, Henry **9**
Tilson Thomas, Michael **24**
Towner, Ralph **22**
Tyner, McCoy **7**
Vangelis **21**
Was, Don **21**
  Also see Was (Not Was)
Washington, Grover, Jr. **5**
Weill, Kurt **12**
Weston, Randy **15**
Whelan, Bill **20**
Whiteman, Paul **17**
Williams, John **9**
Wilson, Cassandra **12**
Winston, George
Winter, Paul **10**
Worrell, Bernie **11**
Yanni **11**
Yeston, Maury **22**
York, Andrew **15**
Young, La Monte **16**

Zimmerman, Udo **5**
Zorn, John **15**
Zappa, Frank **17**
  Earlier sketch in CM **1**

Conductors
Bacharach, Burt **20**
  Earlier sketch CM **1**
Bernstein, Leonard **2**
Britten, Benjamin **15**
Casals, Pablo **9**
Copland, Aaron **2**
Davies, Dennis Russell **24**
Domingo, Placido **20**
  Earlier sketch in CM **1**
Evans, Gil **17**
Fiedler, Arthur **6**
Gould, Morton **16**
Herrmann, Bernard **14**
Ibrahim, Abdullah **24**
Jarrett, Keith **1**
Jones, Hank **15**
Kunzel, Erich **17**
Levine, James **8**
Mancini, Henry **20**
  Earlier sketch in CM **1**
Marriner, Neville **7**
Masur, Kurt **11**
Mehta, Zubin **11**
Menuhin, Yehudi **11**
Nero, Peter **19**
Previn, André **15**
Rampal, Jean-Pierre **6**
Rostropovich, Mstislav **17**
Salonen, Esa-Pekka **16**
Schickele, Peter **5**
Solti, Georg **13**
Tilson Thomas, Michael **24**
Toscanini, Arturo **14**
von Karajan, Herbert **1**
Welk, Lawrence **13**
Williams, John **9**
Zukerman, Pinchas **4**

Contemporary Dance Music
Abdul, Paula **3**
Aphex Twin **14**
Bee Gees, The **3**
B-52's, The **4**
Brown, Bobby **4**
Brown, James **2**
C + C Music Factory **16**
Cherry, Neneh **4**
Clinton, George **7**
Craig, Carl **19**
Deee-lite **9**
De La Soul **7**
Depeche Mode **5**
Earth, Wind and Fire **12**
English Beat, The **9**
En Vogue **10**
Erasure **11**
Eurythmics **6**
Exposé **4**

Fox, Samantha **3**
Fun Lovin' Criminals **20**
Gang of Four **8**
Hammer, M.C. **5**
Harry, Deborah **4**
  Also see Blondie
Ice-T **7**
Idol, Billy **3**
Jackson, Janet **16**
  Earlier sketch in CM **3**
Jackson, Michael **17**
  Earlier sketch in CM **1**
    Also see Jacksons, The
James, Rick **2**
Jones, Grace **9**
Madonna **16**
  Earlier sketch in CM **4**
Massive Attack **17**
Moby **17**
M People **15**
New Order **11**
Orbital **20**
Peniston, CeCe **15**
Pet Shop Boys **5**
Pizzicato Five **18**
Portishead **22**
Prince **14**
  Earlier sketch in CM **1**
Queen Latifah **6**
Rodgers, Nile **8**
Salt-N-Pepa **6**
Shadow, DJ **19**
Shamen, The **23**
Simmons, Russell **7**
Soul II Soul **17**
Sugar Ray **22**
Summer, Donna **12**
Technotronic **5**
TLC **15**
Tricky **18**
2 Unlimited **18**
Vasquez, Junior **16**
Village People, The **7**
Was (Not Was) **6**
Waters, Crystal **15**
Young M.C. **4**

Contemporary Instrumental/New Age
Ackerman, Will **3**
Arkenstone, David **20**
Clinton, George **7**
Collins, Bootsy **8**
Davis, Chip **4**
de Grassi, Alex **6**
Enigma **14**
Enya **6**
Esquivel, Juan **17**
Hedges, Michael **3**
Isham, Mark **14**
Jarre, Jean-Michel **2**
Kitaro **1**
Kronos Quartet **5**
Legg, Adrian **17**
Story, Liz **2**

Summers, Andy **3**
  Also see Police, The
Tangerine Dream **12**
Tesh, John **20**
Winston, George **9**
Winter, Paul **10**
Yanni **11**

Cornet
Armstrong, Louis **4**
Beiderbecke, Bix **16**
Cherry, Don **10**
Handy, W. C. **7**
Oliver, King **15**
Vaché, Jr., Warren **22**

Country
Acuff, Roy **2**
Akins, Rhett **22**
Alabama **21**
  Earlier sketch in CM **1**
Anderson, John **5**
Arnold, Eddy **10**
Asleep at the Wheel **5**
Atkins, Chet **5**
Auldridge, Mike **4**
Autry, Gene **12**
Bellamy Brothers, The **13**
Berg, Matraca **16**
Berry, John **17**
Black, Clint **5**
BlackHawk **21**
Blue Rodeo **18**
Bogguss, Suzy **11**
Bonamy, James **21**
Boone, Pat **13**
Boy Howdy **21**
Brandt, Paul **22**
Brannon, Kippi **20**
Brooks & Dunn **12**
Brooks, Garth **8**
Brown, Junior **15**
Brown, Marty **14**
Brown, Tony **14**
Buffett, Jimmy **4**
Byrds, The **8**
Cale, J. J. **16**
Campbell, Glen **2**
Carpenter, Mary-Chapin **6**
Carter, Carlene **8**
Carter Family, The **3**
Cash, Johnny **17**
  Earlier sketch in CM **1**
Cash, June Carter **6**
Cash, Rosanne **2**
Chesney, Kenny **20**
Chesnutt, Mark **13**
Clark, Guy **17**
Clark, Roy **1**
Clark, Terri **19**
Clements, Vassar **18**
Cline, Patsy **5**
Coe, David Allan **4**
Collie, Mark **15**

Confederate Railroad **23**
Cooder, Ry **2**
Cowboy Junkies, The **4**
Crowe, J. D. **5**
Crowell, Rodney **8**
Cyrus, Billy Ray **11**
Daniels, Charlie **6**
Davis, Linda **21**
Davis, Skeeter **15**
Dean, Billy **19**
DeMent, Iris **13**
Denver, John **22**
  Earlier entry in CM **1**
Desert Rose Band, The **4**
Diamond Rio **11**
Dickens, Little Jimmy **7**
Diffie, Joe **10**
Dylan, Bob **21**
  Earlier sketch in CM **3**
Earle, Steve **16**
Flatt, Lester **3**
Flores, Rosie **16**
Ford, Tennessee Ernie **3**
Foster, Radney **16**
Frizzell, Lefty **10**
Gayle, Crystal **1**
Germano, Lisa **18**
Gill, Vince **7**
Gilley, Mickey **7**
Gilmore, Jimmie Dale **11**
Gordy, Jr., Emory **17**
Greenwood, Lee **12**
Griffith, Nanci **3**
Haggard, Merle **2**
Hall, Tom T. **4**
Harris, Emmylou **4**
Hartford, John **1**
Hay, George D. **3**
Herndon, Ty **20**
Hiatt, John **8**
Highway 101 **4**
Hill, Faith **18**
Hinojosa, Tish **13**
Howard, Harlan **15**
Jackson, Alan **7**
Jennings, Waylon **4**
Jones, George **4**
Judd, Wynonna
  See Wynonna
  See Judds, The
Judds, The **2**
Keith, Toby **17**
Kentucky Headhunters, The **5**
Kershaw, Sammy **15**
Ketchum, Hal **14**
Kristofferson, Kris **4**
Lamb, Barbara **19**
Lang, K. D. **4**
Lawrence, Tracy **11**
LeDoux, Chris **12**
Lee, Brenda **5**
Little Feat **4**
Little Texas **14**
Louvin Brothers, The **12**

Loveless, Patty **21**
 Earlier sketch in CM **5**
Lovett, Lyle **5**
Lynn, Loretta **2**
Lynne, Shelby **5**
Mandrell, Barbara **4**
Mattea, Kathy **5**
Mavericks, The **15**
McBride, Martina **14**
McClinton, Delbert **14**
McCoy, Neal **15**
McCready, Mindy **22**
McEntire, Reba **11**
McGraw, Tim **17**
Miller, Roger **4**
Milsap, Ronnie **2**
Moffatt, Katy **18**
Monroe, Bill **1**
Montgomery, John Michael **14**
Morgan, Lorrie **10**
Murphey, Michael Martin **9**
Murray, Anne **4**
Nelson, Willie **11**
 Earlier sketch in CM **1**
Newton-John, Olivia **8**
Nitty Gritty Dirt Band, The **6**
Oak Ridge Boys, The **7**
O'Connor, Mark **1**
Oslin, K. T. **3**
Owens, Buck **2**
Parnell, Lee Roy **15**
Parsons, Gram **7**
 Also see Byrds, The
Parton, Dolly **24**
 Earlier sketch in CM **2**
Pearl, Minnie **3**
Pierce, Webb **15**
Price, Ray **11**
Pride, Charley **4**
Rabbitt, Eddie **24**
 Earlier sketch in CM **5**
Raitt, Bonnie **3**
Raye, Collin **16**
Reeves, Jim **10**
Restless Heart **12**
Rich, Charlie **3**
Richey, Kim **20**
Ricochet **23**
Rimes, LeAnn **19**
Robbins, Marty **9**
Rodgers, Jimmie **3**
Rogers, Kenny **1**
Rogers, Roy **24**
 Earlier sketch in CM **9**
Sawyer Brown **13**
Scruggs, Earl **3**
Scud Mountain Boys **21**
Seals, Dan **9**
Shenandoah **17**
Skaggs, Ricky **5**
Sonnier, Jo-El **10**
Statler Brothers, The **8**
Stevens, Ray **7**
Stone, Doug **10**
Strait, George **5**

Stuart, Marty **9**
Sweethearts of the Rodeo **12**
Texas Tornados, The **8**
Tillis, Mel **7**
Tillis, Pam **8**
Tippin, Aaron **12**
Travis, Merle **14**
Travis, Randy **9**
Tritt, Travis **7**
Tubb, Ernest **4**
Tucker, Tanya **3**
Twain, Shania **17**
Twitty, Conway **6**
Van Shelton, Ricky **5**
Van Zandt, Townes **13**
Wagoner, Porter **13**
Walker, Clay **20**
Walker, Jerry Jeff **13**
Wariner, Steve **18**
Watson, Doc **2**
Wells, Kitty **6**
West, Dottie **8**
White, Lari **15**
Whitley, Keith **7**
Williams, Don **4**
Williams, Hank, Jr. **1**
Williams, Hank, Sr. **4**
Williams, Lucinda **24**
Willis, Kelly **12**
Wills, Bob **6**
Wynette, Tammy **24**
 Earlier sketch in CM **2**
Wynonna **11**
 Also see Judds, The
Yearwood, Trisha **10**
Yoakam, Dwight **21**
 Earlier sketch in CM **1**
Young, Faron **7**

Dobro
Auldridge, Mike **4**
 Also see Country Gentlemen, The
 Also see Seldom Scene, The
Burch, Curtis
 See New Grass Revival, The
Knopfler, Mark **3**
 Also see Dire Straits
Whitley, Chris **16**

Drums
Aronoff, Kenny **21**
 See **Percussion**
Colaiuta, Vinnie **23**
Starr, Ringo **24**

Dulcimer
Ritchie, Jean **4**

Fiddle
MacIsaac, Ashley **21**
See **Violin**

Film Scores
Anka, Paul **2**
Bacharach, Burt **20**
 Earlier sketch in CM **1**

Badalamenti, Angelo **17**
Berlin, Irving **8**
Bernstein, Leonard **2**
Blanchard, Terence **13**
Britten, Benjamin **15**
Byrne, David **8**
 Also see Talking Heads
Cafferty, John
 See Beaver Brown Band, The
Cahn, Sammy **11**
Cliff, Jimmy **8**
Copeland, Stewart **14**
 Also see Police, The
Copland, Aaron **2**
Crouch, Andraé **9**
Dibango, Manu **14**
Dolby, Thomas **10**
Donovan **9**
Eddy, Duane **9**
Elfman, Danny **9**
Ellington, Duke **2**
Ferguson, Maynard **7**
Froom, Mitchell **15**
Gabriel, Peter **16**
 Earlier sketch in CM **2**
 Also see Genesis
Galás, Diamanda **16**
Gershwin, George and Ira **11**
Gould, Glenn **9**
Grusin, Dave **7**
Guaraldi, Vince **3**
Hamlisch, Marvin **1**
Hancock, Herbie **8**
Harrison, George **2**
Hayes, Isaac **10**
Hedges, Michael **3**
Herrmann, Bernard **14**
Isham, Mark **14**
Jones, Quincy **20**
 Earlier sketch in CM **2**
Knopfler, Mark **3**
 Also see Dire Straits
Lennon, John **9**
 Also see Beatles, The
Lerner and Loewe **13**
Loesser, Frank **19**
Mancini, Henry **20**
 Earlier sketch in CM **1**
Marsalis, Branford **10**
Mayfield, Curtis **8**
McCartney, Paul **4**
 Also see Beatles, The
Menken, Alan **10**
Mercer, Johnny **13**
Metheny, Pat **2**
Montenegro, Hugo **18**
Morricone, Ennio **15**
Nascimento, Milton **6**
Nilsson **10**
Nyman, Michael **15**
Parks, Van Dyke **17**
Peterson, Oscar **11**
Porter, Cole **10**
Previn, André **15**
Reznor, Trent **13**

Richie, Lionel **2**
Robertson, Robbie **2**
Rollins, Sonny **7**
Rota, Nino **13**
Sager, Carole Bayer **5**
Sakamoto, Ryuichi **18**
Schickele, Peter **5**
Shankar, Ravi **9**
Taj Mahal **6**
Waits, Tom **12**
  Earlier sketch in CM **1**
Weill, Kurt **12**
Williams, John **9**
Williams, Paul **5**
Willner, Hal **10**
Young, Neil **15**
  Earlier sketch in CM **2**

Flugelhorn
Sandoval, Arturo **15**
Mangione, Chuck **23**

Flute
Anderson, Ian
  See Jethro Tull
Galway, James **3**
Lateef, Yusef **16**
Mangione, Chuck **23**
Mann, Herbie **16**
Najee **21**
Rampal, Jean-Pierre **6**
Ulmer, James Blood **13**
Wilson, Ransom **5**

Folk/Traditional
Altan **18**
America **16**
Anonymous 4 **23**
Arnaz, Desi **8**
Baez, Joan **1**
Belafonte, Harry **8**
Black, Mary **15**
Blades, Ruben **2**
Bloom, Luka **14**
Blue Rodeo **18**
Brady, Paul **8**
Bragg, Billy **7**
Bromberg, David **18**
Buckley, Tim **14**
Buffalo Springfield **24**
Bulgarian State Female Vocal Choir **10**
Byrds, The **8**
Campbell, Sarah Elizabeth **23**
Caravan **24**
Carter Family, The **3**
Chandra, Sheila **16**
Chapin, Harry **6**
Chapman, Tracy **20**
  Earlier sketch in CM **4**
Chenille Sisters, The **16**
Cherry, Don **10**
Chieftains, The **7**
Childs, Toni **2**
Clannad **23**

Clegg, Johnny **8**
Cockburn, Bruce **8**
Cohen, Leonard **3**
Collins, Judy **4**
Colvin, Shawn **11**
Cotten, Elizabeth **16**
Crosby, David **3**
  Also see Byrds, The
Cruz, Celia **22**
  Earlier sketch in CM **10**
de Lucia, Paco **1**
DeMent, Iris **13**
Donovan **9**
Dr. John **7**
Drake, Nick **17**
Dylan, Bob **3**
Elliot, Cass **5**
Enya **6**
Estefan, Gloria **15**
  Earlier sketch in CM **2**
Fahey, John **17**
Fairport Convention **22**
Feliciano, José **10**
Galway, James **3**
Germano, Lisa **18**
Gibson, Bob **23**
Gilmore, Jimmie Dale **11**
Gipsy Kings, The **8**
Gorka, John **18**
Griffin, Patty **24**
Griffith, Nanci **3**
Grisman, David **17**
Guthrie, Arlo **6**
Guthrie, Woody **2**
Hakmoun, Hassan **15**
Hardin, Tim **18**
Harding, John Wesley **6**
Hartford, John **1**
Havens, Richie **11**
Henry, Joe **18**
Hinojosa, Tish **13**
Ian and Sylvia **18**
Ian, Janis **24**
Iglesias, Julio **20**
  Earlier sketch in CM **2**
Incredible String Band **23**
Indigo Girls **20**
  Earlier sketch in CM **3**
Ives, Burl **12**
Khan, Nusrat Fateh Ali **13**
Kingston Trio, The **9**
Klezmatics, The **18**
Kottke, Leo **13**
Kuti, Fela **7**
Ladysmith Black Mambazo **1**
Larkin, Patty **9**
Lavin, Christine **6**
Leadbelly **6**
Lightfoot, Gordon **3**
Los Lobos **2**
Makeba, Miriam **8**
Mamas and the Papas **21**
Masekela, Hugh **7**
McKennitt, Loreena **24**
McLean, Don **7**

Melanie **12**
Mitchell, Joni **17**
  Earlier sketch in CM **2**
Moffatt, Katy **18**
Morrison, Van **3**
Morrissey, Bill **12**
Nascimento, Milton **6**
N'Dour, Youssou **6**
Near, Holly **1**
Ochs, Phil **7**
O'Connor, Sinead **3**
Odetta **7**
Parsons, Gram **7**
  Also see Byrds, The
Paxton, Tom **5**
Pentangle **18**
Peter, Paul & Mary **4**
Pogues, The **6**
Prine, John **7**
Proclaimers, The **13**
Rankins, The **24**
Redpath, Jean **1**
Ritchie, Jean, **4**
Roches, The **18**
Rodgers, Jimmie **3**
Sainte-Marie, Buffy **11**
Santana, Carlos **1**
Seeger, Pete **4**
  Also see Weavers, The
Selena **16**
Shankar, Ravi **9**
Simon, Paul **16**
  Earlier sketch in CM **1**
  Also see Simon and Garfunkel
Simon and Garfunkel **24**
Snow, Pheobe **4**
Steeleye Span **19**
Story, The **13**
Sweet Honey in the Rock **1**
Taj Mahal **6**
Thompson, Richard **7**
Tikaram, Tanita **9**
Toure, Ali Farka **18**
Van Ronk, Dave **12**
Van Zandt, Townes **13**
Vega, Suzanne **3**
Wainwright III, Loudon **11**
Walker, Jerry Jeff **13**
Watson, Doc **2**
Weavers, The **8**
Whitman, Slim **19**

French Horn
Ohanian, David
  See Canadian Brass, The

Funk
Bambaataa, Afrika **13**
Brand New Heavies, The **14**
Brown, James **2**
Burdon, Eric **14**
  Also see War
  Also see Animals
Clinton, George **7**
Collins, Bootsy **8**

Fishbone **7**
Gang of Four **8**
Jackson, Janet **16**
  Earlier sketch in CM **3**
Khan, Chaka **19**
  Earlier sketch in CM **9**
Mayfield, Curtis **8**
Meters, The **14**
Ohio Players **16**
Parker, Maceo **7**
Prince **14**
  Earlier sketch in CM **1**
Red Hot Chili Peppers, The **7**
Sly and the Family Stone **24**
Stone, Sly **8**
  Also see Sly and the Family Stone
Toussaint, Allen **11**
Worrell, Bernie **11**

Funky
Avery, Teodross **23**
Front 242 **19**
Jamiroquai **21**
Wu-Tang Clan **19**

Fusion
Anderson, Ray **7**
Avery, Teodross **23**
Beck, Jeff **4**
  Also see Yardbirds, The
Clarke, Stanley **3**
Coleman, Ornette **5**
Corea, Chick **6**
Davis, Miles **1**
Fishbone **7**
Hancock, Herbie **8**
Harris, Eddie **15**
Johnson, Eric **19**
Lewis, Ramsey **14**
Mahavishnu Orchestra **19**
McLaughlin, John **12**
Metheny, Pat **2**
O'Connor, Mark **1**
Ponty, Jean-Luc **8**
Reid, Vernon **2**
Ritenour, Lee **7**
Shorter, Wayne **5**
Summers, Andy **3**
  Also see Police, The
Washington, Grover, Jr. **5**

Gospel
Anderson, Marian **8**
Armstrong, Vanessa Bell **24**
Baylor, Helen **20**
Boone, Pat **13**
Brown, James **2**
Caesar, Shirley **17**
Carter Family, The **3**
Charles, Ray **1**
Cleveland, James **1**
Cooke, Sam **1**
  Also see Soul Stirrers, The
Crouch, Andraé **9**
Dorsey, Thomas A. **11**

Five Blind Boys of Alabama **12**
Ford, Tennessee Ernie **3**
4Him **23**
Franklin, Aretha **17**
  Earlier sketch in CM **2**
Franklin, Kirk **22**
Green, Al **9**
Hawkins, Tramaine **17**
Houston, Cissy **6**
Jackson, Mahalia **8**
Kee, John P. **15**
Knight, Gladys **1**
Little Richard **1**
Louvin Brothers, The **12**
Mighty Clouds of Joy, The **17**
Oak Ridge Boys, The **7**
Paris, Twila **16**
Pickett, Wilson **10**
Presley, Elvis **1**
Redding, Otis **5**
Reese, Della **13**
Robbins, Marty **9**
Smith, Michael W. **11**
Soul Stirrers, The **11**
Sounds of Blackness **13**
Staples, Mavis **13**
Staples, Pops **11**
Take 6 **6**
Waters, Ethel **11**
Watson, Doc **2**
Williams, Deniece **1**
Williams, Marion **15**
Winans, The **12**
Womack, Bobby **5**

Guitar
Ackerman, Will **3**
Adé, King Sunny **18**
Allison, Luther **21**
Allman, Duane
  See Allman Brothers, The
Alvin, Dave **17**
Atkins, Chet **5**
Autry, Gene **12**
Barnes, Roosevelt "Booba" **23**
Baxter, Jeff
  See Doobie Brothers, The
Beck **18**
Beck, Jeff **4**
  Also see Yardbirds, The
Belew, Adrian **5**
Benson, George **9**
Berry, Chuck **1**
Berry, John **17**
Bettencourt, Nuno
  See Extreme
Betts, Dicky
  See Allman Brothers, The
Block, Rory **18**
Bloom, Luka **14**
Boyd, Liona **7**
Bream, Julian **9**
Bromberg, David **18**
Brown, Junior **15**

Buck, Peter
  See R.E.M.
Buckingham, Lindsey **8**
  Also see Fleetwood Mac
Burrell, Kenny **11**
Campbell, Glen **2**
Chaquico, Craig **23**
Chesney, Kenny **20**
Chesnutt, Mark **13**
Christian, Charlie **11**
Clapton, Eric **11**
  Earlier sketch in CM **1**
  Also see Cream
  Also see Yardbirds, The
Clark, Roy **1**
Cockburn, Bruce **8**
Collie, Mark **15**
Collins, Albert **19**
  Earlier entry in CM **4**
Cooder, Ry **2**
Cotten, Elizabeth **16**
Cray, Robert **8**
Cropper, Steve **12**
Dale, Dick **13**
Daniels, Charlie **6**
Davis, Reverend Gary **18**
de Grassi, Alex **6**
de Lucia, Paco **1**
Del Rubio Triplets **21**
Denver, John **22**
  Earlier entry in CM **1**
Dickens, Little Jimmy **7**
Diddley, Bo **3**
DiFranco, Ani **17**
Di Meola, Al **12**
Drake, Nick **17**
Earl, Ronnie **5**
  Also see Roomful of Blues
Eddy, Duane **9**
Edge, The
  See U2
Ellis, Herb **18**
Emmanuel, Tommy **21**
Etheridge, Melissa **16**
  Earlier sketch in CM **4**
Fahey, John **17**
Fankhauser, Merrell **24**
Feliciano, José **10**
Fender, Leo **10**
Flatt, Lester **3**
Flores, Rosie **16**
Ford, Lita **9**
Frampton, Peter **3**
Frehley, Ace
  See Kiss
Fripp, Robert **9**
Frisell, Bill **15**
Frith, Fred **19**
Fuller, Blind Boy **20**
Fulson, Lowell **20**
Garcia, Jerry **4**
  Also see Grateful Dead, The
Gatton, Danny **16**
George, Lowell
  See Little Feat

Gibbons, Billy
  See ZZ Top
Gibson, Bob **23**
Gill, Vince **7**
Gilmour, David
  See Pink Floyd
Gorka, John **18**
Green, Grant **14**
Green, Peter
  See Fleetwood Mac
Guy, Buddy **4**
Hackett, Bobby **21**
Haley, Bill **6**
Hardin, Tim **18**
Harper, Ben **17**
Harrison, George **2**
Hatfield, Juliana **12**
  Also see Lemonheads, The
Havens, Richie **11**
Healey, Jeff **4**
Hedges, Michael **3**
Hendrix, Jimi **2**
Hepcat, Harry **23**
Hillman, Chris
  See Byrds, The
  Also see Desert Rose Band, The
Hitchcock, Robyn **9**
Holly, Buddy **1**
Hooker, John Lee **1**
Hopkins, Lightnin' **13**
Howlin' Wolf **6**
Hunter, Charlie **24**
Iommi, Tony
  See Black Sabbath
Ives, Burl **12**
James, Elmore **8**
James, Skip **24**
Jardine, Al
  See Beach Boys, The
Jean, Wyclef **22**
Jefferson, Blind Lemon **18**
Jobim, Antonio Carlos **19**
Johnson, Eric **19**
Johnson, Lonnie **17**
Johnson, Robert **6**
Jones, Brian
  See Rolling Stones, The
Jordan, Stanley **1**
Kantner, Paul
  See Jefferson Airplane
Keith, Toby **17**
King, Albert **2**
King, B. B. **1**
King, Freddy **17**
King, B.B. **24**
Klugh, Earl **10**
Knopfler, Mark **3**
  Also see Dire Straits
Kottke, Leo **13**
Landreth, Sonny **16**
Larkin, Patty **9**
Leadbelly **6**
Legg, Adrian **17**
Lennon, John **9**
  Also see Beatles, The

Lindley, David **2**
Lockwood, Robert, Jr. **10**
Loeb, Lisa **19**
Malmsteen, Yngwie **24**
Marr, Johnny
  See Smiths, The
  See The The
Martino, Pat **17**
Matthews, Eric **22**
May, Brian
  See Queen
Mayfield, Curtis **8**
McClinton, Delbert **14**
McCoury, Del **15**
McDowell, Mississippi Fred **16**
McGuinn, Roger
  See Byrds, The
McLachlan, Sarah **12**
McLaughlin, John **12**
McLean, Dave **24**
McLennan, Grant **21**
McReynolds, Jim
  See McReynolds, Jim and Jesse
McTell, Blind Willie **17**
Metheny, Pat **2**
Mitchell, Joni **17**
  Earlier sketch in CM **2**
Montgomery, Wes **3**
Morrissey, Bill **12**
Mo', Keb' **21**
Muldaur, Maria **18**
Nugent, Ted **2**
Oldfield, Mike **18**
Owens, Buck **2**
Page, Jimmy **4**
  Also see Led Zeppelin
  Also see Yardbirds, The
Parkening, Christopher **7**
Parnell, Lee Roy **15**
Pass, Joe **15**
Patton, Charley **11**
Perkins, Carl **9**
Perry, Joe
  See Aerosmith
Petty, Tom **9**
Phair, Liz **14**
Phillips, Sam **12**
Powell, Baden, **23**
Prince **14**
  Earlier sketch in CM **1**
Raitt, Bonnie **23**
  Earlier sketch in CM 1
Ray, Amy
  See Indigo Girls
Redbone, Leon **19**
Reed, Jimmy **15**
Reid, Vernon **2**
  Also see Living Colour
Reinhardt, Django **7**
Richards, Keith **11**
  Also see Rolling Stones, The
Richman, Jonathan **12**
Ritenour, Lee **7**
Robbins, Marty **9**
Robertson, Robbie **2**

Robillard, Duke **2**
Rodgers, Nile **8**
Rush, Otis **12**
Saliers, Emily
  See Indigo Girls
Sambora, Richie **24**
Santana, Carlos **19**
  Earlier sketch in CM **1**
Satriani, Joe **4**
Scofield, John **7**
Segovia, Andres **6**
Sharrock, Sonny **15**
Shepherd, Kenny Wayne **22**
Shines, Johnny **14**
Simon, Paul **16**
  Earlier sketch in CM **1**
Skaggs, Ricky **5**
Slash
  See Guns n' Roses
Springsteen, Bruce **6**
Stewart, Dave
  See Eurythmics
Stills, Stephen **5**
  Also see Buffalo Springfield
  Also see Crosby, Stills, & Nash
Stuart, Marty **9**
Summers, Andy **3**
  Also see Police, The
Taylor, Mick
  See Rolling Stones, The
Thielemans, Toots **13**
Thompson, Richard **7**
Tippin, Aaron **12**
Toure, Ali Farka **18**
Towner, Ralph **22**
Townshend, Pete **1**
Travis, Merle **14**
Trynin, Jen **21**
Tubb, Ernest **4**
Ulmer, James Blood **13**
Vai, Steve **5**
Van Halen, Edward
  See Van Halen
Van Ronk, Dave **12**
Vaughan, Jimmie **24**
  Also see Fabulous Thunderbirds, The
Vaughan, Stevie Ray **1**
Wagoner, Porter **13**
Waits, Tom **12**
  Earlier sketch in CM **1**
Walker, Jerry Jeff **13**
Walker, T-Bone **5**
Walsh, Joe **5**
  Also see Eagles, The
Wariner, Steve **18**
Waters, Muddy **24**
Watson, Doc **2**
Weir, Bob
  See Grateful Dead, The
Weller, Paul **14**
White, Lari **15**
Whitfield, Mark **18**
Whitley, Chris **16**
Whittaker, Hudson **20**

Wilson, Brian **24**
  Also see Beach Boys, The
Wilson, Nancy
  See Heart
Winston, George **9**
Winter, Johnny **5**
Wiseman, Mac **19**
Wray, Link **17**
Yamashita, Kazuhito **4**
Yarrow, Peter
  See Peter, Paul & Mary
Yoakam, Dwight **21**
Young, Angus
  See AC/DC
Young, Malcolm
  See AC/DC
York, Andrew **15**
Young, Neil **15**
  Earlier sketch in CM **2**
Zappa, Frank **17**
  Also see Buffalo Springfield
  Earlier sketch in CM **1**

Harmonica
Barnes, Roosevelt, "Booba" **23**
Dylan, Bob **3**
Guthrie, Woody **2**
Horton, Walter **19**
Lewis, Huey **9**
Little Walter **14**
McClinton, Delbert **14**
Musselwhite, Charlie **13**
Reed, Jimmy **15**
Thielemans, Toots **13**
Waters, Muddy **24**
  Earlier sketch in CM **4**
Wells, Junior **17**
Williamson, Sonny Boy **9**
Wilson, Kim
  See Fabulous Thunderbirds, The
Wonder, Stevie **17**
  Earlier sketch in CM **2**
Young, Neil **15**
  Also see Buffalo Springfield
  Earlier sketch in CM **2**

Heavy Metal
AC/DC **4**
Aerosmith **22**
  Earlier sketch in CM **1**
Alice in Chains **10**
Anthrax **11**
Black Sabbath **9**
Blue Oyster Cult **16**
Cinderella **16**
Circle Jerks **17**
Danzig **7**
Deep Purple **11**
Def Leppard **3**
Dokken **16**
Faith No More **7**
Fishbone **7**
Ford, Lita **9**
Guns n' Roses **2**
Iron Maiden **10**

Judas Priest **10**
Kilgore **24**
King's X **7**
Led Zeppelin **1**
L7 **12**
Megadeth **9**
Melvins **21**
Metallica **7**
Mötley Crüe **1**
Motörhead **10**
Nugent, Ted **2**
Osbourne, Ozzy **3**
Pantera **13**
Petra **3**
Queensryche **8**
Reid, Vernon **2**
  Also see Living Colour
Reznor, Trent **13**
Roth, David Lee **1**
  Also see Van Halen
Sepultura **12**
Skinny Puppy **17**
Slayer **10**
Soundgarden **6**
Spinal Tap **8**
Stryper **2**
Suicidal Tendencies **15**
Tool **21**
Warrant **17**
Whitesnake **5**
White Zombie **17**

Humor
Borge, Victor **19**
Coasters, The **5**
Dr. Demento **23**
Jones, Spike **5**
Lehrer, Tom **7**
Pearl, Minnie **3**
Russell, Mark **6**
Sandler, Adam **19**
Schickele, Peter **5**
Shaffer, Paul **13**
Spinal Tap **8**
Stevens, Ray **7**
Yankovic, "Weird Al" **7**

Inventors
Fender, Leo **10**
Harris, Eddie **15**
Paul, Les **2**
Scholz, Tom
  See Boston
Teagarden, Jack **10**
Theremin, Leon **19**

Jazz
Adderly, Cannonball **15**
Allen, Geri **10**
Allison, Mose **17**
Anderson, Ray **7**
Armstrong, Louis **4**
Art Ensemble of Chicago **23**
Avery, Teodross **23**
Bailey, Mildred **13**

Bailey, Pearl **5**
Baker, Anita **9**
Baker, Chet **13**
Baker, Ginger **16**
  Also see Cream
Barbieri, Gato **22**
Basie, Count **2**
Bechet, Sidney **17**
Beiderbecke, Bix **16**
Belle, Regina **6**
Bennett, Tony **16**
  Earlier sketch in CM **2**
Benson, George **9**
Berigan, Bunny **2**
Blackman, Cindy **15**
Blakey, Art **11**
Blanchard, Terence **13**
Bley, Carla **8**
Bley, Paul **14**
Blood, Sweat and Tears **7**
Brand New Heavies, The **14**
Braxton, Anthony **12**
  Bridgewater, Dee Dee **18**
Brown, Clifford **24**
Brown, Lawrence **23**
Brown, Ray **21**
Brown, Ruth **13**
  Brubeck, Dave **8**
Burrell, Kenny **11**
Burton, Gary **10**
Calloway, Cab **6**
Canadian Brass, The **4**
Carter, Benny **3**
  Also see McKinney's Cotton Pickers
Carter, Betty **6**
Carter, James **18**
Carter, Regina **22**
Carter, Ron **14**
Chambers, Paul **18**
Charles, Ray **1**
Cherry, Don **10**
Christian, Charlie **11**
Clarke, Stanley **3**
Clements, Vassar **18**
Clooney, Rosemary **9**
Cole, Holly **18**
Cole, Nat King **3**
Coleman, Ornette **5**
Coltrane, John **4**
Connick, Harry, Jr. **4**
Corea, Chick **6**
Davis, Anthony **17**
Davis, Miles **1**
DeJohnette, Jack **7**
Di Meola, Al **12**
Dirty Dozen **23**
Eckstine, Billy **1**
Eldridge, Roy **9**
  Also see McKinney's Cotton Pickers
Ellington, Duke **2**
Ellis, Herb **18**
Evans, Bill **17**
Evans, Gil **17**
Ferguson, Maynard **7**
Ferrell, Rachelle **17**

Fitzgerald, Ella **1**
Flanagan, Tommy **16**
Fleck, Bela **8**
    Also see New Grass Revival, The
Fountain, Pete **7**
Frisell, Bill **15**
Galway, James **3**
Getz, Stan **12**
Gillespie, Dizzy **6**
Goodman, Benny **4**
Gordon, Dexter **10**
Grappelli, Stephane **10**
Green, Benny **17**
Green, Grant **14**
Guaraldi, Vince **3**
Hackett, Bobby **21**
Haden, Charlie **12**
Hampton, Lionel **6**
Hancock, Herbie **8**
Hardcastle, Paul **20**
Hargrove, Roy **15**
Harris, Eddie **15**
Harris, Teddy **22**
Hawkins, Coleman **11**
Hawkins, Erskine **19**
Hedges, Michael **3**
Henderson, Fletcher **16**
Henderson, Joe **14**
Herman, Woody **12**
Hines, Earl "Fatha" **12**
Hirt, Al **5**
Holiday, Billie **6**
Horn, Shirley **7**
Horne, Lena **11**
Humes, Helen **19**
Hunter, Alberta **7**
Hunter, Charlie **24**
Ibrahim, Abdullah **24**
Incognito **16**
Isham, Mark **14**
Jackson, Milt **15**
Jacquet, Illinois **17**
James, Boney **21**
James, Harry **11**
Jarreau, Al **1**
Jarrett, Keith **1**
Jensen, Ingrid **22**
Jobim, Antonio Carlos **19**
Johnson, James P. **16**
Johnson, Lonnie **17**
Jones, Elvin **9**
Jones, Hank **15**
Jones, Philly Joe **16**
Jones, Quincy **20**
 Earlier sketch in CM **2**
Jones, Thad **19**
Jordan, Stanley **1**
Kennedy, Nigel **8**
Kenny G **14**
Kenton, Stan **21**
Kirk, Rahsaan Roland **6**
Kitt, Eartha **9**
Klugh, Earl **10**
Kronos Quartet **5**
Krupa, Gene **13**

Laine, Cleo **10**
Lateef, Yusef **16**
Lee, Peggy **8**
Lewis, Ramsey **14**
Lincoln, Abbey **9**
Israel "Cachao" Lopez **14**
Lloyd, Charles **22**
Lovano, Joe **13**
Mahavishnu Orchestra **19**
Mancini, Henry **20**
    Earlier sketch in CM **1**
Mangione, Chuck **23**
Manhattan Transfer, The **8**
Mann, Herbie **16**
Marsalis, Branford **10**
Marsalis, Ellis **13**
Marsalis, Wynton **20**
    Earlier sketch in CM **6**
Martino, Pat **17**
Masekela, Hugh **7**
McBride, Christian **17**
McFerrin, Bobby **3**
McKinney's Cotton Pickers **16**
McLaughlin, John **12**
McPartland, Marian **15**
McRae, Carmen **9**
Metheny, Pat **2**
Mingus, Charles **9**
Monk, Thelonious **6**
Montgomery, Wes **3**
Morgan, Frank **9**
Morton, Jelly Roll **7**
Mulligan, Gerry **16**
Najee **21**
Nascimento, Milton **6**
Norvo, Red **12**
O'Day, Anita **21**
Oliver, King **15**
Palmer, Jeff **20**
Palmieri, Eddie **15**
Parker, Charlie **5**
Parker, Maceo **7**
Pass, Joe **15**
Paul, Les **2**
Pepper, Art **18**
Peterson, Oscar **11**
Ponty, Jean-Luc **8**
Powell, Bud **15**
Previn, André **15**
Professor Longhair **6**
Puente, Tito **14**
Pullen, Don **16**
Rampal, Jean-Pierre **6**
Redman, Joshua **12**
Reeves, Dianne **16**
Reid, Vernon **2**
    Also see Living Colour
Reinhardt, Django **7**
Rich, Buddy **13**
Roach, Max **12**
Roberts, Marcus **6**
Robillard, Duke **2**
Rodney, Red **14**
Rollins, Sonny **7**
Saluzzi, Dino **23**

Sanborn, David **1**
Sanders, Pharoah **16**
Sandoval, Arturo **15**
Santana, Carlos **19**
    Earlier entry in CM **1**
Schuur, Diane **6**
Scofield, John **7**
Scott, Jimmy **14**
Scott-Heron, Gil **13**
Severinsen, Doc **1**
Sharrock, Sonny **15**
Shaw, Artie **8**
Shorter, Wayne **5**
Silver, Horace **19**
Simone, Nina **11**
Solal, Martial **4**
Strayhorn, Billy **13**
Summers, Andy **3**
    Also see Police, The
Sun Ra **5**
Take 6 **6**
Tatum, Art **17**
Taylor, Billy **13**
Taylor, Cecil **9**
Teagarden, Jack **10**
Terry, Clark **24**
Thielemans, Toots **13**
Threadgill, Henry **9**
Torme, Mel **4**
Tucker, Sophie **12**
Turner, Big Joe **13**
Turtle Island String Quartet **9**
Tyner, McCoy **7**
Ulmer, James Blood **13**
US3 **18**
Vaughan, Sarah **2**
Walker, T-Bone **5**
Washington, Dinah **5**
Washington, Grover, Jr. **5**
Weather Report **19**
Webb, Chick **14**
Weston, Randy **15**
Whitaker, Rodney **20**
Whiteman, Paul **17**
Whitfield, Mark **18**
Whittaker, Rodney **19**
Williams, Joe **11**
Wilson, Cassandra **12**
Wilson, Nancy **14**
Winter, Paul **10**
Witherspoon, Jimmy **19**
Young, La Monte **16**
Young, Lester **14**
Zorn, John **15**

Juju
Adé, King Sunny **18**

Keyboards, Electric
Aphex Twin **14**
Bley, Paul **14**
Brown, Tony **14**
Chemical Brothers **20**
Corea, Chick **6**
Davis, Chip **4**

Dolby, Thomas 10
Emerson, Keith
    See Emerson, Lake & Palmer/Powell
Eno, Brian 8
Foster, David 13
Froom, Mitchell 15
Hammer, Jan 21
Hancock, Herbie 8
Hardcastle, Paul 20
Jackson, Joe 22
    Earlier entry in CM 4
Jarre, Jean-Michel 2
Jones, Booker T. 8
Kitaro 1
Man or Astroman? 21
Manzarek, Ray
    See Doors, The
McDonald, Michael
    See Doobie Brothers, The
McVie, Christine
    See Fleetwood Mac
Orbital 20
Palmer, Jeff 20
Pierson, Kate
    See B-52's, The
Sakamoto, Ryuichi 19
Shaffer, Paul 13
Sun Ra 5
Waller, Fats 7
Wilson, Brian
    See Beach Boys, The
Winwood, Steve 2
    Also see Spencer Davis Group
    Also see Traffic
Wonder, Stevie 17
    Earlier sketch in CM 2
Worrell, Bernie 11
Yanni 11

Liturgical Music
Cooney, Rory 6
Talbot, John Michael 6

Mandolin
Bromberg, David 18
Bush, Sam
    See New Grass Revival, The
Duffey, John
    See Seldom Scene, The
Grisman, David 17
Hartford, John 1
Lindley, David 2
McReynolds, Jesse
    See McReynolds, Jim and Jesse
Monroe, Bill 1
Rosas, Cesar
    See Los Lobos
Skaggs, Ricky 5
Stuart, Marty 9

Musicals
Allen, Debbie 8
Allen, Peter 11
Andrews, Julie 4

Andrews Sisters, The 9
Bacharach, Burt 20
    Earlier sketch in CM 1
Bailey, Pearl 5
Baker, Josephine 10
Berlin, Irving 8
Brightman, Sarah 20
Brown, Ruth 13
Buckley, Betty 16
    Earlier sketch in CM 1
Burnett, Carol 6
Carter, Nell 7
Channing, Carol 6
Chevalier, Maurice 6
Crawford, Michael 4
Crosby, Bing 6
Curry, Tim 3
Davis, Sammy, Jr. 4
Day, Doris 24
Garland, Judy 6
Gershwin, George and Ira 11
Hamlisch, Marvin 1
Horne, Lena 11
Johnson, James P. 16
Jolson, Al 10
Kern, Jerome 13
Laine, Cleo 10
Lerner and Loewe 13
Lloyd Webber, Andrew 6
LuPone, Patti 8
Masekela, Hugh 7
Menken, Alan 10
Mercer, Johnny 13
Moore, Melba 7
Patinkin, Mandy 20
    Earlier sketch in CM 3
Peters, Bernadette 7
Porter, Cole 10
Robeson, Paul 8
Rodgers, Richard 9
Sager, Carole Bayer 5
Shaffer, Paul 13
Sondheim, Stephen 8
Styne, Jule 21
Waters, Ethel 11
Weill, Kurt 12
Yeston, Maury 22

Oboe
Lateef, Yusef 16

Opera
Adams, John 8
Ameling, Elly 24
Anderson, Marian 8
Baker, Janet 14
Bartoli, Cecilia 12
Battle, Kathleen 6
Blegen, Judith 23
Bocelli, Andrea 22
Bumbry, Grace 13
Caballe, Monserrat 23
Callas, Maria 11
Carreras, José 8

Caruso, Enrico 10
Copeland, Stewart 14
    Also see Police, The
Cotrubas, Ileana 1
Davis, Anthony 17
Domingo, Placido 20
    Earlier sketch in CM 1
Fleming, Renee 24
Freni, Mirella 14
Gershwin, George and Ira 11
Graves, Denyce 16
Hampson, Thomas 12
Heppner, Ben 23
Hendricks, Barbara 10
Herrmann, Bernard 14
Horne, Marilyn 9
McNair, Sylvia 15
Norman, Jessye 7
Pavarotti, Luciano 20
    Earlier sketch in CM 1
Price, Leontyne 6
Sills, Beverly 5
Solti, Georg 13
Sutherland, Joan 13
Te Kanawa, Kiri 2
Toscanini, Arturo 14
Upshaw, Dawn 9
von Karajan, Herbert 1
Weill, Kurt 12
Zimmerman, Udo 5

Percussion
Aronoff, Kenny 21
Baker, Ginger 16
    Also see Cream
Blackman, Cindy 15
Blakey, Art 11
Bonham, John
    See Led Zeppelin
Burton, Gary 10
Collins, Phil 20
    Earlier sketch in CM 2
    Also see Genesis
Copeland, Stewart 14
    Also see Police, The
DeJohnette, Jack 7
Densmore, John
    See Doors, The
Dunbar, Aynsley
    See Jefferson Starship
    Also see Journey
    Also see Whitesnake
Dunbar, Sly
    See Sly and Robbie
Fleetwood, Mick
    See Fleetwood Mac
Hampton, Lionel 6
Hart, Mickey
    See Grateful Dead, The
Henley, Don 3
Jones, Elvin 9
Jones, Kenny
    See Who, The
Jones, Philly Joe 16

Jones, Spike **5**
Kreutzman, Bill
  See Grateful Dead, The
Krupa, Gene **13**
Mason, Nick
  See Pink Floyd
Moon, Keith
  See Who, The
Mo', Keb' **21**
N'Dour, Youssou **6**
Otis, Johnny **16**
Palmer, Carl
  See Emerson, Lake & Palmer/Powell
Palmieri, Eddie **15**
Peart, Neil
  See Rush
Powell, Cozy
  See Emerson, Lake & Palmer/Powell
Puente, Tito **14**
Rich, Buddy **13**
Roach, Max **12**
Sheila E. **3**
Starr, Ringo **10**
  Also see Beatles, The
Walden, Narada Michael **14**
Watts, Charlie
  See Rolling Stones, The
Webb, Chick **14**

Piano
Allen, Geri **10**
Allison, Mose **17**
Amos, Tori **12**
Arrau, Claudio **1**
Bacharach, Burt **20**
  Earlier sketch in CM **1**
Ball, Marcia **15**
Basie, Count **2**
Berlin, Irving **8**
Blake, Eubie **19**
Bley, Carla **8**
Bley, Paul **14**
Borge, Victor **19**
Brendel, Alfred **23**
Brickman, Jim **22**
Britten, Benjamin **15**
Bronfman, Yefim **6**
Brubeck, Dave **8**
Bush, Kate **4**
Carpenter, Richard **24**
Charles, Ray **24**
  Earlier sketch in CM **1**
Clayderman, Richard **1**
Cleveland, James **1**
Cliburn, Van **13**
Cole, Nat King **3**
Collins, Judy **4**
Collins, Phil **20**
 Earlier sketch in CM **2**
  Also see Genesis
Connick, Harry, Jr. **4**
Crouch, Andraé **9**
Davies, Dennis Russell **24**
DeJohnette, Jack **7**

Domino, Fats **2**
Dr. John **7**
Dupree, Champion Jack **12**
Ellington, Duke **2**
Esquivel, Juan **17**
Evans, Bill **17**
Evans, Gil **17**
Feinstein, Michael **6**
Ferrell, Rachelle **17**
Flack, Roberta **5**
Flanagan, Tommy **16**
Frey, Glenn **3**
Galás, Diamanda **16**
Glass, Philip **1**
Gould, Glenn **9**
Green, Benny **17**
Grusin, Dave **7**
Guaraldi, Vince **3**
Hamlisch, Marvin **1**
Hancock, Herbie **8**
Harris, Teddy **22**
Helfgott, David **19**
Henderson, Fletcher **16**
Hinderas, Natalie **12**
Hines, Earl "Fatha" **12**
Horn, Shirley **7**
Hornsby, Bruce **3**
Horowitz, Vladimir **1**
Ibrahim, Abdullah **24**
Jackson, Joe **22**
  Earlier entry in CM **4**
James, Skip **24**
Jarrett, Keith **1**
Joel, Billy **12**
 Earlier sketch in CM **2**
John, Elton **20**
 Earlier sketch in CM **3**
Johnson, James P. **16**
Jones, Hank **15**
Joplin, Scott **10**
Kenton, Stan **21**
Kissin, Evgeny **6**
Levine, James **8**
Lewis, Jerry Lee **2**
Lewis, Ramsey **14**
Liberace **9**
Little Richard **1**
Manilow, Barry **2**
Marsalis, Ellis **13**
Matthews, Eric **22**
McDonald, Michael
  See Doobie Brothers, The
McPartland, Marian **15**
McRae, Carmen **9**
McVie, Christine
  See Fleetwood Mac
Milsap, Ronnie **2**
Mingus, Charles **9**
Monk, Thelonious **6**
Morton, Jelly Roll **7**
Newman, Randy **4**
Nero, Peter **19**
Palmieri, Eddie **15**
Perahia, Murray **10**

Peterson, Oscar **11**
Post, Mike **21**
Powell, Bud **15**
Pratt, Awadagin **19**
Previn, André **15**
Professor Longhair **6**
Puente, Tito **14**
Pullen, Don **16**
Rangell, Andrew **24**
Rich, Charlie **3**
Roberts, Marcus **6**
Rubinstein, Arthur **11**
Russell, Mark **6**
Schickele, Peter **5**
Sedaka, Neil **4**
Shaffer, Paul **13**
Solal, Martial **4**
Solti, Georg **13**
Spann, Otis **18**
Story, Liz **2**
Strayhorn, Billy **13**
Sunnyland Slim **16**
Sykes, Roosevelt **20**
Tatum, Art **17**
Taylor, Billy **13**
Taylor, Cecil **9**
Thibaudet, Jean-Yves **24**
Tilson Thomas, Michael **24**
Tyner, McCoy **7**
Vangelis **21**
Waits, Tom **12**
 Earlier sketch in **1**
Waller, Fats **7**
Weston, Randy **15**
Wilson, Brian **24**
Wilson, Cassandra **12**
Winston, George **9**
Winwood, Steve **2**
  Also see Spencer Davis Group
  Also see Traffic
Wonder, Stevie **17**
 Earlier sketch in CM **2**
Wright, Rick
  See Pink Floyd
Young, La Monte **16**

Piccolo
Galway, James **3**

Pop
A-ha **22**
Abba **12**
Abdul, Paula **3**
Adam Ant **13**
Adams, Bryan **20**
 Earlier sketch in CM **2**
Adams, Oleta **17**
Air Supply **22**
All-4-One **17**
Alpert, Herb **11**
America **16**
Amos, Tori **12**
Andrews Sisters, The **9**
Arden, Jann **21**

Arena, Tina **21**
Armatrading, Joan **4**
Arnold, Eddy **10**
Artifacts **23**
Astley, Rick **5**
Atkins, Chet **5**
Avalon, Frankie **5**
Bacharach, Burt **20**
 Earlier sketch in CM **1**
Backstreet Boys **21**
Bailey, Pearl **5**
Baker, Arthur **23**
Bananarama **22**
Bangles **22**
Basia **5**
Beach Boys, The **1**
Beatles, The **2**
Beaver Brown Band, The **3**
Bee Gees, The **3**
Belly **16**
Bennett, Tony **16**
 Earlier sketch in CM **2**
Benson, George **9**
Benton, Brook **7**
B-52's, The **4**
Better Than Ezra **19**
Blige, Mary J. **15**
Blondie **14**
Blood, Sweat and Tears **7**
Blue Rodeo **18**
BoDeans, The **20**
 Earlier sketch in CM **3**
Bolton, Michael **4**
Boo Radleys, The **21**
Booker T. & the M.G.'s **24**
Boone, Pat **13**
Boston **11**
Bowie, David **23**
 Earlier sketch in CM **1**
Boyz II Men **15**
Bragg, Billy **7**
Branigan, Laura **2**
Braxton, Toni **17**
Brickell, Edie **3**
Brooks, Garth **8**
Brown, Bobby **4**
Browne, Jackson **3**
Bryson, Peabo **11**
Buckingham, Lindsey **8**
 Also see Fleetwood Mac
Buckley, Tim **14**
Buffett, Jimmy **4**
Burdon, Eric **14**
 Also see War
 Also see Animals
Cabaret Voltaire **18**
Campbell, Glen **2**
Campbell, Tevin **13**
Cardigans **19**
Carey, Mariah **20**
 Earlier sketch in CM **6**
Carlisle, Belinda **8**
Carnes, Kim **4**
Carpenter, Richard **24**

Carpenters, The **13**
Case, Peter **13**
Chandra, Sheila **16**
Chapin, Harry **6**
Chapman, Tracy **20**
 Earlier sketch in CM **4**
Charlatans, The **13**
Charles, Ray **24**
 Earlier sketch in CM **1**
Checker, Chubby **7**
Cher **1**
Cherry, Neneh **4**
Cherry Poppin' Daddies **24**
Chicago **3**
Chilton, Alex **10**
Clapton, Eric **11**
 Earlier sketch in CM **1**
 Also see Cream
 Also see Yardbirds, The
Clayderman, Richard **1**
Clooney, Rosemary **9**
Coasters, The **5**
Cocker, Joe **4**
Cocteau Twins, The **12**
Cole, Lloyd **9**
Cole, Natalie **21**
 Earlier entry in CM **1**
Cole, Nat King **3**
Cole, Paula **20**
Collins, Judy **4**
Collins, Phil **20**
 Earlier sketch in CM **2**
 Also see Genesis
Color Me Badd **23**
Colvin, Shawn **11**
Commodores, The **23**
Como, Perry **14**
Connick, Harry, Jr. **4**
Cooke, Sam **1**
 Also see Soul Stirrers, The
Cope, Julian **16**
Cornershop **24**
Costello, Elvis **12**
 Earlier sketch in CM **2**
Cranberries, The **14**
Crash Test Dummies **14**
Crenshaw, Marshall **5**
Croce, Jim **3**
Crosby, David **3**
 Also see Byrds, The
 Also see Crosby, Stills, & Nash
Crow, Sheryl **18**
Crowded House **12**
Cure, The **20**
 Earlier sketch in CM **3**
Daltrey, Roger **3**
 Also see Who, The
D'Arby, Terence Trent **3**
Darin, Bobby **4**
Dave Clark Five, The **12**
Davies, Ray **5**
Davis, Sammy, Jr. **4**
Davis, Skeeter **15**
Day, Doris **24**

Dayne, Taylor **4**
DeBarge, El **14**
Del Amitri **18**
Del Rubio Triplets **21**
Denver, John **1**
Depeche Mode **5**
Des'ree **15**
Des'ree **24**
Devo **13**
Diamond, Neil **1**
Dion **4**
Dion, Céline **12**
Doc Pomus **14**
Donovan **9**
Doobie Brothers, The **3**
Doors, The **4**
Droge, Pete **24**
Dubstar **22**
Duran Duran **4**
Dylan, Bob **21**
 Earlier entry in CM **3**
Eagles, The **3**
Earth, Wind and Fire **12**
Easton, Sheena **2**
Edmonds, Kenneth "Babyface" **12**
Electric Light Orchestra **7**
Elfman, Danny **9**
Elliot, Cass **5**
Enigma **14**
En Vogue **10**
Estefan, Gloria **15**
 Earlier sketch in CM **2**
Eurythmics **6**
Everly Brothers, The **2**
Everything But The Girl **15**
Exposé **4**
Fabian **5**
Fatboy Slim **22**
Feliciano, José **10**
Ferguson, Maynard **7**
Ferry, Bryan **1**
Fiedler, Arthur **6**
Fine Young Cannibals **22**
Fisher, Eddie **12**
Fitzgerald, Ella **1**
Flack, Roberta **5**
Fleetwood Mac **5**
Fogelberg, Dan **4**
Fordham, Julia **15**
Foster, David **13**
Four Tops, The **11**
Fox, Samantha **3**
Frampton, Peter **3**
Francis, Connie **10**
Franklin, Aretha **17**
 Earlier sketch in CM **2**
Frey, Glenn **3**
 Also see Eagles, The
Garfunkel, Art **4**
Gaye, Marvin **4**
Gayle, Crystal **1**
Geldof, Bob **9**
Genesis **4**
Gershwin, George and Ira **11**

Gibson, Debbie **1**
  Also see Gibson, Deborah
Gibson, Deborah **24**
  Also see Gibson, Debbie
Gift, Roland **3**
Gin Blossoms **18**
Go-Go's, The **24**
Gong **24**
Goodman, Benny **4**
Gordy, Berry, Jr. **6**
Grant, Amy **7**
Grebenshikov, Boris **3**
Green, Al **9**
Guthrie, Arlo **6**
Hall & Oates **6**
Hammer, M.C. **5**
Hancock, Herbie **8**
Hanson **20**
Harding, John Wesley **6**
Harrison, George **2**
  Also see Beatles, The
Harry, Deborah **4**
  Also see Blondie
Hawkins, Sophie B. **21**
Healey, Jeff **4**
Henley, Don **3**
  Also see Eagles, The
Herman's Hermits **5**
Hitchcock, Robyn **9**
Holland-Dozier-Holland **5**
Hootie and the Blowfish **18**
Horne, Lena **11**
Hornsby, Bruce **3**
Houston, Whitney **8**
Human League, The **17**
Humperdinck, Engelbert **19**
Ian, Janis **5**
Idol, Billy **3**
Iglesias, Julio **20**
  Earlier sketch in CM **2**
Incubus **23**
Indigo Girls **20**
  Earlier sketch in CM **3**
Ingram, James **11**
Ink Spots, The **23**
Isaak, Chris **6**
Isley Brothers, The **8**
Jackson, Janet **16**
  Earlier sketch in CM **3**
Jackson, Joe **22**
  Earlier entry in CM **4**
Jackson, Michael **17**
  Earlier sketch in CM **1**
  Also see Jacksons, The
Jacksons, The **7**
Jam, Jimmy, and Terry Lewis **11**
James **12**
James, Harry **11**
James, Rick **2**
Jarreau, Al **1**
Jayhawks, The **15**
Jefferson Airplane **5**
Jesus Jones **23**
Jodeci **13**

Joel, Billy **12**
  Earlier sketch in CM **2**
Johansen, David **7**
John, Elton **20**
  Earlier sketch in CM **3**
Johnston, Freedy **20**
Jolson, Al **10**
Jones, Quincy **20**
  Earlier sketch in CM **2**
Jones, Rickie Lee **4**
Jones, Tom **11**
Joplin, Janis **3**
Kaye, Carol **22**
Khan, Chaka **19**
  Earlier sketch in CM **9**
King, Ben E. **7**
King, Carole **6**
  Also see Goffin-King
Kiss **5**
Kitt, Eartha **9**
Knight, Gladys **1**
Knopfler, Mark **3**
  Also see Dire Straits
Kool & the Gang **13**
Kraftwerk **9**
Kristofferson, Kris **4**
LaBelle, Patti **8**
Lauper, Cyndi **11**
Lee, Brenda **5**
Leiber and Stoller **14**
Lemper, Ute **14**
Lennon, John **9**
  Also see Beatles, The
Lennon, Julian **2**
Lennox, Annie **18**
Lightning Seeds **21**
  Also see Eurythmics, The
Lewis, Huey **9**
Liberace **9**
Lightfoot, Gordon **3**
Lisa Lisa **23**
Loeb, Lisa **23**
Loggins, Kenny **20**
  Earlier sketch in CM **3**
Lovett, Lyle **5**
Lowe, Nick **6**
Lush **13**
Lynne, Jeff **5**
MacColl, Kirsty **12**
Madonna **16**
  Earlier sketch in CM **4**
Mamas and the Papas **21**
Mancini, Henry **20**
  Earlier sketch in CM **1**
Manhattan Transfer, The **8**
Manilow, Barry **2**
Marley, Bob **3**
Marley, Ziggy **3**
Marsalis, Branford **10**
Martin, Dean **1**
Martin, George **6**
Marx, Richard **21**
  Earlier sketch in CM **3**
Mathis, Johnny **2**
Mazzy Star **17**

McCartney, Paul **4**
  Also see Beatles, The
McFerrin, Bobby **3**
McLachlan, Sarah **12**
McLean, Don **7**
McLennan, Grant **21**
Medley, Bill **3**
Melanie **12**
Michael, George **9**
Midler, Bette **8**
Mighty Mighty Bosstones **20**
Mike & the Mechanics **17**
Miller, Mitch **11**
Miller, Roger **4**
Milli Vanilli **4**
Mills Brothers, The **14**
Minnelli, Liza **19**
Mitchell, Joni **17**
  Earlier sketch in CM **2**
Money, Eddie **16**
Monkees, The **7**
Montand, Yves **12**
Moore, Chante **21**
Morissette, Alanis **19**
Morrison, Jim **3**
Morrison, Van **24**
  Earlier sketch in CM **3**
Morrissey **10**
Mouskouri, Nana **12**
Moyet, Alison **12**
Murray, Anne **4**
Myles, Alannah **4**
Neville, Aaron **5**
  Also see Neville Brothers, The
Neville Brothers, The **4**
New Kids on the Block **3**
Newman, Randy **4**
Newton, Wayne **2**
Newton-John, Olivia **8**
Nicks, Stevie **2**
Nilsson **10**
Nitty Gritty Dirt Band **6**
No Doubt **20**
Nyro, Laura **12**
Oak Ridge Boys, The **7**
Ocasek, Ric **5**
Ocean, Billy **4**
O'Connor, Sinead **3**
Odds **20**
Oldfield, Mike **18**
Orchestral Manoeuvres in the Dark **21**
Orlando, Tony **15**
Osborne, Joan **19**
Osmond, Donny **3**
Page, Jimmy **4**
  Also see Led Zeppelin
  Also see Yardbirds, The
Page, Patti **11**
Parks, Van Dyke **17**
Parsons, Alan **12**
Parton, Dolly **24**
  Earlier sketch in CM **2**
Pendergrass, Teddy **3**
Peniston, CeCe **15**
Penn, Michael **4**

Pet Shop Boys **5**
Peter, Paul & Mary **4**
Phillips, Sam **12**
Piaf, Edith **8**
Pizzicato Five **18**
Plant, Robert **2**
  Also see Led Zeppelin
Pointer Sisters, The **9**
Porter, Cole **10**
Prefab Sprout **15**
Presley, Elvis **1**
Priest, Maxi **20**
Prince **14**
  Earlier sketch in CM **1**
Proclaimers, The **13**
Prodigy **22**
Pulp **18**
Queen **6**
Rabbitt, Eddie **24**
  Earlier sketch in CM **5**
Raitt, Bonnie **3**
Rea, Chris **12**
Redding, Otis **5**
Reddy, Helen **9**
Reeves, Martha **4**
R.E.M. **5**
Republica **20**
Richard, Cliff **14**
Richie, Lionel **2**
Riley, Teddy **14**
Robbins, Marty **9**
Robinson, Smokey **1**
Rogers, Kenny **1**
Rolling Stones **3**
Ronstadt, Linda **2**
Ross, Diana **1**
Roth, David Lee **1**
  Also see Van Halen
Roxette **23**
RuPaul **20**
Ruffin, David **6**
Sade **2**
Sager, Carole Bayer **5**
Sainte-Marie, Buffy **11**
Sanborn, David **1**
Seal **14**
Seals, Dan **9**
Seals & Crofts **3**
Secada, Jon **13**
Sedaka, Neil **4**
Selena **16**
Shaffer, Paul **13**
Shamen, The **23**
Sheila E. **3**
Shirelles, The **11**
Shonen Knife **13**
Siberry, Jane **6**
Simon, Carly **22**
  Earlier entry in CM **4**
Simon, Paul **16**
  Earlier sketch in CM **1**
Sinatra, Frank **23**
  Earlier sketch in CM **1**
Smiths, The **3**

Snow, Pheobe **4**
Sobule, Jill **20**
Sonny and Cher **24**
Soul Coughing **21**
Sparks **18**
Spector, Phil **4**
Spice Girls **22**
Springfield, Dusty **20**
Springfield, Rick **9**
Springsteen, Bruce **6**
Squeeze **5**
Stafford, Jo **24**
Stansfield, Lisa **9**
Starr, Ringo **24**
  Earlier sketch in CM **10**
Steely Dan **5**
Stereolab **18**
Stevens, Cat **3**
Stewart, Rod **20**
  Earlier sketch in CM **2**
  Also see Faces, The
Stills, Stephen **5**
  Also see Buffalo Springfield
  Also see Crosby, Stills, & Nash
Sting **19**
  Earlier sketch in CM **2**
  Also see Police, The
Story, The **13**
Straw, Syd **18**
Streisand, Barbra **2**
Suede **20**
Summer, Donna **12**
Sundays, The **20**
Supremes, The **6**
Surfaris, The **23**
Sweat, Keith **13**
Sweet, Matthew **9**
SWV **14**
Talking Heads **1**
Talk Talk **19**
Taylor, James **2**
Tears for Fears **6**
Teenage Fanclub **13**
Temptations, The **3**
10,000 Maniacs **3**
The The **15**
They Might Be Giants **7**
Thomas, Irma **16**
Three Dog Night **5**
Tiffany **4**
Tikaram, Tanita **9**
Timbuk 3 **3**
TLC **15**
Toad the Wet Sprocket **13**
Tony! Toni! Toné! **12**
Torme, Mel **4**
Townshend, Pete **1**
  Also see Who, The
Turner, Tina **1**
Valli, Frankie **10**
Vandross, Luther **2**
Vega, Suzanne **3**
Velocity Girl **23**
Vinton, Bobby **12**

Walsh, Joe **5**
Warnes, Jennifer **3**
Warwick, Dionne **2**
Was (Not Was) **6**
Washington, Dinah **5**
Waters, Crystal **15**
Watley, Jody **9**
Webb, Jimmy **12**
"Weird Al" Yankovic **7**
Weller, Paul **14**
Who, The **3**
Williams, Andy **2**
Williams, Dar **21**
Williams, Deniece **1**
Williams, Joe **11**
Williams, Lucinda **24**
  Earlier sketch in CM **10**
Williams, Paul **5**
Williams, Vanessa **10**
Williams, Victoria **17**
Wilson, Brian **24**
  Also see Beach Boys, The
Wilson, Jackie **3**
Wilson Phillips **5**
Winwood, Steve **2**
  Also see Spencer Davis Group
  Also see Traffic
Womack, Bobby **5**
Wonder, Stevie **17**
  Earlier sketch in CM **2**
XTC **10**
Young, Neil **15**
  Also see Buffalo Springfield
  Earlier sketch in CM **2**
Young M.C. **4**

Producers
Ackerman, Will **3**
Albini, Steve **15**
Alpert, Herb **11**
Austin, Dallas **16**
Baker, Anita **9**
Bass, Ralph **24**
Benitez, Jellybean **15**
Bogaert, Jo
  See Technotronic
Brown, Junior **15**
Brown, Tony **14**
Browne, Jackson **3**
Burnett, T Bone **13**
Cale, John **9**
Clarke, Stanley **3**
Clinton, George **7**
Collins, Phil **2**
  Also see Genesis
Combs, Sean "Puffy" **16**
Costello, Elvis **2**
Cropper, Steve **12**
Crowell, Rodney **8**
Dixon, Willie **10**
DJ Premier
  See Gang Starr
Dr. Dre **15**
  Also see N.W.A.

Dolby, Thomas **10**
Dozier, Lamont
  See Holland-Dozier-Holland
Edmonds, Kenneth "Babyface" **12**
Enigma **14**
Eno, Brian **8**
Ertegun, Ahmet **10**
Ertegun, Nesuhi **24**
Foster, David **13**
Fripp, Robert **9**
Froom, Mitchell **15**
Gordy, Jr., Emory **17**
Gray, F. Gary **19**
Grusin, Dave **7**
Hardcastle, Paul **20**
Holland, Brian
  See Holland-Dozier-Holland
Holland, Eddie
  See Holland-Dozier-Holland
Jackson, Millie **14**
Jam, Jimmy, and Terry Lewis **11**
Jones, Booker T. **8**
Jones, Quincy **20**
 Earlier sketch in CM **2**
Jourgensen, Al
  See Ministry
Krasnow, Bob **15**
Lanois, Daniel **8**
Laswell, Bill **14**
Leiber and Stoller **14**
Lillywhite, Steve **13**
Lynne, Jeff **5**
Marley, Rita **10**
Martin, George **6**
Master P **22**
Mayfield, Curtis **8**
McLaren, Malcolm **23**
McKnight, Brian **22**
Miller, Mitch **11**
Osby, Greg **21**
Parks, Van Dyke **17**
Parsons, Alan **12**
Post, Mike **21**
Prince **14**
 Earlier sketch in CM **1**
Queen Latifah **24**
 Earlier sketch in CM **6**
Riley, Teddy **14**
Robertson, Robbie **2**
Rodgers, Nile **8**
Rubin, Rick **9**
Rundgren, Todd **11**
Shocklee, Hank **15**
Simmons, Russell **7**
Skaggs, Ricky **5**
Spector, Phil **4**
Sure!, Al B. **13**
Sweat, Keith **13**
Swing, DeVante
 See Jodeci
Too $hort **16**
Toussaint, Allen **11**
Tricky **18**

Vandross, Luther **24**
  Earlier sketch in CM **2**
Vasquez, Junior **16**
Vig, Butch **17**
Walden, Narada Michael **14**
Was, Don **21**
Watt, Mike **22**
Wexler, Jerry **15**
Whelan, Bill **20**
Willner, Hal **10**
Wilson, Brian **24**
  Also see Beach Boys, The
Winbush, Angela **15**
Woods-Wright, Tomica **22**

Promoters
Clark, Dick **2**
Geldof, Bob **9**
Graham, Bill **10**
Hay, George D. **3**
Simmons, Russell **7**

Ragtime
Johnson, James P. **16**
Joplin, Scott **10**

Rap
Anthony, Marc **19**
Arrested Development **14**
Austin, Dallas **16**
Bambaataa, Afrika **13**
Basehead **11**
Beastie Boys, The **8**
Biz Markie **10**
Black Sheep **15**
Bone Thugs-N-Harmony **18**
Busta Rhymes **18**
Campbell, Luther **10**
Cherry, Neneh **4**
Combs, Sean "Puffy" **16**
Common **23**
Coolio **19**
Cypress Hill **11**
Das EFX **14**
De La Soul **7**
Digable Planets **15**
Digital Underground **9**
DJ Jazzy Jeff and the Fresh Prince **5**
Dr. Dre **15**
  Also see N.W.A.
Eazy-E **13**
  Also see N.W.A.
EPMD **10**
Eric B. and Rakim **9**
Franti, Michael **16**
Fugees, The **17**
Gang Starr **13**
Geto Boys, The **11**
Goodie Mob **24**
Grandmaster Flash **14**
Gravediggaz **23**
Hammer, M.C. **5**
Heavy D **10**
House of Pain **14**

Ice Cube **10**
Ice-T **7**
Insane Clown Posse **22**
Jackson, Millie **14**
Kane, Big Daddy **7**
Kid 'n Play **5**
Knight, Suge **15**
Kool Moe Dee **9**
Kris Kross **11**
KRS-One **8**
L.L. Cool J. **5**
Last Poets **21**
Love, G. **24**
MC Breed **17**
MC Lyte **8**
MC 900 Ft. Jesus **16**
MC Serch **10**
Master P **22**
Nas **19**
Naughty by Nature **11**
N.W.A. **6**
Notorious B.I.G. **20**
Pharcyde, The **17**
P.M. Dawn **11**
Public Enemy **4**
Queen Latifah **24**
  Earlier sketch in CM **6**
Rage Against the Machine **18**
Riley, Teddy **14**
Rubin, Rick **9**
Run-D.M.C. **4**
Salt-N-Pepa **6**
Scott-Heron, Gil **13**
Shaggy **19**
Shanté **10**
Shocklee, Hank **15**
Simmons, Russell **7**
Sir Mix-A-Lot **14**
Snoop Doggy Dogg **17**
Snow **23**
Spearhead **19**
Special Ed **16**
Sure!, Al B. **13**
TLC **15**
Tone-L c **3**
Too $hort **16**
Tribe Called Quest, A **8**
Tricky **18**
2Pac **17**
Usher **23**
US3 **18**
Vanilla Ice **6**
Wu-Tang Clan **19**
Young M.C. **4**
Yo Yo **9**

Record Company Executives
Ackerman, Will **3**
Alpert, Herb **11**
Brown, Tony **14**
Busby, Jheryl **9**
Chess, Leonard **24**
Combs, Sean "Puffy" **16**
Davis, Chip **4**

Davis, Clive **14**
Ertegun, Ahmet **10**
Foster, David **13**
Gabriel, Peter **16**
  Earlier sketch in CM **2**
  Also see Genesis
Geffen, David **8**
Gordy, Berry, Jr. **6**
Hammond, John **6**
Harley, Bill **7**
Harrell, Andre **16**
Jam, Jimmy, and Terry Lewis **11**
Knight, Suge **15**
Koppelman, Charles **14**
Krasnow, Bob **15**
LiPuma, Tommy **18**
Madonna **16**
  Earlier sketch in CM **4**
Marley, Rita **10**
Martin, George **6**
Mayfield, Curtis **8**
Mercer, Johnny **13**
Miller, Mitch **11**
Mingus, Charles **9**
Near, Holly **1**
Ostin, Mo **17**
Penner, Fred **10**
Phillips, Sam **5**
Reznor, Trent **13**
Rhone, Sylvia **13**
Robinson, Smokey **1**
Rubin, Rick **9**
Simmons, Russell **7**
Spector, Phil **4**
Teller, Al **15**
Too $hort **16**
Wexler, Jerry **15**
Woods-Wright, Tomica **22**

Reggae
Bad Brains **16**
Big Mountain **23**
Black Uhuru **12**
Burning Spear **15**
Cliff, Jimmy **8**
Dube, Lucky **17**
Inner Circle **15**
Israel Vibration **21**
Marley, Bob **3**
Marley, Rita **10**
Marley, Ziggy **3**
Mystic Revealers **16**
Skatalites, The **18**
Sly and Robbie **13**
Steel Pulse **14**
Third World **13**
Tosh, Peter **3**
UB40 **4**
Wailer, Bunny **11**

Rhythm and Blues/Soul
Aaliyah **21**
Abdul, Paula **3**
Adams, Oleta **17**

Alexander, Arthur **14**
All-4-One **17**
Austin, Dallas **16**
Ballard, Hank **17**
Baker, Anita **9**
Ball, Marcia **15**
Basehead **11**
Belle, Regina **6**
Berry, Chuck **1**
Blackstreet **23**
Bland, Bobby "Blue" **12**
Blessid Union of Souls **20**
Blige, Mary J. **15**
Blues Brothers, The **3**
Bolton, Michael **4**
Booker T. & the M.G.'s **24**
Boyz II Men **15**
Brandy **19**
Braxton, Toni **17**
Brown, James **16**
  Earlier sketch in CM **2**
Brown, Ruth **13**
Brownstone **21**
Bryson, Peabo **11**
Burdon, Eric **14**
  Also see War
  Also see Animals
Busby, Jheryl **9**
C + C Music Factory **16**
Campbell, Tevin **13**
Carey, Mariah **20**
  Earlier sketch in CM **6**
Carr, James **23**
Charles, Ray **24**
  Earlier sketch in CM **1**
Cole, Natalie **21**
  Earlier sketch in CM **1**
Color Me Badd **23**
Commodores, The **23**
Cooke, Sam **1**
  Also see Soul Stirrers, The
Cropper, Steve **12**
Curtis, King **17**
D'Angelo **20**
D'Arby, Terence Trent **3**
DeBarge, El **14**
Des'ree **15**
Dibango, Manu **14**
Diddley, Bo **3**
Domino, Fats **2**
Dr. John **7**
Earth, Wind and Fire **12**
Edmonds, Kenneth "Babyface" **12**
En Vogue **10**
Evora, Cesaria **19**
Fabulous Thunderbirds, The **1**
Four Tops, The **11**
Fox, Samantha **3**
Franklin, Aretha **17**
  Earlier sketch in CM **2**
Gaye, Marvin **4**
Gill, Johnny **20**
Gordy, Berry, Jr. **6**
Green, Al **9**

Hall & Oates **6**
Hayes, Isaac **10**
Holland-Dozier-Holland **5**
Howland, Don **24**
Hurt, Mississippi John **24**
Ike and Tina Turner **24**
Incognito **16**
Ingram, James **11**
Isley Brothers, The **8**
Jackson, Freddie **3**
Jackson, Janet **3**
Jackson, Michael **17**
  Earlier sketch in CM **1**
  Also see Jacksons, The
Jackson, Millie **14**
Jacksons, The **7**
Jam, Jimmy, and Terry Lewis **11**
James, Etta **6**
Jodeci **13**
Jones, Booker T. **8**
Jones, Grace **9**
Jones, Quincy **20**
  Earlier sketch CM **2**
Jordan, Louis **11**
Kelly, R. **19**
Khan, Chaka **19**
  Earlier sketch CM **9**
King, Ben E. **7**
King, B. B. **24**
Knight, Gladys **1**
Kool & the Gang **13**
LaBelle, Patti **8**
Los Lobos **2**
Love, G. **24**
Maxwell **22**
Mayfield, Curtis **8**
McKnight, Brian **22**
Medley, Bill **3**
Meters, The **14**
Milli Vanilli **4**
Mills, Stephanie **21**
Monifah **24**
Mo', Keb' **21**
Moore, Chante **21**
Moore, Melba **7**
Morrison, Van **3**
Ndegéocello, Me'Shell **18**
Neville, Aaron **5**
  Also see Neville Brothers, The
Neville Brothers, The **4**
Ocean, Billy **4**
Ohio Players **16**
O'Jays, The **13**
Otis, Johnny **16**
Pendergrass, Teddy **3**
Peniston, CeCe **15**
Perry, Phil **24**
Pickett, Wilson **10**
Pointer Sisters, The **9**
Priest, Maxi **20**
Prince **14**
  Earlier sketch in CM **1**
Rainey, Ma **22**
Rawls, Lou **19**

Redding, Otis **5**
Reese, Della **13**
Reeves, Martha **4**
Richie, Lionel **2**
Riley, Teddy **14**
Robinson, Smokey **1**
Ross, Diana **6**
  Also see Supremes, The
Ruffin, David **6**
  Also see Temptations, The
Sam and Dave **8**
Scaggs, Boz **12**
Secada, Jon **13**
Shai **23**
Shanice **14**
Shirelles, The **11**
Shocklee, Hank **15**
Sledge, Percy **15**
Sly & the Family Stone **24**
Soul II Soul **17**
Spinners , The **21**
Stansfield, Lisa **9**
Staples, Mavis **13**
Staples, Pops **11**
Stewart, Rod **20**
 Earlier sketch in CM **2**
 Also see Faces, The
Stone, Sly **8**
Subdudes, The **18**
Supremes, The **6**
  Also see Ross, Diana
Sure!, Al B. **13**
Sweat, Keith **13**
SWV **14**
Temptations, The **3**
Third World **13**
Thomas, Irma **16**
TLC **15**
Thornton, Big Mama **18**
Tony! Toni! Toné! **12**
Toussaint, Allen **11**
Turner, Tina **1**
Vandross, Luther **24**
 Earlier sketch in CM **2**
Was (Not Was) **6**
Waters, Crystal **15**
Watley, Jody **9**
Wexler, Jerry **15**
White, Karyn **21**
Williams, Deniece **1**
Williams, Vanessa **10**
Wilson, Jackie **3**
Winans, The **12**
Winbush, Angela **15**
Womack, Bobby **5**
Wonder, Stevie **17**
 Earlier sketch in CM **2**
Zhane **22**

Rock
311 **20**
AC/DC **4**
Adam Ant **13**

Adams, Bryan **20**
 Earlier sketch in CM **2**
Aerosmith **22**
 Earlier sketch in CM **3**
Afghan Whigs **17**
Alarm **2***
Albini, Steve **15**
Alexander, Arthur **14**
Alice in Chains **10**
Alien Sex Fiend **23**
Allman Brothers, The **6**
Alvin, Dave **17**
America **16**
American Music Club **15**
Animals **22**
Anthrax **11**
Aquabats **22**
Archers of Loaf **21**
Art of Noise **22**
Audio Adrenaline **22**
Aztec Camera **22**
Babes in Toyland **16**
Bad Brains **16**
Bad Company **22**
Badfinger **23**
Baker, Ginger **16**
  Also see Cream
Ballard, Hank **17**
Band, The **9**
Barenaked Ladies **18**
Barlow, Lou **20**
Basehead **11**
Beach Boys, The **1**
Beastie Boys, The **8**
Beat Farmers, The **23**
Beatles, The **2**
Beaver Brown Band, The **3**
Beck, Jeff **4**
  Also see Yardbirds, The
Beck **18**
Belew, Adrian **5**
Belly **16**
Ben Folds Five **20**
Benatar, Pat **8**
Berry, Chuck **1**
Bettie Serveert **17**
Bevis Frond **23**
Biafra, Jello **18**
Big Audio Dynamite **18**
Big Head Todd and the Monsters **20**
Bjork **16**
Black Crowes, The **7**
Black, Frank **14**
Black Flag **22**
Black Sabbath **9**
Blackman, Cindy **15**
Blind Melon **21**
Blondie **14**
Blood, Sweat and Tears **7**
Blue Oyster Cult **16**
Blue Rodeo **18**
Blues Traveler **15**
Blur **17**

BoDeans, The **20**
 Earlier sketch in CM **3**
Bon Jovi **10**
Boston **11**
Bowie, David **23**
 Earlier sketch in CM **1**
Brad **21**
Bragg, Billy **7**
Breeders **19**
Brickell, Edie **3**
Browne, Jackson **3**
Buckingham, Lindsey **8**
 Also see Fleetwood Mac
Buckley, Tim **14**
Buffalo Springfield **24**
Buffalo Tom **18**
Burdon, Eric **14**
 Also see War
 Also see Animals
Burnett, T Bone **13**
Bush **18**
Butthole Surfers **16**
Buzzcocks, The **9**
Byrds, The **8**
Byrne, David **8**
 Also see Talking Heads
Cale, J. J. **16**
Cale, John **9**
Camel **21**
Captain Beefheart **10**
Caravan **24**
Cardigans **19**
Cars, The **20**
Catherine Wheel **18**
Cave, Nick **10**
Charlatans, The **13**
Charm Farm **20**
Cheap Trick **12**
Cher **1**
 Also see Sonny and Cher
Chicago **3**
Chumbawamba **21**
Church, The **14**
Cinderella **16**
Circle Jerks, The **17**
Clapton, Eric **11**
 Earlier sketch in CM **1**
 Also see Cream
 Also see Yardbirds, The
Clash, The **4**
Clemons, Clarence **7**
Clinton, George **7**
Coasters, The **5**
Cochrane , Tom **22**
Cocker, Joe **4**
Collective Soul **16**
Collins, Phil **2**
 Also see Genesis
Compulsion **23**
Congo Norvell **22**
Cooder, Ry **2**
Cooke, Sam **1**
 Also see Soul Stirrers, The

Cooper, Alice **8**
Cope, Julian **16**
Costello, Elvis **12**
    Earlier sketch in CM **2**
Cougar, John(ny)
    See Mellencamp, John
Counting Crows **18**
Cracker **12**
Cramps, The **16**
Cranberries, The **14**
Crash Test Dummies **14**
Cream **9**
Creedence Clearwater Revival **16**
Crenshaw, Marshall **5**
Crosby, David **3**
    Also see Byrds, The
Crosby, Stills, and Nash **24**
Crow, Sheryl **18**
Crowded House **12**
Cult, The **16**
Cure, The **20**
    Earlier sketch in CM **3**
Curry, Tim **3**
Curve **13**
Dale, Dick **13**
Daltrey, Roger **3**
    Also see Who, The
Dandy Warhols, The
Daniels, Charlie **6**
Danzig **7**
D'Arby, Terence Trent **3**
Dave Clark Five, The **12**
Dave Matthews Band **18**
Davies, Ray **5**
dc Talk **18**
de Burgh, Chris **22**
Dead Can Dance **16**
Dead Milkmen **22**
Deep Purple **11**
Def Leppard **3**
Deftones **22**
Del Amitri **18**
Depeche Mode **5**
Devo **13**
Diddley, Bo **3**
DiFranco, Ani **17**
Dinosaur Jr. **10**
Dire Straits **22**
Doc Pomus **14**
Dog's Eye View **21**
Dokken **16**
Doobie Brothers, The **3**
Doors, The **4**
Dreamtheater **23**
Duran Duran **4**
Dylan, Bob **3**
Eagles, The **3**
Echobelly **21**
Eddy, Duane **9**
Einstürzende Neubauten **13**
Electric Light Orchestra **7**
Elliot, Cass **5**
Emerson, Lake & Palmer/Powell **5**
Emmet Swimming **24**

English Beat, The **9**
Eno, Brian **8**
Erickson, Roky **16**
Escovedo, Alejandro **18**
Etheridge, Melissa **16**
    Earlier sketch in CM **4**
Eurythmics **6**
Everclear **18**
Extreme **10**
Faces, The **22**
Fairport Convention **22**
Faithfull, Marianne **14**
Faith No More **7**
Fall, The **12**
Ferry, Bryan **1**
fIREHOSE **11**
Fishbone **7**
Flaming Lips **22**
Fleetwood Mac **5**
Flores, Rosie **16**
Fogelberg, Dan **4**
Fogerty, John **2**
        Also see Creedence Clearwater Revival
Foo Fighters **20**
Ford, Lita **9**
Foreigner **21**
Four Seasons, The **24**
Fox, Samantha **3**
Frampton, Peter **3**
Frankie Lymon and The Teenagers **24**
Franti, Michael **16**
Frey, Glenn **3**
    Also see Eagles, The
Front 242 **19**
Froom, Mitchell **15**
Fu Manchu **22**
Fugazi **13**
Gabriel, Peter **16**
    Earlier sketch in CM **2**
    Also see Genesis
Gang of Four **8**
Garcia, Jerry **4**
    Also see Grateful Dead, The
Gatton, Danny **16**
Genesis **4**
Geraldine Fibbers **21**
Ghost **24**
Gift, Roland **3**
Gin Blossoms **18**
Glitter, Gary **19**
Goo Goo Dolls, The **16**
Graham, Bill **10**
Grant Lee Buffalo **16**
Grateful Dead **5**
Grebenshikov, Boris **3**
Green Day **16**
Griffin, Patty **24**
Guess Who **23**
Guided By Voices **18**
Guns n' Roses **2**
Gwar **13**
Hagar, Sammy **21**
Hall & Oates **6**
Harper, Ben **17**

Harrison, George **2**
    Also see Beatles, The
Harry, Deborah **4**
    Also see Blondie
Harvey, Polly Jean **11**
Hatfield, Juliana **12**
    Also see Lemonheads, The
Healey, Jeff **4**
Helmet **15**
Hendrix, Jimi **2**
Henley, Don **3**
    Also see Eagles, The
Henry, Joe **18**
Hiatt, John **8**
Hole **14**
Holland-Dozier-Holland **5**
Hooters **20**
Hootie and the Blowfish **18**
Idol, Billy **3**
INXS **21**
    Earlier sketch in CM **2**
Iron Maiden **10**
Isaak, Chris **6**
Jackson, Joe **22**
    Earlier entry in CM **4**
Jackyl **24**
Jagger, Mick **7**
    Also see Rolling Stones, The
Jane's Addiction **6**
Jars of Clay **20**
Jayhawks, The **15**
Jefferson Airplane **5**
Jesus Lizard **19**
Jesus and Mary Chain, The **10**
Jethro Tull **8**
Jett, Joan **3**
Jimmie's Chicken Shack **22**
Joel, Billy **12**
    Earlier sketch in CM **2**
Johansen, David **7**
John, Elton **20**
    Earlier sketch in CM **3**
Jon Spencer Blues Explosion **18**
Joplin, Janis **3**
Journey **21**
Joy Division **19**
Judas Priest **10**
KMFDM **18**
Kennedy, Nigel **8**
Kidjo, Anjelique **17**
King Crimson **17**
King Missile **22**
Kinks, The **15**
Kiss **5**
Knopfler, Mark **3**
    Also see Dire Straits
Korn **20**
Kravitz, Lenny **5**
Landreth, Sonny **16**
Led Zeppelin **1**
Leiber and Stoller **14**
Lemonheads, The **12**
Lennon, John **9**
    Also see Beatles, The

Lennon, Julian **2**
Less Than Jake **22**
Letters to Cleo **22**
Lindley, David **2**
Little Feat **4**
Little Texas **14**
Live **14**
Living Colour **7**
Loggins, Kenny **20**
  Earlier sketch in CM **3**
Los Lobos **2**
Love and Rockets **15**
Love Spit Love **21**
L7 **12**
Luna **18**
Luscious Jackson **19**
Lush **13**
Lydon, John **9**
  Also see Sex Pistols, The
Lynne, Jeff **5**
Lynyrd Skynyrd **9**
MacIsaac, Ashley **21**
Madder Rose **17**
Marilyn Manson **18**
Martin, George **6**
Marx, Richard **3**
McCartney, Paul **4**
  Also see Beatles, The
McClinton, Delbert **14**
MC5, The **9**
McKee, Maria **11**
McMurtry, James **10**
Meat Loaf **12**
Meat Puppets, The **13**
Megadeth **9**
Mekons, The **15**
Mellencamp, John **20**
  Earlier sketch in CM **2**
Metallica **7**
Midnight Oil **11**
Mighty Mighty Bosstones **20**
Mike & the Mechanics **17**
Miller, Steve **2**
Ministry **10**
Moby Grape **12**
Money, Eddie **16**
Moody Blues, The **18**
Morphine **16**
Morrison, Jim **3**
  Also see Doors, The
Morrison, Van **23**
  Earlier sketch in CM **3**
Murphy, Peter **22**
Mötley Crüe **1**
Motörhead **10**
Mould, Bob **10**
Mudhoney **16**
Muldaur, Maria **18**
Myles, Alannah **4**
Nelson, Rick **2**
New York Dolls **20**
Newman, Randy **4**
Newsboys, The **24**

Nicks, Stevie **2**
  Also see Fleetwood Mac
Nirvana **8**
NRBQ **12**
Nugent, Ted **2**
Oasis **16**
Ocasek, Ric **5**
O'Connor, Sinead **3**
Offspring **19**
Ono, Yoko **11**
Orbison, Roy **2**
Osbourne, Ozzy **3**
Our Lady Peace **22**
Page, Jimmy **4**
  Also see Led Zeppelin
  Also see Yardbirds, The
Palmer, Robert **2**
Pantera **13**
Parker, Graham **10**
Parker, Maceo **7**
Parsons, Alan **12**
Parsons, Gram **7**
  Also see Byrds, The
Pavement **14**
Pearl Jam **12**
Pearls Before Swine **24**
Pere Ubu **17**
Perkins, Carl **9**
Petty, Tom **9**
Phillips, Sam **5**
Phish **13**
Pigface **19**
Pink Floyd **2**
Pixies, The **21**
Plant, Robert **2**
  Also see Led Zeppelin
Pogues, The **6**
Poi Dog Pondering **17**
Poison **11**
Police, The **20**
Pop, Iggy **23**
  Earlier sketch in CM **1**
Presley, Elvis **1**
Pretenders, The **8**
Primal Scream **14**
Primus **11**
Prince **14**
  Earlier sketch in CM **1**
Prine, John **7**
Proclaimers, The **13**
Prong **23**
Pulp **18**
Quasi **24**
Queen **6**
Queensryche **8**
Quicksilver Messenger Service **23**
Radiohead **24**
Rage Against the Machine **18**
Raitt, Bonnie **23**
  Earlier sketch in CM **3**
Ramones, The **9**
Red Hot Chili Peppers, The **7**
Redd Kross **20**

Reed, Lou **16**
  Earlier sketch in CM **1**
  Also see Velvet Underground, The
Reef **24**
Reid, Vernon **2**
  Also see Living Colour
R.E.M. **5**
REO Speedwagon **23**
Replacements, The **7**
Residents, The **14**
Reverend Horton Heat **19**
Reznor, Trent **13**
Richards, Keith **11**
  Also see Rolling Stones, The
Richman, Jonathan **12**
Robertson, Robbie **2**
Rolling Stones, The **23**
  Earlier sketch in CM **3**
Rollins, Henry **11**
Roth, David Lee **1**
  Also see Van Halen
Rubin, Rick **9**
Rundgren, Todd **11**
Rush **8**
Ryder, Mitch **11**
Sambora, Richie **24**
Santana, Carlos **19**
  Earlier entry in CM **1**
Satriani, Joe **4**
Scaggs, Boz **12**
Scorpions, The **12**
Screaming Trees **19**
Scud Mountain Boys **21**
Seal **14**
Seger, Bob **15**
Sepultura **12**
Sex Pistols, The **5**
Shadows, The **22**
Shaffer, Paul **13**
Shannon, Del **10**
Shocked, Michelle **4**
Shonen Knife **13**
Shudder to Think **20**
Silver Apples **23**
Silverchair **20**
Simon, Carly **22**
  Earlier sketch in CM **4**
Simon, Paul **16**
  Earlier sketch in CM **1**
  Also see Simon and Garfunkel
Simon and Garfunkel **24**
Simple Minds **21**
Siouxsie and the Banshees **8**
Skinny Puppy **17**
Slayer **10**
Sleater-Kinney **20**
Smashing Pumpkins **13**
Smith, Patti **17**
  Earlier sketch in CM **1**
Smithereens, The **14**
Smiths, The **3**
Social Distortion **19**
Son Volt **21**
Sonic Youth **9**

Soul Asylum **10**
Soundgarden **6**
Sparks **18**
Specials, The **21**
Spector, Phil **4**
Spencer Davis Group **19**
Spin Doctors **14**
Spinal Tap **8**
Spirit **22**
Sponge **18**
Springsteen, Bruce **6**
Squeeze **5**
Starr, Ringo **10**
   Also see Beatles, The
Starr, Ringo **24**
Steeleye Span **19**
Steely Dan **5**
Steppenwolf **20**
Stevens, Cat **3**
Stewart, Rod **2**
Stills, Stephen **5**
   Also see Buffalo Springfield
   Also see Crosby, Stills, & Nash
Sting **19**
 Earlier sketch in CM **2**
Stone Roses, The **16**
Stone, Sly **8**
Stone Temple Pilots **14**
Straw, Syd **18**
Stray Cats, The **11**
Stryper **2**
Sublime **19**
Sugarcubes, The **10**
Suicidal Tendencies **15**
Summers, Andy **3**
   Also see Police, The
Superdrag **23**
Surfin' Pluto **24**
Tears for Fears **6**
Teenage Fanclub **13**
Television **17**
10,000 Maniacs **3**
Tesla **15**
Texas Tornados, The **8**
The The **15**
They Might Be Giants **7**
Thin Lizzy **13**
Thompson, Richard **7**
Three Dog Night **5**
Throwing Muses **15**
Timbuk 3 **3**
Toad the Wet Sprocket **13**
Tool **21**
Townshend, Pete **1**
   Also see Who, The
Traffic **19**
Tragically Hip, The **18**
T. Rex **11**
Treadmill Trackstar **21**
Trynin, Jen **21**
Tsunami **21**
Turner, Tina **1**
Tuxedomoon **21**

U2 **12**
 Earlier sketch in CM **2**
Ulmer, James Blood **13**
Urge Overkill **17**
Uriah Heep **19**
Vai, Steve **5**
Valens, Ritchie **23**
Valli, Frankie **10**
Van Halen **8**
Vaughan,, Jimmie **24**
Vaughan, Stevie Ray **1**
Velvet Underground, The **7**
Ventures **19**
Veruca Salt **20**
Verve, The **18**
Verve Pipe, The **20**
Vincent, Gene **19**
Violent Femmes **12**
Waits, Tom **12**
 Earlier sketch in CM **1**
Wallflowers, The **20**
Walsh, Joe **5**
   Also see Eagles, The
War **14**
Warrant **17**
Weezer **20**
Weller, Paul **14**
Whitesnake **5**
White Zombie **17**
Whitley, Chris **16**
Who, The **3**
Wilson, Brian **24**
   Also see Beach Boys, The
Winter, Johnny **5**
Winwood, Steve **2**
   Also see Spencer Davis Group
   Also see Traffic
Wray, Link **17**
Wyatt, Robert **24**
X **11**
Yardbirds, The **10**
Yes **8**
Yo La Tengo **24**
Young, Neil **15**
   Also see Buffalo Springfield
 Earlier sketch in CM **2**
Zappa, Frank **17**
 Earlier sketch in CM **1**
Zevon, Warren **9**
Zombies, The **23**
ZZ Top **2**

Rock and Roll Pioneers
Ballard, Hank **17**
Berry, Chuck **1**
Clark, Dick **2**
Darin, Bobby **4**
Diddley, Bo **3**
Dion **4**
Domino, Fats **2**
Eddy, Duane **9**
Everly Brothers, The **2**
Francis, Connie **10**

Glitter, Gary **19**
Haley, Bill **6**
Hawkins, Screamin' Jay **8**
Holly, Buddy **1**
James, Etta **6**
Jordan, Louis **11**
Lewis, Jerry Lee **2**
Little Richard **1**
Nelson, Rick **2**
Orbison, Roy **2**
Otis, Johnny **16**
Paul, Les **2**
Perkins, Carl **9**
Phillips, Sam **5**
Presley, Elvis **1**
Professor Longhair **6**
Sedaka, Neil **4**
Shannon, Del **10**
Shirelles, The **11**
Spector, Phil **4**
Twitty, Conway **6**
Valli, Frankie **10**
Wilson, Jackie **3**
Wray, Link **17**

Saxophone
Adderly, Cannonball **15**
Anderson, Wessell **23**
Ayler , Albert **19**
Barbieri, Gato **22**
Bechet, Sidney **17**
Braxton, Anthony **12**
Carter, Benny **3**
   Also see McKinney's Cotton Pickers
Carter, James **18**
Chenier, C. J. **15**
Clemons, Clarence **7**
Coleman, Ornette **5**
Coltrane, John **4**
Curtis, King **17**
Desmond, Paul **23**
Dibango, Manu **14**
Dorsey, Jimmy
   See Dorsey Brothers, The
Getz, Stan **12**
Golson, Benny **21**
Gordon, Dexter **10**
Harris, Eddie **15**
Hawkins, Coleman **11**
Henderson, Joe **14**
Herman, Woody **12**
Hodges, Johnny **24**
Jacquet, Illinois **17**
James, Boney **21**
Kenny G **14**
Kirk, Rahsaan Roland **6**
Koz, Dave **19**
Lacy, Steve **23**
Lateef, Yusef **16**
Lloyd, Charles **22**
Lopez, Israel "Cachao" **14**
Lovano, Joe **13**
Marsalis, Branford **10**
Morgan, Frank **9**

Mulligan, Gerry **16**
Najee **21**
Osby, Greg **21**
Parker, Charlie **5**
Parker, Maceo **7**
Pepper, Art **18**
Redman, Joshua **12**
Rollins, Sonny **7**
Sanborn, David **1**
Sanders, Pharoah **16**
Shorter, Wayne **5**
Threadgill, Henry **9**
Washington, Grover, Jr. **5**
Winter, Paul **10**
Young, La Monte **16**
Young, Lester **14**
Zorn, John **15**

Sintir
Hakmoun, Hassan **15**

Songwriters
Acuff, Roy **2**
Adams, Bryan **20**
  Earlier sketch in CM **2**
Adams, Yolanda **23**
Aikens, Rhett **22**
Albini, Steve **15**
Alexander, Arthur **14**
Allen, Peter **11**
Allison, Mose **17**
Alpert, Herb **11**
Alvin, Dave **17**
Amos, Tori **12**
Anderson, Ian
  See Jethro Tull
Anderson, John **5**
Anka, Paul **2**
Armatrading, Joan **4**
Astbury, Ian
  See Cult, The
Atkins, Chet **5**
Autry, Gene **12**
Bacharach, Burt **20**
  Earlier sketch in CM **1**
Baez, Joan **1**
Baker, Anita **9**
Balin, Marty
  See Jefferson Airplane
Barlow, Lou **20**
Barrett, (Roger) Syd
  See Pink Floyd
Basie, Count **2**
Becker, Walter
  See Steely Dan
Beckley, Gerry
  See America
Belew, Adrian **5**
Benton, Brook **7**
Berg, Matraca **16**
Berlin, Irving **8**
Berry, Chuck **1**
Bjork **16**
  Also see Sugarcubes, The

Black, Clint **5**
Black, Frank **14**
Blades, Ruben **2**
Blige, Mary J. **15**
Bloom, Luka **14**
Bono
  See U2
Brady, Paul **8**
Bragg, Billy **7**
Brandt, Paul **22**
Brickell, Edie **3**
Brokop, Lisa **22**
Brooke, Jonatha
  See Story, The
Brooks, Garth **8**
Brown, Bobby **4**
Brown, James **16**
  Earlier sketch in CM **2**
Brown, Junior **15**
Brown, Marty **14**
Browne, Jackson **3**
Buck, Peter
  See R.E.M.
Buck, Robert
  See 10,000 Maniacs
Buckingham, Lindsey **8**
  Also see Fleetwood Mac
Buckley, Jeff **22**
Buckley, Tim **14**
Buffett, Jimmy **4**
Bunnell, Dewey
  See America
Burdon, Eric **14**
  Also see War
  Also see Animals
Burnett, T Bone **13**
Burning Spear **15**
Bush, Kate **4**
Byrne, David **8**
  Also see Talking Heads
Cahn, Sammy **11**
Cale, J. J. **16**
Cale, John **9**
Calloway, Cab **6**
Campbell, Sarah Elizabeth **23**
Captain Beefheart **10**
Cardwell, Joi **22**
Carlisle, Bob **22**
Carpenter, Mary-Chapin **6**
Carter, Carlene **8**
Cash, Johnny **17**
  Earlier sketch in CM **1**
Cash, Rosanne **2**
Cetera, Peter
  See Chicago
Chandra, Sheila **16**
Chapin, Harry **6**
Chapman, Steven Curtis **15**
Chapman, Tracy **4**
Chaquico, Craig **23**
Charles, Ray **24**
  Earlier sketch in CM **1**
Chenier, C. J. **15**
Childs, Toni **2**

Chilton, Alex **10**
Clapton, Eric **11**
  Earlier sketch in CM **1**
  Also see Cream
  Also see Yardbirds, The
Clark, Guy **17**
Clements, Vassar **18**
Cleveland, James **1**
Clinton, George **7**
Cochrane, Tom **23**
Cockburn, Bruce **8**
Cohen, Leonard **3**
Cole, Lloyd **9**
Cole, Nat King **3**
Collins, Albert **4**
Collins, Judy **4**
Collins, Phil **2**
  Also see Genesis
Cooder, Ry **2**
Cooke, Sam **1**
  Also see Soul Stirrers, The
Collie, Mark **15**
Cooper, Alice **8**
Cope, Julian **16**
Corgan, Billy
  See Smashing Pumpkins
Costello, Elvis **12**
  Earlier sketch in CM **2**
Cotten, Elizabeth **16**
Crenshaw, Marshall **5**
Croce, Jim **3**
Crofts, Dash
  See Seals & Crofts
Cropper, Steve **12**
Crosby, David **3**
  Also see Byrds, The
Crow, Sheryl **18**
Crowe, J. D. **5**
Crowell, Rodney **8**
Daniels, Charlie **6**
Davies, Ray **5**
  Also see Kinks, the
de Burgh, Chris **22**
DeBarge, El **14**
DeMent, Iris **13**
Denver, John **22**
  Earlier entry in CM **1**
Des'ree **15**
Diamond, Neil **1**
Diddley, Bo **3**
Difford, Chris
  See Squeeze
DiFranco, Ani **17**
Dion **4**
Dixon, Willie **10**
Doc Pomus **14**
Domino, Fats **2**
Donelly, Tanya
  See Belly
  Also see Throwing Muses
Donovan **9**
Dorsey, Thomas A. **11**
Doucet, Michael **8**

Dozier, Lamont
  See Holland-Dozier-Holland
Drake, Nick **17**
Dube, Lucky **17**
Duffy, Billy
  See Cult, The
Dulli, Greg **17**
  See Afghan Whigs, The
Dylan, Bob **21**
  Earlier entry in CM **3**
Earle, Steve **16**
Edge, The
  See U2
Edmonds, Kenneth "Babyface" **12**
Eitzel, Mark
  See American Music Club
Elfman, Danny **9**
Ellington, Duke **2**
Emerson, Keith
  See Emerson, Lake & Palmer/Powell
Emmanuel, Tommy **21**
English, Michael **23**
Enigma **14**
Erickson, Roky **16**
Ertegun, Ahmet **10**
Escovedo, Alejandro **18**
Estefan, Gloria **15**
  Earlier sketch in CM **2**
Etheridge, Melissa **16**
  Earlier entry in CM **4**
Everly, Don
  See Everly Brothers, The
Everly, Phil
  See Everly Brothers, The
Fagen, Don
  See Steely Dan
Faithfull, Marianne **14**
Ferry, Bryan **1**
Flack, Roberta **5**
Flatt, Lester **3**
Fogelberg, Dan **4**
Fogerty, John **2**
  Also see Creedence Clearwater Revival
Fordham, Julia **15**
Foster, David **13**
Frampton, Peter **3**
Franti, Michael **16**
Frey, Glenn **3**
  Also see Eagles, The
Fripp, Robert **9**
Frizzell, Lefty **10**
Gabriel, Peter **16**
  Earlier sketch in CM **2**
  Also see Genesis
Garcia, Jerry **4**
  Also see Grateful Dead, The
Gaye, Marvin **4**
Geldof, Bob **9**
George, Lowell
  See Little Feat
Gershwin, George and Ira **11**
Gibb, Barry
  See Bee Gees, The

Gibb, Maurice
  See Bee Gees, The
Gibb, Robin
  See Bee Gees, The
Gibbons, Billy
  See ZZ Top
Gibson, Bob **23**
Gibson, Debbie **1**
Gift, Roland **3**
Gill, Vince **7**
Gilley, Mickey **7**
Gilmour, David
  See Pink Floyd
Goffin-King **24**
Gold, Julie **22**
Goodman, Benny **4**
Gordy, Berry, Jr. **6**
Gorka, John **18**
Grant, Amy **7**
Green, Al **9**
Greenwood, Lee **12**
Griffin, Patty **24**
Griffith, Nanci **3**
Guthrie, Arlo **6**
Guthrie, Woodie **2**
Guy, Buddy **4**
Haggard, Merle **2**
Hall, Daryl
  See Hall & Oates
Hall, Tom T. **4**
Hamlisch, Marvin **1**
Hammer, M.C. **5**
Hammerstein, Oscar
  See Rodgers, Richard
Hardin, Tim **18**
Harding, John Wesley **6**
Harley, Bill **7**
Harper, Ben **17**
Harris, Emmylou **4**
Harrison, George **2**
  Also see Beatles, The
Harry, Deborah **4**
  Also see Blondie
Hart, Lorenz
  See Rodgers, Richard
Hartford, John **1**
Hatfield, Juliana **12**
  Also see Lemonheads, The
Hawkins, Screamin' Jay **8**
Hayes, Isaac **10**
Healey, Jeff **4**
Hedges, Michael **3**
Hendrix, Jimi **2**
Henley, Don **3**
  Also see Eagles, The
Henry, Joe **18**
Hersh, Kristin
  See Throwing Muses
Hiatt, John **8**
Hidalgo, David
  See Los Lobos
Hillman, Chris
  See Byrds, The
  Also see Desert Rose Band, The

Hinojosa, Tish **13**
Hitchcock, Robyn **9**
Holland, Brian
  See Holland-Dozier-Holland
Holland, Eddie
  See Holland-Dozier-Holland
Holly, Buddy **1**
Hornsby, Bruce **3**
Howard, Harlan **15**
Hutchence, Michael
  See INXS
Hynde, Chrissie
  See Pretenders, The
Ian, Janis **5**
Ice Cube **10**
Ice-T **7**
Idol, Billy **3**
Isaak, Chris **6**
Jackson, Alan **7**
Jackson, Janet **16**
  Earlier sketch in CM **3**
Jackson, Joe **22**
  Earlier entry in CM **4**
Jackson, Michael **17**
  Earlier sketch in CM **1**
  Also see Jacksons, The
Jackson, Millie **14**
Jagger, Mick **7**
  Also see Rolling Stones, The
Jam, Jimmy, and Terry Lewis **11**
James, Rick **2**
Jarreau, Al **1**
Jennings, Waylon **4**
Jett, Joan **3**
Joel, Billy **12**
  Earlier sketch in CM **2**
Johansen, David **7**
John, Elton **20**
  Earlier sketch in CM **3**
Johnson, Lonnie **17**
Johnson, Matt
  See The The
Jones, Brian
  See Rolling Stones, The
Jones, George **4**
Jones, Mick
  See Clash, The
Jones, Quincy **20**
  Earlier sketch in CM **2**
Jones, Rickie Lee **4**
Joplin, Janis **3**
Judd, Naomi
  See Judds, The
Kane, Big Daddy **7**
Kantner, Paul
  See Jefferson Airplane
Kee, John P. **15**
Keith, Toby **17**
Kelly, R. **19**
Ketchum, Hal **14**
Khan, Chaka **19**
  Earlier sketch in CM **9**
King, Albert **2**

King, B. B. **1**
King, Ben E. **7**
King, Carole **6**
  Also see Goffin-King
King, Freddy **17**
Kirkwood, Curt
  See Meat Puppets, The
Knopfler, Mark **3**
  Also see Dire Straits
Kottke, Leo **13**
Kravitz, Lenny **5**
Kristofferson, Kris **4**
Lake, Greg
  See Emerson, Lake & Palmer/Powell
Landreth, Sonny **16**
Lang, K. D. **4**
Larkin, Patty **9**
Lavin, Christine **6**
LeDoux, Chris **12**
Lee, Peggy **8**
Lehrer, Tom **7**
Leiber and Stoller **14**
Lennon, John **9**
  Also see Beatles, The
Lennon, Julian **2**
Lewis, Huey **9**
Lightfoot, Gordon **3**
Little Richard **1**
Llanas, Sammy
  See BoDeans, The
L.L. Cool J **5**
Loeb, Lisa **23**
Loggins, Kenny **20**
  Earlier sketch in CM **3**
Love, Courtney
  See Hole
Love, Laura **20**
Loveless, Patty **5**
Lovett, Lyle **5**
Lowe, Nick **6**
Lydon, John **9**
  Also see Sex Pistols, The
Lynn, Loretta **2**
Lynne, Jeff **5**
Lynne, Shelby **5**
Lynott, Phil
  See Thin Lizzy
MacColl, Kirsty **12**
MacDonald, Barbara
  See Timbuk 3
MacDonald, Pat
  See Timbuk 3
Madonna **16**
  Earlier sketch in CM **4**
Manilow, Barry **2**
Mann, Aimee **22**
Mann, Billy **23**
Manzarek, Ray
  See Doors, The
Marley, Bob **3**
Marley, Ziggy **3**
Marx, Richard **3**
Mattea, Kathy **5**

May, Brian
  See Queen
Mayfield, Curtis **8**
MC Breed **17**
McCartney, Paul **4**
  Also see Beatles, The
McClinton, Delbert **14**
McCoury, Del **15**
McCulloch, Ian **23**
McDonald, Michael
  See Doobie Brothers, The
McGuinn, Roger
  See Byrds, The
McLachlan, Sarah **12**
McLaren, Malcolm **23**
McLean, Don **7**
McLennan, Grant **21**
McMurtry, James **10**
MC 900 Ft. Jesus **16**
McTell, Blind Willie **17**
McVie, Christine
  See Fleetwood Mac
Medley, Bill **3**
Melanie **12**
Mellencamp, John **20**
  Earlier sketch in CM **2**
Mercer, Johnny **13**
Merchant, Natalie
  See 10,000 Maniacs
Mercury, Freddie
  See Queen
Michael, George **9**
Miller, Roger **4**
Miller, Steve **2**
Milsap, Ronnie **2**
Mitchell, Joni **17**
  Earlier sketch in CM **2**
Moffatt, Katy **18**
Morrison, Jim **3**
Morrison, Van **24**
  Earlier sketch in CM **3**
Morrissey **10**
Morrissey, Bill **12**
Morton, Jelly Roll **7**
Mould, Bob **10**
Moyet, Alison **12**
Nascimento, Milton **6**
Ndegéocello, Me'Shell **18**
Near, Holly **1**
Nelson, Rick **2**
Nelson, Willie **11**
  Earlier sketch in CM **1**
Nesmith, Mike
  See Monkees, The
Neville, Art
  See Neville Brothers, The
Newman, Randy **4**
Newmann, Kurt
  See BoDeans, The
Nicks, Stevie **2**
Nilsson **10**
Nugent, Ted **2**
Nyro, Laura **12**

Oates, John
  See Hall & Oates
Ocasek, Ric **5**
Ocean, Billy **4**
Ochs, Phil **7**
O'Connor, Sinead **3**
Odetta **7**
Orbison, Roy **2**
Osbourne, Ozzy **3**
Oslin, K. T. **3**
Owens, Buck **2**
Page, Jimmy **4**
  See Led Zeppelin
  Also see Yardbirds, The
Palmer, Robert **2**
Paris, Twila **16**
Parks, Van Dyke **17**
Parnell, Lee Roy **15**
Parker, Graham **10**
Parsons, Gram **7**
  Also see Byrds, The
Parton, Dolly **24**
  Earlier sketch in CM **2**
Paul, Les **5**
Paxton, Tom **5**
Peniston, CeCe **15**
Penn, Michael **4**
Perez, Louie
  See Los Lobos
Perkins, Carl **9**
Perry, Joe
  See Aerosmith
Petty, Tom **9**
Phair, Liz **14**
Phillips, Sam **12**
Pickett, Wilson **10**
Pierson, Kate
  See B-52's, The
Plant, Robert **2**
  Also see Led Zeppelin
Pop, Iggy **1**
Porter, Cole **10**
Prince **14**
  Earlier sketch in CM **1**
Prine, John **7**
Professor Longhair **6**
Rabbitt, Eddie **24**
  Earlier sketch in CM **5**
Raitt, Bonnie **23**
  Earlier sketch in CM **3**
Ray, Amy
  See Indigo Girls
Rea, Chris **12**
Redding, Otis **5**
Reddy, Helen **9**
Reed, Lou **16**
  Earlier sketch in CM **1**
  Also see Velvet Underground, The
Reid, Charlie
  See Proclaimers, The
Reid, Craig
  See Proclaimers, The
Reid, Vernon **2**
  Also see Living Colour

Rich, Charlie **3**
Richards, Keith **11**
  Also see Rolling Stones, The
Richey, Kim **20**
Richie, Lionel **2**
Richman, Jonathan **12**
Riley, Teddy **14**
Ritchie, Jean **4**
Robbins, Marty **9**
Roberts, Brad
  See Crash Test Dummies
Robertson, Robbie **2**
Robillard, Duke **2**
Robinson, Smokey **1**
Rodgers, Jimmie **3**
Rodgers, Richard **9**
Roland, Ed
  See Collective Soul
Roth, David Lee **1**
  Also see Van Halen
Russell, Mark **6**
Rutherford, Mike
  See Genesis
Ryder, Mitch **23**
Sade **2**
Sager, Carole Bayer **5**
Saliers, Emily
  See Indigo Girls
Sandman, Mark
  See Morphine
Sangare, Oumou **22**
Satriani, Joe **4**
Scaggs, Boz **12**
Schneider, Fred III
  See B-52's, The
Scott-Heron, Gil **13**
Scruggs, Earl **3**
Seal **14**
Seals, Dan **9**
Seals, Jim
  See Seals & Crofts
Secada, Jon **13**
Sedaka, Neil **4**
Seeger, Pete **4**
  Also see Weavers, The
Seger, Bob **15**
Shannon, Del **10**
Sheila E. **3**
Shepherd, Kenny Wayne **22**
Shocked, Michelle **4**
Siberry, Jane **6**
Simmons, Gene
  See Kiss
Simmons, Patrick
  See Doobie Brothers, The
Simon, Carly **22**
  Earlier entry in CM **4**
Simon, Paul **16**
 Earlier sketch in CM **1**
Skaggs, Ricky **5**
Sledge, Percy **15**
Slick, Grace
  See Jefferson Airplane

Smith, Patti **17**
 Earlier sketch in CM **1**
Smith, Robert
  See Cure, The
  Also see Siouxsie and the Banshees
Snoop Doggy Dogg **17**
Sondheim, Stephen **8**
Spector, Phil **4**
Springsteen, Bruce **6**
Stanley, Paul
  See Kiss
Stanley, Ralph **5**
Starr, Ringo **10**
  Also see Beatles, The
Stevens, Cat **3**
Stevens, Ray **7**
Stewart, Dave
  See Eurythmics, The
Stewart, Rod **20**
  Earlier sketch in CM **2**
  Also see Faces, The
Stills, Stephen **5**
  Also see Buffalo Springfield
  Also see Crosby, Stills, & Nash
Sting **19**
  Earlier sketch in CM **2**
  Also see Police, The
Stipe, Michael
  See R.E.M.
Strait, George **5**
Straw, Syd **18**
Streisand, Barbra **2**
Strickland, Keith
  See B-52's, The
Strummer, Joe
  See Clash, The
Stuart, Marty **9**
Styne, Jule **21**
Summer, Donna **12**
Summers, Andy **3**
  Also see Police, The
Sure!, Al B. **13**
Sweat, Keith **13**
Sweet, Matthew **9**
Swing, DeVante
  See Jodeci
Taj Mahal **6**
Taupin, Bernie **22**
Taylor, James **2**
Taylor, Koko **10**
Thompson, Richard **7**
Thornton, Big Mama **18**
Tikaram, Tanita **9**
Tilbrook, Glenn
  See Squeeze
Tillis, Mel **7**
Tillis, Pam **8**
Timmins, Margo
  See Cowboy Junkies, The
Timmins, Michael
  See Cowboy Junkies, The
Tippin, Aaron **12**
Tone-L c **3**
Torme, Mel **4**

Tosh, Peter **3**
Toussaint, Allen **11**
Townshend, Pete **1**
  Also see Who, The
Travis, Merle **14**
Travis, Randy **9**
Treadmill Trackstar **21**
Tricky **18**
Tritt, Travis **7**
Trynin, Jen **21**
Tubb, Ernest **4**
Twain, Shania **17**
Twitty, Conway **6**
2Pac **17**
Tyler, Steve
  See Aerosmith
Vai, Steve **5**
  Also see Whitesnake
Vandross, Luther **24**
  Earlier sketch in CM **2**
Van Halen, Edward
  See Van Halen
Van Ronk, Dave **12**
Van Shelton, Ricky **5**
Van Zandt, Townes **13**
Vedder, Eddie
  See Pearl Jam
Vega, Suzanne **3**
Wagoner, Porter **13**
Waits, Tom **12**
  Earlier sketch in CM **1**
Walden, Narada Michael **14**
Walker, Jerry Jeff **13**
Walker, T-Bone **5**
Waller, Fats **7**
Walsh, Joe **5**
  Also see Eagles, The
Wariner, Steve **18**
Warren, Diane **21**
Waters, Crystal **15**
Waters, Muddy **4**
Waters, Roger
  See Pink Floyd
Watt, Mike **22**
Webb, Jimmy **12**
Weill, Kurt **12**
Weir, Bob
  See Grateful Dead, The
Welch, Bob
  See Fleetwood Mac
Weller, Paul **14**
West, Dottie **8**
White, Karyn **21**
White, Lari **15**
Whitley, Chris **16**
Whitley, Keith **7**
Williams, Dar **21**
Williams, Deniece **1**
Williams, Don **4**
Williams, Hank, Jr. **1**
Williams, Hank, Sr. **4**
Williams, Lucinda **24**
  Earlier sketch in CM **10**

Williams, Paul **5**
Williams, Victoria **17**
Williams, Lucinda **24**
  Earlier sketch in CM **10**
Wills, Bob **6**
Wilson, Brian **24**
  Also see Beach Boys, The
Wilson, Cindy
  See B-52's, The
Wilson, Ricky
  See B-52's, The
Winbush, Angela **15**
Winter, Johnny **5**
Winwood, Steve **2**
  Also see Spencer Davis Group
  Also see Traffic
Womack, Bobby **5**
Wonder, Stevie **17**
  Earlier sketch in CM **2**
Wray, Link **17**
Wyatt, Robert **24**
Wynette, Tammy **24**
  Earlier sketch in CM **2**
Yoakam, Dwight **21**
  Earlier entry in CM **1**
Young, Angus
  See AC/DC
Young, Neil **15**
  Also see Buffalo Springfield
  Earlier sketch in CM **2**
Zappa, Frank **17**
  Earlier sketch in CM **1**
Zevon, Warren **9**

Trombone
Anderson, Ray **7**
Brown, Lawrence **23**
Dorsey, Tommy
  See Dorsey Brothers, The
Miller, Glenn **6**
Teagarden, Jack **10**
Turre, Steve **22**
Watts, Eugene
  See Canadian Brass, The

Trumpet
Alpert, Herb **11**
Armstrong, Louis **4**
Baker, Chet **13**
Berigan, Bunny **2**
Blanchard, Terence **13**

Brown, Clifford **24**
Cherry, Don **10**
Coleman, Ornette **5**
Davis, Miles **1**
Eldridge, Roy **9**
  Also see McKinney's Cotton Pickers
Ferguson, Maynard **7**
Gillespie, Dizzy **6**
Hargrove, Roy **15**
Hawkins, Erskine **19**
Hirt, Al **5**
Isham, Mark **14**
James, Harry **11**
Jensen, Ingrid **22**
Jones, Quincy **20**
  Earlier sketch in CM **2**
Jones, Thad **19**
Loughnane, Lee **3**
Marsalis, Wynton **20**
  Earlier sketch in CM **6**
Masekela, Hugh **7**
Matthews, Eric **22**
Mighty Mighty Bosstones **20**
Miles, Ron **22**
Mills, Fred
  See Canadian Brass, The
Oliver, King **15**
Rodney, Red **14**
Romm, Ronald
  See Canadian Brass, The
Sandoval, Arturo **15**
Severinsen, Doc **1**
Terry, Clark **24**

Tuba
Daellenbach, Charles
  See Canadian Brass, The
Phillips, Harvey **3**

Vibraphone
Burton, Gary **10**
Hampton, Lionel **6**
Jackson, Milt **15**
Norvo, Red **12**

Viola
Dutt, Hank
  See Kronos Quartet
Jones, Michael
  See Kronos Quartet
Killian, Tim

  See Kronos Quartet
Menuhin, Yehudi **11**
Zukerman, Pinchas **4**

Violin
Acuff, Roy **2**
Anderson, Laurie **1**
Bell, Joshua **21**
Bromberg, David **18**
Bush, Sam
  See New Grass Revival, The
Carter, Regina **22**
Chang, Sarah **7**
Clements, Vassar **18**
Coleman, Ornette **5**
Cugat, Xavier **23**
Daniels, Charlie **6**
Doucet, Michael **8**
Germano, Lisa **18**
Gingold, Josef **6**
Grappelli, Stephane **10**
Gray, Ella
  See Kronos Quartet
Harrington, David
  See Kronos Quartet
Hartford, John **1**
Hidalgo, David
  See Los Lobos
Kennedy, Nigel **8**
Krauss, Alison **10**
Lamb, Barbara **19**
Lewis, Roy
  See Kronos Quartet
Marriner, Neville **7**
Menuhin, Yehudi **11**
Midori **7**
Mutter, Anne-Sophie **23**
O'Connor, Mark **1**
Perlman, Itzhak **2**
Ponty, Jean-Luc **8**
Salerno-Sonnenberg, Nadja **3**
Shallenberger, James
  See Kronos Quartet
Sherba, John
  See Kronos Quartet
Skaggs, Ricky **5**
Stern, Isaac **7**
Whiteman, Paul **17**
Wills, Bob **6**
Zukerman, Pinchas **4**

Cumulative Musicians Index

Volume numbers appear in **bold**.

A-ha **22**
Aaliyah **21**
Abba **12**
Abbott, Jacqueline
  See Beautiful South
Abbott, Jude
  See Chumbawamba
Abbruzzese, Dave
Abdul, Paula **3**
Abong, Fred
  See Belly
Abrahams, Mick
  See Jethro Tull
Abrams, Bryan
  See Color Me Badd
Abrantes, Fernando
  See Kraftwerk
AC/DC **4**
Ace of Base **22**
Ackerman, Will **3**
Acland, Christopher
  See Lush
Acuff, Roy **2**
Acuna, Alejandro
  See Weather Report
Adam Ant **13**
Adamendes, Elaine
  See Throwing Muses
Adams, Bryan **20**
  Earlier sketch in CM **2**
Adams, Clifford
  See Kool & the Gang
Adams, Craig
  See Cult, The
Adams, Donn
  See NRBQ
Adams, John **8**
Adams, Mark
  See Specials, The
Adams, Oleta **17**
Adams, Terry
  See NRBQ
Adams, Victoria
  See Spice Girls
Adams, Yolanda **23**
Adcock, Eddie
  See Country Gentleman, The
Adderly, Cannonball **15**
Adderly, Julian
  See Adderly, Cannonball
Adé, King Sunny **18**
Adler, Steven
  See Guns n' Roses

Aerosmith **22**
  Earlier sketch in CM **3**
Afghan Whigs **17**
Afonso, Marie
  See Zap Mama
AFX
  See Aphex Twin
Air Supply **22**
Ajile
  See Arrested Development
Akingbola, Sola
  See Jamiroquai
Akins, Rhett **22**
Alabama **21**
  Earlier sketch in CM **1**
Alarm **22**
Albarn, Damon
  See Blur
Albert, Nate
  See Mighty Mighty Bosstones
Alberti, Dorona
  See KMFDM
Albini, Steve **15**
Albuquerque, Michael de
  See Electric Light Orchestra
Alder, John
  See Gong
Alexakis, Art
  See Everclear
Alexander, Arthur **14**
Alexander, Tim
  See Asleep at the Wheel
Alexander, Tim "Herb"
  See Primus
Ali
  See Tribe Called Quest, A
Alice in Chains **10**
Alien Sex Fiend **23**
Alkema, Jan Willem
  See Compulsion
Allcock, Martin
  See Fairport Convention
  Also see Jethro Tull
Allen, April
  See C + C Music Factory
Allen, Chad
  See Guess Who
Allen, Daevid
  See Gong
Allen, Dave
  See Gang of Four
Allen, Debbie **8**
Allen, Duane
  See Oak Ridge Boys, The

Allen, Geri **10**
Allen, Johnny Ray
  See Subdudes, The
Allen, Papa Dee
  See War
Allen, Peter **11**
Allen, Red
  See Osborne Brothers, The
Allen, Rick
  See Def Leppard
Allen, Ross
  See Mekons, The
All-4-One **17**
Allison, Luther **21**
Allison, Mose **17**
Allman, Duane
  See Allman Brothers, The
Allman, Gregg
  See Allman Brothers, The
Allman Brothers, The **6**
Allsup, Michael Rand
  See Three Dog Night
Alpert, Herb **11**
Alphonso, Roland
  See Skatalites, The
Alsing, Pelle
  See Roxette
Alston, Andy
  See Del Amitri
Alston, Shirley
  See Shirelles, The
Altan **18**
Alvin, Dave **17**
  Also see X
Am, Svet
  See KMFDM
Amato, Dave
  See REO Speedwagon
Amedee, Steve
  See Subdudes, The
Ameling, Elly **24**
Ament, Jeff
  See Pearl Jam
America **16**
American Music Club **15**
Amon, Robin
  See Pearls Before Swine
Amos, Tori **12**
Anastasio, Trey
  See Phish
Anderson, Al
  See NRBQ
Anderson, Andy
  See Cure, The

Anderson, Brett
  See Suede
Anderson, Cleave
  See Blue Rodeo
Anderson, Emma
  See Lush
Anderson, Gladstone
  See Skatalites, The
Anderson, Ian
  See Jethro Tull
Anderson, Jhelisa
  See Shamen, The
Anderson, John 5
Anderson, Jon
  See Yes
Anderson, Keith
  See Dirty Dozen
Anderson, Laurie 1
Anderson, Marian 8
Anderson, Pamela
  See Incognito
Anderson, Ray 7
Anderson, Signe
  See Jefferson Airplane
Anderson, Wessell 23
Andersson, Benny
  See Abba
Andes, Mark
  See Spirit
Andes, Matt
  See Spirit
Andes, Rachel
  See Spirit
Andrews, Barry
  See XTC
Andrews, Julie 4
Andrews, Laverne
  See Andrews Sisters, The
Andrews, Maxene
  See Andrews Sisters, The
Andrews, Patty
  See Andrews Sisters, The
Andrews, Revert
  See Dirty Dozen
Andrews Sisters, The 9
Andy, Horace
  See Massive Attack
Anger, Darol
  See Turtle Island String Quartet
Angus, Colin
  See Shamen, The
Animals 22
Anka, Paul 2
Anointed 21
Anonymous, Rodney
  See Dead Milkmen
Anonymous 4 23
Anselmo, Philip
  See Pantera
Ant, Adam
  See Adam Ant
Anthony, Marc 19
Anthony, Michael
  See Massive Attack

Anthony, Michael
  See Van Halen
Anthrax 11
Anton, Alan
  See Cowboy Junkies, The
Antoni, Mark De Gli
  See Soul Coughing
Antunes, Michael
  See Beaver Brown Band, The
Aphex Twin 14
Appice, Vinnie
  See Black Sabbath
Aquabats 22
Araya, Tom
  See Slayer
Archers of Loaf 21
Arden, Jann 21
Ardolino, Tom
  See NRBQ
Arellano, Rod
  See Aquabats
Arena, Tina 21
Argent, Rod
  See Zombies, The
Arkenstone, David 20
Arm, Mark
  See Mudhoney
Armatrading, Joan 4
Armerding, Jake
  See Northern Lights
Armerding, Taylor
  See Northern Lights
Armstrong, Billie Joe
  See Green Day
Armstrong, Louis 4
Armstrong, Vanessa Bell 24
Arnaz, Desi 8
Arnold, Eddy 10
Arnold, Kristine
  See Sweethearts of the Rodeo
Aronoff, Kenny 21
Arrau, Claudio 1
Arrested Development 14
Art Ensemble of Chicago, The 23
Arthurs, Paul
  See Oasis
Art of Noise 22
Artifacts 23
Ash, Daniel
  See Love and Rockets
Ashcroft, Richard
  See Verve, The
Ashton, Susan 17
Asleep at the Wheel 5
Astbury, Ian
  See Cult, The
Astley, Rick 5
Astro
  See UB40
Asuo, Kwesi
  See Arrested Development
Atkins, Chet 5
Atkinson, Paul
  See Zombies, The

Atkinson, Sweet Pea
  See Was (Not Was)
Audio Adrenaline 22
Auf Der Maur, Melissa
  See Hole
Augustyniak, Jerry
  See 10,000 Maniacs
Auldridge, Mike 4
    Also see Country Gentlemen, The
    Also see Seldom Scene, The
Austin, Cuba
  See McKinney's Cotton Pickers
Austin, Dallas 16
Autry, Gene 12
Avalon, Frankie 5
Avery, Eric
  See Jane's Addiction
Avery, Teodross 23
Avory, Mick
Avory, Mick
  See Rolling Stones, The
  See Kinks, The
Ayers, Kevin
  See Gong
Aykroyd, Dan
  See Blues Brothers, The
Ayler, Albert 19
Ayres, Ben
  See Cornershop
Azorr, Chris
  See Cherry Poppin' Daddies
Aztec Camera 22
B, Daniel
  See Front 242
Baah, Reebop Kwaku
  See Traffic
Babatunde, Don
  See Last Poets
Babes in Toyland 16
Babjak, James
Babyface
  See Edmonds, Kenneth "Babyface"
Bacharach, Burt 20
  Earlier sketch in CM 1
Bachman, Eric
  See Archers of Loaf
Bachman, Randy
  See Guess Who
Backstreet Boys 21
Badalamenti, Angelo 17
Bad Brains 16
Bad Company 22
Badfinger 23
Badger, Pat
  See Extreme
Bad Livers, The 19
Badrena, Manola
  See Weather Report
Baez, Joan 1
Bailey, Mildred 13
Bailey, Pearl 5
Bailey, Phil
  See Earth, Wind and Fire

Bailey, Victor
　　See Weather Report
Bailey, Keith
　　See Gong
Baker, Anita **9**
Baker, Arthur **23**
Baker, Bobby
　　See Tragically Hip, The
Baker, Chet **13**
Baker, Ginger **16**
　　Also see Cream
Baker, Janet **14**
Baker, Jon
　　See Charlatans, The
Baker, Josephine **10**
Balakrishnan, David
　　See Turtle Island String Quartet
Balch, Bob
　　See Fu Manchu
Balch, Michael
　　See Front Line Assembly
Baldursson, Sigtryggur
　　See Sugarcubes, The
Baldwin, Donny
　　See Starship
Baliardo, Diego
　　See Gipsy Kings, The
Baliardo, Paco
　　See Gipsy Kings, The
Baliardo, Tonino
　　See Gipsy Kings, The
Balin, Marty
　　See Jefferson Airplane
Ball, Marcia **15**
Ballard, Florence
　　See Supremes, The
Ballard, Hank **17**
Balsley, Phil
　　See Statler Brothers, The
Baltes, Peter
　　See Dokken
Balzano, Vinnie
　　See Less Than Jake
Bambaataa, Afrika **13**
Bamonte, Perry
　　See Cure, The
Bananarama **22**
Bancroft, Cyke
　　See Bevis Frond
Band, The **9**
Bangles **22**
Banks, Nick
　　See Pulp
Banks, Peter
　　See Yes
Banks, Tony
　　See Genesis
Baptiste, David Russell
　　See Meters, The
Barbarossa, Dave
　　See Republica
Barbata, John
　　See Jefferson Starship

Barber, Keith
　　See Soul Stirrers, The
Barbero, Lori
　　See Babes in Toyland
Barbieri, Gato **22**
Bardens, Peter
　　See Camel
Barenaked Ladies **18**
Bargeld, Blixa
　　See Einstürzende Neubauten
Bargeron, Dave
　　See Blood, Sweat and Tears
Barham, Meriel
　　See Lush
Barile, Jo
　　See Ventures, The
Barker, Paul
　　See Ministry
Barker, Travis Landon
　　See Aquabats
Barlow, Barriemore
　　See Jethro Tull
Barlow, Lou **20**
　　Also see Dinosaur Jr.
Barlow, Tommy
　　See Aztec Camera
Barnes, Danny
　　See Bad Livers, The
Barnes, Micah
　　See Nylons, The
Barnes, Roosevelt "Booba" **23**
Barnwell, Duncan
　　See Simple Minds
Barnwell, Ysaye Maria
　　See Sweet Honey in the Rock
Barr, Ralph
　　See Nitty Gritty Dirt Band, The
Barre, Martin
　　See Jethro Tull
Barrere, Paul
　　See Little Feat
Barrett, Dicky
　　See Mighty Mighty Bosstones
Barrett, (Roger) Syd
　　See Pink Floyd
Barrett, Robert
　　See Goodie Mob
Barron, Christopher
　　See Spin Doctors
Barrow, Geoff
　　See Portishead
Bartels, Joanie **13**
Bartholomew, Simon
　　See Brand New Heavies, The
Bartoli, Cecilia **12**
Barton, Lou Ann
　　See Fabulous Thunderbirds, The
Bartos, Karl
　　See Kraftwerk
Basehead **11**
Basher, Mick
　　See X
Basia **5**
Basie, Count **2**

Bass, Colin
　　See Camel
Bass, Colin
　　See Chumbawamba
Bass, Ralph **24**
Batchelor, Kevin
　　See Big Mountain
　　See Steel Pulse
Batel, Beate
　　See Einstürzende Neubauten
Batiste, Lionel
　　See Dirty Dozen
Batoh, Masaki
　　See Ghost
Batoh, Masaki
　　See Pearls Before Swine
Battin, Skip
　　See Byrds, The
Battle, Kathleen **6**
Bauer, Judah
　　See Jon Spencer Blues Explosion
Baumann, Peter
　　See Tangerine Dream
Bautista, Roland
　　See Earth, Wind and Fire
Baxter, Adrian
　　See Cherry Poppin' Daddies
Baxter, Jeff
　　See Doobie Brothers, The
Bayer Sager, Carole
　　See Sager, Carole Bayer
Baylor, Helen **20**
Baynton-Power, David
　　See James
Bazilian, Eric
　　See Hooters
Beach Boys, The **1**
Beale, Michael
　　See Earth, Wind and Fire
Beard, Frank
　　See ZZ Top
Beasley, Paul
　　See Mighty Clouds of Joy, The
Beastie Boys, The **8**
Beat Farmers **23**
Beatles, The **2**
Beauford, Carter
　　See Dave Matthews Band
Beautiful South **19**
Beaver Brown Band, The **3**
Bechet, Sidney **17**
Beck, Jeff **4**
　　Also see Yardbirds, The
Beck, William
　　See Ohio Players
Beck **18**
Becker, Walter
　　See Steely Dan
Beckford, Theophilus
　　See Skatalites, The
Beckley, Gerry
　　See America
Bee Gees, The **3**

Beers, Garry Gary
  See INXS
Behler, Chuck
  See Megadeth
Beiderbecke, Bix **16**
Belafonte, Harry **8**
Belew, Adrian **5**
  Also see King Crimson
Belfield, Dennis
  See Three Dog Night
Bell, Andy
  See Erasure
Bell, Brian
  See Weezer
Bell, Derek
  See Chieftains, The
Bell, Eric
  See Thin Lizzy
Bell, Jayn
  See Sounds ofBlackness
Bell, Joshua **21**
Bell, Melissa
  See Soul II Soul
Bell, Ronald
  See Kool & the Gang
Bell, Taj
  See Charm Farm
Belladonna, Joey
  See Anthrax
Bellamy, David
  See Bellamy Brothers, The
Bellamy, Howard
  See Bellamy Brothers, The
Bellamy Brothers, The **13**
Belle, Regina **6**
Bello, Frank
  See Anthrax
Bello, Elissa
  See Go-Go's, The
Belly **16**
Belushi, John
  See Blues Brothers, The
Benante, Charlie
  See Anthrax
Benatar, Pat **8**
Benckert, Vicki
  See Roxette
Benedict, Scott
  See Pere Ubu
Ben Folds Five **20**
Bengry, Peter
  See Cornershop
Benitez, Jellybean **15**
Bennett, Brian
  See Shadows, The
Bennett, Tony **16**
  Earlier sketch in CM **2**
Bennett-Nesby, Ann
  See Sounds of Blackness
Benson, George **9**
Benson, Ray
  See Asleep at the Wheel
Benson, Renaldo "Obie"
  See Four Tops, The

Bentley, John
  See Squeeze
Benton, Brook **7**
Bentyne, Cheryl
  See Manhattan Transfer, The
Berenyi, Miki
  See Lush
Berg, Matraca **16**
Bergeson, Ben
  See Aquabats
Berggren, Jenny
  See Ace of Base
Berggren, Jonas
  See Ace of Base
Berggren, Linn
  See Ace of Base
Berigan, Bunny **2**
Berkely, Anthony
  See Gravediggaz
Berlin, Irving **8**
Berlin, Steve
  See Los Lobos
Berndt, Jay
  See Kilgore
Bernstein, Leonard **2**
Berry, Bill
  See R.E.M.
Berry, Chuck **1**
Berry, John **17**
Berry, Robert
  See Emerson, Lake & Palmer/Powell
Berryhill, Bob
  See Surfaris, The
Bessant, Jack
  See Reef
Best, Nathaniel
  See O'Jays, The
Best, Pete
  See Beatles, The
Bettencourt, Nuno
  See Extreme
Better Than Ezra **19**
Bettie Serveert **17**
Bettini, Tom
  See Jackyl
Betts, Dicky
  See Allman Brothers, The
Bevan, Bev
  SeeBlack Sabbath
    Also see Electric Light Orchestra
B-52's, The **4**
Bevis Frond **23**
Bezozi, Alan
  See Dog's Eye View
Biafra, Jello **18**
Big Audio Dynamite **18**
Big Head Todd and the Monsters **20**
Big Mike
  See GetoBoys, The
Big Money Odis
  See Digital Underground
Big Mountain **23**
Bin Hassan, Umar
  See Last Poets

Bingham, John
  See Fishbone
Binks, Les
  See Judas Priest
Biondo, George
  See Steppenwolf
Birchfield, Benny
  See Osborne Brothers, The
Bird
  See Parker, Charlie
Birdsong, Cindy
  See Supremes, The
Birdstuff
  See Man or Astroman?
Biscuits, Chuck
  See Danzig
    Also see Social Distortion
Bishop, Michael
  See Gwar
Biz Markie **10**
BizzyBone
  See Bone Thugs-N-Harmony
Bjelland, Kat
  See Babes in Toyland
Björk **16**
  Also see Sugarcubes, The
Bjork, Brant
  See Fu Manchu
Black, Clint **5**
Black Crowes, The **7**
Black Flag **22**
Black Francis
  See Black, Frank
Black, Frank **14**
Black, Mary **15**
Black Sabbath **9**
Black Sheep **15**
Black Uhuru **12**
Black, Vic
  See C + C Music Factory
BlackHawk **21**
Blackman, Cindy **15**
Blackmore, Ritchie
  See Deep Purple
Blackstreet **23**
Blackwood, Sarah
  See Dubstar
Blades, Ruben **2**
Blake, Eubie **19**
Blake, Norman
  See Teenage Fanclub
Blake, Tim
  See Gong
Blakey, Art **11**
Blanchard, Terence **13**
Bland, Bobby "Blue" **12**
Blegen, Jutith **23**
Blessid Union of Souls **20**
Bley, Carla **8**
Bley, Paul **14**
Blige, Mary J. **15**
Blind Melon **21**
Block, Rory **18**
Blondie **14**

Blood, Dave
  See Dead Milkmen
Blood, Sweat and Tears **7**
Bloom, Eric
  See Blue Oyster Cult
Bloom, Luka **14**
Blue, Buddy
  See Beat Farmers
Bluegrass Patriots **22**
Blue Oyster Cult **16**
Blue Rodeo **18**
Blues, Elwood
  See Blues Brothers, The
Blues, "Joliet" Jake
  See Blues Brothers, The
Blues Brothers, The **3**
Blues Traveler **15**
Blunstone, Colin
  See Zombies, The
Blunt, Martin
  See Charlatans, The
Blur **17**
BoDeans, The **20**
  Earlier sketch in CM **3**
Bob, Tim
  See Rage Against the Machine
Bocelli, Andrea **22**
Boff, Richard
  See Chumbawamba
Bogaert, Jo
  See Technotronic
Bogdan, Henry
  See Helmet
Bogguss, Suzy **11**
Bogle, Bob
  See Ventures, The
Bohannon, Jim
  See Pearls Before Swine
Bolade, Nitanju
  See Sweet Honey in the Rock
Bolan, Marc
  See T. Rex
Bolton, Michael **4**
Bon Jovi **10**
Bon Jovi, Jon
  See Bon Jovi
Bonamy, James **21**
Bonebrake, D. J.
  See X
Bone Thugs-N-Harmony **18**
Bonham, John
  See Led Zeppelin
Bonnecaze, Cary
  See Better Than Ezra
Bonner, Leroy "Sugarfoot"
  See Ohio Players
Bono
  See U2
Bono, Sonny
  See Sonny and Cher
Bonsall, Joe
  See Oak Ridge Boys, The
Boo Radleys, The **21**
Booker T. & the M.G.'s **24**

Books
  See Das EFX
Boone, Pat **13**
Booth, Tim
  See James
Boquist, Dave
  See Son Volt
Boquist, Jim
  See Son Volt
Bordin, Mike
  See Faith No More
Borg, Bobby
  See Warrant
Borge, Victor **19**
Borowiak, Tony
  See All-4-One
Bostaph, Paul
  See Slayer
Boston **11**
Bostrom, Derrick
  See Meat Puppets, The
Bottum, Roddy
  See Faith No More
Bouchard, Albert
  See Blue Oyster Cult
Bouchard, Joe
  See Blue Oyster Cult
Bouchikhi, Chico
  See Gipsy Kings, The
Bowen, Jimmy
  See Country Gentlemen, The
Bowens, Sir Harry
  See Was (Not Was)
Bowie, David **1**
Bowie, Lester
  See Art Ensemble of Chicago, The
Bowie, David **23**
Bowman, Steve
  See Counting Crows
Box, Mick
  See Uriah Heep
Boy Howdy **21**
Boyd, Brandon
  See Incubus
Boyd, Eadie
  See Del Rubio Triplets
Boyd, Elena
  See Del Rubio Triplets
Boyd, Liona **7**
Boyd, Milly
  See Del Rubio Triplets
Boyle, Doug
  See Caravan
Boyz II Men **15**
Bozulich, Carla
  See Geraldine Fibbers
Brad **21**
Bradbury, John
  See Specials, The
Bradshaw, Tim
  See Dog's Eye View
Bradstreet, Rick
  See Bluegrass Patriots
Brady, Paul **8**

Bragg, Billy **7**
Bramah, Martin
  See Fall, The
Brand New Heavies, The **14**
Brandt, Paul **22**
Brandy **19**
Branigan, Laura **2**
Brannon, Kippi **20**
Brantley, Junior
  See Roomful of Blues
Braxton, Anthony **12**
Braxton, Toni **17**
B-Real
  See Cypress Hill
Bream, Julian **9**
Breeders **19**
Brendel, Alfred **23**
Brennan, Ciaran
  See Clannad
Brennan, Enya
  See Clannad
Brennan, Maire
  See Clannad
Brennan, Paul
  See Odds
Brennan, Pol
  See Clannad
Brenner, Simon
  See Talk Talk
Brevette, Lloyd
  See Skatalites, The
Brickell, Edie **3**
Brickman, Jim **22**
Bridgewater, Dee Dee **18**
Briggs, James Randall
  See Aquabats
Briggs, Vic
  See Animals
Briggs, David
  See Pearls Before Swine
Bright, Garfield
  See Shai
Bright, Ronnie
  See Coasters, The
Brightman, Sarah **20**
Briley, Alex
  See Village People, The
Brindley, Paul
  See Sundays, The
Britten, Benjamin **15**
Brittingham, Eric
  See Cinderella
Brix
  See Fall, The
Brockenborough, Dennis
  See Mighty Mighty Bosstones
Brockie, Dave
  See Gwar
Brokop, Lisa **22**
Bromberg, David **18**
Bronfman, Yefim **6**
Brooke, Jonatha
  See Story, The
Brookes, Jon
  See Charlatans, The

Brooks, Baba
   See Skatalites, The
Brooks, Garth **8**
Brooks, Leon Eric "Kix"
   See Brooks & Dunn
Brooks & Dunn **12**
Broonzy, Big Bill **13**
Brotherdale, Steve
   See Joy Division
   Also see Smithereens, The
Broudie, Ian
   See Lightning Seeds
Brown, Bobby **4**
Brown, Brooks
   See Cherry Poppin' Daddies
Brown, Clarence "Gatemouth" **11**
Brown, Clifford **24**
Brown, Donny
   See Verve Pipe, The
Brown, Duncan
   See Stereolab
Brown, George
   See Kool & the Gang
Brown, Harold
   See War
Brown, Heidi
   See Treadmill Trackstar
Brown, Ian
   See Stone Roses, The
Brown, James **16**
   Earlier sketch in CM **2**
Brown, Jimmy
   See UB40
Brown, Junior **15**
Brown, Marty **14**
Brown, Melanie
   See Spice Girls
Brown, Mick
   See Dokken
Brown, Norman
   See Mills Brothers, The
Brown, Rahem
   See Artifacts
Brown, Ray **21**
Brown, Ruth **13**
Brown, Selwyn "Bumbo"
   See Steel Pulse
Brown, Steven
   See Tuxedomoon
Brown, Tim
   See Boo Radleys, The
Brown, Tony **14**
Brown, Lawrence **23**
Brown, Morris
   See Pearls Before Swine
Browne, Jackson **3**
   Also see Nitty Gritty Dirt Band, The
Brownstein, Carrie
   See Sleater-Kinney
Brownstone **21**
Brubeck, Dave **8**
Bruce, Dustan
   See Chumbawamba

Bruce, Jack
   See Cream
Bruford, Bill
   See King Crimson
   Also see Yes
Bruster, Thomas
   See Soul Stirrers, The
Bryan, David
   See Bon Jovi
Bryan, Karl
   See Skatalites, The
Bryan, Mark
   See Hootie and the Blowfish
Bryant, Elbridge
   See Temptations, The
Bryant, Jeff
   See Ricochet
Bryant, Junior
   See Ricochet
Bryson, Bill
   See Desert Rose Band, The
Bryson, David
   See Counting Crows
Bryson, Peabo **11**
Buchanan, Wallis
   See Jamiroquai
Buchholz, Francis
   See Scorpions, The
Buchignani, Paul
   See Afghan Whigs
Buck, Mike
   See Fabulous Thunderbirds, The
Buck, Peter
   See R.E.M.
Buck, Robert
   See 10,000 Maniacs
Buckingham, Lindsey **8**
   Also see Fleetwood Mac
Buckley, Betty **16**
   Earlier sketch in CM **1**
Buckley, Jeff **22**
Buckley, Tim **14**
Buckwheat Zydeco **6**
Budgie
   See Siouxsie and the Banshees
Buerstatte, Phil
   See White Zombie
Buffalo Springfield **24**
Buffalo Tom **18**
Buffett, Jimmy **4**
Bulgarian State Female Vocal Choir, The
   10
Bulgarian State Radio and Television
   Female Vocal Choir, The
   See Bulgarian State Female Vocal Choir,
   The
Bulgin, Lascelle
   See Israel Vibration
Bullock, Craig
   See Sugar Ray
Bumbry, Grace **13**
Bumpus, Cornelius
   See Doobie Brothers, The

Bunker, Clive
   See Jethro Tull
Bunnell, Dewey
   See America
Bunskoeke, Herman
   See Bettie Serveert
Bunton, Emma
   See Spice Girls
Burch, Curtis
   See New Grass Revival, The
Burchill, Charlie
   See Simple Minds
Burden, Ian
   See Human League, The
Burdon, Eric
   See Animals
Burdon, Eric **14**
   Also see War
Burgess, Paul
   See Camel
Burgess, Tim
   See Charlatans, The
Burke, Clem
   See Blondie
Burkum, Tyler
   See Audio Adrenaline
Burnett, Carol **6**
Burnett, T Bone **13**
Burnette, Billy
   See Fleetwood Mac
Burnham, Hugo
   See Gang of Four
Burning Spear **15**
Burns, Bob
   See Lynyrd Skynyrd
Burns, Karl
   See Fall, The
Burr, Clive
   See Iron Maiden
Burrell, Boz
   See Bad Company
Burrell, Kenny **11**
Burrell
   See King Crimson
Burton, Cliff
   See Metallica
Burton, Gary **10**
Burton, Tim
   See Mighty Mighty Bosstones
Busby, Jheryl **9**
Bush **18**
Bush, Dave
   See Fall, The
Bush, John
   See Anthrax
Bush, Kate **4**
Bush, Sam
   See New Grass Revival, The
Bushwick, Bill
   See Geto Boys, The
Busta Rhymes **18**
Butler, Bernard
   See Suede

Butler, Richard
  See Love Spit Love
Butler, Terry "Geezer"
  See Black Sabbath
Butler, Tim
  See Love Spit Love
Butterfly
  See Digable Planets
Butthole Surfers **16**
Buttrey, Kenneth
  See Pearls Before Swine
Buzzcocks, The **9**
Byers, Roddy
  See Specials, The
Byrds, The **8**
Byrne, David **8**
  Also see Talking Heads
Byrne, Dermot
  See Altan
Byrom, Larry
  See Steppenwolf
Byron, David
  See Uriah Heep
Byron, Don **22**
Byron, Lord T.
  See Lords of Acid
C + C Music Factory **16**
Caballe, Monserrat **23**
Cabaret Voltaire **18**
Cachao
  See Lopez, Israel "Cachao"
Caesar, Shirley **17**
Cafferty, John
  See Beaver Brown Band, The
Caffey, Charlotte
  See Go-Go's, The
Cage, John **8**
Cahn, Sammy **11**
Cain, Jonathan
  See Journey
Calderon, Mark
  See Color Me Badd
Cale, J. J. **16**
Cale, John **9**
  Also see Velvet Underground, The
Calhoun, Will
  See Living Colour
California, Randy
  See Spirit
Calire, Mario
  See Wallflowers, The
Callahan, Ken
  See Jayhawks, The
Callas, Maria **11**
Callis, Jo
  See Human League, The
Calloway, Cab **6**
Camel **21**
Cameron, Duncan
  See Sawyer Brown
Cameron, G. C.
  See Spinners, The
Cameron, Matt
  See Soundgarden

Campbell, Ali
  See UB40
Campbell, Glen **2**
Campbell, Kerry
  See War
Campbell, Luther **10**
Campbell, Martyn
  See Lightning Seeds
Campbell, Phil
  See Motörhead
Campbell, Robin
  See UB40
Campbell, Tevin **13**
Campbell, Sarah Elizabeth **23**
CanadianBrass, The **4**
Cantrell, Jerry
  See Alice in Chains
Canty, Brendan
  See Fugazi
Capaldi, Jim
  See Traffic
Cappelli, Frank **14**
Captain Beefheart **10**
Caravan **24**
Cardigans **19**
Cardwell, Joi **22**
Carey, Danny
  See Tool
Carey, Mariah **20**
  Earlier sketch in CM **6**
Carlisle, Belinda **8**
  Also see Go-Go's, The
Carlisle, Bob **22**
Carlos, Bun E.
  See Cheap Trick
Carlos, Don
  See Black Uhuru
Carlson, Paulette
  See Highway 101
Carnes, Kim **4**
Carpenter, Bob
  See Nitty Gritty Dirt Band, The
Carpenter, Karen
  See Carpenters, The
Carpenter, Mary-Chapin **6**
Carpenter, Richard **24**
  Also see Carpenters, The
Carpenter, Stephen
  See Deftones
Carpenters, The **13**
Carr, Ben
  See Mighty Mighty Bosstones
Carr, Eric
  See Kiss
Carr, Martin
  See Boo Radleys, The
Carr, James **23**
Carr, Teddy
  See Ricochet
Carrack, Paul
  See Mike & the Mechanics
  Also see Squeeze
Carreras, José **8**

Carrigan, Andy
  See Mekons, The
Carroll, Earl "Speedo"
  See Coasters, The
Carruthers, John
  See Siouxsie and the Banshees
Cars, The **20**
Carter, Anita
  See Carter Family, The
Carter, A. P.
  See Carter Family, The
Carter, Benny **3**
  Also see McKinney's Cotton Pickers
Carter, Betty **6**
Carter, Carlene **8**
Carter, Helen
  See Carter Family, The
Carter, James **18**
Carter, Janette
  See Carter Family, The
Carter, Jimmy
  See Five Blind Boys of Alabama
Carter, Joe
  See Carter Family, The
Carter, June **6**
  Also see Carter Family, The
Carter, Maybell
  See Carter Family, The
Carter, Nell **7**
Carter, Nick
  See Backstreet Boys
Carter, Regina **22**
Carter, Ron **14**
Carter, Sara
  See Carter Family, The
Carter Family, The **3**
Carthy, Martin
  See Steeleye Span
Caruso, Enrico **10**
Casady, Jack
  See Jefferson Airplane
Casale, Bob
  See Devo
Casale, Gerald V.
  See Devo
Casals, Pablo **9**
Case, Peter **13**
Cash, Johnny **17**
  Earlier sketch in CM **1**
Cash, Rosanne **2**
Cassidy, Ed
  See Spirit
Catallo, Gene
  See Surfin' Pluto
Catallo, Shris
  See Surfin' Pluto
Cates, Ronny
  See Petra
Catherall, Joanne
  See Human League, The
Catherine Wheel **18**
Caustic Window
  See Aphex Twin

Cauty, Jimmy
  See Orb, The
Cavalera, Igor
  See Sepultura
Cavalera, Max
  See Sepultura
Cave, Nick **10**
Cavoukian, Raffi
  See Raffi
Cease, Jeff
  See Black Crowes, The
Cervenka, Exene
  See X
Cetera, Peter
  See Chicago
Chamberlin, Jimmy
  See Smashing Pumpkins
Chambers, Martin
  See Pretenders, The
Chambers, Paul **18**
Chambers, Terry
  See XTC
Champion, Eric **21**
Chance, Slim
  See Cramps, The
Chancellor, Justin
  See Tool
Chandler, Chas
  See Animals
Chandra, Sheila **16**
Chaney, Jimmy
  See Jimmie's Chicken Shack
Chang, Sarah **7**
Channing, Carol **6**
Chapin, Harry **6**
Chapin, Tom **11**
Chapman, Steven Curtis **15**
Chapman, Tony
  See Rolling Stones, The
Chapman, Tracy **20**
  Earlier sketch in CM **4**
Chaquico, Craig
  See Jefferson Starship
Chaquico, Craig **23**
Charlatans, The **13**
Charles, Yolanda
  See Aztec Camera
Charles, Ray **24**
  Earlier sketch in CM **1**
Charm Farm **20**
Chea, Alvin "Vinnie"
  See Take 6
Cheap Trick **12**
Checker, Chubby **7**
Che Colovita, Lemon
  See Jimmie's Chicken Shack
Cheeks, Julius
  See Soul Stirrers, The
Chemical Brothers **20**
Cheng, Chi
  See Deftones
Chenier, C. J. **15**
Chenier, Clifton **6**
Chenille Sisters, The **16**

Cher **1**
  Also see Sonny and Cher
Cherone, Gary
  See Extreme
Cherry, Don **10**
Cherry, Neneh **4**
Cherry Poppin' Daddies **24**
Chesney, Kenny **20**
Chesnutt, Mark **13**
Chess, Leonard **24**
Chevalier, Maurice **6**
Chevron, Phillip
  See Pogues, The
Chicago **3**
Chieftains, The **7**
Childress, Ross
  See Collective Soul
Childs, Toni **2**
Chilton, Alex **10**
Chimes, Terry
  See Clash, The
Chin, Tony
  See Big Mountain
Chisholm, Melanie
  See Spice Girls
Chopmaster J
  See Digital Underground
Chrisman, Andy
  See FourHim
Christ, John
  See Danzig
Christian, Charlie **11**
Christina, Fran
  See Fabulous Thunderbirds, The
  Also see Roomful of Blues
Chuck D
  See Public Enemy
Chumbawamba **21**
Chung, Mark
  See Einstürzende Neubauten
Church, Kevin
  See Country Gentlemen, The
Church, The **14**
Cieka, Rob
  See Boo Radleys, The
Cinderella **16**
Cinelu, Mino
  See Weather Report
Cipollina, John
  See Quicksilver Messenger Service
Circle Jerks, The **17**
Cissell, Ben
  See Audio Adrenaline
Clannad **23**
Clapton, Eric **11**
  Earlier sketch in CM **1**
  Also see Cream
  Also see Yardbirds, The
Clark, Alan
  See Dire Straits
Clark, Dave
  See Dave Clark Five, The
Clark, Dick **2**

Clark, Gene
  See Byrds, The
Clark, Graham
  See Gong
Clark, Guy **17**
Clark, Keith
  See Circle Jerks, The
Clark, Mike
  See Suicidal Tendencies
Clark, Roy **1**
Clark, Steve
  See Def Leppard
Clark, Terri **19**
Clark, Tony
  See Blessid Union of Souls
Clarke, Bernie
  See Aztec Camera
Clarke, "Fast" Eddie
  See Motörhead
Clarke, Michael
  See Byrds, The
Clarke, Stanley **3**
Clarke, Vince
  See Depeche Mode
  Also see Erasure
Clarke, William
  See Third World
Clash, The **4**
Clayderman, Richard **1**
Claypool, Les
  See Primus
Clayton, Adam
  See U2
Clayton, Sam
  See Little Feat
Clayton-Thomas, David
  SeeBlood, Sweat and Tears
Clean, Dean
  See Dead Milkmen
Cleaves, Jessica
  See Earth, Wind and Fire
Clegg, Johnny **8**
Clements, Vassar **18**
Clemons, Clarence **7**
Cleveland, James **1**
Cliburn, Van **13**
Cliff, Jimmy **8**
Clifford, Douglas Ray
  See Creedence Clearwater Revival
Cline, Nels
  See Geraldine Fibbers
Cline, Patsy **5**
Clinton, George **7**
Clivilles, Robert
  See C + C Music Factory
Clooney, Rosemary **9**
Clouser, Charlie
  See Prong
Coasters, The **5**
Cobain, Kurt
  See Nirvana
Cobham, Billy
  See Mahavishnu Orchestra

Cochran, Bobby
  See Steppenwolf
Cochrane, Tom **23**
Cockburn, Bruce **8**
Cocker, Jarvis
  See Pulp
Cocker, Joe **4**
Cocking, William "Willigan"
  See Mystic Revealers
Coco the Electronic Monkey Wizard
  See Man or Astroman?
Cocteau Twins, The **12**
Codenys, Patrick
  See Front 242
Codling, Neil
  See Suede
Coe, David Allan **4**
Coffey, Jeff
  See Butthole Surfers
Coffey, Jr., Don
  See Superdrag
Coffie, Calton
  See Inner Circle
Cohen, Jeremy
  See Turtle Island String Quartet
Cohen, Leonard **3**
Cohen, Porky
  See Roomful of Blues
Colaiuta, Vinnie **23**
Colbourn, Chris
  See Buffalo Tom
Cole, David
  See C + C Music Factory
Cole, Holly **18**
Cole, Lloyd **9**
Cole, Natalie **21**
  Earlier sketch in CM **1**
Cole, Nat King **3**
Cole, Paula **20**
Cole, Ralph
  See Nylons, The
Coleman, Ornette **5**
Collective Soul **16**
Colletti, Dominic
  See Bevis Frond
Colley, Dana
  See Morphine
Collie, Mark **15**
Collin, Phil
  See Def Leppard
Collins, Albert **19**
  Earlier sketch in CM **4**
Collins, Allen
  See Lynyrd Skynyrd
Collins, Bootsy **8**
Collins, Chris
  See Dream Theater
Collins, Judy **4**
Collins, Mark
  See Charlatans, The
Collins, Mel
  See Camel
Collins, Mel
  See King Crimson

Collins, Phil **20**
  Earlier sketch in CM **2**
  Also see Genesis
Collins, Rob
  See Charlatans, The
Collins, William
  See Collins, Bootsy
Colomby, Bobby
  See Blood, Sweat and Tears
Color Me Badd **23**
Colt, Johnny
  See Black Crowes, The
Coltrane, John **4**
Colvin, Shawn **11**
Colwell, David
  See Bad Company
Combs, Sean "Puffy" **16**
Comess, Aaron
  See Spin Doctors
Commodores, The **23**
Common **23**
Como, Perry **14**
Compulsion **23**
Confederate Railroad **23**
Congo Norvell **22**
Conneff, Kevin
  See Chieftains, The
Connelly, Chris
  See KMFDM
Connick, Harry, Jr. **4**
Connolly, Pat
  See Surfaris, The
Connors, Marc
  See Nylons, The
Conti, Neil
  See Prefab Sprout
Conway, Billy
  See Morphine
Conway, Gerry
  See Pentangle
Cooder, Ry **2**
Cook, Greg
  See Ricochet
Cook, Jeffrey Alan
  See Alabama
Cook, Paul
  See Sex Pistols, The
Cook, Stuart
  See Creedence Clearwater Revival
Cook, Wayne
  See Steppenwolf
Cooke, Sam **1**
  Also see Soul Stirrers, The
Cool, Tre
  See Green Day
Coolio **19**
Coomes, Sam
  See Quasi
Cooney, Rory **6**
Cooper, Alice **8**
Cooper, Jason
  See Cure, The
Cooper, Martin
  See Orchestral Manoeuvres in the Dark

Cooper, Michael
  See Third World
Cooper, Paul
  See Nylons, The
Cooper, Ralph
  See Air Supply
Coore, Stephen
  See Third World
Cope, Julian **16**
Copeland, Stewart **14**
  Also see Police, The
Copland, Aaron **2**
Copley, Al
  See Roomful of Blues
Corea, Chick **6**
Corella, Doug
  See Verve Pipe, The
Corgan, Billy
  See Smashing Pumpkins
Corina, Sarah
  See Mekons, The
Cornelius, Robert
  See Poi Dog Pondering
Cornell, Chris
  See Soundgarden
Cornershop **24**
Cornick, Glenn
  See Jethro Tull
Corrigan, Brianna
  See Beautiful South
Cosper, Kina
  See Brownstone
Costello, Elvis **12**
  Earlier sketch in CM **2**
Coté, Billy
  See Madder Rose
Cotoia, Robert
  See Beaver Brown Band, The
Cotrubas, Ileana **1**
Cotten, Elizabeth **16**
Cotton, Caré
  See Sounds of Blackness
Cougar, John(ny)
  See Mellencamp, John
Coughlan, Richard
  See Caravan
Counting Crows **18**
Country Gentlemen, The **7**
Coury, Fred
  See Cinderella
Coutts, Duncan
  See Our Lady Peace
Coverdale, David
  See Whitesnake **5**
Cowan, John
  See New Grass Revival, The
Cowboy Junkies, The **4**
Cox, Andy
  See English Beat, The
  Also see Fine Young Cannibals
Cox, Terry
  See Pentangle
Coxon, Graham
  See Blur

Coyne, Mark
  See Flaming Lips
Coyne, Wayne
  See Flaming Lips
Cracker **12**
Craig, Albert
  See Israel Vibration
Craig, Carl **19**
Crain, S. R.
  See Soul Stirrers, The
Cramps, The **16**
Cranberries, The **14**
Crash Test Dummies **14**
Crawford, Dave Max
  See Poi Dog Pondering
Crawford, Da'dra
  See Anointed
Crawford, Ed
  See fIREHOSE
Crawford, Michael **4**
Crawford, Steve
  See Anointed
Cray, Robert **8**
Creach, Papa John
  See Jefferson Starship
Cream **9**
Creedence Clearwater Revival **16**
Creegan, Andrew
  See Barenaked Ladies
Creegan, Jim
  See Barenaked Ladies
Crenshaw, Marshall **5**
Cretu, Michael
  See Enigma
Criss, Peter
  See Kiss
Crissinger, Roger
  See Pearls Before Swine
Croce, Jim **3**
Crofts, Dash
  See Seals & Crofts
Cronin, Kevin
  See REO Speedwagon
Cropper, Steve
  See Booker T. & the M.G.'s
Cropper, Steve **12**
Crosby, Bing **6**
Crosby, David **3**
  See Byrds, The
  Also see Crosby, Stills, and Nash
Crosby, Stills, and Nash **24**
Cross, Bridget
  See Velocity Girl
Cross, David
  See King Crimson
Cross, Mike
  See Sponge
Cross, Tim
  See Sponge
Crouch, Andraé **9**
Crover, Dale
  See Melvins
Crow, Sheryl **18**
Crowded House **12**

Crowe, J. D. **5**
Crowell, Rodney **8**
Crowley, Martin
  See Bevis Frond
Cruikshank, Gregory
  See Tuxedomoon
Cruz, Celia **22**
  Earlier sketch in CM **10**
Cuddy, Jim
  See Blue Rodeo
Cugat, Xavier **23**
Cult, The **16**
Cumming, Graham
  See Bevis Frond
Cummings, Burton
  See Guess Who
Cummings, Danny
  See Dire Straits
Cummings, David
  See Del Amitri
Cunningham, Abe
  See Deftones
Cunningham, Ruth
  See Anonymous 4
Cuomo, Rivers
  See Weezer
Cure, The **20**
  Earlier sketch in CM **3**
Curless, Ann
  See Exposé
Curley, John
  See Afghan Whigs
Curran, Ciaran
  See Altan
Currie, Justin
  See Del Amitri
Currie, Steve
  See T. Rex
Curry, Tim **3**
Curtis, Ian
  See Joy Division
Curtis, King **17**
Curve **13**
Custance, Mickey
  See Big Audio Dynamite
Cuthbert, Scott
  See Everclear
Cutler, Chris
  See Pere Ubu
Cypress Hill **11**
Cyrus, Billy Ray **11**
D'Angelo **20**
Dacus, Donnie
  See Chicago
Dacus, Johnny
  See Osborne Brothers, The
Daddy G
  See Massive Attack
Daddy Mack
  See Kris Kross
Daellenbach, Charles
  See Canadian Brass, The
Dahlheimer, Patrick
  See Live

Daisley, Bob
  See Black Sabbath
Dale, Dick **13**
Daley, Richard
  See Third World
Dall, Bobby
  See Poison
Dallin, Sarah
  See Bananarama
Dalton, John
  See Kinks, The
Dalton, Nic
  See Lemonheads, The
Daltrey, Roger **3**
  Also see Who, The
Dammers, Jerry
  See Specials, The
Dando, Evan
  See Lemonheads, The
Dandy Warhols **22**
Danell, Dennis
  See Social Distortion
D'Angelo, Greg
  See Anthrax
Daniels, Charlie **6**
Daniels, Jack
  See Highway 101
Daniels, Jerry
  See Ink Spots
Danko, Rick
  See Band, The
Danny Boy
  See House of Pain
Danzig **7**
Danzig, Glenn
  See Danzig
D'Arby, Terence Trent **3**
Darin, Bobby **4**
Darling, Eric
  See Weavers, The
Darriau, Matt
  See Klezmatics, The
Darvill, Benjamin
  See Crash Test Dummies
Das EFX **14**
Daugherty, Jay Dee
  See Church, The
Daulne, Marie
  See Zap Mama
Dave, Doggy
  See Lords of Acid
Dave Clark Five, The **12**
Dave Matthews Band **18**
Davenport, N'Dea
  See Brand New Heavies, The
Davidson, Lenny
  See Dave Clark Five, The
Davie, Hutch
  See Pearls Before Swine
Davies, Dave
  See Kinks, The
Davies, James
  See Jimmie's Chicken Shack

Davies, Ray **5**
  Also see Kinks, The
Davies, Saul
  See James
Davies, Dennis Russell **24**
Davis, Anthony **17**
Davis, Brad
  See Fu Manchu
Davis, Chip **4**
Davis, Clive **14**
Davis, Gregory
  See Dirty Dozen
Davis, John
  See Superdrag
Davis, Jonathan
  See Korn
Davis, Linda **21**
Davis, Michael
  See MC5, The
Davis, Miles **1**
Davis, Reverend Gary **18**
Davis, Sammy, Jr. **4**
Davis, Santa
  See Big Mountain
Davis, Skeeter **15**
Davis, Spencer
  See Spencer Davis Group
Davis, Steve
  See Mystic Revealers
Davis, Zelma
  See C + C Music Factory
Davis, Jody
  See Newsboys, The
Dawdy, Cheryl
  See Chenille Sisters, The
Day, Doris **24**
Dayne, Taylor **4**
dc Talk **18**
de Albuquerque, Michael
  See Electric Light Orchestra
De Borg, Jerry
  See Jesus Jones
Deacon, John
  See Queen
Dead Can Dance **16**
Dead Milkmen **22**
Deakin, Paul
  See Mavericks, The
Deal, Kelley
  See Breeders
Deal, Kim
  See Breeders
  Also see Pixies, The
Dean, Billy **19**
DeBarge, El **14**
de Burgh, Chris **22**
de Coster, Jean Paul
  See 2 Unlimited
Dee, Mikkey
  See Dokken
  Also see Motörhead
Deee-lite **9**
Deep Forest **18**
Deep Purple **11**

Def Leppard **3**
Deftones **22**
DeGarmo, Chris
  See Queensryche
de Grassi, Alex **6**
Deibert, Adam Warren
  See Aquabats
Deily, Ben
  See Lemonheads, The
DeJohnette, Jack **7**
Del Rubio Triplets **21**
Delaet, Nathalie
  See Lords of Acid
De La Soul **7**
DeLeo, Dean
  See Stone Temple Pilots
DeLeo, Robert
  See Stone Temple Pilots
De La Luna, Shai
  See Lords of Acid
de la Rocha, Zack
  See Rage Against the Machine
DeLorenzo, Victor
  See Violent Femmes
Del Amitri **18**
Del Mar, Candy
  See Cramps, The
Delp, Brad
  See Boston
de Lucia, Paco **1**
DeMent, Iris **13**
Demento, Dr. **23**
Demeski, Stanley
  See Luna
De Meyer, Jean-Luc
  See Front 242
Demos, Greg
  See Guided By Voices
Dempsey, Michael
  See Cure, The
Denison, Duane
  See Jesus Lizard
Dennis, Garth
  See Black Uhuru
Denny, Sandy
  See Fairport Convention
Densmore, John
  See Doors, The
Dent, Cedric
  See Take 6
Denton, Sandy
  See Salt-N-Pepa
Denver, John **22**
  Earlier sketch in CM **1**
De Oliveria, Laudir
  See Chicago
Depeche Mode **5**
de Prume, Ivan
  See White Zombie
Derosier, Michael
  See Heart
Desaulniers, Stephen
  See Scud Mountain Boys

Deschamps, Kim
  See Blue Rodeo
Desert Rose Band, The **4**
Desmond, Paul **23**
Des'ree **24**
  Earlier sketch in CM **15**
Destri, Jimmy
  See Blondie
Deupree, Jerome
  See Morphine
Deutrom, Mark
  See Melvins
DeVille, C. C.
  See Poison
Devito, Tommy
  See Four Seasons, The
Devo **13**
Devoto, Howard
  See Buzzcocks, The
DeWitt, Lew C.
  See Statler Brothers, The
de Young, Joyce
  See Andrews Sisters, The
Dexter X
  See Man or Astroman?
Diagram, Andy
  See James
Diamond "Dimebag" Darrell
  See Pantera
Diamond, Mike
  See Beastie Boys, The
Diamond, Neil **1**
Diamond Rio **11**
Di'anno, Paul
  See Iron Maiden
Dibango, Manu **14**
Dickens, Little Jimmy **7**
Dickerson, B.B.
  See War
Dickinson, Paul Bruce
  See Iron Maiden
Dickinson, Rob
  See Catherine Wheel
Diddley, Bo **3**
Diffie, Joe **10**
Difford, Chris
  See Squeeze
DiFranco, Ani **17**
Digable Planets **15**
Diggle, Steve
  See Buzzcocks, The
Diggs, Robert
  See Gravediggaz
Digital Underground **9**
DiMant, Leor
  See House of Pain
Di Meola, Al **12**
DiMucci, Dion
  See Dion
DiNizo, Pat
  See Smithereens, The
Dilworth, Joe
  See Stereolab

Dinning, Dean
  See Toad the Wet Sprocket
Dinosaur Jr. **10**
Dio, Ronnie James
  See Black Sabbath
Dion **4**
Dion, Céline **12**
Dire Straits **22**
Dirks, Michael
  See Gwar
Dirnt, Mike
  See Green Day
Dirty Dozen **23**
Dittrich, John
  See Restless Heart
Dixon, George W.
  See Spinners, The
Dixon, Jerry
  See Warrant
Dixon, Willie **10**
DJ Domination
  See Geto Boys, The
DJ Fuse
  See Digital Underground
DJ Jazzy Jeff and the Fresh Prince **5**
D.J. Lethal
  See House of Pain
D.J. Minutemix
  See P.M. Dawn
DJ Muggs
  See Cypress Hill
DJ Premier
  See Gang Starr
DJ Ready Red
  See Geto Boys, The
DJ Terminator X
  See Public Enemy
Doc Pomus **14**
Doe, John
  See X
Dogbowl
  See King Missile
Dog's Eye View **21**
Doherty, Denny
  See Mamas and the Papas
Dokken **16**
Dokken, Don
  See Dokken
Dolby, Monica Mimi
  See Brownstone
Dolby, Thomas **10**
Dolenz, Micky
  See Monkees, The
Dombroski, Vinnie
  See Sponge
Domingo, Placido **20**
  Earlier sketch in CM **1**
Dominici, Charlie
  See Dream Theater
Domino, Fats **2**
Donahue, Jerry
  See Fairport Convention
Donahue, Jonathan
  See Flaming Lips

Donald, Tony
  See Simple Minds
Donelly, Tanya
  See Belly
  Also see Breeders
  Also see Throwing Muses
Donohue, Tim
  See Cherry Poppin' Daddies
Dorough, Bob
  See Pearls Before Swine
Dott, Gerald
  See Incredible String Band
Doughty, Neal
  See REO Speedwagon
Dream Theater **23**
Droge, Pete **24**
Dufresne, Mark
  See Confederate Railroad
Duggan, Noel
  See Clannad
Duggan, Paidraig
  See Clannad
Duke, John
  See Pearls Before Swine
Duncan, Gary
  See Quicksilver Messenger Service
Dunn, Donald "Duck"
  See Booker T. & the M.G.'s
Dupree, Jimmy
  See Jackyl
Donovan **9**
Donovan, Bazil
  See Blue Rodeo
Don, Rasa
  See Arrested Development
Doobie Brothers, The **3**
Doodlebug
  See Digable Planets
Doors, The **4**
Dorge, Michel (Mitch)
  See Crash Test Dummies
Dorney, Tim
  See Republica
Dorough, Howie
  See Backstreet Boys
Dorsey, Jimmy
  See Dorsey Brothers, The
Dorsey, Thomas A. **11**
Dorsey, Tommy
  See Dorsey Brothers, The
Dorsey Brothers, The **8**
Doth, Anita
  See 2 Unlimited
Doucet, Michael **8**
Doughty, M.
  See Soul Coughing
Douglas, Jerry
  See Country Gentlemen, The
Dowd, Christopher
  See Fishbone
Dowling, Dave
  See Jimmie's Chicken Shack
Downes, Geoff
  See Yes

Downey, Brian
  See Thin Lizzy
Downie, Gordon
  See Tragically Hip, The
Downing, K. K.
  See Judas Priest
Doyle, Candida
  See Pulp
Dozier, Lamont
  See Holland-Dozier-Holland
Drake, Nick **17**
Drake, Steven
  See Odds
Drayton, Leslie
  See Earth, Wind and Fire
Dr. Dre **15**
  Also see N.W.A.
Dreja, Chris
  See Yardbirds, The
Drew, Dennis
  See 10,000 Maniacs
Dr. John **7**
Drozd, Stephen
  See Flaming Lips
Drumbago,
  See Skatalites, The
Drumdini, Harry
  See Cramps, The
Drummond, Don
  See Skatalites, The
Drummond, Tom
  See Better Than Ezra
Dryden, Spencer
  See Jefferson Airplane
Dubbe, Berend
  See Bettie Serveert
Dube, Lucky **17**
Dubstar **22**
Dudley, Anne
  See Art of Noise
Duffey, John
  See Country Gentlemen, The
  Also see Seldom Scene, The
Duffy, Billy
  See Cult, The
Duffy, Martin
  See Primal Scream
Dukowski, Chuck
  See Black Flag
Dulli, Greg
  See Afghan Whigs
Dumont, Tom
  See No Doubt
Dunbar, Aynsley
  See Jefferson Starship
  Also see Journey
  Also see Whitesnake
Dunbar, Sly
  See Sly and Robbie
Duncan, Bryan **19**
Duncan, Steve
  See Desert Rose Band, The
Duncan, Stuart
  See Nashville Bluegrass Band

Dunlap, Slim
  See Replacements, The
Dunn, Holly **7**
Dunn, Larry
  See Earth, Wind and Fire
Dunn, Ronnie
  See Brooks & Dunn
Dunning, A.J.
  See Verve Pipe, The
Dupree, Champion Jack **12**
Duran Duran **4**
Durante, Mark
  See KMFDM
Duritz, Adam
  See Counting Crows
Durrill, Johnny
  See Ventures, The
Dutt, Hank
  See Kronos Quartet
Dyble, Judy
  See Fairport Convention
Dylan, Bob **21**
  Earlier sketch in CM **3**
Dylan, Jakob
  See Wallflowers, The
D'Amour, Paul
  See Tool
E., Sheila
  See Sheila E.
Eacrett, Chris
  See Our Lady Peace
Eagles, The **3**
Earl, Ronnie **5**
  Also see Roomful of Blues
Earle, Steve
  See Afghan Whigs
Earle, Steve **16**
Early, Ian
  See Cherry Poppin' Daddies
Earth, Wind and Fire **12**
Easton, Elliot
  See Cars, The
Easton, Sheena **2**
Eazy-E **13**
  Also see N.W.A.
Echeverria, Rob
  See Helmet
Echobelly **21**
Eckstine, Billy **1**
Eddy, Duane **9**
Eden, Sean
  See Luna
Edge, Graeme
  See Moody Blues, The
Edge, The
  See U2
Edmonds, Kenneth "Babyface" **12**
Edmonton, Jerry
  See Steppenwolf
Edwards, Dennis
  See Temptations, The
Edwards, Edgar
  See Spinners, The

Edwards, Gordon
  See Kinks, The
Edwards, John
  See Spinners , The
Edwards, Johnny
  See Foreigner
Edwards, Leroy "Lion"
  See Mystic Revealers
Edwards, Mark
  See Aztec Camera
Edwards, Michael James
  See Jesus Jones
Edwards, Mike
  See Electric Light Orchestra
Edwards, Nokie
  See Ventures, The
Efrem, Towns
  See Dirty Dozen
Ehran
  See Lords of Acid
Eid, Tamer
  See Emmet Swimming
Einheit
  See Einstürzende Neubauten
Einheit, F.M.
  See KMFDM
Einstürzende Neubauten **13**
Einziger, Michael
  See Incubus
Eisenstein, Michael
  See Letters to Cleo
Eitzel, Mark
  See American Music Club
Ekberg, Ulf
  See Ace of Base
Eklund, Greg
  See Everclear
El-Hadi, Sulieman
  See Last Poets
Eldon, Thór
  See Sugarcubes, The
Eldridge, Ben
  See Seldom Scene, The
Eldridge, Roy **9**
  Also see McKinney's Cotton Pickers
Electric Light Orchestra **7**
Elfman, Danny **9**
Elias, Manny
  See Tears for Fears
Ellefson, Dave
  See Megadeth
Ellington, Duke **2**
Elliot, Cass **5**
Elliot, Joe
  See Def Leppard
Elliott, Cass
  See Mamas and the Papas
Elliott, Dennis
  See Foreigner
Elliott, Doug
  See Odds
Ellis, Bobby
  See Skatalites, The
Ellis, Herb **18**

Ellis, Terry
  See En Vogue
ELO
  See Electric Light Orchestra
Ellis, Arti
  See Pearls Before Swine
Elmore, Greg
  See Quicksilver Messenger Service
Ely, John
  See Asleep at the Wheel
Ely, Vince
  See Cure, The
Emerson, Bill
  See Country Gentlemen, The
Emerson, Keith
  See Emerson, Lake & Palmer/Powell
Emerson, Lake & Palmer/Powell **5**
Emery, Jill
  See Hole
Emmanuel, Tommy **21**
Emmet Swimming **24**
English, Richard
  See Flaming Lips
English Beat, The **9**
English, Michael **23**
Enigma **14**
Eno, Brian **8**
Enos, Bob
  See Roomful of Blues
Enright, Pat
  See Nashville Bluegrass Band
Entwistle, John
  See Who, The
En Vogue **10**
Enya **6**
EPMD **10**
Erasure **11**
Eric B.
  See Eric B. and Rakim
Eric B. and Rakim **9**
Erickson, Roky **16**
Erlandson, Eric
  See Hole
Errico, Greg
  See Quicksilver Messenger Service
Errico, Greg
  See Sly & the Family Stone
Erskine, Peter
  See Weather Report
Ertegun, Ahmet **10**
Ertegun, Nesuhi **24**
Esch, En
  See KMFDM
Escovedo, Alejandro **18**
Eshe, Montsho
  See Arrested Development
Eskelin, Ian **19**
Esler-Smith, Frank
  See Air Supply
Esquivel, Juan **17**
Estefan, Gloria **15**
  Earlier sketch in CM **2**
Estrada, Roy
  See Little Feat

Etheridge, Melissa **16**
  Earlier sketch in CM **4**
Eurythmics **6**
Evan, John
  See Jethro Tull
Evans, Bill **17**
Evans, Dick
  See U2
Evans, Gil **17**
Evans, Mark
  See AC/DC
Evans, Shane
  See Collective Soul
Evans, Tom
  See Badfinger
Everclear **18**
Everlast
  See House of Pain
Everly Brothers, The **2**
Everly, Don
  See Everly Brothers, The
Everly, Phil
  See Everly Brothers, The
Everman, Jason
  See Soundgarden
Everything But The Girl **15**
Evora, Cesaria **19**
Ewen, Alvin
  See Steel Pulse
Exkano, Paul
  See Five Blind Boys of Alabama
Exposé **4**
Extreme **10**
Ezell, Ralph
  See Shenandoah
Fabian **5**
Fabulous Thunderbirds, The **1**
Faces, The **22**
Fadden, Jimmie
  See Nitty Gritty Dirt Band, The
Fagan, Don
  See Steely Dan
Fahey, John **17**
Fahey, Siobhan
  See Bananarama
Fairport Convention **22**
Fairs, Jim
  See Pearls Before Swine
Faithfull, Marianne **14**
Faith No More **7**
Fakir, Abdul "Duke"
  See Four Tops, The
Falconer, Earl
  See UB40
Fall, The **12**
Fallon, David
  See Chieftains, The
Fankhauser, Merrell **24**
Fink, Jr., Rat
  See Alien Sex Fiend
Fisher, Brandon
  See Superdrag
Flannery, Sean
  See Cherry Poppin' Daddies

Fleming, Renee **24**
Forbes, Graham
  See Incredible String Band
Forsi, Ken
  See Surfaris, The
Four Seasons, The **24**
FourHim **23**
Foxwell Baker, Iain Richard
  See Jesus Jones
Frankenstein, Jeff
  See Newsboys, The
Frankie Lymon and The Teenagers **24**
Fredriksson, Marie
  See Roxette
Freiberg, David
  See Quicksilver Messenger Service
Freshwater, John
  See Alien Sex Fiend
Fuller, Jim
  See Surfaris, The
Fuqua, Charlie
  See Ink Spots
Furay, Richie
  See Buffalo Springfield
Furler, Peter
  See Newsboys, The
Fältskog, Agnetha
  See Abba
Fambrough, Henry
  See Spinners, The
Farley, J. J.
  See Soul Stirrers, The
Farndon, Pete
  See Pretenders, The
Farrar, Jay
  See Son Volt
Farrar, John
  See Shadows, The
Farrell, Perry
  See Jane's Addiction
Farris, Dionne
  See Arrested Development
Farris, Tim
  See Israel Vibration
Farriss, Andrew
  See INXS
Farriss, Jon
  See INXS
Farriss, Tim
  See INXS
Fatboy Slim **22**
Fay, Johnny
  See Tragically Hip, The
Fay, Martin
  See Chieftains, The
Fearnley, James
  See Pogues, The
Fehlmann, Thomas
  See Orb, The
Feinstein, Michael **6**
Fela
  See Kuti, Fela
Felber, Dean
  See Hootie and the Blowfish

Felder, Don
  See Eagles, The
Feldman, Eric Drew
  See Pere Ubu
Feliciano, José **10**
Fender, Freddy
  See Texas Tornados, The
Fender, Leo **10**
Fennell, Kevin
  See Guided By Voices
Fennelly, Gere
  See Redd Kross
Fenwick, Ray
  See Spencer Davis Group
Ferguson, Jay
  See Spirit
Ferguson, Keith
  See Fabulous Thunderbirds, The
Ferguson, Maynard **7**
Ferguson, Neil
  See Chumbawamba
Ferguson, Steve
  See NRBQ
Ferrell, Rachelle **17**
Ferrer, Frank
  See Love Spit Love
Ferry, Bryan **1**
Ficca, Billy
  See Television
Fiedler, Arthur **6**
Fielder, Jim
  See Blood, Sweat and Tears
Fields, Johnny
  See Five Blind Boys of Alabama
Fier, Anton
  See Pere Ubu
Finch, Jennifer
  See L7
Finer, Jem
  See Pogues, The
Fine Young Cannibals **22**
Finn, Micky
  See T. Rex
Finn, Neil
  See Crowded House
Finn, Tim
  See Crowded House
fIREHOSE **11**
Fishbone **7**
Fisher, Eddie **12**
Fisher, Jerry
  See Blood, Sweat and Tears
Fisher, John "Norwood"
  See Fishbone
Fisher, Phillip "Fish"
  See Fishbone
Fisher, Roger
  See Heart
Fishman, Jon
  See Phish
Fitzgerald, Ella **1**
Fitzgerald, Kevin
  See Geraldine Fibbers
Five Blind Boys of Alabama **12**

Flack, Roberta **5**
Flaming Lips **22**
Flanagan, Tommy **16**
Flansburgh, John
  See They Might Be Giants
Flatt, Lester **3**
Flavor Flav
  See Public Enemy
Flea
  See Red Hot Chili Peppers, The
Fleck, Bela **8**
  Also see New Grass Revival, The
Fleetwood, Mick
  See Fleetwood Mac
Fleetwood Mac **5**
Fleischmann, Robert
  See Journey
Flemons, Wade
  See Earth, Wind and Fire
Flesh-N-Bone
  See Bone Thugs-N-Harmony
Fletcher, Andy
  See Depeche Mode
Fletcher, Guy
  See Dire Straits
Flint, Keith
  See Prodigy
Flores, Rosie **16**
Floyd, Heather
  See Point of Grace
Flür, Wolfgang
  See Kraftwerk
Flynn, Pat
  See New Grass Revival, The
Fogelberg, Dan **4**
Fogerty, John **2**
  Also see Creedence Clearwater Revival
Fogerty, Thomas
  See Creedence Clearwater Revival
Folds, Ben
  See Ben Folds Five
Foley
  See Arrested Development
Foo Fighters **20**
Forbes, Derek
  See Simple Minds
Ford, Lita **9**
Ford, Mark
  See Black Crowes, The
Ford, Penny
  See Soul II Soul
Ford, Tennessee Ernie **3**
Fordham, Julia **15**
Foreigner **21**
Fortune, Jimmy
  See Statler Brothers, The
Fortus, Richard
  See Love Spit Love
Fossen, Steve
  See Heart
Foster, David **13**
Foster, Malcolm
  See Pretenders, The

Foster, Paul
  See Soul Stirrers, The
Foster, Radney **16**
Fountain, Clarence
  See Five Blind Boys of Alabama
Fountain, Pete **7**
Four Tops, The **11**
Fox, Lucas
  See Motörhead
Fox, Oz
  See Stryper
Fox, Samantha **3**
Frame, Roddy
  See Aztec Camera
Frampton, Peter **3**
Francis, Black
  See Pixies, The
Francis, Connie **10**
Francis, Mike
  See Asleep at the Wheel
Franke, Chris
  See Tangerine Dream
Franklin, Aretha **17**
  Earlier sketch in CM **2**
Franklin, Elmo
  See Mighty Clouds of Joy, The
Franklin, Kirk **22**
Franklin, Larry
  See Asleep at the Wheel
Franklin, Melvin
  See Temptations, The
Franti, Michael **16**
Frantz, Chris
  See Talking Heads
Fraser, Elizabeth
  See Cocteau Twins, The
Frater, Shaun
  See Fairport Convention
Frazier, Stan
  See Sugar Ray
Freese, Josh
  See Suicidal Tendencies
Frehley, Ace
  See Kiss
Freiberg, David
  See Jefferson Starship
French, Mark
  See Blue Rodeo
Freni, Mirella **14**
Frey, Glenn **3**
  Also see Eagles, The
Fricker, Sylvia
  See Ian and Sylvia
Friedman, Marty
  See Megadeth
Friel, Tony
  See Fall, The
Fripp, Robert **9**
  Also see King Crimson
Frisell, Bill **15**
Frishmann, Justine
  See Suede
Frith, Fred **19**
Frizzell, Lefty **10**

Froese, Edgar
  See Tangerine Dream
Front 242 **19**
Front Line Assembly **20**
Froom, Mitchell **15**
Frusciante, John
  See Red Hot Chili Peppers, The
Fugazi **13**
Fugees, The **17**
Fulber, Rhys
  See Front Line Assembly
Fuller, Blind Boy **20**
Fulson, Lowell **20**
Fu Manchu **22**
Fun Lovin' Criminals **20**
Furr, John
  See Treadmill Trackstar
Furuholmen, Magne
  See A-ha
Futter, Brian
  See Catherine Wheel
Gabay, Yuval
  See Soul Coughing
Gabriel, Peter **16**
  Earlier sketch in CM **2**
  Also see Genesis
Gadler, Frank
Gagliardi, Ed
  See Foreigner
Gahan, Dave
  See Depeche Mode
Gaines, Steve
  See Lynyrd Skynyrd
Gaines, Timothy
  See Stryper
Galea, Darren
  See Jamiroquai
Galás, Diamanda **16**
Gale, Melvyn
  See Electric Light Orchestra
Gallagher, Liam
  See Oasis
Gallagher, Noel
  See Oasis
Gallup, Simon
  See Cure, The
Galore, Lady
  See Lords of Acid
Galway, James **3**
Gambill, Roger
  See Kingston Trio, The
Gamble, Cheryl "Coko"
  See SWV
Gane, Tim
  See Stereolab
Gang of Four **8**
Gang Starr **13**
Gannon, Craig
  See Aztec Camera
Gano, Gordon
  See Violent Femmes
Garcia, Dean
  See Curve

Garcia, Jerry **4**
  Also see Grateful Dead, The
Garcia, Leddie
  See Poi Dog Pondering
Gardner, Carl
  See Coasters, The
Gardner, Suzi
  See L7
Garfunkel, Art **4**
  Also see Simon and Garfunkel
Garland, Judy **6**
Garnes, Sherman
  See Frankie Lymon and The Teenagers
Garrett, Peter
  See Midnight Oil
Garrett, Scott
  See Cult, The
Garrett, Amos
  See Pearls Before Swine
Garvey, Steve
  See Buzzcocks, The
Gaskill, Jerry
  See King's X
Gatton, Danny **16**
Gaudio, Bob
  See Four Seasons, The
Gaudreau, Jimmy
  See Country Gentlemen, The
Gaugh, "Bud" Floyd, IV
  See Sublime
Gavurin, David
  See Sundays, The
Gay, Marc
  See Shai
Gayden, Mac
  See Pearls Before Swine
Gaye, Marvin **4**
Gaynor, Mel
  See Simple Minds
Gayol, Rafael "Danny"
  See BoDeans
Gayle, Crystal **1**
Geary, Paul
  See Extreme
Gee, Rosco
  See Traffic
Geffen, David **8**
Geldof, Bob **9**
Genensky, Marsha
  See Anonymous 4
Genesis **4**
Gentling, Matt
  See Archers of Loaf
Gentry, Teddy Wayne
  See Alabama
George, Lowell
  See Little Feat
George, Rocky
  See Suicidal Tendencies
Georges, Bernard
  See Throwing Muses
Georgiev, Ivan
  See Tuxedomoon
Geraldine Fibbers **21**

Germano, Lisa **18**
Gerrard, Lisa
  See Dead Can Dance
Gershwin, George and Ira **11**
Gessle, Per
  See Roxette
GetoBoys, The **11**
Getz, Stan **12**
Ghost **24**
Giammalvo, Chris
  See Madder Rose
Gianni, Angelo
  See Treadmill Trackstar
Gibb, Barry
  See Bee Gees, The
Gibb, Maurice
  See Bee Gees, The
Gibb, Robin
  See Bee Gees, The
Gibbins, Mike
  See Badfinger
Gibbons, Beth
  See Portishead
Gibbons, Billy
  See ZZ Top
Gibbons, Ian
  See Kinks, The
Giblin, John
  See Simple Minds
Gibson, Debbie **1**
Gibson, Wilf
  See Electric Light Orchestra
Gibson, Bob **23**
Gibson, Deborah **24**
Gifford, Katharine
  See Stereolab
Gifford, Peter
  See Midnight Oil
Gift, Roland **3**
  Also see Fine Young Cannibals
Gilbert, Gillian
  See New Order
Gilbert, Nicole Nicci
  See Brownstone
Gilbert, Ronnie
  See Weavers, The
Gilbert, Simon
  See Suede
Giles, Michael
  See King Crimson
Gilkyson, Tony
  See X
Gill, Andy
  See Gang of Four
Gill, Janis
  See Sweethearts of the Rodeo
Gill, Johnny **20**
Gill, Pete
  See Motörhead
Gill, Vince **7**
Gillan, Ian
  See Deep Purple
Gillespie, Bobby
  See Primal Scream

Gillespie, Dizzy **6**
Gilley, Mickey **7**
Gillian, Ian
  See Black Sabbath
Gillies, Ben
  See Silverchair
Gillingham, Charles
  See Counting Crows
Gilmore, Jimmie Dale **11**
Gilmour, David
  See Pink Floyd
Gin Blossoms **18**
Gingold, Josef **6**
Ginn, Greg
  See Black Flag
Gioia
  See Exposé
Gipp, Cameron
  See Goodie Mob
Gipsy Kings, The **8**
Giraudy, Miquette
  See Gong
Gittleman, Joe
  See Mighty Mighty Bosstones
Glass, Eddie
  See Fu Manchu
Glass, Philip **1**
Glasscock, John
  See Jethro Tull
Glennie, Jim
  See James
Glitter, Gary **19**
Glover, Corey
  See Living Colour
Glover, Roger
  See Deep Purple
Go-Go's, The **24**
Gobel, Robert
  See Kool & the Gang
Godchaux, Donna
  See Grateful Dead, The
Godchaux, Keith
  See Grateful Dead, The
Goettel, Dwayne Rudolf
  See Skinny Puppy
Goffin, Gerry
  See Goffin-King
Goffin-King **24**
Gogin, Toni
  See Sleater-Kinney
Goh, Rex
  See Air Supply
Gold, Julie **22**
Golden, William Lee
  See Oak Ridge Boys, The
Golding, Lynval
  See Specials, The
Goldsmith, William
  See Foo Fighters
Goldstein, Jerry
  See War
Golson, Benny **21**
Gong **24**
Goo Goo Dolls, The **16**

Gooden, Ramone Pee Wee
  See Digital Underground
Goodie Mob **24**
Goodman, Benny **4**
Goodman, Jerry
  See Mahavishnu Orchestra
Goodridge, Robin
  See Bush
Gordon, Dexter **10**
Gordon, Dwight
  See Mighty Clouds of Joy, The
Gordon, Jim
  See Traffic
Gordon, Kim
  See Sonic Youth
Gordon, Mike
  See Phish
Gordon, Nina
  See Veruca Salt
Gordy, Berry, Jr. **6**
Gordy, Emory, Jr. **17**
Gore, Martin
  See Depeche Mode
Gorham, Scott
  See Thin Lizzy
Gorka, John **18**
Gorman, Christopher
  See Belly
Gorman, Steve
  See Black Crowes, The
Gorman, Thomas
  See Belly
Gosling, John
  See Kinks, The
Gossard, Stone
  See Brad
  Also see Pearl Jam
Gott, Larry
  See James
Goudreau, Barry
  See Boston
Gould, Billy
  See Faith No More
Gould, Glenn **9**
Gould, Morton **16**
Goulding, Steve
  See Poi Dog Pondering
Grable, Steve
  See Pearls Before Swine
Gracey, Chad
  See Live
Gradney, Ken
  See Little Feat
Graffety-Smith, Toby
  See Jamiroquai
Graham, Bill **10**
Graham, Glen
  See Blind Melon
Graham, Johnny
  See Earth, Wind and Fire
Graham, Larry
  See Sly & the Family Stone
Gramm, Lou
  See Foreigner

Gramolini, Gary
  See Beaver Brown Band, The
Grandmaster Flash **14**
Grant, Amy **7**
Grant, Bob
  See The Bad Livers
Grant Lee Buffalo **16**
Grant, Lloyd
  See Metallica
Grappelli, Stephane **10**
Grateful Dead, The **5**
Gratzer, Alan
  See REO Speedwagon
Gravatt, Eric
  See Weather Report
Gravediggaz **23**
Graves, Denyce **16**
Gray, Del
  See Little Texas
Gray, Ella
  See Kronos Quartet
Gray, F. Gary **19**
Gray, James
  See Blue Rodeo
Gray, James
  See Spearhead
Gray, Luther
  See Tsunami
Gray, Tom
  See Country Gentlemen, The
  Also see Seldom Scene, The
Gray, Walter
  See Kronos Quartet
Gray, Wardell
  See McKinney's Cotton Pickers
Grebenshikov, Boris **3**
Grech, Rick
  See Traffic
Greco, Paul
  See Chumbawamba
Green, Al **9**
Green, Benny **17**
Green, Charles
  See War
Green, David
  See Air Supply
Green Day **16**
Green, Grant **14**
Green, Karl Anthony
  See Herman's Hermits
Green, Peter
  See Fleetwood Mac
Green, Susaye
  See Supremes, The
Green, Willie
  See Neville Brothers, The
Green, Carlito
  See Goodie Mob
Greenhalgh, Tom
  See Mekons, The
Greensmith, Domenic
  See Reef
Greenspoon, Jimmy
  See Three Dog Night

Greenwood, Al
  See Foreigner
Greenwood,Colin
  See Radiohead
Greenwood, Gail
  See Belly
Greenwood, Jonny
  See Radiohead
Greenwood, Lee **12**
Greer, Jim
  See Guided By Voices
Gregg, Paul
  See Restless Heart
Gregory, Bryan
  See Cramps, The
Gregory, Dave
  See XTC
Gregory, Troy
  See Prong
Greller, Al
  See Yo La Tengo
Grey, Charles Wallace
  See Aquabats
Griffin, Bob
  See BoDeans, The
Griffin, Kevin
  See Better Than Ezra
  See NRBQ
Griffin, Mark
  See MC 900 Ft. Jesus
Griffin, Patty **24**
Griffith, Nanci **3**
Grigg, Chris
  See Treadmill Trackstar
Grisman, David **17**
Grohl, Dave
  See Nirvana
Grohl, David
  See Foo Fighters
Grotberg, Karen
  See Jayhawks, The
Groucutt, Kelly
  See Electric Light Orchestra
Grove, George
  See Kingston Trio, The
Grover, Charlie
  See Sponge
Grundy, Hugh
  See Zombies, The
Grusin, Dave **7**
Guaraldi, Vince **3**
Guard, Dave
  See Kingston Trio, The
Gudmundsdottir, Björk
  See Björk
  Also see Sugarcubes, The
Guerin, John
  See Byrds, The
Guess Who **23**
Guest, Christopher
  See Spinal Tap
Guided By Voices **18**
Gunn, Trey
  See King Crimson

Guns n' Roses **2**
Gunther, Cornell
  See Coasters, The
Gunther, Ric
  See Bevis Frond
Guru
  See Gang Starr
Guss, Randy
  See Toad the Wet Sprocket
Gustafson, Steve
  See 10,000 Maniacs
Gut, Grudrun
  See Einstürzende Neubauten
Guthrie, Arlo **6**
Guthrie, Robin
  See Cocteau Twins, The
Guthrie, Woody **2**
Guy, Billy
  See Coasters, The
Guy, Buddy **4**
Guyett, Jim
  See Quicksilver Messenger Service
Gwar **13**
Hacke, Alexander
  See Einstürzende Neubauten
Hackett, Bobby **21**
Hackett, Steve
  See Genesis
Haden, Charlie **12**
Hadjopulos, Sue
  See Simple Minds
Hagar, Regan
  See Brad
Hagar, Sammy **21**
  Also see Van Halen
Haggard, Merle **2**
Hakim, Omar
  See Weather Report
Hakmoun, Hassan **15**
Hale, Simon
  See Incognito
Haley, Bill **6**
Haley, Mark
  See Kinks, The
Halford, Rob
  See Judas Priest
Hall, Bruce
  See REO Speedwagon
Hall, Daryl
  See Hall & Oates
Hall, John S.
  See King Missile
Hall, Lance
  See Inner Circle
Hall, Randall
  See Lynyrd Skynyrd
Hall, Terry
  See Specials, The
Hall, Tom T. **4**
Hall, Tony
  See Neville Brothers, The
Hall & Oates **6**
Halliday, Toni
  See Curve

Halliwell, Geri
  See Spice Girls
Ham, Pete
  See Badfinger
Hamer, Harry
  See Chumbawamba
Hamilton, Arnold
  See Gravediggaz
Hamilton, Frank
  See Weavers, The
Hamilton, Katie
  See Treadmill Trackstar
Hamilton, Milton
  See Third World
Hamilton, Page
  See Helmet
Hamilton, Tom
  See Aerosmith
Hamilton, Tom
  See Aerosmith
Hamlisch, Marvin **1**
Hammer, Jan **21**
  Also see Mahavishnu Orchestra
Hammer, M.C. **5**
Hammerstein, Oscar
  See Rodgers, Richard
Hammett, Kirk
  See Metallica
Hammon, Ron
  See War
Hammond, John **6**
Hammond-Hammond, Jeffrey
  See Jethro Tull
Hampson, Sharon
  See Sharon, Lois & Bram
Hampson, Thomas **12**
Hampton, Lionel **6**
Hancock, Herbie **8**
Handy, W. C. **7**
Hanley, Kay
  See Letters to Cleo
Hanley, Steve
  See Fall, The
Hanna, Jeff
  See Nitty Gritty Dirt Band, The
Hanneman, Jeff
  See Slayer
Hannibal, Chauncey "Black"
  See Blackstreet
Hannon, Frank
  See Tesla
Hannan, Patrick
  See Sundays, The
Hansen, Mary
  See Stereolab
Hanson, Paul
  See Gravediggaz
Hanson **20**
Hanson, Isaac
  See Hanson
Hanson, Taylor
  See Hanson
Hanson, Zachary
  See Hanson

Hardcastle, Paul **20**
Hardin, Eddie
  See Spencer Davis Group
Hardin, Tim **18**
Harding, John Wesley **6**
Hardson, Tre "Slimkid",
  See Pharcyde, The
Hargrove, Kornell
  See Poi Dog Pondering
Hargrove, Roy **15**
Harket, Morten
  See A-ha
Harley, Bill **7**
Harley, Wayne
  See Pearls Before Swine
Harms, Jesse
  See REO Speedwagon
Harper, Ben **17**
Harper, Raymond
  See Skatalites, The
Harrell, Andre **16**
Harrell, Lynn **3**
Harrington, Carrie
  See Sounds of Blackness
Harrington, David
  See Kronos Quartet
Harris, Addie "Micki"
  See Shirelles, The
Harris, Damon Otis
  See Temptations, The
Harris, Eddie **15**
Harris, Emmylou **4**
Harris, Evelyn
  See Sweet Honey in the Rock
Harris, Gerard
  See Kool & the Gang
Harris, James
  See Echobelly
Harris, Jet
  See Shadows, The
Harris, Joey
  See Beat Farmers
Harris, Kevin
  See Dirty Dozen
Harris, Lee
  See Talk Talk
Harris, Mark
  See FourHim
Harris, Mary
  See Spearhead
Harris, R. H.
  See Soul Stirrers, The
Harris, Steve
  See Iron Maiden
Harris, Teddy **22**
Harrison, George **2**
  Also see Beatles, The
Harrison, Jerry
  See Talking Heads
Harrison, Nigel
  See Blondie
Harrison, Richard
  See Stereolab

Harry, Deborah **4**
  Also see Blondie
Hart, Chuck
  See Surfin' Pluto
Hart, Lorenz
  See Rodgers, Richard
Hart, Mark
  See Crowded House
Hart, Mickey
  See Grateful Dead, The
Hart, Robert
  See Bad Company
Hart, Tim
  See Steeleye Span
Hartford, John **1**
Hartke, Stephen **5**
Hartley, Matthieu
  See Cure, The
Hartman, Bob
  See Petra
Hartman, John
  See Doobie Brothers, The
Hartnoll, Paul
  See Orbital
Hartnoll, Phil
  See Orbital
Harvey, Bernard "Touter"
  See Inner Circle
Harvey, Philip "Daddae"
  See Soul II Soul
Harvey, Polly Jean **11**
Harvie, Iain
  See Del Amitri
Harwood, Justin
  See Luna
Haseltine, Dan
  See Jars of Clay
Hashian
  See Boston
Haskell, Gordon
  See King Crimson
Haskins, Kevin
  See Love and Rockets
Haslinger, Paul
  See Tangerine Dream
Hassan, Norman
  See UB40
Hastings, Jimmy
  See Caravan
Hastings, Pye
  See Caravan
Hatfield, Juliana **12**
  Also see Lemonheads, The
Hauser, Tim
  See Manhattan Transfer, The
Havens, Richie **11**
Hawes, Dave
  See Catherine Wheel
Hawkes, Greg
  See Cars, The
Hawkins, Coleman **11**
Hawkins, Erskine **19**
Hawkins, Nick
  See Big Audio Dynamite

Hawkins, Roger
  See Traffic
Hawkins, Screamin' Jay **8**
Hawkins, Sophie B. **21**
Hawkins, Taylor
  See Foo Fighters
Hawkins, Tramaine **17**
Hawkins, Xian
  See Silver Apples
Hay, George D. **3**
Hayes, Isaac **10**
Hayes, Roland **13**
Hayes, Gordon
  See Pearls Before Swine
Haynes, Gibby
  See Butthole Surfers
Haynes, Warren
  See Allman Brothers, The
Hays, Lee
  See Weavers, The
Hayward, David Justin
  See Moody Blues, The
Hayward, Richard
  See Little Feat
Headliner
  See Arrested Development
Headon, Topper
  See Clash, The
Healey, Jeff **4**
Heard, Paul
  See M People
Hearn, Kevin
  See Barenaked Ladies
Heart **1**
Heaton, Paul
  See Beautiful South
Heavy D **10**
Hecker, Robert
  See Redd Kross
Hedford, Eric
  See Dandy Warhols, The
Hedges, Eddie
  See Blessid Union of Souls
Hedges, Michael **3**
Heggie, Will
  See Cocteau Twins, The
Heidorn, Mike
  See Son Volt
Heitman, Dana
  See Cherry Poppin' Daddies
Helfgott, David **19**
Hell, Richard
  See Television
Hellauer, Susan
  See Anonymous 4
Hellerman, Fred
  See Weavers, The
Helm, Levon
  See Band, The
  Also see Nitty Gritty Dirt Band, The
Helmet **15**
Hemingway, Dave
  See Beautiful South

Hemmings, Paul
  See Lightning Seeds
Henderson, Andy
  See Echobelly
Henderson, Billy
  See Spinners, The
Henderson, Fletcher **16**
Henderson, Joe **14**
Hendricks, Barbara **10**
Hendrix, Jimi **2**
Henley, Don **3**
  Also see Eagles, The
Henrit, Bob
  See Kinks, The
Henry, Bill
  See Northern Lights
Henry, Joe **18**
Henry, Kent
  See Steppenwolf
Henry, Nicholas "Drummie"
  See Mystic Revealers
Hensley, Ken
  See Uriah Heep
Hepcat, Harry **23**
Heppner, Ben **23**
Herdman, Bob
  See Audio Adrenaline
Herman, Maureen
  See Babes in Toyland
Herman, Tom
  See Pere Ubu
Herman, Woody **12**
Herman's Hermits **5**
Herndon, Mark Joel
  See Alabama
Herndon, Ty **20**
Heron, Mike
  See Incredible String Band
Herrera, R. J.
  See Suicidal Tendencies
Herrlin, Anders
  See Roxette
Herrmann, Bernard **14**
Herron, Cindy
  See En Vogue
Hersh, Kristin
  See Throwing Muses
Hester, Paul
  See Crowded House
Hetfield, James
  See Metallica
Hetson, Greg
  See Circle Jerks, The
Hewson, Paul
  See U2
Hexum, Nick
  See 311
Hiatt, John **8**
Hickman, Johnny
  See Cracker
Hicks, Chris
  See Restless Heart
Hicks, Sheree
  See C + C Music Factory

Hidalgo, David
  See Los Lobos
Higgins, Jimmy
  See Altan
Higgins, Terence
  See Dirty Dozen
Highway 101 **4**
Hijbert, Fritz
  See Kraftwerk
Hill, Brendan
  See Blues Traveler
Hill, Dusty
  See ZZ Top
Hill, Faith **18**
Hill, Ian
  See Judas Priest
Hill, Lauryn "L"
  See Fugees, The
Hill, Scott
  See Fu Manchu
Hill, Stuart
  See Shudder to Think
Hillage, Steve
  See Orb, The
Hillage, Steve
  See Gong
Hillier, Steve
  See Dubstar
Hillman, Bones
  See Midnight Oil
Hillman, Chris
  See Byrds, The
  Also see Desert Rose Band, The
Hinderas, Natalie **12**
Hinds, David
  See Steel Pulse
Hines, Earl "Fatha" **12**
Hines, Gary
  See Sounds of Blackness
Hinojosa, Tish **13**
Hirst, Rob
  See Midnight Oil
Hirt, Al **5**
Hitchcock, Robyn **9**
Hitchcock, Russell
  See Air Supply
Hitt, Bryan
  See REO Speedwagon
Hodges, Johnny **24**
Hodo, David
  See Village People, The
Hoenig, Michael
  See Tangerine Dream
Hoffman, Guy
  See BoDeans, The
  Also see Violent Femmes
Hoffman, Kristian
  See Congo Norvell
Hoffs, Susanna
  See Bangles
Hogan, Mike
  See Cranberries, The
Hogan, Noel
  See Cranberries, The

Hoke, Jim
  See NRBQ
Holder, Gene
  See Yo La Tengo
Hole **14**
Holiday, Billie **6**
Holland, Brian
  See Holland-Dozier-Holland
Holland, Bryan "Dexter"
  See Offspring
Holland, Dave
  See Judas Priest
Holland, Eddie
  See Holland-Dozier-Holland
Holland, Julian "Jools"
  See Squeeze
Holland-Dozier-Holland **5**
Hollis, Mark
  See Talk Talk
Hollister, Dave
  See Blackstreet
Holly, Buddy **1**
Holmes, Malcolm
  See Orchestral Manoeuvres in the Dark
Holmstrom, Peter
  See Dandy Warhols, The
Holt, David Lee
  See Mavericks, The
Honeyman, Susie
  See Mekons, The
Honeyman-Scott, James
  See Pretenders, The
Hood, David
  See Traffic
Hook, Peter
  See Joy Division
  Also see New Order
Hooker, John Lee **1**
Hoon, Shannon
  See Blind Melon
Hooper, Nellee
  See Soul II Soul
  Also see Massive Attack
Hooters **20**
Hootie and the Blowfish **18**
Hope, Gavin
  See Nylons, The
Hopkins, Doug
  See Gin Blossoms
Hopkins, Lightnin' **13**
Hopkins, Nicky
  See Quicksilver Messenger Service
Hopwood, Keith
  See Herman's Hermits
Horn, Shirley **7**
Horn, Trevor
  See Yes
Horne, Lena **11**
Horne, Marilyn **9**
Horner, Jessica
  See Less Than Jake
Hornsby, Bruce **3**
Horovitz, Adam
  See Beastie Boys, The

Horowitz, Vladimir **1**
Horton, Jeff
  See Northern Lights
Horton, Walter **19**
Hossack, Michael
  See Doobie Brothers, The
Houari, Rachid
  See Gong
House, Kenwyn
  See Reef
House, Son **11**
House of Pain **14**
Houston, Cissy **6**
Houston, Whitney **8**
Howard, Harlan **15**
Howe, Brian
  See Bad Company
Howe, Steve
  See Yes
Howell, Porter
  See Little Texas
Howlett, Liam
  See Prodigy
Howland, Don **24**
Howlett, Mike
  See Gong
Howlin' Wolf **6**
H.R.
  See Bad Brains
Hubbard, Greg "Hobie"
  See Sawyer Brown
Hubbard, Preston
  See Fabulous Thunderbirds, The
  Also see Roomful of Blues
Huber, Connie
  See Chenille Sisters, The
Hubrey, Georgia
  See Yo La Tengo
Hudson, Earl
  See Bad Brains
Hudson, Garth
  See Band, The
Huffman, Doug
  See Boston
Hughes, Bruce
  See Cracker
Hughes, Glenn
  See Black Sabbath
Hughes, Glenn
  See Village People, The
Hughes, Leon
  See Coasters, The
Human League, The **17**
Humes, Helen **19**
Humperdinck, Engelbert **19**
Humphreys, Paul
  See Orchestral Manoeuvres in the Dark
Hunt, Darryl
  See Pogues, The
Hunter, Alberta **7**
Hunter, Mark
  See James
Hunter, Shepherd "Ben"
  See Soundgarden

Hunter, Charlie **24**
Hurley, George
  See fIREHOSE
Hurst, Ron
  See Steppenwolf
Hurt, Mississippi John **24**
Hutchence, Michael
  See INXS
Hutchings, Ashley
  See Fairport Convention
  Also see Steeleye Span
Huth, Todd
  See Primus
Hyatt, Aitch
  See Specials, The
Hyde, Michael
  See Big Mountain
Hyman, Rob
  See Hooters
Hyslop, Kenny
  See Simple Minds
Hütter, Ralf
  See Kraftwerk
Hutton, Danny
  See Three Dog Night
Huxley, Rick
  See Dave Clark Five, The
Hyman, Jerry
  See Blood, Sweat and Tears
Hynde, Chrissie
  See Pretenders, The
Ian, Janis **5**
Ian, Scott
  See Anthrax
Ian and Sylvia **18**
Ian, Janis **24**
Ibbotson, Jimmy
  See Nitty Gritty Dirt Band, The
Ibold, Mark
  See Pavement
Ibrahim, Abdullah **24**
Ice Cube **10**
  Also see N.W.A
Ice-T **7**
Idol, Billy **3**
Iglesias, Julio **20**
  Earlier sketch in CM **2**
Iha, James
  See Smashing Pumpkins
Ike and Tina Turner **24**
Illsley, John
  See Dire Straits
Incognito **16**
Incredible String Band **23**
Incubus **23**
Indigo Girls **20**
  Earlier sketch in CM **3**
Inez, Mike
  See Alice in Chains
Infante, Frank
  See Blondie
Ingram, Jack
  See Incredible String Band
Ingram, James **11**

Ink Spots **23**
Inner Circle **15**
Innes, Andrew
  See Primal Scream
Innis, Dave
  See Restless Heart
Insane Clown Posse **22**
Interior, Lux
  See Cramps, The
INXS **21**
  Earlier sketch in CM **2**
Iommi, Tony
  See Black Sabbath
Iron Maiden **10**
Irons, Jack
  See Red Hot Chili Peppers, The
Isaak, Chris **6**
Isacsson, Jonas
  See Roxette
Isham, Mark **14**
Isles, Bill
  See O'Jays, The
Isley, Ernie
  See Isley Brothers, The
Isley, Marvin
  See Isley Brothers, The
Isley, O'Kelly, Jr.
  See Isley Brothers, The
Isley, Ronald
  See Isley Brothers, The
Isley, Rudolph
  See Isley Brothers, The
Isley Brothers, The **8**
Israel Vibration **21**
Ives, Burl **12**
Ivey, Michael
  See Basehead
Ivins, Michael
  See Flaming Lips
J.
  See White Zombie
J, David
  See Love and Rockets
Jabs, Matthias
  See Scorpions, The
Jackson, Al
  See Booker T. & the M.G.'s
Jackson, Alan **7**
Jackson, Eddie
  See Queensryche
Jackson, Freddie **3**
Jackson, Jackie
  See Jacksons, The
Jackson, Janet **16**
  Earlier sketch in CM **3**
Jackson, Jermaine
  See Jacksons, The
Jackson, Joe **22**
  Earlier sketch in CM **4**
Jackson, Karen
  See Supremes, The
Jackson, Mahalia **8**
Jackson, Marlon
  See Jacksons, The

Jackson, Michael **17**
  Earlier sketch in CM **1**
  Also see Jacksons, The
Jackson, Millie **14**
Jackson, Milt **15**
Jackson, Pervis
  See Spinners , The
Jackson, Randy
  See Jacksons, The
Jackson, Tito
  See Jacksons, The
Jackson 5, The
  See Jacksons, The
Jacksons, The **7**
Jackyl **24**
Jacobs, Christian Richard
  See Aquabats
Jacobs, Jeff
  See Foreigner
Jacobs, Parker
  See Aquabats
Jacobs, Walter
  See Little Walter
Jacox, Martin
  See Soul Stirrers, The
Jacquet, Illinois **17**
Jade 4U
  See Lords of Acid
Jaffee, Rami
  See Wallflowers, The
Jagger, Mick
  See Rolling Stones, The
Jagger, Mick **7**
  Also see Rolling Stones, The
Jairo T.
  See Sepultura
Jalal
  See Last Poets
Jam, Jimmy
  See Jam, Jimmy, and Terry Lewis
Jam, Jimmy, and Terry Lewis **11**
Jam Master Jay
  See Run-D.M.C.
James **12**
James, Alex
  See Blur
James, Andrew "Bear"
  See Midnight Oil
James, Boney **21**
James, Cheryl
  See Salt-N-Pepa
James, David
  See Alien Sex Fiend
James, David
  See Spearhead
James, Doug
  See Roomful of Blues
James, Elmore **8**
James, Etta **6**
James, Harry **11**
James, Onieda
  See Spearhead
James, Richard
  See Aphex Twin

James, Rick **2**
James, Ruby
  See Aztec Camera
James, Sylvia
  See Aztec Camera
James, Jesse
  See Jackyl
James, Skip **24**
James, John
  See Newsboys, The
Jamiroquai **21**
Jamison, Le Le
  See Spearhead
Jane's Addiction **6**
Janovitz, Bill
  See Buffalo Tom
Jansch, Bert
  See Pentangle
Jardine, Al
  See Beach Boys, The
Jarman, Joseph
  See Art Ensemble of Chicago, The
Jarobi
  See Tribe Called Quest, A
Jarre, Jean-Michel **2**
Jarreau, Al **1**
Jarrett, Irwin
  See Third World
Jarrett, Keith **1**
Jars of Clay **20**
Jasper, Chris
  See Isley Brothers, The
Jaworski, Al
  See Jesus Jones
Jay, Miles
  See Village People, The
Jayhawks, The **15**
Jayson, Mackie
  See Bad Brains
Jazzie B
  See Soul II Soul
Jean, Wyclef **22**
 Also see Fugees, The
Jeanrenaud, Joan Dutcher
  See Kronos Quartet
Jeczalik, Jonathan
  See Art of Noise
Jefferson, Blind Lemon **18**
Jefferson Airplane **5**
Jefferson Starship
  See Jefferson Airplane
Jemmott, Gerald
  See Pearls Before Swine
Jenifer, Darryl
  See Bad Brains
Jenkins, Barry
  See Animals
Jennings, Greg
  See Restless Heart
Jennings, Waylon **4**
Jensen, Ingrid **22**
Jerry, Jah
  See Skatalites, The

Jessee, Darren
  See Ben Folds Five
Jessie, Young
  See Coasters, The
Jesus Jones **23**
Jesus and Mary Chain, The **10**
Jesus Lizard **19**
Jethro Tull **8**
Jett, Joan **3**
Jimenez, Flaco
  See Texas Tornados, The
Jimmie's Chicken Shack **22**
Joannou, Chris
  See Silverchair
Jobim, Antonio Carlos **19**
Jobson, Edwin
  See Jethro Tull
Jodeci **13**
Joel, Billy **12**
  Earlier sketch in CM **2**
Joel, Phil
  See Newsboys, The
Johansen, David
  See New York Dolls
Johansen, David **7**
Johanson, Jai Johanny
  See Allman Brothers, The
Johansson, Glenn
  See Echobelly
Johansson, Lars-Olof
  See Cardigans
John, Elton **20**
  Earlier sketch in CM **3**
Johns, Daniel
  See Silverchair
Johnson, Alphonso
  See Weather Report
Johnson, Bob
  See Steeleye Span
Johnson, Brian
  See AC/DC
Johnson, Courtney
  See New Grass Revival, The
Johnson, Danny
  See Steppenwolf
Johnson, Daryl
  See Neville Brothers, The
Johnson, Eric
  See Archers of Loaf
Johnson, Eric **19**
Johnson, Gene
  See Diamond Rio
Johnson, Gerry
  See Steel Pulse
Johnson, James P. **16**
Johnson, Jerry
  See Big Mountain
Johnson, Lonnie **17**
Johnson, Matt
  See The The
Johnson, Mike
  See Dinosaur Jr.
Johnson, Ralph
  See Earth, Wind and Fire

Johnson, Robert **6**
Johnson, Scott
  See Gin Blossoms
Johnson, Shirley Childres
  See Sweet Honey in the Rock
Johnson, Tamara "Taj"
  See SWV
Johnston, Bruce
  See Beach Boys, The
Johnston, Freedy **20**
Johnston, Howie
  See Ventures, The
Johnston, Tom
  See Doobie Brothers, The
JoJo
  See Jodeci
Jolly, Bill
  See Butthole Surfers
Jolson, Al **10**
Jon Spencer Blues Explosion **18**
Jones, Adam
  See Tool
Jones, Benny
  See Dirty Dozen
Jones, Booker T.
  See Booker T. & the M.G.'s
Jones, Booker T. **8**
Jones, Brian
  See Rolling Stones, The
Jones, Busta
  See Gang of Four
Jones, Claude
  See McKinney's Cotton Pickers
Jones, Darryl
  See Rolling Stones, The
Jones, Davy
  See Monkees, The
Jones, Denise
  See Point of Grace
Jones, Elvin **9**
Jones, Geoffrey
  See Sounds of Blackness
Jones, George **4**
Jones, Grace **9**
Jones, Hank **15**
Jones, Jamie
  See All-4-One
Jones, Jim
  See Pere Ubu
Jones, John Paul
  See Led Zeppelin
Jones, Kendall
  See Fishbone
Jones, Kenny
  See Faces, The
Jones, Kenny
  See Who, The
Jones, Marshall
  See Ohio Players
Jones, Maxine
  See En Vogue
Jones, Michael
  See Kronos Quartet

Jones, Mic
  See Big Audio Dynamite
  Also see Clash, The
Jones, Mick
  See Foreigner
Jones, Orville
  See Ink Spots
Jones, Philly Joe **16**
Jones, Quincy **20**
  Earlier sketch in CM **2**
Jones, Rickie Lee **4**
Jones, Robert "Kuumba"
  See Ohio Players
Jones, Ronald
  See Flaming Lips
Jones, Sandra "Puma"
  See Black Uhuru
Jones, Simon
  See Verve, The
Jones, Spike **5**
Jones, Stacy
  See Veruca Salt
Jones, Stacy
  See Letters to Cleo
Jones, Steve
  See Sex Pistols, The
Jones, Terry
  See Point of Grace
Jones, Thad **19**
Jones, Tom **11**
Jones, Will "Dub"
  See Coasters, The
Joplin, Janis **3**
Joplin, Scott **10**
Jordan, Lonnie
  See War
Jordan, Louis **11**
Jordan, Stanley **1**
Jorgensor, John
  See Desert Rose Band, The
Joseph, Charles
  See Dirty Dozen
Joseph, Kirk
  See Dirty Dozen
Joseph-I, Israel
  See Bad Brains
Josephmary
  See Compulsion
Jourgensen, Al
  See Ministry
Journey **21**
Joyce, Mike
  See Buzzcocks, The
  Also see Smiths, The
Joy Division **19**
Judas Priest **10**
Judd, Naomi
  See Judds, The
Judd, Wynonna
  See Judds, The
  Also see Wynonna
Judds, The **2**
Juhlin, Dag
  See Poi Dog Pondering

Jukebox
  See Geto Boys, The
Jungle DJ "Towa" Towa
  See Deee-lite
Jurado, Jeanette
  See Exposé
Kabongo, Sabine
  See Zap Mama
Kahlil, Aisha
  See Sweet Honey in the Rock
Kain, Gylan
  See Last Poets
Kakoulli, Harry
  See Squeeze
Kale, Jim
  See Guess Who
Kalligan, Dick
  See Blood, Sweat and Tears
Kamanski, Paul
  See Beat Farmers
Kaminski, Mik
  See Electric Light Orchestra
Kamomiya, Ryo
  See Pizzicato Five
Kanal, Tony
  See No Doubt
Kanawa, Kiri Te
  See Te Kanawa, Kiri
Kane, Arthur
  See New York Dolls
Kane, Big Daddy **7**
Kane, Nick
  See Mavericks, The
Kannberg, Scott
  See Pavement
Kanter, Paul
  See Jefferson Airplane
Kaplan, Ira
  See Yo La Tengo
Karajan, Herbert von
  See von Karajan, Herbert
Karges, Murphy
  See Sugar Ray
Kath, Terry
  See Chicago
Kato, Nash
  See Urge Overkill
Katunich, Alex
  See Incubus
Katz, Simon
  See Jamiroquai
Katz, Steve
  See Blood, Sweat and Tears
Kaukonen, Jorma
  See Jefferson Airplane
Kavanagh, Chris
  See Big Audio Dynamite
Kay, Jason
  See Jamiroquai
Kay, John
  See Steppenwolf
Kaye, Carol **22**
Kaye, Tony
  See Yes

Kay Gee
  See Naughty by Nature
K-Ci
  See Jodeci
Kean, Martin
  See Stereolab
Keane, Sean
  See Chieftains, The
Kee, John P. **15**
Keelor, Greg
  See Blue Rodeo
Keenan, Maynard James
  See Tool
Keene, Barry
  See Spirit
Keifer, Tom
  See Cinderella
Keitaro
  See Pizzicato Five
Keith, Jeff
  See Tesla
Keith, Toby **17**
Kelly, Charlotte
  See Soul II Soul
Kelly, Kevin
  See Byrds, The
Kelly, Rashaan
  See US3
Kemp, Rick
  See Steeleye Span
Kendrick, David
  See Devo
Kendricks, Eddie
  See Temptations, The
Kennedy, Delious
  See All-4-One
Kennedy, Frankie
  See Altan
Kennedy, Nigel **8**
Kenner, Doris
  See Shirelles, The
Kenny, Bill
  See Ink Spots
Kenny, Clare
  See Aztec Camera
Kenny, Herb
  See Ink Spots
Kenny G **14**
Kenton, Stan **21**
Kentucky Headhunters, The **5**
Kern, Jerome **13**
Kerr, Jim
  See Simple Minds
Kershaw, Sammy **15**
Ketchum, Hal **14**
Key, Cevin
  See Skinny Puppy
Keyser, Alex
  See Echobelly
Khan, Chaka **19**
  Earlier sketch in CM **9**
Khan, Nusrat Fateh Ali **13**
Khan, Praga
  See Lords of Acid

Kibble, Mark
  See Take 6
Kibby, Walter
  See Fishbone
Kick, Johnny
  See Madder Rose
Kid 'n Play 5
Kidjo, Anjelique 17
Kiedis, Anthony
  See Red Hot Chili Peppers, The
Kilbey, Steve
  See Church, The
Kilgallon, Eddie
  See Ricochet
Kilgore 24
Killian, Tim
  See Kronos Quartet
Kimball, Jennifer
  See Story, The
Kimball, Jim
  See Jesus Lizard
Kimble, Paul
  See Grant Lee Buffalo
Kincaid, Jan
  See Brand New Heavies, The
Kinchla, Chan
  See Blues Traveler
King, Albert 2
King, B.B. 1
King, Andy
  See Hooters
King, Ben E. 7
King, Bob
  See Soul Stirrers, The
King, Carole 6
King, Ed
  See Lynyrd Skynyrd
King, Freddy 17
King, Jon
  See Gang of Four
King, Kerry
  See Slayer
King, Philip
  See Lush
King Ad-Rock
  See Beastie Boys, The
King Crimson 17
King Missile 22
King, Jr., William
  See Commodores, The
King, Carole
  See Goffin-King
King, B.B. 24
Kingston Trio, The 9
King's X 7
Kinks, The 15
Kinney, Sean
  See Alice in Chains
Kirk, Rahsaan Roland 6
Kirk, Richard H.
  See Cabaret Voltaire
Kirke, Simon
  See Bad Company

Kirkland, Mike
  See Prong
Kirkwood, Cris
  See Meat Puppets, The
Kirkwood, Curt
  See Meat Puppets, The
Kirtley, Peter
  See Pentangle
Kirwan, Danny
  See Fleetwood Mac
Kiss 5
Kisser, Andreas
  See Sepultura
Kissin, Evgeny 6
Kitaro 1
Kitsos, Nick
  See BoDeans
Kitt, Eartha 9
Klein, Jon
  See Siouxsie and the Banshees
Klezmatics, The 18
Klugh, Earl 10
Kmatsu, Bravo
  See Pizzicato Five
KMFDM 18
Knight, Gladys 1
Knight, Jon
  See New Kids on the Block
Knight, Jordan
  See New Kids on the Block
Knight, Larry
  See Spirit
Knight, Peter
  See Steeleye Span
Knight, Suge 15
Knighton, Willie
  See Goodie Mob
Knopfler, David
  See Dire Straits
Knopfler, Mark 3
  See Dire Straits
Know, Dr.
  See Bad Brains
Knowledge
  See Digable Planets
Knox, Nick
  See Cramps, The
Knox, Richard
  See Dirty Dozen
Knudsen, Keith
  See Doobie Brothers, The
Konietzko, Sascha
  See KMFDM
Konishi, Yasuharu
  See Pizzicato Five
Konto, Skip
  See Three Dog Night
Kool & the Gang 13
Kool Moe Dee 9
Kooper, Al
  See Blood, Sweat and Tears
Koppelman, Charles 14
Koppes, Peter
  See Church, The

Korn 20
Kottke, Leo 13
Kotzen, Richie
  See Poison
Kowalczyk, Ed
  See Live
Kraftwerk 9
Krakauer, David
  See Klezmatics, The
Kramer, Joey
  See Aerosmith
Kramer, Wayne
  See MC5, The
Krasnow, Bob 15
Krause, Bernie
  See Weavers, The
Krauss, Alison 10
Krauss, Scott
  See Pere Ubu
Kravitz, Lenny 5
Krawits, Michael
  See Pearls Before Swine
Krayzie Bone
  See Bone Thugs-N-Harmony
Krazy Drayz
  See Das EFX
Kretz, Eric
  See Stone Temple Pilots
Kreutzman, Bill
  See Grateful Dead, The
Krieger, Robert
  See Doors, The
Kriesel, Greg
  See Offspring
Kris Kross 11
Kristofferson, Kris 4
Krizan, Anthony
  See Spin Doctors
Kronos Quartet 5
Kropp, Mike
  See Northern Lights
KRS-One 8
Krupa, Gene 13
Krusen, Dave
  See Pearl Jam
Kulak, Eddie
  See Aztec Camera
Kulick, Bruce
  See Kiss
Kunkel, Bruce
  See Nitty Gritty Dirt Band, The
Kunzel, Erich 17
Kurdziel, Eddie
  See Redd Kross
Kurihara, Michio
  See Ghost
Kuti, Fela 7
LaBar, Jeff
  See Cinderella
LaBelle, Patti 8
LaBrie, James
  See Dream Theater
LaPread, Ronald
  See Commodores, The

Lack, Steve
  See Veruca Salt
Lacy, Steve **23**
Lady Miss Kier
  See Deee-lite
Ladybug
  See Digable Planets
Ladysmith Black Mambazo **1**
Lafalce, Mark
  See Mekons, The
Lagerburg, Bengt
  See Cardigans, The
Laine, Cleo **10**
Laine, Denny
  See Moody Blues, The
Laird, Rick
  See Mahavishnu Orchestra
Lake, Greg
  See Emerson, Lake & Palmer/Powell
  Also see King Crimson
LaLonde, Larry "Ler"
  See Primus
Lally, Joe
  See Fugazi
Lamb, Michael
  See Confederate Railroad
Lamble, Martin
  See Fairport Convention
Lamm, Robert
  See Chicago
Lancaster, Brian
  See Surfin' Pluto
Landreth, Sonny **16**
Lane, Jani
  See Warrant
Lane, Jay
  See Primus
Lane, Ronnie
  See Faces, The
lang, k. d. **4**
Langan, Gary
  See Art of Noise
Langford, Jon
  See Mekons, The
Langley, John
  See Mekons, The
Langlois, Paul
  See Tragically Hip, The
Langston, Leslie
  See Throwing Muses
Lanier, Allen
  See Blue Oyster Cult
Lanker, Dustin
  See Cherry Poppin' Daddies
Lanois, Daniel **8**
Larkin, Patty **9**
Larson, Chad Albert
  See Aquabats
Larson, Nathan
  See Shudder to Think
Last Poets **21**
Laswell, Bill **14**
Lataille, Rich
  See Roomful of Blues

Lateef, Yusef **16**
Latimer, Andrew
  See Camel
Laughner, Peter
  See Pere Ubu
Lauper, Cyndi **11**
Laurence, Lynda
  See Supremes, The
Lavin, Christine **6**
Lavis, Gilson
  See Squeeze
Lawlor, Feargal
  See Cranberries, The
Lawrence, Tracy **11**
Lawry, John
  See Petra
Laws, Roland
  See Earth, Wind and Fire
Lawson, Doyle
  See Country Gentlemen, The
Layzie Bone
  See Bone Thugs-N-Harmony
LeMaistre, Malcolm
  See Incredible String Band
Leadbelly **6**
Leadon, Bernie
  See Eagles, The
  Also see Nitty Gritty Dirt Band, The
Lear, Graham
  See REO Speedwagon
Leary, Paul
  See Butthole Surfers
Leavell, Chuck
  See Allman Brothers, The
LeBon, Simon
  See Duran Duran
Leckenby, Derek "Lek"
  See Herman's Hermits
Ledbetter, Huddie
  See Leadbelly
LeDoux, Chris **12**
Led Zeppelin **1**
Lee, Beverly
  See Shirelles, The
Lee, Brenda **5**
Lee, Buddy
  See Less Than Jake
Lee, Garret
  See Compulsion
Lee, Geddy
  See Rush
Lee, Peggy **8**
Lee, Pete
  See Gwar
Lee, Sara
  See Gang of Four
Lee, Stan
  See Incredible String Band
Lee, Tommy
  See Mötley Crüe
Lee, Tony
  See Treadmill Trackstar
Leeb, Bill
  See Front Line Assembly

Leen, Bill
  See Gin Blossoms
Leese, Howard
  See Heart
Legg, Adrian **17**
Lehrer, Tom **7**
Leiber and Stoller **14**
Leiber, Jerry
  See Leiber and Stoller
Lemmy
  See Motörhead
Lemonheads, The **12**
Lemper, Ute **14**
Le Mystère des VoixBulgares
  See Bulgarian State Female Vocal Choir,
  The
Lenear, Kevin
  See Mighty Mighty Bosstones
Lenners, Rudy
  See Scorpions, The
Lennon, John **9**
  Also see Beatles, The
Lennon, Julian **2**
Lennox, Annie **18**
  Also see Eurythmics
Leonard, Glenn
  See Temptations, The
Lerner, Alan Jay
  See Lerner and Loewe
Lerner and Loewe **13**
Lesh, Phil
  See Grateful Dead, The
Leskiw, Greg
  See Guess Who
Leslie, Chris
  See Fairport Convention
Lessard, Stefan
  See Dave Matthews Band
Less Than Jake **22**
Letters to Cleo **22**
Levene, Keith
  See Clash, The
Levert, Eddie
  See O'Jays, The
Leverton, Jim
  See Caravan
Levin, Tony
  See King Crimson
Levine, James **8**
Levy, Andrew
  See Brand New Heavies, The
Levy, Ron
  See Roomful of Blues
Lewis, Huey **9**
Lewis, Ian
  See Inner Circle
Lewis, Jerry Lee **2**
Lewis, Marcia
  See Soul II Soul
Lewis, Michael
  See Quicksilver Messenger Service
Lewis, Mike
  See Yo La Tengo

Lewis, Otis
  See Fabulous Thunderbirds, The
Lewis, Peter
  See Moby Grape
Lewis, Ramsey **14**
Lewis, Roger
Lewis, Roger
  See Dirty Dozen
  See Inner Circle
Lewis, Roy
  See Kronos Quartet
Lewis, Samuel K.
  See Five Blind Boys of Alabama
Lewis, Terry
  See Jam, Jimmy, and Terry Lewis
Lhote, Morgan
  See Stereolab
Li Puma, Tommy **18**
Libbea, Gene
  See Nashville Bluegrass Band
Liberace **9**
Licht, David
  See Klezmatics, The
Lifeson, Alex
  See Rush
Lightfoot, Gordon **3**
Lightning Seeds **21**
Ligon, Willie Joe
  See Mighty Clouds of Joy, The
Liles, Brent
  See Social Distortion
Lilienstein, Lois
  See Sharon, Lois & Bram
Lilker, Dan
  See Anthrax
Lilley, John
  See Hooters
Lillywhite, Steve **13**
Lincoln, Abbey **9**
Lindley, David **2**
Lindes, Hal
  See Dire Straits
Linna, Miriam
  See Cramps, The
Linnell, John
  See They Might Be Giants
Lipsius, Fred
  See Blood, Sweat and Tears
Lisa, Lisa **23**
Little, Keith
  See Country Gentlemen, The
Little, Levi
  See Blackstreet
Little Feat **4**
Little Richard **1**
Little Texas **14**
Little Walter **14**
Littrell, Brian
  See Backstreet Boys
Live **14**
Living Colour **7**
Llanas, Sam
  See BoDeans, The
L.L. Cool J. **5**

Lloyd, Charles **22**
Lloyd, Richard
  See Television
Lloyd Webber, Andrew **6**
Locke, John
  See Spirit
Locking, Brian
  See Shadows, The
Lockwood, Robert, Jr. **10**
Lodge, John
  See Moody Blues, The
Loeb, Lisa **23**
Loewe, Frederick
  See Lerner and Loewe
Loggins, Kenny **20**
  Earlier sketch in CM **3**
Lombardo, Dave
  See Slayer
London, Frank
  See Klezmatics, The
Lopes, Lisa "Left Eye"
  See TLC
Lopez, Israel "Cachao" **14**
Lord, Jon
  See Deep Purple
Lords of Acid **20**
Loria, Steve
  See Spirit
Lorson, Mary
  See Madder Rose
Los Lobos **2**
Los Reyes
  See Gipsy Kings, The
Loughnane, Lee
  See Chicago
Louison, Steve
  See Massive Attack
Louris, Gary
  See Jayhawks, The
Louvin Brothers, The **12**
Louvin, Charlie
  See Louvin Brothers, The
Louvin, Ira
  See Louvin Brothers, The
Lovano, Joe **13**
Love, Rollie
  See Beat Farmers
Love and Rockets **15**
Love, Courtney
  See Hole
Love, Gerry
  See Teenage Fanclub
Love, Laura **20**
Love, Mike
  See Beach Boys, The
Love, G. **24**
Loveless, Patty **21**
  Earlier sketch in CM **5**
Lovering, David
  See Cracker
  Also see Pixies, The
Love Spit Love **21**
Lovett, Lyle **5**

Lowe, Chris
  See Pet Shop Boys
Lowe, Nick **6**
Lowell, Charlie
  See Jars of Clay
Lowery, David
  See Cracker
Lozano, Conrad
  See Los Lobos
L7 **12**
Lucas, Trevor
  See Fairport Convention
Luccketta, Troy
  See Tesla
Lucia, Paco de
  See de Lucia, Paco
Luciano, Felipe
  See Last Poets
Luke
  See Campbell, Luther
Lukin, Matt
  See Mudhoney
Luna **18**
Lupo, Pat
  See Beaver Brown Band, The
LuPone, Patti **8**
Lush **13**
Luttell, Terry
  See REO Speedwagon
Lydon, John **9**
  Also see Sex Pistols, The
Lyfe, DJ
  See Incubus
Lymon, Frankie
  See Frankie Lymon and The Teenagers
Lynch, Dermot
  See Dog's Eye View
Lynch, George
  See Dokken
Lyngstad, Anni-Frid
  See Abba
Lynn, Lonnie Rashid
  See Common
Lynn, Loretta **2**
Lynne, Jeff **5**
  Also see Electric Light Orchestra
Lynne, Shelby **5**
Lynott, Phil
  See Thin Lizzy
Lynyrd Skynyrd **9**
Lyons, Leanne "Lelee"
  See SWV
Ma, Yo-Yo **24**
  Earlier sketch in CM **2**
MacColl, Kirsty **12**
MacDonald, Eddie
  See Alarm
Macfarlane, Lora
  See Sleater-Kinney
MacGowan, Shane
MacIsaac, Ashley **21**
MacKaye, Ian
  See Fugazi

Mack Daddy
 See Kris Kross
Mackey, Steve
 See Pulp
MacNeil, Michael
 See Simple Minds
MacPherson, Jim
 See Breeders
Madan, Sonya Aurora
 See Echobelly
Madder Rose **17**
Madonna **16**
 Earlier sketch in CM **4**
Mael, Ron
 See Sparks
Mael, Russell
 See Sparks
Magehee, Marty
 See FourHim
Maghostut, Malachi Favors
 See Art Ensemble of Chicago, The
Maginnis, Tom
 See Buffalo Tom
Magnie, John
 See Subdudes, The
Magoogan, Wesley
 See English Beat, The
Maïtra, Shyamal
 See Gong
Maher, John
 See Buzzcocks, The
Mahoney, Tim
 See 311
Maida, Raine
 See Our Lady Peace
Maimone, Tony
 See Pere Ubu
Makeba, Miriam **8**
Malcolm, Hugh
 See Skatalites, The
Malcolm, Joy
 See Incognito
Male, Johnny
 See Republica
Malherbe, Didier
 See Gong
Malins, Mike
 See Goo Goo Dolls, The
Malkmus, Stephen
 See Pavement
Malley, Matt
 See Counting Crows
Mallinder, Stephen
 See Cabaret Voltaire
Malmsteen, Yngwie **24**
Malo, Raul
 See Mavericks, The
Malone, Tom
 See Blood, Sweat and Tears
Malone, Tommy
 See Subdudes, The
Mamas and the Papas **21**
Mancini, Henry **20**
 Earlier sketch in CM **1**

Mandrell, Barbara **4**
Maness, J. D.
 See Desert Rose Band, The
Mangione, Chuck **23**
Manhattan Transfer, The **8**
Manilow, Barry **2**
Mann, Aimee **22**
Mann, Herbie **16**
Man or Astroman? **21**
Mann, Billy **23**
Manuel, Richard
 See Band, The
Manzarek, Ray
 See Doors, The
March, Kevin
 See Shudder to Think
Marie, Buffy Sainte
 See Sainte-Marie, Buffy
Marilyn Manson **18**
Marini, Lou, Jr.
 See Blood, Sweat and Tears
Marley, Bob **3**
Marley, Rita **10**
Marley, Ziggy **3**
Marr, Johnny
 See Smiths, The
 Also see The The
Marriner, Neville
Mars, Chris
 See Replacements, The
Mars, Derron
 See Less Than Jake
Mars, Mick
 See Mötley Crüe
Marsalis, Branford **10**
Marsalis, Ellis **13**
Marsalis, Wynton **20**
 Earlier sketch in CM **6**
Marsh, Ian Craig
 See Human League, The
Marshal, Cornel
 See Third World
Marshall, Jenell
 See Dirty Dozen
Martin, Barbara
 See Supremes, The
Martin, Carl
 See Shai
Martin, Christopher
 See Kid 'n Play
Martin, Dean **1**
Martin, Dewey
 See Buffalo Springfield
Martin, George **6**
Martin, Greg
 See Kentucky Headhunters, The
Martin, Jim
 See Faith No More
Martin, Jimmy **5**
 Also see Osborne Brothers, The
Martin, Johnny
 See Mighty Clouds of Joy, The
Martin, Phonso
 See Steel Pulse

Martin, Sennie
 See Kool & the Gang
Martin, Tony
 See Black Sabbath
Martinez, Anthony
 See Black Flag
Martinez, S. A.
 See 311
Martini, Jerry
 See Sly & the Family Stone
Martino, Pat **17**
Marvin, Hank B.
 See Shadows, The
Marx, Richard **21**
 Earlier sketch in CM **3**
Mascis, J
 See Dinosaur Jr.
Masdea, Jim
 See Boston
Masekela, Hugh **7**
Maseo, Baby Huey
 See De La Soul
Masi, Nick
 See Four Seasons, The
Mason, Dave
 See Traffic
Mason, Nick
 See Pink Floyd
Mason, Steve
 See Jars of Clay
Mason, Terry
 See Joy Division
Masse, Laurel
 See Manhattan Transfer, The
Massey, Bobby
 See O'Jays, The
Massive Attack **17**
Mastelotto, Pat
 See King Crimson
Master P **22**
Masur, Kurt **11**
Material
 See Laswell, Bill
Mathis, Johnny **2**
Mathus, Jim
 See Squirrel Nut Zippers
Matlock, Glen
 See Sex Pistols, The
Mattacks, Dave
 See Fairport Convention
Mattea, Kathy **5**
Matthews, Chris
 See Shudder to Think
Matthews, Dave
 See Dave Matthews Band
Matthews, Eric **22**
Matthews, Ian
 See Fairport Convention
Matthews, Simon
 See Jesus Jones
Matthews Band, Dave
 See Dave Matthews Band
Matthews, Quinn
 See Butthole Surfers

Matthews, Scott
  See Butthole Surfers
Maunick, Bluey
  See Incognito
Maurer, John
  See Social Distortion
Mavericks, The **15**
Maxwell **22**
Maxwell, Charmayne
  See Brownstone
Maxwell, Tom
  See Squirrel Nut Zippers
May, Brian
  See Queen
Mayall, John **7**
Mayfield, Curtis **8**
Mays, Odeen, Jr.
  See Kool & the Gang
Mazelle, Kym
  See Soul II Soul
Mazibuko, Abednigo
  See Ladysmith Black Mambazo
Mazibuko, Albert
  See Ladysmith Black Mambazo
Mazzola, Joey
  See Sponge
Mazzy Star **17**
MCA
  See Yauch, Adam
McAloon, Martin
  See Prefab Sprout
McAloon, Paddy
  See Prefab Sprout
McArthur, Keith
  See Spearhead
McBrain, Nicko
  See Iron Maiden
MCBreed **17**
McBride, Christian **17**
McBride, Martina **14**
McCabe, Nick
  See Verve, The
McCabe, Zia
  See Dandy Warhols, The
McCall, Renee
  See Sounds of Blackness
McCarrick, Martin
  See Siouxsie and the Banshees
McCarroll, Tony
  See Oasis
McCartney, Paul **4**
  Also see Beatles, The
McCarty, Jim
  See Yardbirds, The
MC Clever
  See Digital Underground
McCary, Michael S.
  See Boyz II Men
McClary, Thomas
  See Commodores, The
McClinton, Delbert **14**
McCluskey, Andy
  See Orchestral Manoeuvres in the Dark

McCollum, Rick
  See Afghan Whigs
McConnell, Page
  See Phish
McCook, Tommy
  See Skatalites, The
McCoury, Del **15**
McCowin, Michael
  See Mighty Clouds of Joy, The
McCoy, Neal **15**
McCracken, Chet
  See Doobie Brothers, The
McCready, Mike
  See Pearl Jam
McCready, Mindy **22**
McCulloch, Andrew
  See King Crimson
McCullough, Danny
  See Animals
McCuloch, Ian **23**
McD, Jimmy
  See Jimmie's Chicken Shack
McDaniel, Chris
  See Confederate Railroad
McDaniels, Darryl "D"
  See Run-D.M.C.
McDermott, Brian
  See Del Amitri
McDonald, Barbara Kooyman
  See Timbuk 3
McDonald, Ian
  See Foreigner
  Also see King Crimson
McDonald, Jeff
  See Redd Kross
McDonald, Michael
  See Doobie Brothers, The
McDonald, Pat
  See Timbuk 3
McDonald, Steven
  See Redd Kross
McDorman, Joe
  See Statler Brothers, The
McDougall, Don
  See Guess Who
McDowell, Hugh
  See Electric Light Orchestra
McDowell, Mississippi Fred **16**
McEntire, Reba **11**
MC Eric
  See Technotronic
McEuen, John
  See Nitty Gritty Dirt Band, The
McFarlane, Elaine
  See Mamas and the Papas
McFee, John
  See Doobie Brothers, The
McFerrin, Bobby **3**
MC5, The **9**
McGee, Brian
  See Simple Minds
McGee, Jerry
  See Ventures, The

McGeoch, John
  See Siouxsie and theBanshees
McGinley, Raymond
  See Teenage Fanclub
McGinniss, Will
  See Audio Adrenaline
McGrath, Mark
  See Sugar Ray
McGraw, Tim **17**
McGuigan, Paul
  See Oasis
McGuinn, Jim
  See McGuinn, Roger
McGuinn, Roger
  See Byrds, The
M.C. Hammer
  See Hammer, M.C.
McGuire, Mike
  See Shenandoah
McIntosh, Robbie
  See Pretenders, The
McIntyre, Joe
  See New Kids on the Block
McJohn, Goldy
  See Steppenwolf
McKagan, Duff
  See Guns n' Roses
McKay, Al
  See Earth, Wind and Fire
McKay, John
  See Siouxsie and the Banshees
McKean, Michael
  See Spinal Tap
McKee, Maria **11**
McKee , Julius
  See Dirty Dozen
McKeehan, Toby
  See dc Talk
McKenna, Greg
  See Letters to Cleo
McKennitt, Loreena **24**
McKenzie, Christina "Licorice"
  See Incredible String Band
McKenzie, Derrick
  See Jamiroquai
McKenzie, Scott
  See Mamas and the Papas
McKernarn, Ron "Pigpen"
  See Grateful Dead, The
McKinney, William
  See McKinney's Cotton Pickers
McKinney's Cotton Pickers **16**
McKnight, Brian **22**
McKnight, Claude V. III
  See Take 6
McLachlan, Sarah **12**
McLagan, Ian
  See Faces, The
McLaren, Malcolm **23**
McLaughlin, John **12**
  Also see Mahavishnu Orchestra
McLean, A. J.
  See Backstreet Boys
McLean, Don **7**

McLean, Dave **24**
McLennan, Grant **21**
McLeod, Rory
  See Roomful of Blues
MC Lyte **8**
McLoughlin, Jon
  See Del Amitri
McMeel, Mickey
  See Three Dog Night
McMurtry, James **10**
McNabb, Travis
  See Better Than Ezra
McNair, Sylvia **15**
McNeilly, Mac
  See Jesus Lizard
MC 900 Ft. Jesus **16**
McNew, James
  See Yo La Tengo
McPartland, Marian **15**
McQuillar, Shawn
  See Kool & the Gang
McRae, Carmen **9**
M.C. Ren
  See N.W.A.
McReynolds, Jesse
  See McReynolds, Jim and Jesse
McReynolds, Jim
  See McReynolds, Jim and Jesse
McReynolds, Jim and Jesse **12**
MC Serch **10**
McShane, Ronnie
  See Chieftains, The
McShee, Jacqui
  See Pentangle
McTell, Blind Willie **17**
McVie, Christine
  See Fleetwood Mac
McVie, John
  See Fleetwood Mac
McWhinney, James
  See Big Mountain
McWhinney, Joaquin
  See Clannad
  See Big Mountain
Mdletshe, Geophrey
  See Ladysmith Black Mambazo
Meat Loaf **12**
Meat Puppets, The **13**
Medley, Bill **3**
Medlock, James
  See Soul Stirrers, The
Meehan, Tony
  See Shadows, The
Megadeth **9**
Mehta, Zubin **11**
Meine, Klaus
  See Scorpions, The
Meisner, Randy
  See Eagles, The
Mekons, The **15**
Melanie **12**
Melax, Einar
  See Sugarcubes, The

Mellencamp, John **20**
  Earlier sketch in CM **2**
Melvins **21**
Mendel, Nate
  See Foo Fighters
Mengede, Peter
  See Helmet
Menken, Alan **10**
Menuhin, Yehudi **11**
Menza, Nick
  See Megadeth
Mercer, Johnny **13**
Merchant, Jimmy
  See Frankie Lymon and The Teenagers
Merchant, Natalie
  See 10,000 Maniacs
Mercier, Peadar
  See Chieftains, The
Mercury, Freddie
  See Queen
Mertens, Paul
  See Poi Dog Pondering
Mesaros, Michael
  See Smithereens, The
Messecar, Dek
  See Caravan
Messina, Jim
  See Buffalo Springfield
Metallica **7**
Meters, The **14**
Methembu, Russel
  See Ladysmith Black Mambazo
Metheny, Pat **2**
Meyer, Eric
  See Charm Farm
Meyers, Augie
  See Texas Tornados, The
Mhaonaigh, Mairead Ni
  See Altan
Michael, George **9**
Michaels, Bret
  See Poison
Michel, Prakazrel "Pras"
  See Fugees, The
Michel, Luke
  See Emmet Swimming
Middlebrook, Ralph "Pee Wee"
  See Ohio Players
Middleton, Mark
  See Blackstreet
Midler, Bette **8**
Midnight Oil **11**
Midori **7**
Mighty Clouds of Joy, The **17**
Mighty Mighty Bosstones **20**
Mike & the Mechanics **17**
Mike D
  See Beastie Boys, The
Mikens, Dennis
  See Smithereens, The
Mikens, Robert
  See Kool & the Gang
Milchem, Glenn
  See Blue Rodeo

Miles, Chris
  See Northern Lights
Miles, Richard
  See Soul Stirrers, The
Miles, Ron **22**
Millar, Deborah
  See Massive Attack
Miller, Charles
  See War
Miller, Glenn **6**
Miller, Jacob "Killer" Miller
  See Inner Circle
Miller, Jerry
  See Moby Grape
Miller, Mark
  See Sawyer Brown
Miller, Mitch **11**
Miller, Rice
  See Williamson, Sonny Boy
Miller, Roger **4**
Miller, Steve **2**
Milli Vanilli **4**
Mills Brothers, The **14**
Mills, Donald
  See Mills Brothers, The
Mills, Fred
  See Canadian Brass, The
Mills, Harry
  See Mills Brothers, The
Mills, Herbert
  See Mills Brothers, The
Mills, John, Jr.
  See Mills Brothers, The
Mills, John, Sr.
  See Mills Brothers, The
Mills, Sidney
  See Steel Pulse
Mills, Stephanie **21**
Milsap, Ronnie **2**
Milton, Doctor
  See Alien Sex Fiend
Mingus, Charles **9**
Ministry **10**
Miss Kier Kirby
  See Lady Miss Kier
Mitchell, Alex
  See Curve
Mitchell, John
  See Asleep at the Wheel
Mitchell, Joni **17**
  Earlier sketch in CM **2**
Mitchell, Keith
  See Mazzy Star
Mitchell, Mitch
  See Guided By Voices
Mitchell, Roscoe
  See Art Ensemble of Chicago, The
Mittoo, Jackie
  See Skatalites, The
Mize, Ben
  See Counting Crows
Mizell, Jay
  See Run-D.M.C.
Moby **17**

Moby Grape **12**
Modeliste, Joseph "Zigaboo"
  See Meters, The
Moerlen, Pierre
  See Gong
Moffatt, Katy **18**
Moginie, Jim
  See Midnight Oil
Mohr, Todd
  See Big Head Todd and the Monsters
Molland, Joey
  See Badfinger
Monifah **24**
Montana, Country Dick
  See Beat Farmers
Moore, Archie
  See Velocity Girl
Moore, Kevin
  See Dream Theater
Morrison, Van **24**
Moss, Jason
  See Cherry Poppin' Daddies
Moye, Famoudou Don
  See Art Ensemble of Chicago, The
Mo', Keb' **21**
Molloy, Matt
  See Chieftains, The
Moloney, Paddy
  See Chieftains, The
Monarch, Michael
  See Steppenwolf
Money B
  See Digital Underground
Money, Eddie **16**
Monk, Meredith **1**
Monk, Thelonious **6**
Monkees, The **7**
Monroe, Bill **1**
Montand, Yves **12**
Montenegro, Hugo **18**
Montgomery, John Michael **14**
Montgomery, Wes **3**
Monti, Steve
  See Curve
Montoya, Craig
  See Everclear
Montrose, Ronnie **22**
Moody Blues, The **18**
Moon, Keith
  See Who, The
Mooney, Tim
  See American Music Club
Moore, Alan
  See Judas Priest
Moore, Angelo
  See Fishbone
Moore, Chante **21**
Moore, Johnny "Dizzy"
  See Skatalites, The
Moore, LeRoi
  See Dave Matthews Band
Moore, Melba **7**
Moore, Sam
  See Sam and Dave

Moore, Thurston
  See Sonic Youth
Morand, Grace
  See Chenille Sisters, The
Moraz, Patrick
  See Moody Blues, The
  Also see Yes
Moreira, Airto
  See Weather Report
Morello, Tom
  See Rage Against the Machine
Moreno, Chino
  See Deftones
Moreve, Rushton
  See Steppenwolf
Morgan, Frank **9**
Morgan, Lorrie **10**
Morley, Pat
  See Soul Asylum
Morphine **16**
Morricone, Ennio **15**
Morris, Keith
  See Circle Jerks, The
Morris, Kenny
  See Siouxsie and the Banshees
Morris, Nate
  See Boyz II Men
Morris, Stephen
  See Joy Division
  Also see New Order
  Also see Pogues, The
Morris, Wanya
  See Boyz II Men
Morrison, Bram
  See Sharon, Lois & Bram
Morrison, Claude
  See Nylons, The
Morrison, Jim **3**
  Also see Doors, The
Morrison, Sterling
  See Velvet Underground, The
Morrison, Van **3**
Morrissett, Paul
  See Klezmatics, The
Morrissey **10**
  Also see Smiths, The
Morrissey, Bill **12**
Morrissey, Steven Patrick
  See Morrissey
Morton, Everett
  See English Beat, The
Morton, Jelly Roll **7**
Morvan, Fab
  See Milli Vanilli
Mosbaugh, Garth
  See Nylons, The
Mosely, Chuck
  See Faith No More
Moser, Scott "Cactus"
  See Highway 101
Mosher, Ken
  See Squirrel Nut Zippers
Mosley, Bob
  See Moby Grape

Mothersbaugh, Bob
  See Devo
Mothersbaugh, Mark
  See Devo
Mouzon, Alphonse
  See Weather Report
Moyse, David
  See Air Supply
Murphy, Michael
  See REO Speedwagon
Murray, Jim
  See Quicksilver Messenger Service
Mutter, Anne-Sophie **23**
Myung, John
  See Dream Theater
Mötley Crüe **1**
Motörhead **10**
Motta, Danny
  See Roomful of Blues
Mould, Bob **10**
Moulding, Colin
  See XTC
Mounfield, Gary
  See Stone Roses, The
Mouquet, Eric
  See Deep Forest
Mouskouri, Nana **12**
Moyet, Alison **12**
M People **15**
Mr. Dalvin
  See Jodeci
Mudhoney **16**
Mueller, Karl
  See Soul Asylum
Muir, Jamie
  See King Crimson
Muir, Mike
  See Suicidal Tendencies
Muldaur, Maria **18**
Mulholland, Dave
  See Aztec Camera
Mullen, Larry, Jr.
  See U2
Mullen, Mary
  See Congo Norvell
Mulligan, Gerry **16**
Murcia, Billy
  See New York Dolls
Murdock, Roger
  See King Missile
Murph
  See Dinosaur Jr.
Murphy, Brigid
  See Poi Dog Pondering
Murphy, Dan
  See Soul Asylum
Murphy, Peter **22**
Murphey, Michael Martin **9**
Murray, Anne **4**
Murray, Dave
  See Iron Maiden
Murray, Dee
  See Spencer Davis Group

Mushroom
　See Massive Attack
Musselwhite, Charlie **13**
Mustaine, Dave
　See Megadeth
　　Also see Metallica
Mwelase, Jabulane
　See Ladysmith Black Mambazo
Mydland, Brent
　See Grateful Dead, The
Myers, Alan
　See Devo
Myles, Alannah **4**
Mystic Revealers **16**
Nadirah
　See Arrested Development
Naftalin, Mark
　See Quicksilver Messenger Service
Nagler, Eric **8**
Najee **21**
Nakai, R. Carlos **24**
Nakamura, Tetsuya "Tex"
　See War
Nakatami, Michie
　See Shonen Knife
Narcizo, David
　See Throwing Muses
Nascimento, Milton **6**
Nash, Graham
　See Crosby, Stills, and Nash
Nashville Bluegrass Band **14**
Nastanovich, Bob
　See Pavement
Naughty by Nature **11**
Navarro, David
　See Jane's Addiction
Nawasadio, Sylvie
　See Zap Mama
N'Dour, Youssou **6**
Ndegéocello, Me'Shell **18**
Ndugu
　See Weather Report
Near, Holly **1**
Neel, Johnny
　See Allman Brothers, The
Negron, Chuck
　See Three Dog Night
Negroni, Joe
　See Frankie Lymon and The Teenagers
Neil, Chris
　See Less Than Jake
Neil, Vince
　See Mötley Crüe
Nelson, Brian
　See Velocity Girl
Nelson, David
　See Last Poets
Nelson, Errol
　See Black Uhuru
Nelson, Rick **2**
Nelson, Shara
　See Massive Attack
Nelson, Willie **11**
　Earlier sketch in CM **1**

Nesbitt, John
　See McKinney's Cotton Pickers
Nesmith, Mike
　See Monkees, The
Ness, Mike
　See Social Distortion
Neufville, Renee
　See Zhane
Neumann, Kurt
　See BoDeans
Nevarez, Alfred
　See All-4-One
Neville, Aaron **5**
　Also see Neville Brothers, The
Neville, Art
　See Meters, The
　Also see Neville Brothers, The
Neville, Charles
　See Neville Brothers, The
Neville, Cyril
　See Meters, The
　Also see Neville Brothers, The
Neville Brothers, The **4**
Nevin, Brian
　See Big Head Todd and the Monsters
New Grass Revival, The **4**
New Kids on the Block **3**
Newman, Randy **4**
Newmann, Kurt
　See BoDeans, The
New Order **11**
New Rhythm and Blues Quartet
　See NRBQ
Newsboys, The **24**
Newson, Arlene
　See Poi Dog Pondering
Newton, Paul
　See Uriah Heep
Newton, Wayne **2**
Newton-Davis, Billy
　See Nylons, The
Newton-John, Olivia **8**
New York Dolls **20**
Nibbs, Lloyd
　See Skatalites, The
Nicholas, James Dean "J.D."
　See Commodores, The
Nicholls, Geoff
　See Black Sabbath
Nichols, Gates
　See Confederate Railroad
Nichols, Todd
　See Toad the Wet Sprocket
Nicks, Stevie **2**
　Also see Fleetwood Mac
Nico
　See Velvet Underground, The
Nicol, Simon
　See Fairport Convention
Nicolette
　See Massive Attack
Nielsen, Rick
　See Cheap Trick

Nilija, Robert
　See Last Poets
Nilsson **10**
Nilsson, Harry
　See Nilsson
Nirvana **8**
Nisbett, Steve "Grizzly"
　See Steel Pulse
Nishino, Kohji
　See Ghost
Nitty Gritty Dirt Band, The **6**
Nobacon, Danbert
　See Chumbawamba
Nocentelli, Leo
　See Meters, The
No Doubt **20**
Nolan, Jerry
　See New York Dolls
Nomiya, Maki
　See Pizzicato Five
Noone, Peter
　See Herman's Hermits
Norica, Sugar Ray
　See Roomful of Blues
Norman, Jessye **7**
Norman, Jimmy
　See Coasters, The
Norris, Jean
　See Zhane
Northey, Craig
　See Odds
Norum, John
　See Dokken
Norvell, Sally
　See Congo Norvell
Norvo, Red **12**
Notorious B.I.G. **20**
Novoselic, Chris
　See Nirvana
Nowell, Bradley James
　See Sublime
NRBQ **12**
Nugent, Ted **2**
Nunn, Bobby
　See Coasters, The
N.W.A. **6**
Nutter, Alice
　See Chumbawamba
Nylons, The **18**
Nyman, Michael **15**
Nyolo, Sally
　See Zap Mama
Nyro, Laura **12**
Oakes, Richard
　See Suede
Oakey, Philip
　See Human League, The
Oakley, Berry
　See Allman Brothers, The
Oak Ridge Boys, The **7**
Oasis **16**
Oates, John
　See Hall & Oates

O'Brien, Derek
   See Social Distortion
O'Brien, Dwayne
   See Little Texas
O'Bryant, Alan
   See Nashville Bluegrass Band
Ocasek, Ric
   See Cars, The
Ocasek, Ric **5**
Ocean, Billy **4**
Oceans, Lucky
   See Asleep at the Wheel
Ochs, Phil **7**
O'Connell, Chris
   See Asleep at the Wheel
O'Connor, Billy
   See Blondie
O'Connor, Daniel
   See House of Pain
O'Connor, Mark **1**
O'Connor, Sinead **3**
O'Day, Anita **21**
Odds **20**
Odetta **7**
O'Donnell, Roger
   See Cure, The
Odmark, Matt
   See Jars of Clay
Ofwerman, Clarence
   See Roxette
Ofwerman, Staffan
   See Roxette
Ogino, Kazuo
   See Ghost
Ogletree, Mike
   See Simple Minds
Ogre, Nivek
   See Skinny Puppy
O'Hagan, Sean
   See Stereolab
Ohanian, David
   See Canadian Brass, The
O'Hare, Brendan
   See Teenage Fanclub
Ohio Players **16**
O'Jays, The **13**
Oje, Baba
   See Arrested Development
Olafsson, Bragi
   See Sugarcubes, The
Olander, Jimmy
   See Diamond Rio
Olaverra, Margot
   See Go-Go's, The
Oldfield, Mike **18**
Oldham, Jack
   See Surfaris, The
Oldham, Sean
   See Cherry Poppin' Daddies
Olds, Brent
   See Poi Dog Pondering
Oliver, Joe
   See Oliver, King
Oliver, King **15**

Olson, Jeff
   See Village People, The
Olson, Mark
   See Jayhawks, The
Olsson, Nigel
   See Spencer Davis Group
Onassis, Blackie
   See Urge Overkill
Ono, Yoko **11**
Orange, Walter "Clyde"
   See Commodores, The
Orb, The **18**
Orbison, Roy **2**
Orbital **20**
Orchestral Manoeuvres in the Dark **21**
O'Reagan, Tim
   See Jayhawks, The
Orff, Carl **21**
Orlando, Tony **15**
O'Riordan, Cait
   See Pogues, The
O'Riordan, Dolores
   See Cranberries, The
O'Brien, Darrin Kenneth
   See Snow
O'Brien, Marty
   See Kilgore
O'Brien,, Ed
   See Radiohead
Örn, Einar
   See Sugarcubes, The
Örnolfsdottir, Margret
   See Sugarcubes, The
Orr, Benjamin
   See Cars, The
Orr, Casey
   See Gwar
Orrall, Frank
   See Poi Dog Pondering
Orzabal, Roland
   See Tears for Fears
Osborne, Bob
   See Osborne Brothers, The
Osborne, Buzz
   See Melvins
Osborne, Sonny
   See Osborne Brothers, The
Osborne Brothers, The **8**
Osbourne, Ozzy **3**
   Also see Black Sabbath
Osby, Greg **21**
Oskar, Lee
   See War
Oslin, K. T. **3**
Osman, Mat
   See Suede
Osmond, Donny **3**
Ostin, Mo **17**
Otis, Johnny **16**
Ott, David **2**
Our Lady Peace **22**
Outler, Jimmy
   See Soul Stirrers, The

Owen, Randy Yueull
   See Alabama
Owens, Buck **2**
Owens, Campbell
   See Aztec Camera
Owens, Ricky
   See Temptations, The
Oyewole, Abiodun
   See Last Poets
Page, Jimmy **4**
   Also see Led Zeppelin
   Also see Yardbirds, The
Page, Patti **11**
Page, Steven
   See Barenaked Ladies
Paice, Ian
   See Deep Purple
Palmer, Bruce
   See Buffalo Springfield
Palmer, Carl
   See Emerson, Lake & Palmer/Powell
Palmer, Clive
   See Incredible String Band
Palmer, David
   See Jethro Tull
Palmer, Jeff **20**
Palmer, Keeti
   See Prodigy
Palmer, Phil
   See Dire Straits
Palmer, Robert **2**
Palmer-Jones, Robert
   See King Crimson
Palmieri, Eddie **15**
Paluzzi, Jimmy
   See Sponge
Pamer, John
   See Tsunami
Pankow, James
   See Chicago
Panter, Horace
   See Specials, The
Pantera **13**
Papach, Leyna
   See Geraldine Fibbers
Pappas, Tom
   See Superdrag
Parazaider, Walter
   See Chicago
Paris, Twila **16**
Park, Cary
   See Boy Howdy
Park, Larry
   See Boy Howdy
Parkening, Christopher **7**
Parker, Charlie **5**
Parker, Graham **10**
Parker, Kris
   See KRS-One
Parker, Maceo **7**
Parker, Tom
   See Animals
Parkin, Chad
   See Aquabats

Parks, Van Dyke **17**
Parnell, Lee Roy **15**
Parsons, Alan **12**
Parsons, Dave
  See Bush
Parsons, Gene
  See Byrds, The
Parsons, Gram **7**
  Also see Byrds, The
Parsons, Ted
  See Prong
Parsons, Tony
  See Iron Maiden
Parton, Dolly **24**
  Earlier sketch in CM **2**
Partridge, Andy
  See XTC
Pasemaster, Mase
  See De La Soul
Pash, Jim
  See Surfaris, The
Pasillas, Jose
  See Incubus
Pass, Joe **15**
Pastorius, Jaco
  See Weather Report
Paterson, Alex
  See Orb, The
Patinkin, Mandy **20**
  Earlier sketch CM **3**
Patti, Sandi **7**
Patton, Charley **11**
Patton, Mike
  See Faith No More
Paul, Alan
  See Manhattan Transfer, The
Paul, Les **2**
Paul, Vinnie
  See Pantera
Paul III, Henry
  See BlackHawk
Paulo, Jr.
  See Sepultura
Pavarotti, Luciano **20**
  Earlier sketch in CM **1**
Pavement **14**
Paxton, Tom **5**
Payne, Bill
  See Little Feat
Payne, Scherrie
  See Supremes, The
Payton, Denis
  See Dave Clark Five, The
Payton, Lawrence
  See Four Tops, The
Pearl, Minnie **3**
Pearl Jam **12**
Pearls Before Swine **24**
Pearson, Dan
  See American Music Club
Peart, Neil
  See Rush
Pedersen, Herb
  See Desert Rose Band, The

Peduzzi, Larry
  See Roomful of Blues
Peek, Dan
  See America
Peeler, Ben
  See Mavericks, The
Pegg, Dave
  See Fairport Convention
  Also see Jethro Tull
Pegrum, Nigel
  See Steeleye Span
Pelletier, Mike
  See Kilgore
Pence, Jeff
  See Blessid Union of Souls
Pendergrass, Teddy **3**
Pengilly, Kirk
  See INXS
Peniston, CeCe **15**
Penn, Michael **4**
Penner, Fred **10**
Pentangle **18**
Pepper, Art **18**
Perahia, Murray **10**
Pere Ubu **17**
Peretz, Jesse
  See Lemonheads, The
Perez, Louie
  See Los Lobos
Perkins, Carl **9**
Perkins, John
  See XTC
Perkins, Percell
  See Five Blind Boys of Alabama
Perkins, Steve
  See Jane's Addiction
Perlman, Itzhak **2**
Perlman, Marc
  See Jayhawks, The
Pernice, Joe
  See Scud Mountain Boys
Perry, Brendan
  See Dead Can Dance
Perry, Doane
  See Jethro Tull
Perry, Joe
  See Aerosmith
Perry, John G.
  See Caravan
Perry, Steve
  See Journey
Perry, Steve
  See Cherry Poppin' Daddies
Perry, Virgshawn
  See Artifacts
Perry, Phil **24**
Persson, Nina
  See Cardigans
Peter, Paul & Mary **4**
Peters, Bernadette **7**
Peters, Dan
  See Mudhoney
Peters, Joey
  See Grant Lee Buffalo

Peters, Mike
  See Alarm
Petersen, Chris
  See Front Line Assembly
Peterson, Debbi
  See Bangles
Peterson, Garry
  See Guess Who
Peterson, Oscar **11**
Peterson, Vicki
  See Bangles
Petersson, Tom
  See Cheap Trick
Petra **3**
Pet Shop Boys **5**
Petty, Tom **9**
Petrucci, John
  See Dream Theater
Pfaff, Kristen
  See Hole
Phair, Liz **14**
Phantom, Slim Jim
  See Stray Cats, The
Pharcyde, The **17**
Phelps, Doug
  See Kentucky Headhunters, The
Phelps, Ricky Lee
  See Kentucky Headhunters, The
Phife
  See Tribe Called Quest, A
Phil, Gary
  See Boston
Philbin, Greg
  See REO Speedwagon
Philips, Anthony
  See Genesis
Phillips, Chris
  See Squirrel Nut Zippers
Phillips, Chynna
  See Wilson Phillips
Phillips, Glenn
  See Toad the Wet Sprocket
Phillips, Grant Lee
  See Grant Lee Buffalo
Phillips, Harvey **3**
Phillips, John
  See Mamas and the Papas
Phillips, Mackenzie
  See Mamas and the Papas
Phillips, Michelle
  See Mamas and the Papas
Phillips, Sam **5**
Phillips, Sam **12**
Phillips, Shelley
  See Point of Grace
Phillips, Simon
  See Judas Priest
Phish **13**
Phungula, Inos
  See Ladysmith Black Mambazo
Piaf, Edith **8**
Piazzolla, Astor **18**
Picciotto, Joe
  See Fugazi

Piccolo, Greg
  See Roomful of Blues
Pickering, Michael
  See M People
Pickett, Wilson **10**
Pierce, Marvin "Merv"
  See Ohio Players
Pierce, Webb **15**
Pierson, Kate
  See B-52's, The
Pilatus, Rob
  See Milli Vanilli
Pilson, Jeff
  See Dokken
Pinder, Michael
  See Moody Blues, The
Pine, Courtney
  See Soul II Soul
Pink Floyd **2**
Pinkus, Jeff
  See Butthole Surfers
Pinnick, Doug
  See King's X
Pirner, Dave
  See Soul Asylum
Pirroni, Marco
  See Siouxsie and the Banshees
Pixies, The **21**
Pizzicato Five **18**
Plakas, Dee
  See L7
Plant, Robert **2**
  Also see Led Zeppelin
Ploog, Richard
  See Church, The
P.M. Dawn **11**
Pogues, The **6**
Poi Dog Pondering **17**
Poindexter, Buster
  See Johansen, David
Point of Grace **21**
Pointer, Anita
  See Pointer Sisters, The
Pointer, Bonnie
  See Pointer Sisters, The
Pointer, June
  See Pointer Sisters, The
Pointer, Ruth
  See Pointer Sisters, The
Pointer Sisters, The **9**
Poison **11**
Poison Ivy
  See Rorschach, Poison Ivy
Poland, Chris
  See Megadeth
Polce, Tom
  See Letters to Cleo
Police, The **20**
Pollard, Jim
  See Guided By Voices
Pollard, Robert, Jr.
  See Guided By Voices
Pollock, Courtney Adam
  See Aquabats

Polygon Window
  See Aphex Twin
Pomus, Doc
  See Doc Pomus
Ponty, Jean-Luc **8**
  Also see Mahavishnu Orchestra
Pop, Iggy **23**
  Earlier sketch in CM **1**
Popper, John
  See Blues Traveler
Porter, Cole **10**
Porter, George, Jr.
  See Meters, The
Porter, Tiran
  See Doobie Brothers, The
Portishead **22**
Portman-Smith, Nigel
  See Pentangle
Portnoy, Mike
  See Dream Theater
Posdnuos
  See De La Soul
Post, Louise
  See Veruca Salt
Post, Mike **21**
Potts, Sean
  See Chieftains, The
Powell, Billy
  See Lynyrd Skynyrd
Powell, Bud **15**
Powell, Cozy
  See Emerson, Lake & Palmer/Powell
Powell, Kobie
  See US3
Powell, Paul
  See Aztec Camera
Powell, William
  See O'Jays, The
Powell, Baden **23**
Powers, Congo
  See Cramps, The
Powers, Kid Congo
  See Congo Norvell
Prater, Dave
  See Sam and Dave
Prefab Sprout **15**
Presley, Elvis **1**
Pretenders, The **8**
Previn, André **15**
Price, Alan
  See Animals
Price, Leontyne **6**
Price, Louis
  See Temptations, The
Price, Mark
  See Archers of Loaf
Price, Ray **11**
Price, Rick
  See Electric Light Orchestra
Pride, Charley **4**
Priest, Maxi **20**
Prima, Louis **18**
Primal Scream **14**

Primettes, The
  See Supremes, The
Primus **11**
Prince **14**
  Earlier sketch in CM **1**
Prince Be
  See P.M. Dawn
Prince, Prairie
  See Journey
Prine, John **7**
Prior, Maddy
  See Steeleye Span
Proclaimers, The **13**
Prodigy **22**
Professor Longhair **6**
Prong **23**
Propatier, Joe
  See Silver Apples
Propes, Duane
  See Little Texas
Prout, Brian
  See Diamond Rio
Public Enemy **4**
Puente, Tito **14**
Pullen, Don **16**
Pulp **18**
Pulsford, Nigel
  See Bush
Pusey, Clifford "Moonie"
  See Steel Pulse
Pyle, Andy
  See Kinks, The
Pyle, Artemis
  See Lynyrd Skynyrd
Pyle, Pip
  See Gong
Q-Tip
  See Tribe Called Quest, A
Quaife, Peter
  See Kinks, The
Quasi **24**
Queen **6**
Queen Ida **9**
Queen Latifah **24**
  Earlier sketch in CM **6**
Queensryche **8**
Querfurth, Carl
  See Roomful of Blues
Quicksilver Messenger Service **23**
REO Speedwagon **23**
Rabbitt, Eddie **24**
  Earlier sketch in CM **5**
Rabin, Trevor
  See Yes
Radiohead **24**
Raffi **8**
Rage Against the Machine **18**
Raheem
  See GetoBoys, The
Rainey, Ma **22**
Rainey, Sid
  See Compulsion
Raitt, Bonnie **23**
  Earlier sketch in CM **3**

Rakim
  See Eric B. and Rakim
Raleigh, Don
  See Squirrel Nut Zippers
Ralphs, Mick
  See Bad Company
Ramone, C. J.
  See Ramones, The
Ramone, Dee Dee
  See Ramones, The
Ramone, Joey
  See Ramones, The
Ramone, Johnny
  See Ramones, The
Ramone, Marky
  See Ramones, The
Ramone, Ritchie
  See Ramones, The
Ramone, Tommy
  See Ramones, The
Ramones, The **9**
Rampal, Jean-Pierre **6**
Ramsay, Andy
  See Stereolab
Ranaldo, Lee
  See Sonic Youth
Randall, Bobby
  See Sawyer Brown
Raney, Jerry
  See Beat Farmers
Rangell, Andrew **24**
Ranglin, Ernest
  See Skatalites, The
Ranken, Andrew
  See Pogues, The
Rankin, Cookie
  See Rankins, The
Rankin, Heather
  See Rankins, The
Rankin, Jimmy
  See Rankins, The
Rankin, John Morris
  See Rankins, The
Rankin, Raylene
  See Rankins, The
Ranking, Roger
  See English Beat, The
Rankins, The **24**
Rapp, Tom
  See Pearls Before Swine
Rarebell, Herman
  See Scorpions, The
Raven, Paul
  See Prong
Ray, Amy
  See Indigo Girls
Raybon, Marty
  See Shenandoah
Raye, Collin **16**
Raymonde, Simon
  See Cocteau Twins, The
Rea, Chris **12**
Read, John
  See Specials, The

Reagon, Bernice Johnson
  See Sweet Honey in the Rock
Redding, Otis **5**
Redd Kross **20**
Reddy, Helen **9**
Red Hot Chili Peppers, The **7**
Redman, Don
  See McKinney's Cotton Pickers
Redman, Joshua **12**
Redpath, Jean **1**
Reece, Chris
  See Social Distortion
Reed, Jimmy **15**
Reed, Lou **16**
  Earlier sketch in CM **1**
  Also see Velvet Underground, The
Reef **24**
Reese, Della **13**
Reeves, Dianne **16**
Reeves, Jim **10**
Reeves, Martha **4**
Reich, Steve **8**
Reid, Charlie
  See Proclaimers, The
Reid, Christopher
  See Kid 'n Play
Reid, Craig
  See Proclaimers, The
Reid, Delroy "Junior"
  See Black Uhuru
Reid, Don
  See Statler Brothers, The
Reid, Ellen Lorraine
  See Crash Test Dummies
Reid, Harold
  See Statler Brothers, The
Reid, Janet
  See Black Uhuru
Reid, Jim
  See Jesus and Mary Chain, The
Reid, Vernon **2**
  Also see Living Colour
Reid, William
  See Jesus and Mary Chain, The
Reifman, William
  See KMFDM
Reinhardt, Django **7**
Reitzell, Brian
  See Redd Kross
Relf, Keith
  See Yardbirds, The
R.E.M. **5**
Renbourn, John
  See Pentangle
Reno, Ronnie
  See Osborne Brothers, The
Replacements, The **7**
Republica **20**
Residents, The **14**
Restless Heart **12**
Revell, Adrian
  See Jamiroquai
Rex
  See Pantera

Reyes, Andre
  See Gipsy Kings, The
Reyes, Canut
  See Gipsy Kings, The
Reyes, Nicolas
  See Gipsy Kings, The
Reynolds, Nick
  See Kingston Trio, The
Reynolds, Robert
  See Mavericks, The
Reynolds, Sheldon
  See Earth, Wind and Fire
Reznor, Trent **13**
Rhodes, Nick
  See Duran Duran
Rhodes, Philip
  See Gin Blossoms
Rhodes, Todd
  See McKinney's Cotton Pickers
Rhone, Sylvia **13**
Rich, Buddy **13**
Rich, Charlie **3**
Richard, Cliff **14**
Richard, Zachary **9**
Richards, Edward
  See Shamen, The
Richards, Keith **11**
  Also see Rolling Stones, The
Richardson, Geoffrey
  See Caravan
Richardson, Kevin
  See Backstreet Boys
Richey, Kim **20**
Richie, Lionel
  See Commodores, The
Richie, Lionel **2**
Richling, Greg
  See Wallflowers, The
Richman, Jonathan **12**
Richrath, Gary
  See REO Speedwagon
Rick, Dave
  See King Missile
Ricochet **23**
Riebling, Scott
  See Letters to Cleo
Rieckermann, Ralph
  See Scorpions, The
Rieflin, William
  See Ministry
Riles, Kelly
  See Velocity Girl
Riley, Teddy **14**
Riley, Teddy "Street"
  See Blackstreet
Riley, Timothy Christian
  See Tony! Toni! Toné!
Rippon, Steve
  See Lush
Ritchie, Brian
  See Violent Femmes
Ritchie, Jean **4**
Ritenour, Lee **7**
Roach, Max **12**

Roback, David
  See Mazzy Star
Robbins, Charles David
  See BlackHawk
Robbins, Marty **9**
Roberts, Brad
  See Crash Test Dummies
Roberts, Brad
  See Gwar
Roberts, Dan
  See Crash Test Dummies
Roberts, Ken
  See Charm Farm
Roberts, Marcus **6**
Roberts, Nathan
  See Flaming Lips
Robertson, Brian
  See Motörhead
  Also see Thin Lizzy
Robertson, Ed
  See Barenaked Ladies
Robertson, Robbie **2**
  Also see Band, The
Robeson, Paul **8**
Robillard, Duke **2**
  Also see Roomful of Blues
Robinson, Arnold
  See Nylons, The
Robinson, Chris
  See Black Crowes, The
Robinson, David
  See Cars, The
Robinson, Dawn
  See En Vogue
Robinson, R.B.
  See Soul Stirrers, The
Robinson, Rich
  See Black Crowes, The
Robinson, Romye "Booty Brown"
  See Pharcyde, The
Robinson, Smokey **1**
Robinson, Cynthia
  See Sly & the Family Stone
Roche, Maggie
  See Roches, The
Roche, Suzzy
  See Roches, The
Roche, Terre
  See Roches, The
Roches, The **18**
Rockenfield, Scott
  See Queensryche
Rocker, Lee
  See Stray Cats, The
Rockett, Rikki
  See Poison
Rockin' Dopsie **10**
Rodford, Jim
  See Kinks, The
Rodgers, Jimmie **3**
Rodgers, Nile **8**
Rodgers, Paul
  See Bad Company

Rodgers, Richard **9**
Rodney, Red **14**
Rodriguez, Rico
  See Skatalites, The
  Also see Specials, The
Rodriguez, Sal
  See War
Roe, Marty
  See Diamond Rio
Roeder, Klaus
  See Kraftwerk
Roeser, Donald
  See Blue Oyster Cult
Roeser, Eddie "King"
  See Urge Overkill
Roessler, Kira
  See Black Flag
Rogers, Dan
  See Bluegrass Patriots
Rogers, Kenny **1**
Rogers, Norm
  See Jayhawks, The
Rogers, Roy **24**
  Earlier sketch in CM **9**
Rogers, Willie
  See Soul Stirrers, The
Roland, Dean
  See Collective Soul
Roland, Ed
  See Collective Soul
Rolie, Gregg
  See Journey
Rolling Stones, The **23**
  Earlier sketch in CM **3**
Rollins, Henry **11**
  Also see Black Flag
Rollins, Sonny **7**
Rollins, Winston
  See Jamiroquai
Romano, Ruben
  See Fu Manchu
Romm, Ronald
  See Canadian Brass, The
Ron, Wood
  See Rolling Stones, The
Ronstadt, Linda **2**
Roomful of Blues **7**
Roper, De De
  See Salt-N-Pepa
Rorschach, Poison Ivy
  See Cramps, The
Rosas, Cesar
  See Los Lobos
Rose, Axl
  See Guns n' Roses
Rose, Johanna Maria
  See Anonymous 4
Rose, Michael
  See Black Uhuru
Rosen, Gary
  See Rosenshontz
Rosen, Peter
  See War

Rosenshontz **9**
Rosenthal, Jurgen
  See Scorpions, The
Rosenthal, Phil
  See Seldom Scene, The
Ross, Diana **1**
  Also see Supremes, The
Ross, Malcolm
  See Aztec Camera
Rossdale, Gavin
  See Bush
Rossi, John
  See Roomful of Blues
Rossington, Gary
  See Lynyrd Skynyrd
Rostill, John
  See Shadows, The
Rostropovich, Mstislav **17**
Rota, Nino **13**
Roth, C. P.
  See Blessid Union of Souls
Roth, David Lee **1**
  Also see Van Halen
Roth, Ulrich
  See Scorpions, The
Rotheray, Dave
  See Beautiful South
Rotsey, Martin
  See Midnight Oil
Rotten, Johnny
  See Lydon, John
  Also see Sex Pistols, The
Rourke, Andy
  See Smiths, The
Rowberry, Dave
  See Animals
Rowe, Dwain
  See Restless Heart
Rowlands, Bruce
  See Fairport Convention
Rowlands, Tom
  See Chemical Brothers
Rowntree, Dave
  See Blur
Roxette **23**
Rubin, Mark
  See Bad Livers, The
Rubin, Rick **9**
Rubinstein, Arthur **11**
Rucker, Darius
  See Hootie and the Blowfish
Rudd, Phillip
  See AC/DC
Rue, Caroline
  See Hole
Ruffin, David **6**
  Also see Temptations, The
Ruffy, Dave
  See Aztec Camera
Rundgren, Todd **11**
Run-D.M.C. **4**
RuPaul **20**
Rush **8**

Rush, Otis **12**
Rushlow, Tim
  See Little Texas
Russell, Alecia
  See Sounds of Blackness
Russell, Graham
  See Air Supply
Russell, John
  See Steppenwolf
Russell, Mark **6**
Russell, Mike
  See Shudder to Think
Rutherford, Mike
  See Genesis
  Also see Mike & the Mechanics
Rutsey, John
  See Rush
Ryan, David
  See Lemonheads, The
Ryan, Mark
  See Quicksilver Messenger Service
Ryan, Mick
  See Dave Clark Five, The
Ryder, Mitch **23**
  Earlier sketch in CM **11**
Ryland, Jack
  See Three Dog Night
Rzeznik, Johnny
  See Goo Goo Dolls, The
Sabo, Dave
  See Bon Jovi
Sade **2**
Sadier, Laetitia
  See Stereolab
Saffery, Anthony
  See Cornershop
Saffron,
  See Republica
Sager, Carole Bayer **5**
Sahm, Doug
  See Texas Tornados, The
St. Hubbins, David
  See Spinal Tap
St. John, Mark
  See Kiss
St. Marie, Buffy
  See Sainte-Marie, Buffy
St. Nicholas, Nick
  See Steppenwolf
Sainte-Marie, Buffy **11**
Sakamoto, Ryuichi **19**
Salerno-Sonnenberg, Nadja **3**
Saliers, Emily
  See Indigo Girls
Salisbury, Peter
  See Verve, The
  Also see Pizzicato Five
Salmon, Michael
  See Prefab Sprout
Saloman, Nick
  See Bevis Frond
Salonen, Esa-Pekka 16
Salt-N-Pepa **6**

Saluzzi, Dino **23**
Sam, Watters
  See Color Me Badd
Sam and Dave **8**
Sambora, Richie **24**
  Also s ee Bon Jovi
Sammy, Piazza
  See Quicksilver Messenger Service
Sampson, Doug
  See Iron Maiden
Samuelson, Gar
  See Megadeth
Samwell-Smith, Paul
  See Yardbirds, The
Sanborn, David **1**
Sanchez, Michel
  See Deep Forest
Sanctuary, Gary
  See Aztec Camera
Sanders, Ric
  See Fairport Convention
Sanders, Steve
  See Oak Ridge Boys, The
Sandman, Mark
  See Morphine
Sandoval, Arturo **15**
Sandoval, Hope
  See Mazzy Star
Sands, Aaron
  See Jars of Clay
Sanford, Gary
  See Aztec Camera
Sangare, Oumou **22**
Sanger, David
  See Asleep at the Wheel
Santana, Carlos **20**
  Earlier sketch in CM **1**
Santiago, Herman
  See Frankie Lymon and The Teenagers
Santiago, Joey
  See Pixies, The
Saraceno, Blues
  See Poison
Sasaki, Mamiko
  See PulpSanders, Pharoah **16**
Satchell, Clarence "Satch"
  See Ohio Players
Satriani, Joe **4**
Savage, Rick
  See Def Leppard
Savage, Scott
  See Jars of Clay
Sawyer Brown **13**
Sawyer, Phil
  See Spencer Davis Group
Saxa
  See English Beat, The
Saxon, Stan
  See Dave Clark Five, The
Scaccia, Mike
  See Ministry
Scaggs, Boz **12**
Scanlon, Craig
  See Fall, The

Scarface
  See Geto Boys, The
Schmid, Daniel
  See Cherry Poppin' Daddies
Schock, Gina
  See Go-Go's, The
Schramm, Dave
  See Yo La Tengo
Schelhaas, Jan
  See Camel
  Also see Caravan
Schemel, Patty
  See Hole
Schenker, Michael
  See Scorpions, The
Schenker, Rudolf
  See Scorpions, The
Schenkman, Eric
  See Spin Doctors
Schermie, Joe
  See Three Dog Night
Scherpenzeel, Ton
  See Camel
Schickele, Peter **5**
Schlitt, John
  See Petra
Schloss, Zander
  See Circle Jerks, The
Schmelling, Johannes
  See Tangerine Dream
Schmit, Timothy B.
  See Eagles, The
Schmoovy Schmoove
  See Digital Underground
Schneider, Florian
  See Kraftwerk
Schneider, Fred III
  See B-52's, The
Schnitzler, Conrad
  See Tangerine Dream
Scholten, Jim
  See Sawyer Brown
Scholz, Tom
  See Boston
Schon, Neal
  See Journey
Schrody, Erik
  See House of Pain
Schroyder, Steve
  See Tangerine Dream
Schulman, Mark
  See Foreigner
Schulz, Guenter
  See KMFDM
Schulze, Klaus
  See Tangerine Dream
Schuman, William **10**
Schuur, Diane **6**
Sclavunos, Jim
  See Congo Norvell
Scofield, John **7**
Scorpions, The **12**
Scott, Ronald Belford "Bon"
  See AC/DC

Scott, George
  See Five Blind Boys of Alabama
Scott, Howard
  See War
Scott, Jimmy **14**
Scott, Sherry
  See Earth, Wind and Fire
Scott-Heron, Gil **13**
Scruggs, Earl **3**
Scud Mountain Boys **21**
Seal **14**
Seales, Jim
  See Shenandoah
Seals, Brady
  See Little Texas
Seals, Dan **9**
Seals, Jim
  See Seals & Crofts
Seals & Crofts **3**
Seaman, Ken
  See Bluegrass Patriots
Sears, Pete
  See Jefferson Starship
Secada, Jon **13**
Secrest, Wayne
  See Confederate Railroad
Sedaka, Neil **4**
Seeger, Pete **4**
  Also see Weavers, The
Seger, Bob **15**
Segovia, Andres **6**
Selway, Phil
  See Radiohead
Seldom Scene, The **4**
Selena **16**
Sen Dog
  See Cypress Hill
Senior, Milton
  See McKinney's Cotton Pickers
Senior, Russell
  See Pulp
Sensi
  See Soul II Soul
Sepultura **12**
Seraphine, Daniel
  See Chicago
Sermon, Erick
  See EPMD
Setzer, Brian
  See Stray Cats, The
Severin, Steven
  See Siouxsie and the Banshees
Severinsen, Doc **1**
Sex Pistols, The **5**
Sexton, Chad
  See 311
Seymour, Neil
  See Crowded House
Shabalala, Ben
  See Ladysmith Black Mambazo
Shabalala, Headman
  See Ladysmith Black Mambazo
Shabalala, Jockey
  See Ladysmith Black Mambazo

Shabalala, Joseph
  See Ladysmith Black Mambazo
Shadows, The **22**
Shaffer, Paul **13**
Shai **23**
Shakespeare, Robbie
  See Sly and Robbie
Shakur, Tupac
  See 2Pac
Shallenberger, James
  See Kronos Quartet
Shamen, The **23**
Shane, Bob
  See Kingston Trio, The
Shanice **14**
Shankar, Ravi **9**
Shannon, Del **10**
Shannon, Sarah
  See Velocity Girl
Shanté **10**
Shapiro, Jim
  See Veruca Salt
Shapps, Andre
  See Big Audio Dynamite
Sharon, Lois & Bram **6**
Sharp, Dave
  See Alarm
Sharpe, Matt
  See Weezer
Sharrock, Chris
  See Lightning Seeds
Sharrock, Sonny **15**
Shaw, Adrian
  See Bevis Frond
Shaw, Artie **8**
Shaw, Martin
  See Jamiroquai
Shea, Tom
  See Scud Mountain Boys
Shearer, Harry
  See Spinal Tap
Sheehan, Bobby
  See Blues Traveler
Sheehan, Fran
  See Boston
Sheila E. **3**
Shelley, Peter
  See Buzzcocks, The
Shelley, Steve
  See Sonic Youth
Shenandoah **17**
Shepherd, Kenny Wayne **22**
Sheppard, Rodney
  See Sugar Ray
Sherba, John
  See Kronos Quartet
Sherinian, Derek
  See Dream Theater
Sherman, Jack
  See Red Hot Chili Peppers, The
Shines, Johnny **14**
Shirelles, The **11**
Shirley, Danny
  See Confederate Railroad

Shively, William
  See Big Mountain
Shocked, Michelle **4**
Shock G
  See Digital Underground
Shocklee, Hank **15**
Shogren, Dave
  See Doobie Brothers, The
Shonen Knife **13**
Shontz, Bill
  See Rosenshontz
Shorter, Wayne **5**
  Also see Weather Report
Shovell
  See M People
Shudder to Think **20**
Siberry, Jane **6**
Sice
  See Boo Radleys, The
Sidelnyk, Steve
  See Aztec Camera
Siegal, Janis
  See Manhattan Transfer, The
Sikes, C. David
  See Boston
Sills, Beverly **5**
Silva, Kenny Jo
  See Beaver Brown Band, The
Silver Apples **23**
Silverchair **20**
Simien, Terrance **12**
Simmons, Gene
  See Kiss
Simmons, Joe "Run"
  See Run-D.M.C.
Simmons, Patrick
  See Doobie Brothers, The
Simmons, Russell **7**
Simmons, Trinna
  See Spearhead
Simms, Nick
  See Cornershop
Simon and Garfunkel **24**
Simon, Carly **22**
  Earlier sketch in CM **4**
Simon, Paul **16**
  Earlier sketch in CM **1**
  See also Simon and Garfunkel
Simone, Nina **11**
Simonon, Paul
  See Clash, The
Simons, Ed
  See Chemical Brothers
Simins, Russell
  See Jon Spencer Blues Explosion
Simple Minds **21**
Simpson, Denis
  See Nylons, The
Simpson, Derrick "Duckie"
  See Black Uhuru
Simpson, Mel
  See US3
Simpson, Ray
  See Village People, The

Simpson, Rose
See Incredible String Band
Sims, David William
See Jesus Lizard
Sims, Neil
See Catherine Wheel
Sin, Will
See Shamen, The
Sinatra, Frank **23**
Earlier sketch in CM **1**
Sinclair, David
See Camel
See Caravan
Sinclair, Gord
See Tragically Hip, The
Sinclair, Richard
See Camel
See Caravan
Sinfield, Peter
See King Crimson
Singer, Eric
See Black Sabbath
Singh, Talvin
See Massive Attack
Singh, Tjinder
See Cornershop
Sioux, Siouxsie
See Siouxsie and the Banshees
Siouxsie and the Banshees **8**
Sir Mix-A-Lot
Sir Rap-A-Lot
See Geto Boys, The
Sirois, Joe
See Mighty Mighty Bosstones
Siverton
See Specials, The
Sixx, Nikki
See Mötley Crüe
Sixx, Roger
See Less Than Jake
Skaggs, Ricky **5**
Also see Country Gentlemen, The
Skatalites, The **18**
Skeoch, Tommy
See Tesla
Skillings, Muzz
See Living Colour
Skinny Puppy **17**
Sklamberg, Lorin
See Klezmatics, The
Skoob
See Das EFX
Slash
See Guns n' Roses
Slayer **10**
Sleater-Kinney **20**
Sledd, Dale
See Osborne Brothers, The
Sledge, Percy **15**
Sledge, Robert
See Ben Folds Five
Slick, Grace
See Jefferson Airplane

Slijngaard, Ray
See 2 Unlimited
Sloan, Eliot
See Blessid Union of Souls
Slovak, Hillel
See Red Hot Chili Peppers, The
Sly and Robbie **13**
Sly & the Family Stone **24**
Small, Heather
See M People
Smalls, Derek
See Spinal Tap
Smart, Terence
See Butthole Surfers
Smashing Pumpkins **13**
Smear, Pat
See Foo Fighters
Smith, Adrian
See Iron Maiden
Smith, Bessie **3**
Smith, Brad
See Blind Melon
Smith, Chad
See Red Hot Chili Peppers, The
Smith, Charles
See Kool & the Gang
Smith, Curt
See Tears for Fears
Smith, Debbie
See Curve
Smith, Debbie
See Echobelly
Smith, Fran
See Hooters
Smith, Fred
See Blondie
Smith, Fred
See MC5, The
Smith, Fred
See Television
Smith, Garth
See Buzzcocks, The
Smith, Joe
See McKinney's Cotton Pickers
Smith, Kevin
See dc Talk
Smith, Mark E.
See Fall, The
Smith, Michael W. **11**
Smith, Mike
See Dave Clark Five, The
Smith, Parrish
See EPMD
Smith, Patti **17**
Earlier sketch in CM **1**
Smith, Robert
See Cure, The
Also see Siouxsie and the Banshees
Smith, Robert
See Spinners, The
Smith, Shawn
See Brad
Smith, Smitty
See Three Dog Night

Smith, Steve
See Journey
Smith, Tweed
See War
Smith, Wendy
See Prefab Sprout
Smith, Willard
See DJ Jazzy Jeff and the Fresh Prince
Smithereens, The **14**
Smiths, The **3**
Smyth, Gilli
See Gong
Smyth, Joe
See Sawyer Brown
Sneed, Floyd Chester
See Three Dog Night
Snoop Doggy Dogg **17**
Snow **23**
Snow, Don
See Squeeze
Snow, Phoebe **4**
Soan, Ashley
See Del Amitri
Sobule, Jill **20**
Solal, Martial **4**
Soloff, Lew
See Blood, Sweat and Tears
Solti, Georg **13**
Sondheim, Stephen **8**
Sonefeld, Jim
See Hootie and the Blowfish
Sonic Youth **9**
Sonnenberg, Nadja Salerno
See Salerno-Sonnenberg, Nadja
Sonni, Jack
See Dire Straits
Sonnier, Jo-El **10**
Sonny and Cher **24**
Son Volt **21**
Sorum, Matt
See Cult, The
Sosa, Mercedes **3**
Soucie, Michael
See Surfin' Pluto
Soul Asylum **10**
Soul Coughing **21**
Soul Stirrers, The **11**
Soul II Soul **17**
Soundgarden **6**
Sounds of Blackness **13**
Sousa, John Philip **10**
Southerland, Bill
See Kilgore
Spampinato, Joey
See NRBQ
Spampinato, Johnny
See NRBQ
Spann, Otis **18**
Sparks **18**
Sparks, Donita
See L7
Special Ed **16**
Specials, The **21**
Spector, Phil **4**

Speech
  See Arrested Development
Spellman, Jim
  See Velocity Girl
Spence, Alexander "Skip"
  See Jefferson Airplane
  Also see Moby Grape
Spence, Cecil
  See Israel Vibration
Spence, Skip
  See Spence, Alexander "Skip"
Spencer, Jeremy
  See Fleetwood Mac
Spencer, Jim
  See Dave Clark Five, The
Spencer, Jon
  See Jon Spencer Blues Explosion
Spencer, Thad
  See Jayhawks, The
Spice Girls 22
Spinal Tap 8
Spin Doctors 14
Spinners, The 21
Spirit 22
Spitz, Dan
  See Anthrax
Spitz, Dave
  See Black Sabbath
Sponge 18
Spring, Keith
  See NRBQ
Springfield, Dusty 20
Springfield, Rick 9
Springsteen, Bruce 6
Sproule, Daithi
  See Altan
Sprout, Tobin
  See Guided By Voices
Squeeze 5
Squire, Chris
  See Yes
Squire, John
  See Stone Roses, The
Squires, Rob
  See Big Head Todd and the Monsters
Squirrel Nut Zippers 20
Stacey, Peter "Spider"
  See Pogues, The
Stacy, Jeremy
  See Aztec Camera
Staehely, Al
  See Spirit
Staehely, J. Christian
  See Spirit
Stafford, Jo 24
Staley, Layne
  See Alice in Chains
Staley, Tom
  See NRBQ
Stanier, John
  See Helmet
Stanley, Ian
  See Tears for Fears

Stanley, Paul
  See Kiss
Stanley, Ralph 5
Stansfield, Lisa 9
Staples, Mavis 13
Staples, Neville
  See Specials, The
Staples, Pops 11
Starcrunch
  See Man or Astroman?
Starling, John
  See Seldom Scene, The
Starr, Mike
  See Alice in Chains
Starr, Ringo 24
  Earlier sketch in CM 10
  Also see Beatles, The
Starship
  See Jefferson Airplane
Statler Brothers, The 8
Stead, David
  See Beautiful South
Steaks, Chuck
  See Quicksilver Messenger Service
Steel, John
  See Animals
Steele, Billy
  See Sounds of Blackness
Steele, David
  See English Beat, The
  Also see Fine Young Cannibals
Steel Pulse 14
Steele, Jeffrey
  See Boy Howdy
Steele, Michael
  See Bangles
Steely Dan 5
Stefani, Gwen
  See No Doubt
Steier, Rick
  See Warrant
Stein, Chris
  See Blondie
Steinberg, Lewis
  See Booker T. & the M.G.'s
Steinberg, Sebastian
  See Soul Coughing
Stephenson, Van Wesley
  See BlackHawk
Steppenwolf 20
Sterban, Richard
  See Oak Ridge Boys, The
Stereolab 18
Sterling, Lester
  See Skatalites, The
Stern, Isaac 7
Stevens, Cat 3
Stevens, Ray 7
Stevens, Roger
  See Blind Melon
Stevenson, Bill
  See Black Flag
Stevenson, Don
  See Moby Grape

Steward, Pat
  See Odds
Stewart, Dave
  See Eurythmics
Stewart, Derrick "Fatlip"
  See Pharcyde, The
Stewart, Freddie
  See Sly & the Family Stone
Stewart, Ian
  See Rolling Stones, The
Stewart, Jamie
  See Cult, The
Stewart, John
  See Kingston Trio, The
Stewart, Larry
  See Restless Heart
Stewart, Rod 20
  Earlier sketch in CM 2
  Also see Faces, The
Stewart, Sylvester
  See Sly & the Family Stone
Stewart, Tyler
  See Barenaked Ladies
Stewart, Vaetta
  See Sly & the Family Stone
Stewart, William
  See Third World
Stewart, Winston "Metal"
  See Mystic Revealers
Stiff, Chris
  See Jackyl
Stills, Stephen 5
  See Buffalo Springfield
  Also see Crosby, Stills, and Nash
Sting 19
  Earlier sketch in CM 2
  Also see Police, The
Stinson, Bob
  See Replacements, The
Stinson, Tommy
  See Replacements, The
Stipe, Michael
  See R.E.M.
Stockman, Shawn
  See Boyz II Men
Stoll
  See Clannad
  See Big Mountain
Stoller, Mike
  See Leiber and Stoller
Stoltz, Brian
  See Neville Brothers, The
Stoltzman, Richard 24
Stonadge, Gary
  See Big Audio Dynamite
Stone, Curtis
  See Highway 101
Stone, Doug 10
Stone Roses, The 16
Stone, Sly 8
Stone Temple Pilots 14
Stookey, Paul
  See Peter, Paul & Mary
Story, Liz 2

Story, The **13**
Stradlin, Izzy
   See Guns n' Roses
Strain, Sammy
   See O'Jays, The
Strait, George **5**
Stratton, Dennis
   See Iron Maiden
Stravinsky, Igor **21**
Straw, Syd **18**
Stray Cats, The **11**
Strayhorn, Billy **13**
Street, Richard
   See Temptations, The
Streisand, Barbra **2**
Strickland, Keith
   See B-52's, The
Stringer, Gary
   See Reef
Strummer, Joe
   See Clash, The
Stryper **2**
Stuart, Mark
   See Audio Adrenaline
Stuart, Marty **9**
Stuart, Peter
   See Dog's Eye View
Stubbs, Levi
   See Four Tops, The
Styne, Jule **21**
Subdudes, The **18**
Sublime **19**
Such, Alec Jon
   See Bon Jovi
Suede **20**
Sugar Ray **22**
Sugarcubes, The **10**
Suicidal Tendencies **15**
Sulley, Suzanne
   See Human League, The
Sullivan, Jacqui
   See Bananarama
Sullivan, Kirk
   See FourHim
Summer, Donna **12**
Summer, Mark
   See Turtle Island String Quartet
Summers, Andy **3**
   Also see Police, The
Sumner, Bernard
   See Joy Division
   Also see New Order
Sundays, The **20**
Sun Ra **5**
Sunnyland Slim **16**
Super DJ Dmitry
   See Deee-lite
Superdrag **23**
Supremes, The **6**
Sure!, Al B. **13**
Surfaris, The **23**
Surfin' Pluto **24**
Sutcliffe, Stu
   See Beatles, The

Sutherland, Joan **13**
Svenigsson, Magnus
   See Cardigans
Svensson, Peter
   See Cardigans
Svigals, Alicia
   See Klezmatics, The
Swarbrick, Dave
   See Fairport Convention
Sweat, Keith **13**
Sweet, Matthew **9**
Sweet, Michael
   See Stryper
Sweet, Robert
   See Stryper
Sweethearts of the Rodeo **12**
Sweet Honey in the Rock **1**
Swing, DeVante
   See Jodeci
SWV **14**
Sykes, John
   See Whitesnake
Sykes, Roosevelt **20**
Sylvain, Sylvain
   See New York Dolls
Tabac, Tony
   See Joy Division
Tabor, Ty
   See King's X
TAFKAP (The Artist Formerly Known as Prince)
   See Prince
Taggart, Jeremy
   See Our Lady Peace
Tait, Michael
   See dc Talk
Taj Mahal **6**
Tajima, Takao
   See Pizzicato Five
Takac, Robby
   See Goo Goo Dolls, The
Takanami
   See Pizzicato Five
Takemitsu, Toru **6**
Take 6 **6**
Takizawa, Taishi
   See Ghost
Talbot, John Michael **6**
Talcum, Joe Jack
   See Dead Milkmen
Talking Heads **1**
Tandy, Richard
   See Electric Light Orchestra
Tangerine Dream **12**
Taree, Aerle
   See Arrested Development
Tate, Geoff
   See Queensryche
Tatum, Art **17**
Taupin, Bernie **22**
Taylor, Andy
   See Duran Duran
Taylor, Billy **13**
Taylor, Cecil **9**

Taylor, Chad
   See Live
Taylor, Courtney
   See Dandy Warhols, The
Taylor, Dave
   See Pere Ubu
Taylor, Dick
   See Rolling Stones, The
Taylor, Earl
   See Country Gentlemen, The
Taylor, James **2**
Taylor, James "J.T."
   See Kool & the Gang
Taylor, John
   See Duran Duran
Taylor, Johnnie
   See Soul Stirrers, The
Taylor, Koko **10**
Taylor, Leroy
   See Soul Stirrers, The
Taylor, Melvin
   See Ventures, The
Taylor, Mick
   See Rolling Stones, The
Taylor, Philip "Philthy Animal"
   See Motörhead
Taylor, Roger
   See Duran Duran
Taylor, Roger Meadows
   See Queen
Taylor, Teresa
   See Butthole Surfers
Teagarden, Jack **10**
Tears for Fears **6**
Technotronic **5**
Teenage Fanclub **13**
Te Kanawa, Kiri **2**
Television **17**
Teller, Al **15**
Tempesta, John
   See White Zombie
Temple, Michelle
   See Pere Ubu
Temptations, The **3**
Tennant, Neil
   See Pet Shop Boys
10,000 Maniacs **3**
Terminator X
   See Public Enemy
Terrell, Jean
   See Supremes, The
Terry, Boyd
   See Aquabats
Terry, Clark **24**
Tesh, John **20**
Tesla **15**
Texas Tornados, The **8**
Thacker, Rocky
   See Shenandoah
Thain, Gary
   See Uriah Heep
Thayil, Kim
   See Soundgarden
The The **15**

They Might Be Giants **7**
Thibaudet, Jean-Yves **24**
Thielemans, Toots **13**
Thin Lizzy **13**
Third World **13**
Thomas, Alex
  See Earth, Wind and Fire
Thomas, David
  See Pere Ubu
Thomas, David
  See Take 6
Thomas, David Clayton
  See Clayton-Thomas, David
Thomas, Dennis "D.T."
  See Kool & the Gang
Thomas, George "Fathead"
  See McKinney's Cotton Pickers
Thomas, Irma **16**
Thomas, Mickey
  See Jefferson Starship
Thomas, Olice
  See Five Blind Boys of Alabama
Thomas, Ray
  See Moody Blues, The
Thomas, Rozonda "Chilli"
  See TLC
Thompson, Chester
  See Weather Report
Thompson, Danny
  See Pentangle
Thompson, Dennis
  See MC5, The
Thompson, Les
  See Nitty Gritty Dirt Band, The
Thompson, Mayo
  See Pere Ubu
Thompson, Porl
  See Cure, The
Thompson, Richard
  See Fairport Convention
Thompson, Richard **7**
Thomson, Kristin
  See Tsunami
Thorn, Christopher
  See Blind Melon
Thorn, Stan
  See Shenandoah
Thorn, Tracey
  See Everything But The Girl
  Also see Massive Attack
Thornalley, Phil
  See Cure, The
Thornhill, Leeroy
  See Prodigy
Thornton, Big Mama **18**
Thornton
  See Color Me Badd
Thornton, Willie Mae
  See Thornton, Big Mama
Threadgill, Henry **9**
311 **20**
3-D
  See Massive Attack
Three Dog Night **5**

Throwing Muses **15**
Thunders, Johnny
  See New York Dolls
Tickner, George
  See Journey
Tiffany **4**
Tikaram, Tanita **9**
Tilbrook, Glenn
  See Squeeze
Tiller, Mary
  See Anointed
Tillis, Mel **7**
Tillis, Pam **8**
Tilson Thomas, Michael **24**
Timbuk 3 **3**
Timmins, Margo
  See Cowboy Junkies, The
Timmins, Michael
  See Cowboy Junkies, The
Timmins, Peter
  See Cowboy Junkies, The
Timms, Sally
  See Mekons, The
Tinsley, Boyd
  See Dave Matthews Band
Tippin, Aaron **12**
Tipton, Glenn
  See Judas Priest
TLC **15**
Toad the Wet Sprocket **13**
Toback, Jeremy
  See Brad
Todd, Andy
  See Republica
Tolhurst, Laurence
  See Cure, The
Tolland, Bryan
  See Del Amitri
Toller, Dan
  See Allman Brothers, The
Tone-L c **3**
Tontoh, Frank
  See Aztec Camera
Tony K
  See Roomful of Blues
Tony! Toni! Toné! **12**
Too $hort **16**
Toohey, Dan
  See Guided By Voices
Took, Steve Peregrine
  See T. Rex
Tool **21**
Toomey, Jenny
  See Tsunami
Topham, Anthony "Top"
  See Yardbirds, The
Tork, Peter
  See Monkees, The
Torme, Mel **4**
Torres, Hector "Tico"
  See Bon Jovi
Toscanini, Arturo **14**
Tosh, Peter **3**
Toure, Ali Farka **18**

Tourish, Ciaran
  See Altan
Toussaint, Allen **11**
Towner, Ralph **22**
Townes, Jeffery
  See DJ Jazzy Jeff and the Fresh Prince
Townshend, Pete **1**
  Also see Who, The
Tragically Hip, The **18**
Travers, Brian
  See UB40
Travers, Mary
  See Peter, Paul & Mary
Travis, Merle **14**
Travis, Randy **9**
Treach
  See Naughty by Nature
T. Rex **11**
Treadmill Trackstar **21**
Tribe Called Quest, A **8**
Tricky
  See Massive Attack
Tricky **18**
Trimm, Rex
  See Cherry Poppin' Daddies
Tritsch, Christian
  See Gong
Tritt, Travis **7**
Trotter, Kera
  See C + C Music Factory
Trucks, Butch
  See Allman Brothers, The
Trugoy the Dove
  See De La Soul
Trujillo, Robert
  See Suicidal Tendencies
Truman, Dan
  See Diamond Rio
Trynin, Jen **21**
Tsunami **21**
Tubb, Ernest **4**
Tubridy, Michael
  See Chieftans, The
Tucker, Corin
  See Sleater-Kinney
Tucker, Moe
  See Velvet Underground, The
Tucker, Sophie **12**
Tucker, Tanya **3**
Tufnel, Nigel
  See Spinal Tap
Tull, Bruce
  See Scud Mountain Boys
Turbin, Neil
  See Anthrax
Turgon, Bruce
  See Foreigner
Turner, Big Joe **13**
Turner, Erik
  See Warrant
Turner, Joe Lynn
  See Deep Purple
Turner, Mike
  See Our Lady Peace

Turner, Steve
  See Mudhoney
Turner, Tina **1**
Turner, Ike
  See Ike and Tina Turner
Turner, Tina
  See Ike and Tina Turner
Turpin, Will
  See Collective Soul
Turre, Steve **22**
Turtle Island String Quartet **9**
Tutton, Bill
  See Geraldine Fibbers
Tutuska, George
  See Goo Goo Dolls, The
Tuxedomoon **21**
Twain, Shania **17**
Twist, Nigel
  See Alarm
Twitty, Conway **6**
2 Unlimited **18**
23, Richard
  See Front 242
2Pac **17**
  Also see Digital Underground
Tyagi, Paul
  See Del Amitri
Tyler, Steve
  See Aerosmith
Tyner, McCoy **7**
Tyner, Rob
  See MC5, The
Tyson, Ian
  See Ian and Sylvia
Tyson, Ron
  See Temptations, The
UB40 **4**
US3 **18**
Ulmer, James Blood **13**
Ulrich, Lars
  See Metallica
Ulvaeus, Björn
  See Abba
Um Romao, Dom
  See Weather Report
Unruh, N. U.
  See Einstürzende Neubauten
Uosikkinen, David
  See Hooters
Upshaw, Dawn **9**
Urge Overkill **17**
U2 **12**
  Earlier sketch in CM **2**
Usher **23**
Utley, Adrian
  See Portishead
Vaché, Jr., Warren **22**
Vachon, Chris
  See Roomful of Blues
Vai, Steve **5**
  Also see Whitesnake
Valens, Ritchie **23**
Valenti, Dino
  See Quicksilver Messenger Service

Valentine, Gary
  See Blondie
Valentine, Hilton
  See Animals
Valentine, Rae
  See War
Valentine, Kathy
  See Go-Go's, The
Valenzuela, Jesse
  See Gin Blossoms
Valli, Frankie **10**
  See Four Seasons, The
Valory, Ross
  See Journey
van Dijk, Carol
  See Bettie Serveert
Van Gelder, Nick
  See Jamiroquai
Van Hook, Peter
  See Mike & the Mechanics
Van Rensalier, Darnell
  See Shai
Vandenburg, Adrian
  See Whitesnake
Vander Ark, Brad
  See Verve Pipe, The
Vander Ark, Brian
  See Verve Pipe, The
Vandross, Luther **2**
Van Halen **8**
Van Halen, Alex
  See Van Halen
Van Halen, Edward
  See Van Halen
Vandross, Luther **24**
Vanilla Ice **6**
Van Ronk, Dave **12**
Van Shelton, Ricky **5**
Van Vliet, Don
  See Captain Beefheart
Van Zandt, Townes **13**
Van Zant, Johnny
  See Lynyrd Skynyrd
Van Zant, Ronnie
  See Lynyrd Skynyrd
Vasquez, Junior **16**
Vaughan, Jimmie **24**
  See Fabulous Thunderbirds, The
Vaughan, Sarah **2**
Vaughan, Stevie Ray **1**
Vedder, Eddie
  See Pearl Jam
Vega, Bobby
  See Quicksilver Messenger Service
Vega, Suzanne **3**
Velocity Girl **23**
Velvet Underground, The **7**
Ventures, The **19**
Verlaine, Tom
  See Television
Verta-Ray, Matt
  See Madder Rose
Veruca Salt **20**
Verve, The **18**

Verve Pipe, The **20**
Vettese, Peter-John
  See Jethro Tull
Vicious, Sid
  See Sex Pistols, The
  Also see Siouxsie and the Banshees
Vickrey, Dan
  See Counting Crows
Victor, Tommy
  See Prong
Vienna Boys Choir **23**
Vig, Butch **17**
Village People, The **7**
Vincent, Vinnie
  See Kiss
Vincent, Gene **19**
Vinnie
  See Naughty by Nature
Vinton, Bobby **12**
Violent Femmes **12**
Virtue, Michael
  See UB40
Visser, Peter
  See Bettie Serveert
Vito, Rick
  See Fleetwood Mac
Vitous, Mirslav
  See Weather Report
Voelz, Susan
  See Poi Dog Pondering
Volz, Greg
  See Petra
Von, Eerie
  See Danzig
von Karajan, Herbert **1**
Vox, Bono
  See U2
Vudi
  See American Music Club
Waaktaar, Pal
  See A-ha
Wade, Adam
  See Shudder to Think
Wade, Chrissie
  See Alien Sex Fiend
Wade, Nik
  See Alien Sex Fiend
Wadenius, George
  See Blood, Sweat and Tears
Wadephal, Ralf
  See Tangerine Dream
Wagoner, Faidest
  See Soul Stirrers, The
Wagoner, Porter **13**
Wahlberg, Donnie
  See New Kids on the Block
Wailer, Bunny **11**
Wainwright III, Loudon **11**
Waits, Tom **12**
  Earlier sketch in CM **1**
Wakeling, David
  See English Beat, The
Wakeman, Rick
  See Yes

Walden, Narada Michael **14**
Walford, Britt
  See Breeders
Walker, Clay **20**
Walker, Colin
  See Electric Light Orchestra
Walker, Ebo
  See New Grass Revival, The
Walker, Jerry Jeff **13**
Walker, T-Bone **5**
Wallace, Bill
  See Guess Who
Wallace, Ian
  See King Crimson
Wallace, Richard
  See Mighty Clouds of Joy, The
Wallace, Sippie **6**
Waller, Charlie
  See Country Gentlemen, The
Waller, Fats **7**
Wallflowers, The **20**
Wallinger, Karl **11**
Wallis, Larry
  See Motörhead
Walls, Chris
  See Dave Clark Five, The
Walls, Denise "Nee-C"
  See Anointed
Walls, Greg
  See Anthrax
Walsh, Joe **5**
  Also see Eagles, The
Walters, Robert "Patch"
  See Mystic Revealers
War **14**
Ward, Andy
Ward, Andy
  See Bevis Frond
  See Camel
Ward, Andy
  See Chumbawamba
Ward, Bill
Ward, Michael
  See Wallflowers, The
  See Black Sabbath
Ware, Martyn
  See Human League, The
Wareham, Dean
  See Luna
Wariner, Steve **18**
Warner, Les
  See Cult, The
Warnes, Jennifer **3**
Warrant **17**
Warren, George W.
  See Five Blind Boys of Alabama
Warren, Mervyn
  See Take 6
Warwick, Clint
  See Moody Blues, The
Warwick, Dionne **2**
Was, David
  See Was (Not Was)

Was, Don **21**
  Also see Was (Not Was)
Wash, Martha
  See C + C Music Factory
Washington, Chester
  See Earth, Wind and Fire
Washington, Dinah **5**
Washington, Grover, Jr. **5**
Was (Not Was) **6**
Wasserman, Greg
  See Offspring
Waters, Crystal **15**
Waters, Ethel **11**
Waters, Muddy **4**
Waters, Roger
  See Pink Floyd
Waters, Muddy **24**
Watkins, Christopher
  See Cabaret Voltaire
Watkins, Tionne "T-Boz"
  See TLC
Watley, Jody **9**
Watson, Doc **2**
Watson, Guy
  See Surfaris, The
Watson, Ivory
  See Ink Spots
Watt, Ben
  See Everything But The Girl
Watt, Mike **22**
  Also see fIREHOSE
Watts, Bari
  See Bevis Frond
Watts, Charlie
  See Rolling Stones, The
Watts, Eugene
  See Canadian Brass, The
Watts, Lou
  See Chumbawamba
Watts, Raymond
  See KMFDM
Watts, Todd
  See Emmet Swimming
Weaver, Louie
  See Petra
Weavers, The **8**
Webb, Chick **14**
Webb, Jimmy **12**
Webb, Paul
  See Talk Talk
Webber, Andrew Lloyd
  See Lloyd Webber, Andrew
Webber, Mark
  See Pulp
Webster, Andrew
  See Tsunami
Wedgwood, Mike
  See Caravan
Wedren, Craig
  See Shudder to Think
Weezer **20**
Weider, John
  See Animals

Weiland, Scott
  See Stone Temple Pilots
Weill, Kurt **12**
Weir, Bob
  See Grateful Dead, The
Weiss, Janet
  See Sleater-Kinney
Weiss, Janet
  See Quasi
Welch, Bob
Welch, Bruce
  See Shadows, The
Welch, Mcguinness
  See Fleetwood Mac
  Also see Lords of Acid
Welch, Sean
  See Beautiful South
Welk, Lawrence **13**
Weller, Paul **14**
Wells, Cory
  See Three Dog Night
Wells, Junior **17**
Wells, Kitty **6**
Welnick, Vince
  See Grateful Dead, The
Welty, Ron
  See Offspring
Wenberg, Erik
  See Emmet Swimming
West, Brian
  See Cherry Poppin' Daddies
West, Dottie **8**
West, Steve
  See Pavement
Westerberg, Paul
  See Replacements, The
Weston
  See Orb, The
Weston, Randy **15**
Wetton, John
  See King Crimson
Wexler, Jerry **15**
Weymouth, Tina
  See Talking Heads
Whalen, Katharine
  See Squirrel Nut Zippers
Wheat, Brian
  See Tesla
Wheeler, Audrey
  See C + C Music Factory
Wheeler, Caron
  See Soul II Soul
Wheeler, Harriet
  See Sundays, The
Wheeler, Robert
  See Pere Ubu
Whelan, Bill **20**
Whelan, Gavan
  See James
Whitaker, Rodney **20**
White, Alan
  See Oasis
White, Alan
  See Yes

White, Barry **6**
White, Billy
White, Chris
　See Dire Straits
　See Zombies, The
White, Dennis
　See Charm Farm
　See Dokken
White, Clarence
　See Byrds, The
White, Dave
　See Warrant
White, Freddie
　See Earth, Wind and Fire
White, Lari **15**
White, Mark
　See Mekons, The
White, Mark
　See Spin Doctors
White, Maurice
　See Earth, Wind and Fire
White, Ralph
　See Bad Livers, The
White, Roland
　See Nashville Bluegrass Band
White, Verdine
　See Earth, Wind and Fire
Whitehead, Donald
　See Earth, Wind and Fire
Whiteman, Paul **17**
Whitesnake **5**
White Zombie **17**
Whitfield, Mark **18**
Whitford, Brad
　See Aerosmith
Whitley, Chris **16**
Whitley, Keith **7**
Whittaker, Hudson **20**
Whitten, Chris
　See Dire Straits
Whitwam, Barry
　See Herman's Hermits
Who, The **3**
Wichnewski, Stephen
　See Yo La Tengo
Widenhouse, Je
　See Squirrel Nut Zippers
Wiedlin, Jane
　See Go-Go's, The
Wiggins, Dwayne
　See Tony! Toni! Toné!
Wiggins, Raphael
　See Tony! Toni! Toné!
Wiggs, Josephine
　See Breeders
Wikso, Ron
　See Foreigner
Wilborn, Dave
　See McKinney's Cotton Pickers
Wilburn, Ishmael
　See Weather Report
Wilcox, Imani
　See Pharcyde, The

Wilde, Phil
　See 2 Unlimited
Wilder, Alan
　See Depeche Mode
Wilk, Brad
　See Rage Against the Machine
Wilkeson, Leon
　See Lynyrd Skynyrd
Wilkie, Chris
　See Dubstar
Wilkinson, Geoff
　See US3
Wilkinson, Keith
　See Squeeze
Williams, Andy **2**
Williams, Boris
　See Cure, The
Williams, Cliff
　See AC/DC
Williams, Dana
　See Diamond Rio
Williams, Deniece **1**
Williams, Don **4**
Williams, Eric
　See Blackstreet
Williams, Fred
　See C + C Music Factory
Williams, Hank, Jr. **1**
Williams, Hank, Sr. **4**
Williams, James "Diamond"
　See Ohio Players
Williams, Joe **11**
Williams, John **9**
Williams, Lamar
　See Allman Brothers, The
Williams, Lucinda **10**
Williams, Marion **15**
Williams, Milan
　See Commodores, The
Williams, Otis
　See Temptations, The
Williams, Paul **5**
　See Temptations, The
Williams, Phillard
　See Earth, Wind and Fire
Williams, Terry
　See Dire Straits
Williams, Vanessa **10**
Williams, Victoria **17**
Williams, Walter
　See O'Jays, The
Williams, Wilbert
　See Mighty Clouds of Joy, The
Williams, William Elliot
　See Artifacts
Williams, Lucinda **24**
Williamson, Robin
　See Incredible String Band
Williamson, Sonny Boy **9**
Willie D.
　See Geto Boys, The
Willis, Clarence "Chet"
　See Ohio Players
Willis, Kelly **12**

Willis, Larry
　See Blood, Sweat and Tears
Willis, Pete
　See Def Leppard
Willis, Rick
　See Foreigner
Willis, Victor
　See Village People, The
Willner, Hal **10**
Wills, Bob **6**
Wills, Aaron (P-Nut)
　See 311
Wills, Rick
　See Bad Company
Willson-Piper, Marty
　See Church, The
Wilmot, Billy "Mystic"
　See Mystic Revealers
Wilson, Anne
　See Heart
Wilson, Brian
　See Beach Boys, The
Wilson, Carl
　See Beach Boys, The
Wilson, Carnie
　See Wilson Phillips
Wilson, Cassandra **12**
Wilson, Chris
　See Love Spit Love
Wilson, Cindy
　See B-52's, The
Wilson, Don
　See Ventures, The
Wilson, Dennis
　See Beach Boys, The
Wilson, Eric
　See Sublime
Wilson, Jackie **3**
Wilson, Kim
　See Fabulous Thunderbirds, The
Wilson, Mary
　See Supremes, The
Wilson, Nancy **14**
　See Heart
Wilson, Patrick
　See Weezer
Wilson, Ransom **5**
Wilson, Ricky
　See B-52's, The
Wilson, Robin
　See Gin Blossoms
Wilson, Ron
　See Surfaris, The
Wilson, Shanice
　See Shanice
Wilson, Wendy
　See Wilson Phillips
Wilson Phillips **5**
Wilson, Brian **24**
Wilson-James, Victoria
　See Shamen, The
Wilton, Michael
　See Queensryche

Wimpfheimer, Jimmy
  See Roomful of Blues
Winans, Carvin
  See Winans, The
Winans, Marvin
  See Winans, The
Winans, Michael
  See Winans, The
Winans, Ronald
  See Winans, The
Winans, The **12**
Winbush, Angela **15**
Winfield, Chuck
  See Blood, Sweat and Tears
Winston, George **9**
Winter, Johnny **5**
Winter, Kurt
  See Guess Who
Winter, Paul **10**
Winwood, Muff
  See Spencer Davis Group
Winwood, Steve **2**
  Also see Spencer Davis Group
  Also see Traffic
Wiseman, Bobby
  See Blue Rodeo
WishBone
  See Bone Thugs-N-Harmony
Withers, Pick
  See Dire Straits
Wolstencraft, Simon
  See Fall, The
Womack, Bobby **5**
Wonder, Stevie **17**
  Earlier sketch in CM **2**
Wood, Chris
  See Traffic
Wood, Danny
  See New Kids on the Block
Wood, Ron
  See Faces, The
  Also see Rolling Stones, The
Wood, Roy
  See Electric Light Orchestra
Woods, Gay
  See Steeleye Span
Woods, Terry
  See Pogues, The
Woodson, Ollie
  See Temptations, The
Woodward, Keren
  See Bananarama
Woody, Allen
  See Allman Brothers, The
Woolfolk, Andrew
  See Earth, Wind and Fire
Worley, Jeff
  See Jackyl
Worrell, Bernie **11**
Wray, Link **17**
Wreede, Katrina
  See Turtle Island String Quartet
Wren, Alan
  See Stone Roses, The

Wretzky, D'Arcy
  See Smashing Pumpkins
Wright, Adrian
  See Human League, The
Wright, David "Blockhead"
  See English Beat, The
Wright, Heath
  See Ricochet
Wright, Hugh
  See Boy Howdy
Wright, Jimmy
  See Sounds of Blackness
Wright, Norman
  See Country Gentlemen, The
Wright, Rick
  See Pink Floyd
Wright, Simon
  See AC/DC
Wright, Tim
  See Pere Ubu
Wurzel
  See Motörhead
Wyatt, Robert **24**
Wyman, Bill
  See Rolling Stones, The
Wynette, Tammy **24**
  Earlier sketch in CM **2**
Wynne, Philippe
  See Spinners, The
Wynonna **11**
  Also see Judds, The
X **11**
XTC **10**
Xefos, Chris
  See King Missile
Ya Kid K
  See Technotronic
Yamamoto, Hiro
  See Soundgarden
Yamano, Atsuko
  See Shonen Knife
Yamano, Naoko
  See Shonen Knife
Yamashita, Kazuhito **4**
Yamauchi, Tetsu
  See Faces, The
Yamazaki, Iwao
  See Ghost
Yankovic, "Weird Al" **7**
Yanni **11**
Yardbirds, The **10**
Yarrow, Peter
  See Peter, Paul & Mary
Yates, Bill
  See Country Gentlemen, The
Yauch, Adam
  See Beastie Boys, The
Yearwood, Trisha **10**
Yella
  See N.W.A.
Yes **8**
Yeston, Maury **22**
Yo La Tengo **24**

Yoakam, Dwight **21**
  Earlier sketch in CM **1**
Yoot, Tukka
  See US3
York, Andrew **15**
York, John
  See Byrds, The
York, Pete
  See Spencer Davis Group
Yorke, Thom E.
  See Radiohead
Young, Adrian
  See No Doubt
Young, Angus
  See AC/DC
Young, Faron **7**
Young, Fred
  See Kentucky Headhunters, The
Young, Gary
  See Pavement
Young, Grant
  See Soul Asylum
Young, Jeff
  See Megadeth
Young, La Monte **16**
Young, Lester **14**
Young, Malcolm
  See AC/DC
Young, Neil **15**
  Earlier sketch in CM **2**
  Also see Buffalo Springfield
Young, Paul
  See Mike & the Mechanics
Young, Richard
  See Kentucky Headhunters, The
Young, Robert "Throbert"
  See Primal Scream
Young M.C. **4**
Yo Yo **9**
Yow, David
  See Jesus Lizard
Yseult, Sean
  See White Zombie
Yule, Doug
  See Velvet Underground, The
Zander, Robin
  See Cheap Trick
Zankey, Glen
  See Bluegrass Patriots
Zap Mama **14**
Zappa, Frank **17**
  Earlier sketch in CM **1**
Zawinul, Josef
  See Weather Report
Zender, Stuart
  See Jamiroquai
Zevon, Warren **9**
Zhane **22**
Zilinskas, Annette
  See Bangles
Zimmerman, Udo **5**
Zombie, Rob
  See White Zombie
Zombies, The **23**

Zoom, Billy
  See X
Zorn, John **15**
Zoyes, Dino
  See Charm Farm
Zuccaro, Steve
  See Charm Far
Zukerman, Pinchas **4**
Zulu, Ras I
  See Spearhead
ZZ Top **2**